Energy-Conserving Site Design

E. GREGORY McPHERSON

Editor

A Publication of the
American Society of
Landscape Architects

The Landscape Architecture Foundation
wishes to express its gratitude to
the
AMERICAN CONSERVATION ASSOCIATION, INC.
and
Consolidated Edison Company of New York, Inc.
for their financial assistance
without which this book would not be possible.

Printed in Providence, Utah by Keith W. Watkins & Sons Inc.

Published in the United States in 1984 by the
American Society of Landscape Architects,
1733 Connecticut Avenue, N.W.
Washington, D.C. 20009

Library of Congress Catalog Card Number: 84-72817
ISBN: 0-941236-07-2

To my parents
who taught me to believe
that we can create a better future

Preface

AMERICANS learned from the energy crisis of the 1970s that the price and availability of energy affects our lives in many ways. Likewise, we also learned that our behavior affects energy supply, consumption, and cost. Daily decisions made by landscape architects, architects, planners, and developers have short- and long-term implications for energy use. In fact, most decisions have energy implications. Land-use planning affects amounts of energy used for transportation and construction. Infrastructure design decisions result in differing levels of embodied-energy use. Determinations regarding siting of structures affect energy consumption for space conditioning, lighting, and water heating. Planting and landscape design decisions also influence amounts of energy required to heat and cool buildings, pump irrigation water, and maintain landscapes.

The need to recognize how site design decisions influence energy consumption has become even more widely acknowledged in recent years. Developers are concerned with increasing their market leverage by investing in energy-conserving projects. Builders recognize a growing trend among home buyers to invest in structures that are economical to heat and cool. Energy-conscious architects realize that buildings cannot be separated from the landscapes around them and that both must be designed as one to achieve greatest energy savings. Local governments more frequently require minimum shading levels for parking lots, shadow pattern plans, southerly orientation of homes, and limited use of water-consuming vegetation. Federal and state regulations now influence the inclusion of energy concerns in the site design process. Energy conservation measures have become standard components of almost every development program. This trend will continue because energy efficiency is economically beneficial to everyone; conservation is cheaper than developing new energy supplies.

Energy-Conserving Site Design owes its inception to frustration at having to collect a cumbersome stack of publications for a course I was teaching on this topic. The absence of a textbook that provided current information and useful design tools on these topics hindered the educational process and was motivation for this effort.

This book, like the course, focuses on residential development. It encompasses design scales ranging from the individual residence to the community and planned unit development. Procedures and techniques described may be applied to other types of development. The book fills a void in the professional literature and should be useful to teachers, students, and practitioners.

Rather than reading the book from cover to cover, practicing professionals may prefer to use it as a reference manual, browsing to locate topic areas most relevant to current practice. Numerous design tools located throughout the book can be abstracted for use in solving practical design problems. The list of references and annotated bibliography will direct the interested reader to sources of related information.

The eleven contributing authors differ in background and profession; some are practicing architects and landscape architects, some are scientists, some are teachers. This collection of essays emphasizes the fact that communication between professions and an interdisciplinary team approach are essential to resolving complex planning and design problems often encountered today.

Energy-Conserving Site Design contains four sections arranged to reflect the site design process. The first section provides an overview of energy-efficient site design. In Chapter One, "A History of Microclimatic Modification: 1600 to 1980," John Stilgoe provides historical perspective on the use of landscape design principles to improve human comfort, and more recently, to conserve energy. His account begins with a description of the sensitive siting of early North American farmsteads to protect work areas, shade the home, and extend the growing season. The chapter concludes with a glimpse of the future, suggesting that as energy prices rise home grounds will acquire more significance and Americans will continue to modify microclimates through landscape design to create enjoyable outdoor spaces and conserve energy.

In the second chapter, "Benefits and Costs of Energy-Conserving Site Design," Greg McPherson reviews literature dealing with the economic effects of various energy conserving site design options. This chapter outlines energy supply and consumption patterns to illustrate areas where design can achieve greatest savings. Major findings are presented from three Department of Energy-sponsored site and neighborhood development case studies. The chapter then summarizes the energy conservation potential for landscaping of individual dwelling units.

The final chapter in Section 1, "Planning the Energy-Conserving Development," also by McPherson, describes procedures for integrating energy concerns into the traditional site design and planning process. Attention focuses on developing a program that contains energy-related goals and objectives. A description of data collection and analysis techniques especially relevant to subsequent design of energy-efficient development is provided. Specific methods for generating and evaluating energy-conserving site design options are presented.

Section 2, "Analysis and Site Planning," was written with the assumption that readers are familiar with traditional site analysis procedures. The four chapters in this section present a more in-depth treatment of site analysis and planning for energy conservation than provided in Section One. Chapters Four and Five, by Lee Herrington, emphasize climatic analysis as a prerequisite to energy-conserving site design. Chapter Four, "Climatic Variables," introduces micrometerology and explains such terms as solar radiation, conduction, and latent heat transfers— terms several authors use later in the text. Herrington uses a simple energy bucket model to explore differences in the microclimates of soils, forests, and cities. He concludes the chapter with a description of methods for estimating human thermal comfort for design purposes.

In Chapter Five, "Climatic Analysis," Herrington builds on an understanding of climatic variables gained from Chapter Four and explains the meanings of common climatic data descriptors that are sometimes misleading and often misunderstood. He presents sources of climatic data and describes when and how climatic data collected at one site can be extrapolated to another. Methods used to analyze radiation, wind, and temperature data to find typical conditions for design purposes also are described.

In Chapter Six, "Master Planning," James Zanetto presents site design principles for conserving energy that apply to the overall site as well as to groups of buildings. Zanetto examines several prototypical neighborhood patterns to provide a conceptual basis for structuring energy-efficient communities and neighborhoods. He outlines a number of building strategies (e.g., solar systems, earthsheltering, insulation, and daylighting) and their implications for planning, emphasizing key solar planning principles of solar access and building orientation because they apply to all housing types. Zanetto then specifies siting guidelines for conventional and solar housing (detached, clustered, and attached), mobile homes, and earthsheltered housing.

Robert Thayer, in "Planning for Solar Access," states that solar access can provide "a central organizing pattern for energy-efficient community landscapes of the future." He provides principles and tools by which planners and designers can explore new design forms. He explains solar access as a simple geometric and spatial concept, then describes techniques for protecting solar access: siting structures, street and lot orientation, bulk plane height limits, shadow pattern mapping, and height limit contour mapping. Thayer emphasizes the need for balancing solar access with solar control.

In Section 3, "Landscape Design," the focus shifts from community and neighborhood site planning to landscape design at the scale of the cluster or individual structure. In Chapter Eight, "Solar Control Planting Design," Greg McPherson describes ways in which a building gains heat. Some of the ways in which trees, shrubs, and vines can provide passive cooling are summarized. Research results are presented that document the effects of vegetative shading on energy consumption. The chapter then focuses on design application, providing guidelines for locating and selecting plants to shade structures. Chapter Eight concludes with four prototypical designs that illustrate key planting design principles mentioned earlier.

In Chapter Nine, "Planting Design for Wind Control," Gordon Heisler proceeds from a brief discussion of heat transfer processes in buildings to ways in which windbreaks affect wind flow and air temperature. With this background, the chapter surveys windbreak effects on energy savings and breeze control. Recommendations are made for windbreak design that include evaluation of wind climatology, tree density, tree spacing, space requirements, and species selection. Two design examples illustrate these recommendations.

In Chapter Ten, "Water-Conserving Landscape Design," Robert Thayer and Thomas Richman explore the relation between water used to maintain landscapes and energy consumption costs. The authors define characteristics of community and residential water use and emphasize how consumers' perceptions and attitudes toward water consumption act to fashion a collective vision of the "ideal landscape." They describe the concept of hydrozonic landscaping and techniques for implementing and managing each hydrozone. Finally, three examples are provided that illustrate application of the hydrozone concept to everyday design problems.

The final chapter in Section 3, "Conservation of Embodied Energy through Landscape Design," by David Pitt, examines methods used to quantify and reduce fossil fuel consumed in the manufacturing of landscape materials and in the processes of implementing and maintaining design solutions. Embodied energy is defined. The difference between direct and indirect energy consumption is also explained. Pitt provides tables that outline the embodied energy requirements of various site design components. He notes that spaces receiving intensive human use require more resilient landscape materials. The higher the resiliency of a landscape material, the greater are its embodied-energy requirements. A residential case study describes a process of accounting for the embodied-energy requirements in site design. Pitt concludes with the observation that the designer can achieve sizable energy savings by first examining the level of use intensity in the landscape and then designing accordingly.

Section 4, entitled "Alternative Futures," places energy-conserving site design within the context of the future. In Chapter Twelve, "Community Design Case Study: Oak Hills," Greg McPherson, Robert Hrabak, and David Socwell compare costs associated with site development, embodied energy, and operational energy consumption for an 800-acre conventional site design and a redesigned energy plan. Procedures are delineated for quantifying the effects of reducing road widths, parking areas, and driveways on site development costs and embodied-energy consumption. Effects of improved building and window orientation, and of massing of buildings on annual space heating costs also are examined. Energy-conserving site design

principles enumerated by authors throughout the book are graphically portrayed.

In Chapter Thirteen, "The Ecological City: Closing the Loop," David Morris presents an encompassing view of the dynamic interaction between energy policy and social change. He explains how cheap energy and low transportation costs resulted in a fractured society, where production, consumption, and disposal took place many miles apart. He describes how communities throughout the country are taking actions to achieve greater local self-reliance and mend their economies. Morris observes that we are moving full circle: from an economy based on iron ore and petroleum to one based on agriculture. However, technology now allows us to expand our economy through the rapid transfer of information. The chapter concludes by stating that our future depends upon our willingness to use our technological capacity to devise new ways to conserve our dwindling natural resources, and describes the vital role site planners can play in shaping the community of the future.

Appendices in *Energy-Conserving Site Design* provide additional technical information for interested readers. They include a comprehensive list of energy-conserving options, solar radiation and soil temperature equations, and further discussion and examples of precision planting for solar control and solar access.

This comprehensive book provides landscape architects, architects, planners, developers, students, and the layman with a sound guide to energy-efficient site planning and design. It will, we hope, contribute to a greater understanding of the important role energy conservation can play in the site design process. Garrett Eckbo has stated in "Is Landscape Architecture?" that ". . . [o]ur challenge is to search for answers that will generate new forms and relations between people and nature, and to express those new relations in architecture and landscape." Eckbo's challenge is met by the authors of this volume, and the results should stimulate and further challenge individuals who share the desire to contribute to the evolution of landscape planning and design.

I would be remiss to not extend my appreciation to those individuals whose assistance has played an important role in the development of this book. Ted Andra served as technical editor, and the consistency of style and structure that makes this book more than a collection of disjointed articles is largely due to his diligent scrutiny and skillful rewriting. His contribution has been invaluable. Robert Thayer reviewed the entire manuscript and offered thoughful suggestions throughout the duration of the project. Adair

McPherson also made important editorial contributions to the book. Sherry Barndollar, Al Massoni, and Gerry Patten successfully coordinated my efforts with those of the Landscape Architecture Foundation and the American Society of Landscape Architects. Faculty and staff associated with the Forest Resources Department and Department of Landscape Architecture and Environmental Planning at Utah State University provided the opportunity, time, and support necessary to make this book a reality.

Greg McPherson
Logan, Utah
March, 1984

Contents

Overview of Energy-Conserving Site Design 1

CHAPTER ONE
A History of Microclimatic Modification:
1600 to 1980

JOHN R. STILGOE
Harvard University
Cambridge, Massachussetts

WHAT did our ancestors really know about energy-saving, resource-conserving site design? Were they masters of microclimatic manipulation, able to redirect prevailing winds, shift sunlight, and retain moisture? Were they the lore-educated experts remembered now by energy-short Americans? A backward scrutiny of the domestic site design of past generations suggests not only the complexity of such questions, but the near impossibility of arriving at definite conclusions.

Site Selection and Design Heritage

Europeans arrived in the New World carrying with them a sort of baggage of site-design folklore. The typical European peasant had had scant opportunity to colonize virgin territory; for generations, fathers handed sons long-worked farms (Mayhew, 1973). Consequently, many colonists knew little about site-locating, but a great deal about improving existing farmsteads and fields. Nevertheless, agriculturists had definite ideas about the rudiments of site selection.

Perhaps the finest explication of early seventeenth-century site locating and site manipulation, Charles Estienne's *Maison rustique or The Countrey Farme,* covers a wealth of western European traditional practice. The massive folio, translated into English in 1616, remains one of the most detailed handbooks of agriculture ever compiled. No other work better describes the thought of American colonists.

Estienne explained site-locating chiefly in regard to prosperous farming and only secondarily in regard to building the complex of farm structures called a farmstead. "You must make choice of a place far from marshes, far from the sea shore, and where neither the southern nor northern winds do ordinarily blow," he began, "and which lies not altogether open to the south sun, nor yet unto the north: but principally see that it be placed near unto some good and honest neighbor." Such directives complicate the understanding of early American site-location practice. Clearly Estienne considered a good neighbor as important as a site sheltered from north winds. He also carefully integrated the design of the structures, and particularly of the farm house and barn, into a larger theory of location. "If there ever be a hill, build upon the edge thereof, making choice to have your lights toward the east; but if you be in a cold country, open your lights also on the south side, and little or nothing towards the north," he counseled in a long passage explaining the different uses of "lights" (permanently set panes of glass designed only to admit sunlight) and "windows" (shuttered openings intended to admit fresh air). A wise builder, according to Estienne, chooses the side of a hill to "recoup the liberty of the air, and a goodly prospect," to "be safe from the annoyances of foggy mists" and to avoid "cold in winter." On such a site, a house should present its chief lights "upon the sun-rising in the months of March and September," but the barn and stables "shall be open toward the sunset, in respect of their greatest lights," and should front their windows on the south. In an age well aware of the expensive luxury of glass and terrified of diseases caused by night air or fog, Estienne emphasized the healthfulness of the perfect hillside site — and did not forget the rewards of a good view.

Of more importance to Estienne, and to most of his contemporaries too, microclimatic manipulation engrossed the attention of husbandmen unable to move to better sites. *Maison rustique* devotes much attention to improving local climates, sometimes assuming that such improvements might take generations to accomplish their work. "Over against the North, you shall procure some row or tuft of trees for to be a mark unto you of your place, and defense also for the same against the northern winds in the winter," Estienne suggested, realizing the equal importance of marking boundary lines and deflecting winds. "But if you be in a hot country, you must set your said tuft of trees on the south side, against such winds and heat of sun as come from there." He warned of the necessity of putting kitchen gardens south of an effective windbreak, and near the farmhouse to save the steps of the housewife. And he noted the usefulness of the garden as a beautiful space, calculated to refresh the eye, and consequently worth locating near the farmyard. His immense, minutely detailed guidebook ranges over hundreds of site-manipulation details, considering the best ways to conserve water resources, ventilate barns, and protect vineyards. Not all of his good advice took root in the colonies, however.

Understanding site-location and site-design practice in the American colonies, including the Spanish colonies, requires an understanding of the practice of shaping entire landscapes (Stilgoe, 1982a). It also requires an understanding of major climatic and resource differences between western Europe and most of North America. Beyond doubt, English colonists found New England winters to be far colder than those of home, just as English people learned that summer in Virginia meant high temperatures and violent thunderstorms unlike anything in their experience. On the other hand, colonists discovered a bountiful supply of firewood. "It may be objected that it is too cold a country for our Englishmen, who have been accustomed to a warmer climate," noted William Wood in 1634 in *New England's Prospect*. "To which it may be answered, there is wood good store and better, cheap to build warm houses and make good fires, which makes the winter less tedious." Such circumstances lessened the authority of tradition and of European experts like Estienne. Old World site-locating theory and site-manipulation practice always implied a scarcity of such resources as firewood. In the colonies, where trees grew so thick that settlers burned huge piles of felled timber simply to make fields, builders cared less about windbreaks and more about

effective chimneys. Virginians immersed in raising tobacco and cotton, two plants wholly alien to European tradition, likewise dispensed with much suddenly "old fashioned" practice.

Early Farmsteads and Homes

Almost every North American colonist farmed. From the Spanish settlements in California to the French villages in Louisiana to the British towns in New England, almost all site design revolved around the growing of crops, and often of crops foreign to North America. Farming efficiency also preoccupied the settlers; a few minutes saved from a particular chore, or a chore eliminated from daily or seasonal work freed farmer and farmwife for other, more profitable labors. While colonists quickly abandoned much of their Old World heritage, they retained or invented remarkably efficient site design practices.

Almost every colonial farmyard reflected male-female job segregation. Men worked in fields and in the farmyard tending large livestock; women worked in the kitchen "ell" and in the kitchen garden. Every structure and space in and around the farmyard reflected the job segregation and the urge toward efficiency. According to several experts, a farmwife ought to be able to see her clothesline from her kitchen window, just as a farmer ought to be able to step from the stall-area of his barn into a harness room (Allen, 1852; Stilgoe, 1982a). In cold regions, almost always north of the Mason-Dixon line, the barn typically stood north of the farmhouse, not to shelter the house and reduce its fuel requirements, but to create a sort of court or yard in which outdoor work could be done year round. In northern New England, farmers often connected houses to barns by building a long, shed-like structure that enabled them to move from house to barn without venturing outdoors (Hubka, 1977). Of more importance, however, was the ability of the "connected barn" to act as a vast windscreen for the farmyard; the farmwife could tend chickens and the "family pig" secure from most winter winds (Figure 1-1). An almost identical arrangement of farm buildings, the *casa-corral,* evolved in present-day New Mexico; the courtyard sheltered by farm buildings and adobe walls provided a sun-trap perfect for outdoor winter work. The farmyard represented the one place on the farm in which both farmer and farmwife shared space, and it materially helped the efficiency of both workers, chiefly by stretching the duration of weather warm enough to perform outdoor activities.

Figure 1 1. Connecting farm buildings, Attleboro, Mass., 1980 (photograph by the author).

The *typical* American farm had acquired by 1800 very definite characteristics. Wherever possible, the farmstead stood on the side of a south-facing hill, the barn to the north and several sheds making up a screen around the barnyard. The kitchen garden usually stood to the west to obtain some shelter from the structures, and fields stretched away from the farmstead in all directions. Often a woodlot stood at the north end of the holding, acting as a sort of windbreak, and sometimes one or two deciduous trees shaded the farmhouse south facade (Figure 1-2). Locating a farm on a hillside meant avoiding the cold air that hangs in valleys, and avoiding too the mists that farmers believed carried disease; of course, slope

Figure 1-2. Amish farmstead nestled in a south-facing hollow, with windbreak of trees to the northwest, near Red Lion, Pa. (photograph by the author).

5

soil is rarely as rich as bottom-land, so the hillside farmer traded a longer growing season against richer soil. Everywhere in the new Republic, farm families avoided the north slopes of hills, knowing that such exposure produces a much shorter growing season. North-slope farms often failed, and today the astute observer traveling in upstate New York, for example, often finds prosperous farms on south-facing hillsides and only timber on the north-facing slopes.

Landscape historians know that many farms violated many of the typical characteristics. For a multitude of reasons, farm families often abandoned New World practice. Some families feared the health hazard implicit in the odors forever drifting from barns to houses; siting barns to the windward of houses meant living forever with the stench of manure and the possibility of disease. Other families put pure water highest on their list of desires, and located houses and wells on the highest ground. Below that level, they sited barns, stables, and other structures sheltering livestock. In the age before piped-in water, locating the kitchen very near the well saved the farmwife hours of walking. A pure spring, flowing freely even in droughts, proved a powerful attraction to any family looking for farmland; in water-short regions, such a spring made a north-facing hillside seem nearly perfect. In other locations, the children and grandchildren of original settlers, having had the chance to grow intimately familiar with local climate, built farms organized according to winter winds prevailing from the west, for example, or winter storms from the northeast. Deciphering the wisdom of such site-designers is now difficult; in some cases the hills remain and still deflect storms, but often the nineteenth-century woodlots have vanished, and the massive trees that once shaped air flow no longer guide local storms. Much research remains to be done concerning the intentions of uneducated but wise builders; many farmhouses have north-facing lights and/or windows simply because barns stood north of houses and farmwives wanted to watch their husbands, especially when the men did such dangerous work as splitting wood. But where families sited barns to the west or east of their houses, the houses often have only one or two north-facing windows, and often reveal a long roof sloping almost to the ground on the north side. Such roofs, designed to direct winter winds over the structure, nowadays point in directions difficult to understand. It is possible that over two or more centuries weather patterns have changed or else that tree-felling has caused winds to move in new paths.

In the humid South, houses quickly revealed their occupants' awareness of blistering heat and heavy rainfall. The deep porch, sometimes extending totally around the house, not only sheltered the family from rain; it sheltered the interior of the house from sun while providing semi-outdoor space that could be efficiently used. In winter, for example, the low sun fell directly into the south-facing porch sheltered by the house from northern winds; in summer, the north porch provided a shady, often breezy place for the farmwife to work. Partly because of slavery, many southerners worried little about designing houses for coolness; slave cooks, for example, freed planter-class wives from the necessity of working next to wood-fueled stoves in summer. Such simple architectural features as high ceilings, over-hanging porches, balconies, and the free-standing "summer" kitchen did contribute to the coolness of southern houses.

Almost everywhere in North America, at least until the 1950s, builders of "common" houses and farms — those structures not designed by professionally trained architects or by experiment-minded agricultural reformers — toyed with the wisdom of planting deciduous trees just south of their houses. Such trees shaded roofs in summer and, when they lost their leaves, permitted welcome sunlight to warm roofs. Sometimes the trees existed for largely ornamental reasons, but many families feared the effect of prolonged shade on wood-shingled roofs (Stilgoe, 1982a). Beyond that, shading one or more sides of a house sometimes increased insect nuisances; mosquitoes shun sunlight and, in the era before the invention of window screening, sunlight proved more endurable than shady, insect-filled porches and kitchens. Asphalt shingles, tin roofing, and window screens helped popularize the "colonial" notion of using deciduous trees to cool and heat a farmhouse.

If Estienne's *Maison rustique* marks the highpoint of the early seventeenth-century European site-locating and site-design practice carried to the New World, perhaps S.W. Johnson's *Rural Economy* (1806) marks the epitome of "traditional American" practice. "A farmhouse should be built on the most healthy spot on the farm," Johnson counsels, "open to the south and southwestern breezes, which prevail in the summer; and well sheltered from the northwest and northeast in the winter, by trees either of natural growth, or cultivated on purpose, and set as near the center of the farm as convenient." Johnson summarizes the early American attitude toward pure water, good drainage, prevailing winds, and crop-growing requirements. Within 30 years, however, much of his information had become almost antiquated, and Americans had begun to discard centuries of lore.

6

Energy Shortages and Architectural Adaptations

In the winter of 1637-38, North American colonists experienced their first fuel crisis. The settlers of Boston, after only seven years of occupancy, had nearly exhausted their supply of firewood. "We at Boston were almost ready to break up for want of wood," wrote Governor John Winthrop of the near catastrophe (Rutman, 1967). Of course, the settlers quickly solved the problem by buying firewood from off-peninsula farmers and by restricting the cutting of trees within the settlement. Nevertheless, a handful of settlers did understand something of the limitations of North American natural resources. Not for more than 150 years did Americans worry about firewood shortages. In the year 1800, a typical New England farm family burned about 15 cords of wood, although 20 made for a more comfortable winter (Brown, 1948). Assuming that a cord of wood is the equivalent of three-fifths of a standing acre, the typical family consumed about 10 acres of woodland annually to cook, process farm produce, and keep warm. The population of Massachusetts consumed approximately 2 million cords, or roughly 2,000 square miles of timber in 1800. The firewood consumption taxed and overtaxed the capacity of farm woodlots and distant forests, already strained by demands for fence and building timber and for charcoal for the new nation's young iron industry (Stilgoe, 1982a).

Several areas of the country encountered severe fuel shortages earlier than most. Cape Cod, for example, had been almost totally deforested by 1800, presenting an almost desert-like appearance to travelers (Stilgoe, 1981). By the middle of the nineteenth century when Thoreau's *Cape Cod* was published (1865), its inhabitants were reduced to purchasing almost all firewood and scavenging for the rest. "Almost all the wood used for fuel is imported by vessels or currents, and of course all the coal," Thoreau remarked. "I was told that probably a quarter of the fuel and a considerable part of the lumber used in North Truro was driftwood. Many get *all* their fuel from the beach." As early as the beginning of the century, however, Cape Codders had begun manipulating microclimates to conserve fuel.

Much of the manipulation involved architectural innovation. The "Cape Cod" house (Figure 1-3), a one and a half story, compact structure focused on a central chimney, incorporated dozens of energy-saving features. Its low ceilings offered only 6 or 6½ ft. of headroom, but made rooms easy to heat; its small windows, often strategically located to capture sun

Figure 1-3. Energy-efficient house, Massachusetts, 1848. From: (Barber, 1848).

and avoid prevailing northern winds, reduced infiltration of cold air. Cape Codders experimented with a variety of insulation materials before settling on a mixture of crushed clamshells and dried seaweed, an inflammable but highly efficient barrier against cold. The central chimney warmed the two upper chambers and enabled "zone control" of heating; many Cape Codders closed off the parlor and perhaps one other room during the depths of the winter, and lived in a warm kitchen and "back room." The little houses impressed Thoreau, who eventually determined that "houses near the sea are generally low and broad." He found too that the houses of the typical Cape Codder seemed somehow to fit better into the landscape than those of the well-to-do who could afford to buy firewood and coal. "Generally, the old-fashioned and unpainted houses on the Cape looked more comfortable, as well as picturesque, than the modern and more pretending ones, which were less in harmony with the scenery, and less firmly planted," he wrote in *Cape Cod.* Thoreau devoted little attention to the peculiar siting of Cape Cod houses, but other travelers did.

In the early nineteenth century, Timothy Dwight rode along the sandy Cape and marveled at the small houses, noting in his travels in New England and New York (1821) that "generally, they exhibit a tidy, neat aspect in themselves and in their appendages, and furnish proofs of comfortable living." Dwight noted that almost every such house stood "surrounded by a fence enclosing a small piece of ground," and that in most such enclosures "were orchards of apple trees, defended from the sea winds by a barrier of cherry trees or locusts," which permitted meadow grass to grow in the dry, sandy, but sheltered soil. Such houses, Dwight noted again and again, usually stood in valleys or hollows, where their inhabitants "find a better soil and security from the violence of the winds." Shelter dramatically reduced fuel requirements, provided a microclimate favorable to orchard and garden crops, and shielded cows and other livestock and the family well from windblown sand. Combined with the architectural changes, the Cape Cod house site proved remarkably energy-efficient.

While Cape Codders struggled to adjust to a dramatically dimished firewood supply, pioneers settling the treeless plains confronted life with almost no firewood at all. Women cooked over fires made of grass and dried buffalo dung, and longed for the time when their families could afford a precut house shipped west from Michigan or Chicago. In the meantime, they made do with sod houses.

The dug-out or sod house, sometimes called a "soddie," is a remarkable adaptation to the plains.

Homesteaders dug into a south-facing slope and increased the wall height by piling up great blocks of prairie sod around the perimeter. The sod house endured far longer than one or two years (Ise, 1936; Dick, 1937; Henderson, 1978). The thick balks of sod resisted wind infiltration; if a family had the luck to find enough cottonwood or other trees to make a log roof, blocks of sod often formed the roof covering too. While not wholly waterproof, in the High Plains where rainfall is limited, the sod-roofed house trapped heat from the fire that often burned on an open hearth and protected its inhabitants against snow, cold, and damp.

Despite its immediate attractions, among which the most favored was its minimal cost, the sod house irritated most inhabitants. Life in a dug-out meant unending toil for the housewife, who fought a losing battle against insects, dust, and dirt (women usually preferred canvas roofs over log-and-sod roofs simply because the more permanent sod roofs forever dropped earth onto food, bedding, and furniture). Lining walls and ceiling with newspaper helped prevent falling dirt, but did little to retard the depredations of insects. Sod houses built wholly above ground lasted only as long as the bottom row of sod balks retained its shape; in a heavy rain, or after days of light rain, the blocks of sod could soften and without warning suddenly collapse the entire dwelling.

Not surprisingly, plains families hoped to prosper after a few years and order a knocked-down house from the many suppliers of such structures. Little is known about the popular reaction to the two-, three-, and four-room houses shipped by rail from major cities, brought by wagon to sites next to the sod houses, and then assembled by farmers or hired carpenters. Certainly their immense popularity suggests the common reaction, but the homesteaders had little other choice, since most lacked timber for fencing, let alone building.

The demise of the sod-house occurred, however, in the decades following the Civil War. Farm families obtaining good profits from their massive wheat and corn harvests found it possible to abandon traditional house-siting wisdom, at least for a moment. The sod house — and the Cape Cod house — represent a popular adaptation to energy shortage; what replaced the sod house reflected massive changes in the American way of life.

Modernization

When George G. Hill published *Practical Suggestions for Farm Buildings,* a 1901 United States Department of Agriculture Farmer's Bulletin, most Americans no longer thought much of the farm-siting lore recounted by Estienne. Hill, in fact, only briefly mentions the importance of windbreaks, and then chiefly as a way of improving the comfort of outdoor workers, not as important to household economy. His lack of attention is not at all unique; writers in the *Cyclopedia of American Agriculture* (Bailey, 1907), for example, devote scarcely any more attention. Between about 1850 and 1900, farm families — and the families of storekeepers, physicians, fishermen, and others — had changed their lives.

Iron stoves and, within a few years, coal revolutionized American housekeeping (wood-burning stoves consume far less fuel than open fireplaces). From Benjamin Franklin's prototype to the efficient "air-tight" stoves of the 1890s, the progress of American stove-making drastically decreased the pressure on the nation's timber resources. Stoves altered family habits too, however, and reshaped notions of personal comfort.

Stoves can be moved. Nineteenth-century Americans discovered that a wood stove could be moved from the kitchen onto the back porch or into a free-standing summer kitchen in the backyard. In summer, the housewife found herself cooking amidst breezes that made her chores less onerous, and the rest of the family enjoyed a house free of cookstove heat. In winter, the stove could be moved back into the kitchen, placed against the now sealed-up fireplace, and made to heat large spaces. Well-to-do families sometimes splurged on a second stove, usually located in the "parlor" and lit only on special occasions, but the typical American family living in a single-family house relied on one large cast-iron combination heating- and cooking-appliance often equipped to boil water for bathing and other purposes. A little tinkering enabled the cast-iron monster to heat upstairs rooms; a hole cut in a ceiling or wall improved the flow of hot air. On bitter windy nights, families sat in kitchens, reading, talking, and doing schoolwork not by the fire-light of the 1820s but by the whale-oil (and later kerosene) lamps of the contemporary period.

Coal soon supplanted wood, particularly in the regions deforested or where remaining timber proved more useful for making fence rails. Railroads transported coal everywhere, and eventually even to such poverty-stricken places as Cape Cod. For the housewife, coal meant easier cooking; a coal-stove fire could be more easily and finely regulated than a wood one, and coal was easier to handle. By 1900, suburban families had discovered the usefulness of furnaces carefully placed in basements. In regions where gas enabled housewives to discard coal-burning stoves, furnaces evenly warmed large houses, and families dispersed away from kitchens.

Other inventions helped Americans forget tradition. Tar paper, perhaps the most lowly invention of all, helped prevent wind infiltration. To some writers of the period, only tar paper made possible life in the High Plains (Smalley, 1893). Along with the popularization of cement, cinder block, air-moving fans, and hot-water radiators, tar paper helped convince Americans that comfortable houses could be built anywhere, even atop hills. So long as coal remained plentiful — and very cheap — American house siting departed further from earlier tradition.

Instead of nestling in hollows facing roughly south, late-nineteenth-century American houses usually face roads. Instead of offering only one or two windows to the north, such houses frequently show substantially more north glass area, partly in an attempt to achieve evenness of lighting, partly in an attempt to enjoy good views. Roofs no longer adjusted to prevailing microclimate winds; instead they followed styles dictated by eastern architects. Such houses speak of firm faith in modern industrialism, of a faith in such effective equipment as the gravity-fed furnace. In 1915, a housewife could easily raise the temperature of her house by simply moving a lever on the kitchen wall; below, in the cellar, the elevated hopper dumped coal onto the fire, dampers opened, and valves moved — all with a flick of the wrist. While husbands remained enslaved by the duty to remove ashes and load the coal hopper, housewives and children lived snugly in the clean, draft-free rooms upstairs. Only farmers kept alive the old lore, and then only because their crops needed protection.

Windbreaks and Shelterbelts

Throughout the period of rapid modernization and even more rapid social change, American farmers kept alive time-tested techniques of microclimate manipulation and even invented new ones. Now and then their expertise attracted the scrutiny of landscape architects and other nonagricultural designers, but only rarely. The web of lore, invention, and seat-of-the-pants wisdom is immensely complicated, but the history of windbreaks, while only one small part of the entire web, illustrates the finesse of American agriculturists.

"The face of the country is becoming denuded, and wintry winds and summer storms sweep our farms with more fury than formerly," commented one agricultural editor in 1866 in the *Illustrated Annual Register*. "Young plants of grass and winter grain, after heaving by frost, are beaten about and

9

sometimes torn out by the action of the winds upon them." By the 1850s, American farmers clearly understood the microclimate changes brought about by the diminishing size of farm woodlots (Stilgoe, 1982a). Railroad companies consumed vast quantities of wood for fuel and ties; steamboat firms purchased cordwood for fuel, too. But farmers forced to replace miles of rail or post-and-rail fencing, rebuild barn and house sills, and keep families warm caused most of the timber consumption. A farmer might clear-cut his woodlot for cash or home consumption and suddenly discover his crops "blasted" by storms. Even worse, his neighbors might learn the detrimental effects too, as their own crops suddenly failed. Thus as farmers ceased to rely on homegrown timber and cordwood and began to purchase stovewood shipped by rail or else buy several tons of coal, they embarked on a long struggle to build windbreaks — for the sake of their crops. "Land owners who have planted belts of evergreens have found that the protection they afford has amounted on an average to an increase in the crops raised within the range of their shelter, of about fifty percent more than where fully exposed," continued the editor (Figure 1-4).

Figure 1-4. In July, 1938, the Norway spruce windbreak planted by one Cortland County, New York farmer for wind and snow protection was forty years old and functioning well (courtesy of United States Forest Service).

Mid-nineteenth-century windbreaks took two forms. One type derived from careful cutting of forests; farmers left standing mature trees 70 or 80 feet tall. Such "leftover" windbreaks figure in many paintings of American farms, and are sometimes mistaken for vaguely European looking hedgerows. The more common type of windbreak — aside from the strategically located woodlot — began as a row of small saplings (Figure 1-5). "By selecting thrifty growers, such as the Norway spruce and the Scotch larch, a growth of 25 to 30 feet high will be reached in about ten years, if they are properly cultivated; and 50 feet in twenty-five years," wrote the editor of the *Illustrated Annual Register* in 1866. Agricultural periodicals of

the era devote much attention to the proper siting, cultivation, and thinning of such windbreaks. The typical farmer planted twice as many windbreaks as he needed, since young trees protect much less ground than tall ones. After 15 or 20 years, he felled every other windbreak, using the timber for fence repair and fuel, because the maturing trees protected more area.

Figure 1-5. In the spring of 1937, one South Dakota family planted a farm windbreak: within two years the small trees had made good progress (courtesy of United States Forest Service).

Experts disagreed about the best trees to plant. Some argued that elms and other trees known for sprawling root systems ought not be planted near field crops and suggested oaks and black birch instead. Others specified bordering every field on the farm with "shade or timber trees," partly to divert wind, but largely to provide building timber and firewood. (*Illustrated Annual Register,* 1880). Other experts counseled farmers to plant evergreen windbreaks, although they realized that such softwood would be of little fuel value. Of chief importance in the literature, however, is the implied assumption that farmers would think about long-term benefits. Again and again, authors speak of 15- or 20-year periods preceding the era of real microclimate improvement. Farmers intending to leave their farms better than they found them, perhaps to sons and daughters, perhaps to unknown purchasers, planted windbreaks for the future, not the present. Between 1800 and 1860, American farmers learned the value of windbreaks and woodlots, and relearned the caution offered by Estienne and other seventeenth-century writers.

Science and pipe dreams furthered the windbreak-planting efforts of thousands of farmers, especially in the plains states. By the middle of the nineteenth century, scientists like George Perkins Marsh had begun studying the climatic effects of trees and forests. Marsh's opus, *Man and Nature: Or, Physical Geography as Modified by Human Action* (1864), investigates windbreaks in two ways. First, it addresses "trees as a shelter to ground to the leeward," noting the local climatic effects of trees. Second, and more importantly, it analyzes the regional effects of forests. Marsh concluded after studying the large-scale climatic effects of forest removal in western and south-central Europe, "It is evident that the effect of the forest, as a mechanical impediment to the passage of the wind, would extend to a very considerable distance above its own height, and hence protect while standing, or lay open when felled, a much larger surface than might at first thought be supposed." Eventually, he extrapolated from his findings and, while aware of "the slender historical evidence," announced that "almost every treatise on the economy of the forest adduces numerous facts in support of the doctrine that the clearing of the woods tends to diminish the flow of springs and the humidity of the soil." Along with other foresters and ecologists, Marsh unwittingly stimulated a grand American pipe dream.

"Rain follows the plow," a motto that heartened farm families settling the High Plains, derived partly from scientific efforts at understanding rainfall patterns and their relationship to ground cover, and partly from the hope of homesteaders that quasi-arid regions would grow eastern crops like corn. In the first decades of pioneering, the motto seemed true, but gradually the ground water drawn up by continuous plowing — "dry farming" as it came to be known — began to lessen. Agricultural experts counseled farmers to plant windbreaks to decrease evaporation as well as to divert winds and provide fuel. At least one landscape architect, H.W.S. Cleveland, advocated planting windbreaks to change the regional rainfall of the West. Commenting on the western soil in *Landscape Architecture as Applied to the Wants of the West* (1873), Cleveland indicated that "Where such grasses will grow, trees will grow, and with the growth

of trees in sufficient quantity will come the increase of humidity and the modification of the storms, floods, and other excesses of natural phenomena, which are fatal to the success of extended agricultural operations." Cleveland cared little about the varieties of trees planted in the windbreaks he suggested should be set along railroad lines and around farms; he wanted trees set out at once. "Plant those that *will* grow, and in time they will serve as screens for more valuable kinds, as is done on the sea shore, where the worthless silver poplar (abele) will grow luxuriantly and in a few years form a screen behind which more delicate deciduous and evergreen trees will grow as readily as if they were unaware of the vicinity of the ocean." Farmers did encounter difficulty in nursing along the saplings, however, and sporadic years of drought sometimes killed windbreaks just as they withered acres of wheat and other grain. Clearly, rain did not necessarily follow the movement of farming into land previously used only for ranching. Windbreaks did not dramatically increase regional rainfall, and many farms failed.

Marsh, Cleveland, and other experts, while perhaps wrong about the regional effects of mass windbreak planting, unknowingly predicted the dramatic catastrophe of the dust-bowl years of the 1920s and 30s. In response to the blowing dust, the federal government urged farmers to plant windbreaks, partly to control evaporation of ground moisture, partly to stop the dust, and partly to counter the effect of wind sweeping uninterrupted over miles of farms surrounded by barbed wire. Nearly two decades after the first plantings, Joseph H. Stoeckeler and Ross A. Williams in a 1949 *Yearbook of Agriculture* article entitled "Windbreaks and Shelterbelts," summed up the advantages of the maturing belts of trees: Well-maintained windbreaks decreased farmhouse fuel requirements by roughly one-fourth, and in almost every case helped farm families harvest far more produce from vegetable gardens. They made possible growing fruit where winter storms had previously killed orchards. But the results of shelterbelts, windbreaks planted to protect field crops, proved even more cheering. Between the middle of the nineteenth century, when reformers first began urging farmers to plant them, and 1949, some 123,191 miles of shelterbelts had been established. Privately planted shelterbelts frequently consisted of osage orange trees, whose large thorns helped confine wandering livestock. Those planted by the Forest Service, which between 1932 and 1942 set out more than 18,000 miles of trees in farm and ranch country hit by drifting dust, and by farmers following expert advice consisted of such

11

species as Siberian elm, green ash, hackberry, honeylocust, cottonwood (see Figure 1-6), white and golden willow, chokecherry, ponderosa pine, and others (Stoeckeler & Williams, 1949). But the true extent of the actual results of the tree-planting can never be known, for in the dust-bowl years farmers discovered the advantages of deep-well irrigation, and sometimes dismissed shelterbelts as of secondary value, if that.

Figure 1-6. A turn-of-the-century cottonwood windbreak adjoining an alfalfa field in Chaves County, New Mexico (courtesy of United States Forest Service).

Gardeners, on the other hand, had used windbreaks continuously from the time of Estienne to the dust-bowl years. Everywhere in the United States, vegetable and flower growers screened their gardens with plantings of trees (Figure 1-7). Turn-of-the-century magazines aimed at the ever-growing population of the nation's suburbs directed attention again and again to the many advantages of windbreaks. Some articles explained what famous Americans had done to their grounds; a 1905 *Country Life* (Maynard) article examining the country home of Horace Greeley

Figure 1-7. The author's vegetable garden, shielded by a windbreak on the north side, Norwell, Mass., 1982.

notes the publisher's effective use of windbreaks: "At the northern end of the plot selected for the garden, he planted a windbreak of evergreens. He planted four rows of them — pines and firs, bought at a nursery, and hemlocks and cedars transplanted from the adjoining woods. Under the shelter of the wind-break he built a good-sized greenhouse, and near by planted strawberries and other small fruits" (Capen, 1905). Perhaps Greeley made such good use of windbreaks because he understood something of High Plains agriculture, but thousands of other suburbanites learned from how-to-do-it essays.

Henry Troth's "Wind-Breaks for Country Homes," another 1905 *Country Life* article, notes that "a wind-break saves coal, makes many a house habitable or comfortable that would otherwise be vacant or cheerless in winter, permits the summer home to be occupied in time for the first spring flowers as well as the last autumn colors, and gives the garden a chance to yield fresh vegetables two weeks or more earlier than unprotected gardens" (Figure 1-8, see next page). Troth called the white spruce "the best tree of all for wind-breaks," but he recognized the peculiar difficulties of planting windbreaks along the ocean—for example, where salt spray harmed many species—and in other locations, and advised readers about the planting of Scotch and Austrian pine, black walnut, lindens, and other species. American gardening and suburban-life magazines always devoted some attention to the care of windbreaks, not so much to save home-heating fuel, but to give gardens some protection against late-spring winds and summer dry spells. Of course, the articles shifted focus over the decades. By 1939, for example, *Real Gardening* understood the new notion of backyard privacy; Donald Wyman's "Natural Screens and Windbreaks" includes an analysis of climbing vines that help to screen houses and protect gardeners from neighbors' eyes. In 1961, *Horticulture* published a brief article detailing the fuel-saving advantages of windbreaks adjacent to suburban houses and emphasizing their ability to control drifting snow (Plimpton, 1961). The many articles concerning siting maintaining gardens often mention windbreaks, but by the 1960s, most advice concerned only their use in lengthening growing seasons.

Not all microclimatic manipulation focused on reducing cold winds; indeed farmers worried as much about controlling evaporation, or did until engine-driven, deep-well pumps seemingly freed them from rainfall and evaporation worries. Too, Americans tried to retain coolness throughout the summer, and sometimes wondered about the summertime effect of windbreaks that might cut off soothing breezes.

Figure 1-8. On Arbor Day, 1939, the children enrolled in Erdlicher School, about two miles northwest of Casselton, North Dakota, planted a windbreak to further protect their schoolbuilding (courtesy United States Forest Service).

Natural Cooling

Planting for cooling and moisture retention never preoccupied Americans. Other factors than the worry about roofing deterioration caused farmers to keep trees away from their houses. Nurturing saplings in or near barnyards proved immensely difficult; manure and urine frequently killed those saplings that survived attacks by hungry livestock. In 1864, *The Country Gentleman* advised planting apple trees instead of cherry trees, only because "apple trees will bear a much larger amount of manure." Many farm families planted an apple tree on the site of a disused privy, but did so largely for the crop value (Stilgoe, 1982). Only the advent of synthetic roofing, primarily tar paper and "combination" shingles, encouraged householders to plant trees designed to shade houses.

Moisture retention received even less effort. The popularization of the windmill made possible vegetable gardening in the High Plains, and windmills often pumped enough water to fill troughs for cattle stricken by drought (Webb, 1931). A windmill-powered well pump is at least somewhat ecologically sound, since it pumps only when the wind, which hastens evaporation, blows. Self-regulating windmills (Figure 1-9), designed to pump steadily even as wind speeds increased, freed housewives from the nerve-wracking chore of adjusting the ever-squeaking blades, and provided an even flow of water intended first for household use, then for livestock watering, then finally for garden—but not field—irrigation.

Figure 1-9. Self-regulating windmill, built ca. 1880, Clive, Iowa (photograph by the author).

13

Irrigation ditches encouraged volunteer plants, including trees, to grow along them, and provided cool places to sit or swim, but nineteenth-century Americans devoted little time to relaxing. The windmill remains a little-known factor in microclimatic manipulation, largely because contemporary agricultural periodicals analyzed the machines, not their uses.

If Americans embraced any one technique intended to retain moisture and provide coolness, they embraced the planting of vines, and particularly of grapevines. Wisteria and other ornamental vines frequently shaded front and back porches, dooryards, and summerhouses, tea houses, and gazebos. Grapevines proved more popular, simply because they produced an edible crop, not one fit only for wild birds. "The grapevine is an ideal covering for the pergola near the house, for it gives shade in summer and light in winter," noted Mary P. Cunningham in a 1922 *House Beautiful* article. "It has more stability and flatness as a top covering than the rampant bittersweet or actinidia, and is darker and better in color that the yellow-green wisteria". By 1922, of course, many suburbanites no longer cared to make their own wine or jelly, and the grapevine became an ornamental plant used chiefly for shading patios and other places intended for relaxation. The grape arbors that decorated farmhouses existed for a more "useful" purpose, of course, and the fact that they provided shady bowers for the family to enjoy in rare moments of leisure struck most agricultural experts as a pleasant but scarcely important consideration.

Why did Americans not make better use of moisture-retaining, air-cooling planting? The answer lies partly in the national preoccupation with agriculture. Farming required long hours of arduous work, and the isolation of farms prompted many families to devote Sundays to visiting. Everywhere in agricultural America, from the panhandle of Florida to the plains of Montana, summer meant a time of hard work, and coolness arrived, if it came at all, at sundown. A vine-shaded, west- or east-facing porch, its floor freshly "washed" with several buckets of water flung hastily over it, seemed as cool as it might be. To sit beneath the several fully-grown maples before the house, to enjoy a Fourth of July picnic by the creek lined with cottonwoods — such was the search for coolness in rural America.

In suburban America, particularly in the East, well- and municipal-water enabled suburbanites to maintain green lawns in all but the worst droughts, and soon electricity powered fans. Until the 1930s nonfarming Americans remained an essentially indoor people, at least at home; only gradually, as new sports like swimming changed living habits around the home, did suburban Americans begin a new epoch in microclimatic manipulation. That epoch emphasized planting for outdoor enjoyment, and prompted a reevaluation of time-tested climate controls and the discovery of new ones.

The Era of Abundant Energy

Cheap energy fueled the transformation of the American built environment, including the form of new houses and yards (Fitch, 1972). Air cooling, called "air conditioning" in advertisements and eventually in popular American speech, seemingly solved the problem of cooling interior space; no longer did ivy-shaded walls seem vital. Oil-fueled furnaces, particularly those forcing hot air throughout houses, encouraged householders to fell windbreaks and to install massive "picture windows" facing in any direction. Water struck most Americans as an inexhaustible resource, and enabled the making of ever greener lawns, even in the arid Southwest. Cheap energy saved energy. The husband, who formerly devoted hours to shifting coal, discovered how much human energy an oil-fire furnace conserved; the housewife using an electric clothes dryer discovered long hours freed from the chore of hanging laundry on outdoor clotheslines. Children no longer pumped well water or stacked cordwood or carried kindling from woodshed to kitchen. Americans discovered enormous amounts of "free time," something their grandparents had never had, and devoted themselves to working a second job, working outside the home, going to night school, and relaxing. And relaxation led to much microclimatic manipulation.

The transformation of American domestic space by the "recreational mood" that swept the nation in the years following 1945 is a little-studied, often condemned one, but in its time it struck most observers as entirely laudable. A nation tired of economic depression, world war, and political tension hoped to relax outdoors.

No series of articles better explains the transformation than those published by *House Beautiful* in 1949 and 1950. In October 1949, the magazine began its "Climate Control" series, "a continuing project to show you how to manipulate the design and materials of old or new houses to reduce the stresses and strains of climate on Man and Materials." The lengthy series of articles began partly as an attempt to familiarize readers with "scores of new techniques and materials" developed in the 20 years preceding the issue, and also to help readers design more comfortable houses. The last concept is immensely important for our own era as well. The editor, Elizabeth Gordon, intended the project as something much more than a how-to-save-money series emphasizing ways to conserve fuel, build more cheaply, and rehabilitate obsolescent houses. Emphasizing "better living and better health" and focusing on climate understanding and climate modification, the *House Beautiful* series remains one of the finest collaborations ever undertaken by climatologists, ecologists, architects, and landscape architects.

The exceptionally well-illustrated, well-researched series included a number of articles emphasizing microclimatic manipulation by careful siting and planting. Articles such as "Good Site Planning Can Double Your Outdoor Living," "How to Pick Your Private Climate," "How to Fix Your Private Climate," and "Here, Climate Control Began with a Tree" emphasize the overall nature of microclimate control. Wolfgang Langewiesche (1950) and other authors asserted that families should plan grounds for sunshine to extend the season of outdoor living, should erect fences to screen views and modify air circulation, and should make use of every sort of plant to improve their "private" climates. "You can doctor your climate. (You can also spoil it.) Country people have always known that," wrote Langewiesche (1949) in an article about improving microclimates. "They have always used windbreaks, shade trees, hedges, garden walls, L-shaped houses, houses built around a court." His comments are the beginning of the "wise countryman" theme, which asserts that agricultural people know the most about climate modification. "But we city people have forgotten such things," he continued in a description of a sun-pocket. He stressed the usefulness of converting rural knowledge into suburban practice, giving as examples the wonders worked by white-painted garages and fences on dark rooms needing reflected light, the way a gate at the bottom of a walled garden releases cold air down hill, and the different temperature-keeping qualities of different colored paving. One *House Beautiful* 1949 "Pace-Setter House," a sort of ideal house designed for Orange, N.J., developed most of the general themes outlined in the first part of the series. A scarcely more energy-efficient, well-planted house and site cannot be found in design periodicals today, if one excludes solar-heating attachments.

Other articles in the series detailed specific modifications. "How to Control the Sun," "Good Lawns Keep You Cool," "Vines: Climate Control Device for Summer Coolness," "How to Manipulate Sun and Shade" all focus on the need for well-designed spaces for outdoor recreation. "Climate Control is no *substitute* for good architecture and good engineering, but it is the most significant *supplement* to them made during the Twentieth Century," announced James Marston Fitch in a 1949 article entitled "How You Can Use *House Beautiful's* Climate Control Project." Fitch lamented the spread of Cape Cod houses "all over the U.S.A." "This is a good climate-control design for the long winters and short cool summers of New England," he noted. "But it has no business in Alabama or Kansas." So much speculator-built housing struck experts as poorly designed and sited that *House Beautiful* hoped to improve buyers' ability to recognize good and bad sites and to improve the bad. Written by experts but addressed to laymen, often to laymen newly arrived in suburbs from cities, the articles remain a wonderfully useful tool.

A third type of article in the series focused on climate problems in particular parts of the country. Buford L. Pickens' "How to Live at Peace with the Gulf Coast Climate" (1950), exemplifies this type. Well-illustrated with climate maps, carefully researched, and accompanied by a companion article detailing a model home, the article represents an attempt to end standardized house-building by showing prospective buyers wonderfully more pleasant houses available at similar costs. The integration of architecture and landscape architecture at every level, from site selection to patio design, produced "model regional houses" of grace and — perhaps more important — of usefulness to a generation anxious to live outdoors.

Interpreting the *House Beautiful* series and its model homes by today's standards proves difficult, but it is clear that the message so well defined and illustrated went largely unheeded. Overall, typical house and garden design varied little from an increasingly energy-dependent path. Suburbanites in the 1950s and 1960s indeed enjoyed cheap electricity, oil, gas, and gasoline prices, along with plentiful water supplies, and they certainy wasted them, keeping houses exceptionally warm in winter, for example. They also enjoyed energy-saving inventions of a type other than that analyzed by *House Beautiful* — a type little studied today, involving new social inventions, which continue to haunt Americans.

Until the 1940s, for example, upper-class people prized pale skin; farmers worked in the fields, and became deeply tanned, but the American "leisure class" carried parasols, wore straw hats, and showed its freedom from manual, outdoor work by its paleness. Industrialism changed the social rules; factory workers laboring indoors 10 or more hours each day exhibited a genuine palor, and gradually the upper class began to prefer a suntan, even to the point of going south for wintertime vacations. In the years between 1900 and 1950, consequently, shady places, particularly the vine-covered gazebo, lost much of their prestige. Space for sunbathing became vastly more important, and gradually outdoor coolness came to mean either a leafy tree under which a child might read or fix his bicycle, or some sort of swimming pool. Perhaps the most common replacement of the "arbor" or "tea-house," the "sun deck" came to symbolize the new social attitudes. The whole social adaptation to what *House Beautiful* called "outdoor living" remains uninvestigated but important, for it emphasized sunlight, warmth, and leisure, things seemingly lacking in the "energy-short" 1980s.

The Future

Americans have indeed manipulated their microclimates, but always with differences from one generation to another. Essentially, the guiding rule seems to have been this: manipulate for one or two dominant reasons. The Cape Codder and the High Plains settler manipulated to save fuel; the established High Plains farmer manipulated to lengthen his growing season. A single manipulation undertaken for one reason had expected secondary effects — the High Plains farmer lengthened his growing season and realized some saving in fuel for heating his house. In the 1980s and 1990s, two needs will dominate microclimatic manipulation by site modification.

First, Americans will strive to conserve "purchased" mechanical energy, particularly energy used for heating. Site design that lowers winter fuel bills — and perhaps lengthens gardening time — will prove particularly important (Stilgoe, 1982b). Windbreaks especially will return in popularity, and perhaps ivy, grapevines, and other plant screening in the humid South. Proper placement of shade trees will accompany a growing increase in use of solar energy features in new homes.

Second, Americans will continue to desire outdoor living. Landscape architects must recognize that the creation of *enjoyable* outdoor places, places to be used as long and as much as possible each year, will attract clients in every part of the nation. So many "energy-efficient" houses are simply unimaginative — but superbly engineered — overinsulated boxes surrounded by uninspired, ugly, *useless* grounds. Their inhabitants save on fuel bills, but often lament their lack of "old-fashioned" luxuries like patios, sun decks, and shady places. The continuing desire for healthful, gracious outdoor spaces makes the 1949-50 *House Beautiful* point of view as historically important as anything written by Estienne, Dwight, or Thoreau. Climatically effective grounds can be beautiful and useful, even as they conserve water, deflect fuel-wasting winds, and stop drifting snow.

The past holds no secret microclimatic manipulation keys. Americans have manipulated climate for important reasons, and they have always understood the reasons before beginning replanting and other tasks. New materials like tar paper and new machines like electric air coolers have altered national goals, but the connection between reason and design change has always been misunderstood. In the decades ahead, fuel and water conservation will be of equal value with pleasant, useful outdoor recreational spaces.

The energy crisis has only begun. Predictions of severe gasoline shortages and drastic price increases suggest to any thoughtful individual that the decades ahead will witness a new appreciation of stay-at-home living. It will be too expensive to drive far, too expensive to go to restaurants, movie theaters, or covered shopping malls to escape the heat or cold. The efficient design of homes and surrounding grounds will acquire greater and greater significance as energy prices rise (Stilgoe, 1982b). Now is the time to learn from the past, and plan for the energy-short future.

CHAPTER TWO
Benefits and Costs of Energy-Conserving Site Design

E. GREGORY McPHERSON
Utah State University
Logan, Utah

DURING the past decade, meteorologists, engineers, urban foresters, architects, and landscape architects have conducted numerous research projects in an effort to quantify the energy-conserving potential of various site-design strategies. Invariably, clients are concerned with payback periods and benefit-cost analyses as critical input in the investment decision process. Increasingly they demand that designers justify their products economically as well as aesthetically and functionally. If energy-conserving designs are going to be accepted and implemented, designers must be able to document the expected costs and potential benefits of the conservation strategies inherent in their plans.

This chapter describes benefits and costs that have been calculated for projects designed on a variety of scales. An examination of the relationships between energy supply and consumption follows to provide a basis for understanding why and how energy-conserving site design can have a beneficial effect upon our nation's energy future.

Energy Supply

Energy supply generally equals but frequently exceeds energy consumed because of generation and transmission losses. In 1983 total energy supply was 74.2 quadrillion Btu (74.2 Quads), and 70.5 Quads were consumed. Nearly four Quads of energy were exported (DOE/EIA-0383, 1984). Net energy imported from outside the U.S. constituted 12% of the total energy consumed in 1983. The Energy Information Administration (EIA) projects that net oil imports will increase with continued growth in the U.S.

economy. Stobaugh and Yergin (1979) have maintained that "it would be very much in the nation's interest to reverse the trend toward more oil imports. But contrary to popular impression, domestic oil production is unlikely to be the way to do it. Geology denies that possibility" (p. 16).

In 1983, the United States derived only about 4% of its energy supplies from renewable resources (hydroelectric power, wood, solar). Nonrenewable resources — principally oil, natural gas, coal, and uranium — supplied the remaining 96% of U.S. energy consumption (DOE/EIA-0383, 1984). The reserves of these nonrenewable resources are sufficient to supply consumption at current rates for only a relatively few years. In late 1980, known domestic oil reserves were equal to only 10 years of production at current rates (DOE/EIA-173, 1982). New discoveries will be made, but resources of oil, natural gas, coal, and uranium are finite. Table 2-1 (see next page) shows the estimates of the number of years left before the world's recoverable energy reserves will be depleted.

The figures in Table 2-1 vividly demonstrate that the energy crisis is no myth. Projections of fossil fuel reserves vary widely and are a subject of great debate. However, all authorities concur that the costs of extracting and producing energy will increase. Hayes (1977) stated:

> We are not running out of energy. However, we are running out of cheap oil and gas. We are running out of money to pay for doubling and redoubling an already vast energy supply system. We are running out of political willingness to ac-

Table 2-1. World Recoverable Energy Reserves

Estimate of life (years) based on 1974 consumption (72.8 quadrillion BTU)	Coal	Oil	Natural Gas	Others[a]	Total
Highest estimate	1600	123	238	98	586
Average estimate	677	65	87	35	250
Lowest estimate	43	28	24	30	32
Estimate of life (years) based on a 5% growth in rate of usage					
Highest estimate	88	40	53	34	65
Average estimate	72	26	32	21	52
Lowest estimate	25	18	15	19	20

aOthers include uranium, shale, tarsand and other minor fossil-fuel resources. From: (O'Callaghan, 1978).

cept the social costs of continued rapid energy expansion. We are running out of the environmental capacity needed to handle the waste generated in energy production. And we are running out of time to adjust to these new realities. (p. 207)

By modifying the quantity and rate of energy consumption, we can buy the time needed to reduce dependence upon a limited supply of nonrenewable resources. The next section examines energy-consumption patterns and specifically notes where and how landscape architects can significantly affect energy consumption.

Energy Consumption Trends

Figure 2-1 illustrates the historical and future net energy demands projected by the EIA. Note that a dramatic change from trends in energy consumption occurred between 1973 and 1975, and after 1979. During the 1950s and 1960s, oil and natural gas were abundant and preferred to other fuels because they were clean, convenient, and economical. However, as the consumption of oil and natural gas continued to

grow, domestic production began to level off and decline. The nation's dependence on imported energy became vividly apparent in 1973 when OPEC embargoed oil shipments to the United States. As a result of the embargo, oil consumption and imports declined during the next two years and Americans realized their vulnerability to foreign producers. Although consumption began to grow rapidly in 1976, that growth ceased in 1979, when oil prices doubled.

The EIA projects that total energy consumption will increase at an average rate of 1.1% per year, due in part to the projected stability of world oil prices. "That growth is expected to continue beyond 1985 despite increasing world oil prices because of projected increases in industrial production, personal income, and population, and diminished opportunities for energy conservation" (DOE/EIA-0173, 1982, pp. 24-25).

Energy Consumption by Sectors

Energy consumption is often analyzed by examining how much energy various sectors of the economy use. Energy-consumption sectors include industrial, transportation, commercial, and residential demands. Once designers and planners know what amounts of energy are consumed in each sector, they can then more accurately predict where their efforts can have the greatest impact on reducing energy use.

Industrial Demands

The industrial sector consists of agriculture, construction, mining, and manufacturing. Historically, this sector has been the largest end-use consumer of energy in the economy, accounting for about 40% of the energy consumed in the United States.

The EIA projects that the industrial sector's relative share of energy consumption will increase because of relatively larger conservation potentials in the residential, commercial, and transportation sectors.

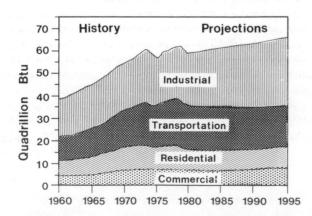

Figure 2-1. Energy consumption by industrial, transportation, residential, and commercial sectors: history and projections. From: (DOE/EIA-0173, 1982)

Nevertheless, a serious commitment to conservation through the use of such measures as recycling of materials and heat (cogeneration), reclaiming of scrap iron, and returning to more labor-intensive production could reduce industrial energy consumption by up to 10%. Landscape architects could influence energy use for construction through application of energy-conserving site design principles.

Transportation Demands

The transportation sector uses energy to transport people and commodities via five major modes of travel: highway, rail, air, marine, and pipeline. In 1983, the transportation sector consumed 35% of all energy and more than half of the petroleum (DOE/EIA-0383, 1984). Petroleum meets 97% of this sector's energy requirements. Conservation in energy used for transportation can thus have a significant effect on aggregate U.S. oil requirements.

However, the EIA projects that energy consumption in the transportation sector will decline in the future, reversing the trend that began in 1965 when energy use in transportation began growing faster than energy use in other sectors. Two factors are primarily responsible for the projected decline: increased automobile fuel efficiency, a direct result of increased gasoline costs; and a projected decrease in automobile travel. Vehicle miles traveled per capita and personal vehicle registrations are projected to increase at a slower rate than occurred during the past 17 years. The anticipated net effect of these trends is about 30% lower gasoline consumption in 1995 than in recent years (DOE/EIA-173,1982).

One of our most promising opportunities to reduce transportation energy consumption and conserve other resources lies in the use of mass transit systems in highly populated metropolitan areas. Wasiutynaski (1982) has reported that subways, buses, and streetcars are two to three times more energy efficient than automobiles. They are also more durable. While an automobile typically wears out in about 100,000 miles, the service life of a railcar is often more than a million miles. Perhaps the most important benefit of mass transportation is that it encourages land-use patterns that reduce overall energy use. Cities without mass transit exhibit uncontrolled urban sprawl, while those with transit systems have denser concentrations of development along the transportation corridors. High-density development not only reduces automobile use but also results in less energy consumed for space heating and cooling. Wasiutynaski has pointed out that "in New York City, which grew up around its transit system, per-capita consumption

of energy for all purposes (including bright lights, heating, and air-conditioning as well as transportation) averages 180 million Btu's annually; roughly half of the U.S. national average of 346 million Btu's per capita (1979 figures)" (p. 30).

Site planners can influence transportation energy use at several different project scales. At the neighborhood scale, they can design transportation systems that discourage automobile use and encourage pedestrian traffic, for example, by creating foot paths and bicycle ways separated from streets and linking residences with on-site schools, shops, workplaces, and mass transit/pedestrian routes that service off-site destinations. Clustering housing and locating residences near workplaces and other major destinations also reduces automobile use and gasoline consumption. During site selection, the site planner should consider how the proximity of the proposed site to major destinations will affect transportation energy use. A solar subdivision located 30 miles from workplaces, schools, and shopping facilities may cost far more in terms of transportation energy than it saves through conservation in the residential sector. Finally, planners involved in regional and transportation planning can promote various energy-saving options. Car pooling, park-and-ride, and rapid, light-rail systems have proven feasible and will continue to be so as petroleum prices increase.

Commercial Demands

The commercial sector consumed slightly over 10% of total energy consumption in 1983 (DOE/EIA-0383, 1984). A small upward trend in energy use for this sector is projected as commercial floorspace increases due to the projected growth in population and general expansion of the economy. This relatively small increase in energy consumption is attributed to the great opportunity for improved efficiency in the commercial sector. Energy use per square feet is forecast to decrease.

Opportunities to improve the thermal integrity of commercial buildings are numerous. In recent years only 27% of existing buildings have added insulation, 36% have added weatherstripping, and only 23% have added shading (DOE/EIA-0173, 1982). In addition, mandated conservation programs and more efficient end-use equipment will result in greater energy savings.

Natural gas, which is more economical, convenient, and available than oil, is the predominant fuel used in the commercial sector. The commercial sector uses more electricity than the residential sector because commercial activity generates more demands for air conditioning, lighting, and electromechanical uses.

Commercial electricity consumption is projected to increase substantially, with electricity supplying 35% of the commercial energy needs in 1995, compared to 27% in 1979. This is because air conditioning, lighting, and other end uses requiring electricity are expected to increase as the opportunities for equipment efficiency or structural efficiency improvements are reduced with time. Also, relatively small increases are projected in electricity prices as utilities switch from oil- to coal-powered generation. However, because of the heavy demand for space heating, natural gas is expected to remain the dominant fuel in the commercial sector, while oil will supply a dwindling percentage of energy for space heating.

Designers can have a significant impact on commercial sector energy use. Vegetation can provide exterior shading to reduce the large demand for electricity required to provide air conditioning. This demand can be further lessened through sensitive siting and architectural design to promote natural daylighting, which reduces internal heat loads generated by

lighting, as well as electricity consumed directly by the lighting systems. Optimum location and orientation of commercial structures can cut cooling and heating costs. Commercial areas also require extensive parking areas. Widespread use of smaller cars now makes it feasible to reduce the size of parking lots by as much as 25%, thus reducing large amounts of energy embodied in asphalt and concrete. These and other site design options can also be applied effectively to conserve energy in the residential sector.

Residential Demands

The residential sector consumes 17% of the energy in the United States. Table 2-2 presents results from the *Residential Energy Consumption Survey* (DOE/EIA-0262, 1981) for April 1979 through March 1980. During this period, winter and summer weather was slightly cooler than long-term normals for the country as a whole (95 more heating degree days and 174 fewer cooling degree days). Although more energy than normal was used for space heating, less was required for space cooling; so total energy consumption approached that of a normal year.

Table 2-2. Total Residential Energy Consumption and Expenditures April 1979 through March 1980

Household characteristics	Total households (millions)	Av. amount consumed per household (MMBtu)	Av. expended per household ($)
Total households	77.5	126	815
Type of structure			
Single family detached	50.1	138	896
Single family attached	3.3	135	795
2-4 unit building	9.3	129	764
5+ unit building	10.6	77	548
Mobile home	4.1	86	649
Other	0.1	125	894
Household members			
One	15.4	89	538
Two	26.8	116	764
Three	13.2	135	873
Four	11.9	153	1003
Five or more	10.2	163	1073
Census region			
Northeast	17.2	145	1033
North Central	20.7	168	924
South	24.9	92	744
West	14.7	100	527
Year house built			
1939 or earlier	25.5	148	885
1940 to 1949	6.9	123	773
1950 to 1959	14.7	127	817
1960 to 1964	7.5	122	827
1965 to 1969	7.8	101	712
1970 to 1974	8.1	108	781
1975 to 1979	7.1	98	742

From: (DOE/EIA-0262, 1981)

As Table 2-2 shows, the average amount of energy consumed per household in 1979-80 was 126 million Btu (MMBtu), which amounts to an average expenditure of $815 per year. Single-family detached homes, which comprise 65% of the housing stock, consume 71% of the total amount of energy used by the residential sector, or 12% of total U.S. energy consumption. Less energy per household is consumed in attached buildings than in detached structures, and energy consumption per unit decreases as the number of units in the building increases. Residential energy consumption per household increases as the number of household members increase and generally is greater in older structures than in new homes. Households located in northern climates, where heating requirements far exceed cooling needs, expend larger sums for energy than those situated in the less extreme climates of the South and West.

Figure 2-2 shows the end-use energy consumption for a typical individual home. Percentages will vary depending upon such things as structural type, primary fuel type, geographic location, etc. Energy consumed for space conditioning (both heating and cooling) represents approximately two-thirds of the total energy consumed in the typical home and roughly 11% of total U.S. energy consumption.

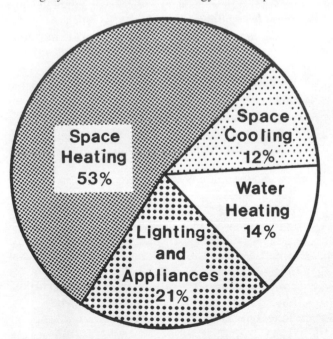

Figure 2-2. End-use energy consumption for a typical U.S. residence. From: (Carroll, Hathans, Palmedo, & Stern, 1976)

Space heating, accounting for about 53% of all energy consumed by households, is an important aspect of residential energy use. Although natural gas

is the primary fuel used for space heating today, this has not always been the case. Figure 2-3 illustrates the percentage of households using different types of fuels for space heating. Over one-third of the existing housing stock was built prior to 1940, when few or no standards for insulation existed. Many homes were heated with coal or wood. Over the past 30 years, old homes have been converted to, and new homes have been built with, oil, gas, and electric heating systems. This shift in residential fuel types is due to "changes in the types and sizes of residential structure, the introduction of many new electricity-consuming appliances, the extension of natural gas service to a greater number of residences, and the massive movement of population from metropolitan and rural areas to the suburbs. The combined effect, together with the availability of inexpensive supplies of natural gas and oil, has led to a dramatic change in the mix of residential fuels" (DOE/EIA-0173, 1982, p. 32).

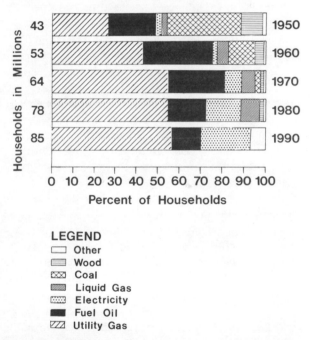

Figure 2-3. Percentages of households using different types of energy for heating purposes: history and projections. From: (DOE/EIA-1973, 1982)

Energy costs play a major role in the consumer's choice of fuel for household space heating. Historically, residential electricity has been most expensive, while natural gas has been least expensive per Btu. However, between 1980 and 1982, the residential prices of both electricity and natural gas rose sharply at nearly double the rate of inflation (12.3%). Residential electricity prices increased about 45% from 4.5 cents per kilowatt hour (kwh) in 1980 to 6.5 cents/kwh in 1982. Increased oil prices were primarily responsible. Residential natural gas prices increased about 43%, from $3.50 to $5.00 per 1000 ft³. Natural gas deregulation policies are expected to sustain this trend (DOE/EIA-0202, 1982). EIA projects that between 1983 and 1995 residential prices for fuel oil, natural gas, and electricity will increase at average annual rates of 3.7%, 5.2%, and 0.5%, respectively (DOE/EIA-0383, 1984). Natural gas, electricity, and other energies such as solar will be used to heat a larger percentage of homes by 1990, while the use of fuel oil, liquid gas, and coal will diminish.

Space heating choices are also related to geographical factors and population distribution in rural and metropolitan areas. Natural gas is less readily available and, along with electricity, more expensive in the Northeast than in other regions of the country. Natural gas and electricity are the predominant heating fuels in metropolitan areas, whereas fuel oil, liquid gas, and wood are used more frequently in rural areas (DOE/EIA-0173, 1982).

Energy in this sector is projected to be used less for heating and more for nonheating purposes. Construction of more homes in warmer climates, increasing multifamily housing which requires less heating per unit, and increasing prices for fuel oil and natural gas account for this trend. Because electricity provides most nonheating services, consumption is projected to increase at an average rate of about 2.4% from 1983 to 1995, while total residential energy consumption will remain stable.

Water heating accounts for about 14% of all energy consumed by households (Figure 2-2). The type of space-heating fuel often determines the choice of fuel for water heating — builders or consumers who choose gas or electric space-heating systems usually favor gas or electric water-heating systems as well.

Space cooling consumes an average of 12% of the total energy used in a home. This amount can vary widely depending upon geographic location and the type of mechanical cooling system used. The three most common mechanical cooling systems are central air conditioning, room air conditioners, and evaporative coolers. Electricity is the primary fuel used to provide energy for space cooling. Central air-conditioning systems are notoriously consumptive, especially when compared with evaporative coolers. Evaporative coolers use from three to five times less energy (depending upon type and coefficient of performance) than central cooling systems. The efficiency of evaporative coolers declines rapidly, however, when relative humidity is over 30%, a factor that limits their usefulness to semiarid and arid regions. The relatively high cost of electricity as compared to natural gas and the large quantities of electricity used to operate central air-conditioning systems explains why space-cooling costs can exceed space-heating costs in climates with more heating degree days than cooling degree days. For example, in Utah the average homeowner with a central air-conditioning system in 1980 spent $306.00 for space cooling (4838 kwh) and $396.00 for space heating. However, Salt Lake City has on the average 5983 heating degree days and only 927 cooling degree days (McPherson, 1981).

Appliances and lighting consume about 21% of the energy used in a typical residence. The refrigerator/freezer, clothes dryer, and range with oven are the most consumptive home appliances.

The EIA projects that household energy use will decrease from 120 million Btu per household in 1980 to 89 million Btu in 1990 — a decline of 26% (DOE/EIA-0173, 1982). Total residential energy consumption is expected to remain relatively stable as the increased demand for energy by new households is offset by a decreasing amount of energy used annually per household. Central to this thesis is the assumption that the prices of all heating fuels will continue to increase through 1995 (with electricity increasing at the slowest rate). Rising energy prices will stimulate consumers to continue replacing less efficient space-conditioning systems and appliances with more efficient units and to improve the thermal performance of both old and new homes.

Working together, architects and landscape architects can promote increased energy efficiency in new residential construction. Just as architects are exploring new design forms more responsive to climate and inhabitants than hermetic buildings with massive plants for manufacturing the air and light, so landscape architects are becoming more adept in their use of vegetation, earthforms, and other design elements to conserve energy. If a new energy-efficient structure is to function well, the landscape in which it rests must be designed to enhance rather than detract from its thermal performance. For example, by providing solar access to a solar hot-water collector system in the summer while at the same time shading other portions of the structure, auxiliary energy used for both water heating and space cooling can be minimized.

This analysis of energy-consumption patterns suggests that energy-conscious site planners can achieve the greatest impact by directing their efforts at reducing energy used primarily for space conditioning of residential and commercial buildings. Thirty-six percent of U.S. energy consumption is used to heat, air-condition, light, and provide hot water for homes, commercial buildings, and factories (Stobaugh & Yergin, 1979). Some general design options, which if used properly can contribute to reductions in energy used for space conditioning include site selection, structural orientation, building form, ensuring solar access, and the use of vegetation, landforms, water bodies, structures, and other landscape elements for microclimatic improvement. Regional planners can achieve substantial reductions in energy used for transportation through appropriate land-use planning. However, this book focuses on savings obtainable at the neighborhood scale, where smaller reductions in transportation energy use are likely to result from implementation of most energy-conserving site design options.

Projections indicate that the price of fuels will continue to escalate as energy consumption increases and energy supplies become more scarce and costlier to recover. Energy-conserving site design offers businesses, industries, and especially homeowners a variety of opportunities to reduce energy consumption and cut energy costs.

Potential for Energy Conservation

Energy conservation is best conceptualized as a form of energy production — an alternative energy source. A conservation measure can be compared to other energy sources in terms of payback, ease of recovery, and environmental effects. As Hayes (1977) has pointed out,

> In both industrialized and rural societies, a dollar invested in energy conservation can make more net energy available than a dollar invested in developing new energy sources. Eric Hirst calculates, for example, that investments in improving air conditioner efficiency can save ten times as much electricity as similar investments in new power plants can produce. Arjun Makhaijani has shown how a $10 investment in improved stove efficiency can cut an Indian family's wood consumption in half — saving $10 to $25 per year. Neither example entails a loss of benefit or comfort. (p. 85)

Planners and designers might then ask which is cheaper and safer — a barrel of foreign oil with the risk of a dramatic price increase or a barrel of oil saved by windbreaks and shade trees?

The potential impact conservation could have upon energy consumption is great. Yergin (1979) has stated that "if the United States were to make a serious commitment to conservation, it might well consume 30 to 40 percent less energy that it now does, and still enjoy the same or even higher standard of living" (p. 136). Ross and Williams (1977) have used a physical model-

ing approach to substitute energy-conservation techniques for conventional technologies. Their results indicate that the same U.S. living standard in 1973 could theoretically have been delivered with 40% less energy. The fact that Sweden and West Germany, with about the same GNP per capita as the U.S., use about half as much fuel per capita further confirms the assumption that much less energy than is now being consumed is actually required to meet our needs (Hayes, 1977). Energy conservation requires the curtailment of energy waste, not the curtailment of vital services.

Although energy conservation is not a long-term answer to the energy problem, it does offer a number of short-term solutions. A comprehensive energy-conservation program will allow the world's finite supply of fossil fuels to be stretched. A portion of the fossil-fuel base can be reserved for home-energy uses: drugs, lubricants, and other materials. Energy consumption can immediately be reduced with a minimal impact on the stability of our social, political, and economic systems. Thus, energy conservation can permit the world to make the transition into a new era without tumultuous upheavals. An enlightened energy-conservation program can bolster employment levels and the economy in general by reducing our dependence on uncertain oil imports and the concomitant draining of energy dollars from our economy. Finally, energy conservation can help to minimize the environmental degradation associated with such current energy-conversion technologies as nuclear and coal-fired generation plants, off-shore oil drilling, and strip mining.

> Conservation may well be the cheapest, safest, most productive energy alternative readily available in large amounts. By comparison, conservation is a quality energy source. It does not threaten to undermine the international monetary system, nor does it emit carbon dioxide into the atmosphere, nor does it generate problems comparable to nuclear waste. And contrary to the conventional wisdom, conservation can stimulate innovation, employment and economic growth. (Stobaugh and Yergin, 1979, p. 137)

Three D.O.E. Case Studies of Energy Conservation in Community Development

In 1978, the Department of Energy Community Systems Program awarded five grants to local developers and their design and engineering support personnel as part of the Site and Neighborhood Design program. The goal was to prepare and compare energy-conservation plans and design schemes with conventional design schemes. The objectives of the case studies were to:

1. Obtain, through participation in the actual development planning process, a better understanding of how conservation of energy can be factored into the series of trade-offs and decisions in the project planning and design process.
2. Demonstrate how variations in design options, including energy system selection and site planning can meet functional needs while simultaneously minimizing or reducing energy consumption.
3. Evaluate through actual case studies how design/development decisions affect energy demand, how decisions might be modified to achieve greater energy efficiencies, and how the feasibilities of the various options are assessed in specific circumstances.

Each case study was a real project involving new multibuilding development at scales ranging from 50 to 500 acres. The sites were in different climatic regions, used different marketing programs, and were designed and evaluated in a variety of ways. Because of these major differences, it is impossible to make direct quantitative comparisons between the case studies. The unifying feature of the case studies is the program plan. In each case study, a five-step program plan was used as a guide for rational and efficient decision-making:

1. Preliminary identification of the potential energy conservation options at the site and neighborhood design scale.
2. Categorization and organization of the options.
3. Evaluation of the potential options for application on a specific site.
4. Selection of the site or case specific options appropriate to the specific location.
5. Application or incorporation of the appropriate options into an energy-conserving plan.

The following summarizes the design principles employed and energy savings projected to result from three of the five case studies. Copies of the case studies or the summary report, *Site and Neighborhood Design for Energy Conservation: Five Case Studies* (Center for Landscape Architectural Education and Research, 1981), from which much of this text is excerpted, can be obtained from the National Technical Information Service. Chapter Twelve, "Community Design Case Study: Oak Hills" provides a more detailed discussion of methods and results from a similar case study approach.

Radisson, N.Y.

Radisson, located 12 miles northeast of Syracuse, is a 2,850-acre new community being developed by the New York State Urban Development Corporation. Approximately 46% of the new community, including more than 500 dwelling units, had been developed before the study began. The technical team prepared plans for a Town Center site and a 92-acre residential site. For this chapter only the development plans for the residential site are examined.

Two energy-conserving plans were developed based on the following criteria:

1. Selection of building sites should be based on climatological data whenever possible.
2. Structures should be sited and grouped for maximum winter wind protection and solar orientation to reduce space-heating loads.
3. Roads and utilities should be designed to reduce embodied energy costs and financial costs for site development. (Embodied energy is energy expended in the manufacturing and, in some cases, installation of materials.)

Energy Plan 1 increased site density over the Conventional Plan by 28% primarily through the use of townhouse and cluster housing along a system of private drives and auto courts (Figure 2-4, see next page). Energy Plan 2 was a response to the developers' concern over the marketability of an extensive cluster-housing plan in an untested market area. In this plan, the number of housing clusters was limited and only single-family detached housing were clustered. Table 2-3 (see next page) presents the development characteristics of the three plans.

The Conventional and the two Energy Plans for the residential site were compared according to embodied energy differences, variation in development costs, and operational energy savings. Embodied energy is the sum total of energy expended in obtaining raw materials, manufacturing materials, and construction activity. Site development costs (including embodied energy costs) describe dollar amounts paid for site preparation. Both these costs may or may not include costs associated with construction of the buildings. Operational energy costs may be expressed in dollar amounts or Btu. These are costs associated with operation and maintenance after installation and construction are completed.

Estimates of embodied-energy savings for site development were calculated based upon measured differences of infrastructure requirements between the plans. Table 2-4 shows that both energy plans consume about the same amount of embodied energy as the Conventional Plan. However, the more densely

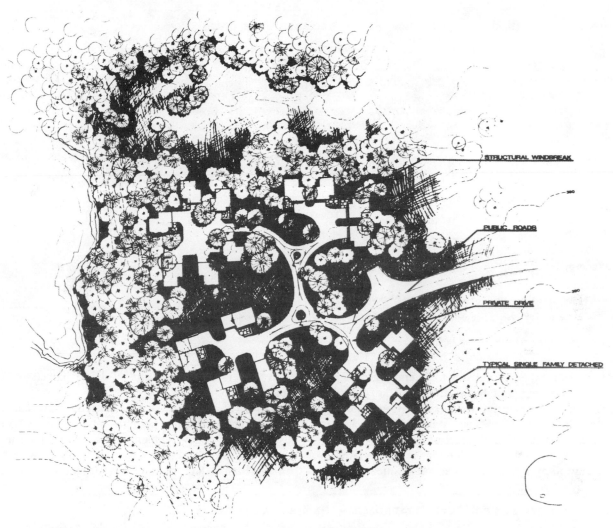

STRUCTURAL WINDBREAK

PUBLIC ROADS

PRIVATE DRIVE

TYPICAL SINGLE FAMILY DETACHED

Figure 2-4. Single-family detached cluster from the Radisson Energy Plan #1. From: (Reimann Buechner Partnership, 1979)

Table 2-3. Development Characteristics — Radisson Case Study

	Conventional plan	Energy plan #1	Energy plan #2
Total number of dwelling units	343	401(+17%)	362 (+6%)
Gross site density (units/acre)	2.6	3.3(+28%)	2.8 (+8%)
Unit distribution:			
Multifamily	142	142( )	142 ( )
Single family detached	135		116(+10%)
Single family cluster	– – –	132(-2%)	32
Town house	66	127(+92%)	72 (+9%)
Total no. of protected units	64	193(+201%)	168 (+162%)
Public and private roadways (linear ft)	10,950	11,830(+8%)	10,900 ( )

From: (Reimann Buechner Partnership, 1979)

Table 2-4. Embodied Energy Comparison — Radisson Case Study

	Conventional plan 201 DU	Energy plan 1 259 DU	Energy plan 2 220 DU	
Roads/driveways	7,975.60 40/DU	7,550.81 29/DU	7,885.60 36/DU	
Water	4,277.50 22.	3,700.00 14.	4,217.70 19.	
San. sewers	3,435.00 17.	3,500.00 14.	3,319.30 15.	
Drainage:				
Piping	3,688.30 18.	4,700.00 18.	3,053.60 14.	
Ditching[a]	28.00 .14	28.00 .11	28.00 .13	
Walkways	600.00 3.	600.00 2.	600.00 3.	
Contingencies	3,000.00 15.	3,011.00 12.	2,865.00 13.	
Total energy	23,004.00 114.	23,090.00 89.	21,970.00 100.	Total per unit

Note: All quantities shown are given in millions of Btu (MMBtu).

[a]Difference in cost between piping and ditching operations is due to increased pipe size for energy plans required because of increased density.

From: (Reimann Beuchner Partnership, 1979)

---

developed energy plans consume less embodied energy on a per dwelling unit basis. Energy Plan #1 saved 25.29 million Btu per unit (22%). This is equivalent to 4.4 barrels of oil or an energy savings of $132 per dwelling unit assuming a barrel of oil costs $30 (1985 projected value).[1] When this savings is extrapolated to all 401 dwelling units, the conservation measures are equivalent to the production of 1,765 barrels of oil worth $52,950.

Embodied-energy savings translate into reduced development costs on a per unit basis as Table 2-5 illustrates. Total development costs per dwelling unit are 18% lower for Energy Plan 1 and 9% lower for Energy Plan 2 than for the Conventional Plan. These

Table 2-5. Development Cost Comparison — Radisson Case Study

	Conventional plan 201 DU	Energy plan 1 259 DU	Energy plan 2 220 DU	
Roads/driveways	$593,000 $ 2,950	$530,000 $ 2,046	$577,000 $ 2,622	
Water	$238,000 $ 1,184	$236,000 $ 911	$231,000 $$ 1,050	
San. sewers	$425,000 $ 2,114	$462,000 $ 1,784	$420,000 $ 1,909	
Drainage:				
Piping	$160,000 $ 796	$291,000 $ 1,124	$177,000 $ 804	
Ditching[a]	$ 52,000 $ 258	$ 52,000 $ 258	$ 52,000 $ 258	
Walkways	$225,000 $ 1,119	$225,000 $ 1,119	$225,000 $ 1,119	
Contingencies	$253,950 $ 1,263	$269,000 $ 1,038	$252,300 $ 1,146	
Totals	$1,946,950 9,686	$2,065,000 7,972	$1,934,300 8,793	Total per DU

[a]Difference in cost between piping and ditching operations is due to increased pipe size for energy plans required because of increased density.

From: (Reimann Buechner Partnership, 1979)

[1]There are 5.82 million Btu's in a barrel of crude oil.

reductions can be attributed to design modifications that reduce the costs of installing roads, driveways, water lines, and sanitary sewers. Savings associated with site development costs are absorbed directly by the developer and indirectly by the subsequent homeowner due to lower purchase prices. However, the homeowner may pay quality of life costs. For example, reductions in road costs may be a result of reduced road length, which implies higher densities and perhaps less privacy; or narrow roads, which may slow traffic or impede emergency vehicle access. While quality of life costs are difficult to quantify, they cannot be ignored.

Estimates of operational energy savings were computed based on a 25% average reduction for heating loads for homes protected from prevailing winter winds. A comparative analysis of meter readings for existing single family dwellings in Radisson indicated that this was the average energy savings for protected structures. Heating loads and cost savings for each building type were projected against the total number of protected dwelling units to obtain an estimate of load and cost savings. Figure 2-5 shows a typical buffering technique recommended for structures in Radisson. Only 32% of the dwelling units in the Conventional Plan were protected, whereas 75% and 80% of those in Energy Plans 1 and 2, respectively, were protected.

The researchers found that,

> Modeling of reduced heating load due to wind protection identified potential annual savings of between 6% to 9% on both energy plans for single family detached units and up to 13% for town house units. This reduction represents a savings in annual operating costs of $27 annually for single family detached units and $44 annually for town house units. (Reimann Buechner Partnership, 1979, p. 2)

The Radisson case study results indicate that a 28% increase in development density can save approximately 20% on front-end embodied-energy and development costs. Careful siting and planning to reduce air infiltration can be expected to reduce operational energy consumption for space heating by approximately 10% in cold climate zones.

Burke Center, Va.

Burke Center is a 1,218-acre new community located in Fairfax County within commuting distance of Washington, D.C. Of the total acreage, six undeveloped parcels, which totaled 218 acres, were selected for the case study. The Town Center site contained 124 acres in the middle of the project and had

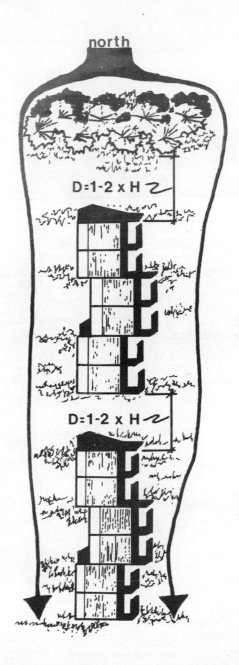

Figure 2-5. Buffering of townhouse units by a single row of evergreens and siting of a cluster 1½ to 2 times the height of the protected cluster upwind. Adapted from: (Reimann Buechner Partnership, 1979)

access off primary internal collector roads. The development program included retail, office, and commercial recreation space together with garden and high-rise apartment structures. Energy-conserving solutions used at the Town Center site provide good examples of how site designers can reduce commercial, residential, and transportation sector energy use (Figure 2-6).

27

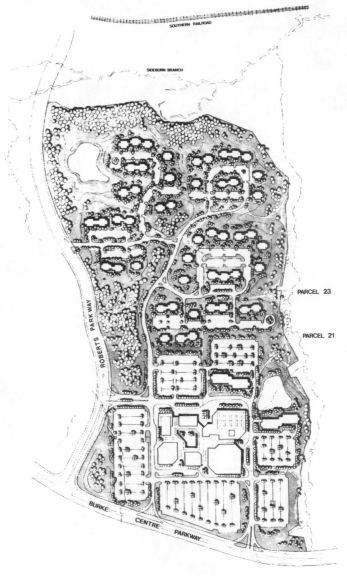

Figure 2-6. Town Center Energy Plan — Burke Center. From: (Land Design/Research, Inc., 1979)

The first design option consolidated office space in large multilevel structures placed on a central court (Figure 2-7, see next page). This provided easy access to all commercial uses on three sides. Residential units, including two high-rise structures, were sited along the fourth edge, providing easy access for singles and couples seeking urban conveniences. In the Energy Plan, nearly all of the structures were oriented for southern exposure which resulted in a 24% increase of wall surface exposed to winter sun and a 50% decrease of wall surface exposed to summer heat compared to the Conventional Plan. Nine acres of natural vegetation located to the north and west were retained to protect the structures from winter winds. All of the

commercial buildings were sunk a half level below grade to reduce surface wall exposure. These measures and other in-building modifications (groundwater heat pumps) translated into a projected annual operational energy savings of 7 billion Btu, or a 27% ($50,000) reduction over the Conventional Plan.

The technical team calculated that of the total energy consumed by the community, 57% went to off-site transportation needs. This assumes the destination of all work trips was downtown Washington, D.C. The consolidation of commercial structures provided room for a 277-space parking lot to facilitate a park-and-ride mass transit system for commuters. Implementation of this system could save 45,000 gallons of gasoline annually, assuming most commuters use the transit system. On-site transportation energy use was reduced by 25% through the reduction of friction points (stops and lights) in the road system. A path system for bicyclists and pedestrians connected the residential and commercial areas in hope that 20% of the auto trips would be replaced by walking, thus saving 1,500 gallons of gasoline per year. "Taking all of the transportation savings into account, the total annual savings of gasoline for the same level of usage would be an estimated 26,400 gallons" (Land Design/Research, Inc., 1979, p. 13).

Table 2-6 summarizes the site development costs for both the Conventional Plan and Energy Plan. In the Energy Plan, these cost savings are $1.2 million or about 20% lower than for the Conventional Plan. The largest reductions stemmed from reduced earth moving and lesser amounts of paving, curbs, and utility construction.

Energy-conserving site design measures significantly reduced residential energy use in the high-rise and garden apartment units on the Town Center site. The high-rise units were expected to consume 20 MM-Btu/unit/year less as a result of proper site orientation, the use of water-to-air heat pumps, and water-conserving devices. That savings amounts to a $220 cost reduction per year for each of the 336 units. When applied to the entire Town Center site, this form of productive conservation would save energy equivalent to 1155 barrels of oil annually worth about $34,650 (1985 projected value). The cost of wells, equipment, and other items associated with the water-to-air pump system is approximately $725,000. However, the annual savings are projected to be $298,000, a return of 41% per year.

For the total study area, the Energy Plan projected a 20% reduction in site development energy consumption and a 33% reduction in building energy consumption over the Conventional Plan.

Table 2-6. Site Development Costs — Burke Center Case Study
Town Center Site

Item/Description	Conventional Plan		Energy Plan	
	Quantity	Total Price ($000)	Quantity	Total price ($000)
Site preparation	107 ac.	$ 268	110 ac.	$ 275
Earthwork	N/A C.Y.	1,754	N/A C.Y.	1,402
Erosion control	Lump Sum	16	Lump Sum	13
Site drainage	11,040 L.F.	472	11,200 L.F.	414
Sanitary sewer	14,900 L.F.	285	12,125 L.F.	230
Waterline	20,260 L.F.	389	12,160 L.F.	233
Pavement	204,500 S.Y.	2,831	178,540 S.Y.	2,471
Curb	68,340 L.F.	547	25,000 L.F.	200
Shade trees	1,005	176	1,457	255
Evergreen trees	76	6	138	10
Shrubs	936	19	936	19
		$6,762		$5,522

Energy Plan Savings: $1,240,000.
From: (Land Design/Research Inc., 1979)

Greenbriar, Va.

The 415-acre Greenbriar study area is to be the initial phase of a larger planned unit development in Chesapeake, Va. The study area contains a shopping center, office buildings, two schools, a fire station, 2,758 residential units, and an 18-hole golf course. Consultants for the Greenbriar project divided the energy-conservation options into four separate

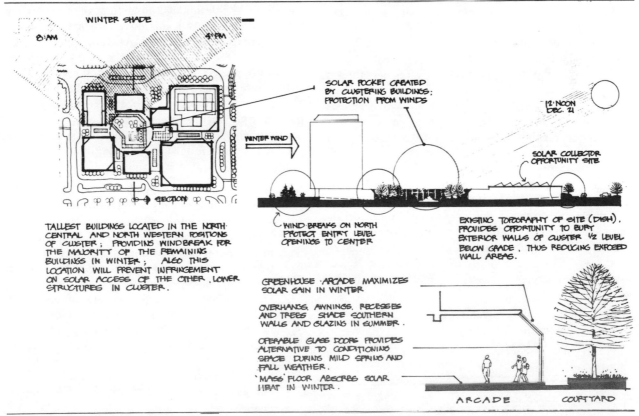

Figure 2-7. Plan view and sections of energy-conserving features — Town Center Energy Plan. From: (Land Design/Research, Inc., 1979)

categories: 1) land-planning applications, 2) architectural applications, 3) mechanical applications, and 4) community systems applications. The research team first determined how much energy was consumed in the production and operation of the Conventional Plan. They then evaluated a number of conservation options, each evaluated for its performance in conserving energy, its capital requirement, commercial applicability, its legality, and its market acceptance. The conservation options selected form the basis of the Energy Plan and are summarized as follows.

The research team found that a reduction in street widths from 28 ft to 24 ft reduced the total square footage of road per lot by 144 ft^2. They calculated that this resulted in an embodied energy savings of 3.8 MMBtu per lot which translates into an oil equivalent savings of about $20 per lot (at 1985 price, $30/bbl).

The embodied energy in asphalt is 55% less than that contained in poured-in-place concrete. The technical team found that 4.0×10^{10} Btu could be saved by changing 4-in. concrete sidewalk slabs to 2-in. asphalt slabs. Changing the curb and gutter from concrete to asphalt could result in a slightly smaller energy savings of 2.9×10^{10} Btu. These savings translate into a reduction of $75 for each dwelling unit (at 1985 price, $30/bbl). The study did not address the implications of these changes on long-term maintenance costs.

A computer simulation of a 2,100 ft^2 conventional residence indicated that a 4.4% annual reduction in energy consumption was possible by reorientating a structure facing east/west to face south. A 9% to 11% savings was projected if the distribution of windows were altered as well. The designers increased the number of north/south facing lots by 12.2% and decreased east/west facing lots by 4.8% in the Energy Plan. This improved the efficiency of lot to infrastructure and permitted the addition of 25 lots with no increase in investment for infrastructure.

At Greenbriar, dense shade from deciduous trees on the east and west facades of the house resulted in a typical daily reduction of 85,000 Btu, a potential annual savings of over $78 per dwelling unit or 11% of typical cooling costs (based on a 1979 rate of 3.5 cents/kwh).

Following are other architectural and mechanical options included in the Energy Plan:

- "Arkansas" construction (2 x 6 studs-24 in. on center, sealed toe plates and corner joints)
- Insulated slab on grade foundation
- Groundwater source heat pump
- Domestic hot water-heat reclaimer
- Greenhouse

"In the Energy Plan the capital investments of $200 to $3,150 per dwelling unit reduced estimated operating energy consumption by 54.7%. This represents an energy savings to the consumer of 21,575 kwh per year. Over a 30-year conventional mortgage period, this represents a savings of $22,338 per house at current energy costs of 3.5 cents per kwh [1985 price is 7.5 cents per kwh]" (Greenbriar Associates, 1980, p. 64).

The Greenbriar case study demonstrates again that relatively simple and straightforward modifications in land planning and architectural design can result in substantial savings in both embodied energy associated with site development and annual operational costs for space conditioning.

Conclusions of DOE Case Studies
Each of the previous studies indicates that substantial energy can be saved through modifying site designs during the development process. The largest savings in annual operational energy consumption ranged from 30% to 50% in Burke Center and Greenbriar, where sophisticated mechanical systems reduced in-building energy use. More modest potential energy savings of 10% to 20% were reported at Radisson and Greenbriar when only site design and building envelope modifications were used. At Radisson a 22% savings in embodied energy was projected. At Radisson and Burke Center an 18% to 20% savings in site development costs were projected. Savings of embodied-energy and site development costs were primarily due to reduced earth moving, improved infrastructure design (less paving and utility construction), and increased development density. Energy-conscious site designers should keep the following two additional findings in mind:

1. As the thermal efficiency of building envelopes improves, the orientation and protection of glazing becomes more critical since it accounts for a larger and larger percentage of heat gain and loss. Therefore, the marginal energy contribution of correct siting and planting becomes increasingly significant.
2. Developers are generally aware of embodied-energy costs because they reflect site development costs. Over 3 to 5 years, the annual operating costs will equal the initial embodied-energy costs. Thus, over a 30-year project life, an initial reduction of 6 to 10 Btu in embodied energy is equivalent to a 1 Btu annual reduction in operating cost.

Hrabak (Argonne National Laboratory, 1979)

identified three general levels of design options associated with these case studies:

Level 1: Passive design. Level 1 includes employment of options such as careful placement of structures with respect to microclimate, and optimal orientation, lot configuration, use of vegetation, distribution of glazing, infrastructure design, etc. Costs associated with implementing these options are minimal.

Level 2: Independent active systems. Level 2 includes not only solar collectors and other readily available "alternative" technologies, but also other active mechanical and building systems (e.g., groundwater heat pumps) that interact with the sun, wind, water, and other forms of low-grade energy on the site. Most in-building active systems increase cost $500 to $2000 per unit and have a 3- to 5-year payback period.

Level 3: Community energy systems. Level 3 design options examine economies of scale and efficiency in meeting multibuilding energy requirements from centralized power facilities. Large capital outlays for these technologies requires a thorough analysis to determine whether they are appropriate.

The potential for greater energy savings improves with each subsequent design level, while at the same time the required capital expenditures and investment risks increase. The design levels build sequentially on the savings generated at the previous level. For example, incorporating solar collectors in a design is difficult if the structures are oriented east/west or vegetation is restricting solar access. Thus, good passive site design provides a basis for the implementation of other energy-conserving design options that offer potentially greater energy savings.

Energy Conservation Potential for Individual Dwelling Units

A substantial percentage of the community-scale energy savings just described results from specific landscape design options implemented around individual structures. Many studies report measured improvements of energy efficiency for various landscape designs around individual dwelling units. Research results documenting potential energy savings are reviewed thoroughly in chapters comprising Section Three "Landscape Design" (also see Hutchison, Wendt, Taylor, and The Critical Review Panel, 1982). Thus, only a summary of findings will be presented here.

Estimates of actual fuel reductions from windbreaks range from 3% to 30% (DeWalle, 1978a). DeWalle, Heisler, and Jacobs (1983) have reported a 12% reduction in fuel used to heat a mobile home when it is protected by a windbreak located one tree height upwind. No quantitative studies document the effectiveness of vegetation planted next to building walls in reducing space-heating costs.

Shading of structures by vegetation can virtually eliminate the need for mechanical cooling in cold and temperate zones (McPherson, 1981a). In warmer climate zones, shade can reduce by one-half the energy required for air conditioning (Parker, 1981). Thayer, Zanetto, and Maeda (1983) report that deciduous trees to the south of a solar home slightly reduce cooling costs but markedly increase heating costs due to solar access blockage by bare winter branches.

Energy consumption associated with landscape maintenance can be substantially reduced through the use of drough-tolerant and disease-resistant species, ground covers instead of extensive turf grass areas, and the appropriate use of materials such as mulches, pavements, and wood decking (Parker, 1982; Pitt, Gould, & Green, 1982a, b).

In summary, authorities conclude that the initial investment in energy-conserving landscape design need not exceed that of more traditional design that does not consciously incorporate energy concerns. In addition, the potential for savings is great in the long term because, while energy prices increase with time, the energy-conserving performance of vegetation also increases as it matures. Vegetation also offers numerous benefits at the same time it conserves energy by cleansing the air, reducing erosion, suppressing noise, creating privacy, and attracting wildlife. We can and must begin to provide Americans with landscape designs that are no more costly to install and maintain than typical current designs, and at the same time are not only esthetic, functional, and compatible with user needs, but also offer sizable long-term energy savings.

Finally, it is important to consider the national economic benefits that may accrue from widespread application of energy-conserving landscape design. DeWalle (1978b) has reported that landscape design incorporating existing energy-conservation design criteria could reduce space-conditioning energy consumption in the residential and commercial sectors by about 10%. This amounts to a 1.4% net reduction in total U.S. energy consumption, equivalent to a savings of over 500,000 barrels of oil each day. At current oil prices of $30 a barrel, this represents a daily savings of 15 million dollars. Hutchison et al. (1982) found that this projected energy savings was significant: "Landscaping for energy conservation should be an attractive energy conservation option in a nation plagued with chronic energy short-fall induced balance-of-trade deficits" (p. 55). Thus, energy-conserving landscape design can play a significant role in freeing the country from dependence on uncertain energy imports as well as providing economic benefits to home and other building owners.

Acknowledgments
The author thanks Gordon Heisler and Larry Wegkamp for their critical reviews of this chapter.

CHAPTER THREE
Planning the Energy-Conserving Development

E. GREGORY McPHERSON
Utah State University
Logan, Utah

THIS chapter illustrates how energy-conserving development can become a part of the traditional planning/development process. First, an initial overview will provide a description of the traditional process and the changes and additions that can be made to make it more adequately reflect energy concerns. A more detailed investigation of specific parts of the process follows. Energy-related decisions regarding programming are discussed; the development program affects potentials for energy conservation in fundamental ways. Data collection and analysis procedures necessary to the design of energy-conserving sites are also described. Finally, ways in which energy-conserving development options can be generated, evaluated, and given three-dimensional form are presented.

The Planning Process and Energy Conservation

Most site designers employ one form or another of a traditional planning/design process described in the literature (e.g., Lynch, 1971; McHarg, 1969; Steinitz, Parker, & Jordan, 1976; Toth, 1974). Figure 3-1 (see next page) illustrates an example of the traditional or "Baseline Planning/Development Process" developed by Barton-Aschman Associates, Inc. (1980).

Before describing how the process can be modified to reflect concern for energy management it should be noted that the process described in this chapter is oriented to large-scale private development, such as a large planned unit development (PUD) or new town. Development at this scale, ideally, would take place within a framework of comprehensive planning that would attempt to conserve and increase the efficiency of energy use, in balance with other objectives related to environmental protection, market demands, and public interests. Energy concerns such as solar access, reductions of embodied energy, and potential for on-site energy generation would be recognized early enough in the development process to affect decisions regarding the size and location of development, the mix of land uses, and the choice of basic service systems. Today, development is occurring in only a few areas of the country on a scale large enough to make it feasible to inject energy conservation as a central consideration in every phase of the process. However, landscape architects involved with smaller-scale land development projects may still employ all or part of the process outlined below and consider a range of energy-conserving options for implementation as opportunities arise.

The following is excerpted from the Barton-Aschman (1980) report and describes the first six planning phases with emphasis upon modification for energy conservation. Table A-1, located in Appendix A, provides a more detailed list of potential modifications to the generic planning process.

Phase I: Project Initiation

Project initiation assumes that no key decisions regarding the site, development program, or market have been made, which is all too often not the case when landscape architectural services are retained. During this phase the team is assembled, general development objectives are identified, and work programs are established. It is important that someone familiar with energy-conservation techniques be included on the original team and that basic energy-related objectives are established.

Phase II: Basic Reconnaissance/Inventory
Many developers complete the Reconnaissance/Inventory phase before they begin Phase I. However, formal work in this phase is often required for larger projects, and should be completed before major land acquisition or similar financial commitments are made.

Some of the most fundamental decisions regarding the role of energy conservation in the planning/design process will be made on the basis of information assembled during this phase. For example, data collected on slope, aspect, and land cover are used to evaluate the potential for solar-energy utilization and to assess development densities. Measurements of wind speed and direction are needed to evaluate the feasibility of using wind power for various purposes. Relatively more detailed information will be needed regarding factors important in energy planning and the governmental or control framework involved than is the case when energy conservation is not a concern.

Phase III: Establish Needs/Program
This is perhaps the most critical phase in the process because basic decisions made here determine when energy conservation measures will be feasible or even can be considered. During this phase the development

program is formulated, feasibility of major options is determined, site selection is accomplished, and key financial commitments are obtained. For large-scale projects key decisions regarding basic systems and land-use mixes will greatly affect potentials for energy conservation.

Energy considerations should play a major role in this phase. The following steps can be followed provided appropriate data is collected in Phase II.

1. Identify potential major energy-saving options. These may be classified into similar groups as shown in Appendix A-2.
2. Evaluate energy performance of selected options.
3. Make financial analyses of proposed energy-conservation measures as part of overall project analysis.
4. Conduct further testing of marketability.
5. Evaluate parts of the site in terms of their ability to serve project goals and to help meet energy concerns.

Although basic program and site decisions are made at this phase some can be considered only tentative and many issues remain to be resolved. For example, changes in energy prices, interest rates, consumer demand, and the marketability of energy options can occur during the planning process. These changes can affect the feasibility of many energy-saving measures that are part of the development program. The key here is to establish a development program that includes as many energy-conservation options as possible, even though some may be excluded as a result of additional evaluation.

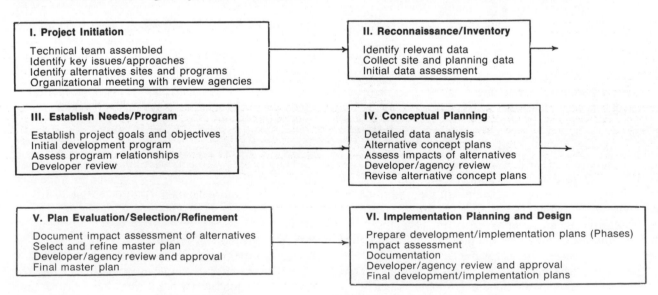

Figure 3-1. Baseline planning/development process. Adapted from: (Barton-Aschman, 1980)

Phase IV: Concept or Schematic Planning

The energy-conscious landscape architect's participation in creating the development team, preparing the development program, and in selecting a site provides a strong point of departure for energy-conscious concept planning. However, on many occasions it is not possible to begin planning for energy conservation at the program or site selection level. The problem is then one of deriving and implementing appropriate energy-conservation measures on an incremental basis. Such planning may begin in this phase and much can still be accomplished.

Typically, work done during schematic planning includes collecting specific site-related data, analyzing these data to identify the best locations for various land uses on the sites, and generalizing alternative design concepts based on "prototypical building blocks."

Energy-related planning requires collecting some special data as well as suitability/vulnerability analyses for any special energy conservation/generation features included in the program. These may include evaluating of microclimatic assets and liabilities, such as windbreaks and frost pockets, and identifying of the best locations for tapping groundwater, constructing a central heating-cooling plant, and siting of solar-tempered homes.

Beyond this, initial design concepts must be developed to reflect the key energy-conservation concepts appropriate for the project. Alternative plans should be prepared that include different arrangements and mixes of energy-conserving features, or perhaps no special energy features, to provide a basis for evaluation and comparison.

Phase V: Plan Evaluation/Selection/Refinement

The final product of Plan Evaluation/Selection/Refinement is a master plan which meets developer goals and objectives for the project and which receives public agency approval. Depending on the scale of the project, the plan could be quite general, simply defining basic systems, development areas, and open spaces, or it could be relatively detailed, showing building, parking, and road layouts, as well as major landscape features. In this phase alternative plans developed in Phase IV are compared and evaluated. One is selected and refined to reflect needs for change identified in the evaluation process, for example, to reduce costs, mitigate undesired impacts, and further increase energy savings. Public agencies and the developer may require some form of an impact-assessment document, and a more detailed impact assessment of the most promising conservation alternatives may improve the likelihood of obtaining public agency approval.

Phase VI: Implementation Planning and Design

Once required agency approvals are obtained, a carefully phased coordination of different segments of the actual development process is needed to promote a smooth transition to actual project implementation. Consequently, this step involves identifying individual development phases which make sense as marketing and financial units. Appropriate schedules for financing, contracting, site preparation, materials purchase, and contract coordination are also developed. Selected energy options must be integrated into detailed development programs, which are typically oriented to other financing or construction constraints.

Final decisions to implement energy options are made in this phase. Designers responsible for detailing basic plans may make many of these decisions, which significantly affect the level of conservation ultimately achieved.

Establishing the Framework for Energy-Conserving Site Design

Energy-conscious site design may not be successful if the appropriate decision-making framework is not established prior to conceptual design. Particularly relevant issues are creation of the development team, formulation of the development program, and site selection. Integration of energy concerns into each of these initial steps of the development process requires some modifications and unique considerations that landscape architects should be aware of.

Creating the Project Team

Planning of projects with emphasis on effective energy conservation and use generally requires application of a wider range of skills and areas of experience than conventional projects. In many cases, individual team members can provide several of the additional skills needed, and, in some instances, input from consultants is necessary. However, if the fullest possible consideration is to be given to energy conservation, the technical team should have at least one member who is able to assess and integrate energy-conservation criteria into the decision-making process from project conception to conclusion.

Skill and experience areas often needed for large-scale energy-sensitive development planning are listed below (Barton-Aschman, 1980). Special contributions and responsibilities of each are also noted.

35

- *Economic, market, or finance specialists* can provide information regarding the awareness, receptivity, and capability of the market to support energy-sensitive projects. They can also assess the likelihood of financing project proposals, including various energy options.
- *Geology/soils specialists* can provide information regarding use of groundwater, feasibility of earth-sheltered housing, and use of special earth forms which affect planning of energy-conserving development.
- *Climatology expertise* is needed to extrapolate available mesoclimatic data to a specific site and to evaluate the effects of natural and man-made features on human comfort and energy use.
- *Land-planning and site-design specialists* can evaluate site locations and potentials to reduce energy use, sites most appropriate for development, and possible mixes of land use.
- *Building design skills* can help identify and develop energy-sensitive building designs and materials appropriate to the site and market.
- *Building system specialists* can identify heating, ventilating, air conditioning, utilities, communications, and security systems most appropriate for the building types being considered. They can also design and evaluate alternative systems.
- *Energy systems analysts/utility coordinators* can provide information on appropriate energy systems and technologies. Their expertise is needed to determine the sources and types of energy that may be used in the project, including feasibility for on-site generation and storage. Coordination may also be required to plan for energy-efficient distribution and supply facilities.
- *Transportation specialists* can evaluate the effects of alternative plans on transportation energy use and propose energy-conserving transportation plans.
- *Legal expertise* can address questions regarding zoning, covenants, building codes, and joint development and multiple-use problems or potentials.

Figure 3-2 (see next page) shows members of the decision-making and technical teams participating in the Radisson case study. In this study, the decision-making team plays a key role because they decide on the acceptability of any development proposal based upon the criteria of program, market, and compatibility with existing development. Clear channels of communication within and between both teams must be established at the beginning of the project and maintained throughout to prevent costly delays in gaining approvals.

Program Development and Site Selection

Programming and site selection are closely inter-related. "Purpose [program] cannot be precisely stated until site limitations are known. The site cannot be thoroughly analyzed until purposes are set forth. Clients set the purpose, but purpose also helps determine the relevant clients" (Lynch, 1971, p. 4). As Lynch notes, these initial phases of the development process are looping and cyclical. In the Baseline Planning/Development Process previously described, a preliminary program is developed and a site selected in Phase I (Project Initiation). The initial program and site-selection decisions are evaluated during Phase III (Needs Analysis) in light of more detailed information generated from data inventoried during Phase II. The nonlinear nature of the process also applies to energy-sensitive land development. However, differences do exist. The goals, objectives, and methods delineated at the earliest stages of the development process affect the degree to which energy-conserving options are generated, evaluated, and implemented. Thus, a consensus that defines the degree of commitment to energy conservation must be forged between members of the technical and decision-making teams. This consensus is usually reflected in the development program or a statement of goals and objectives.

Setting goals and objectives. The objectives of a project should respond to the needs of the client and the user. The clients' needs will always include a return on investment factor, which translates into development densities, landscaping budgets, and amenity values. Clients may have other needs that should be represented in the program, such as the desire to promote energy efficiency.

The designer has a responsibility to represent the interest of the eventual user as well as that of the client and should gain an understanding of those for whom the site is being planned and assess to what extent the user can become a part of the planning/design process. The inclusion of energy-related concerns into the development program will have a significant impact on the user. For example, site designs discouraging use of automobiles may be accepted by young families, but rejected by older citizens living in cold climates.

Program objectives should provide guidance without dictating specific solutions. If they are too general, compliance cannot be discerned, but if they are too specific, design options are needlessly restricted. For example, "a comfortable environment" is too general an objective, but "all south and west facades to be shaded by trees" is a specific solution generated before design has even begun. Lynch (1971, p. 4) asserts that "to maintain indoor summer temperatures within the human comfort range" is a preferred statement because it is testable and can be accomplished in a variety of ways.

Development objectives result from interaction between the technical team and the developer or decision-making team. The developer's concern with the market, financing, and project scale must be recognized, as must the oftentimes voiceless concerns of the user. The degree to which energy-related goals and objectives can be incorporated will vary with each project. The following example (Corbett, 1981) illustrates energy-related goals and objectives that may be developed for a large development with a strong emphasis on resource and energy conservation.

Two broad goals for "holistically designed settlements" are defined:

1. To meet basic human material needs, largely from within the settlement . . . in a diversity of ways all consistent with the preservation of a healthy and stable ecosystem.
2. To promote and support a way of life that permits satisfaction of psychological needs and simplifies the task of satisfying material needs.

Objectives for developing energy- and resource-conserving living environments are:

- Reduction of automobile dependence.
- Local employment and local production of consumer goods.
- Self-sufficiency in energy as nearly as possible.
- Wise water management.
- Agricultural production through efficient land use.
- Opportunities for all income groups.

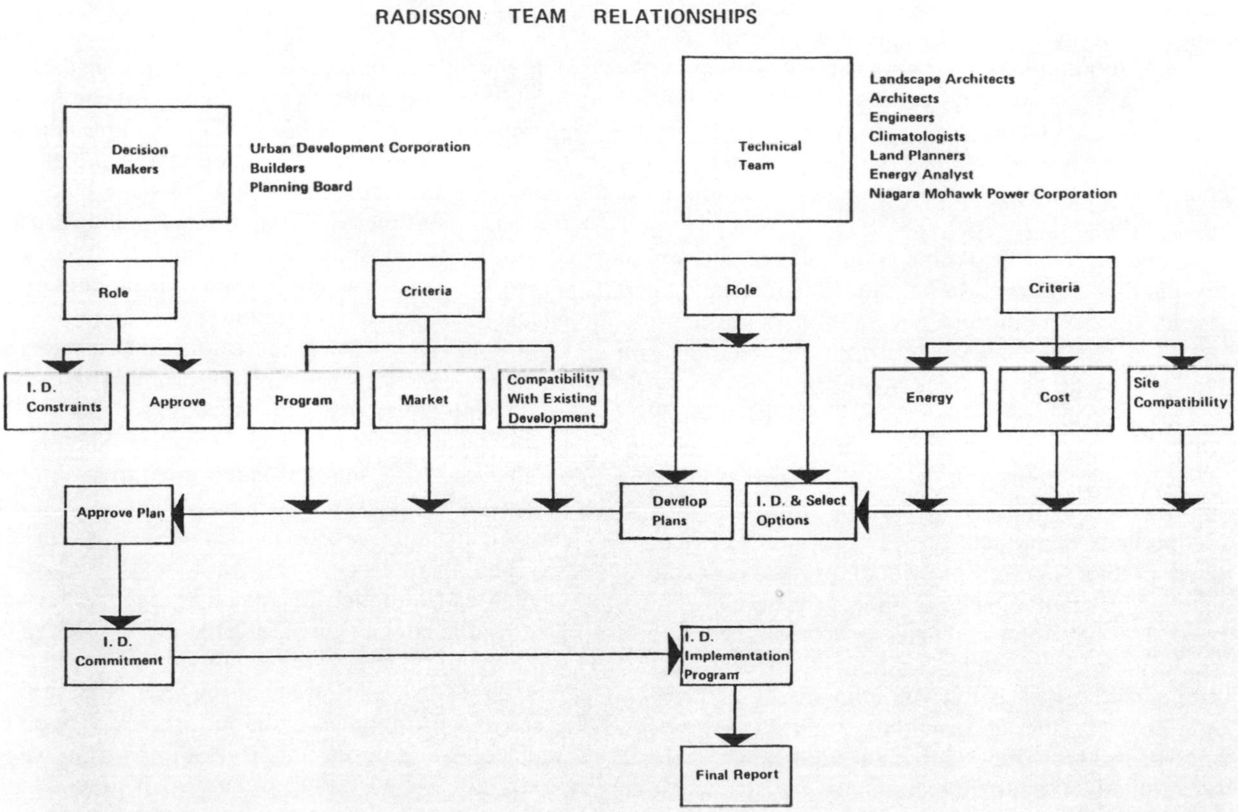

RADISSON TEAM RELATIONSHIPS

Figure 3-2. Team relationships from the Radisson case study. From: (CLAER, 1981)

- Efficient provision of educational and governmental services.
- Physical environment that fosters a healthy, non-consumptive, social environment.
- Participatory planning process including design review.

Selecting a methodology. Methodology is another component of the program which takes on additional significance once a decision has been made to promote energy conservation. Will energy conservation be considered in every step of the process or only on a case-by-case basis when the benefits appear obvious?

Ideally, energy-related decisions should be made at almost every point in the process. This *top-down* approach (Barton-Aschman Associates, 1980) involves planning for a project comprehensively and from its inception. The top-down approach is most effective when the scale of development is large. For example, the scale of a large PUD or new town provides opportunities for making many functional and locational decisions and coordinating and integrating a variety of energy-saving techniques. This approach can also be applied to smaller-scale developments; however, the range of energy-conserving options is generally related to the size and scale of the project. Adoption of the top-down approach implies that energy conservation is a major goal of the development project. Appendix A-1 is a very useful tool for organizing and integrating energy factors into the design process if a comprehensive approach is desired.

In reality, most landscape architects consider or apply energy conservation measures individually or a few at a time. At present few developers are committed to a comprehensive approach, so decisions are typically made on an incremental basis.

This second approach may be termed *bottom-up* (Barton-Aschman Associates, 1980). It involves considering and adopting or rejecting energy-conserving options one at a time, with little effort directed to comprehensive application. This approach can be applied to the smallest individual project and can be focused on areas of special interest to developers, the market, or public agencies, such as benefit-cost analysis of reduced residential street widths. Implementing most options, individually or in small combinations, can occur without significant loss of effectiveness. However, individual application may not take full advantage of the cumulative or synergistic effect of the more comprehensive top-down approach. In most cases, the technical team will use a bottom-up approach. In either case, programming should include consideration of the approach taken to integrate energy conservation into the development process.

Another more specific methodological question pertains to the way in which data will be collected and analyzed to evaluate the feasibility of implementing certain energy options. Typically, landscape architects use an analytical approach whereby data on various physical and cultural factors are collected and combined to analyze suitability and vulnerability (Figure 3-3). This process provides a consistent level of information about the site as a whole.

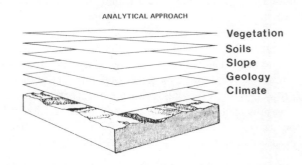

ANALYTICAL APPROACH

Vegetation
Soils
Slope
Geology
Climate

Figure 3-3. Analytical approach to site analysis. From: (CLAER, 1981)

Frequently, it is necessary to have more specific information to quantitatively assess the benefits of an energy-conservation measure. For example, the decision to retain existing vegetation or remove and then replant in residential areas requires quite detailed information on species composition, stand structure, canopy densities, microclimatic conditions under the canopies and in the open, and energy-use characteristics of the residences and users. A prototypical approach (Figure 3-4, see next page) may be better suited to solving this problem than is the analytical approach. In this case use of the prototypical approach would require identifying a small area of the site that is representative of a much larger area. If the site is so heterogeneous that it is impossible to find a prototype then this approach is unsuitable. A prototypical residential unit is also needed. Computer simulation of annual energy use for space heating and cooling given forested and unforested conditions could then provide data used to guide decision-making for similar areas throughout the site. The merit of this approach is that efforts are focused on a smaller-scale subject and thus the analysis can be much more detailed than when the entire site is assessed analytically. Accurate modeling of energy consumption requires detailed establishment of site parameters, which is made possible by using the prototypical approach.

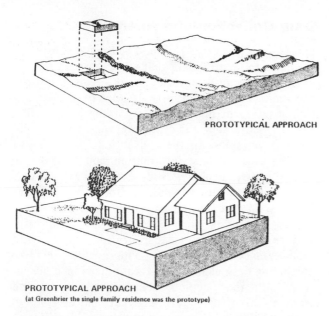

PROTOTYPICAL APPROACH

PROTOTYPICAL APPROACH
(at Greenbrier the single family residence was the prototype)

Figure 3-4. Prototypical approach to site analysis. From: (CLAER, 1981)

Both of these approaches can be combined. An analytical approach may be used to divide the site into parcels having high degrees of similarity. Each area is then analyzed in greater detail using the prototypical approach. The individual parts are then put back together to form a complete energy-conservation plan for the entire site.

The choice of methodological approach is important because it affects the type and way the data are collected, how energy-conservation options are developed, and the analysis tools utilized to assess implementation feasibility. For these reasons the technical team and developer should decide whether a top-down or bottom-up approach will be used to consider energy options. The technical team should also determine whether an analytical, prototypical, or hybrid approach is best suited to its needs for data collection and analysis.

Some general programming options. Following are general programming options that have implications for energy conservation (Zanetto, 1983). Efforts should be made to incorporate as many of these types of land-use and site-selection concerns into the program as is appropriate. Specific design solutions can then be evaluated and those that do not work eliminated.

Location of and proximity to services and goods are often pivotal issues related to programming specific land uses. For example, the decision to program shopping areas, schools, services, and recreation should be based in part on the proximity of these ex-

isting facilities to the project site. A large percentage of a typical suburban household energy budget is used for transportation (Land Design/Research, Inc., 1979). Society as a whole devotes 35% of the energy it consumes to moving people and freight.

Studies indicate that the *location* of housing (how far it is from common destinations) is more critical in terms of net energy use than whether or not housing is solar (Calthorpe & Benson, 1979). This indicates that the surrounding area must be inventoried for key uses (e.g., shopping, recreation, employment, schools, and services). If these facilities are not provided within an easy walking or bicycling distance (2 to 3 miles maximum), they should be programmed into the neighborhood, provided the development is sufficiently large to support them. These facilities must be linked to the larger community to make them economically viable. Other additional land uses not only reduce energy use but also add to neighborhood vitality and stability, which is uncommon in many of today's suburban subdivisions. The following are among these programming options and facilities:

- *Schools:* elementary schools within ½ mile (safe) walk or bike ride for children (De Chiara & Koppelman, 1975). Ten neighborhoods can easily share an elementary facility.
- *Neighborhood commercial and services:* small grocery, office space for doctors and other professionals, workshops for a variety of small businesses, sandwich shops, day care centers, home businesses, etc.
- *Recreational and social facilities:* play fields, natural play areas and playgrounds, a swimming pool (one for the whole neighborhood), a meeting space for the residents' association and for classes, presentations, weddings, performances, religious services, etc.
- *Housing:* a variety of types and densities for all household types, incomes, and age groups. Owner/builder groups can work together as teams with professional guidance for construction and money management. Housing should be clustered in small units that foster social exchange and shared facilities.
- *Range of circulation/transportation alternatives:* especially bike and pedestrian paths within the neighborhood. A central link to existing public transportation systems such as buses and carpooling centers for commuters and/or a neighborhood vehicular service scheduled to deliver people to their destinations should be considered. Vehicular traffic should be sited and aligned in deference to pedestrian and bicycle cir-

culation. Through traffic should be avoided in the neighborhood. Autos should be kept to the perimeter as much as possible, but emergency vehicle penetration and trash collection allowed. Efficient mail distribution should be planned.

- *Local (or dispersed) energy systems:* the potential for neighborhood or community-scale systems such as wind power, biomass production, geothermal and hydroelectric generation, and solar ponds should be utilized if feasible. Unit-specific energy systems include solar space heating, solar hot-water heating, passive and hybrid cooling, and photovoltaics.
- *Gardening/agricultural space:* a hierarchy of gardening spaces from the individual household, to the small cluster, to neighborhood-owned and managed orchards, vineyards, and fuel woodlots.
- *Water management:* land for on-site sewerage systems with shared septic tanks draining into common-area leach fields for subsurface irrigation of fruit trees and biomass crops. Large-scale recycling systems and graywater recycling to homes, community gardens, and for landscape irrigation should be considered. Land for open drainage systems should be allowed which provide on-site retention and percolation of storm water runoff beneficial to the local water table, surrounding plants, and to the city storm-water system as a whole.

When energy-conservation strategies such as these are part of the development program from the outset, the result can be a well-integrated environmental community, such as La Vereda Compound in Santa Fe. Developer and designer Wayne Nichols describes the concept behind this innovative condominium project.

At La Vereda, we refined our basic market mix for an environmental community — energy conservation through passive solar, water conservation, and low-impact land planning. The key is that passive solar is only one part of a total mix. The buyer doesn't see the solar separated from the total real estate product. Site development that preserves the existing vegetation communicates a sensitivity and responsibility of the developer that weighs as heavily as good solar design and quality construction. Saving the beauty of the land, saving our scarce water resource, as well as saving energy are all part of a single philosophy. These must be welded together to form a single finished product. That product is a community. A buyer doesn't just purchase a home. The home sits on a street and the street is part of a larger neighborhood. People purchase neighborhoods. Solar must fit into the neighborhood as well as into a single house. (McAdams, 1983, p. 36)

Data Collection and Analysis

Once a program exists it should be evaluated by team members to identify data that will be needed for site analysis. Because data collection can be time-consuming and costly, efforts are often focused on collecting pertinent information regarding limiting factors, trigger factors, and other important physical and cultural variables. In the conventional site-analysis process much of the information collected is site related (e.g., geology, soil, topography, surface hydrology, vegetation, wildlife, climate, etc.). Other information that is often critical and therefore inventoried includes data related to land use, culture/demography, transportation, views, and finance/markets/economics. Data analysis involves combining data elements to create maps or other information that depicts relative suitability and vulnerability of the site to different land uses.

In planning for energy conservation, some different kinds of data are needed to perform analyses that locate areas most suitable for energy-efficient site design. The degree of detail needed will vary depending upon the intended use of the data. Generally, data collected to assist in selecting an overall site for development need not be as detailed as that required to select the best specific site for a particular land use or to evaluate the feasibility of implementing specific energy options.

The following section describes procedures for collecting and analyzing site, development, regulatory, and energy-related data often used during the energy-conserving development process. Landscape architects typically utilize site-related data and often collect development- and regulatory-related data. Use of energy-related data is less common but necessary to informed decision-making if conservation of energy is a recognized goal.

Collecting Site-Related Data
Physical factors affecting energy-conserving site design include climate, topography, surface cover, surface water, and groundwater.

Climate. Energy-efficient site design implies designing with climate to reduce energy needs for space conditioning. Thus, design strategies should follow from thorough climatic analysis based upon the collection of appropriate data. Chapters Four and Five describe how to collect, analyze, and extrapolate mesoclimatic data to the site in question. These chapters emphasize the need to collect temperature, solar radiation, wind velocity and direction data that depict typical diurnal patterns for each month or season. Appendix C presents an easy way to determine approximate two-hourly temperatures for a typical day of each month from mean maximum and minimum monthly temperatures.

Other climatic data less frequently used but which may be significant include

- *Monthly heating and cooling degree days:* necessary input for some energy-load computer simulation models.
- *Mean monthly total snowfall:* influences ground temperature which affects earth-sheltered housing and may also influence siting of roads, buildings, and vegetation to reduce snow-removal costs.
- *Mean monthly dewpoint temperature and sky cover:* affects feasibility of cooling via radiation to total global radiation: affects collector performance and shading effectiveness.
- *Diffuse fraction, or ratio of diffuse radiation to total global radiation:* affects collector performance and shading effectiveness.

Topography. Data on percentage of slope, slope aspect (or orientation), and winter shading by landforms are essential to subsequent analysis of available solar energy. Usually a separate map is made for each factor. Figure 3-5 shows use of a terrain model and heliodon to determine shadow patterns cast by landforms.

Surface cover. Existing vegetation and productivity of the site influence feasibility of utilizing biomass forests as a renewable energy resource. Shading from buildings and trees may limit solar access. Albedo (surface reflectivity) of earth, vegetation, water and man-made objects affects air and ground temperatures and performance of solar collection systems. Table 3-1 shows the albedo of various surfaces.

Table 3-1. Albedo of Various Surfaces

Surface	Percent
Water surfaces	3-10
Dark cultivated soils	7-10
Coniferous forests	10-15
Asphalt	15
Deciduous forests	15-20
Densely built-up areas	15-25
Meadows and fields	12-30
Sandy soil	15-40
Dirty firm snow	20-50
Brick	23-48
Light sand dunes	30-60
Old snow cover	40-70
Fresh snow cover	75-95

From: (Sterling, Carmody, & Elnicky, 1981) and (McClenon & Robinette, 1977).

Surface water. The amount and availability of surface water influences energy costs for irrigation and culinary water supply. Data on flow rates and head (vertical drop) are needed to assess hydropower generation potential. Bodies of surface water also affect microclimate through cooling and warming effects.

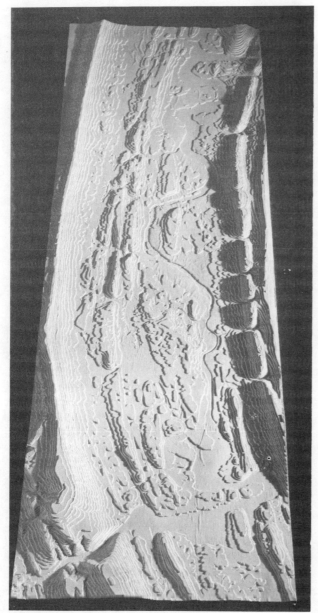

Figure 3-5. Shadows cast by landforms depicted on a three-dimensional model. (Photograph courtesy of Daniel Montgomery).

Groundwater. Groundwater temperature indicates if a geothermal resource is present and is important in assessing feasibility of groundwater heat pumps and earth-sheltered housing (coincides with soil temperatures for near-surface sources). The expense of waterproofing and building construction are influenced by groundwater conditions. Well-water temperature data (National Well Water Association, undated) have been mapped for the U.S. and are the only measured data available. A set of groundwater temperature tables was synthesized by a theoretical model of ground temperature variation. Figure 3-6 shows the average temperature of an undisturbed soil profile ranging in depth from 2 to 12 ft for July 21. Numbers in italics show the normal daily maximum dew-point temperature for the same day. The difference between earth and dew-point temperatures provides a comparable regional index of condensation likelihood. Large differences, both positive (as in the arid Southwest) and negative (throughout the Northeast), indicate greater likelihood of condensation (Labs, 1981).

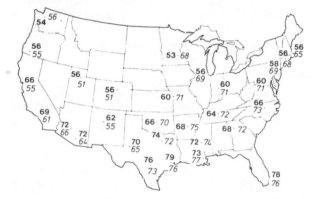

Figure 3-6. Well-water temperatures, July 21. Bold face indicates earth temperatures at 2-12-ft depth. Italics indicate daily maximum dew point. From: (Labs, 1981)

Analyzing Site-Related Data

Comprehensive analysis of site-related data is the backbone of sound ecological planning. Typical overlay maps used to generate a development composite are shown in Figure 3-7. Areas most suitable for conventional housing and other land uses are easily recognized on the development composite. Designers and planners involved with site design for energy-efficient development must generate suitability composites that incorporate energy-related factors as well. Mesoclimatic, microclimatic, topographic, and surface-cover data are usually considered during the traditional site analysis and design process. However, their importance increases when planning for energy-conserving residential development.

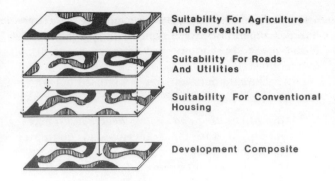

Suitability For Agriculture And Recreation

Suitability For Roads And Utilities

Suitability For Conventional Housing

Development Composite

Figure 3-7. Typical overlay process.

Mesoclimatic data analysis. Interpretation of mesoclimatic data can be used as input for analysis of the site's microclimates if extrapolations can be conducted with confidence. Another use of these data is to develop design priorities that can be used later to evaluate the feasibility of specific design options. *Houses and Climate . . . An Energy Perspective for Florida Builders* (Bureau of Research, 1979) provides an excellent example of how climatic data can be graphically portrayed and analyzed to develop design priorities. Figure 3-8 (see next page) illustrates how the climatic summary for one month is presented.

Figure 3-9 (see next page) illustrates how these data can be interpreted in terms of the average monthly temperature/humidity effect on comfort. Values in the temperature/humidity matrix indicate the percentage of time a given temperature/humidity condition occurs. Percentages are based on hourly data, which require access to typical day data for each month. This can be obtained from the Typical Meteorological Year (TMY) weather tapes or manual calculations from Local Climatological Data (see Appendix B-4). The matrix allows the designer to see what conditions must be overcome to achieve comfort. For example, if conditions are predominantly hot and humid the designer can then refer to typical day wind data to see when winds are sufficiently strong to improve this condition.

Compilation of monthly values results in a matrix showing average annual temperature humidity effect on comfort (Figure 3-10, see next page). Once existing temperature/humidity conditions are known, the relative requirements for mechanical cooling and heating can be calculated. For example, in Orlando, Fla., cooling is needed 48.2% of the year and heating is required 38.7% of the year (from Figure 3-10). Potential savings due to natural ventilation, mechanical ventilation, humidification, dehumidification, solar-radiation gain, and solar control can be estimated

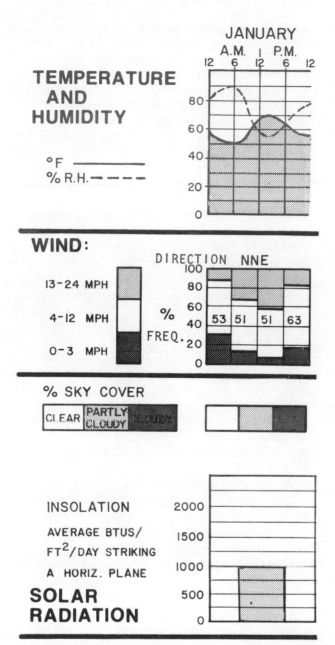

Figure 3-8. Climatic summary: January, Orlando, Fla. From: (Bureau of Research, 1979)

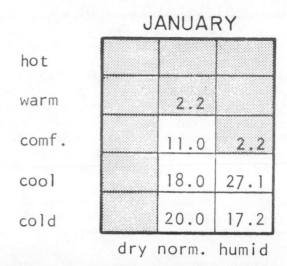

JANUARY

	dry	norm.	humid
hot			
warm		2.2	
comf.		11.0	2.2
cool		18.0	27.1
cold		20.0	17.2

Figure 3-9. Average monthly temperature/humidity effect on comfort: January, Orlando, Fla. From: (Bureau of Research, 1979)

AV'GE. ANNUAL TEMP./HUMID. EFFECT ON COMFORT (%)

	0 — 30%	30% — 80%	80% — 100%
85°F	0.0 hot/dry	10.1 hot/normal	0.5 hot/humid
80°F	0.1 warm/dry	6.4 warm/normal	5.0 warm/humid
70°F	0.2 dry	12.6 comfortable	26.1 humid
55°F	0.3 cool/dry	9.7 cool/normal	18.7 cool/humid
	0.1 cold/dry	5.3 cold/normal	4.6 cold/humid

<u>NOTE:</u> Upper limit of 80% R.H. in Normal range.

Figure 3-10. Average annual temperature/humidity effect on comfort: Orlando, Fla. From: (Bureau of Research, 1979)

based upon characteristics of the structure, HVAC system, and landscaping. Potential savings estimates generally require computer simulation.

Design priorities are also derived from the mesoclimatic analysis using the annual and monthly matrices. General design priorities developed from the Orlando data are as follows:

Cooling
1. Optimize orientation
2. Provide shading
3. Move air

Heating
1. Maximize solar gain

Specific design solutions for each priority could also be included as part of this analysis.

Collecting and interpretating mesoclimatic data may appear at first to be excessively time consuming and unjustifiably expensive. This may be the case if the results can only be applied to a single project of modest dimension. However, many firms conduct the largest amount of their work within a discrete region and may find that the information resulting from such a study applies to numerous projects. More information on the approach described above is contained in other works by Vivian Loftness (1977) including *Identifying Climatic Design Regions and Assessing Climatic Impact On Residential Building Design.*

Microclimatic data analysis. Mapping of microclimatic data is notoriously difficult because of their multidimensional nature. One can only approximate the results of complex microclimatic variables which interact in different ways through changing space and time. In most cases the goal of doing so is to identify (1) areas where microclimatic factors are conducive to development, (2) areas where development could occur provided that measures are taken to mitigate microclimate, and (3) areas where development should be avoided due to microclimatic extremes.

Sterling, Carmody, and Elnicky (1981) suggest that microclimatic data be transposed onto three maps that are then overlayed to create an Energy-Related Composite for the site. Contents of each map include the following:

1. orientation factors — solar orientation
2. land-related factors
   a. cold winter winds
   b. cooling summer breezes
   c. slope exposure
   d. shading by land
   e. air drainage/ambient air
   f. leeward zone (leeward and adjacent to water bodies)
   g. snowdrop zone
3. land-management factors
   a. relative albedo
   b. shading by vegetation
   c. shading by land
   d. other thermal effects

A subjective rating system is used for the various energy-related factors. In the final composite, orientation factors are weighted three times as heavily as land-related factors, which are weighted twice as heavily as land-management factors. The composite is optimized to show areas with potential for greatest energy savings during the winter season because areas that are least energy efficient in the winter are least desirable for development in cold climates. The authors have presented a very comprehensive analytical approach which, however, may be overly elaborate for smaller-scale projects.

Important microclimatic data can often be recorded on two maps. The first map depicts relative availability of solar radiation, usually the most important energy-related site selection factor. Site data on aspect and slope are integrated using a matrix technique similar to that presented in Chapter Twelve to show which parts of the site receive the most sunlight assuming absence of tall vegetation. Data on surface cover can then be added to give a more accurate representation. In southern latitudes, areas shaded by deciduous vegetation may be most desirable for development. In northern latitudes open areas that retain snow and reflect sunlight into south-facing windows may be preferred. This map of relative solar flux at the earth's surface should be generated for the season when mechanical space conditioning costs are greatest.

A second map identifies other important microclimatic effects, such as air flow patterns, areas protected and exposed from winds, snowdrop zones, frost pockets, and other thermal phenomena.

Suitability for energy-conserving residential development. Figure 3-11 shows how maps containing

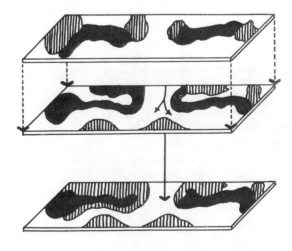

Figure 3-11. Microclimate composite map.

Solar Flux
Dark areas receive most insolation during winter.

Wind, Precipitation, Thermal Factors
Dark areas are most protected and warmest.

Microclimate Composite
Microclimate factors most favorable for energy efficient development.

microclimate data are overlayed to create a composite map showing the effects of microclimate on the relative suitability of areas on the site for energy-efficient development.

The microclimate composite is then incorporated into the synthesis of other overlays typically used to create the development composite. Figure 3-12 shows maps that may be used to create a final energy-conserving development composite.

Buildable areas on the final composite can be segregated into several classes based on associated energy-related benefits or, alternatively, the degree to which design modifications will be needed to achieve energy-efficient design (Sterling et al., 1981). Areas designated as most suitable will be characterized by more intensive land use and higher levels of energy conservation than those deemed less suitable.

As can be seen, incorporating energy-related factors into the traditional overlay process is relatively simple. More emphasis is placed on collecting and analyzing climatic data. This provides information needed to locate land uses where climatic factors can be used to advantage and helps avoid areas where climate is a liability that results in unpleasant conditions and excessive energy use. Chapters Four and Five provide more detailed information on the subjects of climate and design.

Collecting and Analyzing Development-Related Data

Energy-conserving development often entails innovations unfamiliar to potential markets and lending institutions. Therefore, before any energy-conserving design option is implemented its marketability should be assessed. Data collected on marketing needs and innovation acceptance levels will be useful later when approval strategies are devised and energy options evaluated.

Marketing needs and limitations. The National Association of Home Builders (1974) outlines an investigation and decision-making process to assess the likelihood and strength of consumer acceptance. The process includes market and consumer research, competitive evaluation, and market-oriented design. Although this approach indicates typical consumer preferences, prejudices, and budgets, it may not forecast how willing the potential market is to accept nontraditional land-use patterns and dwelling configurations. A marketing and design strategy which aims at the energy- and resource-concerned sector of the home-buying public may limit the project's appeal, but if the project is a true alternative within the housing market, then its sales record may be vigorous. Sterling et al. (1981) have discussed the marketing issue concerning earth-sheltered housing, which they describe as an "alternative housing solution." Their key question was whether the potential home-buyer will assign a value to energy-saving features in homes equal to the cost of providing those features. Because the media is now devoting much attention to energy-conservation innovations, the key to consumer acceptance may be to show a visually appealing product (site design, building exteriors, and layout of interior spaces) coupled with either a simulation or log of dwelling performance (projected utility costs at present and future energy costs). A narrative description of neighborhoodwide as well as dwelling-specific energy features is also effective (e.g., Real Estate Research Corp's. *Selling the Solar Home,* 1971).

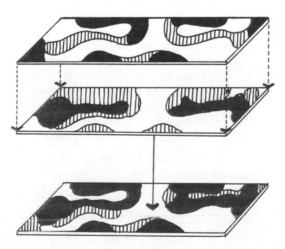

Development Composite
(see Fig. 3-7)

Microclimate Composite
(see Fig. 3-11)

Energy Conserving Development Composite

Figure 3-12. Energy-conserving development composite map.

Innovation acceptance levels. Information on the degree of innovation that consumers, lenders, and regulatory bodies find acceptable can be collected in a casual or scientific manner. Casual techniques, the most frequently employed, take the form of questions posed during informal conversations, meetings, and interviews. However, questionnaires and other types of formal surveys can result in more reliable information on innovation acceptance provided appropriate sampling procedures are followed. Borg and Gall (1979), Dillman (1979), Ferber (1974), and Schoner and Uhl (1975) provide more information on survey and marketing research design. Surveys of consumer-acceptance levels will be most valuable because these data can then be used to demonstrate to lenders and regulatory agencies what the market will accept.

Collecting and Analyzing Regulatory-Related Data

Depending upon the size and location of the proposed development one or more regulatory bodies will review the design. Before a strategy to gain regulatory approval can be formulated, information pertaining to the local project review process, local energy-related development regulations, and energy regulation alternatives should be collected.

Local project review process. Information on the review process may be obtained from the local planning and zoning commission or city/county planning officials. A time line showing when formal reviews are required should be developed and integrated with the work plan. In many cases proposed energy conserving developments represent a new experience for developers and regulatory bodies. To insure that the "government is on your side" it is important to begin working with the regulating body at the earliest possible time.

Local energy-related development regulations. An interview with local planning officials is also needed to determine what regulatory barriers and incentives to energy-conserving development currently exist.

Common development regulations and design standards that obstruct energy conservation include the following (Erley & Mosena, 1980):

- Aesthetic regulations which prohibit installation of solar collectors.
- Setback and lot layout specifications in subdivision ordinances and zoning which limit flexibility in passive siting of buildings.
- Excessive design standards (e.g., street width requirements) which promote energy waste.

Some communities have revised and/or added regulatory incentives to encourage energy conservation as in these examples:

- Bonus points that allow increased density or increased development permits are awarded for energy-conserving amenities to competing developers.
- Priority processing of proposals containing energy-conserving features can significantly speed up the development process.
- Decreased development fees are awarded to energy-efficient proposals.

Incentives to promote energy conservation may also be present at the federal and state levels:

- The Public Utilities Regulatory Policies Act (PURPA) requires states to set buy-back rates for on-site electric generation.
- State and federal tax credits are available to those who purchase solar systems, insulation, and other energy-conserving items.
- Subsidies are available in some states in the form of low-interest loans for products such as solar-powered pumps.

The technical team should be familiar with regulations mandating energy conservation that require energy-conserving development practices. Below are examples of required restrictions:

- Solar access legislation which restricts building height and setback or curtails blocking vegetation.
- Proper lot and building orientation which affects street and lot layout.
- Landscaping ordinances which require increased levels of landscaping for parking lots and commercial development sites.
- Solar domestic hot-water mandation in new construction.

Local energy-related regulations can be categorized into three types depending upon whether they represent (1) barriers to energy conservation, (2) encourage energy conservation, or (3) mandate energy conservation.

Energy regulation alternatives. If significant barriers to energy-conserving development exist, it may be useful to review how other communities have modified similar ordinances or design standards to facilitate energy-efficient design. Gaining approvals may be easier if case study examples of alternatives are cited.

The American Planning Association's *Energy*

Conserving Development Regulations: Current Practice (Erley & Mosena, 1980) cites results from a survey of over 1,400 planning agencies to identify communities that adopted development regulations designed to save energy. The publication provides an annotated description of each energy-conserving development regulation identified in the survey. Development regulations in the report address the four major areas and associated design options listed below.

1. Reduce heat and cooling needs
   - Natural solar heating
   - Natural cooling
   - Wind protection
   - Housing design
2. Reduce transportation needs
   - Increase housing density
   - Integrate land uses
   - Encourage bicycling/walking/mass transit
   - Create efficient traffic flow
3. Reduce embodied-energy needs
   - Develop in higher density
   - Reduce street width
   - Reduce car parking area
   - Develop areas already served by streets and utilities
   - Reuse existing buildings
4. Use alternative energy sources and systems
   - Facilitate use of district heating (heat supplied to buildings from a central source) or other production and distribution systems by developing at appropriate densities with greater integration of uses.
   - Facilitate use of solar-energy systems by planning development so that solar access is assured.
   - Substitute technologies that use renewable energy sources (e.g., solar, wind) for conventional nonrenewable sources (e.g., oil, coal) whenever feasible.

Another good source of information on regulations and programs communities have adopted to promote use of renewable energy resources is *Energy-Efficient Community Planning: A Guide to Saving and Producing Power at the Local Level* (Ridgeway, 1979).

Gaining financial, regulatory, and consumer approval. Once important development and regulatory related data are collected and analyzed a strategy for gaining financial, regulatory, and consumer approval should be developed. Two approaches should be a part of any approval strategy. The first is to identify and contact key decision-makers early in the development process. The second is to identify potential impediments to implementation before they occur.

When developing an approval strategy it is important to understand the vested interest of each decision-maker. The utility company may limit what their representative can do. Local communities may be encouraging or discouraging development in specific locations. Lenders may face a very tight money market and may be in a position to encourage or discourage innovation through their lending policies. All of these factors point to the need to identify and establish communication with decision-makers early in the planning process and to then determine potential impediments to energy-conserving site design strategies.

Collecting and Analyzing Energy Data

Information on energy supply and consumption patterns of existing land uses on or near the site provide base line data against which alternatives can be compared. Collecting energy data is often tedious, but necessary if energy options are to be screened using quantitative measures.

Energy-use profile. Energy profiles estimate the amount of operational energy required annually for different program components and provide a base line for evaluating energy performance of proposed alternatives. Table 3-2 shows estimated energy requirements of five systems in the Burke Center case study (Land Design/Research, Inc., 1979).

Table 3-2. Systems Energy Profile: Burke Center Case Study.

Base Plan Energy Use

	Annual site energy use, 10^9 Btu/yr.	Total %
HVAC, lighting, appliances, and hot water	137.1	21.0
Transportation:		
On-site	96.2	15.0
Off-site	361.2	57.0
Potable water treatment	15.1	2.0
Wastewater treatment	27.1	4.0
Refuse collection and disposal	2.9	1.0
Total Base Plan Energy Use	639.6	100.0

From (CLAER, 1981)

Table 3-3. Building Energy Use Profile by End Use: Burke Center Case Study.

Base plan total energy use of buildings in the Burke Center study area x 10⁹ Btu/yr.

	Resid.[a] energy-use totals	Rec.[b] energy-use totals	Com.[c] energy-use totals	Study area energy-use totals
Total floor area, ft² x 10³	2,298	81.7	323.9	2,703.6
Heating	24.1	2.8	2.7	29.6
Cooling	21.3	3.6	6.3	31.2
Lighting	6.2	1.8	3.2	11.2
Appliances and and equipment	23.3	0.4	1.0	24.7
Hot water	31.5	2.8	2.1	40.4
TOTAL	110.4	11.4	15.3	137.1
Energy cost, $10³/yr.	1,325	107	163	1,595
Energy use index (EUI) Btu/ft²/yr.	48,042	139,935	47,237	50,710

[a]High rise apts., garden apts., cluster units, four/plex units, townhouses. [b]Bowling alley, health & racquet club, roller skating rink, neighborhood & community, meetings & pool bathhouse. [c]Dinner theatre, office bldgs. 1, 2, & 3, commercial/retail bldgs. 1, 2, & 3.
From: (CLAER, 1981)

Table 3-3 shows end use energy profiles for buildings segregated according to end use. End use data such as this can be evaluated to determine where greatest savings can be achieved. For example, end-use percentages for buildings in the Burke Center case study are as follows:

- Heating, 22%
- Cooling, 23%
- Lighting, 8%
- Appliances, 18%
- Hot water, 29%

Preliminary analysis of these data suggests that options aimed at reducing energy used for hot water and cooling might have the most pronounced benefit.

Actual data on energy use are most easily acquired from local utility companies. Monthly or bimonthly utility bills provide totals for electricity, natural gas, fuel oil, etc. Unfortunately, no universal formula exists that can be applied to extrapolate end-use data (i.e., how much electricity is used for space cooling versus lighting versus appliances). Local utility representatives can often provide general figures for buildings of different sizes and types (e.g., all electric versus natural gas as primary heating fuel). Utilities

also have information regarding the timing and magnitude of peak-load power demand. These data can serve as a base line when the effects of energy options on peak loads are evaluated.

Energy-use profiles may already be available in the form of energy audits conducted by local utilities or other researchers. Utility representatives, local energy coordinators, and personnel in the State Energy Office may be of assistance in obtaining this information.

Energy-costs information as well as energy-use patterns should be obtained from local utilities. Data on present fuel rates should also include the possibility of a rate hike in the near future. Most utilities have or are planning to submit rate hike proposals to public service commissions, and these are usually approved. Data on future energy costs are useful when evaluating life-cycle costs of energy-conservation options.

A good source of general information on residential energy consumption are reports available from the National Energy Information Center (NEIC). A series of reports entitled *Residential Energy Consumption Survey: Consumption and Expenditures* (DOE/EIA-0321/1, 1983) contain national and regional (DOE/EIA-0321-2, 1984) data (Northeast, North Central, South, West) regarding consumption of various fuels and energy-related characteristics of households. A similar report (DOE/EIA-0431, 1983) presents estimates of residential energy consumption by end use.

Energy flow. Calculations of energy flow use a systems approach to quantify the amount of energy input to the site, subsequent energy use on the site, and the amount that leaves the site. Figure 3-13 (see next page) depicts energy flow through Burke Center. Energy-flow values can be calculated from energy profile data to provide a comprehensive view of energy demand and consumption.

Energy flows are of limited value for most development projects. For developments of modest scale the expense of collecting the data needed to generate the models often outweighs the value of the product. However, at the scale of large PUDs or new towns, which require energy planning for large transportation, water, and solid-waste subsystems, energy-flow diagrams of conventional systems can be used as base lines. Comparisons can then be made with options not normally a part of conventional systems, such as material recycling, heat recovery, and on-site energy-generation systems.

Because most landscape architects will not have occasion to develop energy-flow diagrams, data collection and analysis procedures will not be described in detail here. For more information interested readers

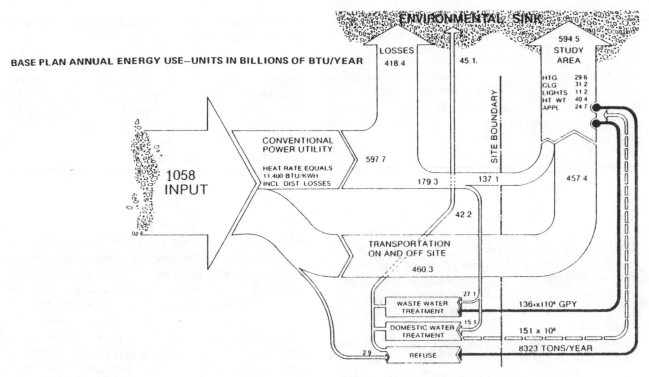

BASE PLAN ANNUAL ENERGY USE—UNITS IN BILLIONS OF BTU/YEAR

Figure 3-13. Energy flow diagram of the Burke Center case study base plan. From: (CLAER, 1981)

are referred to works by H.T. Odum and others in bioenergetics and network analysis (Odum, 1976; Odum & Bayley, 1975; Zuccheto, 1975).

Alternative energy sources. Data collection may include information needed to assess the feasibility of potential energy sources on the site. On-site energy generation most commonly uses solar radiation (solar energy), water (hydroelectric power), and wind (wind power), and biomass (methane gas, cogeneration, fuel oil, ethyl alcohol). Information pertinent to data collection and analysis for each of these energy sources is outlined below along with additional references. Most of the data required are site-related and can be collected at the same time other data are inventoried.

The amount of solar radiation available is usually expressed in Langleys, Btu/ft^2, or watts/m^2 (solar radiation equations and conversion factors are located in Appendix B-2). Areas receiving mean daily solar radiation averaging less than 300 Langleys a year have low solar potential. However, because different types of collector systems have different operational efficiencies it is impossible to pinpoint a single profitable performance threshold, but once the amount of solar radiation and performance specifications for the solar system in question are known, feasibility can be quantitatively assessed. Solar radiation data are available from state energy offices and

the *Climatic Atlas of the United States* (NOAA, 1979). Three other excellent references are *The Solar Radiation Energy Resource Atlas of the United States* (Hulstrom, 1981), the *Insolation Data Manual* (Knapp, Stoffel, & Whitaker, 1980), and its addendum, the *Direct Normal Solar Radiation Data Manual* (Knapp & Stoffel, 1982).

On-site solar-energy measurements are best made with pyranometers (Star, Eppley, and Kipp are commonly used). The effects of shading from surrounding buildings or vegetation can be quite accurately assessed manually. Mazria (1979) describes how to make and use the solar-radiation calculator for this purpose. "Rating the Site Survey Tools" (*Solar Age,* 1983) is an excellent review of four popular solar site-survey instruments now on the market.

Hydropower potential is assessed by measuring flow rate and head or the vertical distance between the water source and proposed intake location. Flow rate is measured by constructing a weir across the stream and then noting the water mark on a depth gauge driven into the stream bed upstream of the weir. The vertical distance the water falls is easily determined by surveying procedures. Flow rates in particular have already been measured for many larger streams throughout the country. The state hydrologist or energy office will indicate if the data are available. Kohler (1983) provides a simple explanation of flow and head measurement techniques and other information useful for assessing microhydro potential.

Areas with consistent winds greater than 10 mph have high wind-power potential. Because wind characteristics are extremely site dependent, on-site measurements over an extended period of time (a year or more) are recommended if large systems or wind farms are proposed. Battelle's Pacific Northwest Laboratory recently completed the *Wind Energy Resource Atlas* (1981), a 12-volume work depicting in tabular, graphic, and narrative form the wind resource on a regional and state level. Recorded wind data and computer mapping techniques were used to estimate wind-power density across the country. More information on siting wind-energy systems is contained in *A Wind Resource Prospecting Study for Indiana* (Otawa, Schoen, & Justham, 1982), *A Siting Handbook for Small Wind Energy Conservation Systems* (Wegley, Montie, & Drake, 1980), and "Meterological and Topographical Indicators of Wind Energy for Regional Assessments" (Elliott, 1979). Gipe (1981a) and Gipe (1981b) present simple techniques for approximating wind power and the potential energy available from particular wind machines, as well as other sources of wind data.

Organic matter or biomass can be used in a number of ways to create power for human use. Trees have traditionally provided fuel for heating homes and continue to do so. Thinnings from a 1-acre wood lot can provide one-half to one cord of wood annually. Biomass forests utilize short rotations and intensive silviculture to provide fuel for central power generation facilities. Further information on forest management principles for biomass and primary production data are contained in works by Cannell (1982), McMillin (1978), and Inman, Salo, and McGurk (1977).

Wood and agricultural waste products can fuel electric generators (wood chips) or be fermented to produce ethyl alcohol for gasohol. Residual agricultural waste can be combined with animal and human waste to produce methane gas and nitrogen-rich fertilizer. Methane can be used to fuel compressors for refrigeration, combustion engines to move people and freight, and as a cooking fuel or lamp gas. Organic refuse and very high temperatures (500F) in the absence of oxygen yield low-grade oil in a process called pyrolysis. One ton of organic material yields about one barrel of oil that can be used as boiler fuel. Numerous sources (Goodman & Love, 1981; Robinson, 1980; White & Plaskett, 1981) contain information on technology and application associated with biomass energy production of various types.

Generating and Evaluating Energy Conserving Options

The decision to consider the possibility of adopting a particular energy-conservation option is not a simple undertaking, for this entails costs for the technical team and those who must review these decisions. The potential for cost savings must appear to be high, and/or there must be considerable pressure to explore these potentials before an energy-saving option is selected for consideration and subsequent evaluation (Barton-Aschman, 1980).

Generating Energy Options

Energy options are typically raised for considerations in two ways. The first and most common is through the developer's activities. This includes options generated by the developer or the technical team. The second way is through community-based efforts to implement what are perceived to be important public objectives. Options both the public and private sector deem feasible and desirable are usually readily accepted. Frequently, however, it is necessary to devise a list of options that are screened to remove unacceptable ones.

Energy-conservation design options for a specific site can be developed in several ways. A common way is for members of the team to brainstorm and select options that appear logical. Sometimes review of energy-use profiles and energy-flow studies results in identifying feasible options. An examination of energy use at each scale of development (dwelling unit, cluster, neighborhood, community) is another sensible way to identify and categorize promising options.

One of the best ways to generate energy options is to review literature describing how options in question work, if they have been implemented, and what their associated costs and benefits are. The five Department of Energy sponsored case studies (CLAER, 1981) provide much of the currently available information on design options, as do other sources cited throughout this book. Appendix A-2 contains a listing and classification of over 100 energy-conserving options (Barton-Aschman, 1981).

Categorization of energy-saving options into subgroups facilitates generation and evaluation procedures. As shown in Appendix A-2 Barton-Aschman (1981) subdivided energy options into five major groups with subgroups for each. These are the major groups:

1. Functions (e.g., land-use patterns)
2. Services (e.g., waste collection)
3. Systems (e.g., utilities)

4. Site features (e.g., landscape planting/materials)
5. Buildings (e.g., design)

An alternative classification scheme follows:

1. Embodied energy (e.g., road width)
2. Land and site planning (e.g., landforms)
3. Architecture (e.g., location/arrangement)
4. Transportation (e.g., parking)
5. Community systems (e.g., district heating)

Both schemes show few differences. The point is that classification systems can be based upon the scale of the project and the relative importance energy-conserving options will have in the design process.

Evaluating Energy Options

Once a list of potential energy-conservation options is generated, a screening or evaluation process must be developed to judge the feasibility of implementing each option. Evaluations often needed to assess implementation feasibility include screening for energy performance, economic feasibility, and marketability. The nature and form of the data required to evaluate options depend upon the role of the developer, community, and consumer in the screening process. Cost or economic data are usually most important to developers, who must take the initiative to include energy options in the development. Data supplied to them must be of the highest quality so that they believe in the validity of and need for certain energy options. Data most important to communities often center on secondary economic or environmental impacts. Consumers are primarily concerned with the short- and long-term costs and benefits of selected energy options.

This section provides an overview of assessment tools used to evaluate options. Obviously, it is beyond the scope of this chapter to describe in detail how each tool is applied. Further information can be obtained from sources referred to in this chapter and the book's bibliography.

Evaluating energy performance. Before the implementation feasibility of any option can be determined the amount of energy savings associated with that option should be known. Landscape architects will be most concerned with quantifying the energy performance of options related to building/site design, embodied energy, and transportation systems.

Energy performance at the building level combines consideration of in-building subsystems with occupant, building envelope, and site characteristics. A typical procedure for calculating energy performance is to select for testing a small set of buildings representing the different building types. Results can then be projected to the entire development. This procedure was used in the case study described in Chapter Twelve and requires quantity takeoffs from preliminary site and architectural plans. Energy analysis can then be pursued through sensitivity analyses using computer simulation or through sampling and comparative procedures.

Sensitivity analyses involve successive computer runs made on the test group to evaluate the effects various design options such as orientation, percent glass, ventilation rates, shading, and wind protection have on energy consumption. Implications regarding both energy use and economic factors can be determined. Options deemed to be cost effective can then be applied to all buildings to assess potential overall savings.

Building energy-analysis software is available for hand calculators, microcomputers, and mainframe computers. The complexity and flexibility of these programs generally increases as more sophisticated hardware is required. Software packages for microcomputers are well suited to the needs of most landscape architects as in the examples listed below:

CALPAS 3 (contact Berkeley Solar Group, 3140 Grove, Berkeley, CA 94703)

MICROPAS (contact ENERCOMP, 2655 Portage Bay Ave., Davis, CA 95616)

NEATWORK (contact Princeton Energy Group, 575 Ewing St., Princeton, NF 08540)

SUNMAT and SUNOP (contact Solarsoft, Box 124, Snowmass, CO 81654)

Software for mainframes is best suited for analyzing large-scale projects that include commercial or industrial facilities. These are some examples:

BLAST (contact U.S. Army Construction Engineering Research Lab, P.O. Box 4005, Champaign, IL 61820)

DOE 2.1 (contact Lawrence Berkeley Laboratories, Berkeley, CA 94720)

TRNSYS (contact Solar Energy Laboratory, University of Wisconsin, 1500 Johnson Drive, Madison, WI 53706)

The above programs represent only some of those available. Each has distinct capabilities, costs, and is available for use on a limited range of computer models. For further information, free brochures entitled *Analysis Methods for Solar Heating and Cooling Applications* (Nordham, 1981, Pub. No. SERI/SP-35-232R) and *Microcomputer Methods for Solar Design and Analysis* (SERI, 1980, Pub. No. SERI/SP-722-1127) are available from the Solar

Energy Research Institute, 1617 Cole Blvd., Golden, CO 80401. Another excellent overview of computer applications for passive solar design is presented by Klein (1983).

Sampling and comparative procedures are also used to assess energy performance. For example, in the Radisson case study (Reimann Buechner Partnership, 1979) estimates of energy consumption were calculated by comparative analysis to existing development within the Radisson new town. The purpose of the study was to establish a correlation between unit siting characteristics and heating-energy consumption. Meter-reading data, obtained from the local utility, identified the heating-fuel type and bimonthly energy use for a two-year period for each unit. Siting characteristics for 75 electrically served units were then developed through analysis of aerial photographs and site visits. The type and quality of vegetative protection and solar orientation were recorded for each unit. A comparative summary of meter readings results and site characteristics revealed that existing protected units with either north/south or east/west orientations consume 28% to 33% less energy than unprotected existing units. The results of this energy-performance evaluation were translated into design strategies affecting building location and orientation, planting design, and use of landforms to reduce air infiltration.

Computer simulation allows numerous options to be tested; however, input parameters and the model itself must be accurate for the results to provide a valid approximation of reality. Field data on energy consumption depict actual energy use but may be confounded by differing user characteristics. There is a need for further post design evaluation to verify these estimates of energy savings.

An important attribute of energy-performance studies is that results can later be used as marketing aids. They also have high acceptability with developers, builders, regulatory bodies, and the lay public during the project review process.

Embodied energy is generally taken to mean the total energy invested in the building and site-improvement process, including the energy expended in obtaining raw materials, manufacturing building materials, and in construction activity (Swanson, 1980). Recent studies (CLAER, 1981; Chapter Twelve) indicate that while savings in embodied energy are not as great as those associated with other types of modifications in building and landscape design, they can contribute significantly to overall energy savings. However, obtaining sufficient reliable data is the major difficulty in quantifying the impacts

of different design options on embodied energy. Principal original sources of information for estimating embodied energy are *Energy in Building Construction* (Center for Advanced Computation, R.G. Stein and Associates, undated), *Energy Use in Building Construction* (Hannon et al., 1977) and *Energy Use in Contract Construction Industry* (Tetra Rech Inc., 1975). Reference to secondary sources (Stein, 1977a, 1977b) and/or independent studies by the technical team usually necessary to collect data applicable to situations other than those incorporated in the original studies (e.g., energy costs for transportation of materials to the site).

Embodied energy use can be estimated for the following types of development activities:

- Site preparation
- Buildings
- Infrastructure
- Landscape design

Typically the first step in estimating embodied-energy use is to determine the area of the subject under study (e.g., square feet of road surface). This requires quantity takeoffs and detailed estimates of material quantities, which in turn implies that a certain level of design specificity is needed before calculation can commence. The second step is to multiply this figure by an estimate of energy embodiment per unit area (e.g., Btu per square foot). The result is total energy embodied in a given design option. This figure can be converted into comparable economic terms using oil equivalents because the price of oil is widely regarded as a good indicator of current energy costs (There are 5.82 million Btu in a barrel of crude oil). Examples of how these procedures are applied are documented in Chapters Eleven and Twelve.

The calculations required to estimate embodied energy use are generally simple and straightforward. The real work lies in collecting information regarding energy embodiment per unit area because the study of embodied energy is a comparatively new area of inquiry. As new studies are conducted and reported, a more thorough data base should evolve, thus making the assessment task less costly and simpler to conduct.

Energy consumption for transportation can account for a large percentage of overall energy use. It is therefore highly desirable to estimate energy performance of the transportation networks for alternative plans. Estimations of energy consumption on these networks should include travel to, from, and within the project, and may also include energy embodied in roadway construction, manufacturing of vehicles, and maintenance. Figure 3-14 shows basic energy components of transportation networks. The following summarizes the Woodlands case study (Swanson, 1980) process for estimating transportation related energy consumption:

1. Three categories of energy use were selected for study: propulsion energy, energy embodied in roadway and car-park construction, and indirect energy (maintenance energy).
2. Land-use data were tabulated by building parcel. The density and character of these land uses form the basis for determining trip generation rates to and from the development.
3. Roadway networks were described in terms of operating speeds, access points, locations of land use, distances along each roadway link, and external connections.
4. A computer model was used to generate, distribute, and assign traffic to the roadway network. The Urban Transportation Planning System (UTPS) is a computer program available for this purpose (U.S. Department of Transportation, 1977).

5. Traffic assignments were reviewed for accuracy and then analyzed to determine the resulting land requirements on each roadway section.
6. Other transportation modes which might efficiently serve the reconfigured land-use plan and result in a net energy savings were included to form a complete system.
7. Total energy consumption for the entire transportation system was then calculated. Two publications by Hirst (1974a, 1974b) provided the data needed to estimate energy use.

This procedure can be used to test a wide variety of transportation options. Common design options that receive testing include different modes of transportation, reconfiguration of path and roadway systems, and the effects of land-use modifications on energy consumption for transportation.

Evaluating economic costs and benefits. Techniques of benefit-cost analysis are commonly used to assess economic feasibility of energy options. Costs of implementing any option can be calculated manually

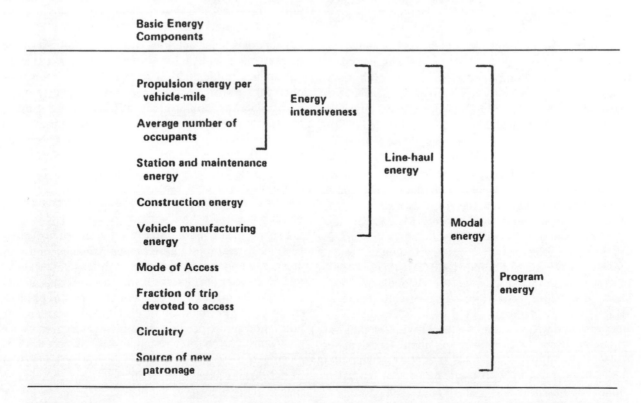

ENERGY COMPONENTS REQUIRED
TO DETERMINE BTU PER PASSENGER MILES FOR VARIOUS MODES

Basic Energy Components

Propulsion energy per vehicle-mile

Average number of occupants

Station and maintenance energy

Construction energy

Vehicle manufacturing energy

Mode of Access

Fraction of trip devoted to access

Circuitry

Source of new patronage

Energy intensiveness

Line-haul energy

Modal energy

Program energy

Figure 3-14. Basic energy components of the transportation network. From: (Congressional Budget Office, 1977)

53

or simulated with a computer. Options or site plans can be compared (see Chapter Twelve). It is often necessary to use different techniques to evaluate different options. For example, savings due to smaller parking lots may be expressed as a one time reduction in capital costs in the absence of information on long-term maintenance costs. However, economic benefits and costs of in-building subsystems (e.g., trombe wall) may be subjected to a more extensive life-cycle cost analysis. Techniques for economic comparison made between similar options should be consistent even though a variety of techniques may be used to assess all options contained in the alternative plans.

Life-cycle costing is a preferred economic assessment tool because it recognizes all costs (operation, maintenance, and replacement) associated with a particular cost expenditure during its "life-cycle" or the life-cycle of the project. Guidelines for life-cycle costing for energy conservation are contained in works published by the Energy Research and Development Administration (ERDA) (ERDA, 1977) and the National Bureau of Standards (Ruegg, McConnaughey, Sav, & Hockenberry, 1978).

A second common index of economic performance is the discounted payback period. This method of analysis provides a measure of the relationship between capital costs and annual savings to be derived from a particular option. A discount rate and energy escalation or inflation rate must be assumed. However, results do not usually express benefits associated with the option after the payback period is reached. Options with payback periods of seven years or less are generally considered cost effective. Further information on calculating the discounted payback period is contained in a short article by Lunde (1982).

Economic feasibility analyses may be used to assess individual options or to determine cumulative effects at the community scale. Costs associated with a single design option can be calculated manually, but computer simulation is often used for life-cycle costing for project analysis and evaluation. Microcomputer software such as SUPERCALC and VISICALC provide the sophistication necessary to conduct such analysis. ENERCALC and L3MODEL are cost-analysis programs used by the Woodlands and Shenandoah case study teams, respectively. The L3-MODEL uses the total net present value of costs method to compare costs of alternative plans on an equivalent basis. Data required as input to calculate project costs on an annual basis over the expected life of the project varies with each model, but basically consist of (1) project parameters, (2) development costs, and (3) energy consumption. In the Shenandoah

case study (Shenandoah Development, Inc., 1980) construction costs, development costs (site and lot), and annual energy costs were computed from unit costs scaled and inflated to produce an annual series of costs for the entire development.

It is important to note that while individual payback periods can be calculated for each energy option based on energy saved versus costs incurred, cumulative results may be different because of the ways options interact. For example, the effect of vegetational shading of west walls versus increasing wall insulation: the two payback periods will differ if taken separately versus cumulatively.

Results of economic feasibility analysis can serve a number of purposes: individual design options can be assessed and compared with other alternatives; results can be useful in gaining approvals from key decision-makers and regulatory bodies; and they can be an important component of the marketing program.

Evaluating marketability. Once an option is determined to save energy and is economically feasible to implement, a check should be made to assure that it is legally implementable. When the option is assumed to be legally implementable or can be made so, the screening advances to a second stage of evaluation: assessment of marketability.

Every developer operates within the confines of the market place and his own financial and managerial resources. "While building and land use design principles can be significantly influenced [by energy-conservation considerations], their ultimate manifestation is a product of market demand and usually becomes a function of negotiation between what the developer would like to achieve and what the builder can actually sell" (CLAER, 1981, p. 287). Developers are dependent on the builders and consumers to determine what the actual end products will be.

Evaluation of marketability requires extensive experience in real estate development, finance, management, and marketing. Typically, four general product-related factors are assessed: the specifications of the product, the price it can demand and costs of production, how the product will be distributed, and plans for promotion of the product. If implementation risks are great, in-depth market research may be necessary.

The scope of this work does not permit description of the various assessment tools that are used to gauge marketability; however, at least one member of the technical team should have expertise in this area.

Evaluating implementation feasibility. Thus far, three criteria have been described for evaluating and selecting energy-conserving options. Other criteria (CLAER, 1981) affecting implementation feasibility that could be incorporated into the screening process are listed below:

- Functional planning — the achieving of efficient site-plan operation through minimization of time delays, congestion, human stress, etc.
- Environmental — preservation and maintenance of the natural environment.
- Socioeconomic — effects on human behavior, human needs, and man-environment relations.
- Technical feasibility — probability of technical feasibility at the time of implementation.
- Legal-political — compliance with current laws and procedures and probability of political acceptance.
- Financing — probability of financing through public and private sources or grants.
- Aesthetics — consideration of building mass, location, materials, color, landscaping, etc.

One aspect complicating the selection of options is that evaluation criteria often overlap and are interdependent. For example, marketability in part depends on economic feasibility, which in turn is dependent upon energy performance, among other things. Another problem is that to accurately evaluate an option the evaluator must have access to specific information on how the option works and how it will be implemented. A cost-analysis expert with insufficient information on solar hot-water heaters may interpret their value quite differently from another individual who is experienced in their construction and installation.

A selection strategy closely related to the feasibility of implementation, outlined by CLAER (1981), separates all screened energy options into one of three categories:

1. Options that can be directly implemented by the developer.
2. Options that are reasonably feasible but cannot be implemented until certain constraints are overcome.
3. Options that are not feasible to implement because of poor marketability, high costs, poor energy performance or other factors.

To assess implementation feasibility, members of the technical team evaluate each energy option using appropriate criteria. All potential constraints to implementation are listed for each energy-conserving option. Those options found feasible and without any

known constraints are incorporated into the site plan. Options found reasonably feasible but not implementable because of present constraints are included in the plan if implementation is likely to be feasible within the "build-out" period. Of course, options found not feasible are not included in the plan. This process simplifies final selection of energy-saving options by relating it directly to implementation.

Designing Energy-Conserving Developments

The chief design challenge confronting the energy-conscious landscape architect is that of integrating new energy-related design components with time honored design principles and forms. Energy options cannot be merely tacked onto a conventional design, but should blend and harmonize with all aspects of the design making it more efficient, more functional, more attractive, and more habitable. Unfortunately, to date there are not many examples of good site design wherein energy conservation is an important goal and has been successfully integrated into the design process. Chapter Six provides a number of examples for the reader searching for new forms that incorporate energy concerns. When a designer is attempting to integrate and create new forms it is important to remember Kevin Lynch's (1971, p. 272) observation that "the automatic use of previous solutions and the automatic worship of innovation are both irrational." He asserts that designers must first understand stereotypic forms (design prototypes) and know when to apply them. They must also be able to recognize problems for which an adapted solution will do and those which call for innovation. In most cases, energy-conserving site design will be incremental in nature; small and subtle modifications that improve energy performance will improve design solutions. Available stereotypes will undergo gradual and almost imperceptible changes as they are adapted to accommodate the need for energy conservation. As these newly modified stereotypes develop and as more knowledge about the consequences of their implementation grows, designers should begin to develop libraries or files that document findings. The sheer number of these design stereotypes and their complex interrelationships suggest that they be recorded in similar groups rather than individually. The Barton-Aschman (1980) report contains an excellent example of how such a library might be organized to facilitate incorporation of data and experience into the state-of-the-art. Stereotypes are grouped into the five major categories as shown in Appendix A-2. The following information is presented for each design stereotype:

- Objectives
- Application (design scale)
- Data and analysis requirements
- Methods/examples of calculating benefits and costs

Examples for more than a dozen stereotypes are given in the report and represent a good summary of critical findings contained in the five DOE case studies. Collecting, documenting, and evaluating evolving forms may appear spurious and mundane, but without a library that contains descriptions of each new form much information is lost and time wasted when later duplication of effort occurs.

Optimizing is another design approach that can reveal form requirements of different energy options. Lynch (1971, p. 274) notes that "one can learn a great deal about the requirements of a particular function by optimizing for it, while holding other requirements subordinate." Optimization forces the designer to really understand the option under study. This understanding may lead to innovation in form giving, because old design stereotypes may be found inappropriate. However, the danger with optimization occurs when it becomes a design end rather than a means to an integrated end. This often leads to unworkable solutions that fail to adequately address other issues of equal or greater concern than energy conservation.

Translation of design options into environmental forms often begins as a series of experimental probes that familiarize the designer with potentials and constraints inherent in implementing the option. The designer should explore as many alternatives as is possible, for those which at first seem impractical may later be preferable because they do not compromise other objectives. New alternatives should be periodically evaluated as information, criteria, and objectives are revised. Design and evaluation should be simultaneous to result in finely tuned solutions that reflect stated goals and objectives and meet the needs of the client and users.

Perhaps most crucial to successful design integration of energy conserving options is continuous communication during the design process. The importance of communication with key decision-makers has already been stressed as related to gaining approvals. It is equally important that designers share information among themselves, consultants, clients, users, and those responsible for implementation. Effective communication between these parties improves project results because the planning/design process is one of constant revision and adaption. For example, program alterations frequently necessitate concomitant changes in land-use allocations, the site plan, and even detailing of specific plan components. Effective communication enhances the design team's flexibility to adapt and integrate better ideas into the project. Without it, a design's potential to evolve into a successful solution that blends man and nature with energy conservation is greatly reduced.

Conclusion

The process of site analysis and design has evolved from procedures that were primarily based on intuition to those based more on empiricism and advanced technology. This reflects other similar trends in our society. Nevertheless, personal creativity and intuition has and always will lie at the heart of exemplary site design. This chapter has presented an overview of the site-planning process and described ways in which considerations related to energy-conserving development can be made a part of this process. Attention has been mainly focused upon program development, data collection and analysis, and techniques for generating and evaluating energy-conserving options. It is hoped that information contained herein will assist landscape architects and planners in their efforts to provide clients with the many benefits associated with energy-efficient development and at the same time promote exploration of new environmental forms that express a greater understanding of the natural rhythms of life around us.

Acknowledgment

The author is deeply indebted to Larry Wegkamp, Craig Johnson, Jim Zanetto, Daniel Montgomery, and Ted Andra for their assistance in developing and refining this chapter.

Analysis and Design 2

CHAPTER FOUR
Climatic Variables

LEE PIERCE HERRINGTON
State University of New York
Syracuse, New York

Climate and Energy

THE earth is a gigantic thermodynamic system powered by thermal energy from the sun that continually flows into, through, and out of the system. This energy pours into the system as *solar* or *shortwave* radiation and as *longwave* radiation. The amount of energy leaving must exactly equal the amount of energy arriving for the temperature of the earth to remain constant. If the rate at which the earth absorbs solar energy exceeds the rate at which energy leaves by infrared radiation, then the temperature of the earth will rise because the energy excess must be stored as thermal energy within the earth. This storage causes the temperature of the earth to increase. This idea that,

energy in – energy out = energy stored

is basic to an understanding of the operation of the earth system and, as a result, the climate of earth. This balance of energy flow and storage is called the *energy budget,* and as with a financial budget which accounts for the inflow and outflow of money, so the energy budget accounts for the inflow and outflow of energy. In fact, the balance in a bank account is analogous to heat content or temperature. A paycheck is the input and the bills, when paid, are the outputs. Similarly, energy flows into and out of a system via conduction, convection, and radiation, terms that will be defined later.

The concept of the energy budget can be illustrated by examining the energy budget of a pot of water on a stove. When the burner is first turned on, the pot and its water are at room temperature. The pot starts to warm because the input of energy from the burner exceeds the energy being lost from the pot by radiation (infrared) and convection. At a certain temperature, the energy losses equal the energy input from the burner, and the pot reaches an equilibrium temperature. It will stay at this temperature as long as none of the inputs or outputs of energy change. If the rate of heat loss by convection is increased by blowing air over the pot, the temperature of the pot would decrease to a new equilibrium. Turning the burner up would result in a higher equilibrium temperature. The rate of heat loss from the pot must be proportional to the pot's temperature. If this were not the case, the pot would never come to equilibrium since heat loss could not catch up to heat gain.

Size is also important; a small pot reaches equilibrium much faster than a large pot. The rate at which an object changes temperature is in direct proportion to the ratio of the rate of energy gain (or loss) to the mass of the object.

What has all this to do with climate? The flow of energy through the earth's system — or any small part of it — will have a strong influence on its climate, particularly its thermal climate which is the fundamental climatic variable. All the other variables used to characterize climate — humidity, precipitation, wind, etc. — can be derived from the thermal climate. Knowledge of the thermal climate is, of course, particularly important to the creation of energy-efficient designs.

The earth's surface does not receive heat energy

steadily. The sun supplies energy only during the day whereas the infrared radiation loss continues 24 hours a day. The result of this for any given area of the earth's surface is that the temperature changes during the course of the day and over the seasons of the year. Over time — day and season — a balance of energy input and output does not occur. The balance we have been discussing occurs only over long periods of time, a year or more.

The term *weather* is used when such variables as temperature, humidity, wind speed, etc., are averaged over a short period of time, say minutes. The term *climate* refers to averages of these variables taken over longer periods of time. The climatic *normals* used by the National Oceanic and Atmospheric Administration (NOAA) are 30-year averages.

Climate can also pertain to averages of climatic variables over an area. Microclimate is the average weather of a small area — an ant hill or a hillside. Mesoclimate is usually the climate of an area between 1 and 18 square miles, city climate for example. Synoptic climate pertains to the climate of areas tens to hundreds of miles on a side — about the dimensions of weather systems. Macroclimate is the climate of continents. The climate at one scale is an average of the climates of smaller scales.

Not all microclimates are the same. Indeed, the average of any climatic variable does not reveal the whole story: San Francisco and Boston have about the same average temperatures but hardly the same climates. A person with one foot in boiling water and one foot in ice water is, on the average, comfortable — a nice 90F (32C). However, the environment of each foot is quite different and the temperature range (difference between maximum and minimum) is large. Climatic data collected to represent the synoptic scale, as found in NOAA's *Local Climatological Data* and the *Climatic Atlas of the United States* (NOAA, 1977), is an average of a number of meso- and microclimates, but it does not tell very much about the individual microclimate, and it is microclimate we are interested in for energy-efficient design.

However, this idea can be turned around: microclimate can be thought of as a *variation* in mesoclimate which is, in turn, a variation in the synoptic climate. That is, the larger scale of climate sets the stage for the smaller scales. Predicting how a given site will modify the synoptic climate is easier than estimating what the microclimate will be on an absolute basis. This chapter and the next form the basis for making such predictions. Energy and energy flow will be examined throughout this and the following chapters. The terms and definitions listed in Table 4-1 should be memorized for more efficient reading.

Table 4-1. Heat Flow Terms

Term	CGS Units	SI Units	Definition
Heat	Cal	Joule	Amount of heat used to raise temperature of 1 g of water 1 C
Flux	Cal/min	Watt	Flow of heat per unit time
Flux density	Cal/cm²/min	Watt/cm²	Flow of heat per unit area per unit time

Throughout the discussion CGS units will be used for clarity of presentation. Most modern texts use SI units. Conversion factors are presented in Appendix B-1.

The Energy Budget

The concept of the energy budget has been used to explain how the flow of energy to and from a physical body controls its temperature. This section uses this concept to explain why certain microclimates are the way they are — why, for example a parking lot in summer is a hot environment but air temperature is not much higher than surrounding lawns and green areas, why concrete benches are so uncomfortable, why metal pump handles should not be kissed in the winter, or why the forest environment is quite different from the city environment.

The energy-budget concept requires that the energy flowing into a system must equal that flowing out of the system *plus* that stored. That is,

energy in = energy out + energy stored

The Bucket Model

An easy way to visualize an energy budget is to think of filling a bucket which has a hole in the bottom. If the hole is big enough, the bucket is impossible to fill. Figure 4-1 (see next page) shows water entering the bucket. At a particular water level, the inflow will equal the outflow and the system will be in equilibrium. If the flow into the system is reduced, the head will drop until the pressure is just enough to again cause outflow to equal inflow. Figure 4-2 (see next page) shows what would happen if the rate of inflow is increased or decreased if the hole in the bottom is made smaller or larger.

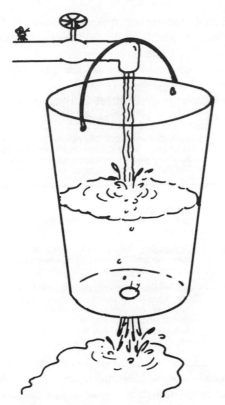

Figure 4-1. A water bucket with a hole models the energy budget. If heat flowing out is greater than heat flowing in the temperature (water level) will drop until equilibrium is reached.

As previously noted, increasing head (pressure) increases the outflow. For heat transfer, the larger the

temperature difference between two points in a body, the larger the flow of heat. That is,

the flow of heat is proportional to the temperature difference per inch.

This sounds suspiciously like the difference in pressure between the top of the water in the bucket and the hole. In the model system, temperature is then analogous to head or height of the water in the bucket. A rising water level in the model is analogous to a rising temperature difference and visa versa.

The analogy can be carried one step further. Figure 4-3 (see next page) compares the water level changes in a narrow and a wide bucket. Both have the same inflow of energy and the same size hole. The narrow bucket reaches equilibrium more quickly, but both achieve the same equilibrium water levels. The pressure is determined only by the height of the water, and this will be the same in both cases. The area of the bucket models the heat capacity (heat storage).

In summary:
1. Rate of flow of water is analogous to rate of flow of energy.
2. Water pressure, or head, is analogous to temperature.

Heat Transfer Terminology
Before applying this model to understanding microclimate, some terminology must be defined. For

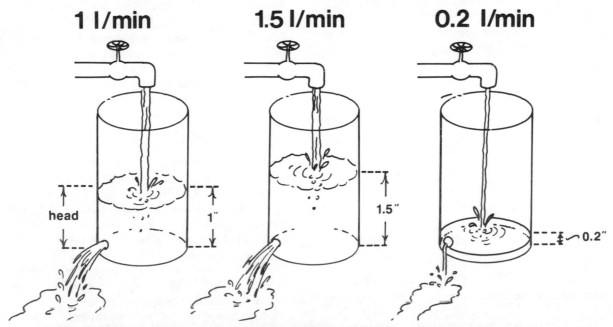

Figure 4-2. The height of water in a bucket is proportional to the rate of inflow and outflow of water, just as the flow of heat is proportional to temperature difference.

our purposes here, there are two kinds of heat: *sensible* and *latent*.

sensible heat is basically heat that can be felt.

latent heat is heat that cannot be felt and is associated with changes in state, such as freezing, evaporation, sublimation, etc. The evaporation of water requires heat. This is why a pot of boiling water stays at 212F (100C) until all the water is evaporated. The evaporation of each gram of water at 100C requires 540 calories of heat. As long as the pot contains water that can be evaporated, the temperature of the water remains at 100C or 212F. When the steam condenses on a window or some other cold surface, the reverse occurs. Latent heat is released and the surface is warmed by what is called vaporization.

These two forms of heat can be transferred by the following methods:

- *Conduction* — sensible heat transfer by molecular transfer of the vibration of molecules, plays a role in liquids and gases, but is especially important in solids.
- *Convection* — sensible heat transfer by the movement of mass. The bubbles which rise to the surface of cooking oatmeal, for example, are convecting heat from the bottom of the pot to the top of the oatmeal. This cannot take place in solids.
- *Evaporation* — latent heat transfer similar to convection. That is, a movement of mass is required for the movement of water vapor.

Heat transfer between an object and its surroundings is incorporated into the bucket model by creating 3 faucets on the bottom of the bucket (Figure 4-4, see next page) rather than one hole. The rate of

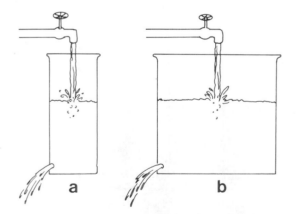

Figure 4-3. The height of water in a bucket is *not* related to the size of the bucket when the system is at equlibrium (inflow = outflow). Differences in heat-storage characteristics of materials will affect the rate at which an equilibrium temperature is reached, but eventually the temperatures will be the same.

energy (water) flow out of the bucket is now regulated by the faucets and is separated into the three different streams of heat loss. The various input and output features of our model are defined in Table 4-2.

Table 4-2. Energy Budget Components

Faucet No.	Transfer process
1	Net radiation input into system — balance of solar radiation, IR radiation in from sky and IR radiation out from ground. The net radiation is absorbed right at the ground-air interface.
2	Conduction — transfer of sensible heat into and out of the ground.
3	Convection — transfer of sensible heat into and from the atmosphere.
4	Evaporation — transport of latent heat from the ground to the atmosphere (note that condensation and dew formation transport latent heat from the atmosphere to the ground).

The model now has all of the energy-flow components needed to explain microclimate. However, one last but very important aspect of the model must be understood before the model is useful: The various flows of energy (water) interact. Suppose that the bucket is in equilibrium (inflow equal to outflow) with about one-third of the total outflow flowing through each of faucets 2, 3, and 4. When faucet 2 is shut off, the water level (temperature) and the flow through faucets 3 and 4 change. The water level rises (increasing temperature) and the flow through each of the open faucets increases by one-sixth of the total. Closing faucet 2 effectively decreases the size of the "hole" thereby requiring a higher pressure (head) for outflow to equal inflow; therefore the water level has to rise. In other words, when there is a temperature gradient between two objects and conductive heat flow from the warmer object to the cooler object is reduced, the temperature gradient will increase (water level rises). The rate of heat flow out of the warmer object by convection and evaporation will then increase until the temperatures of both objects are the same.

This simple model exhibits almost all of the features of energy flow in real situations. Because the water in a bucket is easier to visualize than the energy flowing through a system, in the following sections the bucket model will be used to introduce various aspects of microclimate. First it will be used to study the microclimate of bare soil surfaces; then it will be used to determine the effect of several cover types (grass, forest, city) on microclimate. However, more detail on radiation must first be provided.

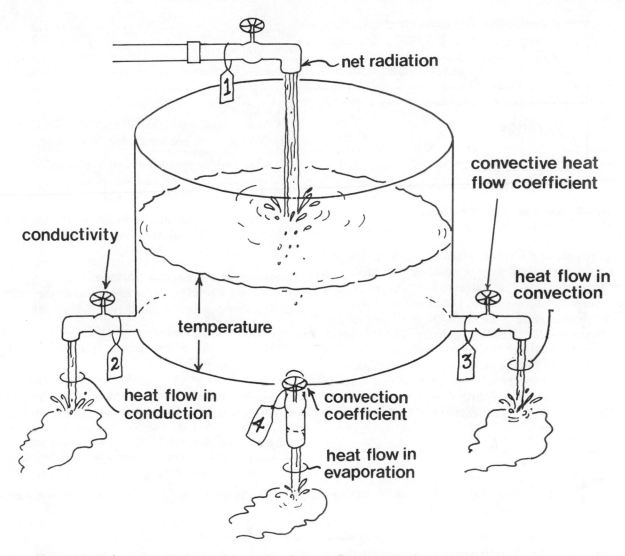

Figure 4-4. The complete bucket model contains all energy-flow components.

Radiation

Radiant-heat transfer is the transfer of heat from one body to another by electromagnetic waves. This covers a wide range of types of radiation — from atomic radiation to radio waves. In micrometeorology and microclimatology the important radiation is that associated with the sun — shortwave or visible radiation — and that associated with the emission of radiation from the earth, the atmosphere, and other bodies with temperatures like those found on earth. This latter radiation is called longwave or infrared (IR) radiation. To understand what controls the flow of energy into and out of a given piece of land or building, some of the physics of radiation must be understood. This section will develop the ideas important to this understanding.

Basic Radiation Physics

A basic law of physics states that all bodies radiate electromagnetic radiation. As a wave phenomenon this radiation can be described by (1) its energy content and (2) its predominant wavelength. Wavelength is the distance between successive troughs or ridges of a moving wave as is found by dividing the period of the wave by the velocity of movement (Figure 4-5). The result is a length usually expressed in microns or micrometers (10,000/cm), nanometers (10,000,000/cm), or Angstrom units (100,000,000/cm). In some cases the reciprocal of the wavelength, the wavenumber, is used. The energy content of the radiation is related to the *amplitude* of the wave and is a function of the fourth power of the temperature of the body. The wavelength of the radiation is inversely

63

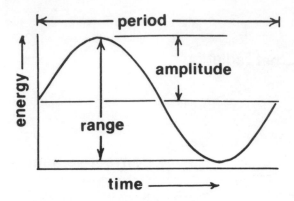

Figure 4-5. Waves are defined by period and amplitude or range (range = 2 x amplitude).

proportional to the temperature of the body. The sun at 6000K (degrees Kelvin or absolute) radiates at its surface about 100,000 cal/cm²/min at wavelengths centered at about ½ micron. The earth and things on it have a temperature of about 300K and hence radiate at a wavelength of about 10 microns with an energy content at the surface of about 0.6 cal/cm²/min. Thus, climatologists use the term *shortwave* radiation for the radiation from the sun and the term *longwave* for the radiation from the earth. These two streams of radiation are so different that they can be treated as separate entities.

A second important law of physics states that radiation emitted from a surface spreads spherically with the result that the energy content of the radiation decreases with distance. Table 4-3 shows the flux density from a small source of radiation.

Table 4-3. The Relationship between Distance and Flux Density

Distance		Flux density
meters	ft	cal/cm²/min
2	6.56	0.2500
4	13.12	0.0625
6	19.68	0.0280
8	26.24	0.0156
10	32.80	0.0100
20	65.60	0.0025

The energy content of the radiation measured per unit area perpendicular to the beam drops off rapidly with distance because of the spreading of the energy over a larger and larger area.

A third important law is that of the *cosine*. When a beam of energy impinges perpendicularly on a surface, the maximum amount of radiant energy is absorbed per unit area by the surface. As the angle of incidence (the angle between the radiation beam and a perpendicular to the surface) increases, the amount of energy absorbed *per unit of surface area* decreases, reaching zero when the ray of radiation is parallel to the surface. Mathematically,

$$\text{radiation absorbed} = \text{beam radiation} \times \cos(Z)$$

where Z is the zenith angle or angle between the beam and a line perpendicular to the surface.

A fourth basic law is that all the energy incident on a surface must be accounted for. It must be:

1. absorbed by the surface, or
2. reflected from the surface, or
3. transmitted through the body.

The fractional parts of the beam of radiation absorbed, reflected, and transmitted must add up to 1.00.

Radiation at the Earth's Surface

On the earth's surface, or for any object on the earth's surface, the sources of radiant energy input are:

1. *Direct beam shortwave* (DBS) — shortwave radiation that comes directly from the sun. DBS is always positive.
2. *Diffuse shortwave* (DS) — solar radiation reflected and scattered by atmospheric particles and clouds. Diffuse radiation comes from all parts of the sky. DS is always positive.
3. *Reflected shortwave* (RS) — shortwave radiation reflected from the earth or any other object. RS is always negative.

On a given land area, then, the *net shortwave radiation* is the sum of:

    direct beam
  + diffuse
  + (–) reflected
    _____
    net shortwave

Note: (–) means that the term is a negative quantity. Net shortwave radiation is always positive.

The longwave balance is made up of:

1. *Atmospheric longwave* (AL) — longwave radiation emitted from the molecules in the atmosphere, coming down from the sky. AL is always positive. The flux density of this radiation can be computed from knowledge of the temperature and humidity of the lower atmosphere.
2. *Ground longwave* (GL) — longwave radiation emitted from the earth's surface (or any other object being studied). GL is always negative and is computed from the temperature of the surface.

64

The *net longwave radiation* is the sum of:

atmospheric
+ (–) ground
_____
net longwave

NOTE: The net longwave radiation can be either positive or negative, that is, radiant energy can be flowing toward or away from the surface. However, the balance is usually zero (AL= GL) or negative (GL>AL).

The total net radiation on the surface is:

net shortwave
+ net longwave
_____
net radiation

The sign of the net radiation is:

+ during the day
0 at sunrise and sunset
– during clear nights
0 or slightly – on cloudy nights

Thus during the day the stream of energy from the sun provides an excess of energy to the surface whereas at night the radiation balance is controlled by the longwave radiation balance. Table 4-4 illustrates these components of the radiation balance in a convenient format. Many of the relationships discussed in this section can be seen in these data.

A number of factors control the amount of solar radiation that impinges on a given piece of the earth's surface. These can be divided into several categories: geometric, atmospheric, and surface.

1. *Geometric factors*. These determine the angle between the solar beam and the surface which is receiving the radiation. They are:
   - *time of year*, which determines the *declination*

angle of the sun above or below the equator. This is the angle between the planes of the sun and the equator (+22.5 at the summer solstice, –22.5 at the winter solstice) in the northern hemisphere (note differences between summer and winter sun angle in Table 4-4).
   - *latitude of surface*, which together with the declination angle, determines the path of the sun through the sky and the maximum height of the sun above the horizon at solar noon. This angle is called the solar altitude:

   noon altitude = latitude – declination

   - *time of day*, which determines the position of the sun on the arc of the sun's path. *Hour angle* is the term given to this position in solar coordinates. The hour angle is measured from south, – to the east, + to the west, 15 degrees for each hour from solar noon.
   - *slope and aspect angles*, which determine the angle of the sun's beam to a sloped surface. Both the slope of the surface and the direction it faces (measured from the south) are necessary for calculation of the angle of incidence of the solar beam with the surface. A surface facing directly south with a slope angle of:

   slope (degrees) = 90 – (latitude – declination)

   from the horizontal will be perpendicular to the sun's rays at solar noon.

2. *Atmospheric factors*. Although the geometric factors are complex, they can be accurately computed. Atmospheric factors that absorb radiation are readily understandable but are almost impossible to compute for any particular place. The term usually used to describe the opacity of the atmosphere is *transmissivity*. Transmissivity varies with the amount of moisture and pollutants in the atmosphere. Clouds obviously reduce

Table 4-4. Radiation Balance of a Meadow for Summer (S) and Winter (W) Days (24 Hours).

Direction		Shortwave S	W	Longwave S	W	Total S	W
Down From Space	DBS	248	12	-	-	-	-
Down From Atmos.	DS	218	39	728	528	1194	623
Up From Ground	RS	-93	-18	-809	-621	902	637
		Net shortwave		Net longwave		Net	
Total		373	33	83	39	292	-6

From: (Reifsnyder & Lull, 1965).

the amount of solar radiation that reaches the surface. If the sun were at the zenith (that is, straight up), the atmosphere would have a relative thickness of 1.0. As the sun approaches the horizon, the thickness of the atmosphere through which the sun's rays must pass increases, resulting in a greatly reduced amount of radiation reaching the surface. This reduction is not due to a change in transmissivity but to a thickening of the effective atmosphere. When the sun is near the horizon, more opportunity exists for the solar beam to be scattered. For this reason the percentage of diffuse radiation in the total solar radiation is higher when the sun is near the horizon than when it is nearly overhead.

3. *Surface factors.* Very few natural surfaces absorb all the radiation incident upon them. Even the best solar collectors will reflect some small percentage of the radiation. The reflectivity of a surface, that is, the amount of radiant energy reflected expressed as a percent of the total incident radiant energy, is often called the *albedo* (100 x RS/(DBS + DS). The winter data in Table 4-4 is for snow-covered grass. Note that a higher albedo occurs in winter than in summer.

Appendix B-2 gives equations from which these angles and the final angle of incidence can be computed.

Summary
Radiant energy can be considered the driving force behind microclimate. During the day the shortwave radiation from the sun, both direct beam and diffuse, provides a positive net radiation to the surface — energy accumulates in the surface and must be disposed of somehow. At night the sky is at a lower temperature than the ground, and longwave or infrared radiation is lost to the sky. Energy is lost from the surface and must be supplied from some other source.

The amount of radiation received from the sun is determined by geometric, atmospheric, and surface factors whereas the radiation lost by longwave radiation is determined by surface temperature and the cloudiness of the sky.

The balance sheet of radiation streams provides the net radiation which is the driving force behind climate.

Microclimate of the Bare Soil System

The bare soil system is the simplest of the systems to be analyzed. It is used here to introduce many of the heat transfer concepts which apply also to the grass, forest, and city systems.

The bare soil system is a horizontal flat surface of a homogeneous soil body. The operation of a dry system, one without any evaporation or condensation taking place, is described first. Thus only the physics of conduction and convection of heat are applicable. In this system, during the day net radiation is the input, and conduction and convection are the outputs. The task is to discover what properties of the soil and atmosphere control the temperature of the surface and the subsurface regions.

Conduction Heat Transfer
Visualize a flat, dry soil at a uniform temperature throughout — say 0C. As the sun rises in the sky, the radiation balance becomes strongly positive and heat accumulates in the surface (the bucket is filling up because none of the faucets have been opened yet). If the soil has a low *heat capacity* (remember, this is modeled as a narrow bucket), its surface temperature rises very quickly. On the other hand, if it has a high heat capacity, the surface temperature will rise much more slowly (wide bucket). As mentioned earlier, this rise in temperature is analogous to a rise in head in the bucket. A driving force is being created by the accumulation of heat (water).

A very common equation in physics states that,

flow of $S = K$ x change in S over distance

where S is any scalar quantity and K is a constant. In terms of heat flow, and more cryptically,

$$Q/At = -K \text{ x } (T_2 - T_1)/(d_2 - d_1)$$

where

Q	=	amount of heat	cal
A	=	area through which heat flows	cm^2
t	=	time	min
K	=	thermal conductivity	cal/cm^2-degree/cm
$T_2 - T_1$	=	temperature difference	degree
$d_2 - d_1$	=	distance over which heat flows	cm

The accumulation of heat in the soil surface results in a temperature gradient being established in the soil which in turn causes a certain amount of heat to flow per unit time per unit area into the soil, with the result that the soil body warms. The exact amount of heat to flow will depend on the conductivity (K) of the material (soil). Study of this equation shows that heat flow will increase if:

1. The thermal conductivity (K) of the material is increased.

2. The temperature difference is increased.
3. The thickness of the material is decreased.

As heat builds up in the soil surface (water pours into the bucket), the difference in temperature between the surface and the layers deeper in the soil increases. Heat flows from the surface into the soil at a rate determined by the conductivity of the soil and the temperature difference between the surface and deeper layers. In the bucket model (Figure 4-4) the rate of flow of water through the conduction faucet is determined by (1) the head, and (2) the opening of the faucet. Thus the magnitude of the faucet's opening is analogous to the conductivity of the soil.

Now, compare two different soil bodies with the same input of radiation (input faucets set the same) and the same heat capacity (buckets with the same cross-sectional area). One, however, has its conduction faucet open twice as much as the other. The soil with the lower conductivity (faucet half open) becomes hotter (higher head). If the two soils are similar except that one has twice the heat capacity of the other, then both soils come to the *same* equilibrium temperature. However, the soil with the lower heat capacity comes to equilibrium much faster than the one with the higher heat capacity.

Inclusion of heat capacity in the model adds the dimension of time. The input of radiation is more or less sinusoidal over time. It rises to a maximum at solar noon then decreases to some slightly negative value during the night. Soils with low heat capacity respond to this changing input of energy more rapidly than soils with high heat capacities. A wooden bench warms much more rapidly than a concrete bench.

In this simple situation only conduction loss has been considered. Both the conductivity of the soil and its heat capacity have been shown to play important roles in determining surface temperature. In summary, during the day:

1. Increasing conductivity will decrease surface temperatures.
2. Increasing heat capacity will decrease response time and may decrease maximum temperatures.

Convective Heat Transfer

The situation described above is not actually realistic. All natural systems on earth have more than one sink for heat. The atmosphere always provides a convective heat transfer route from the soil surface to the outer atmosphere. The process of convection can be described generally by an equation similar to that used to describe heat conduction. The difference is that whereas in a solid conductivity remains the same, in the atmosphere the "conductivity" changes with con-

ditions. Conductivity, however, is really not the right term to use for describing the ability of the air to transport heat. The correct technical term is *eddy diffusivity* and the equations describing heat flow are a little different. Nevertheless, the basic idea is the same. For a given temperature gradient $(T_2 - T_1)/(d_2 - d_1)$, the eddy diffusivity determines the amount of heat transferred per unit area per unit time.

In convection, heat is transferred by circulating masses of air. If a parcel of air is warmed by a hot soil surface and moves upward because of buoyancy forces, then a convection of heat away from the surface occurs (heat loss). Similarly, if a parcel of cold air settles on the surface, a convective heat loss also occurs since heat is extracted from the surface to warm the air (cold air downward is the same as warm air upward). The amount of heat moved is related to the amount of air moved around — wind. Generally, as the wind speed increases, so does the diffusivity of the atmosphere (this is one reason we blow on our soup to cool it). As wind speed increases, so too does the mechanical turbulence (stirring) of the flow of air. This turbulence results in more parcels of air being carried up and down and hence more heat transfer.

Turbulence can also be created by heat — thermal turbulence. If the air is still and the soil surface is heated, the warmer parcels of air rise to be replaced by cooler parcels of air — convection. When the ground is warmer than the air (air temperature decreases upward), the meteorologist says that *lapse* or *unstable* conditions exist and thermal turbulence may be present. If a wind is present, the thermal turbulence and the mechanical turbulence combine. If the atmosphere is *stable* — that is, if the air temperature increases with height (an inversion) — then the atmosphere tends to smooth out the turbulence and the air flow is very smooth and heat transfer is low. The process during the day is summarized as follows:

1. Surface temperature will *increase* as,
   - wind speed *decreases*.
   - turbulence *decreases*.
2. Surface temperature will *decrease* as,
   - wind speed *increases*.
   - turbulence *increases*.

As in the water-bucket model, the faucet for convection opens wider when the wind blows harder and/ or when the wind is turbulent. Thus, if all other heat flow out of a system remains the same, increasing wind or turbulence lowers the temperature (water level).

These factors interact. If the sun goes behind a cloud, net radiation input to the ground is reduced and less thermal turbulence exists. The first effect results in less energy flowing into the system, while the second results in less heat being transferred away from the soil to the air. Usually the first effect outweighs the second and the soil surface temperature drops. To summarize:

1. The thermal properties of soils determine how they react to the environment relative to one another. Soils with a low heat capacity and a low conductivity such as peat, loess, dry fine sand, bark chips, and other soils with low bulk densities have higher daytime temperatures than similarly exposed soils with high heat capacity and conductivity.

2. The input of radiation (net radiation) and the state of the atmosphere determine how a given soil responds to the changing environment. In conditions with low solar radiation and high-velocity turbulent winds, the soil surfaces have lower daytime temperatures than similar soils in situations in which the net radiation is high and the winds are low and not turbulent.

So far only daytime conditions have been described. If the soil is exposed to solar radiation and protected from wind during the day, the soil surface becomes very warm by midafternoon. At night this soil surface experiences strong negative net radiation since it is losing heat to the cold sky by infrared or longwave radiation. The soil cools below air temperature causing heat to flow from the air to the soil surface — the opposite of what happens during the day. Usually a situation which leads to high daytime temperatures, such as a clear sky, also leads to low nighttime temperatures and vice versa.

Frost and dew form when the temperature of a surface — car, grass, or other surface — falls below the dew point temperature of the air. That is, the surface is so cold that the air in close contact with it becomes supersaturated and the water condenses or sublimes onto the surface.

Clear nights with low winds and cold air from the north cause concern among orchard owners because these conditions cause their trees and fruit to freeze. One method of preventing this is to burn smudge pots. Contrary to popular belief this is *not* done to add heat to the air (hot air rises and will not stay around to warm the fruit). The smoke from the pots reduces the radiation loss to the cold sky and thus reduces the chance of freezing. The radiation loss is reduced since the cloud of smoke is much warmer than the clear sky.

These descriptions of nocturnal situations illustrate that what happens at night is the opposite of what happens during the day. Soils which get very hot during

the day get relatively cold at night. The bucket model can be applied to daytime conditions with the assumption that the opposite occurs at night.

Table 4-5 summarizes the effects discussed so far. In most cases conditions which lead to increasing daytime temperatures also lead to decreasing nighttime temperatures.

Table 4-5. Effect of Changing Environment or Soil Property on Soil Surface Temperature.

Energy budget component	Temperature change	
	Day	Night
Net shortwave	+	0
Net longwave	+	+
Conduction into soil	−	
Out of soil		+
Convection to air	−	−
From air	+	+
Latent heat		
Evaporation	−	
Dew formation		+
Secondary effects		
Darken color of soil	+	0
Increase soil moisture	−	+
Increase wind speed	−	+
Increase wind turbulence	−	+

+ denotes increasing temperature.
− denotes decreasing temperature.
0 denotes no effect on temperature.

Temperatures below the Soil Surface

Thus far only the factors which control temperature at the surface of the soil have been described. During the day heat is stored within the soil body and is released by the surface at night. If heat is flowing into and out of the surface, temperatures then vary within the soil body.

During the day the soil surface becomes warmer than the soil beneath the surface. Therefore, heat flows into the soil body. This is the heat that is stored in the soil. This heat also causes the soil to change temperature beneath the surface. The temperature wave on the surface of the soil may be considered almost a sinusoidal wave when plotted over time (Figure 4-6, see next page). A basic law of physics states that the frequency or period of a sinusoidal signal cannot be changed. Therefore the period of the temperature wave beneath the surface is the same as that on the surface. Think of the soil as being layered, then imagine a process whereby some of the heat flowing into the soil is used to heat each succeedingly deeper layer of soil until essentially no heat is left. If each layer extracts a constant percentage of the heat, less heat is available to raise the temperature of the next lower layer. The same thing happens when heat flows out of the soil. More heat flows to the surface from the layers closer to the surface. Therefore the maximum and minimum temperatures of each succeedingly deeper layer are closer together. More temperature variation occurs near the surface than deeper in the soil.

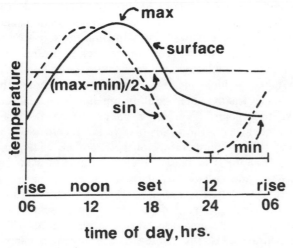

Figure 4-6. Variation of soil surface temperature over time and a similar sinusoidal variation.

At any one soil depth, the temperature pattern over time has the same shape as the surface wave but has a smaller range. In addition, because it takes time for the heat to flow into or out of the soil, the temperature waves within the soil lag behind those of the surface wave. That is, the times of maximum and minimum soil temperatures occur later in the day. The lag time increases with depth into the soil.

The series of figures (Figure 4-7) located in the upper right of the next several pages show temperature profile variations in the same soil. The movement of the temperature wave into the soil can be seen by flipping the pages rapidly.

The surface temperature of a soil is governed by its conductivity and heat capacity. In fact, a soil's range of surface temperatures will be inversely related to both heat capacity (C) and conductivity (K). Or, mathematically,

$$\text{temperature range} :: 1/\sqrt{C \times K}$$

A soil with a high conductivity, such as a moist loam, transfers heat to deeper soil depths more efficiently than one with a low conductivity, such as dry peat. As pointed out above, this leads to lower surface temperatures. It also leads to higher temperatures

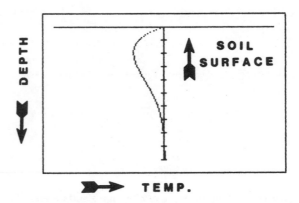

Figure 4-7. Temperatures vary in the soil with both depth and time. "Flipping" these pages will demonstrate how the variation in surface temperature decreases with depth in the soil. The first graph is for noon (12 hrs.). The surface of the soil is warmer than the underlying soil. As the day progresses the surface warms and then cools.

within the soil because more heat gets farther down when the soil is warming. A soil with a high heat capacity, such as wet peat, does not get very warm at the surface or lower down since a great deal of heat is needed to cause a temperature change of even 1 degree. Therefore, the temperature within the soil is inversely related to heat capacity. Mathematically,

$$\text{temperature range in soil} :: 1/\sqrt{K/C}$$

The above equation states that the temperature range at any depth within the soil is directly proportional to the thermal conductivity of the soil and inversely proportional to its heat capacity. Figure 4-8 (see next page) compares the temperature at a depth of 25 cm (0.8 ft) in a sandy soil and in dry peat. Both soils have the same surface temperature pattern. Because of the low ratio of conductivity to heat capacity for the peat ($K/C = 0.0003$, see Table 4-6), its temperature range at 25 cm is much less than that in the sand ($K/C = 0.0023$) at the same depth. The maxima and minima of the variation in the peat occur later than in sand. Dry peat would have a temperature range of 37% of the surface wave at a depth of 3.3 cm (1.3 in.) while the sand would have a similar range in temperature at a depth of 8 cm (3.14 in.). Increasing the moisture content of either soil causes an increase in the 37% depth (Table 4-6).

The temperature wave in the soil also varies with the period of the applied wave. The longer the wave, the deeper it penetrates. Short-period waves, like those due to cloud passage, penetrate only a few centimeters whereas those of a year can penetrate more than a meter.

Soil scientists often use the term *damping depth* to describe the thermal behavior of soils. This is the depth at which the temperature range equals 37% of the temperature range of the surface wave, maxima

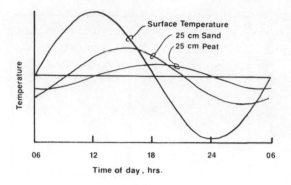

Figure 4-8. Soil temperature profiles at the surface and 25 cm for sandy soil and dry peat.

and minima occurring about 4 hours after those at the surface. Mathematically,

$$\text{damping depth} = 1/\sqrt{PK/C}$$

where P is the period of the temperature wave in seconds. Thus, for two soils with the same surface temperature, the one with the deeper damping depth has a larger temperature range at any given depth (because it has the same temperature range at a deeper depth). The equations used to predict the temperature patterns in soils are rather complex and are given in Appendix B-3. Table 4-6 shows the properties of several different soils which can be used with these equations to gain some insight into the behavior of different soils.

Evaporation and Condensation

If a soil is wet or even damp, some evaporation from the soil occurs. Evaporation, if it occurs, provides a huge avenue for heat loss. On the stove a pot of water at room temperature, 20C (68F), requires only 80 cal per gram of water to bring the water to 100C. An additional 540 cal are needed to evaporate each gram of water. Condensation of the water vapor releases the latent heat. Evaporation and condensation are thus very important elements of the energy budget of natural surfaces.

The process of evaporation and the convective loss of the water vapor emitted by the soil is very similar to the process of sensible heat convection. The driving force is the vapor pressure (e) gradient $(e2-e1)/(d2-d1)$ rather than the temperature gradient $(T2-T1)/(d2-d1)$,

where e = vapor pressure
d = distance
T = temperature

Consider a closed chamber which contains only water and water vapor. At any given temperature a certain number of water molecules leave the water surface to become water vapor. In time there will be so many molecules of water vapor over the water that some of the molecules will reenter the water. When the number of molecules entering the water equals the number leaving, then equilibrium has been reached. At this point, a pressure gauge attached to the chamber reads the *saturation vapor pressure* of the water. If the temperature of the chamber, water, and water vapor is increased, then the vapor pressure increases and visa versa. Figure 4-9 shows the curve of saturation vapor pressure for different temperatures. It does not matter if other gases are present in the chamber. The increase in pressure due to water evaporation is the same as the pressure change measured within the chamber containing only water vapor.

The atmosphere is usually not saturated. Figure 4-9 shows the actual vapor pressures for relative humidities (RH) of 25%, 50%, and 100%. At a temperature of 25C (77F) the saturation vapor pressure (E_s) is 23.75 mmHg. If the actual vapor pressure (E_a) is 11.88 mmHg then the relative humidity is,

$$\text{RH} = 100(E_a/E_s) = 100(11.88/23.75) = 50\%$$

Although common and convenient, it is incorrect to say that "the air holds one half of the water it could," since it is not necessary that any air be present (see above). Now, if the air temperature were reduced to

Table 4-6. Properties of Several Different Soils

Soil type	Water content %	Period = 1 day Thermal conductivity, (K), cal/cm²/sec	Heat capacity, (C), cal/cm³/°C	Damping depth, cm
Sand	0	0.0007	0.3	8.0
	20	0.0042	0.7	14.3
Clay	0	0.0006	0.3	7.4
	40	0.0038	0.7	12.2
Peat	0	0.0001	0.3	3.3
	40	0.0007	0.8	5.1
Snow*	—	0.0017	0.5	9.7

* porosity 0.5
After: (Van Wijk, 1963)

20C, the relative humidity would become 68% [100 (11.88/17.52) = 68%]. At what temperature then would the RH equal 100%? Follow the line for constant Ea marked A on Figure 4-9 to the left until it intersects the 100% RH curve. The temperature at this point is the *dew point,* defined as the temperature at which the air will become saturated (RH = 100%) when it is cooled.

Returning to the soil problem, suppose that the soil has a temperature of 20C and the atmosphere has a RH of 50% and a temperature of 25C. If the soil is wet, the vapor pressure (Es soil) is 17.52 mmHg while that in the air is 11.88 mmHg. Thus a vapor-pressure gradient exists between the soil and the atmosphere

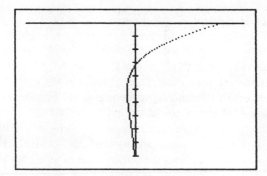

Figure 4-7. 17 hours. 5:00 p.m.

and therefore water vapor moves from the soil to the atmosphere. This convective movement of the water

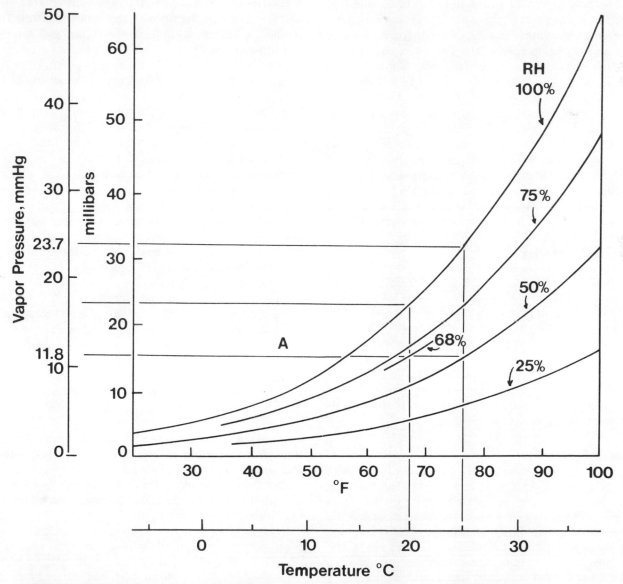

Figure 4-9. Psychrometric chart showing the relation between air temperature and atmospheric moisture at various relative humidities.

vapor is controlled by the same factors that control heat convection: wind speed and turbulence. However, as previously indicated, the driving force, the vapor-pressure gradient, is not directly related to temperature and must be evaluated from knowledge of soil moisture and temperature as well as the vapor pressure of the atmosphere.

Another example. If the vapor pressure of the air is 15.77 mmHg at a temperature of 20C (68F) (RH = 90%) and the soil has a temperature of 15C (59F) (E_s = 12.78 mmHg) due to loss of heat by radiation at night, condensation occurs on the soil surface because the vapor pressure at the soil surface is less than that in the atmosphere. Thus the water vapor would move from the atmosphere to the soil. As condensation at the surface removes water vapor from the atmosphere, the gradient within the atmosphere increases because moisture is being removed at the lower boundary.

Now it is easy to understand why a moist soil is cooler by day and warmer by night than a similar dry soil. This evaporative effect is enhanced because wet soils have a higher bulk density and therefore tend to have a more moderate temperature range.

Returning to the water bucket as an analogy to the energy budget, it can now be seen that including moisture in the model has effectively added a third faucet (evaporation) to the bottom of the water bucket. This provides more opportunity for variation in and control of surface temperature (water level).

Other Systems

Bare soil is a relatively simple surface compared to the complex three-dimensional "surface" that characterizes grass, croplands, forests, and cities. Grass, croplands, and forests are similar in that they are composed of vegetative elements whereas cities consist predominantly of high-density man-made material arranged in a coarse array, compared to most vegetative systems. However, the basic ideas of the energy budget model can be applied to the analysis of these systems.

Grass Systems

A grass system includes any surface covered with relatively short vegetation: lawns, crops, prairies, etc. In contrast to bare soil, grass absorbs shortwave incoming radiation throughout the volume occupied by the grasses above the ground. In grass ecosystems the biomass per unit volume usually increases downward. Almost all of the incoming radiation is absorbed above the ground surface by material characterized by a low density and a very large surface area relative to

ground area. The low density results in little heat storage and high daytime temperatures in the grass canopy. The large surface area results in a very efficient exchange of heat by any of the methods previously discussed. Figure 4-10 (see next page) shows different ways energy is exchanged between a small plant and the surrounding environment.

Applying the law of physics which states that the rate of heat flow is proportional to area, temperature, and time, then if the surface area of one system is twice that of another, the first will require only one-half the temperature gradient to transfer the same amount of heat. This surface area factor then tends to make the maximum temperatures of the vegetation lower than those of a bare soil with the same thermal properties (and the minimum temperatures higher, of course). The low density has the opposite effect: It results in higher daytime temperatures and lower nighttime temperatures.

The rough "hair brush" structure of grass makes it a very efficient absorber of radiation. The albedo of a field is much less than that of an individual leaf. Therefore a relatively high percentage of solar radiation is absorbed. There is little or no effect on the infrared radiation emitted by the grass in relation to that emitted by a flat surface. This tends to increase daytime maximum temperatures and has little effect on nighttime minimums.

If the vegetation is green and if the stomates of the plants are open, transpiration from the vegetation will occur. (Stomates are very small holes in the leaves which allow moisture to pass from the leaf to the atmosphere — an evaporation process.) However, the opening of the stomates is controlled by the water status of the plant and by the light intensity. They tend to be open in the morning and evening and closed at night and during the middle part of the day. If the plant is wilting, or under a moisture stress, the stomates are closed and very little or no transpiration takes place. If the plant is transpiring, the evaporation "faucet" opens, resulting in lower maximum temperatures during the day, or at least part of the day.

Wind does not blow over a vegetative cover, it blows through it. Therefore, air will flow over the entire surface area provided by the vegetation. The wind thus makes the atmosphere a very efficient sink or source of heat. This tends to decrease maximum and increase minimum temperatures.

Because of the relatively low mass of material in the plant canopy, very little heat is stored in the canopy, and most of the heat input during the day is lost through convection, transpiration, and infrared radiation. Because the canopy does not store much heat, it cools very quickly when the radiation balance is negative. The result is higher maximum and lower minimum temperatures than would be found on bare ground. Because the soil is cooler than the upper reaches of the grass canopy during the day, radiation and convection transfer heat from the canopy and the soil surface. Thus some of the input heat is stored in the soil, the amount depending on the amount of vegetation — the more dense the canopy, the less heat reaches the surface.

Forest Systems

A forest system is very similar to a grass system. However, the forest really has two climates, one in the canopy and one in the stem space. Since people are only 1 to 2 m high, the term *forest climate* usually refers only to the climate in the stem space.

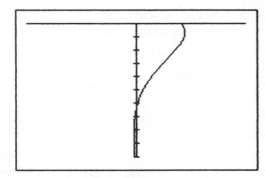

Figure 4-7. 22 hours. 10:00 p.m.

A forest system is similar to the bare soil surface system and the grass system, with the canopy space behaving much like the grass canopy since it has many of the same properties and similar structure. In effect

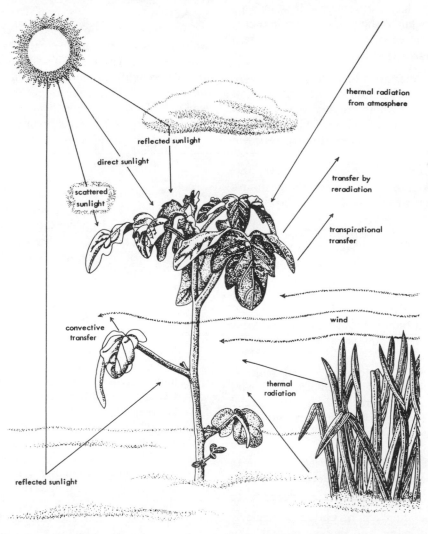

thermal radiation from atmosphere

reflected sunlight

direct sunlight

scattered sunlight

transfer by reradiation

transpirational transfer

wind

convective transfer

thermal radiation

reflected sunlight

Figure 4-10. Exchange of energy between a small plant and its environment. From: (Gates, 1980) with permission of the publisher.

it insulates the stem or trunk space. The below-canopy climate, however, is characterized by:

1. Much less solar radiation present than in the open.
2. Protection from infrared loss to the sky by the canopy.
3. Wind speeds roughly 20% of the winds in the open.

These differences result in a more moderate climate in the stem space than that in the open, with lower maximum temperatures and higher minimum temperatures.

City Systems

A city system is characterized by large amounts of very high-density material — concrete, stone, macadam, etc. It also has a structure, at least in large cities, somewhat similar to the grass system in that it has many tall spindlelike structures. The city system can be further characterized by:

1. High-density materials which do not heat very much during the day but do store a large amount of heat due to their high conductivity (the conduction faucet is open wide). This results in lower maximum and higher minimum temperatures.
2. A lack of vegetation and bare soil (the evaporation faucet is shut off). Therefore maximum temperatures are higher and minimum temperatures are lower.
3. Usually low to moderate regional winds leading to low city winds which result in higher maximum and lower minimum temperatures. Under these conditions the mechanical and thermal properties of the city surface result in a strong drag on air flow. However, at high regional wind speeds the wind blows through the city canyons and convective heat transfer can be an important factor.
4. Heat produced by automobiles and building heating/air conditioning which are significant anthropogenic heat sources. These sources tend to increase both maximum and minimum temperatures.

Applying the energy budget analysis technique to the above yields the city climate, characterized by:

1. Daytime temperatures a little warmer than those of the surrounding countryside, particularly when the wind is low and the sky is clear.
2. Nighttime temperatures higher than those of the surrounding countryside, particularly when the wind is low and the sky is clear.

In short, the city simply does not cool off at night as does the surrounding countryside. The warm city is referred to as the *urban heat island*.

For temperate cities, solar radiation is the major cause of the summer urban heat island, whereas anthropogenic heat is the major cause of the winter heat island.

Application of Energy Budget to Real Situations

The bucket model has been used to explain the general nature of the microenvironment of several common surface types. The same model can also be used to attempt to predict the departure of the microclimate of a piece of land from the synoptic climate as published by NOAA.

Climatic data are collected by sensors mounted in white boxes located at a height of 1 m over grass at many airports. Therefore, if a site looks like an airport *and is in roughly the same topographic position as the site of climatic data collection*, then the climatic data would apply to the site. If this is not the case, then the following steps must be completed:

1. Evaluate the radiation balance (note that output of infrared radiation will be similar regardless of site):
   - Estimate the direct-beam solar radiation input. How will it vary during the day, the season? How does reflectivity differ between the site and the airport?
   - Estimate the differences in infrared radiation balance between the design site and the airport. How much infrared will be lost to the cold sky? How much infrared will be gained from surrounding high-density surfaces?
2. Evaluate the surface properties. Is the bulk density of the surface (including vegetation, if any) higher or lower than that at the airport?
3. Evaluate the differences in evapo-transpiration between the site and the airport. Is the surface moist? Do the plants have adequate moisture? How do plant density and structure differ?
4. Evaluate the wind. Airport winds are almost always higher than those found at other sites because of a long, uninterrupted fetch upwind of the measuring instruments. Usually the wind is lower than that recorded at the airport, particularly when in the city, suburbs, or under a forest canopy.

A mental bucket model can now be constructed to determine if the daytime temperatures (head) will be higher or lower than those at the airport. The night-time temperatures can be assumed to be the opposite of the daytime pattern. The details of climatic data extrapolation will be discussed in the following chapter.

Biometeorology

Animals, including people, exchange energy with their surroundings in exactly the same way as other objects, the major difference being that all animals convert most of the food they eat into heat. This heat must be lost to the environment. Even in the coldest climate the body must lose exactly the same heat it produces *otherwise body temperature will change*. The human body operates at a constant interior body temperature of 98.6F (37C). Comfort, however, is sensed mainly as skin temperature, and in warm situations it is influenced by skin "wettedness." For warm situations, that is, for situations where you feel warm, the bucket model applies if one more *input* faucet is added for heat produced within the body by metabolism.

From this model it is obvious why we begin to feel hot if we increase our activity level when in a comfortable environment. The inflow from the metabolism faucet is increased and thus the water level rises so that the outflow can equal the inflow. Our skin temperature rises so that convective and radiational heat losses from the skin can increase without changing the deep body temperature. Only the skin temperature rises, not the deep body temperature. Another difference between passive objects and animals with active control of their internal systems and, in some cases, their environments is that active control allows changes to be made before the deep body temperature changes. Thus, in hot situations our body physiologically senses that things are getting warmer and opens the skin's capillaries, allowing more warm blood to flow to the surface and increasing the skin's conductivity. Both actions allow more heat to be lost from the body. If body temperature continues to rise, the physiological system starts perspiration, a powerful mechanism for losing heat. Thus the harder the body works, the greater the perspiration.

On the cold side of comfort similar things happen. When heat loss is first sensed, the body closes the skin capillaries thus reducing blood flow to and heat loss from the skin. If heat loss continues, shivering begins, which produces heat by mechanical action (metabolism), and the body tends to "curl up" to reduce the area of heat loss. (Cats and dogs curl up when the weather is cold and stretch out when the weather is hot.)

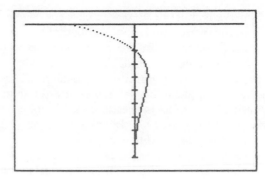

Figure 4-7. 3 hours. 3:00 a.m.

Wind has the same effect on people as it does on the other systems we have studied. Increasing wind speed increases heat transfer. The "wind-chill factor" is an attempt to include in weather reporting the idea that increasing wind speed causes increasing heat loss. A wind-chill temperature of -30F (-34C) when the air temperature is 10F (-12C) means that moving air causes a heat loss equivalent to that which would occur in still air (no wind) at -30F (-34C). As the basic heat-transfer equation indicates, heat transfer can be increased by increasing either the temperature difference *or* the heat-transfer coefficient. When the wind-chill temperature is -30F (-34C), more clothes are necessary to insulate the skin from the environment. This effectively reduces the temperature of the outer layer and thereby reduces the temperature gradient between clothes and air. A perfect insulator can't be used because the body *must* lose the heat produced through metabolism.

In warm situations clothes are taken off, essentially removing insulation so that heat loss is maximized. When as much clothing as possible has been removed, the next step is to blow air over the skin to remove heat by convection. Skin "wet" with perspiration is an effective cooling measure since increasing wind speed will increase the rate of evaporation of perspiration. If a person is not perspiring or if the perspiration cannot evaporate for some reason, then blowing air over the skin will result only in transferring heat to the skin (assuming that the air temperature is higher than skin temperature, which it will usually be in hot situations). Skin temperature must normally be below the deep body temperature of 98.6F (37C) because there must be a gradient of temperature between the deeper parts of the body and the skin for heat transfer to take place. Skin temperatures normally vary between 70F (21C) and 90F (32C).

Several methods can be used to determine whether people will be comfortable in a given environment (Fanger, 1970). Most of these methods are based on experiments with office and factory workers. Thus these methods must be used with care for people outdoors whose expectations concerning thermal comfort are quite different from those of the office worker. The use of complex mathematical models like Fanger's is not appropriate for landscape design, because the applicability of the results in terms of perception of comfort is questionable. Graphic design guides like Olgyay's (1963) Bioclimatic Chart (Figure 4-11), however, are usable instruments. These devices are usually a graph with the temperature on the vertical scale and the relative humidity (RH) on the horizontal scale. On the graph are plotted regions of human thermal comfort for people doing sedentary or light work while dressed in light clothing. Adjustments can be made for wind and solar radiation. The comfort zone is located between roughly 68F and 85F (20C and 30C) depending on wind speed and between 15% and 80% RH. As RH percentage increases, the temperature range for comfort narrows because as the RH of the air increases, its evaporative power decreases. Thus the upper limit of temperature at which a person can be comfortable decreases as RH increases.

Although the bioclimatic chart is one of the easiest

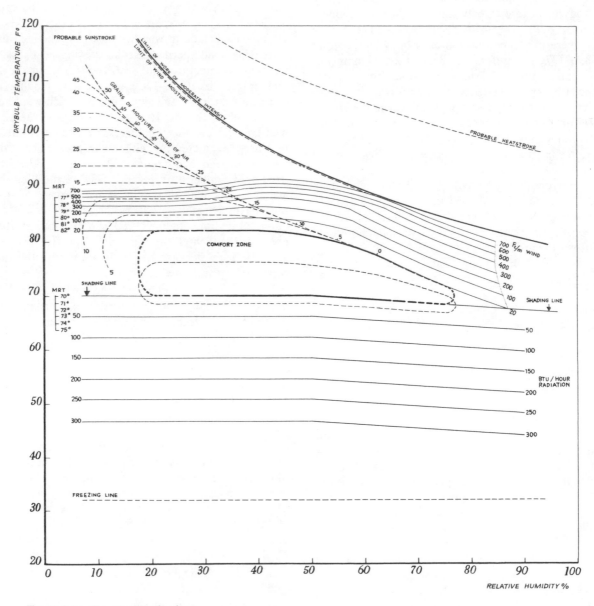

Figure 4-11. The bioclimatic chart.
From: (Olgyay, 1963) with permission of the publisher.

76

devices to use for forecasting human thermal comfort, it should be used with care. Data from the usual climatic stations do not necessarily apply to a given site away from the station. Also, experiments have shown that when outdoors, people do not have the same comfort requirements that they have indoors. People sunning themselves on the beach would be uncomfortable according to most prediction methods. However, since they came there expecting to be hot they will say they are comfortable. In addition, outdoor climatic data does not necessarily apply to the interiors of buildings.

The physiological state of a person can be calculated to any desired degree of accuracy using a variety of methods. However, until data are published relating the sensation of comfort to the physiological state of people outdoors, the techniques developed for the office and factory will have limited use outdoors.

Summary

The thermal state of an ecosystem or organism has been shown to be a result of the flows of energy between the system, ecosystem, or organism and its environment. The analysis of the energy budget of a system — that is, the balance between energy into the system and energy out of the system — has been shown to be useful in explaining and forecasting regional climate, microclimates, and human thermal comfort. I have found that the techniques proposed above work in about 80% of the cases I have studied. Of the remaining 20%, more detailed measurements have been necessary.

The basic procedure advocated is as follows:

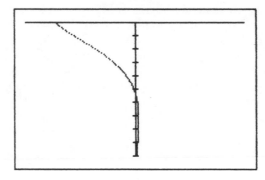

Figure 4-7. 8 hours. 8:00 a.m.

1. Evaluate the radiation budget to determine the amount of energy available to the system. Consider this energy flow to be the driving force.
2. Evaluate the interacting conductive, convective, and evaporative energy flows to arrive at an estimate of the temperature patterns in the system under study.

Because of the interactive nature of the flows in (2), the water-bucket analogy to daytime thermal behavior was introduced. Use of this analogy makes it much easier to evaluate the interaction of the flows and their contolling factors.

Once the physics of microclimate and biometeorology are understood climatic data can be sensibly used in design. But this can only be done if the user understands just what climatic data are and how to extrapolate these data to sites not located where the climatic data are collected. The next chapter examines the uses of climatic data and develops more fully the techniques which can be used to extrapolate the climatic data.

CHAPTER FIVE
Climatic Analysis

LEE PIERCE HERRINGTON
State University of New York
Syracuse, New York

Introduction

CHAPTER Four described the physical basis of microclimate in some detail. One of the basic ideas presented was that the microclimate of a given site is a local modification of the regional climate. This modification is directly related to the physical properties of the surface at the site of interest. In this chapter the sources of regional climatic data, their reliability, and the problems associated with relating them to the meso- or microclimate at the site will be discussed. However, first the terminology peculiar to climate quantification will be defined. The final part of the chapter will present some analyses used to convert published climatic data into usable design information.

Climatic Data Descriptors

Climate can be defined as the "average weather" of a particular place. The average used is the mean value, the sum of the temperatures measured during the day divided by the number of temperatures. Such averages do not tell the whole story, however. Boston (U.S.) and Oxford (England) have the same mean annual temperature (49F) but do not have the same temperature climate. Boston has hot summers and cold winters (Table 5-1) whereas Oxford has a much smaller range in temperature (44F vs. 14F). Spitsbergen Island (78N, 14E), in a tundra climate, has the same range in temperature as Boston but a quite different mean annual temperature. At least

both means and ranges must be used to characterize climate.

The climatic descriptors are usually presented as means and ranges based on an annual, seasonal, monthly, and daily period. Tables will often show maximum and minimum values for the period covered. As Table 5-1 (see next page) shows, Boston has a maximum monthly mean temperature of 71F (21C). Maximum and minimum values are often tabulated under the heading "extremes."

Quite often a statistic called "departure from normal" is included in tables of climatic data. This number is the difference between the value for the particular period tabulated and a very long averaging period — usually 30 years or the length of record for that station. For instance, the mean annual temperature for Boston may have been 51F in a particular year. In this case the departure from normal — the mean annual temperature — would have been listed as 2F. The term *"normal"* is misleading, however. Successive or overlapping 30 year means may be different from one another.

The climatic variables usually included in the set of descriptors used to define climate are:

- *Air temperature* — usually measured in white instrument shelters located about 3 ft (1 m) above the ground in a clearing (airport), expressed in degrees F or C.
- *Air humidity* — can be expressed in several ways as described in Chapter Four.

79

Table 5-1. Mean Monthly, Annual (Yr), and Range (R) in Temperature (F), for Selected Places

Place	J	F	M	A	M	J	J	A	S	O	N	D	Yr	R
Boston	27	28	35	45	57	66	71	69	63	52	41	32	49	44
Oxford	38	40	42	47	53	59	62	61	57	49	44	40	49	14
Spitsbergen	4	-2	-2	8	23	35	42	40	32	22	11	6	18	44

Adapted from: (Trewartha, 1968).

- *Wind speed* — usually measured at a height of 20 ft (6.1 m) above the ground in an open space (airports).
- *Wind direction* — measured at the same place as wind speed, in degrees of azimuth divided by 10 or points of the compass.
- *Precipitation* — measured in depth of water in inches or millimeters on the surface. Snow depth is usually reduced to an equivalent water depth.
- *Hours of sun* — expressed as minutes of sunshine and/or as a percentage of hours possible (time between sunrise and sunset for the day in question).
- *Cloud cover* — percentage of the sky obscured by cloud.
- *Frost-free period or growing season* — the period in days between the last killing frost in spring and the first killing frost in fall.
- *Heating degree-days (HDD)* — represented for a particular day by the number of degrees F by which the average outdoor air temperature on that day falls below a certain threshold level (65F in the U.S.). For example, a day with an average temperature of 50F has 15 heating degree-days (65 – 50 = 15), while one with an average temperature of 65F or above has none. Normally heating is not required in an average building when the average outdoor daily temperature is above 65F because internal temperatures are higher than those out of doors. The number of heating degree-days through a cold season is a summation of degree-days, and it expresses the duration and severity of the cold climate. Areas with more than 5,500 HDD's a year have long cold winters. Those with less than 2,000 HDD's have very mild winters.
- *Cooling degree-days (CDD)* — the number of degrees the daily average outdoor temperature is above a certain threshold level (65F and often 75F in the U.S.). The calculation is identical to that used for heating degree-days except cooling degree-days are measured above the threshold level. Cooling degree-days express the severity and extent of the cooling season. Areas with more than 1500 CDD's have long hot summers and

substantial cooling requirements. Those with less than 500 CDD's a year have mild summers and little need for mechanical cooling.

Sources of Climatic Data

In the United States the National Oceanographic and Atmospheric Administration (NOAA) is the primary source of climatic data. The basic document, a monthly publication called *Local Climatological Data*, contains the detailed monthly data for each of the approximately 300 first-order weather stations maintained by NOAA. An example is included in Appendix B-4. Measurements at these stations are taken at three-hour intervals. The time of these measurements, always listed in Local Standard Time (LST), vary from time zone to time zone since they are taken synoptically — all at the same time — throughout the world. The report includes:

1. For each three-hour measurement period for each day of the month:
   sky cover
   air temperature
   dew point
   wet bulb
   relative humidity (%)
   wind speed
   wind direction
2. For each day of the month:
   mean daily temperature
   daily maximum and minimum temperature
   departure of mean temperature from normal
   mean dew point temperature
   degree days (heating and cooling)
   precipitation:
      water equivalent
      snow depth
   mean daily atmospheric pressure
   wind data:
      resultant direction
      resultant speed
      mean speed
      maximum speed
      direction of maximum wind speed
   mean sky cover day and night

3. For the month:
   monthly means of:
     temperature
     maximum temperature
     minimum temperature:
       departure from normal temperature
     percentage of possible sunshine
     resultant and average wind
   monthly totals for:
     heat and cooling degree days
     precipitation
     minutes of sunshine
     monthly resultant wind speed and direction
     date of maximum wind

When the data from these reports are used, the following cautions should be considered: The three-hour wind speed is reported in knots whereas the average wind data are reported in miles per hour (1 knot = 1.1516 mph). Wind direction is reported in degrees from north divided by 10. A reported wind direction of 27 means that the wind is from 270 degrees azimuth or west. The resultant wind is *not* a simple average; it is the mean wind vector for that day. The mean wind vector is the wind which results from averaging the N-S and E-W components of the wind vector. If the wind blows from the north at 10 mph for four periods and then from the south at 10 mph for four periods, the resultant wind speed will be 0 and the resultant wind direction will be undefined. The resultant wind for a 10 mph N wind and a 10 mph W wind would be a wind from the NW at 14 mph ($\sqrt{200}$).

If the data presented in *Local Climatological Data* are not detailed enough, NOAA *Form FM-1 10A & 10B*, which contains more detailed information, can be ordered from the National Climatic Center. This is the form weather observers use to record the measured data and contains more information than is presented in the *Local Climatological Data* report. Each year the data in *Local Climatological Data* are summarized for the year and compared to the current long-term average or normal. Comparisons are made by listing "departures from normal" for most of the climatic descriptors.

The data in *Local Climatological Data* are further summarized in a number of publications available in libraries or from NOAA; three of the most common of these are:

• *Climatological Data* — published monthly by NOAA for each state (or combinations of states) for first-order stations and a number of other classes of stations, the number often exceeding 200. The data includes daily precipitation, daily maximum and minimum temperatures, daily snowfall and snow-on-the ground. It may contain statistics on wind, evaporation, and soil temperature for some locations.

• *Climatological Data, National Summary* — published monthly by NOAA. This publication contains summaries of general weather and river and flood conditions, basic weather data for selected stations, summary tables of temperature and precipitation extremes, storms, cooling and heating degree-days, and solar radiation.

• *Airport Climatological Summary* — published irregularly by NOAA as part of *Climatography of the United States* and available only for selected airports for which local climatological data are available. It contains a wealth of information not available elsewhere, such as mean number of days with occurrences of various weather phenomenon, frequency of wind direction and weather phenomenon, and wind rose information.

These data are presented as mean monthly and mean annual data.

In addition to the NOAA sources, other sources of climatic information can be very useful for determining the climate of a given site. These sources are listed below:

1. Environmental impact statements for large projects such as flood control, power dams and stations, large shopping malls, etc. can provide a wealth of information. These reports must be critically evaluated, however, since many of these documents contain poor data.

2. Air-quality monitoring stations run by both state and local governmental agencies can often supply quality temperature, solar-radiation, wind, and humidity data.

3. Local airstrips can quite often tell how the weather at their strip compares to that at a nearby first-order station.

4. For areas around bodies of water, sailors can provide good information concerning winds during the seasons when sailing is possible.

5. Every community has at least one person who is very interested in weather and may even have wind and temperature records. These people can sometimes be found through the local TV stations because the stations often use them for sources of local information.

6. Local chapters of the American Meteorological Society can often provide assistance in locating sources of climatological data. Current issues of the *Bulletin of the American Meteorological Society* list active chapters and their officers.

Extrapolation of Climatic Data

Climatic data are easily available but are also easily misused. The major problem is that the location of the climatic station is not near the site to which it is to be applied. Furthermore, the process of extrapolating the available data to the site is complex and, in many cases, may require the services of a professional meteorologist with a great deal of experience with climatic analysis. Nevertheless, the following guidelines can help determine the suitability of extant climatic data to a building site. However, climatic data are only applicable to areas similar to that in which they are measured.

1. *Surface properties.* Most climatic information is collected at airport weather stations. These sites are characterized by grass ground cover and large fetch — that is, there are no obstructions to the wind close to the place of measurement. The more the building site appears to be like an airport, the more closely the data will fit the site. The largest effect will be on the wind. Because of the large fetch, airport winds are usually higher than those measured on a more enclosed site. As a result of the increased wind, air temperatures may be slightly lower at the airport. However, not all climatic stations are located at airports. It pays to visit the measurement site to evaluate its characteristics before trying to extrapolate.

2. *Topography.* Except as noted below, climatic data apply over a wide area as long as the topography is similar. Rochester, N.Y., for example, is located on the old lake plain to the south of Lake Erie and the data for Rochester Airport are applicable to an area extending for several tens of miles in an east-west direction. To the north, the effect of the lake must be considered, whereas to the south the rise of the Allegheny plateau will affect the applicability of the Rochester data. In general, the rougher the topography, the more care must be exercised in extrapolation. Several topographic or physiographic features have predictable effects:

   • *Elevation.* The temperature of the air changes 5.4F/1000 ft (1C/100 m) as it is forced upward or downward. Lifting the air upward results in the lowering of temperature while forcing air downward causes a warming. Thus if the building site is downwind and at a higher elevation than the measurement station, the temperatures at the site will be lower on the average than those reported for the station. Although the change will not usually be as much as 5.4F/1000 ft of change in elevation, this figure will usually suffice.

   • *Shape-of-country.* The general character of the topography can have profound effects on wind. In some cases the shape of the land will steer the wind; in other cases of wind direction and atmospheric stability the land form will not control the wind. If wind is an important part of a building plan, the services of a consulting meteorologist are certainly necessary. The forecasting of wind is not work for amateurs; a great deal of knowledge and experience is required.

   • *Water bodies.* The presence of large bodies of water near either the measurement station or the building site when the other is not so situated can make the extrapolation of climatic data very difficult. The water will modify almost all variables describing the region's climate. Since the water is well stirred it will not change temperature as quickly as the land. As a result areas near the water will have warmer temperatures in the cold seasons than locations remote from the water and visa versa in the warm season. The temperature differences caused by the presence of the water will, in turn, cause differences in wind patterns. Near the water, the regional winds are modified by the land and sea-breeze system. The changes in temperature and wind result in differences in humidity and perhaps cloudiness. In general, the larger the body of water, the larger the magnitude and extent of effect. Professional assistance will usually be required to extrapolate climatic data when water is involved.

   • *Urbanization.* Urban areas are characterized by large amounts of high-density material. The climate of such places in relation to the surrounding rural climates has been described by Peterson (1969), Landsberg (1981), and others. Urban areas usually show the differences listed in Table 5-2 (see next page).

In summary, if the building site is similar in surface properties, enclosure, and topographic position and it lies in the same physiographic region as the climatological measurement station, the climatic data then can probably be applied without too much concern. The more the site varies from that at the climatic station, the more difficult the extrapolation of the climatic data will be.

82

Table 5-2. Changes in Climate Due to Urbanization

Climatic variable	Change
Temperature	
Annual mean	1.0-1.5F (0.6-0.8C) higher
Winter minima	2.0-3.0F (1.1-1.7C) higher
Solar Radiation	15-20% less
Relative humidity	6% less
Wind speed	20-30% less
High rural wind speed	Winds in city may be higher
Low rural wind speed	Winds in city lower
Wind direction	Channeling by buildings

After: (Peterson, 1969)

Methods of Climatic Analysis

The data available from the various climatic sources listed above are seldom entirely useful for design work. The following sections of this chapter explain various methods of analyzing and summarizing climatic data, and the following chapters explain specific application of these techniques.

Radiation

The radiation data found in the most common climatological data are not very useful since they are given in terms of minutes and/or percent of available sunshine. Averaged over the day or a longer period, this information has limited value because it does not indicate when, on the average, the sun is shining — and this can make quite a difference. For instance, Syracuse, N.Y., during the winter, has some periods of sunshine. However, these periods are concentrated in the early morning because as the day progresses winds increase and stability decreases, resulting in increased cloudiness. In winter, therefore, solar radiation is strongest in the morning, but this information can only be discovered by studying the local climatological data sheets. Thus, if the timing of solar radiation is important, the local data may have to be analyzed.

In some cases the amount of radiation being absorbed by various surfaces important to a design may have to be calculated. As pointed out in Chapter Four, the geometric part of this calculation is relatively straightforward and reliable. The adjustments needed to account for the transmissivity of the atmosphere, however, are not easy to make since the climatology of the variables used to calculate transmissivity is hard to find.

Solar radiation data do apply over fairly wide areas, however. When extrapolating measured values is attempted, consideration must be given to the climatology of the cloud cover (as in the Syracuse example) and to fog, a major consideration along the West Coast and in low lying areas.

Wind

As mentioned above, wind data are usually available as the *resultant* direction and speed and the average speed. These data, frankly, are not of much use in designing to take advantage of the wind or protect against it. Since the resultant wind vector is computed from the average north-south and east-west components of the wind, any winds from opposite directions with the same speed will cancel, so what is seen is the "left-over" wind. The larger the difference between the resultant and average wind speeds, the more likely this is to be the case.

The solution to this problem is to find wind rose data — that is, information about the frequency of winds of different velocities from at least the 16 compass points. Such data are available from the National Climatic Center for First-Order Stations. Regional or state air-quality measuring stations can be good sources because people working with air pollution are very interested in the probability of wind from various directions.

The program WIND produced the data in Figure 5-1 and 5-2 (see next page) from *Local Climatological Data* for Syracuse, N.Y.[1] Tabular wind rose data such as these may also be converted into polar graphs, which are easy to read and interpret. The division of the wind at 8.6 mph (9.7 knots) is an approximate division between winds correlated with stable and unstable atmospheric conditions. As the figures show, the frequency of the winds in these two groups can be quite different.

The data in the two wind rose tabulations for Syracuse illustrate the importance of analyzing information concerning the relative wind velocities from various directions. The climatological average wind for Syracuse for April 1982 and January 1983 is shown in Table 5-3. Ideally this type of data would be generated for each season from monthly data. Design strategies would then be based on the mean wind rose for each season. The seasonal means should be constructed from a number of years of data.

---

[1] WIND, TYPICAL, and TANAL are available for Apple II computers from: Forestry Software Associates, 507 E. Fayette St., Syracuse, NY 13202.

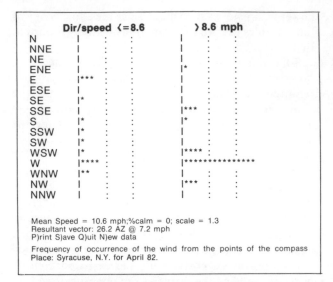

Mean Speed = 10.6 mph;%calm = 0; scale = 1.3
Resultant vector: 26.2 AZ @ 7.2 mph
P)rint S)ave Q)uit N)ew data
Frequency of occurrence of the wind from the points of the compass
Place: Syracuse, N.Y. for April 82.

Figure 5-1. Linear "wind rose" for Syracuse, N.Y., April 1982, produced by the program WIND. The relative probability of winds in two velocity classes (greater than and less than 8.6 mph) are shown for each of the compass points by rows of asterisks. The relative frequency of the high velocity winds from the west is 15/27 or 55%. There were no calm days. The resultant wind was from the west (262 degrees azimuth) at 7.2 mph while the arithmetic average wind speed was 10.6 mph.

```
          Dir/speed  <=8.6            )8.6 mph
N         |*     :     :        |     :     :
NNE       |*     :     :        |     :     :
NE        |**    :     :        |     :     :
ENE       |*********  :         |     :     :
E         |      :     :        |     :     :
ESE       |      :     :        |     :     :
SE        |      :     :        |     :     :
SSE       |      :     :        |     :     :
S         |*     :     :        |     :     :
SSW       |      :     :        |     :     :
SW        |**    :     :        |*    :     :
WSW       |****  :     :        |***  :     :
W         |**    :     :        |***  :     :
WNW       |*     :     :        |*    :     :
NW        |**    :     :        |     :     :
NNW       |      :     :        |     :     :

Mean speed = 7 mph; %calm = 0;scale = 1
Resultant vector: 43.8 AZ @ 2.5 mph
P)rint S)ave Q)uit N)ew data
Frequency of occurrence of the wind from the points of the compass
Place: Syracuse, N.Y. for January 83
```

Figure 5-2. Linear "wind rose" for Syracuse, N.Y. January, 1983. See Figure 5-1 for explanation.

Table 5-3. Comparison of Wind Data

	Jan. 83	Apr. 82
Average wind speed, mph	8.4	12.5
Resultant wind speed, mph	2.6	7.2
Resultant wind direction	W	W

The wind rose data indicate that there is indeed a strong probability for westerly winds with speeds greater than 8.6 mph. However, for April (Figure 5-1) 19% of the high winds are from the E-SSE, a good 135 degrees counterclockwise from west. The January data (Figure 5-2) show that low and high winds appear to have distinctly different distributions — low velocity winds tend to come out of the N to NE whereas the high velocity winds are from the W to WSW.

Temperature

Most climatological tables provide the mean maximum and minimum temperatures for the averaging period. The mean temperature is usually computed as the average of the maximum and minimum.

These data can be misleading if the individual measurements show a large range. This leads to the idea of using "typical" rather than average data. "Typical" means *most common*. Typical temperatures can be quite different from average temperatures if the frequency distribution of temperatures is not strictly normal. In some areas, such as San Francisco, the idea of typical climatic data has also been applied to wind. I have developed the technique of computing the typical climate from knowledge of the frequency of the range (max-min) and the mean temperatures. The program TYPICAL generated the data in Table 5-4 from *Local Climatological Data* for April 1982 at Syracuse, N.Y. The table shows the frequency of occurrence of

Table 5-4. Frequency of Occurrence of Daily Temperature (F) Range (max-min) and Daily Average (min + range/2) for Syracuse, N.Y. for April, 1982.

Range		Average	
Interval (F)	Frequency %	Interval (F)	Frequency%
0-5	0	16-20	3
6-10	3	21-25	7
11-15	20	26-30	7
16-20	30	31-35	3
21-25	13	36-40	17
26-30	13	41-45	17
31-35	13	46-50	20
36-40	7	51-55	3
41-45	0	56-60	10
	—	61-65	13
	99		—
			100

Value	Normals and Typicals Normal (F)	Typicals (F)
Max	54.9	56.25 (56)
Min	32.8	38.75 (39)
Average	43.9	47.50 (48)
Range	22.1	17.50 (18)
100		

temperature ranges and means in 5 degree F ranges. From this information the most common range (18F) and a mean of 48F are selected. The 48F mean was chosen because there was no clear-cut typical value as there was for the range. If a set of data showed two distinct peaks, then the data could be further investigated and two or more typical days described. This procedure removes the influence of uncommon weather conditions, but is, however, not easy to carry out and the data are not available in published tables. The program TYPICAL eliminates these problems. It is easy to use and can quickly compute the frequencies from data in *Local Climatological Data.*

To apply the temperature data to design problems, further analysis must be carried out. One procedure that balances complexity and usefulness is the one proposed by Novell (1981) and modified by McPherson (1983). The procedure is basically one of converting the published mean maximum and minimum temperatures (or typical maximums and minimums) into average (typical) daily temperature variations for the month. This is done by multiplying the mean temperature range by a factor (*S*) and adding the result to the mean minimum. Novell used the ASHRAE "*S*" values. McPherson constructed his own set of *S* values for different months from the climatological data for Salt Lake City, Utah. His technique takes into account the effect of varying day length on the time/temperature curve. Table 5-5 shows these values. A blank table is located in Appendix B-5. When the predicted temperatures for each hour of the day (or two-hour period) are tabulated, the yearly variation is the time over which heating, shading, and cooling are needed. Lines are drawn at the temperatures which separate heating and cooling. In this case 70F separates the underheated period when heating is needed from the overheated period when cooling is needed.

The program TANAL generated the data presented in Table 5-5 from temperature data for Salt Lake City, Utah. It can provide designers and planners with a time-saving tool for climatic analysis.

Analysis Using Combinations of Variables

Another technique for finding typical conditions is to compute joint frequency distributions. For example, Table 5-6 shows the joint frequency distribution for wind and temperature for Syracuse in January 1983 (also see Figure 5-2). This chart shows that for January 1983 the most common wind-temperature combination was 31 to 35F and 6 to 10 mph, probably because Syracuse winter storms are quite often associated with warm air. In Syracuse high winds are sometimes mistakenly thought to be associated with low temperatures. Actually, the high winds are well distributed over the temperature range. The tendency for low temperature to be associated with lower wind speeds is probably because many of Syracuse's lower temperatures result from radiational cooling.

Table 5-5. Typical 2-Hourly Temperatures for Salt Lake City, Utah

MONTHS		JAN	FEB	MAR	APR	MAY	JUN	JUL	AUG	SEP	OCT	NOV	DEC
T MAXIMUM		37	42	51	62	72	82	92	90	80	66	49	40
T MINIMUM		18	23	30	37	45	52	61	59	50	39	28	23
AVERAGE RANGE		19	19	21	25	27	30	31	31	30	27	21	17

S VALUES — 2 hourly Temp. = Tmin + (S × Range)

TIME	J,N,D / AP,AU	E,MA,S,O / MY,JN,JL	JAN	FEB	MAR	APR	MAY	JUN	JUL	AUG	SEP	OCT	NOV	DEC
1 a.m.	.13 / .17	.13 / .12	20	25	33	41	48	56	65	64	54	43	31	25
3 a.m.	.07 / .10	.06 / .08	19	24	31	40	47	54	63	62	52	41	29	24
5 a.m.	.04 / 0	0 / 0	19	23	30	37	45	52	61	59	50	39	29	24
7 a.m.	0 / .10	.07 / .26	18	24	31	40	52	60	69	62	52	41	28	23
9 a.m.	.16 / .49	.38 / .60	21	30	38	49	61	70	80	74	61	49	31	26
11 a.m.	.55 / .77	.68 / .82	28	36	44	56	67	77	86	83	70	57	40	32
1 p.m.	.83 / .95	.89 / .93	34	40	49	61	70	80	90	88	77	63	45	37
3 p.m.	1 / 1	1 / 1	37	42	51	62	72	82	92	90	80	66	49	40
5 p.m.	.69 / .94	.91 / .96	31	40	49	61	71	81	91	88	77	64	42	35
7 p.m.	.38 / .71	.62 / .75	25	35	43	55	65	75	84	81	73	56	36	29
9 p.m.	.25 / .41	.32 / .37	23	29	37	47	55	63	72	71	60	48	33	27
11 p.m.	.19 / .27	.20 / .22	22	27	34	44	51	59	69	67	56	44	32	26

Table 5-6. Joint Frequency Distribution of Wind and Temperature, Syracuse, N.Y. January, 1983.

Temperature group, F	Wind group (MPH)			
	0-5	6-10	11-15	16-20
36-40	1	-	4	-
31-35	2	6	1	1
26-30	1	1	1	-
21-25	2	1	1	1
16-20	-	3	1	1
11-15	1	1	-	-
6-10	-	-	1	-
0-5	1	-	-	-
-4-0	-	1	-	-

It takes about five minutes to construct the wind-temperature frequency diagram and is well worth the effort. The January wind rose data (Figure 5-2) show that low velocity winds usually come from the ENE, whereas the high velocity winds are from the W-WSW. These high velocity winds are usually associated with temperatures greater than 30F (-1.1C). Therefore, designing for cold winter winds from the northwest is inappropriate. In fact, since the really cold temperatures are associated with low wind speeds, it would appear that breaks should be placed to the W to SW since 30F is still cold.

This technique can, of course, be applied to other useful combinations of variables, such as:

- Wind vs. temperature (described above).
- Relative humidity (RH%) vs. temperature when plotted on a bioclimatic chart will indicate the frequency of occurrence of comfortable and uncomfortable conditions. See Novell (1981) for more information on determining two-hourly relative humidity values for a typical day of each month.
- Solar radiation vs. temperature will show if high temperatures and solar radiation are correlated.

The Bioclimatic Chart described in Chapter Four can be used to obtain a general idea of the comfort conditions in an area. This is done by plotting on the chart the average, maximum and minimum, or typical values of temperature and RH. However, outdoor comfort can be quite different from what this chart predicts because of differences between microclimate and climate.

Summary

Site designers often are too precise with data that usually have to be extrapolated over space in order to suggest climate at the site, and they do not review the information critically and carefully to determine how well it fits the building site.

This chapter has presented various methods of obtaining and manipulating climatological data to make them useful for design. It has stressed that "average" data can be misleading, and several techniques are presented for other types of analysis. The idea of "typical" data is introduced as an alternative to "average" data.

CHAPTER SIX
Master Planning

JAMES ZANETTO
Architect and Planner
Davis, California

MASTER planning is the activity that logically follows programming, site selection, and site analysis. Programming and site selection define types of land uses and associated energy-use patterns. Site analysis identifies and abstracts the site's natural and social processes into readily perceived patterns. Master planning, however, defines and coordinates patterns for the built environment with those of the site and surrounding area. During master planning, two levels (or degrees of detail) are studied: One is the site as a whole, with its internal and external relationships, and the other is groupings of buildings including general massing and siting strategies. This chapter will explore principles of master planning at both levels.

Figure 6-1. Pueblo community masterplanned for thermal comfort in a harsh environment.

A basic premise of neighborhood planning for energy conservation is to develop a sense of community, whereby a range of energy-efficient housing types are integrated with public transportation systems, employment, shopping, service, agriculture, and social and recreational facilities. Planners have always been concerned with the issue of "community" (e.g., see Mumford, 1965), but seldom before has energy conservation been used as a principal criterion for achieving a cohesive social environment. The first section of this chapter examines several development approaches that provide a conceptual basis for structuring energy-efficient communities and neighborhoods.

Prototypical Neighborhood Patterns

The Garden City

Ebenezer Howard (1902), framer of the "Garden Cities" concept and an early influential community planner, cited the continuing concentric growth of the major European capitals as a cause of increased substandard housing and inadequate waste removal. He found disproportionate gains in social amenities with increasing city size. He also perceived that the problems of a rural society with its loss of the best youth to urban centers resulted from relatively lower farm income. Howard's remedy was to integrate urban and rural life and in so doing give each access to the other's best qualities while minimizing their most negative aspects (due, he felt, largely to their isolation from each other). Mumford (1965) outlines Howard's main concepts:

- the provision of a permanent belt of open land, to be used for agriculture as an integral part of the city;
- the use of this land to limit the physical spread of the city from within, or encroachments from urban development not under control at the perimeter;
- the permanent ownership and control of the entire urban tract by the municipality itself and its disposition by means of leases into private hands;

- the limitation of population to the number originally planned for the area;
- the reservation for the community of the unearned increment from the growth and prosperity of the city, up to the limits of growth fixed;
- the moving into the new urban area of industries capable of supporting the greater part of its population;
- the provision for founding new communities as soon as the existing land and social facilities are occupied.

Howard presented a clear approach to community development, administration, and management. The impact of his writing on the future of energy-conserving community planning cannot be underestimated.

The Neighborhood Unit

Clarence Perry (1929) developed the concept of the "neighborhood unit," which "embraces all the public facilities and conditions required by the average family for its comfort and proper development within the vicinity of its dwellings." Perry's guidelines for the physical environment were:

- *size* — a population large enough to support an elementary school, yet not be more than ½ mile in radius;
- *boundaries* — clearly defined and limiting through-traffic;
- *open spaces* — an internal system of parks and recreational facilities;
- *institutional sites* — centrally located school, church, and community center;
- *local shops* — perimeter-located facilities shared with adjacent neighborhoods;
- *internal street system* — controlled vehicular and separated pedestrian traffic.

Perry also advocated that a neighborhood association be incorporated into the planning process to fulfill a number of social (and political) needs. The "neighborhood unit" advanced by Perry has obvious implications for energy conservation in the local community.

In contrast, Richman and Chapin (1977) suggest that because of complex social patterns, divergence of values, and the increased mobility of people, Perry's concept that facilities located within the neighborhood will serve as the focal point of residents' activities and social contacts is unlikely to be achieved. They believe that planning is moving away from providing physical facilities to providing for psychological needs as interpreted by the future users themselves or by plann-

ing based on perceived social responses. Richman and Chapin's objectives (shelter, security, child rearing, leisure, social interaction and participation, and symbolic identification) can be effectively implemented, especially in suburban situations, by proper interpretation of Perry's physical elements (size, boundaries, open spaces, institutional sites, local shops, and an internal street system). The key distinction is that in the more modern context these basic psychological needs, and the actual process of determining how best to implement them for a specific user group, remain the main focus of the work. In essence, housing, especially for a group, is a process, not merely a static product.

Successful neighborhood planning for energy and resource conservation involves fulfilling three criteria: providing the essential physical elements; using clear marketing practices that present the neighborhood's organizing concepts, benefits, and responsibilities to potential residents; and establishing a residents' association with adequate decision-making authority. All three contribute to increasing the potential for a self-reliant, low-impact energy-conserving living environment.

Examples of Integrated Neighborhood Design

At the same time Perry was developing the neighborhood-unit concept, Clarence Stein (1957) and Henry Wright were implementing it at Radburn, N.J., America's first attempt at integrating the garden city concept with an automobile society. The Radburn plan used a layout which separated pedestrians and autos. Safe, low-volume cul-de-sac streets, housing oriented towards pedestrian greenbelts, and a school for the central focal point were other important elements of the Radburn plan. The key to their plan was the "superblock" — a neighborhood unit or subunit formed by peripheral vehicular access and central greenbelt networks adjacent to each dwelling. Figure 6-2 (see next page) shows how homes are sited to open onto greenbelts.

A reinterpretation of the Radburn plan is Village Homes in Davis, Calif., designed and developed by Michael Corbett (Figure 6-3). Recognizing the inherent social values of the superblock/greenbelt planning concept, Corbett extended these and incorporated a number of energy and resource-conservation features into the neighborhood. The relatively low-density development of 70 acres has 196 homes, 30 rental units, 12 acres of agricultural land (primarily orchards, vineyards, and garden plots), a central playfield and community center/pool, and a small commercial center housing a number of profes-

Figure 6-2. "Superblock" from Radburn, N.J., plan by Clarence Stein and Henry Wright.

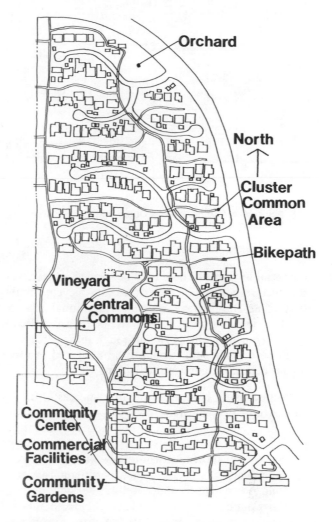

Figure 6-3. Village Homes, Davis, Calif.; a neighborhood designed for social interaction as well as energy conservation. After: (Corbett, 1981).

sional offices. The commercial development center's next phase includes a small restaurant/inn and some workspaces.

All houses are sited and designed for passive solar gain in winter and for natural cooling during the hot Davis summers. As Figure 6-3 shows, the narrow, sinuous cul-de-sac roadways generally run east/west, allowing for north/south orientation of dwellings. Location of houses on the lots, carports and garages, private outdoor spaces, entrances, etc., are all planned for maximum winter solar access. A variety of energy-efficient house designs have been built, ranging from water-wall designs to ducted greenhouse systems to earth-sheltered and active solar designs. All houses have some type of solar domestic hot-water system. (See Bainbridge, Corbett, & Hofacre, 1979, for examples of house designs.)

Circulation is planned to promote pedestrian movement through inclusion of a convenient and extensive bike and pedestrian network that links to the city system. Paralleling the pathways is an open drainage system which virtually eliminates underground pipes by substituting a series of swales controlled by weirs. This allows percolation of storm water into the ground and minimizes the project's impact on the city storm system.

A three-level hierarchy of land ownership exists beginning with fee simple title to individual lots, shared title by each cluster to the adjacent common area/greenbelt, and ownership by the community association of the main playfield, community center, and agricultural areas. A subsidiary corporation owns the commercial center. Corbett clearly planned for on-site employment, food production, recreation, social

life, and for solar heating and natural cooling of the buildings (see Thayer, 1977; Corbett & Corbett, 1979; Corbett, 1981). Village Homes continues to serve as a major example of energy-conserving neighborhood development; however, many other examples are noteworthy.

The Dutch have developed the "Woonerf" concept (Figure 6-4), a residential area in which traffic is not allowed to dominate and the special layout and street furniture emphasizes the street's function as a place in which one lives and has one's home (Royal Dutch Touring Club, 1978). Pedestrians and playing children are acceptable throughout the Woonerf since cars are driven at a walking pace due to the overall layout. Traffic control devices are designed to be usable elements for the residents. Trees, bollards, paving material alternation, benches, and play areas are interwoven to create multiuse zones. The energy-savings

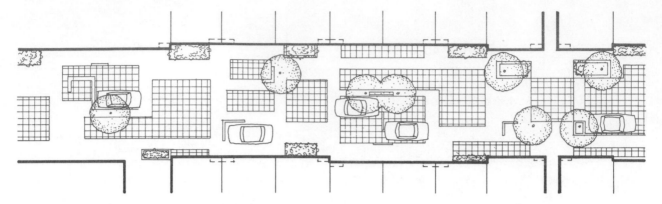

Figure 6-4. "Woonerf" — a Dutch method of utilizing auto access areas as focal points and use areas for surrounding homes.

potential in terms of land area developed is clear, as is the encouragement of pedestrian and bicycle circulation. The Dutch have spent an additional 50% on roadway development costs in Woonerf areas (Royal Dutch Touring Club, 1978), although some percentage of these costs would probably be allocated to other areas in a more conventional plan.

Cumbernauld is an example of a successful British garden city project. The town center/regional shopping center is surrounded by housing that in turn is penetrated by greenbelts. Industrial uses are closely related to transportation routes. A Radburn-like circulation hierarchy consists of a perimeter ring road filtering down to neighborhood cul-de-sacs. In addition to a public bus system, all central area homes are within 10 minutes walk of the town center on separated pathways. All these features reduce energy consumed in transportation.

Laurie (1975) has noted several key factors in residential site design at Cumbernauld, which are illustrated in Figure 6-5. One is coordinating housing type and size with topography. Desired densities are achieved primarily with two-story attached housing with individual gardens. On steeper slopes (above 8.5%) split-level designs without gardens are used. A second concept successfully used is the separation of pedestrians from autos where possible. This leads to many "walk-in" dwellings apart from parking. Apparently, the residents have responded well to this feature. A third factor, analogous to planning for solar access, is planning for daylighting. Provisions for daylighting are especially important in high latitudes where sunlight is often limited. Planning relies primarily on building layout, spacing, and window orientation to achieve the required daily period of sunlight and reduce consumption of electricity.

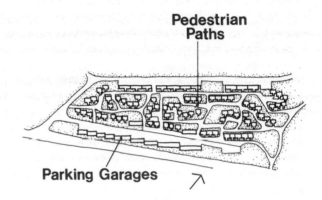

Figure 6-5. Detail of Cumbernauld new town. After: (Laurie, 1975). Note perimeter vehicular access to housing clusters.

The PUD as a Basic Planning Tool

All four of these projects have used planning concepts that extend beyond the lot-by-lot limitations of traditional zoning regulations. All four are, in essence, planned unit developments, or PUDs. PUD is a mechanism provided by many regulatory agencies to allow developments to respond to unique site conditions or to provide a comprehensive grouping of land uses in a single, holistically planned project. Often a developer proposes a project to the regulatory agency, leading to a series of negotiations during which both groups try to implement their broad goals. Many energy-conservation goals can be implemented through the PUD, including:

- Mixed land uses to provide a wide range of facilities within walking distances.
- Alternative circulation systems to maximize bike and pedestrian circulation.
- Flexible siting of streets, lots, buildings, and street trees to achieve optimum solar access.
- Clustering of dwellings to facilitate higher densities, common walls, and shared facilities.

90

Each of the projects just described has combined a series of basic planning concepts (controlled size, mixed land uses, emphasis on pedestrian circulation, local shopping and employment, and controlled vehicular access) to achieve a self-reliant "community" living environment.

Schematic Planning

The schematic planning phase, often referred to as "bubble-diagramming," is the first graphic step in the master planning process. During this phase the planner needs to maintain an overview of project interrelationships and often relies heavily on the program statement and site analysis graphics. The goal is to coordinate abstract patterns of functional relationships with the natural and man-made patterns of the site and surrounding area. Schematic planning, if done well, significantly reduces future energy impacts through achievement of the most beneficial fit between site and program.

The scale of base maps has significant influence on the planner's thought process. Two base maps are recommended. One map is of the site itself, prepared at a size (not larger than 18 by 24 in.) that allows the viewer seated at a drawing board to grasp the whole site at once. The second map, approximately the same size, shows the larger area surrounding the site. This would be a district in an urban situation or an ecosystem unit (such as a watershed) in a rural situation. The scale to which these maps are drawn is not critical (1 in. = 200 ft or 1 in. = 20 ft); however, the ability to see the whole project in its context at a glance is.

The schematic planning process is essentially one of taking the program requirements (land uses and activities) and fitting them to the site (Figure 6-6). Key decisions pertain to determining the requirements needed to create appropriate and efficient interrelationships between the land uses and activities on the site and those on surrounding sites, and creating a harmonious relationship with the natural processes of the site.

Ian McHarg (1969) has developed the best known method of site analysis and site planning with natural systems. Simply stated, the general principle is to avoid excessive initial development and future maintenance/energy costs by having a clear under-

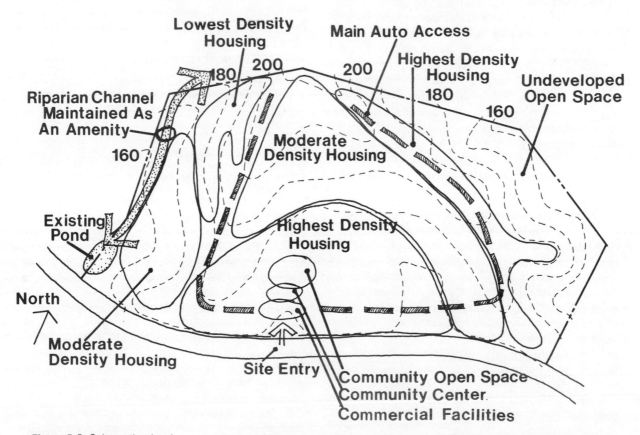

Figure 6-6. Schematic plan for a prototype mobile home community, Oceanside, Calif. After: (Thayer and Zanetto, 1982).

91

standing of the limiting factors of the site's natural processes, and by designing and siting facilities so as to minimize impacts on those limiting factors (see also Belknap & Furtado, 1968; McHarg & Sutton, 1975). Planning methods such as this inherently conserve energy and natural resources. The potential energy impacts of ill-planned development are tremendous, ranging from unnecessarily hot, cold, or dark interior spaces to flooded or sliding buildings and roadways.

McHarg noted that for large-scale projects the resulting land-use map is not a plan. It is a statement of goals. It provides the overall structure or framework for activities to occur. This same principle applies to all levels of planning for residential neighborhoods. The planner must leave certain decisions unmade. The residents of the project need to have an appropriate degree of autonomy to plan their own environment.

Developing an Overall Structure

Knowles (1974) and Corbett (1981) have written on the issue of the community's role in planning. In *Energy and Form* Ralph Knowles describes in historical terms how major developments evolved and what key factors decided their success and social acceptance. Primitive man's responses to environmentally stressful situations evolved from "relocation" (moving to a more hospitable site as seasons change) to "transformation," (modifying an appropriate site to satisfy needs). Transformation requires less land per person but a higher concentration of effort, leading to a greater impact on natural processes. This is now manifested in greater public participation in the planning process.

Corbett (1981) states that an overall structure, based on mutually accepted goals, is critical for neighborhood design:

> The planning process offers the greatest potential if the overall layout is designed in advance, including basic systems such as circulation, energy management, waste management, and major social services. Then, as the settlement is developed, the more detailed design of individual buildings and neighborhoods is left to smaller planning groups including residents and potential residents, under guidelines laid down by the overall planning entity. Approached this way, design could be an incredibly rich and satisfying process for everybody involved, and could restore our feeling that our neighborhoods are truly our own. It would also permit enough diversity and experimentation in neighborhood design to teach us what works and what doesn't.

The residents of such a neighborhood must be aware of the planning principles that are used in the design of their environment. Hamrin (1978) has made a comparative study of the behavior and energy-use patterns of residents of two neighborhoods designed for energy conservation. She found that a development designed and marketed as a total energy and resource conservation system will attract residents who will live in and enhance their dwellings in the most energy-conserving manner.

Moving from the Schematic to Master Plan by "Pattern Language"

The site planner progresses from program statement and site analysis to the schematic plan through the use of a composite suitability (or potentials and constraints) map. The master plan is prepared by continuing refinement of the schematic plan.

One clear method of organizing and presenting master planning concepts, especially within a group, is to use the "Pattern Language" approach of Christopher Alexander (Alexander, Ishikawa, Silverstein, Jacobson, Fiksdahl-King, Angel, 1977; Alexander, 1979). This is the epitome of a preorganized method whereby the logical progression of elements toward a mutually desired goal is a visible and flexible tool, both in the current design work and in future phases. The patterns approach recognizes that

> any town and any building gets its character from those . . . patterns of events . . . which happen there most; and that the patterns of events are linked to (environmental) space.
>
> the patterns 'depend on culture'.
>
> so long as people of a society are separated from the language which is being used to shape their (environments), the (environments) cannot be alive. (Alexander, 1979)

This approach has the ability to balance a deterministic philosophy (occurrences are caused by their environment) with the more "open-ended" view that the residents can continually shape their environment to their own ends.

The planner's goal is to develop a design process that can be left as a written and diagrammatic display. In the initial stages of work the technical team does the majority of the decision-making and establishes the overall framework of the development. This information can be continually passed down to planners and designers of the smaller components (down to the residents themselves) to minimize contradictions in the built environment. A common example of such a contradiction is the blocking of solar access to (passive solar) south-facing windows by vegetation, fences, and other structures. Although simple solar rights restrictions in the deed can remedy the problem, the higher value of a shared public understanding of the basic concept of solar access should be emphasized (see Chapter Seven).

The patterns presented below, excerpted primarily from Alexander (1977), provide a link between the program statement and detailed design and will enhance the planner's and future resident's image of the neighborhood. They are important issues that planners of residential projects frequently address. If followed, these patterns increase the likelihood of energy saving behaviors due to maximization of social "fit" in the environment.

Plan an identifiable neighborhood. A social unit should consist of about 500 people maximum.

Limit penetration of major roads into the neighborhood. Instead, create a ring road collector if topography allows, with small-scale (perhaps cul-de-sac) streets providing access into the site.

Carefully create the boundary. Collector/arterial streets work well for boundary definition. Locate the few neighborhood shops and offices on this edge. Turn houses inward, away from the edge. Important to neighborhood identity is the quality of access into the development. Use gateways to mark the boundary, such as bridges, narrow passages between buildings, an opening through a border of trees, etc. Consider the boundary zone as a meeting place between neighborhoods with parks, small parking lots, work communities, and other functions shared with the adjacent neighborhoods. Also try defining the boundary with vegetation buffers which can be used as windbreaks and fuel sources. In smaller, more dense neighborhoods, begin the pedestrian scale at the boundary. Allow residents and visitors to leave their cars immediately.

Scatter work. Distribute employment opportunities into and throughout each neighborhood. Allow for individually or cooperatively owned small office/workshop clusters (functioning as "work communities") and home trades, each sited to maximize its livelihood. Cafes, inns, and small markets can set up very desirable activity patterns in the neighborhood. The energy implications of a local inn are significant: Nearby dwellings can forego the seldom used "guest room" yet visitors can stay within walking distance; it can serve as a local "evening retreat" for entertaining guests without anyone's having to drive; it can be a source of income if operated by

the neighborhood; and it provides local employment for residents.

Create a web of shopping. Map the locations of and distances to services from the neighborhood. Where adequate consumer demand exists, locate new shops to fill the service gap; locate a new shop next to the largest cluster of other shops.

Provide a focal point, activity node, landmark, or visible center such as a commons, green, playfield, or public square for the neighborhood. Public greens should be very close to (about a three-minute walk) and highly visible from housing clusters. The edge of the public square should be in the boundary zone with the square as the focus of its neighborhood. Locate the square at a natural activity node where many paths cross and community facilities and mutually supporting shops can be located. This location is ideal for a community center/meeting/recreation facility; combine it with an outdoor room for good weather, a place for safe, comfortable public transit links, and provide it with appropriate seating throughout.

Maintain a clear bike/pedestrian circulation system leading to the focal point, neighborhood center, and city bikeway system with as few street crossings as possible. On long straight sections of pathway, where bikes pick up speed, separate pedestrians by pavement type or color if not by physical separation. Provide convenient bike parking facilities. When streets serve only a few dwellings, consider allowing pathways to coincide with streets. At higher traffic volumes, provide pathway networks that overlay at right angles to the streets.

Identify and set aside features and amenities (especially water and mature trees) that are of value to the neighborhood (or larger community) as public assets. Avoid parceling up linear elements such as stream channels; use them as linear common spaces with developed public access appropriate to the preservation and enhancement of the resource.

Lay out housing in terms of "density rings." Locate those who wish most contact with shops and services or other amenities in most dense situations. More distant locations have lower densities. On sites with varying levels of development capability or suitability, vary density accordingly. These rings will typically be eccentric if based on neighborhood boundary features.

Lay out the housing in clusters with the public land between them jointly owned. Size the clusters from about five to 10 households, the scale of face-to-face meetings and decision-making. Keep cluster configurations loose enough for connection to adjacent ones, but keep individual cluster identities clear. Allow for common facilities. Such clusters will tend to police themselves.

Where appropriate, provide space for small children's play areas, usually within sight of the houses. Allow residents to develop the space, perhaps with a budget from land sales or rental fees.

Plan sunny south-facing "positive" outdoor spaces. These will be used more than north-facing spaces in northern latitudes. Avoid labeling fragmentary, leftover spaces between buildings as "use areas." Carefully plan the amount of enclosure appropriate to the use.

Strive for a mix of household types. Mix building types within the neighborhood and within each cluster so that one-person households, couples, families with children, and group households are intermixed. This implies a mix of income and age groups as well.

Plan a "children's home" or day-care center in the neighborhood. Provide a place where children can stay at any hour of the day, for an hour or a week. This "home" functions as a "second family" for the children, allowing them comfortable, close access to full-time adult supervision within the child's own familiar surroundings.

Integrate housing "into the fabric" of uses that would otherwise tend to be nonresidential and have a life only during the day. This includes areas of shops, small industry, and public service.

Allow space near every household for vegetable gardens and, if possible, for fruit and nut trees. These may be most successful on common land where annual tilling and maintenance chores can be shared.

Provide green streets. Minimize paving on low volume cul-de-sacs and driveways. Consider using paving stones or paved wheel tracks. Such streets will minimize storm runoff and humanize the whole character of the neighborhood.

Use off-street parking to allow minimum pavement widths. Consider parking bays or small scattered lots well planted with shade trees. Share parking space at every opportunity, such as with daytime commercial and evening recreation/entertainment uses.

Clearly, a cohesive thread interweaves the work of Howard, Perry, Stein, Mumford, McHarg, Knowles, Corbett, and Alexander. The process of designing residential environments for people should respond to known recurring natural processes and should use broad social principles that become physical planning elements structured in a preorganized but open-ended manner. This provides for tremendous diversity, freedom, and evolution on the smaller scale by allowing residents to plan and build for themselves within a clearly perceived and accepted framework. The result is a more energy-efficient environment with increased sense of community and resident satisfaction.

Building Strategies

Energy-conservation strategies used for individual buildings will affect the way they are planned into larger complexes and how they will fit the site. The following describes a number of these strategies and emphasizes their implications for planning. The principal areas covered deal with a variety of solar collector systems and energy-efficient housing types. These strategies should be applied appropriately to a given climate.

Active and Passive Solar Systems

The use of solar energy is one of the most basic energy-conservation strategies. Two basic types of solar energy systems are commonly used today: active and passive. The majority of well-designed houses use both types of systems for distinct functions. "Hybrid" systems use both active and passive components for a single function, such as space heating.

Active or indirect systems employ a collector — often a glass-covered box painted black on the interior and faced towards the sun (Figure 6-7). Either water or air circulates through the collector, extracting the built-up heat caused by sunlight penetrating the glass. The heat is transferred to a storage medium such as an

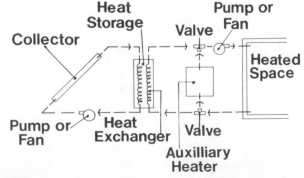

Figure 6-7. Schematic diagram of an active solar energy system.

94

insulated water tank or bed or rocks for use when needed. These systems are similar to conventional heating systems with the sun used as a heat source as opposed to traditional fuels. The term "active" or "indirect" is used to describe these systems because the heat must be moved from collector, to storage, to its final heating application by means of mechanical pumps or fans.

Passive or direct solar systems use the building itself as both collector and storage medium (Figure 6-8). South-facing windows or skylights allow sunlight to enter the building on sunny cold days. The sunlight is allowed to strike some material (termed "thermal mass") such as a concrete floor which stores the heat. During sunless periods insulating drapes or shutters ("movable insulation") cover the windows to prevent trapped heat from escaping. The heat stored in the building is slowly released helping to keep the interior spaces warm.

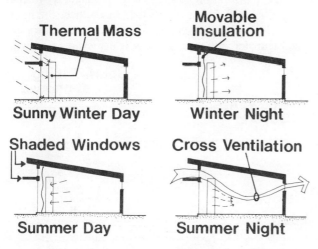

Figure 6-8. Passive system components and operation.

Passive system components also work well to naturally cool interior spaces in the hot season. On summer nights the building is well ventilated with air cooling the thermal mass. Daytime heat gain is minimized by covering windows with movable insulation. As interior temperatures rise during the day, the cooled thermal mass absorbs much of the heat, effectively moderating the air temperature. These systems are called passive or direct since no mechanical devices are required to transfer heat from collector to storage to use area.

The most common residential combination of systems uses passive strategies for the majority of space-heating and cooling demands and an active system for heating domestic water. Many other combinations are popular including solar with conventional or wood-heating back-up systems.

Passive systems for space heating and cooling are widely used because of their cost effectiveness and simplicity of design, operation, and maintenance. Since windows serve as collectors, window orientation is critical. Siting the building and planning its interior (and exterior) spaces for maximum south window area gives the building designer optimum flexibility. (Actual window area must be calculated as a function of the climate, the amount of thermal mass employed, and other factors.) Most glass should be located on the building's south exposure whereas windows oriented east and west should be minimized. East and west windows have very limited application as cold season collectors, but are sources of unnecessary heat gain in the hot season. The primary energy-related functions of north windows are for hot-season cross ventilation and for daylighting.

A building's overall shape and exposed surface area also affect its thermal performance due to heat transfer through the building's skin during difficult weather conditions. Compact building forms are well suited to extreme climates, especially extremely cold climates. The designer has more flexibility in creative housing forms for temperate climates.

Earth sheltering

Earth sheltering is a strategy which combines the thermal mass qualities of earth and the concept of reduced surface area to provide high levels of thermal performance in climates with appropriate soil temperatures. This type of energy-conserving building can be successfully applied in most United States' climates. Figure 6-9 gives an indication of stable ground temperatures in the continental U.S. Only in southern Florida where ground temperatures approach uncomfortably warm levels is earth sheltering limited in cost effectiveness. Although northern and Rocky Mountain temperatures are quite cool, these temperatures

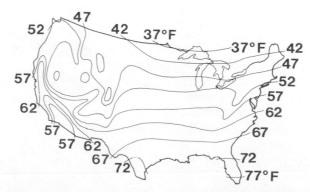

Figure 6-9. Approximate soil temperatures (at depth) based on well-water temperatures and known soil temperature data. After: (Labs, 1979).

can be used to great advantage during the cold season and also for cooling during the hot months.

Preliminary studies (Zanetto & Harding, 1981) indicate that soil temperatures at various depths adjacent to house walls in bermed housing are similar to soil temperatures measured on an undisturbed site. This means that earth-sheltered housing built at grade level and employing berms can have performance levels similar to excavated housing sunk into the site. (Bermed housing can usually be built at a lower cost than excavated designs.)

In addition to orientation, building structure and drainage are the most important site selection and planning factors for earth-sheltered housing. Structural requirements are a function of the soil and underlying bedrock conditions. Slope stability must be quantified by a soils or geotechnical engineer. Where a cut occurs to accept the new building, the building must support the uphill load. Earthquake conditions must be anticipated. Weathered bedrock at the level of the building's footings is desirable to support the heavy roof and wall loads, but very dense rock is difficult to excavate. Impervious rock can cause a perched water table, compounding drainage requirements and structural loading due to hydrostatic pressure.

Drainage should be considered for areas such as those below the building's floor, at the perimeter walls, and at the finish grade surrounding the building. Drainage swales are a typical item in earth-sheltered grading plans.

In addition to reduced-space heating and cooling demands, earth-sheltered buildings can significantly reduce both the amount of storm-water runoff and the visual impacts of development due to the increased land area available for planting. Low-maintenance native planting on berms and rooftops can also increase wildlife habitat. Sod roofs as use areas for the residents should be considered — people generally enjoy planted roofs (Figure 6-10).

Double-Envelope or Convective-Loop Design

Double-envelope design combines passive solar principles with a continuous circulating plenum or surrounding air chamber to achieve comfortable, stable interior temperature and humidity conditions. The collector is an attached greenhouse or sun space. (Figure 6-11). Heated greenhouse air naturally rises (convects) into the plenum which is formed by the attic, a special passageway constructed in the building's north wall, and the subfloor cavity. As the heated air convects through this loop, it transfers its heat to the building and to the earth beneath the floor. During sunless periods air in the convective loop effectively draws upon stored heat to maintain comfortable temperatures.

Figure 6-11 shows a north-wall passageway formed by a double-framing technique. In essence, the house is enclosed by two envelopes minimizing unwanted heat transfer. Summer cooling is achieved by drawing

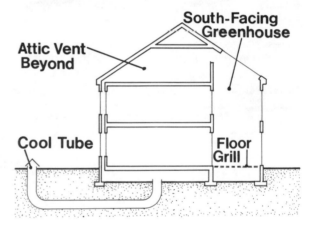

Figure 6-11. Section through a double-envelope space.

Figure 6-10. Zanetto earth-sheltered house, 1979. Inset shows north side.

96

outside air through buried "cool tubes" and exhausting warm air through an attic vent. The greenhouse space may require full shading during the hot season in many climates. Fire dampers are also required in the north wall to reduce flame spread potential. Site planning for double-envelope designs is similar to that of more conventional passive solar designs.

Roof Ponds

Radiative and evaporative roof-pond systems are an innovative cooling strategy most effectively used in arid and semiarid climates. These ponds of water are shaded during the day (in the hot season) and dissipate stored heat from the building's interior by radiation alone or by a combination of radiation and evaporation at night. Radiant systems dissipate heat directly to the north and/or night sky through water in enclosed plastic bags. Evaporative systems, although more powerful as coolers, must contend with dirt and insect problems associated with exposed water surfaces. Ponds are shaded from daytime sun by either movable insulated panels (Skytherm ©) or by stationary louvers (Cool Pool ©) as Figure 6-12 illustrates.

Roof pond systems can also provide effective solar heating. Reflectors are usually employed with heating systems because the horizontal pond surface makes a poor collector during winter's low-angle sun conditions.

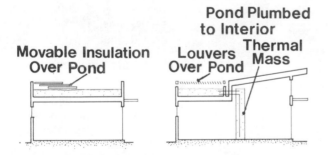

Figure 6-12. Roof-pond radiative and evaporative cooling systems.

Daylighting

Daylighting is the provision of natural light to interior architectural spaces. It is an energy-conservation strategy that can be employed with most building types. Incandescent lighting inefficiently converts electricity into light; about 95% of the energy is converted to heat. Although fluorescent lighting is much more efficient, all lighting adds heat to interior spaces, especially in commercial and institutional buildings where larger numbers of people add significantly to the internal heat load.

Three basic techniques can be used to design for daylighting: graphic techniques, computation, and physical models. Physical models are already used extensively by designers and have the advantage of giving both quantitative and qualitative information. Models need to be large, ½ to 1 in. to 1 ft (Bryan, 1982) and adequately detailed on the interior to allow placement of appropriately designed remote sensors for light meters.

The principal site-planning factors that affect daylighting are building form (to allow adequate window placement for good light penetration to interior spaces) and location of potential daylight obstructions such as adjacent structures and vegetation.

Photovoltaics

Photovoltaic panels convert sunlight directly to electricity by means of wafer-thin silicon cells. At present the technology is cost effective only for remote sites where power-line hook-up costs are excessive. The economics of photovoltaic systems may improve dramatically in the next few years as new methods of producing silicon cells reach commercial stages.

The two main planning considerations to allow future retrofits of solar electrical systems are collector placement and solar access. Photovoltaic collectors require large surface areas to meet the needs of a building and its users; typically the whole south-facing roof surface is covered. North-facing shed roofs or other designs which minimize south-facing surfaces are not appropriate unless detached collectors are used. Detached collector locations include ground surfaces, garages, and adjacent buildings. Photovoltaic collectors also require solar access all year. Rooftop locations have minimal shading conflicts relative to lower collector locations.

Superinsulation

Superinsulation is an example of a nonsolar building strategy offering very good energy-conservation potential in the coldest and cloudiest climates. As its name implies, its key characteristic is the use of abundant amounts of insulation; R-30 walls and R-60 ceilings are common. Reduced window area and movable window insulation complement the strategy of controlled-heat flows.

High levels of insulation can be obtained by using 2 x 6 studs with R-19 batt insulation and rigid insulation boards attached to the exterior, and sometimes interior, surfaces. Since rigid insulation is costly, some builders use deeper wall and roof-framing systems to allow greater depths of batt insulation.

Other common energy conservation techniques often used with superinsulation are interior vapor barriers, insulated foundations, thorough weatherstripping, and air-to-air heat exchangers for introducing fresh air into the building. Superinsulation is an example of a building strategy requiring no special site planning.

Hybrid Strategies

All of these building strategies have a number of variations. Combinations of strategies, such as earth sheltering the lower portion of a double envelope structure, are common and can be termed "hybrid" designs.

The best way to choose an energy-conservation building strategy for a particular application is to coordinate the building's energy requirements with the demands of the local climate and the availability and cost of local labor and materials. For example, attached greenhouses with their extensive collector areas are most suited to cooler climates or locations with low levels of winter sunlight. Greenhouses in hot climates can cause overheating unless costly shading and ventilation components are used.

The energy requirements of different building uses within a neighborhood can also call for different planning strategies. For example, daylighting becomes an important factor in well-used spaces such as meeting halls and classrooms, especially in warm to hot climates. In such spaces, heat from lights, appliances, and humans is often more than enough to supply building heat loads, and strategies then shift to emphasize cooling.

Climatic Adaptation

Climatic adaptation in site planning and building design involves coordinating site features, building massing, and architectural components to take advantage of natural energy flows. Controlled energy flows can create, or help create, conditions of physical (thermal) and psychological comfort for people in outdoor and indoor spaces.

Climatic evaluation techniques involve an analysis of the regional and local climate, including typical weather patterns, to determine which climatic elements cause comfort or discomfort. As Chapter Five points out, it is also necessary to know when (both time of year and time of day) these elements influence comfort.

Alternative planning and design strategies are then compared to find a combination which maximizes beneficial energy flows and minimizes those which are undesirable. This was the method used to develop the Davis, Calif., energy-conservation building code.

An Energy Conservation Building Code

Building-permit requirements in Davis are based on a climatic analysis. The building must either incorporate a series of specified features, or its thermal performance must be calculated to meet set standards. For example, the standard for a single-family detached residence of 1500 ft^2 is a maximum winter heat loss of 208 Btu/ft^2/day and a maximum summer heat gain of 98 Btu/ft^2/day.

The following condensed and abstracted list gives minimum levels for the set of specified features. A number of builders commonly exceed these requirements to maximize energy efficiency. (These levels apply only to the Davis climate.)

Walls	— R-11 insulation, and light color or shaded
Roof/ceilings; ceiling/attics	— R-19 insulation, and roof color light or shaded in midsummer, or R-25 insulation
Floors	— R-11 insulation for suspended floors over an unheated space
Glazing area	— exterior glazing may not exceed 12½% of floor area if single pane, 17½% of floor area if double pane
	— glazing area may be increased if
	* it is south facing
	* it is tilted up at least 30° from the horizontal
	* it is clear
	* it receives direct sun from 10 a.m. to 2 p.m. on December 21
	* the building contains exposed thermal mass with a storage capacity of 750 Btu/day ft^2 of glass
Glazing shading	— most glazing (except north facing) must be shaded from direct sun from 8 a.m. to 4 p.m. on August 21, or must have reflective, insulated interior shutters

exterior shades must be permanent, and intercept 100% of sun during the specified hours, or have a shading coefficient of 0.2 or less

— shades may be temporary if their function will be replaced by plantings

Summer night cooling — windows providing adequate cross ventilation or a mechanical system supplying 15 air changes per hour

A number of well-designed Davis homes achieve 100% natural cooling and approximately 80% solar heating by careful application of the code. The need for an air-conditioning system is eliminated and heating requirements are met with an air-tight wood stove fueled from local orchard prunings or scrap construction lumber.

Separate ordinances require all new housing to provide solar domestic hot-water systems, low-flow shower heads, and new parking lots to provide a tree canopy giving 50% shading of the surface within 15 years. These are further examples of energy- and resource-conservation strategies appropriate to the local climate.

Related Publications

A number of available publications present both climatically oriented planning strategies and evaluation techniques. Olgyay's *Design with Climate* (1963), considered a classic, contains a Bioclimatic Chart which is duplicated in Chapter Four and used to evaluate climate data relative to human comfort. The AIA Research Corporation's *Regional Guidelines for Building Passive Energy Conserving Homes* (1978) defines a number of climate zones in the continental U.S. and ranks a series of energy-conservation options for each. Watson and Lab's *Climatic Design: Energy Efficient Building Principles and Practices* (1983) devotes a section to site-planning principles.

Most of these works rely on historic vernacular architectural forms which evolved over centuries in response to climatic conditions. Examples exist in all parts of the world with similar climates. Rudofsky's delightful *Architecture Without Architects* (1964) gives solutions 1,000 years old. State-of-the-art solutions are used in buildings that place high in regional energy-conservation design competitions.

Computer Simulation

Computer simulation is a nearly indispensable tool for assessing the fitness between building and local climate. Generalized prototype dwellings can be modeled quite inexpensively and key heat-loss/gain components identified. Once the basic structure has been programmed, such simple modifications as amount of insulation, window layout, or thermal mass to south glass proportions can be quickly modeled. The resulting programs are not only design tools but also marketing aids. Such programs are now widely available for popular personal microcomputers. Sources of information on computer simulations are presented in Chapter Three.

Solar Planning Principles

Solar planning principles can give the planner a broad conceptual base for siting specific housing types. The key considerations of solar access and building orientation are applicable to virtually all forms of housing.

Solar Access and Solar Collectors

Solar access for collectors is the most basic solar planning principle. Site planners are often handicapped by an overly narrow concept of just what solar collectors are. For example, some unfortunately still have difficulty envisioning south windows as "collectors." A solar collector is any object, surface, or space which uses the sun's energy to reduce the imported energy needs of a building. The amount of solar access required and various techniques for design and protection of solar access are described in detail in Chapter Seven, "Planning for Solar Access." Generally solar access needs are dependent on a collector's "skyview" requirement. The amount of unobstructed sky a collector must "see" to operate effectively is called its skyview and is shown in Figure 6-13. Collectors with different functions and different seasonal needs for sun have different skyviews.

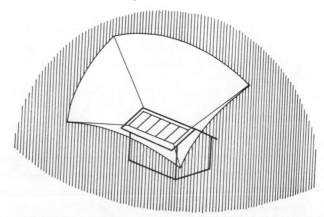

Figure 6-13. "Skyview"—the amount of unobstructed sky a collector must see to operate effectively.

| Winter | Spring / Fall | Summer |

Figure 6-14. Variation in sun path and shadow length with seasons.

Consider the sunlight needs of a domestic hot-water collector, a space-heating collector, and a swimming-pool collector. Domestic hot-water systems require sun all year, space-heating systems require sun in the cold season only, and a swimming-pool collector requires sun only during the warm swimming months. Each of these collectors would have a differently shaped skyview determined by the seasonal limits of the apparent sun paths across the sky.

The amount of sunlight (and consequently heat) a collector receives is dependent on the angle at which light strikes its surface. More sunlight is absorbed as the "angle of incidence" becomes more nearly perpendicular. Five factors influence the angle of incidence: season, time of day, latitude, collector tilt, and collector orientation.

Seasons are a result of different sunlight incidence angles on the earth's surface. The steepest incidence angles occur in the hot season. Seasonal angles also affect shadow length as Figure 6-14 shows.

Time of day specifies the sun's location along the seasonal sun path shown in Figure 6-14. At noon (solar time) the sun is due south in the sky in the northern hemisphere.

Latitude, or angular distance from the equator, affects sunlight angles and therefore shadow patterns of objects. Figure 6-15 illustrates that incident angles decrease as latitude increases. Longer shadows result.

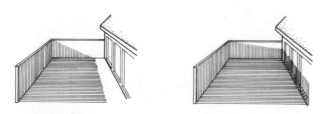

Figure 6-15. Variation in shadow length with latitude. Both conditions show a 6-ft fence 15 ft south of a building on December 21. The left example is San Diego, Latitude 32.5°N; on the right is Pittsburgh, 41°N.

Collector orientation and tilt can be planned to take best advantage of available sunlight during the collector's use period. Some sophisticated systems employ moving collectors to track the sun whereas others use reflective surfaces to catch a range of incident angles. Generally, collectors tilted up toward the vertical and facing due south receive the most winter sun. More horizontal collectors oriented toward the east or west collect most sun in summer. Collectors for year-round use usually face south and have a tilt angle (as measured from the horizontal plane) approximating their latitude angle.

Solar access requirements may not impose significant limitations on building siting for low buildings, with low densities, at low latitudes. Taller buildings, higher densities, and trees can limit sunlight to collectors. The shadow planning techniques presented in Chapter Seven help define limits on acceptable building (and tree) form and location. Some siting potentials and limitations are also inherent in the housing type.

Building Orientation

Optimum orientation of buildings that act as collectors or have collectors mounted on their surfaces is of primary concern to the site planner. Specifying a building's orientation tells a planner which of its sides is most exposed to such climatic factors as sun, wind, and rain, and gives a quick indication of a building's actual or potential thermal performance. Usually a building's orientation refers to the direction faced by the wall that contains the largest amount of window area. For detached rectangular buildings, this is commonly one of the longer walls. Attached dwelling units often have windows located on their shorter end walls to facilitate higher densities. Newer model mobile homes sometimes have a majority of their window area located on an end wall. Where a building's walls have a relatively equal distribution of windows, the building's orientation can be described as the directions faced by the two longer walls. Square, multifaceted, or dome-shaped buildings with an equal distribution of windows have no clear orientation for broad planning purposes.

Windows and doors are also the building components most influenced by winds and breezes. Indeed, windows are clearly the most critical planning factor for today's adequately constructed and insulated housing. Virtually all windows allow infiltration of cool air and escape of warm interior air during cold windy conditions. Appropriate operable window orientation is critical for taking advantage of cooling summer breezes. Adequate cross ventilation is difficult without proper window design and positioning. Windows (including double or triple glazed insulating windows) have the lowest thermal resistance (R value) of any element of the building's skin. This low resistance al-

lows substantial conductive heat gain and heat loss unless movable insulation is used.

Olgyay's Sol-Air concept. Perhaps the most widely known theory on building orientation for human comfort is Victor Olgyay's Sol-Air concept, an approach describing how solar-radiation and air-temperature values can be studied in combination to derive optimum building orientation. Hourly average outdoor air temperatures for the locality are categorized as either too cold, too hot, or within the comfort range for all months of the year. Solar radiation data for vertical surfaces oriented toward the sun are compared to the comfort categorizations. The optimum orientation maximizes cold period sun and minimizes hot period sun. Olgyay reported these results for the four principal climate zones in the continental U.S. as shown in Figure 6-16. Three building configurations

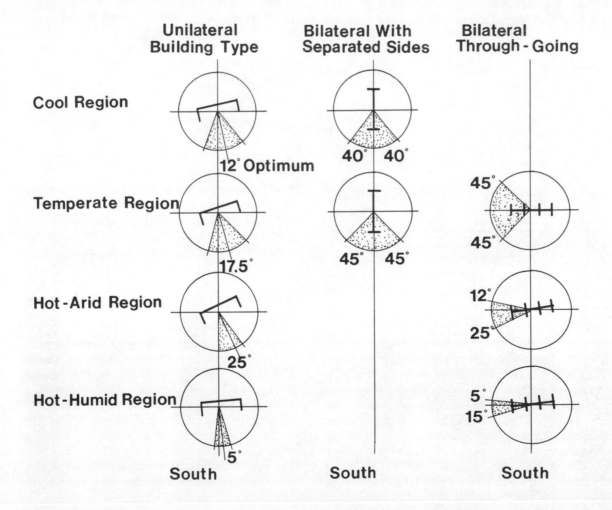

Figure 6-16. Regional building orientation chart. After: (Olgyay, 1963). Blank spaces indicate nonrecommended options.

are presented: unilateral — one long wall glazed; bilateral with separated sides — two unilateral units attached back to back; and bilateral through-going — attached units glazed on opposite walls. Some configurations are not recommended in certain climates.

One weakness of the Sol-Air approach applies to hot/arid climates where broad daily temperature ranges can have extremes on both sides of comfort limits. In a Sol-Air analysis, during the early morning hours of the hot season, a well-ventilated house will have interior air temperatures somewhat below comfort levels. This would call for admitting warming sunlight into the building. As the air temperature rises to comfort levels, the sunlight is blocked and remains blocked for the rest of the hot day. Although this will give maximum comfort during the early morning, this added heat may cause overheated conditions by late afternoon.

Another questionable recommendation is the orientation shift to the east for winter heating purposes. Although the early morning warming is clearly desirable, for a well-designed solar home it may not give best total performance. A house with adequate thermal mass should be sufficiently warm on a winter morning (assuming sunny weather in the past) to "wait" for incoming sun. A house with due-south orientation will capture and store maximum total solar gain for the day. This effect may outweigh the extra bit of early morning heat gain experienced by the house oriented to the east.

The key distinction in orientation criteria between this author's approach and that of Olgyay is that solar gain should be based on the day-long dominant condition instead of hourly need. That is, maximum possible solar gain on a cold day should be provided for, as should minimum possible solar gain on a dominantly hot day. For mild climates or moderate weather conditions, this distinction is obviously not critical.

Wind and breeze effects. Where wind and breeze have a significant impact on building thermal performance, building orientation and design must respond. The most direct method is to compare optimum solar orientation with optimum breeze collection and wind-protection orientations. A long building wall should be oriented for optimum year-round solar effects and adjusted appropriately to the local climate for winds and breezes.

However, many wind protection strategies are still subject to debate. Olgyay (1963) presents these guidelines: (1) Turn the "back side" (most windowless side) to the wind; (2) turn a narrow end, with least surface area, to the wind; or (3) position the building at a 45° angle to the wind. The 45° position reduces winds on the building to 50% to 60% of their velocity. In contrast, another study (Buckley, Harrje, Knowlton, & Heisler, 1978) conducted to measure air infiltration rates (the primary cause of heat loss due to winds) of model homes in a wind tunnel indicates that a 45° orientation to the wind results in the *highest* infiltration levels.

Olgyay finds that parallel rows of buildings shelter downwind rows. The main wind stream tends to rise above the units after the first row. Positioning a windbreak upwind of the first row will give maximum overall protection. Staggering units tends to maximize breeze penetration. Where cold winter winds and cooling summer breezes come from directions 90° apart, buildings can be positioned so that cold winds face parallel rows, yet cool breezes strike staggered buildings.

For housing or any type of site planning in areas exposed to very high winds, the best results may be obtained by modeling the site and alternative building and shelter-belt configurations in a wind tunnel. The ability of wind tunnels to simulate the actual site conditions make them a valuable tool. Detailed information on wind control is contained in Chapter Nine.

Orientation criteria for energy-efficient housing must include flexibility. The planner wants to know not only the "optimum" orientation but also the consequences of using other similar orientations to achieve other program requirements. Goals such as maintaining view corridors, creating pleasant outdoor spaces, facilitating pedestrian and vehicular circulation, and increasing density may all be enhanced if the planner uses a flexible approach to building siting. Generally, the milder the climate, the greater the opportunity for flexibility.

Siting Guidelines for Specific Housing Types

The following section describes the general strategies for siting three residential building types: conventional/solar, mobile homes, and earth sheltered. Detached, attached, and multifamily forms are discussed for each housing type. The overall approach is to present the key planning elements in the "conventional/solar housing" section and to note how the other housing types differ from these basic conditions. The goal is to present an image of a viable "housing ecosystem" in which a number of energy-related factors interact.

Conventional/Solar Housing
Conventional and solar housing are discussed together

since the energy-conscious planner will lay out all housing as if it were "solar." Two basic reasons justify this. The first is that lot layout and building siting can have significant impacts on thermal performance of the buildings and their associated outdoor spaces. The orientation of streets, for example, usually results in most dwelling windows oriented either toward the street or toward the rear yard of the lot. As discussed earlier, the orientation of windows is perhaps the most critical single factor relative to energy use for new, adequately built, and insulated housing. In this case the layout of one element, streets, can serve to facilitate a modest level of solar performance for conventional housing.

The second reason for using solar siting practices for all types of housing is to accommodate and encourage energy-conservation retrofits in the future. While many home and apartment owners debate whether to install solar domestic hot-water and swimming-pool systems, American and Japanese firms are rapidly developing cost-effective photovoltaic (solar electricity) systems. The buildings with ample south-facing roof surfaces will be the first to be retrofitted and will achieve the most cost-effective energy savings.

Key planning principles. True energy-conserving neighborhoods are more than aggregations of south-facing dwellings. As discussed earlier, the occupants' lifestyle significantly influences their household energy consumption. Therefore, the planner must consider a wide range of elements in addition to site conditions when siting dwellings, among which should include:

- resident's use patterns
- dwelling type
- privately owned land including shape, orientation
- outdoor spaces including a hierarchy of private to shared spaces
- dwelling entry
- automobile factors such as storage, access to dwelling, and road layout
- street trees
- pedestrian and bike circulation
- shared facilities
- grading and drainage

Successful plans are seldom developed through a one-at-a-time checklist approach. The pattern shown in Figure 6-17 has been used in one form or another since Stein and Wright's Radburn development. It shows a grouping of dwellings forming a small social unit within the larger neighborhood.

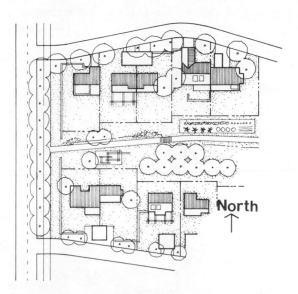

Figure 6-17. Housing cluster forms a small social unit.

This pattern's key planning elements are discussed below to explore their potentials, limitations, and possible variations. This discussion also pertains to all temperature regions; either very hot or very cold climates may require other criteria. Rather than begin with street and lot layout and then work down to smaller-scale considerations as is typically done, the planner may begin by envisioning the resident's needs and work outward.

Small homes should be considered even for the higher-priced market. Smaller spaces require less energy to heat, cool, and maintain, and they consume less material and land in their construction. As our society evolves, more singles and smaller families will require housing. Two- and three-bedroom homes can be built at 1,000 ft^2 incorporating finer materials and detailing than is possible with larger structures. Recent economic trends have tended toward emphasis on smaller dwelling units.

The dwelling should generally be slightly elongated on the east/west axis to maximize south glazing potential and minimize east/west windows. Private outdoor spaces function best on the dwelling's south side. Frank Lloyd Wright called this the "living side." The south side has the option of solar access at any season and can be shaded during the hot season.

Houses with extensive south glass will have minimal privacy concerns if a private outdoor space is located adjacent to the building's south wall. The layout of interior spaces should recognize the benefits of a south exposure. The most commonly used spaces are most successful when located on the south side of the building. Spaces requiring less heat should be located on the north exposure. Bedrooms often function well on the north side of the dwelling, but individual use patterns will give the best criteria. For example, children's bedrooms often double as play spaces and can benefit from south exposure.

The next group of planning elements to consider relate to the automobile, its access to the dwelling, its storage, and the resulting road layout. Does each dwelling, for example, require daily auto access "to its front door," or is a walk of 100 to 200 ft acceptable? Freeing the dwelling from immediate contact with the auto gives great flexibility to the site planner and can result in significant savings in pavement costs as Figure 6-18 shows. Emergency vehicle access is mandatory and can be provided by pathways of suitable width and strength specifications that can also serve residents' infrequent needs for vehicular access for moving heavy items.

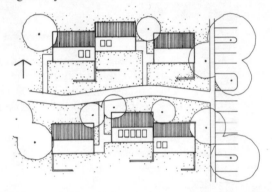

Figure 6-18. Parking at east or west end of a cluster creates car-free zones.

When residents desire direct auto access on a daily basis and a garage or carport is used, the site planner has a number of options. The most common is to attach the garage to the house. Locating the garage/carport on the north side of the dwelling is frequently preferred because it maintains the privacy of the south yard by requiring a north or east/west main entry to the dwelling. Locating the garage to the east or west of the house is beneficial in that it protects those walls from undesirable hot season sun. An attached south location should be avoided because it prevents the opportunity for solar gain. Each of these options has a strong influence on overall street and lot layout.

The two most basic street-orientation alternatives are east/west and north/south. Topographic limitations aside, the planner can choose between these street alternatives by deciding what basic individual lot plans are desired. In more extreme hot or cold climates attaching the garage on the east or west side of the dwelling is beneficial. In hot climates the sun is blocked and maximum cross ventilation is maintained. In cold climates the direct access to the house

is gained without blocking solar access. This pattern can result in north/south streets. To minimize development costs and to maintain efficient land use, lots should be shaped by solar access requirements as discussed in Chapter Seven. Figure 6-19 shows the method and resulting plan. Solar access is preserved to the entire south wall. Other levels of solar access could be planned for as well.

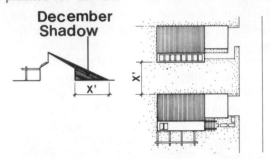

Figure 6-19. Building siting for south-wall solar access.

Locating the garage on the north is generally good practice, though some cross ventilation is blocked. A key limitation is that houses on the north side of the street will have south auto access. Detaching the south garage/carport far enough from the south wall to avoid shading conflicts can be a successful solution especially in milder climates.

Lot configurations can be refined by considering broader land-use possibilities. In a typical subdivision the individual's image of his lot is of a public front yard, a private enclosed back yard, and narrow side yards serving primarily for circulation, storage, or pets. Figure 6-20a (see next page) shows that the street serves as the focal area for the block. In contrast is the pattern in which a shared commons becomes the focal area, a car-free space formed by limiting the depth of individual lots and combining ownership of what would have been back yards in a typical subdivision (Figures 6-20b and c). Streets function more as alleys — narrow, with fenced private yards abutting them, as intraneighborhood circulation emphasizes the bike and pedestrian pathways in the common areas rather than car use along roadways. Roads serve as individual fingers from the perimeter while pathways give quick access to all points from the interior of the neighborhood. Pathways minimize the need to cross streets to move from one area to another. Common area land uses as planned by the adjacent residents include children's play areas, vegetable gardens, fruit and nut orchards, ponds, arbors, "outdoor rooms," firepits, gardening sheds, and laundry facilities.

Front, rear, and side yard setbacks are influenced by these patterns. Orientation is more important than

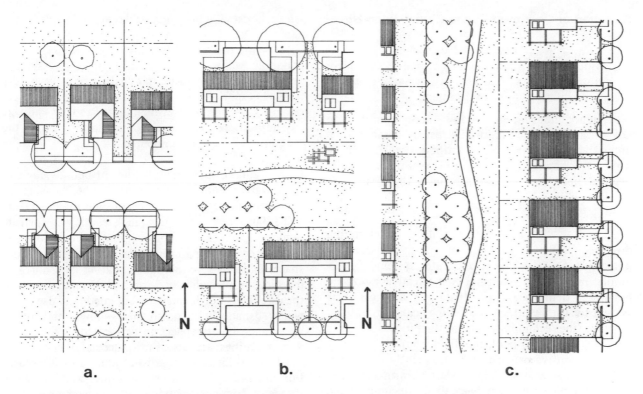

Figure 6-20. Typical subdivision: (a) fenced back yards leave street as the focal area; (b) combining unfenced "backyards" to form a cluster focal area; (c) cluster focal area with north-south streets.

"front" or "back" designation. Figure 6-20b shows that south yard setbacks are generous to allow adequate solar access and outdoor uses. North yard setbacks are minimal. In effect, all buildings are located far to the north on their lots. Side yards are eliminated where possible to give "zero-lot-line" attached units with superior thermal performance to detached units. This duplex configuration gives more usable space on the open sideyard and permits planting trees for summer shade. A larger side yard also allows for side entries to dwellings. However, to be successful side yard entrances must be designed so that they are clearly visible from both street and open spaces. House plans with side entries can work well on both north and south sides of streets if garages are detached. Figure 6-20c shows that the same approach can be used with north/south streets. A key advantage is that south window walls face onto private yards rather than streets or common areas.

Grading and drainage are planning elements offering energy-savings potential. In "open" or "natural" drainage systems lots slope away from roadways into open landscaped swales with occasional weirs to control storm water runoff. The weirs form ponds during heavy rains maximizing on-site percolation and groundwater recharge. This delays and often eliminates discharge into the city storm-water system.

Percolation adds to the water table and reduces energy needed for well pumps. In addition to minimizing environmental impact, the cost savings on storm-system infrastructure and associated savings of embodied energy can be significant. One developer completely landscaped his project from money saved by using the open drainage system.

Street trees are another key planning element. Too often broad deciduous trees are specified, the energy-conservation goal being to maximize summer shade and provide adequate winter solar access through bare branches, a strategy no longer acceptable for solar buildings. Bare deciduous trees commonly block fifty percent of winter sunlight from reaching collectors (Hammond, Zanetto, & Adams, 1981). Street trees' characteristics should match the energy-conservation needs of adjacent buildings (Zanetto & Thayer, 1983). Chapter Seven discusses this aspect of solar access planning in more detail.

The foregoing discussion of conventional and solar housing is intended to give a broad series of guidelines for master planning. The aim is for the planner to begin at the scale of the individual dwelling and to develop a plan which utilizes principles of energy-conserving site design to achieve housing patterns that are both energy efficient and highly liveable.

Attached or Clustered Conventional/Solar Housing

The term "cluster" suggests a positive image of a living association of similar parts, a type of symbiosis. Planning attached or cluster housing has the responsibility of creating this environment.

Attached housing has many energy-conservation advantages. Reduced thermal stress on the individual unit is well documented (Harwood, 1977). Sharing walls, floors, and ceilings with other units essentially negates heat loss or gain through these surfaces, resulting in significant energy savings for heating and cooling.

Shared use of facilities, enhanced by clustering dwellings, offers a number of energy-conservation potentials. Solar domestic hot-water systems, for example, may have a marginal cost effectiveness where hot-water demand is low. Installing a single solar system for use by attached dwellings can substantially improve the economics. Other facilities such as a laundry, swimming pool, playfield, shop or gym may be too expensive or used too infrequently to warrant individual ownership. Neighborhoods, with a swimming pool in virtually every back yard are common and very wasteful of energy. Many homeowners recognize this, but because of neighborhood layout or lack of neighborhood organization a shared pool is not feasible.

Increased density is another significant energy-conservation advantage of clustering. Many sites or portions of sites call for moderate densities due to their proximity to facilities. These facilities are key travel destinations such as employment, shopping or educational centers, or perhaps public amenities such as developed open space. Allowing residents to walk, bike, or take public transit to these facilities saves more energy than providing remote housing with solar systems (Calthorpe & Benson, 1979).

Increased density also conserves land. Unfortunately, flat fertile valley bottom land often gives higher investment returns in development than agriculture. Farming relocates to poorer quality land distant from consumers of its produce. More energy-intensive practices are required to farm such land and to transport its products.

The principal cluster planning problem is to maintain development efficiencies of clustered development while retaining the identity of the individual dwelling. Privacy is a measure of this identity. Both visual and noise privacy are critical. Properly designed and constructed common walls can actually give more visual and noise privacy than is possible with windows of adjacent houses facing each other across narrow side yards.

In Figure 6-17 (p. 103) many of the dwellings share common walls with adjacent units. Interspersed among detached houses, this feature may be hardly noticed, especially if the attached dwellings vary in design. Variation in individual units can lead to diversity both in the visual image of the housing and in the type of resident accommodated.

Key planning principals. The principal energy-conservation planning factors for attached housing are similar to those for detached housing: major glazing and solar access to the dwelling's south wall, private outdoor space (usually on the south), entry location (usually on the north) separate from private outdoor space, and cross ventilation. Locating cars north of dwellings is advisable, because it gives ready access to the dwelling's north entry, makes good land use of the winter "shade belt" north of dwellings, and allows views and activity spaces to be located to the south. Tree plantings are also most successful just to the north of dwellings as Figure 6-21 illustrates. This location maximizes solar access, provides a living screen for views from north windows, shades parking areas in summer, and blocks north winter winds where they occur. Wind direction, visual screening needs, and the type of land use to the north will influence selection of evergreen or deciduous trees.

Figure 6-21. Attached housing with parking to the north and collectors and use areas on the south.

The south facade of an attached housing mass requires special attention to avoid solar access conflicts. Variation in setbacks between individual units creates diversity, interest, and identity for each dwelling but may cause detrimental shading of south windows as Figure 6-22 shows. South rooftops may also receive

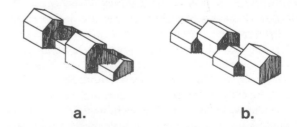

a.   b.

Figure 6-22. (a) One-story recessed plan gives poor solar access; (b) recessing two-story units provides good solar access.

unacceptable amounts of shading where variations in roof lines occur. Alternative collector locations should be considered when wall and roof variations are used.

Many successful housing clusters utilize a focal point or activity center to organize the layout. For solar housing this focus may be more linear than usual because of the need to retain an approximate south exposure for the dwellings. Focal areas often function best where cars are excluded, leading to two basic patterns: one where car parking is at the north and south ends of a cluster, and a second where cars are parked east and west of the cluster (Figure 6-23). A central common area between building massings creates conditions similar to detached housing where some dwellings have public entries on the south exposure.

A central activity area is usually favored for housing of families with children or elderly and for housing in moderate climates where outdoor spaces are well used. At higher densities, or for certain residential types, limited incorporation of cars into the focal area can be successful and maximizes density as well.

Housing clusters using two distinct building forms, as Figure 6-24a shows, can provide diversity of building massing and diversity of outdoor spaces created by the buildings. This technique gives each dwelling a strong identity due to its unique position in the cluster. Roof-level clerestory windows can be quite effective as passive space-heating collectors and can free the site planner of providing south-wall solar access to all dwellings. This building type can also allow north-south street alignment with no energy penalty. Figure 6-24b shows the Suncatcher (developed by Living Systems of Winters, California), which uses reflective roof surfaces to enhance heat gain through the clerestory window, and collects 50% more sunlight than is collected through a typical south window.

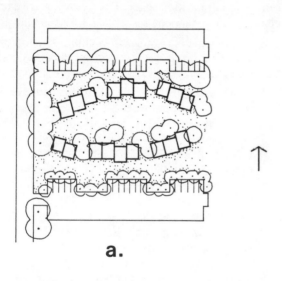

a.

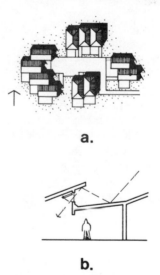

a.

b.

Figure 6-24. Using clerestory solar access to provide diversity in building layout and massing.

South-facing clerestory windows can also be used where attached dwellings share a north/south common wall or where a double-loaded corridor complex would otherwise limit south windows. (The Uniform Building Code should however be noted.) Cross ventilation is another energy-conservation problem with double-loaded corridors. Ventilation can be achieved by locating vents into the corridor and venting the corridor ceiling or end walls. Vents require soundproof shutters to conserve privacy.

Patio housing, commonly overlooked in the United States, usually consists of one-story dwellings with as

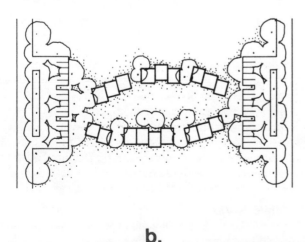

b.

Figure 6-23. Creating car-free focal areas by locating cars either (a) north and south of housing, or (b) east and west.

many as three attached walls (Figure 6-25). The typical "L" shaped building wraps around a private outdoor patio that becomes the focus of the house. Because of the limited area of exposed south wall and the high degree of shading of that south wall by adjacent walls, this housing form has most applications in either mild or overheated climates where solar access needs are minimal. Active rooftop mounted collectors or rooftop clerestory windows can mitigate the solar access problem, however.

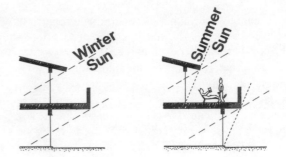

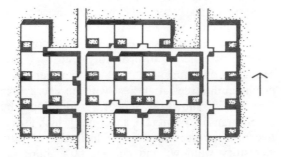

Figure 6-25. Patio housing. After: (Untermann & Small, 1977).

Rotating buildings away from due south can achieve more flexible and diverse site plans. The limits of acceptable rotation are largely a function of the local climate. "South" windows oriented as much as 25 to 45 degrees east or west of due south can serve adequately as collectors. Although such windows create a risk of overheating, they are easily shaded in the summer (although sometimes expensively) by a range of new products such as shade screens, exterior roll down shades, or movable insulation. Computer simulation of dwelling thermal performance is perhaps the best tool to determine acceptable orientation limits. Caution should be used in laying out this type of plan, for densities can diminish relative to a rectilinear plan.

The private sunny garden is a basic amenity of attached housing throughout the world. It is more difficult to provide with two-story attached dwellings because of the overview problem from second story windows. Figure 6-26 shows one solution: placing the private garden on the second floor, perhaps with a stepped-back south facade to avoid shading conflicts with first floor windows.

Rooftops are another potential location for private outdoor spaces, gardens, greenhouses, and play yards. Where solar access to south walls is difficult, rooftops may be the best location for active collector systems. Upper-story greenhouse spaces can have multiple functions as sun rooms, food producers, and as collectors with heated air ducted to living spaces below. However, humidity and temperature conflicts may

Figure 6-26. Stepping back second story decks improves lower floor solar access.

preclude use of sun spaces for both plant propagation and space heating and should be avoided.

Attached or cluster housing often requires concentrated car parking space. The following are energy-conservation practices associated with parking lots:

- Shade parking areas in the hot season. Wide broad trees located between every fourth car will provide good shade.
- Avoid extensive parking lots which can create extreme microclimates (while the trees are young) adding to the thermal stress of adjacent buildings, and pedestrians.
- Use double-loaded parking layouts; they are more efficient than single-loaded ones.
- Use good quality materials and detailing to avoid energy-intensive resurfacing. Consider porous surface materials such as "turf block," decomposed granite, or other locally available products to minimize environmental (especially hydrologic) impacts where appropriate.
- Use low-use turn-around areas to double as game space for youths.

Attached housing can also be connected to uses such as retail outlets, professional offices, and workshops. Figure 6-27 (see next page) depicts an urban/suburban mix of land uses at the neighborhood edge. This area serves as the focal point of the neighborhood where commercial, employment, public transit, and recreational facilities are located. The neighborhood's highest density dwelling complexes are adjacent to the center. Parking is shared with the community center building.

Mobile Homes

One of the most ambiguous aspects of site planning for mobile homes is that the side with most windows varies between the long side in some models to the short end in many newer models. A recent tendency has been to place major windows on the short end to

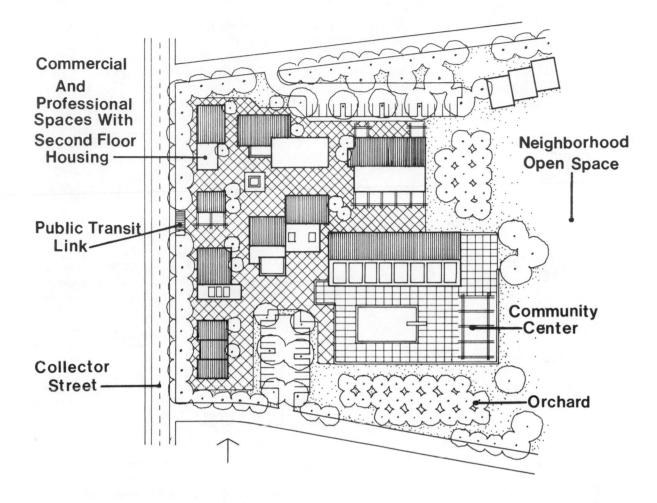

Commercial And Professional Spaces With Second Floor Housing

Public Transit Link

Collector Street

Neighborhood Open Space

Community Center

Orchard

Figure 6-27. Neighborhood commercial/community center.

afford views to the street (the usual activity area) instead of into a very narrow side yard and the neighbor's windows. The planner should be familiar with the kind of mobile home to be sited. Better yet, the planner should go to a manufacturer willing to make custom units with specified window areas, insulation (including movable insulation), and south patio covers that can roll up in winter to allow solar access to windows. Thermal mass, in the form of water tanks or phase-change materials, can be designed into the unit.

The planner should also become familiar with mobile home owners. Residents of mobile home parks in many Sun Belt states, for example, are retirees with distinctive lifestyles and energy needs. These one- or two-occupant residences generally have a low hot-water demand per unit, thus affecting solar domestic hot-water system economies.

Elderly residents may also have unique transportation needs. Lots without car storage space could be designed, transportation provided instead by a

neighborhood-to-downtown shuttle service with frequently scheduled trips to common destinations and/or a "dial-a-ride" service to unique locations. These services could be the responsibility of a residents' association. Considerable energy savings could be gained by operating, maintaining, and housing only a few well-used vehicles instead of a minor fleet of individual cars. Visitor parking spaces would be required, of course.

Where private cars are used, parking and garage facilities should be clustered to achieve both solar access and solar control goals. Carports can be located on the east or west ends of mobile homes to provide shade during the hot season yet maximize south sun to the home and its side yard in the winter. Too often densely packed mobile homes have carports to their north or south, the canopies of which inevitably block solar access. Position of the home's entry door will significantly influence possible carport locations.

The most efficient individual lot plan positions a

109

home with most of its windows on a long side. In Figure 6-28 this side faces south across a sunny outdoor living area. A trellis or arbor with deciduous vines or a canopy with a roll-up cover provide hot-season shade. The home is placed near its north property line (a pattern quite similar to solar housing on north/south streets).

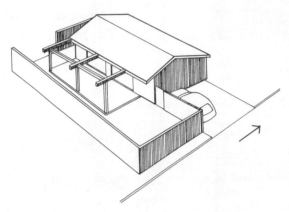

Figure 6-28. Solar access site plan for a mobile home.

Other mobile home modifications may also affect siting. Greenhouses, a popular energy-conservation retrofit for conventional housing, may be used successfully with mobile homes, and as more options become available, greenhouse kits may become commonplace. Built-in thermal mass tanks are also possible if, during manufacture, additional structural supports and appropriately placed windows are incorporated. Since these tanks are filled with water when the home is sited, subsequent relocations of the home would merely require draining the tanks and refilling them at the new site. Another modification is the thermosiphoning air panel attached to an exterior wall. In this device solar energy preheats air to be circulated in the mobile home. Shared solar domestic hot-water systems can also be located on carport rooftops with storage tanks adjacent to one another (distribution lines to each unit require adequate insulation). The resulting hot water can also be used in fan-coil and radiant space-heating systems. Each of these modifications results in solar collector locations that will influence siting of adjacent structures and trees.

The mobile home's interior floor level should be established as close to grade as possible to allow sunlight to ground areas, to minimize tall narrow spaces between units, and to reduce the passage of extreme-temperature air below the floor (skirting will help achieve the last objective).

The conventional siting pattern of equally spaced homes placed perpendicular to the access road can be varied as Figure 6-29 illustrates. Every third unit

could be oriented parallel to the road to provide central common areas among the units. (Too often "common areas" are virtually useless 10-ft wide strips running between the ends of coaches.) Density is hardly affected by this siting strategy. The net density of the plan shown in Figure 6-29 is 7.25 units per acre.

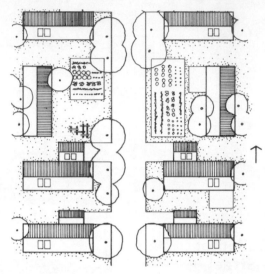

Figure 6-29. Variations in orientation of mobile homes correspond to window layout of specific units. Units parallel to the road have most windows on south-end wall.

Most "mobile" homes never leave their initial site locations. If planning for permanent siting is appropriate in a given situation, greater siting flexibility can result. The homes illustrated in Figure 6-30 have

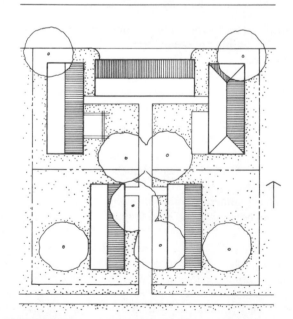

Figure 6-30. Siting options based on permanent siting of off-street homes.

110

major windows on their south-facing end walls. This deep lot pattern can achieve significant savings in street pavement per unit.

Topography is especially critical in siting mobile homes because of their long narrow shape and the inability to vary their floor plan to step-down slopes. Siting the coach along existing contours will reduce the need for retaining walls and the continuing maintenance of earthwork terracing.

Attached modular units are now being marketed. Passive solar and natural cooling features may be available as integrated structural features rather than retrofit options. These higher density units should be located adjacent to the neighborhood's central facilities.

Earth-Sheltered Housing

Earth-sheltered housing conserves significant amounts of energy for space heating and cooling because the interior spaces are tempered by stable moderate earth temperatures. Winter heat loss and summer heat gain are minimized, and heat loss due to winds is much reduced over conventional housing. Earth temperatures in the United States are usually low enough that even well-insulated earth-sheltered homes lose more heat than is generated by the residents' activities (see Figure 6-9). Therefore, solar orientation remains an important goal for the energy-conscious site planner.

Development costs can be a good indicator of the amount of embodied energy. Earth-sheltered development costs are likely to be somewhat higher than costs for conventional housing. Where difficult site conditions are present, costs can escalate substantially. Nevertheless, the site analysis work of a geotechnical engineer can be quite cost effective because the preliminary data will allow the structural engineer to estimate structural system costs that can determine project feasibility. A single earth-sheltered residence may be built on a marginally acceptable site, but construction of a whole complex of earth-sheltered dwellings on a questionable site will result in energy expenditures for heavy equipment and materials that may never be offset by reduced space-conditioning energy

usage. The moral is thus to choose and evaluate the site carefully. However, a "hidden" site-planning factor is the Uniform Building Code's requirement for a direct emergency exit from all habitable rooms (skylights do not fulfill this need). This exit requirement may be critical to the layout of interior spaces and consequently affect overall building configuration and siting of earth-sheltered homes.

Figure 6-31 shows three basic configurations of earth-sheltered buildings: elevational, penetrational, and atrium (Underground Space Center, 1978). The elevational design buries the unit on three sides with all windows concentrated on what is usually the south side. The penetrational design has this same configuration except that some north windows are provided for cross ventilation. The atrium design buries or berms the entire unit with a central core open to the sky. Atrium designs may have less potential for solar access than other earth-shelter options. Shading of the south-facing wall may be caused by the opposite wall or by adjacent walls. Atrium designs also have a greater potential for more exposed surface area. For site-planning purposes elevational and penetrational types can usually be combined.

Key planning principles. Both pedestrian and vehicular access to earth-sheltered dwellings requires careful planning. Privacy concerns for the south exposure of elevational designs are similar to those previously discussed for solar houses. The solutions are more limited for earth-sheltering because fewer alternate entry locations are possible. Corner entries with the major portion of the south wall and yard screened from view are often successful. Where only one elevation is available for entering the building, the traditional "back door" providing direct access to the kitchen or coat room may require some visual cues to keep it from being confused with the main entry. (The main entry and back door can also be combined with a clear separation of circulation occurring within the dwelling.)

Atrium designs may provide an entryway through one of the surrounding berms. Stairs will be necessary if the floor level is recessed below grade. A stairway

Elevational Design   **Penetrational Design**   **Atrium Design**

Figure 6-31. Elevational, penetrational and atrium designs for earth-sheltered housing.

111

down into the central courtyard may intrude too directly on the residents' privacy. Another form of access in submerged designs is to raise a portion of the structure above grade level to house a garage, entry, and other spaces, as Figure 6-32 illustrates.

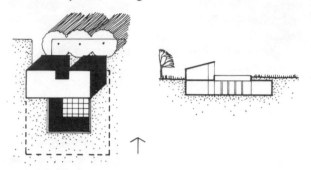

Figure 6-32. Atrium design with above grade access. After: (Sterling, Carmody & Elnicky, 1981).

In a cluster of completely submerged atrium designs, cars and their storage areas become the dominant visual element. If the cars are stored at the roadway, the visual problem is minimized but the resident may not be satisfied in extreme climates. Figure 6-33 shows a bermed rather than submerged atrium design. Car and pedestrians gain access through one berm, making this an atrium/elevational hybrid plan.

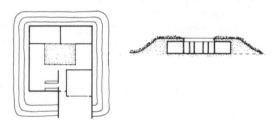

Figure 6-33. Atrium/elevational design. After: (Sterling, et al., 1981).

Detached earth-sheltered homes, unless of submerged atrium design, may require large lots to accommodate berms and drainage swales. Continuing berms between adjacent units can save as much as 50 ft (15 m) of width per lot (Sterling, Carmody, & Elnicky, 1981) and seems virtually mandatory for an economical moderate income design.

As Figure 6-35 shows, attaching units can result in significant additional savings in land area and structural costs. The thermal performance difference between detached and attached earth-sheltered designs can be roughly estimated by comparing the

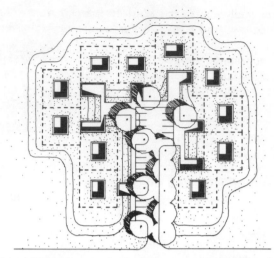

Figure 6-34. Atrium designs have more siting flexibility since solar orientation is less critical. After: (Sterling, et al., 1981).

soil temperatures at various depths with estimated temperatures of the interior spaces of adjacent units. For example in Davis, Calif., soil temperatures at the 8-ft (2.4 m) depth vary between an annual low of 60F (15.5C) in March and a high of 72F (22C) in September. Assuming a neighbor's interior space ranges between 68F (20C) and 80F (26.6C), there is some hot-season advantage but no cold-season advantage to detached versus attached earth-sheltered units. This same basic pattern should apply in climates colder than Davis.

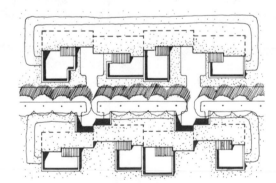

Figure 6-35. Attached earth-sheltered housing has thermal performance similar to detached earth-sheltered housing. After: (Sterling, et al., 1981).

Perhaps the most significant planning factor with attached elevational earth-sheltered dwellings is that densities can increase as slopes increase. Maintaining the original slope of the land allows dwellings to be spaced more closely. With remote parking, slopes up to 40% are acceptable (Sterling, et al., 1981). Figure 6-36 shows how units can be stepped up steep slopes. This significantly reduces structural loading on the lower wall relative to two-story earth-sheltered con-figurations, and gives a better unit-to-site fit.

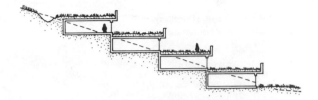

Figure 6-36. Attached elevational earth-sheltered housing can increase in density as slopes increase. After: (Sterling, et al., 1981).

Conclusion

The master planning process results in the project's overall development scheme. Many costs and energy issues can now be quantitatively evaluated and modifications and alternatives to the plan suggested by members of the technical team, and eventually by regulatory agencies. *This may be the last cost-effective planning phase for broad evaluation of the project;* subsequent energy-saving features are likely to be achieved at a more detailed design scale. Chapter Three presented technical evaluation methods. Table 6-1 presents another project evaluation guide by Kern, Kern, Mullan, and Mullan (1982). An extension of Malcolm Well's "Wilderness Scale," it is not an exact method but a subjective one that allows the energy-and resource-conscious planner to keep broad goals in mind. The considerations are developed for single-family housing but generally apply to all scales of work.

Table 6-1. Site Planning and Building Design Guidelines

Energy conserving	Energy expending
Materials	
Site-available and site-processed	Manufactured and imported
Recycled or renewable resource	Limited, nonrenewable resource
Low-energy content (e.g., adobe)	High energy content (e.g., aluminum)
Little handling and no packaging	Much handling and wasteful packaging
Natural, nontoxic materials	Excessive use of solvents, glues, foams, and other toxic substances
Construction phase	
Used hand tools	Required heavy machinery
Benign process, little safety equipment needed	Unsafe, noisy, toxic workplace Protective devices necessary
Process-enhanced health	Hazardous process rusulted in injury
Preserved soil and plants	Undue damage to plants, soil compaction, residue damage from concrete, solvent and paint cleanup, etc.
Knowledge and skills bank of local community increased	Specialized work force imported, contributing nothing to local richness and diversity
Included participation of children	Excluded family and friends
The house	
Small, compact, efficient	Extravagant waste of space
Areas have many uses	Single function spaces
Durable, long-lasting	Will not survive 30-year mortgage
Easily maintained	Difficult or unsafe maintenance
Repairable	Planned obsolescence
Final disposition recyclable or compostable	Toxic material or waste disposal problem
Increases flora and fauna diversity by creating special alcoves and microclimates for multipurpose plants	Monoculture, vulnerable to disease and pest
Personal, cultural, and worldwide ramifications	
Low cost	Enslaved to mortgage
Cash outlay to local craftspeople or local industry	Concentrated wealth outside local community, contributed to exploitation in Third World
Close to workplace, schools, social life, supplies	Suburban home or rural retreat burdening community services

(Continued on next page)

Table 6-1. Site Planning and Building Design Guidelines (Continued)

Personal, cultural, and worldwide ramifications

Energy conserving	Energy expending
Captures solar energy for space heating, hot water, lighting, electricity; part of decentralized energy grid of moderate value, self-reliant and easily defendable, does not require military capability to defend	Dependent on electrical grid, imported oil, nuclear power, gas pipelines; depends on expensive centralized facilities and complex transmission system, vulnerable to breakdown, saboteur or vandal, requiring military defense, paramilitary presence for protection
Promotes clarity, contentment, simplicity, centeredness, joy	Complications and problems create irritation and frustration, encourages self-indulgence and egoism, creates anxiety from indebtedness

———————

After: (Kern, Kern, Mullan, & Mullan, 1982)

CHAPTER SEVEN
Planning for Solar Access

ROBERT L. THAYER, JR., ASLA
University of California, Davis
Davis, California

SOLAR energy represents a critical contribution to the energy future of the nation as noted by Stobaugh and Yergin in their book *Energy Future* (1979). Direct use of solar energy for space heating, domestic hot water, clothes drying, creation of electricity, and general outdoor comfort is a safe, sustainable, and relatively impact-free means of reducing dependency upon irreplaceable fossil fuels. However, collecting useful solar energy, whether dispersed among the many houses in a neighborhood or concentrated in one area of a downtown commercial center, requires an adequate and perpetual supply of incident sunlight available to solar collectors. Physical blocking of radiation from solar devices results in their lowered efficiency and reduced economic usefulness (Kohler & Lewis, 1981). Thus, if solar energy is to be effectively utilized, the means of protecting access of sunlight to collectors, or "solar access," must be assured.

Solar Access Concepts and Challenges

Solar access — the means of protecting incident sunlight to collectors — is both a physical and technological problem as well as a legal and planning policy challenge. As designers, landscape architects will be most concerned with design techniques that guarantee solar access through direct manipulation of design elements: buildings, trees, landforms, structures, and other vegetation. However, since sunlight necessary for operating a solar collector does not come from directly overhead but passes diagonally across land as the earth rotates, sunlight can easily be blocked by vegetation and structures existing or planned on neighboring property. As a result, a considerable body of legal debate and research has developed concerning how best to protect the solar access of one property owner while perpetuating the property rights of another (Gergacz, 1982; Hayes, 1979; Jaffe, 1980). Some of the legal means and planning devices for protecting solar access will be discussed here. Emphasis will be given, however, to planning for solar access through *direct design*.

Solar Access as a Physical/Spatial Concept

Landscape architects who design for protecting solar access must be familiar with the three-dimensional, temporal relationship between the sun and the earth. Although the earth is obviously orbiting around the sun, a solar collector "sees" the sun in terms of paths across the sky from morning to evening. These solar paths change during the year as the angle of the earth's axis changes from summer to winter with respect to the sun. The position of the sun relative to the earth can be precisely determined if the latitude and longitude of the observer and the time of day are known. Position of the sun with respect to the earth is measured by the *azimuth*, or horizontal angle the sun makes with respect to due south, and the *altitude*, or vertical angle describing the height of the sun relative to the horizon (Figure 7-1). For the northern hemisphere, the sun rises in the east, sets in the west, and is approximately due south at noon at an altitude angle dependent upon latitude. In summer, the sun rises slightly north of due east and sets slightly north of due west and achieves a relatively high altitude angle with respect to the horizon. In winter, the sun

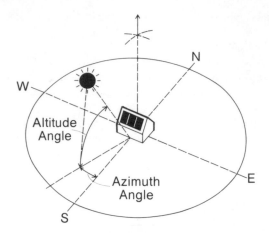

Figure 7-1. Postion of the sun with respect to a structure as defined by azimuth and altitude angles.

rises south of east, sets south of west, and follows a path much closer to the southern horizon — a lower altitude angle. On noon of March 21 and Sept. 21, the sun is in the equinox position, or midway in elevation between the winter low and summer high altitudes. Also at this time, the sun rises and sets precisely due east and west, respectively. Figure 7-2 shows the sun's path during the spring/fall equinox and summer and winter solstice.

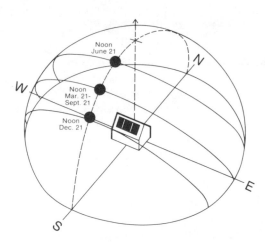

Figure 7-2. Sun paths for December 21 (winter solstice), June 21 (summer solstice), and March/September 21 (spring and fall equinox).

"Skyspace" refers to that portion of space adjacent to the collector surface which must be kept free of obstruction for maximum operating efficiency. A skyspace can be identified from a knowledge of the motion of the sun with respect to earth and an understanding of the characteristics of a particular solar collector. In the northern hemisphere, this space is generally above and to the south of the collector, as

Figure 7-3 indicates. Specific boundaries of the skyspace relative to the ground will depend on:

1. Whether the collector is fixed or movable.
2. The spatial orientation of the collector.
3. The height of the collector above the ground.
4. The latitude (and, to a minor degree, longitude) of the collector.
5. The function of the collector (i.e., heating space, heating water, electrical production, etc.).
6. The slope of the land under and near the collector.

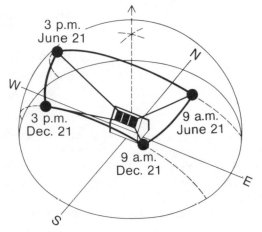

Ⓐ Critical Solar Skyspace

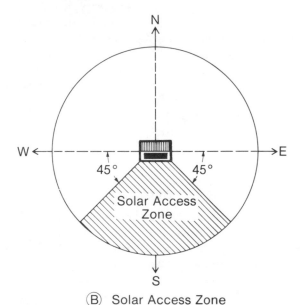

Ⓑ Solar Access Zone

Figure 7-3. Critical solar skyspace translated into a solar access zone. In this zone, trees, buildings, and other objects should be critically evaluated for potential solar access blockage.

If the collector moves to follow the sun, a much larger skyspace is required than if the collector is fix-

116

ed, since movable collectors can "track" the sun as it moves, maintaining a more efficient orientation throughout the day. However, most collectors are fixed. Sun angles striking a fixed collector obliquely result in very little heat gain and can be obstructed without significant loss of collector efficiency (Berdahl, Grether, Martin, & Wahlig, 1978; Erley & Jaffe, 1979). Although south is the most beneficial orientation for collectors, a 35° orientation to the southwest or southeast can be 90% as efficient if the skyspace is skewed slightly to the west or east, respectively (Barnaby, Caesar, Wilcox, & Nelson, 1977).

If the collector surface is located high above the ground, the critical skyspace moves higher. This allows taller structures and vegetation underneath without blocking critical sunlight. If the collector is sited on a north-facing slope, height restrictions on potentially obstructing elements are more severe than on a south-facing slope where buildings and trees can be taller without obstructing collectors.

Skyspace configuration also depends on latitude. A collector mounted 10-ft high in Maine will result in a shallower skyspace than the same 10-ft high collector located in Texas, as Figure 7-4 illustrates.

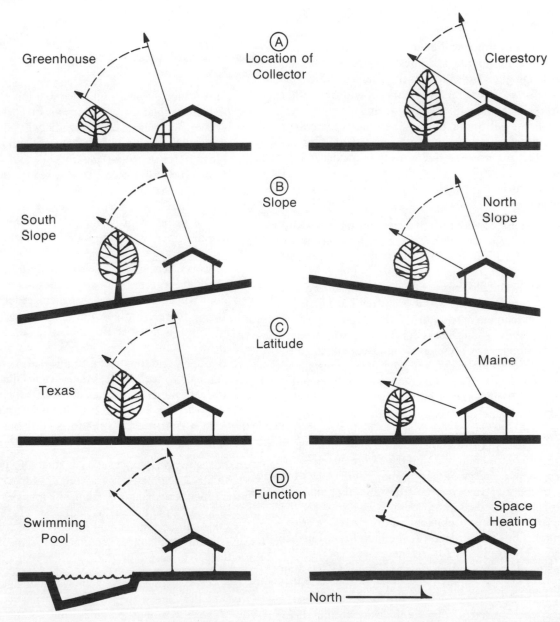

Figure 7-4. Solar skyspace configuration dependent upon a variety of factors, including collector location and function, slope, and latitude.

117

If the collector is used for space heating in buildings, the skyspace has a narrower vertical dimension since summer sun angles are not critical and could be blocked without negative effect on performance. However, collectors that must operate year-round, such as domestic water heaters, should be free from obstruction during the summer as well as winter. Thus, the upper sector of the skyspace becomes as critical as the lower. The critical skyspace for swimming pools needing heat only from April through September or October is opposite that required for space-heating systems. High-angle summer sun must strike collectors to heat the pool. Winter sunlight is not needed.

Often solar homes will have multiple collector surfaces, most commonly a domestic water heater and south-facing glass for space heating, each of which has different solar access requirements. In addition, other outdoor areas such as swimming-pool decks, greenhouses, patios, or clotheslines must sometimes be considered solar "collectors" in need of solar access protection because their utility may depend on adequate sunlight. Figure 7-4 illustrates how the solar skyspace varies in response to the factors just described.

Solar access considerations arise in many types of development. Landscape architects will be primarily involved in protecting solar access through siting of buildings, structures, and vegetation. On occasion, landscape architects may be consulted during the design of buildings, but will more often have little influence on choice or design of the solar collection devices. Ideally, solar access can best be protected by (1) assembling a team including landscape architects, architects, solar engineers, and energy specialists, and (2) designing the project site completely as a team, including the design and siting of solar structures and the design of plantings so that for the lifetime of the project, no solar access conflicts will occur (see Chapter Three). In the construction of new projects such as residential planned-unit developments, this approach is easy and can result in maximum utilization of solar energy. However most design situations will, unfortunately, be less than ideal, because of (1) the role of the landscape architect and time when he or she is brought into the project, (2) the inability to predict the solar features of future structures, or (3) the presence of complicating factors such as existing buildings or trees. Landscape architects may be called in to help solve solar access problems of property owners who are retrofitting solar devices to buildings in neighborhoods where solar energy was never originally considered. Large mature trees may inhibit

collector location or block it altogether; buildings on adjacent property may undergo changes in use or character which affect shadows. In some cases, the landscape architect may have to weigh the potential for solar access against the benefit of large shade trees on energy conservation by reducing cooling load — a topic to be addressed later in the chapter. Landscape architects familiar with solar access planning and design techniques may be able to assist in the development plans for solar structures on infill or vacant lots in existing developed areas. This often requires sophisticated site analysis and shadow-casting techniques to determine the extent of existing solar access and best possible locations for collectors. Regardless of the type of development situation, landscape architects need to ask certain questions and assess specific conditions:

1. How much natural sunlight is available? Is there seasonal cloud cover? Morning or evening fog?
2. How much solar access already exists due to the nature of the physical site? Do trees on buildings block solar access at present?
3. How much solar access is required for the collectors in question?
4. Are there nonenergy-related amenities that would suffer by provision of solar access such as visual screening, food production, historic trees, etc.?
5. Are existing structures or vegetation, such as shade trees in parking lots, windbreaks stopping cold winds, etc., already reducing energy use?
6. Is the future configuration of buildings known, or must a nonspecific level of solar access be provided?
7. Should deciduous trees be allowed to penetrate solar skyspace? What is their branch density out-of-leaf? When do they gain and lose their leaves?
8. Are surrounding land uses likely to change and cause detrimental shadows on the site in question?

Landscape architects must ask such questions and, as with other land design parameters, address solar access through a rigorous program/site analysis process. Protection of solar access through design is essentially a rational, three-dimensional process of the type landscape architects handle commonly in professional practice.

Solar Access as a Legal/Planning Challenge

Occasionally landscape architects will become involved with regional planning for solar access or development of public policy with respect to solar access protection. However, a number of factors complicate the planning process, necessitating a brief historic and legal background.

There existed in England a doctrine of "ancient lights" that protected a person's right to continuous sunlight shining in a window across the property of another if the first person had been receiving this sunlight for an uninterrupted period of time (Hayes, 1979). However, most U.S. courts have rejected this doctrine as legal precedent and, consequently, no *automatic* rights to sunlight exist merely by prior appropriation. In 1957, an historic court case occurred in Miami, Fla.:

> The Eden Roc Hotel sued the rival Fontainebleau when the latter proposed to build a fourteen-story tower that would shade the cabana, swimming pool and sunbathing areas of the Eden Roc from two o'clock or during busy winter months . . . . Yet the District Court of Appeals of Florida supported the right of the Fontainebleau to shade the Eden Roc property. (Hayes, 1979, p. 183)

In this case, the court found no legal precedent giving one property owner the right to sunlight falling upon his property over the property of another without some contractual or statutory obligation. Public policy clearly favored full development of land. When solar emerged as a potential energy source in the 1970s, a legal debate began as to how best to guarantee solar access and still respect property rights (Eisenstadt, 1982; Jaffe, 1980). Primarily at issue was whether the protection of solar rights of one property owner consituted a "taking" of constitutional property rights of another. The issue is under debate (Kosloff, 1982).

Free-market mechanism. Some planners and economists insist that governmentally imposed solar access controls are unnecessary because the marketplace will directly influence environmental design when oil prices rise and solar energy becomes more economically advantageous. The limitations of this approach should be obvious.

State law. Several states have passed solar access laws which establish means of protecting sunlight to collectors. New Mexico's Solar Rights Act (Kerr, 1979) establishes the right to sunlight through beneficial use and prior appropriation (following western water law as a model). If a property owner establishes a collector and uses it to actually save energy, the right to sun becomes automatic. California passed the Solar Rights Act in 1978 which amends certain existing codes to require developers to provide passive and

natural solar heating and cooling opportunities in planning subdivisions and establishes the right to solar easements (see below). The California Solar Shade Control Act, also passed in 1978, is based upon public nuisance law and restricts the planting or growth of vegetation that blocks solar skyspace for qualifying collectors (Thayer, 1981a).

Zoning. Some cities, such as Los Angeles, are considering using zoning powers to protect solar access (Los Angeles, 1980). Solar zoning grows directly out of height and setback regulations embodied in zoning law. Knowles (1981) has described a process termed "solar envelope" zoning (Figure 7-5) which defines the physical volumetric limits of a building on a specific parcel that will shade surroundings at specific times of the day. Solar envelopes could be established as a zoning overlay on existing land use controls. Other zoning

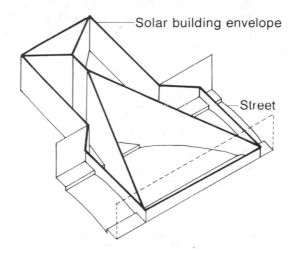

Figure 7-5. A solar envelope: the buildable space derived from a solar zoning approach. From: (Knowles, 1981).

changes to preserve solar access might include setbacks (Fregonese, 1980), height limits, zero-lot line regulations, and other adaptions of traditional development controls. Some planners favor zoning because it extends familiar and legally acceptable methods to solar access protection and applies to all land in a universal and somewhat "democratic" process (Jaffe & Erley, 1979). It is criticized because it subjects property owners with no interest in solar utilization to another layer of development restriction (SolarCal, 1981).

Solar easements. A solar easement is a private contractual agreement between two property owners granting the right to unobstructed sunlight to one property owner across property of another (Burke &

119

Lemons, 1980). Presumably, the grantor of the easement is paid a sum of money to keep obstructions on his property from shading the collector of the grantee. Easements are favored because they are private agreements applying only to parties affected and are not superimposed by a government bureaucracy on unwilling citizens. They can apply to both new and existing development and have little cost to local governments. However, one property owner in a typical suburban neighborhood may need to purchase solar easements from several adjacent landowners. If these persons establish solar collectors and wish to purchase protective solar easements of their own, the area could become a web of tangled overlapping private easements difficult to comprehend by all but the most skilled lawyer. Other criticisms of solar easements pertain to timing (most easements would be established when conflict had already arisen) and possible windfall profit (selling an easement even though one had no plans to develop into the neighbor's skyspace) (SolarCal, 1981). Figure 7-6 illustrates several types of solar easements.

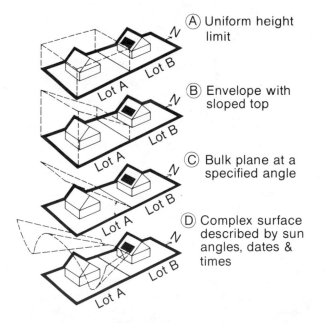

(A) Uniform height limit

(B) Envelope with sloped top

(C) Bulk plane at a specified angle

(D) Complex surface described by sun angles, dates & times

Figure 7-6. Solar easements: Various physical descriptions of protected skyspace can be established in the legal language.

Recordation/prior appropriation. One method of local protection of solar access is that of recordation of prior appropriation (similar to the New Mexico State Act). A property owner wishing to guarantee solar access would register his existing (or proposed) solar system with the local government agency, which in turn would check any future building permits in the area to ensure that none resulted in solar access

blockage to the registrant. Pros and cons of this method are similar to those for solar easements (Oregon Appropriate Technology, Inc., 1982).

Codes, covenants, and restrictions (CC&Rs). Subdivisions usually have a set of binding restrictions on the use of individual lots within the subdivision. CC&Rs can be extended to promote solar energy systems and to prohibit blocking of solar access (Thayer, 1981a, c). Local agencies can require developers to include provision for solar access in CC&Rs as a condition for approval of the subdivision. CC&Rs have the advantages of being attachable to the deed and can remain with the property if it is sold. They involve little government involvement and, unlike some zoning laws, can be used to regulate vegetation. The major disadvantages of CC&Rs are that they are buried in the "fine print" at the sale or resale of property and can be easily overlooked.

A principal point of controversy exists over how best to control development for protection of solar access: Should a broad democratic zoning approach be established that applies to all property whether or not it now utilizes solar energy systems, or should solar access be guaranteed on an individual case-by-case basis affecting only concerned parties, even if potential solar access on some sites is ultimately lost through benign neglect? Virtually all possible alternatives are being explored today (Eisenstadt, 1982). The appropriate solar access protection method will inevitably vary with the physical, social, and political context.

Protecting Solar Access through Direct Design

When possible, protecting solar access by direct design is most desirable. Direct planning and design of structures, landforms, and vegetation to protect solar access initially and as vegetation grows will avoid possibility of legal conflict in the future.

Solar Radiation Analysis

The process of solar access begins with a thorough analysis. Of particular importance are the solar data: solar intensity and azimuth and altitude angles at various dates of the year and times of day. This information is found in climatic data manuals, computerized on climate data input tapes, or obtained from skycharts and sun-angle calculators:

Solar data manuals. Some states offer solar data in document form. *The California Solar Data Manual* (Berdahl, et al., 1978), published by the state's energy commission, contains a wealth of information on radiation cloud cover; percent possible sunshine; solar altitudes and azimuths for various locations, dates, and times; standard weather and climate data (rainfall, wind, temperature, and humidity); and information on performance and costs of solar collectors. Another valuable source of information is the *Climatic Atlas of the United States* (NOAA, 1977), a volume containing monthly values for mean percentages of possible sunshine, mean total hours of sunshine, mean percentage sky cover, and mean daily solar radiation.

Computer input data tapes. Several sources of computerized weather and solar data exist for various regions of the country. Most well known are the weather files produced by the National Oceanic and Atmospheric Administration (NOAA), available for major cities across the country.

Skycharts. A skychart is a polar-coordinate graph of sun altitudes plotted with respect to solar azimuth angles and covers the range of sun paths from summer solstice (June 21) through spring/fall equinox (March 22, Sept. 21), to winter solstice (Dec. 21). By picking the chart corresponding to the latitude of the location in question, a designer can obtain basic data on sun angles at various times of the day, month, and year. Figure 7-7 shows a sample skychart for 41° north latitude (Berhdahl, et al., 1978).

41° Latitude

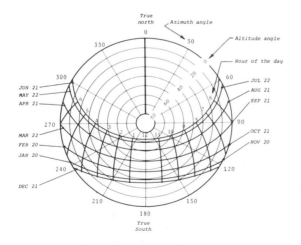

Figure 7-7. Skychart for 41° north latitude. From: (Berdahl, et al., 1978).

Sun-angle calculators. Libbey-Owens-Ford, Inc. manufactures an inexpensive sun-angle calculator consisting of several cardboard sky-chart templates (one for each 4° latitude from 24°N to 52°N), a plastic overlay template showing profile angles (useful in projecting shadows from roof overhangs) and angles of incidence (useful for calculating solar collector orientation efficiency), and a clear plastic cursor showing true altitude angle of the sun at any azimuth. The device is a quick "slide rule" extremely valuable to landscape architects and other environmental designers.

Skyspace Configuration

A critical step in designing for solar access is to determine the general configuration of the skyspace needed for efficient collector operation. The top and bottom surfaces of the skyspace of a particular collector are primarily determined by the times of year when the collector must be free of obstruction. This will vary between the surface defined by the Dec. 21 sun path as a minimum and that defined by the June 21 sun path as a maximum. Not all collectors, however, will need the skyspace entirely clear from the low in December to the high in June. For example, let us examine a house in a temperate zone of the United States, an area with moderately cold winters, yet moderately hot summers. Figure 7-8 (see next page) shows that the house has a solar greenhouse for space heating, a domestic solar water heater, and a solar-heated swimming pool, each of which has different solar access requirements. The greenhouse needs unobstructed sun only during the winter heating season, so the sun paths between Dec. 21 and March/Sept. 21 will roughly define its skyspace boundaries. The collector for the domestic water heater, providing hot water for laundry, showers, dishes, and the like, needs clear sun all year; the Dec. 21 and June 21 sunpaths will define its skyspace boundaries. The swimming pool is used most heavily in the summer, but could be used in the spring and fall if it could be kept warm. Therefore, collectors providing solar heat to the swimming pool need only be free from obstruction between March 21 and Sept. 21. Low-angle sun striking the swimming pool collector between September and March could be blocked with no loss of operating efficiency if the swimming pool is not used in winter (Figure 7-8).

The lateral surfaces of the skyspace required for a collector are most dependent upon two factors: the orientation of the collector with respect to south and the time of day. Since sunlight striking a solar collector at an oblique (i.e., shallow) angle is less useful than sunlight striking nearly perpendicular to the collector,

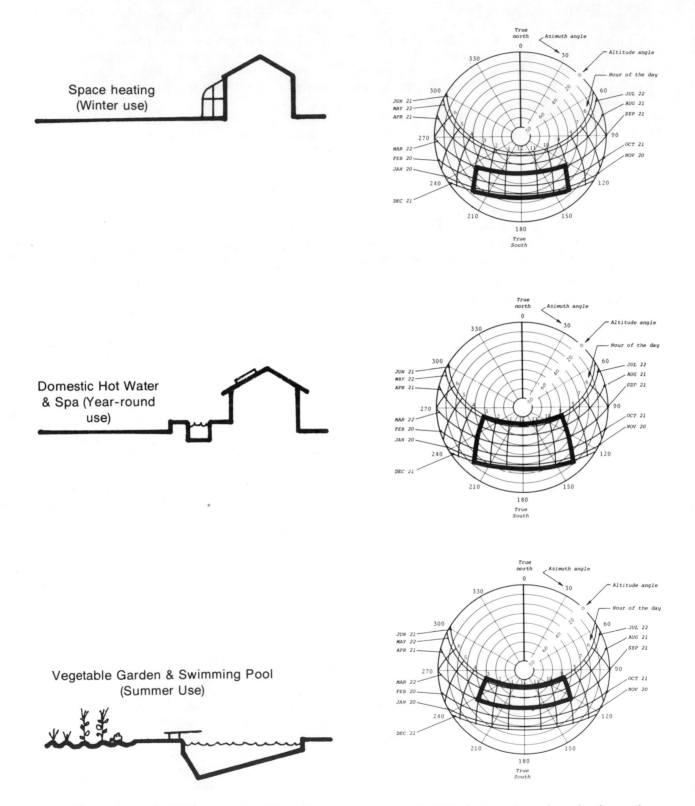

Figure 7-8. Specific skyspace configurations for solar space heating, domestic hot-water and spa heating, and swimming-pool heating.

122

early morning and late afternoon sun are less critical to solar collector performance than midday sun. A collector oriented to the south will receive 90% of the available radiation between *9:00 a.m.* and *3:00 p.m.* on *Dec. 21* (Barnaby et al., 1977). Therefore, sunlight hitting the collector before or after respective morning threshold times can be obstructed with little measurable loss in collector efficiency. For most situations, azimuth angles of plus and minus 45^0 from due south (i.e., approximately southeast and southwest) define the lateral boundaries of the skyspace or solar access zone. A more liberal or less solar-efficient boundary would be plus and minus 30^0 from due south, or roughly between 10:00 a.m. and 2:00 p.m. on Dec. 21. If a collector is oriented significantly west or east of due south, the lateral boundaries of skyspace can be slightly realigned up to 10^0 more in the direction of primary collector alignment (i.e., up to $+55^0$ azimuth). A wide solar access zone, defined by 60^0, is warranted for collectors requiring unblocked summer sun, such as those heating swimming pools, because summer sun azimuth angles sweep a wider arc for the same amount of elapsed time than they do in the winter.

Profile views. While three-dimensional conceptualization of solar access is essential, a simple profile view can be drawn (usually from the east or west) for quick analysis. This view would show the solar collector or house, any potentially obstructing elements, and the shadows projected (i.e., sun altitude angles) for 12:00 noon on various design days, such as Dec. 21, June 21, or March/Sept. 21. Figure 7-9 shows how profile views can be used to estimate setbacks for trees or structures in terms of beneficial or detrimental shade. They can be developed without sophisticated equipment or complex analysis.

Shadow templates. Another useful design technique that complements the profile view is the shadow template, a plan-view composite of the shadow cast by a tree or structure during all times critical to solar access protection (Figure 7-10, see next page). Shadow templates can be made for trees, buildings, or any other obstructions, either for detrimental winter shade, beneficial summer shade, or isolated situations during any time of day or year. Very accurate shadow templates can be constructed for trees or buildings by assuming that every critical point on the surface of a tree crown or building roof is a pole of a given height and a specific horizontal location. Each pole's shadow is then projected at a series of critical sun altitude and azimuth angles for a number of design times and dates, resulting in a highly accurate composite shadow (Erley & Jaffe, 1979). Such a process is time consuming and most often not warranted. Assumptions can be made regarding the shapes of buildings and the form of trees which make shadow template construction much simpler and accurate enough for most solar access analysis situations.

Building shadow templates are most useful in determining whether an existing building will shade a collector, but are also useful in siting buildings to preserve solar access. A building shadow template can be very concise if the building shape is simple and the orientation is known. A highly complex building shape which may be sited in any number of directional orientations may necessitate more than one shadow template. For steeply pitched roofs (i.e., 4/12 and above), projection of the *ridgeline* of the roof will yield the most extreme shadows because of low sun altitude angles during critical solar periods. For flat roofs and shallow-pitched roofs, projection of the northern-most edge of the roof eave will create the shadow template's extremities. Therefore, projecting points other than

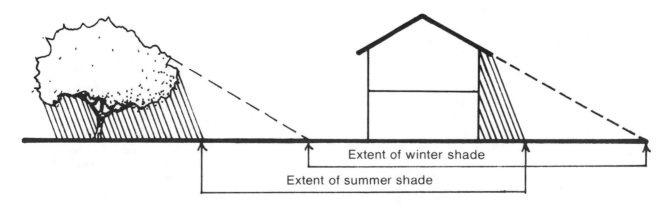

Figure 7-9. Profile views that provide a quick method for estimating extent of beneficial summer shade and detrimental winter shade.

123

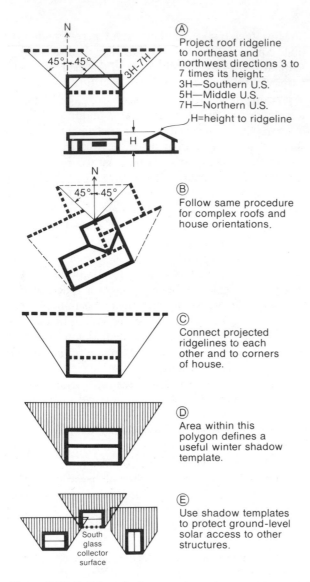

(A) Project roof ridgeline to northeast and northwest directions 3 to 7 times its height:
3H—Southern U.S.
5H—Middle U.S.
7H—Northern U.S.
H=height to ridgeline

(B) Follow same procedure for complex roofs and house orientations.

(C) Connect projected ridgelines to each other and to corners of house.

(D) Area within this polygon defines a useful winter shadow template.

(E) Use shadow templates to protect ground-level solar access to other structures.

South glass collector surface

Figure 7-10. Building shadow templates that provide a quick method for solar access estimation in site design.

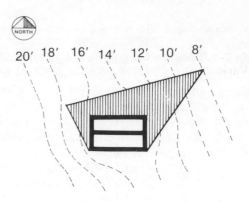

20' 18' 16' 14' 12' 10' 8'

Figure 7-11. Composite winter shadows created by a building on a sloped site: Downhill shadows are lengthened, uphill shadows are shortened.

these on the building is not usually necessary. For winter-shading templates (i.e., detrimental shade to be kept away from collectors), projecting the ridgeline (or northern roof edge for flat-roofed structures) a specified distance to the north, northeast, and northwest, as Figure 7-10 shows, will generate a template revealing the extent of detrimental shade between 9:00 a.m. and 3:00 p.m. on Dec. 21 *on a flat surface.* A shadow projection cast upon the roof of another building or up a rising slope is shorter than if cast upon flat ground (Figure 7-11). The shadow will be longer than the template if cast downhill or into a sunken area. In such cases it is best to develop profile views showing the appropriate increase or decrease in the shadow template due to elevation changes.

However, for sloped sites, tables can be used to determine north shadow-projection distances as a ratio of the vertical height of the shadow-casting object. Table 7-1 (see next page) shows the range of ratios of horizontal shadow distance to vertical height of the shading object for slopes in the eight compass directions on Dec. 21 at 40° N latitude. The table gives values for morning shadow distance (to the northwest), noon (to the north), and afternoon (to the northeast). For example, on a 5% NE slope a 10-ft high pole will cast a 48-ft shadow to the northwest in the morning, a 22-ft shadow to the north at noon, and a 62-ft shadow to the northeast in the afternoon, as Figure 7-11 shows. Table 7-2 (see next page) shows ratios of north projections of shadow length to height of shadow-casting objects for various north and south slopes only for a range of latitudes in the United States. For example, a 10-ft high pole at latitude 35° will cast a 16-ft horizontal shadow on a 20% south slope, a 25-ft shadow on a flat site, and a 48-ft shadow on a 20% north slope at noon.

Because shadow templates are shown in plan view, they are useful tools to aid site planners in locating separated units so that an unobstructed skyspace is provided to the south walls of northerly units at ground level. If a designer wishes to preserve only solar access to collectors mounted 10-ft high and is unconcerned with ground-level access, the shadow templates can be shortened an amount in plan view corresponding to the increased height of the collectors times the shadow-projection ratio, as Figure 7-12 shows (see page 126).

Tree shadow templates are necessarily less sharply defined. Not only are the precise form and growth rate of a specific tree hard to predict, but the mature size of the tree is always a subject of debate. Any specifically sized tree-shadow template assumes a "frozen" size for the tree. In reality, of course, the tree will grow to

Table 7-1. Shadow Length Ratios (Horizontal Length of Shadow of an Object One-Unit High) for Various Orientations and Degrees of Slope at 40° N Latitude.

40° NORTH LATITUDE

	N			NE			E			SE		
SLOPE	AM	NOON	PM	AM	NOON	PM	AM	NOON	PM	AM	NOON	PM
0%	4.8	2.0	4.8	4.8	2.0	4.8	4.8	2.0	4.8	4.8	2.0	4.8
5%	5.7	2.2	5.7	4.8	2.2	6.2	4.1	2.0	5.7	3.8	1.9	4.8
10%	7.2	2.5	7.2	4.8	2.3	9.1	3.6	2.0	7.2	3.2	1.8	4.8
15%	9.6	2.9	9.6	4.8	2.6	16.6	3.2	2.0	9.1	2.8	1.7	4.8
20%	14.5	3.4	14.5	4.8	2.8	97.5	2.8	2.0	14.5	2.4	1.6	4.8

	S			SW			W			NW		
SLOPE	AM	NOON	PM	AM	NOON	PM	AM	NOON	PM	AM	NOON	PM
0%	4.8	2.0	4.8	4.8	2.0	4.8	4.8	2.0	4.8	4.8	2.0	4.8
5%	4.1	1.8	4.1	4.8	1.9	3.8	5.7	2.0	4.1	6.2	2.2	4.8
10%	3.6	1.7	3.6	4.8	1.8	3.2	7.2	2.0	3.6	9.1	2.3	4.8
15%	3.2	1.6	3.2	4.8	1.7	2.8	9.6	2.0	3.2	16.6	2.6	4.8
20%	2.8	1.5	2.8	4.8	1.6	2.4	14.5	2.0	2.8	97.5	2.8	4.8

From: (Jaffe & Erley, 1979)

Table 7-2. Shadow Length Ratios for North and South-Oriented Slopes at Various Latitudes.

	South Slope	20%	15%	10%	5%	Flat	5%	10%	15%	20%	North Slope
N. Latitude	25°	1.1	1.2	1.3	1.4	1.5	1.6	1.8	1.9	2.1	
	30°	1.4	1.5	1.6	1.7	1.9	2.1	2.3	2.6	3.0	
	35°	1.6	1.8	2.0	2.2	2.5	2.8	3.3	3.9	4.8	
	40°	2.0	2.3	2.5	2.9	3.4	4.0	5.1	6.8	10.2	
	45°	2.5	2.9	3.4	4.1	5.1	6.8	10.4	21.5	—	
	48°	2.9	3.5	4.2	5.3	7.2	11.2	25.4	—	—	

From: (Jaffe & Erley, 1979)

"maturity" over a period of time. These imprecise parameters combined with the complexities of leaf periods and sunlight penetration values both in leaf and out-of-leaf create a rather inexact shading shadow template compared to that of a building, which is precise, immediate, and theoretically permanent.

Due partly to the difficulty in specifying tree canopy parameters, trees have become even more controversial challenges to solar access than structures, since less regulation exists governing their placement (Thayer, 1981a). Almost anyone can plant a tree almost anywhere without a permit. Furthermore, trees are almost universally appreciated, while some buildings may be despised. Any attempt to curtail tree growth or placement may prove very unpopular. The result for landscape architects and other tree planners is the need to make careful, realistic predictions about the size and shape of trees for solar access protection (Zanetto, 1978; Zanetto & Thayer, 1983). Although the shape of the shadow template generated is dependent upon the form and size of the tree, certain generalizations can be made in constructing tree-shadow templates to save tedious work otherwise leading to minute and inconsequential differences in solar access. The most direct method is to establish a "design maturity" — perhaps not the ultimate size of the tree but one that represents the average size over its useful life. Once this rather risky estimate has been completed, a corresponding estimate of the spread of the tree can be made and, together, the two dimen-

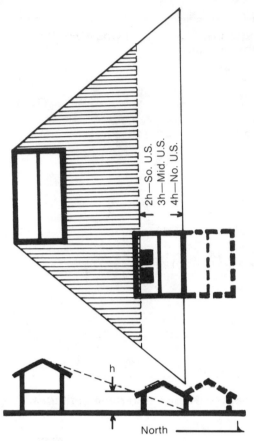

Figure 7-12. Building shadow template shortened to protect only rooftop solar access.

sions can adequately describe the tree for physical shading purposes (Figure 7-13). The resulting template can be used to site buildings near the shade of existing trees or trees in relation to existing or planned structures.

As with building-shadow templates, tree-shadow templates can be adjusted for different levels of solar access protection (i.e., winter sun, summer sun, etc.) in relation to critical solar altitude and azimuth angles. Of most use will be the winter shadow template created by the crown (bare branches if the tree is deciduous), but templates based on other times may be critical as well. A summer tree-shadow template useful for protecting swimming pools and associated pool-heating collectors can be developed by shortening the length of the northwest and northeast according to the higher solar altitude angles (most likely the March/Sept. 21 date). Also, a more liberal winter shadow template protecting slightly less solar access earlier in the morning and later in the afternoon can be developed using 30° azimuths instead of 45°. The narrower winter template favors development, the wider winter template favors solar access. At 40° north latitude on Dec. 21, the wider template protects roughly 90% of useful sunlight falling on a collector in a given day, whereas the narrow template at the same latitude protects only about 70% (Jaffe & Erley, 1979).

Where continuous rows of trees are planted suf-

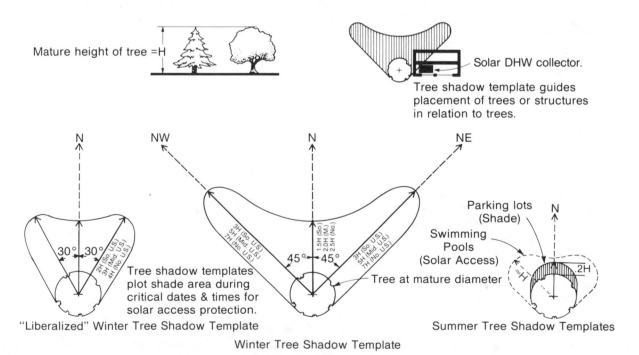

Figure 7-13. Tree-shadow templates for solar access protection and summer shade.

ficiently close together, a simple, continuous shadow pattern emerges making repeated composite templates cumbersome (Figure 7-14). Such is the case with rows of identical street trees on a straight street of constant direction. In such cases a solar profile or section view at 9:00 a.m., 12:00 noon, or 3:00 p.m. will give a meaningful distance for projecting shadows.

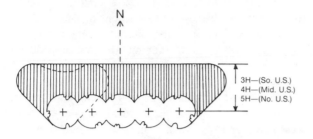

Figure 7-14. Continuous tree-row shadow pattern for winter solar access.

Solar viewing devices. Several manufacturers now offer solar viewers, most often combinations of optical lenses used in conjunction with clear plastic templates showing the paths of the sun at critical date and times (Figure 7-15). An observer can see elements which may obstruct valuable sunlight by setting up a solar viewer at the existing or future location of a solar collector. Many derivatives of the solar viewer or optical solar skychart are now commercially available.

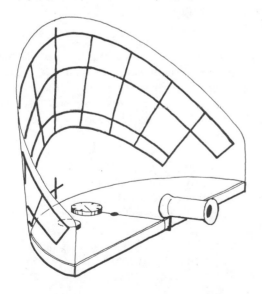

Figure 7-15. The solar site selector: one of several devices useful in first-hand estimation of solar access conditions.

Heliodons. One existing tool for three-dimensional investigation of building-vegetation-solar relationships is the heliodon, a three-dimensional model consisting of a hypothetical ground plane, a light source representing the sun, and some mechanism to maneuver the light source or ground plane to simulate the sun's movement across the site (Figure 7-16). A model of the building or environment is produced and located on the ground plane and the resultant shadows from the model "sun" are analyzed. Heliodons can give the designer the necessary connection between two and three dimensions to make fine adjustments to design or siting. However, the actual sun's rays are parallel and resultant shadows quite sharp, whereas the heliodon sun is a finite distance away from the model. As a result, unrealistic distortions in shadows usually occur because the model cannot be infinitely small and the distance from the model to the light source is limited by the size of the heliodon. Because of their relatively large size, heliodons are most often custom made and not commonly available in the marketplace.

Figure 7-16. Conceptual illustration of a simple heliodon.

Computer simulation. Within the near future, computer systems will be used to analyze and perhaps optimize solar access for collectors in relation to vegetation and structures. Schiler (1979), Knowles (1981), Thayer (1981a), Wager (1982), and Westergaard (1982), have all experimented with computer-based graphic analyses relating to solar access. One program, SUNDIAL (Fregonese, 1983) operates on popular microcomputers and computes shadow patterns for trees and buildings. The program is interactive and output consists of shadow pattern templates useful in solar access planning. The author (Thayer, In Preparation) is currently developing a microcomputer-based, interactive graphics program for use in generating tree-height limit contour maps. Within five years, it may be possible for the average landscape architecture firm to digitize site information into a small office computer and manipulate different plant/structure relationships via a keyboard and accompanying graphic screen to offer various perspective views of each solar access alternative (Figure 7-17). Until such graphic/computer capabilities are within limits of cost and time budgets, planners and designers must rely however, on simple drawing-board graphic techniques based on existing solar reference data.

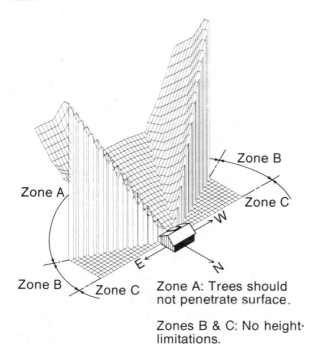

Figure 7-17. Computer-generated surface representing maximum allowable height of trees for solar access protection. From: (Thayer, 1981a).

Site-Design Techniques for Solar Access

Many techniques exist for maximizing solar access through design; several have been mentioned in previous chapters. Techniques include manipulating street and lot orientation, lot dimensions, structure siting, setbacks, and establishing height limitations.

Street and lot orientation. For most types of residential development, alignment of the street in a general east-west direction will facilitate solar access to the south walls of most units (Figure 7-18a, see next page). Since placement of the narrower dimension of the lot along the street increases the number of lots accessible per linear foot of street frontage, east-west streets create lots with the long dimensions running north and south, decreasing the chances of buildings being sited too close to each other in the north-south

direction. The streets themselves act as solar access buffer strips between east-west rows or clusters of units.

An exception is extremely long narrow units such as mobile homes which, because of unique proportions, should most often be sited with the long axis east-west. Figure 7-18b shows that this would require streets which run north-south to serve the most mobile-home lots. Where multiple-unit apartment or condominium units attach to one another, their attachment is best on east and west sides, leaving the south side unobstructed for potential solar heat-gaining surfaces (Figure 7-18c). Thus, in most cases, east-west streets serve the most number of attached units and preserve the most solar access to each unit. Low-angle east and west summer sun, which is most often detrimental to energy conservation, only falls on the end units in an attached cluster. Many of these concepts are discussed at length in Chapter Six.

Lot dimensions. As previously implied, lot dimensions optimum for solar access relate directly to street orientation and building type. Although lots narrowest on the east-west dimension parallel to the street are favored, extremely narrow lots for detached buildings will necessitate narrow structures that may not have optimal surface-to-mass ratios or may have too little potential solar collector surfaces to the south. This will be particularly acute if large side setbacks are required or if extremely cold climates call for large heat-gaining surfaces.

Siting structures. A lot slightly longer in the north-south dimension will, however, make it possible to site a detached unit farther to the north on the lot so that the most critical solar access zone is within the owner's lot and not on a bordering property. This might eliminate the need to enter into a solar easement or to establish another complex solar access control. A situation whereby parallel east-west streets serve lots slightly longer in the north-south direction, with units sited to the north of each lot, offers the greatest solar access protection with the least possible conflicts between neighbors.

At this point it must be noted that most existing solar communities today have adhered almost too rigidly to this particular format to the point of over-monotonizing the site plan (Figure 7-19a). In fact, the fear of creating "barracks"-type communities has caused some developers and planners to abandon plans to construct solar houses and neighborhoods. Solar houses can be oriented up to 25° either side of due south and still achieve a 95% efficiency. Figure 7-19b shows that streets need not "march" rigidly east

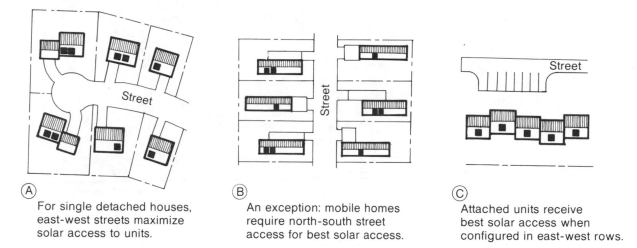

(A) For single detached houses, east-west streets maximize solar access to units.

(B) An exception: mobile homes require north-south street access for best solar access.

(C) Attached units receive best solar access when configured in east-west rows.

Figure 7-18. Optimal street, lot, and unit orientations for various solar housing types.

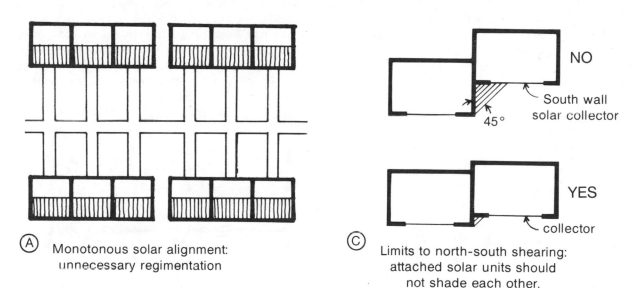

(A) Monotonous solar alignment: unnecessary regimentation

(B) A visually diverse solar housing cluster increases spatial quality.

(C) Limits to north-south shearing: attached solar units should not shade each other.

Figure 7-19. Solar housing developments: Variations in orientation and shearing to create visual interest.

and west, but can meander in a general east-west direction with plenty of curves to offset the more controlled orientation of units themselves. North-south "shearing" of attached units with south solar access can also help diversify the space articulation of a solar neighborhood, although there are limits to shearing based upon self-shading (Figure 7-19c). Generally, a unit must not extend southward of an adjacent unit beyond that point where it begins to block solar access during the morning or evening sun azimuths (usually about 45°), whichever the case may be.

When neighborhoods with multiple-height structures are planned, an obvious practice is to place the

129

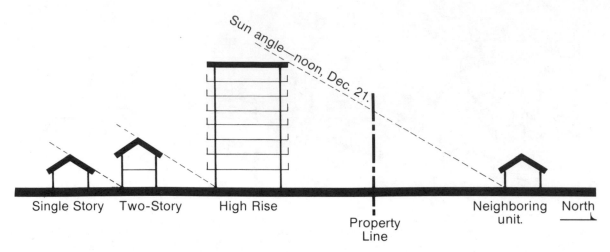

Single Story Two-Story High Rise

Property Line

Neighboring unit. North

Figure 7-20. Planned developments showing how solar access to building surfaces is maximized if taller structures are placed to the north, provided no shade is cast upon structures occupying property bordering on the north.

lowest units to the south of the taller high-rise units, thus assuring solar access to the most building surfaces (Figure 7-20). Care should be taken in many cases not to site very tall structures to the extreme north of a property bounded on the north by lower structures immediately beyond the property line. Such a situation invites solar access problems with northern neighbors. Land uses such as parking lots, golf courses, or other utilitarian and open spaces can act as appropriate buffers to the north of tall structures, and shadows can fall on these spaces with little ill effect.

Figure 7-21 shows that on land sloping southward, units may be placed closer together in a north-south direction and still preserve solar access. In contrast, developments on north-facing slopes will require more north-south distance between units to preserve solar access. Thus, north slopes are also best for open spaces, parking, low structures, low-density development, or other land uses where solar access is not critical.

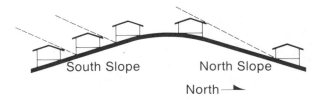

South Slope North Slope

North →

Figure 7-21. Comparison shows south slopes allow greater densities than north slopes for siting multiple-unit solar structures.

Setbacks. In some cases, setback regulations for fences, carports, or other auxiliary structures can be made more flexible to allow such elements to be

placed out of the solar access zone. Some planning jurisdictions in the United States have already begun relaxing front, side, and rear setbacks to allow more flexible unit siting to conform to the demands of solar-energy utilization without decreasing buildable area or density (Kosloff, 1982). Developers can be given density "bonuses" if they establish solar access protection through design or restrictive covenant. Figure 7-22 il-

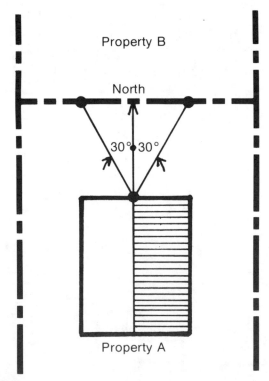

Property B

North

30° 30°

Property A

Figure 7-22. The Ashland, Ore., solar setback; new structures must be sited so that a north property line setback is met that guarantees solar access to northerly property. From: (Fregonese, 1980).

130

lustrates a "solar setback" that prohibits structures from being built too close to the south property line of a northerly neighbor (Fregonese, 1980).

Bulk-plane height limits. Unfortunately, much solar development may occur after streets, lots, and units are fixed and essentially permanent. Because solar is not currently utilized in most existing buildings, a great deal of solar development occurring in the future will be retrofitted or modified to existing structures and landscapes. Furthermore, landscape architects may not be called into the design process early enough to effect changes at the building design, redesign, or siting phases and must therefore confront solar access as a last-minute challenge. Landscape architects may be called upon to prepare planting plans for new or recently retrofitted solar buildings or neighborhoods, or they may be engaged to develop planning techniques to assure solar access to structures yet to be built. If the locations and positions of solar collectors are known, very specific solar envelopes or bulk planes restricting vegetation height can be established (Riordon & Hiller, 1980). The simplest method of determining bulk planes for solar access is by means of the following formulae also shown in Figure 7-23:

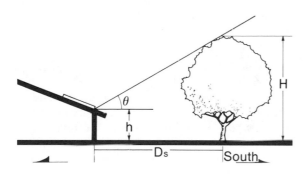

$$H = D_s \tan\theta + h$$

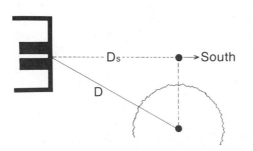

Figure 7-23. Bulk-plane height limits for solar access by formula.

$$H = D_s \tan\theta + h$$

where H = maximum height of tree or structure to south of a collector

D_s = southerly component of distance to tree or structure

θ = profile altitude angle of the sun at noon on December 21

h = height to bottom of collector

This equation becomes:

$H = 0.4D_s + h$ for northern U.S. (approx. 44° N.L.)

$H = 0.5D_s + h$ for midlatitude states (approx. 40° N.L.)

$H = 0.6D_s + h$ for southern U.S. (approx. 32° N.L.)

When the collector surface extends to ground level, as in south-wall glass or greenhouses, the equation for the midlatitude states, for example, would be:

$$H = 0.5D_s$$

In this example, any tree or structure greater than one-half as tall as the distance to the collector would potentially obstruct some of the collector surface on Dec. 21. These simple formulae merely define a bulk plane in space extending upward and southward at angles of about 22°, 26°, and 30° for northern, middle, and southern states, respectively. Such planes would establish conservative limits to height of trees, structures, and other potentially obstructing objects. The amount of detrimental effect such obstructions might have on collectors would depend upon how high and how broadly they interrupt the bulk plane. Also, these formulae prescribe solar access protection for winter space heat and represent a low threshold of penetration of the skyspace. For space-heating collectors, an additional plane can be established at a *steeper* angle originating from the *highest* point of a collector that defines the top surface of the solar skyspace, *below* which trees or structures cannot penetrate. In Appendix C, McPherson has advocated planting of trees so that major branching occurs *above* an angle corresponding to this top-inclined surface, therefore obstructing little beneficial winter sunlight. Figure 7-24 shows that this planting approach may prove impractical for protecting solar access to critical collector surfaces, especially if those surfaces are mounted on the roofs of structures. In such cases, it would be next to impossible to plant trees that would branch high enough and, even so, trees will most certainly block solar access while growing to maturity. Few structures would be able to clear an upper threshold without penetrating the lower bulk plane and obstructing solar access, although in certain cases

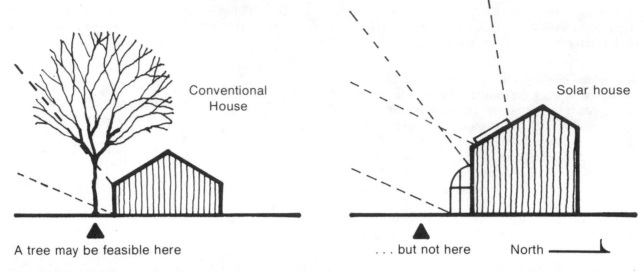

Conventional House

Solar house

A tree may be feasible here

. . . but not here   North ————⌐

Figure 7-24. A deciduous tree placed for solar control interferes with solar access to collectors in winter.

precision solar control with shade trees can be accommodated with minimal solar access interference.

Height-limit contour maps. Bulk-plane templates can be combined for each fixed collector known to exist to create a composite height limitation map for protecting solar access in solar subdivisions. Such a process was completed for the Delta Gardens solar subdivision in Yolo County, Calif. (Thayer, 1981c). Streets, lots, and houses were designed for optimal solar utilization prior to establishing the landscape plan. For each solar house, a bulk plane was established which protected solar access to all second-story south glass and rooftop collectors (ground-floor glazing was exempted, being less plentiful because of garage location). Tree-height "contour" lines, representing innermost acceptable locations of 30-, 40-, 50-ft trees, were drawn across each solar access zone in plan view and the result was a composite, tree-height contour limitations map (Figure 7-25, see next page). The map defined an imaginary surface over the subdivision beyond which trees could not penetrate without interrupting critical solar skyspace for at least one collector. The map was used in the master planting plan to position trees. For any given location, no tree was specified which had an estimated mature height greater than that shown on the tree height-limit map. For example, no 40-ft shade trees were specified inside (i.e., to the north of) the 40-ft height contour line. The map was also used as a legal document in conjunction with a protective covenant as part of the deed restrictions requiring homeowners to refrain from planting trees with mature heights greater than

the location on the map allows. The "official" reference established to determine expected mature height of trees is the current edition of the Sunset *New Western Garden Book* (Williamsen, 1979), the most authoritative guide to landscape vegetation in the western United States.

Obviously, bulk planes and limit maps are somewhat crude. Actual surfaces described by the motion of the sun are more complex, being shallower at the 10:00 a.m. and 2:00 p.m. azimuths than at 12:00 noon. Also, some argument exists as to whether a bulk plane need be the absolute lowest altitude angle, as on Dec. 21, or whether a slightly higher altitude angle will suffice. Also questionable is the necessity of curtailing *any* tree which may *ever* penetrate the skyspace even with *leafless* branches. Obviously, vegetation presents a far greater solar access challenge for landscape architects than structures, which are generally concise and immediate (i.e., within one solar year) in terms of their impact upon shadows. A tree may never achieve its mature height; it may take years before doing so, and may block little sunlight when out of leaf even when skyspace penetration occurs. All of these factors should be considered when planning for solar access. One way to "liberalize" the amount of vegetation allowable is to increase the angle of the bulk plane upward as Figure 7-26a indicates(see page 134). Another is to maintain the same angle but raise the entire plane by a uniform height (Figure 7-26b, see page 134). In discussions relating to the solar envelope, Knowles (1981) mentions the possibility of having two top surfaces to the envelope, one for evergreen vegetation and a parallel higher surface for deciduous vegetation.

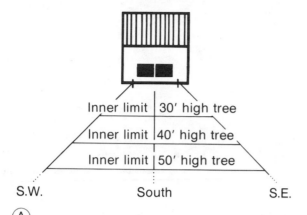

Inner limit | 30' high tree

Inner limit | 40' high tree

Inner limit | 50' high tree

S.W.　　　　South　　　　S.E.

(A)
Tree height limit templates are determined for each housing unit.

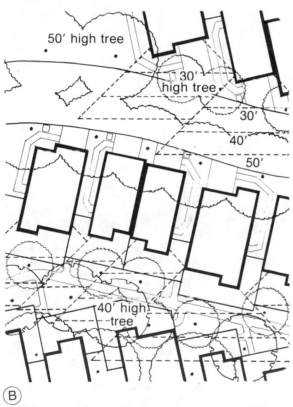

50' high tree

30' high tree

30'

40'

50'

40' high tree

(B)
Templates are combined to form a composite height limit contour map guiding placement of trees.

Figure 7-25. A procedure for establishing maximum tree height limits in solar subdivisions.

Balancing Solar Access and Solar Control

A rationale has been given for the liberalization of solar access constraints in favor of more blockage by trees and structures. However, equally credible justification exists for strict adherence to solar access protection measures. First, many cities, counties, and states have passed or are considering solar access laws that restrict vegetation. California's Solar Shade Control Act does so very stringently, so any liberalizing of solar access configurations in California would result in earlier and more dramatic infringement of the law (Thayer, 1981a). Once solar access is lost, it may be extremely hard to regain, and the resultant solar contribution toward energy savings can no longer be counted upon in the future. While public attitudes currently favor shade trees in almost all regions of the United States, mounting evidence suggests that some alteration in the way the public configures its neighborhood tree canopies to protect solar access is warranted. Kohler and Lewis (1981) present evidence that efficiency of solar collectors decreases in relative direct proportion to the percentage of collector surface shaded from incident radiation (Figure 7-27, see next page). Common sense suggests that solar collection systems to heat water, air, or provide electricity not be sized any larger than necessary in the most cost-efficient manner. Even a 10% reduction in insolation due to tree shade could render a solar system cost ineffective. Although benefit-cost ratios are improving, most solar systems installed today are only marginally economical. Also, houses with solar collectors are apt to have less air leakage and better insulation than nonsolar houses and would benefit less from solar control by shade trees. While the following chapter deals with controlling unwanted sunlight by use of trees, careful tradeoffs must occur in balancing solar control needs with solar access needs of a particular dwelling.

Issues surrounding relative need for shade and solar access are many. For example, some would argue that trees provide shade in the summer and therefore lower the need for late afternoon air conditioning, which uses expensive electricity and places peak-power demands on utilities. Reduction of peak-power loads enables utility companies to avoid increasing generating capacity at great expense to customers. Therefore, shading of buildings by trees is an understandable conservation goal for utilities in areas where summer air conditioning is necessary (McPherson, 1981).

On the other hand, trees which provide shade may block solar access, thereby reducing savings in heating energy (Buffington, 1978). In some southern states where the need for cooling energy far outweighs the need for heating, shade trees may be more beneficial for summer cooling than they are detrimental to solar access. Conversely, in cold northerly climates shade

133

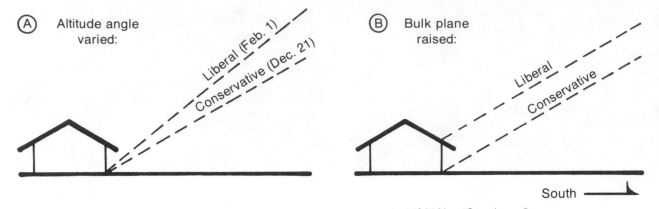

Ⓐ Altitude angle varied:

Liberal (Feb. 1)
Conservative (Dec. 21)

Ⓑ Bulk plane raised:

Liberal
Conservative

South

Figure 7-26. Procedures for "liberalizing" solar access restrictions on vegetation in relation to structures.

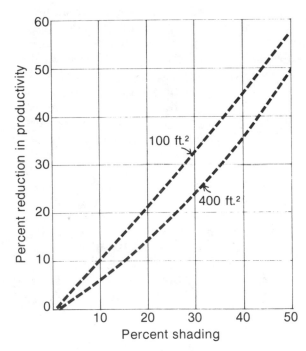

Figure 7-27. Percent reduction in productivity of a solar collector as a function of percentage of the solar aperture shaded for Nashville, Tennessee.
From: (Kohler & Lewis, 1981)

trees may be a luxury and a distinct drawback to solar energy utilization. Over much of the United States, however, there is considerable need for both heating energy in winter and cooling energy in summer. In such areas the balance between conservation in heating and cooling and, hence, the proper role of trees in providing shade or allowing solar access must be carefully considered.

Popular literature has often advocated energy conservation through placement of deciduous shade trees to the direct south of houses on the premise that shade and sunlight penetration are naturally moderated according to the appropriate season. The advent of residential solar energy development casts con-

siderable doubt on the absolute wisdom of such a planting approach. Several studies (Hammond, Zanetto & Adams, 1981; Heisler, 1982; Westergaard, 1982; and others) have now established that considerable sunlight is blocked by common deciduous trees when *out of leaf*. Also, periods when trees are in and out of leaf may not correspond that well to house heating and cooling periods. If misplaced or poorly chosen, deciduous trees can cause considerable reduction in the natural heat gain of houses and solar collectors in winter (Figure 7-28). Chapter Eight aptly discusses these issues.

Figure 7-28. Deciduous tree branches blocking considerable incident sunlight to collectors.

In an attempt to examine tradeoffs between solar access and solar control needs, a computer simulation study was initiated for the Sacramento area in California (Thayer, Zanetto, & Maeda, 1983). Several common landscape trees were measured for canopy density (both in and out of leaf) and foliation period. Four trees were hypothetically "placed" in a dense

134

east-west row at distances of 15 ft, 25 ft, then 35 ft, to the direct south of a test house. Three test houses were utilized: one energy-efficient solar house with passive space heating and rooftop solar panels for domestic hot water, one "standard" house with no particular solar or energy-conserving features, and a third house similar to the standard house after retrofitting with a solar domestic hot-water system. In each combination of tree species, tree position, and house type, the computer program modeled the thermodynamics of the house and calculated monthly solar heating, natural cooling, and domestic hot-water contributions and monthly energy costs assuming current Sacramento rates. Figure 7-29 describes the configuration of the simulations. In each case, no vegetation other than the row of trees in question was assumed. Shade-tree canopy densities were entered as input data to the program, and geometrical algorithms were established to determine hourly shading coefficients on critical buildings' surfaces resulting from tree shadows.

Results, shown in Table 7-3 (see next page), yield some surprises. Deciduous trees had a decidedly negative effect on annual energy costs for the solar house when compared to the same house with no trees. *While deciduous trees lowered the annual cooling costs of the solar house somewhat, that savings was more than offset by inefficiencies in solar gain due to solar access blockage by bare winter branches.* A similar, though less dramatic pattern was revealed for the standard house with the solar DHW retrofit. For the totally nonsolar standard house annual energy savings were never substantially increased or decreased under any tree or setback conditions. Results indicate that for the particular solar house, climate, and trees

in question, placement of deciduous trees in the solar access zone *costs* money.

A future study is being undertaken to examine this tradeoff for a wider range of climate zones, house types, and tree canopies. Until such work is completed, however, it may be unwise to translate the results of this limited study directly into design policy. Also, it would be wrong to interpret the results of this study as evidence that shade trees are inappropriate for energy conservation. Obviously, they are quite beneficial, especially when blocking low-angle, morning and evening sun from east and west walls and windows or high summer sun from noncritical collector surfaces or roof areas. However, the study previously described adds another level of legitimate concern for planning street trees and other shade trees.

Findings and assumptions previously discussed were incorporated into a test project to retrofit whole streets in Davis, Calif., with shade-tree canopies that maximized shading of pavement while protecting solar access. Figure 7-30 (see page 137) shows a simple method of constructing profile views showing both detrimental winter and beneficial summer shade used to select and locate trees for a proper balance of shade and solar access (Zanetto & Thayer, 1982).

Conclusions

Solar access is a simple geometric and spatial concept made more complex by the legal, social, and economic implications surrounding its protection. Maximum energy conservation through preservation of solar access can best be achieved through *direct design* by a coordinated team of landscape architects, architects, and energy specialists who respond sensitively to

Street tree crowns modelled as a continuous truncated cylinder.

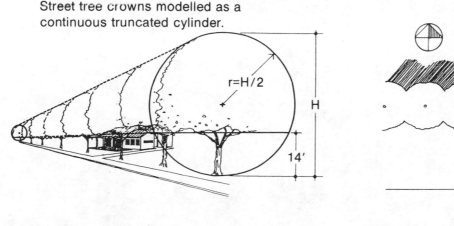

Setback varies—

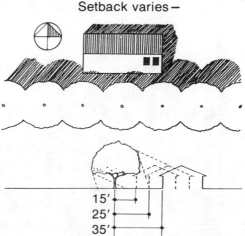

Figure 7-29. Spatial geometry for computer simulation of the effects of street trees placed in east-west rows to the south of solar and conventional houses.
From: (Thayer, et. al., 1983)

Table 7-3. Computer-Generated Energy Costs for Three Test Houses under Various Tree Species and Setback Conditions.

	Conventional house			Conventional house with solar domestic hot water			Solar house		
	15'	25'	35'	15'	25'	35'	15'	25'	35'
Koelreuteria bipinnata	$766.23 H = 358.53 C = 285.11 W = 122.59	$786.58 H = 354.99 C = 309.00 W = 122.59	$788.20 H = 351.90 C = 313.71 W = 122.59	$688.86 H = 358.53 C = 285.11 W = 45.21	$702.67 H = 354.99 C = 309.00 W = 38.68	$699.30 H = 351.90 C = 313.71 W = 33.69	$217.20 H = 109.46 C = 62.53 W = 45.21	$219.13 H = 111.39 C = 69.06 W = 38.68	$210.40 H = 106.56 C = 70.15 W = 33.69
Celtis australis	$765.03 H = 357.14 C = 285.30 W = 122.59	$772.89 H = 357.50 C = 292.80 W = 122.59	$785.00 H = 353.46 C = 308.95 W = 122.59	$697.51 H = 357.14 C = 285.30 W = 55.08	$697.05 H = 357.50 C = 292.80 W = 46.75	$702.82 H = 353.46 C = 308.95 W = 40.40	$223.45 H = 105.85 C = 62.53 W = 55.08	$219.07 H = 107.07 C = 65.25 W = 46.75	$217.22 H = 107.80 C = 69.02 W = 40.40
Pistacia chinensis	$777.18 H = 369.22 C = 285.31 W = 122.59	$777.94 H = 370.04 C = 285.31 W = 122.59	$792.89 H = 369.08 C = 301.22 W = 122.59	$733.94 H = 369.22 C = 285.37 W = 79.35	$718.56 H = 370.04 C = 285.31 W = 63.22	$725.01 H = 369.08 C = 301.22 W = 54.71	$274.02 H = 132.12 C = 62.56 W = 79.35	$259.78 H = 134.04 C = 62.53 W = 63.22	$254.34 H = 132.63 C = 67.00 W = 54.71
Eucalyptus melliodora	$782.46 H = 374.57 C = 285.30 W = 122.59	$783.35 H = 375.45 C = 285.31 W = 122.59	$798.45 H = 374.64 C = 301.22 W = 122.59	$740.54 H = 374.57 C = 285.30 W = 80.67	$725.10 H = 375.45 C = 285.31 W = 64.34	$731.26 H = 374.64 C = 301.22 W = 55.39	$288.00 H = 144.80 C = 62.53 W = 80.67	$273.75 H = 146.89 C = 62.53 W = 64.34	$268.24 H = 145.84 C = 67.00 W = 55.39
No Tree		$773.14 H = 335.84 C = 314.71 W = 122.59			$681.60 H = 335.84 C = 314.71 W = 31.05			$170.17 H = 68.76 C = 70.36 W = 31.05	

$ = total annual energy cost.
H = annual space heating cost
C = annual space cooling cost
W = annual water heating cost
(Note: All costs rounded to nearest $0.01)

From: (Thayer, Zanetto, & Maeda, 1983)

136

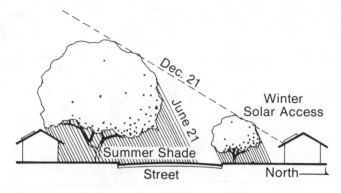

Figure 7-30. Balancing shade and solar access conditions for street trees on east-west streets.

specific site and program needs. Inevitably, the need for solar access will not disappear, but may become increasingly critical as costs of energy rise and the efficiency, cost, and technical feasibility of various solar energy utilization systems increase. A time may soon come when increased utility costs justify widespread retrofitting of photovoltaic arrays to produce electricity for existing houses and structures. Such a situation will dramatically accelerate the need for protecting present and future solar access.

Solar access can be looked upon as a clear necessity in the landscape — a natural factor which need not stifle design creativity but rather provide a central organizing pattern for energy-efficient community landscapes of the future (Figure 7-31).

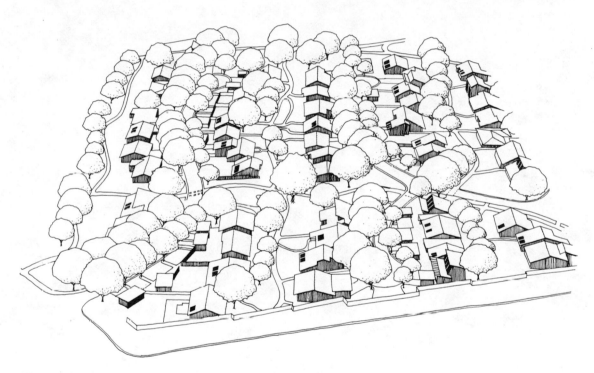

Figure 7-31. Bird's eye view of a solar subdivision with trees placed in response to solar access requirements.

Landscape Design 3

CHAPTER EIGHT
Planting Design
for Solar Control

E. GREGORY McPHERSON
Utah State University
Logan, Utah

PLANTING for solar control implies purposeful arrangement of trees, shrubs, and vines to moderate incident solar radiation. Because insolation is a principal parameter of the energy budget (see Chapter Four), its control is requisite to the design of landscapes that conserve energy and create comfortable outdoor spaces. In keeping with the focus of this book, the following chapter explores ways in which landscape architects can use plant materials to reduce energy consumption for space cooling. They will also use solar control techniques for other purposes not emphasized in this chapter, such as microclimatic improvement of outdoor living spaces; and they will use solar control devices other than plant materials.

This chapter first describes the mechanisms by which a building gains heat, then briefly summarizes the various ways that vegetation can provide passive cooling. It presents research results documenting the effects of vegetative shading on energy consumption to acquaint the reader with potential benefits associated with solar control plantings. The next two sections focus on design application and provide guidelines for locating and selecting plants to shade structures. Prototypical designs for four different climates illustrate key principles and conclude the chapter.

Heat Gain

The purpose of passive cooling with vegetation is to minimize heat gain and promote heat loss during the overheated period. Olgyay (1963) has defined the overheated period as the period when air temperatures are 70F (21C) or above.

Pathways of Heat Transfer

The pathways by which heat is gained between the interior living spaces and the external climate are defined in Chapter Four and illustrated in Figure 8-1. Direct solar radiation generally contributes the largest amount of heat energy to residences. Insolation on the roof and walls results in outside surface temperatures that are greater than those inside wall surfaces. The magnitude of this temperature gradient and the thermophysical properties of the building envelope control the rate of heat transfer to interior spaces. Diffuse radiation from the sky becomes more important in

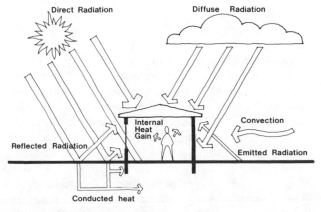

Figure 8-1. Heat gain pathways.

areas with frequent cloud cover or other forms of atmospheric turbidity, such as particulates. Diffuse

141

radiation may contribute as much as 50% of the total annual radiation load in such areas. Albedo of the reflective surface and angle of incidence determine the amount of insolation due to reflected solar radiation. In northern regions, the high albedo of new-fallen snow and low solar altitude angles combine to contribute 11-50% more insolation on south-facing vertical surfaces than predicted in tables for low ground albedo (Montgomery, Heisler, & Keown, 1982).

Infiltration can result in heat gain if the outside air is warmer than inside air. When moving air strikes a building, pressure gradients develop that cause cool inside air located near the floor to be drawn out of the building. At the same time, warm outside air infiltrates through openings near the ceiling creating a convective loop. This form of convective heat transfer is discussed in more detail in Chapter Nine. Convective heat transfer also occurs when a wall is shaded and thereby cooler than the air moving across it. If nearby ground surfaces are neither vegetated nor shaded, the air above the earth can be much warmer than the surface temperature of the shaded wall due to emission of longwave radiation. The wall is warmed by the passing air and conduction may then transfer this heat into the building. If the earth's temperature is warmer than that of the adjacent wall or slab, conduction of heat to the interior can occur. The final heat gain pathway is internal heat gain generated by appliances, lighting, and people. Internal heat gain plays a significant and substantially greater role in commercial buildings than in residences.

Before planting for solar control, the landscape architect should consider the relative importance of the structure's building components with respect to heat gain. Windows, which readily transmit solar radiation but are almost opaque to longwave radiation, account for the greatest amount of heat entering a building. Generally, conduction through the roof and walls is next in importance. Vegetation located to shade the windows, roof, and walls will provide the greatest protection from heat gain for a typical home. However, the relative importance of each component will vary depending on the structure's characteristics. For example, a building with poorly insulated black walls and a well ventilated and insulated attic may benefit more from shade cast on the walls than on the roof. Each building should be analyzed to determine how effective shading on different surfaces of a structure will be (this type of analysis is described later in the chapter).

Heat loss pathways particularly relevant to solar control are radiation and convection. A building is cooled when heat is radiated to cooler objects around it. Radiation is especially effective on cloudless evenings that promote heat loss via radiation to the cool night sky. However, foundation plantings and foliage overhanging the roof create an insulating envelope that reduces heat loss because less of the night sky is "seen" by the building. Heat loss via convection can also be reduced by solar control plantings that slow or deflect cool breezes that might otherwise strike the building. For these reasons, landscape architects should consider the impact of their designs on heat loss as well as heat gain.

Sol-Air Impacts

Solar radiation and air temperature act together to warm the exterior of a structure. Heat is transferred to the interior spaces through the pathways just described. The relative impact of these factors varies seasonally and daily. Before designers can know how to best use vegetation for cooling, they must know how these factors affect the building envelope.

Solar load. Figure 8-2 shows daily solar heat gain for different orientations (except north) of window exposures at 40° north latitude. During the summer, when the need for shading is greatest, more than twice as much insolation strikes east- and west-facing surfaces as strikes south-oriented surfaces. The horizontal surface receives the largest amount of radiation, while the north-facing wall receives the least. However, in more southern latitudes north-facing walls can receive a substantial amount of insolation. Thus, to provide the best protection from undesirable summertime solar load, the designer should locate vegetation to shade the east- and west-facing surfaces as well as the roof.

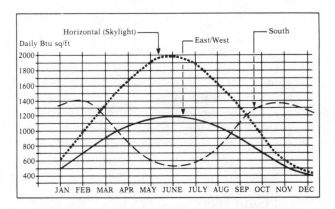

Figure 8-2. Daily solar heat gain for different orientation of window exposures at 40° north latitude. North orientation is not shown since the quantities are relatively small (less than 200 Btu/sq. ft.). From: (Daryanani & Lull, 1982)

During the fall and spring transition periods, total insolation on the south wall is slightly more than on the east and west walls due to lower solar altitude angles and a more southerly sun path than occurs during the summer. In areas with very long overheated periods, vegetative shading of the south wall may be warranted since overhangs may not be entirely effective at obstructing low-angle insolation.

Insolation on the east and west walls in winter is much less than that recorded for the south wall. In most parts of the U.S., solar heat gain through south-facing windows is desirable, so vegetation must be positioned to promote heat gain during the underheated period.

Air temperature or ambient load. Although the solar load on a south wall or horizontal surface is symmetrical around solar noon, as Figure 8-3a shows, the ambient load reaches its maximum at approximately 3:00 p.m. This delay is due to the heat lag effect of the earth, which also explains why annual maximum temperatures occur about a month after the summer solstice, the time of maximum solar radiation. The ambient load also differs from the solar load in that at any one moment it is relatively the same on every surface. The ambient load gradually increases on all walls until it reaches a peak at 3:00 p.m. The heat lag effect of the building's thermal mass results in a peak interior ambient load several hours later, even though the ambient load on the exterior surface of the wall is declining. Figure 8-3b illustrates this point.

The surface of a building cannot discriminate between the solar and ambient loads. It "senses" a thermal load that is the net effect of both. Olgyay (1963) describes the combined sol-air effect depicted in Figure 8-3c in more detail. The sol-air impact on a building surface is greatest at 3:00 p.m., when air temperatures are warmest and insolation is passing through windows to heat the interior because of lower, and consequently more favorable, angles of incidence than during the midday hours. The building's thermal mass and resistance to heat transfer will determine how quickly interior temperatures respond to warming of the exterior surface. Vegetation located to shade east- and southeast-facing surfaces keeps walls cooled during the night from absorbing large amounts of heat during the day, which would warm the living spaces. This keeps the interior from becoming uncomfortably hot early in the day and allows it to remain cool as the sol-air impact increases. Shade on the roof and southwest- and west-facing walls and windows can significantly reduce maximum inside air temperatures and hasten early evening cooling. The following section examines the mechanisms by which vegetation promotes passive cooling of a structure.

How Cooling Is Achieved

Vegetation provides a form of passive cooling by two means. First, shade cast by plants reduces the conversion of radiant energy to sensible heat, thereby reducing the surface temperatures of shaded objects. Second, evapotranspiration at the leaf surface results in cooling the leaf and adjacent air due to the exchange of latent heat. Before exploring these cooling effects

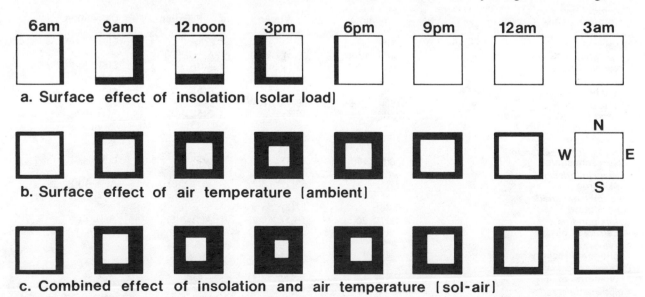

6am 9am 12 noon 3pm 6pm 9pm 12am 3am

a. Surface effect of insolation (solar load)

b. Surface effect of air temperature (ambient)

c. Combined effect of insolation and air temperature (sol-air)

Figure 8-3. Solar, ambient, and sol-air impacts on a building. a. Solar load, b. Ambient load, c. Sol-air load. Adapted from: (Knowles, 1974).

143

on the thermal environment of a building, it is necessary to describe briefly how heat energy is partitioned when solar radiation interacts with a plant.

Solar Radiation and Vegetation

The amount of incident solar radiation absorbed by the woody biomass and leaves of a plant ranges from 60% to 90% depending on the following (Reifsnyder & Lull, 1965):

1. Density of woody biomass.
2. Location of leaves on the plant (their orientation with respect to the sun and proximity to trunks or canopy edge).
3. Angle of presentation of leaves to the sun.
4. Location of the sun.

Almost all of this absorbed energy is converted to sensible heat. A portion is reradiated as longwave radiation from the canopy, particularly at night. Another portion heats the air by convection. Most of the radiation absorbed and not radiated is consumed by evapotranspiration, provided there is adequate soil moisture. A small amount is stored, warming the plant and surrounding soil.

According to Reifsnyder and Lull (1965), a dense forest reflects 10-20% of the incident solar radiation depending on surface albedo. Light penetrating the canopy receives repeated or multiple reflection, which accounts for the high interception of light in some species with low canopy closure values.

Incident solar radiation that is not absorbed or reflected is transmitted to the surface below. The transmissivity of plants varies with species as a result of twig and leaf density and foliage development. Table 8-3 lists recorded values for selected ornamental and shade trees. While a typical canopy strongly reduces short wave radiation, it readily transmits near-infrared radiation. This phenomenon is primarily due to the spectral properties of leaves (Gates, 1980). The ability of vegetation to significantly reduce transmission of shortwave radiation is most propitious when the primary goal is cooling because shortwave radiation contains more heat energy than does longwave radiation. For example, sunflecks that dapple the ground beneath trees with direct solar radiation can contribute a large amount of heat energy to the surface they strike. Waggoner, Pack, and Reifsnyder (1959) have measured temperature changes of as much as 16C (29F) in litter on a forest floor within twenty minutes as a large sunfleck moved across the sensor. Landscape architects concerned with passive cooling can use the ability of vegetation to selectively absorb shortwave solar radiation and optimize results by selecting species that transmit the least amount of heat energy.

Table 8-3. Calculated Shading Coefficients and Foliation Periods for Selected Trees

| Botanical name Common name | Shading coefficients (% transmission) | | Foliation Periods | |
	Summer	Winter	Foliation	Defoliation
Acer ginnala Amur Maple	.09(6)		E(8)	E(8)
Acer platanoides Norway Maple	.14(1), .14(3) .10(5), .10(6)	.65(1), .75(6) .75(6), .61(7)	A(1), E(5) A(8)	A(1), A(5) E(8)
Acer rubrum Red Maple	.17(6)	.75(4), .82(6) .63(7)	A(8)	E(8)
Acer saccharinum Silver Maple	.18(1), .11(5) .21(6)	.66(1), .87(4) .59(7)	A(5), A(8)	A(1), A(5)
Acer saccharum Sugar Maple	.16(6)	.82(4), .56(7)	A(5), L(8)	E(8)
Aesculus hippocastanum Horsechestnut	.08(5), .15(6)	.73(4)	A(5)	L(5)
Albizzia julibrissin Silk Tree	.17(1)	.63(1), .73(7)	A(1), L(8)	A(1), A(8)
Amelanchier canadensis Shadblow	.23(6)	.57(7)		
Betula pendula European Birch	.15(1), .20(5) .19(6)	.48(1), .60(2) .88(4), .52(7)	A(1), A(5) A(8),	A(1), E(5) L(8)
Carya ovata Shagbark Hickory	.23(6)	.66(7)		
Catalpa speciosa Western Catalpa	.24(6)	.83(4), .52(7)	L(5)	
Celtis australis European Hackberry	.08(1)	.53(1)	E(1)	A(1)

(Continued on next page)

Table 8-3. Calculated Shading Coefficients and Foliation Periods for Selected Trees (Continued).

Botanical name / Common name	Shading coefficients (% transmission)		Foliation Periods	
	Summer	Winter	Foliation	Defoliation
Celtis occidentalis Common Hackberry	.12(5)		A(5)	A(5)
Crataegus laevigata English Hawthorn	.14(5)		A(5), E(8)	L(5), A(8)
Crataegus lavallei Carrier Hawthorn	.11(5)		A(8)	L(8)
Crataegus phaenopyrum Washington Hawthorn	.24(5)			A(1), A(5)
Elaeagnus angustifolia Russian Olive	.13(5)		A(5)	L(5)
Fagus sylvatica European Beech	.12(6)	.83(5)	L(8)	L(8)
Fraxinus excelsior European Ash	.14(1), .15(5)	.59(1)	A(1), L(5)	E(1), A(5)
Fraxinus holotricha 'Moraine' Moraine Ash	.22(1)	.50(2)	E(1)	A(1)
Fraxinus pennsylvanica Green Ash	.13(5), .20(6)	.71(6), .70(7)	L(5), A(8)	E(5), E(8)
Ginkgo biloba Maidenhair Tree	.20(1), .16(5) .22(6)	.55(1), .72(6)	E(1), A(5)	A(1), E(5)
Gleditsia triacanthos inermis Honey Locust	.32(1), .30(5) .38(6)	.48(1), .85(2)	E(1), L(5) A(8)	E(1), A(5) E(8)
Gymnocladus dioicus Kentucky Coffee Tree	.14(5)		L(5)	
Juglans nigra Black Walnut	.09(5)	.55(2), .72(7)	L(5)	E(5)
Koelreuteria bipinnata Chinese Flame Tree	.10(1)	.70(1)	E(1)	L(1)
Koelreuteria paniculata Goldenrain Tree	.25(1), .13(5)	.42(1)	A(1), A(5) E(8)	A(1), E(5) A(8)
Liquidamber styraciflua Sweetgum	.18(1)	.70(1), .84(4) .65(7)	A(1), L(8)	A(1), L(8)
Liriodendron tulipifera Tulip Tree	.10(5)	.78(4), .69(7)	L(5), E(8)	A(1), L(5) A(8)
Malus spp. Crabapple	.15(1), .15(5)	.85(1)	A(1), E(5) E(8)	L(1), A(5)
Parkinsonia aculeata Jerusalem Thorn	.15(1)	.27(1)	A(1)	L(1)
Pistachia chinensis Chinese Pistache	.15(1)	.38(1)	E(1)	A(1)
Platanus acerifolia London Plane Tree	.17(1), .14(3) .11(5)	.64(1), .46(3)	A(1), L(5)	A(1), L(5)
Platanus racemosa California Sycamore	.09(1)	.45(1), .60(2)	E(1)	L(1)
Populus deltoides Cottonwood	.15(6)	.68(7)	E(5)	A(5)
Populus tremuloides Quaking Aspen	.20(5), .31(6)		E(5)	A(5)
Pyrus communis Common Pear	.20(6)	.60(7)		
Quercus alba White Oak	.25(6)			
Quercus palustris Pin Oak	.15(1), .30(3)	.63(3), .88(4)	A(1), L(8)	L(1), L(8)
Quercus robur English Oak	.19(6)	.83(6)	L(8)	L(8)
Quercus rubra Red Oak	.19(6)	.79(4), .81(6) .70(7)		A(1)
Sapium sebiferum Chinese Tallow Tree	.17(1)	.63(1)	E(1)	A(1)
Sophora japonica Japanese Pagoda Tree	.20(1), .24(5) .22(6)	.35(1)	A(1), L(5)	E(1), E(5)
Tilia cordata Littleleaf Linden	.07(1), .13(5) .17(6)	.46(1), .70(6) .62(7)	A(1), L(8)	L(1), A(5), E(8)

(Continued on next page)

145

Table 8-3. Calculated Shading Coefficients and Foliation Periods for Selected Trees (Continued).

Botanical name Common name	Shading coefficients (% transmission)		Foliation Periods	
	Summer	Winter	Foliation	Defoliation
Ulmus americana American Elm	.13(5)	.89(4), .63(7)	A(5)	A(5)
Ulmus pumila Siberian Elm	.15(1), .15(5)	.29(1), .50(4)	A(1), E(5) E(8)	A(1), A(5), A(8)
Zelkova serrata Japanese Zelkova	.15(1), .24(6)	.54(1), .78(6) .74(7)	A(1), A(8)	A(1), L(8)

References (shown in parentheses in table)	Instrumentation	Foliation	Defoliation
1. Hammond, Zanetto, and Adams, 1980	Light meter	E=March 1-31 A=After April 1	E=Sept.-Oct. 31 A=Nov. 1-30 L=After Dec. 1
2. Erley and Jaffee, 1979	Light meter		
3. Heisler, 1982	Arrays of Pyranometers		
4. Jennings, 1982	Photographs analyzed with light meter		
5. McPherson, 1981 (c); (Foliation periods, 1980)	Pyranometer	E=April 15-30 A=May 1-15 L=After May 15	E=Oct.-Nov. 15 A=Nov. 16-30 L=After Dec. 1
6. Schiler, 1979	Photographs and Optical Scanner		
7. Westergaard, 1982	Photographs and Optical Scanner		
8. Ticknor, 1981		E=Feb. 26-Mar. 31 L=After May 15	E=Oct. 12-Nov. 5 L=After Dec. 1

Attenuation of Solar Radiation

The floor, walls, and roof of a building combine to create an envelope that reduces the temperature extremes inside the structure by protecting this space from external climatic conditions. Vegetation functions similarly by forming a secondary envelope that obstructs direct, diffuse, and reflected solar radiation. For example, the outside surface temperature of a shaded east-facing wall at 10:00 a.m. can be as much as 43F (22C) cooler than an identical unshaded surface (McPherson, 1980). Cooler inside wall temperatures in the shaded structure result. Thus, a vegetative canopy transfers the active heat-absorbing surface from the building envelope, which readily absorbs and stores heat energy, to a living crown surface, which readily loses heat to the surrounding air. The net result of shading is a reduction in heat gain via conduction of sensible heat through walls and ceilings as well as via transmission of solar radiation through glazed openings.

Not only can shading reduce peak temperatures inside a structure, but it can also induce a lag in the building heating rate. Deering (1950) and McPherson (1981a) have reported that the peak inside air temperatures of densely shaded structures can be 8.7F (4.8C) to 20F (11C) lower than the peak temperatures in identical but unshaded structures. They also report that peak temperatures are reached 1½ to 3½ hours later in the shaded structures. This delay can be attributed to the inside temperatures of the shaded structure being primarily responsive to outside ambient temperatures. Shading minimizes the effect of the solar load. In contrast, the unshaded structure is affected both by solar load and ambient load. This heat lag effect might be used to shift cooling energy demands to off-peak periods, thereby reducing costly demands on utilities and the need for supplemental energy generating facilities.

As previously noted, vegetation planted close to the walls and overhanging the roof can offset some of the cooling effect created by shading. The result may be a delayed onset of temperature decline (one to three hours) and slightly warmer inside air temperatures 1F to 2F (.6C to 1C) if convective cooling is not employed (McPherson, 1981a). However, in terms of net energy savings, the benefits associated with reduced heat gain from vegetative shading far surpass the harmful aspects of delayed and reduced nocturnal heat loss.

Vegetation can also lessen reflected solar radiation through the placement of shrubs, vines, and low branching trees between the reflective surface and the building envelope. Effectiveness will depend upon the amount of reflected solar radiation that is blocked, which results from (1) plant placement with respect to the angle of reflection, (2) solar radiation intensity, (3) albedo of the reflective surface, and (4) canopy density of the plant.

Transpirational Cooling

Transpirational cooling occurs when large amounts of energy are used to change water from a liquid to a vapor at the leaf surface. The magnitude of cooling provided depends on the amount of transpiring surface area and evapotranspiration rate. Available soil moisture is frequently a limiting factor that reduces the transpirational cooling effect. In humid areas where irrigation water is plentiful, the result of increased transpiration is higher humidity, which may not improve human comfort. The increased humidity associated with transpirational cooling is not as undesirable in hot arid regions; however, the water required to irrigate plants is becoming increasingly expensive and requires considerable energy to deliver to the landscape (see Chapter Ten).

The cooling affected by vegetational transpiration is negligible for an open grown tree, although it has been compared with the cooling capacity of five average-sized room air conditioners operating 20 hours a day (Federer, 196). Hutchison, Taylor, Wendt, and the Critical Review Panel (1982) have stated that while calculations used to arrive at this conclusion are correct, the widely accepted belief that a single tree will provide cooling to a home that is equivalent to many air conditioners is wrong:

> The rapid mixing of the layer of the atmosphere near the surface of the earth that results from wind and temperature differences causes the cooling effect of a single tree to be rapidly diffused, and therefore diluted, into the comparatively infinite volume of air adjacent to the earth's surface. The end result is that no measurable cooling results from this LE exchange [latent heat flux] in the immediate vicinity of the tree or anywhere else, despite a substantial alteration of the surface energy budget. (pp. 17-18)

While the transpirational cooling of air within the canopy of a single tree has little influence on the thermal environment of a nearby building, the collective effect of large numbers of transpiring trees and well-watered ground covers can reduce air temperatures and air conditioning requirements at a meso-scale. Duckworth and Sandberg (1954) have found temperatures in San Francisco's lush Golden Gate park to average about 14F (8C) cooler than the less vegetated urban areas nearby. Although some experts question whether this effect is due to the presence of vegetation alone or to the combined effect of ocean and vegetative influences, most agree that large vegetated areas can have a significant evaporative cooling effect, which may extend beyond the borders of the vegetated area (Hutchison et al., 1982).

To promote effective transpirational cooling, designers usually have to implement vegetation planning and management at the neighborhood or community scale. However, cooling resulting from shading can be successfully implemented at the microscale (the scale of the individual building). Henceforth, this chapter will be concerned primarily with ways of achieving passive cooling through the use of shading, because shading is more effective and easier to control than is transpirational cooling.

Potential Energy Savings

Research results indicate that shading by vegetation can contribute to substantial reductions in electricity used for air conditioning. Three factors influence the magnitude of energy savings. First is the quantity and quality of shading, which are important in terms of shade density, the area of coverage, and the part of the structure shaded. Second, structural characteristics influence the effect. For example, shading a mobile home that has less insulation and thermal mass than a permanent home would result in a more pronounced effect because of larger diurnal temperature swings and a shorter lag time. Another structural consideration concerns the type of mechanical cooling system used. Because evaporative coolers use one-fourth to one-fifth less energy per unit of cooling delivered than central air conditioning systems, net energy savings due to shading will be less for a building that is evaporatively cooled than for a similar one with a central cooling system, assuming other factors are held constant. Third, geographic location will modify the shading effect. Owners of buildings in hot climate zones where mechanical cooling is a necessity for a large part of the year benefit more from shading than those in temperate and cold regions. Also, homeowners in arid climates benefit more than those in humid climates. Solar radiation loads are larger in arid lands due to less atmospheric water vapor. Large diurnal temperature fluctuations characteristic of arid climates permit use of nocturnal convective cooling in association with thermal mass to reduce early morning temperatures inside the home. Dense shading can then maintain cooler daytime temperatures than would result in a humid climate where nocturnal temperatures often remain well above the comfort level. Landscape architects should consider the influence these factors have on potential energy savings when assessing use of vegetative shading as a design option and also in evaluating the research results that follow.

Cooling in Mobile Homes

Two studies have documented actual energy savings in mobile homes as a result of vegetative shading. In the 1950s, considerable interest was shown in energy-conserving planting design. In 1956, Deering performed a series of experiments with a 20x60-ft mobile home to quantify cooling effects from tree shade. The mobile home was located on three different sites: Site A had full sun and bare ground; Site B was east of and adjacent to a grove of eucalyptus trees; and Site C was beneath a grove of dense fig trees. Peak inside temperatures within the structure were 20F (11C) cooler in the shade of the fig grove (Site C) than when the same mobile home was located in the open (Site A). Deering also reported that the inside temperatures reached 75F (24C) 3½ hours later under the fig trees and dropped to the same temperature 2¾ hours earlier at that site than at the open unshaded site. Thus, he found that tree shade not only reduced maximum temperatures but also reduced the period that temperatures exceeded a comfort level of 75F (24C) by more than six hours. Deering was the first to quantitatively validate the commonly accepted notion that tree shading can result in sizable temperature reductions and energy savings. If anyone deserves the title "Father of Solar Control," it is Professor Deering.

A more recent study by Parker (1981) examined the effects of shading on electricity consumed to air condition a double-wide mobile home used as a day-care center in Miami, Fla. Parker's analysis of energy use patterns before landscaping revealed that in April, not a particularly hot month, 71.6% of the total amount of electricity used in the structure was for cooling. Landscaping was installed to shade the walls and windows of the structure and to direct warm breezes away from and over the structure, thereby reducing infiltration of hot air and removing sensible heat resulting from the absorption of solar radiation by the roof. Energy use in the structure was again monitored two years after landscaping. Comparisons of energy use before and after landscaping were then made for periods of similar weather conditions. Average external air temperatures for time periods during four days before landscaping were found similar to those occurring during the same time periods for seven days after landscaping. The results of these quantitative comparisons indicate that a 60-65% reduction in energy used for air conditioning occurred on hot summer days. During the hot afternoon hours, shading reduced energy consumption from 8.65 kwh to 3.67 kwh — a 57.6% reduction. Parker noted that this savings corresponds to an average reduction in power demand of 4.98 kilowatts during the peak demand period. In most areas of the U.S., peak load demands occur in the summer because of extensive air conditioning needs. Because electrical generating capacities are generally adequate to meet all but the peak load demands, a reduction of this magnitude during the peak demand period may reduce the need for costly additional generating capabilities.

In summarizing his results and other benefits associated with solar control plantings, Parker indicated that,

> Throughout the course of a cooling season, an extensive vegetative landscape should reduce a

$600 air conditioning bill to about $360. Since a landscape comparable to the one described in [the] experiments can be commercially installed for about $1000, the landscape will have a pay back period of about four years. Obviously, a much shorter pay back can be achieved by the homeowner installing the trees and shrubs himself. It shold of course be noted that this pay back will not begin until the plants have achieved significant growth (usually 3 to 5 years). All economic pay back calculations of this type should also include the increased value of the residential property associated with the installed landscaping and should consider the fact that significant funds are generally spent on landscaping purely for aesthetic reasons. (p. 2-11)

Bray (1982) has recently calculated the energy conserving effectiveness of a dense planting around a small trailer in Athens, Ga. Bray used heat transfer formulas to determine hour-by-hour heat gain (6 a.m. to 6 p.m.) on July 23 for an optimally landscaped and an unlandscaped trailer. Assuming that vegetation around the landscaped trailer was 5 years old, Bray then calculated a 51.6% reduction in heat gain for the shaded trailer as compared to the unlandscaped trailer. The results of this simulation correspond quite closely with data collected by Parker in the field.

Cooling in Permanent Structures

Buffington (1978) has used a computer simulation of heat extraction rates (the rate at which an air conditioner removes heat from a building) to determine the effectiveness of different combinations of theoretically uniform shade on the walls and roof of a concrete block control house in central Florida. To evaluate the economic effectiveness of this shading, Buffington later (1979) analyzed the simulated yearly savings for space conditioning, the expense for each landscaping modification, and the present worth calculations — all based on given interest and energy cost escalation rates.

Table 8-1 illustrates that heavily shaded east- and west-facing walls result in greater savings for cooling than does a heavily shaded roof due to a longer period of exposure to solar radiation and more favorable angles of incidence during all but the midday summer hours. Heavily shaded walls and roof results in a 14% reduction in annual cooling costs — equivalent to $100. However, shading from bare branches during the heating period increases heating costs by 8%, resulting in a net savings of only $93 per year. This illustrates the importance of providing solar access as well as solar control, even in a climate with a relatively short underheated period. A heavily shaded wall and roof structure could save $1,205 more in future energy

Table 8-1. Effectiveness of Wall and Roof Shading in Central Florida

	% Savings for cooling	Annual cooling savings	Annual heating expense	Net annual savings	Present worth of future energy savings[c]
Control house	0	$535[b]	$179[b]	$714[b]	$ 0
Shading modifications[a]					
Wall shading					
Light shading	6	42	7	35	
Heavy shading	11	86	12	74	959
Roof shading					
Light shading	3	13	2	11	
Heavy shading	6	25	3	22	285
Full shading	9	39	5	34	
Wall and roof shading					
Heavy wall and roof shading	14	108	15	93	1,205

* [a]Light, heavy, and full shading correspond to 33%, 67%, and 100% shading, respectively, during the cooling season, and 10%, 20%, and 25% shading, respectively, during the heating season.
* [b]These figures are annual costs for the east-facing control house based upon current price estimates of the utilities (1979).
* [c]Assumes a 10% annual energy cost escalation rate and 15% interest rate for an assumed 20 year life.
* From: (Buffington, 1978, 1979)

than an unshaded one, and this amount saved in utilities for space conditioning over 20 years could be spent for the shaded structure. Results such as those can provide landscape architects with useful information to help determine the economic feasibility of various vegetative shading strategies.

The author (McPherson, 1981c) has constructed two identical one-eighth scale model homes to assess the affects of morning and afternoon shade and shade from trees with different canopy densities on outside and inside wall and air temperatures. The models were calibrated with each other and the prototypic home after which they were designed. They were found to have similar rates of heat gain, heat loss, and heat lag. The models were not ventilated, which caused their inside temperatures to be slightly warmer later in the day than occurred in the prototype home. Dense shade from Norway maples cast on the east elevation of a test model resulted in cooler morning and early afternoon inside air temperatures than was recorded simultaneously for the unshaded model. At 1:00 p.m. the air temperature inside the shaded model was 12.7F (7C) cooler. Dense shade cast on the west elevation resulted in lower late afternoon and early evening temperatures, as well as an earlier onset of temperature decline. A 11.7F (6.5C) lower temperature was recorded at 6:00 p.m., and peak temperatures were reached four hours earlier and began to drop 3½ hours earlier in the shaded model. Energy savings of 55% and 57% were calculated for the models with shaded east and west elevations, respectively, on the day measurements were made.

Results also indicated that full shade from trees with both dense and open canopies effectively lowers inside air temperatures, although dense-canopied trees provide more cooling. Outside wall temperature of the model fully shaded by a honey locust (28% transmission) were 3.6F to 5.4F (2C to 3.5C) higher than those simultaneously recorded on the identical model situated under full shade of a dense Norway maple (10% transmission). This translated into a 5.4F (3C) warmer maximum temperature inside the model under locust shade (McPherson, 1981b). Another experiment showed that the maximum temperature inside the model under full maple shade was 74.3F (23.5C), whereas that of the unshaded model was 83F (28.25C). McPherson concluded that dense full shade could virtually eliminate the need for mechanical cooling in northern Utah because inside temperatures remained within the comfort zone (mid-seventies) even when ambient air temperatures were in the high eighties. By eliminating the need to air condition a home, the homeowner with a central air conditioning system in Utah could save about $300 a year and reduce annual space conditioning costs by 37%. The homeowner could acquire three 10- to 15-ft trees with this same amount of money, and with time, the trees' size would increase and their performance improve. At the same time, the cost of electricity will increase. Thus, the initial investment becomes even more beneficial in the long run.

These and other studies (Center for Environmental Studies, 1977; DeWalle, Heisler, & Jacobs, 1983; Hansen & Mandraes, 1979; Laechelt & Williams, 1976) all have confirmed that a number of benefits can be derived from vegetative shading:

1. Improved human comfort in structures without mechanical cooling.

2. Reduced air conditioning energy consumption in buildings with mechanical cooling systems.
3. Reduced peak load demands on utilities.
4. Reduced foreign imports with associated benefits to the U.S. economy.
5. Relatively short payback periods and sizable long term savings.

Most landscape architects, planners, developers, and homeowners are not aware of the benefits that can be derived from solar control plantings. In most cases, they select and locate vegetation with little consideration of its effect on space conditioning costs, often resulting in landscapes that increase rather than decrease these costs. Numerous and significant benefits can result from solar control plantings, even though the costs are minimal.

Locating Vegetation

The process of locating vegetation for solar control should not be approached haphazardly or the design may result in greater energy costs than savings. At the same time, a "cook book" approach should not be used because the critical factors will vary with each problem. The following discussion addresses various questions designers should answer before locating plants for solar control and presents general guidelines for use in locating trees, shrubs, and vines. A more technical approach to precision planting for solar control and solar access is included in Appendix C for those seeking to optimize their designs for passive cooling.

When to Shade

A review of the climatic analysis readily indicates whether cooling is needed and, if so, what its relative importance as a design priority is to be. Assuming that cooling is required, the next question to consider is, "For what time period is cooling needed?" This question must be answered before locating vegetation for shade because one must first know where the sun is in the sky when shading is desired. Once the designer determines when to shade, it is relatively easy to find the sun's location and then position the plant so that its canopy will block insolation during the time period when cooling is desired.

If the aim of solar control is to improve human comfort indoors, then shading is needed when conditions become uncomfortably hot and mechanical cooling is used for relief. Olgyay (1963) has defined the period when cooling measures are needed as the Overheated Zone, and has located the shading line at the 70F (21C) point along the bottom of the Comfort Zone on the Bioclimatic Chart (see Chapter Four).

This means that when outdoor temperatures are above 70F (21C), shading is needed. While this definition is practical, it is also somewhat inaccurate since it does not consider the effect of humidity on human thermal comfort. Residents of Tucson, Ariz., for example, may not feel a need for shading until ambient temperatures reach 75F (24C) or higher because of the low relative humidity. Despite this omission, designers generally accept and use Olgyay's definition. Table 8-2 lists the overheated days for selected U.S. cities. A method for determining the overheated period of cities not included is presented in Appendix C.

Table 8-2. Extent of the Overheated Period for Selected U.S. Cities

City	First day	Last day	Total days
Atlanta	April 12	Oct. 23	194
Boston	May 26	Sept. 22	119
Fresno	March 28	Nov. 9	226
Houston	March 5	Nov. 28	268
Los Angeles	June 15	Nov. 15	153
Miami	All year		365
Minneapolis	May 22	Sept. 18	119
Philadelphia	May 6	Oct. 6	153
Phoenix	Feb. 15	Dec. 2	290
Portland	June 1	Sept. 26	118
Salt Lake City	May 9	Oct. 6	150
St. Louis	April 28	Oct. 15	170

One answer to the question "When to shade?" is simply, "When ambient temperatures are 70F (21C) or above." When it may be aesthetically, economically, or otherwise unfeasible to locate enough plants to shade a structure during the entire overheated period, a second question arises: "When should one plan to shade a structure for optimal cooling effect and energy savings?"

Placing vegetation between a building and the sun during the peak of the cooling period can maximize the vegetation's cooling effectiveness. As air temperatures increase to their peak and energy consumption for air conditioning reaches a maximum, shading from vegetation provides the largest temperature reductions and the greatest energy savings (Parker, 1981). The period during which cooling demands are the greatest varies from region to region, but generally coincides with the period of maximum air temperature. Parker, an advocate of peak load landscaping, has argued that designers are incorrect in using June 22 as the design date. His analysis of the climatic records for Miami, Fla., has indicated that maximum ambient temperatures are reached around Aug. 6, and the period of peak power demand for air conditioning occurs around Aug. 5. The peak system loading for the local utility in Utah, however, occurs one to two weeks before maximum air temperatures

(July 28) due to large power demands for irrigation as well as air conditioning. The design date should generally coincide with the day that air temperatures are greatest.

On the design date, peak electrical power demand occurs near 5:30 p.m., because of high heat gains during the preceding afternoon hours and the activation of mechanical cooling systems when people return home from work (Parker, 1981). The design hour is determined by estimating the thermal capacitance or heat lag effect of the residence. Generally a two- to three-hour delay occurs before heat energy on the exterior walls transfers inside and affects the air conditioning load. Thus, the deisgn hour for a typical residence is 3:00 p.m., which corresponds closely to the time of maximum daily temperature.

The concept of peak load landscaping is simple and useful. Although the precise design date and hour will vary from region to region and with the thermodynamic characteristics of the structure, in most instances the variations will not be great enough to warrant additional calculations. Precisely positioning a tree for peak load reduction is more complex, especially if solar access is provided, as Figure 8-4 shows. The plan views show the azimuth angles along which a tree must be located to shade a one story home in Salt Lake City and Miami at 3:00 p.m. on Aug. 1. Differences in latitude affect tree location. The shaded region in each section depicts canopy height required for shade at this time. However, a tree must be taller than this if shade is also desired between June 22 and Aug. 1, when the altitude angle of the sun is greater (to 53° in Salt Lake City and 65° in Miami on June 22). Salt Lake City temperatures are not always above 70F (21C) when the sun is at a 255° azimuth bearing. The lowest altitude angle of the sun

is 13° when temperatures are 70F (21C) or above. To provide solar access during the underheated period, the area below a line drawn at a 13° angle from the top of the window should be free of foliage, as shown in the diagram. In Miami, temperatures are always above 70F (21C) when the sun is due west (270° azimuth), and therefore the tree may branch to the ground because solar access is not a concern. See Appendix C for more information on calculating canopy dimensions for peak load landscaping in various regions.

Where to Shade

The previous discussion illustrates that if the designer knows when to shade (the design date and hour) then he or she can readily solve the problem of where to shade through use of the appropriate design tools. However, suppose he or she wants to locate vegetation to provide cooling during overheated periods other than when cooling requirements are greatest. First, the designer should conduct a structural analysis to determine through what parts of the building's envelope the greatest heat gain occurs, prioritizing these areas in terms of relative shading needs. Plants are then located to shade those portions of the structure most responsible for heat gain. In this manner, the designer can assure the greatest possible energy savings from use of a limited number of plants.

Structural analysis: Heat gain. The interaction between sol-air impacts and thermophysical properties of the building envelope determine the relative amount of heat gain through any portion of the structure. Important factors to consider include the following:

1. *Orientation.* The orientation of the building influences the amount of surface area exposed to insolation at a given time and the angle at which the sun's rays strike the walls, windows, and roof. Orientation affects the amount and rate at which various building surfaces gain and lose heat. An east- or west-facing structure presents large areas of wall and glazing to the low-angle morning and afternoon sun. If these surfaces are not shaded, the structure will warm up early, remain warm through the afternoon, and then gain more heat before sunset. A structure oriented to the south presents relatively less surface area to the low-angle summer sun, but the south-facing roof may become a major source of heat gain if the attic space and ceiling below it are poorly insulated. However, most attics and ceilings are usually better insulated than are the walls.

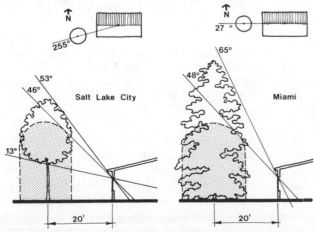

Figure 8-4. Canopy dimensions of trees located for solar control in Salt Lake City and Miami. The shaded region indicates tree height required for peak load landscaping.

2. *Window location.* Since approximately three-quarters of total heat gain comes through the windows, their location must be noted with respect to the sun's angle of incidence during the period when shading is desired.

3. *Heat capacitance and conductivity of walls and roof.* Structures made from materials that store but do not readily transfer heat will not benefit from shading as much as buildings or parts of buildings that readily gain and lose heat. For example, experiments on the temperature effects of different types of roofing materials indicate that white cedar shakes stay 10-20F (5.6-11C) cooler during the day than do white asphalt shingles (Living Systems, 1977). It is thus not as important to shade a cedar shake roof to the same degree as a shingle roof.

4. *Surface color and texture.* Dark or rough-textured surfaces absorb more solar radiation than do light-colored or smooth surfaces. Tests by Living Systems (1977) have shown that a black asphalt shingle roof reaches a maximum temperature of 150F (65.5C) while the maximum temperature of the same asphalt shingle roof painted white is only 110F (43.3C). Surfaces that are not reflective need shading more than those that have a high albedo.

5. *Solar access.* The location of areas where winter heat gain is desired should be noted. This would typically include south-facing windows, roof-mounted solar collectors, greenhouses, and perhaps the entire south wall.

Figure 8-5 illustrates how an analysis of the relative amount of heat gain might be graphically presented.

Structural analysis: Use areas. In addition to using the heat gain analysis to record the relative need for shading various parts of the building envelope, the relative need for cooling in the different living spaces also must be considered. This need is dependent on the following variables:

1. *Amount of use.* Frequently used rooms (kitchen, dining, and living rooms) have a higher cooling need than seldom used ones (bathrooms and utility rooms).

2. *Time of use.* Activity areas heavily used when sol-air impacts are greatest require more cooling than those seldom used during the same period. Again, kitchen, dining, and living rooms are frequently used in late afternoon when cooling is needed most.

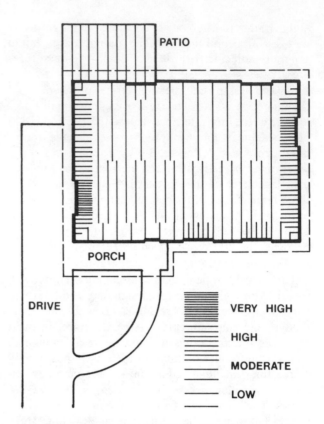

Figure 8-5. Structural analysis: Heat gain.

3. *Location.* A room's location with respect to the sol-air impacts on its walls should be considered. For example, a bedroom located on the west side of a home has a higher relative need for cooling than one on the east side. If unshaded, the wall of the west room may radiate heat well into the night, thus making it difficult to sleep. The unshaded bedroom to the east becomes warmest in the late morning, when it is not being occupied, and is not warmed by the solar load later in the day.

To determine the relative cooling need of each use area, the designer must evaluate the effect of each of these variables. A matrix or graphic analysis as Figure 8-6 (see next page) illustrates may assist in determining relative cooling needs of use areas.

Structural analysis: Shading composite. Heat gain analysis indicates areas of the building skin that have the greatest need for shading. The use area analysis identifies places within or outside the structure that have the highest relative cooling need. The synthesis of these analyses results in a composite that depicts the relative shading need of every part of the building envelope. The shading composite in Figure 8-7 illustrates which areas of a structure are most impor-

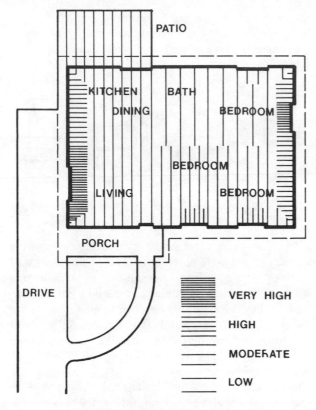

Figure 8-6. Structural analysis: Use areas.

PATIO

KITCHEN | BATH
DINING | BEDROOM
BEDROOM
LIVING | BEDROOM

PORCH

DRIVE

VERY HIGH
HIGH
MODERATE
LOW

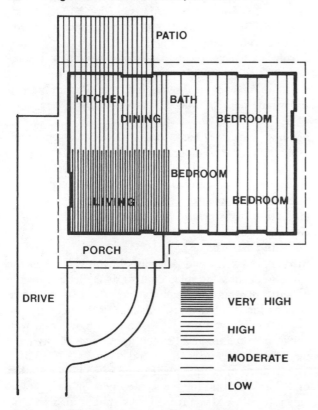

Figure 8-7. Structural analysis: Shading composite.

PATIO

KITCHEN | BATH
DINING | BEDROOM
BEDROOM
LIVING | BEDROOM

PORCH

DRIVE

VERY HIGH
HIGH
MODERATE
LOW

tant to shade. Once a hierarchy of areas to be shaded is determined, it is easier to incorporate effective solar control design into the planting design process. By locating vegetation to shade areas of highest priority, the designer can maximize energy savings.

Locating Trees

Recommendations for locating trees, shrubs, and vines follow. These guidelines are somewhat general because a wide range of shading geometries, structural characteristics, and vegetation types exists in the U.S. The purpose of presenting guidelines is to provide the reader who is casually interested in solar control with the information needed to avoid unwittingly making serious mistakes, which can result in energy-consuming landscapes.

Planting near the structure. The closer a tree is located to a structure, the sooner energy savings will be realized. This is especially true for trees located to shade the south roof or wall. Trees placed too far to the south of the building do not provide shade during the overheated period (Figure 8-8), but do shade the

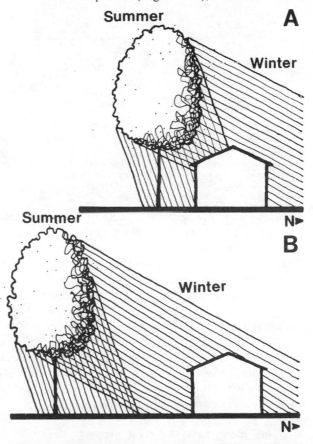

Figure 8-8. Proper (A) and improper (B) placement of trees to the south of a home. Tree located too far to the south shades home during the winter. Tree located close to the home provides shade in summer and solar access to the south wall during the winter.

153

south elevation during the winter when the sun is lower in the sky. Trees located to the south should be relatively close to the structure and pruned high enough to allow maximum insolation during the underheated period. Another benefit of close planting is that the south roof will be shaded sooner.

Trees located to shade east and west elevations will provide more daily shade for a longer period if they are closer to the wall. Figure 8-9 shows that a tree 25 ft (7.6m) high and 15 ft (4.6m) wide planted 10 ft (3m) from the west wall shades 47% of the exposed surface between the hours of 3 p.m. and 7 p.m. An identical tree placed 20 ft (6.1m) from the wall only shades 27% of the wall during these hours.

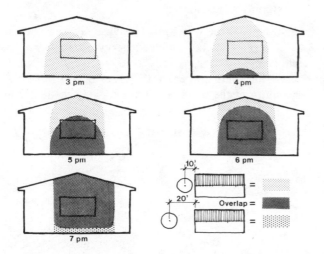

Figure 8-9. Trees located close to east and west facing walls for greater shading. Shaded areas represent shadow patterns cast on west walls by a typical tree located 10 and 20 feet from a home on August 8 in Gainesville, Florida.

Trees should not be planted close to structures if the soil has high shrink-swell characteristics. Dehydration and rehydration of expansive soils may result in damage to the foundation and walls. Also, trees with shallow or invasive root systems and species that are susceptible to storm damage should not be selected.

Using trees to shade windows. Window shade provided by an arching tree canopy is preferable to shade from shrubs or shutters. The canopy can effectively block solar radiation while still permitting a view to the outside, even when the tree is in full leaf. Trees should be located to shade east- and west-facing windows.

Planting along east and west property lines. When buildings are sited, their ability to shade adjacent structures should be considered. Trees located near the east or west property lines in higher density developments may shade one structure in the morning

and another in the late afternoon. Figure 8-10 illustrates the siting of residential units and trees to maximize shading of east and west facades.

Figure 8-10. Vegetation located along east and west property lines for shading in both the morning and afternoon.

In many cases narrow side yards severely limit the amount of available planting space for trees along east and west property lines. One solution to this dilemma is to use trees with fastigiate or upright and narrow forms. For example, two common cultivars of Norway maple ('Erectum' and 'Columnare') exhibit this form and can be used successfully in foundation plantings to shade east and west walls.

Shading the air conditioning unit. Shading and transpirational cooling can significantly lower the operating temperature of an air conditioning unit and increase its operating efficiency by at least 4% (Parker, 1981). Trees should be positioned to shade the air conditioner during the entire cooling season. Shrubs may be needed to obstruct low-angle insolation. The surrounding vegetation should be pruned so it will not restrict air flow to and from the unit but will still shade nearby walls and windows.

Shading exterior heat sinks. Extensive concrete, asphalt, brick, and other hard surfaces can absorb and radiate large amounts of heat. Shading these surfaces reduces the ambient heat load on the adjacent structure and also creates conditions more conducive to utilization of exterior living spaces.

Locating Shrubs

Most researchers and designers have overlooked the value of shrubs for solar control as evidenced by the paucity of data on canopy density and foliation periods for shrub species. Parker (1981) has reported that a single five-foot-tall shrub shading an east wall between 9:00 a.m. and 12:00 p.m. reduces the average temperature of the wall behind it by 24.3F (13.5C). This reduction is equivalent to an effective insulation or R value of 14.0 for the shaded portion of a typical concrete block structure. Shrubs should also be considered for solar control use because of the following:

154

1. Significant reductions in heat gain through walls and windows can be quickly realized with shrubs because they become established more quickly after transplanting than do trees.
2. Shrubs are less expensive to purchase than trees and can be more easily installed and maintained.
3. The roots of most shrubs will not harm utilities or foundations, and the threat of property damage due to broken limbs is minimal.
4. Shrubs require less space than do trees.

Shading east and west walls and windows. Tall shrubs located close to the east and west walls will effectively reduce insolation. In areas with long overheated periods (five months or more), evergreen shrubs may be used along the west wall without sacrificing heat gain during the underheated period. Large shrubs planted to either side of east- and west-facing windows allow less radiation to penetrate into the home than do smaller shrubs, as Figure 8-11 shows.

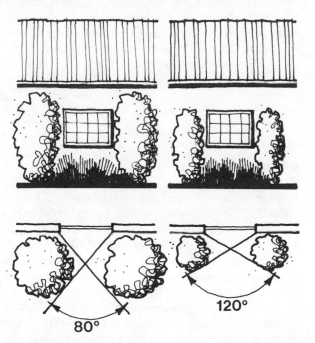

Figure 8-11. Large shrubs reduce the azimuth range from which insolation may strike a window more than do smaller shrubs.

Shading south walls. It is preferable to locate shrubs instead of trees to the south of a building if solar access must be preserved. It is very difficult to locate trees that will not at some time during their lifespan cast shade on south glazing or a roof-mounted solar collector. Shrubs, on the other hand, do not grow large enough to shade a roof and can be easily pruned to avoid shading windows. Parker (1981) recommends

angle pruning of shrubs and hedges, as Figure 8-12 illustrates (see next page). The dead air space behind the pruned plant traps heat and may elevate wall temperatures during the coldest months. New growth in the spring will gradually diminish the sun pocket and provide additional shading.

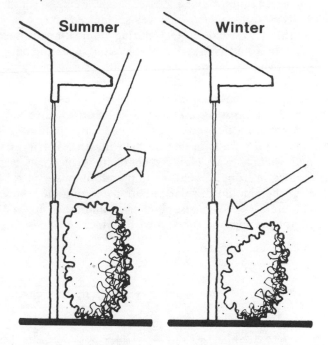

Figure 8-12. Angle pruning in late fall creates a winter heat trap next to the wall. Adapted from: (Parker, 1981).

Locating shrubs for breeze control. Landscape architects should be aware of the effects solar control plantings will have on air flow patterns. When possible, shrubs and trees should facilitate the flow of cool breezes and dissipate or divert hot winds from buildings and outdoor living spaces. Chapter Nine presents techniques for achieving these ends.

Locating Vines

Surprisingly little research has been conducted to quantify the cooling effectiveness of vines. A vine-covered wall is protected from direct solar radiation by the leaves, and transpirational cooling accentuates the cooling effect created by shading. The result is a relatively stable boundary layer between the foliage and wall, which maintains slightly cooler temperatures than would occur on a similar unshaded wall surface. It is anticipated but undocumented that cooler inside temperatures would result. The following design guidelines present a few common ways vines can be used for passive cooling (see Spirn & Santos, *Plants for Passive Cooling*, 1981, for more detailed discussion of design applications).

Locating vines to shade walls, windows, and exterior spaces. Deciduous vines are best used on south- and east-facing walls where winter heat gain is accommodated by leaf abscission. Evergreen vines provide year-round shade for north and west walls in northern latitudes. In regions with long overheated periods, evergreen vines may be located on the east and south walls as well. Vine-covered trellises located to the east, south, or west can protect glazing from summertime insolation and create a cool, pleasant space for outdoor living. However, trellises south of windows and walls can block solar access if large structural supports and dense latticing are used. Vines may be located to grow up a lattice or cable attached to the overhang. Lattices or cables can be located in front of windows or walls as Figure 8-13 illustrates. Hinged and window wall planters containing vines can be located in front of windows to permit manual control over the amount of solar radiation entering the home (Figure 8-14). Annuals, perennials, and other flowering plants may be substituted for vines.

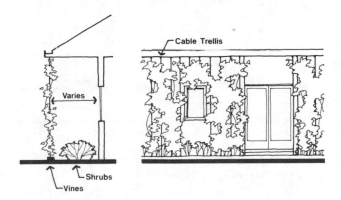

Figure 8-13. Vines growing on cables for solar control. Adapted from: (Spirn & Santos, 1981).

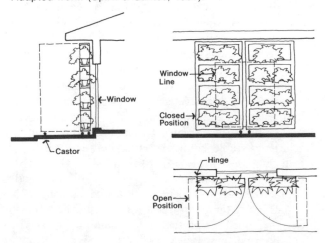

Figure 8-14. Hinged planter for manual control of window shading. Adapted from: (Spirn & Santos, 1981).

Selecting the appropriate type of vine for each location. Climbing vines will grow up textured surfaces without support. However, some vigorous growing species can cause damage by separating aluminum siding from the wall. Twining vines require support and are best used in conjunction with ramadas, trellises, cables, and other sturdy support structures. Shrub-type vines also require support and entail more maintenance than climbing or twining-type vines.

Selecting Vegetation

Landscape designers can increase energy savings by selecting tree, shrub, and vine species whose characteristics are best suited to a conservation task. Traditionally, the primary criteria upon which plant selection is based include adaptability to site conditions, ornamental features, and maintenance requirements. Landscape architects and other researchers have recently gathered information on new criteria for plant selection, such as canopy density. Energy-conscious designers should consider these criteria along with those they have traditionally used when evaluating the value of individual plant species for use in energy-conserving landscapes. The following sections describe the significance of these plant characteristics in the context of solar control and provide references so that regionally specific data can be obtained.

Canopy Density

Research results (Buffington, 1978; Heisler, Halverson, & Zisa, 1981, McPherson, 1981c) have indicated that canopy density is one of the most important variables to consider when selecting a plant for solar control. Bare-branch canopy density is also important if solar access is a concern. In both cases, shading effectiveness can be expressed as the shading coefficient, which describes the fraction of incident solar radiation that is transmitted through the canopy. As generally expressed, it can vary from 1.0 (all solar energy transmitted) to 0.0 (no solar energy transmitted). Canopy density is sometimes expressed as a percentage of the incident solar radiation that is blocked (in the case of solar control) or transmitted (in the case of solar access). To avoid confusion, the shading coefficient concept will be used henceforth.

Studies measuring actual shading coefficients for plants in leaf have not been extensive, limited only to trees. Johnson, McBee, and Tasselli (n.d.) in Virginia; Gardner (1982) in Ohio; Heisler, Halverson, and Zisa (1981) in Pennsylvania; and McPherson (1981c) in Utah, have used pyranometers to measure solar radiation transmitted through the leafy canopy as a percentage of that available in the open. However, instrument location and measurement techniques varied, thus making comparisons difficult. Schiler (1979) has reported the visual density of 19 tree species in leaf, while Westergaard (1982) has given the visual density of 52 leafless tree species calculated through optical scanning of photographs. Visual density is defined as the silhouette density expressed directly as the ratio of occluded area to total area. Table 8-3 lists the calculated shading coefficients of selected ornamental and shade trees. Figure 8-15 and 8-16 show differences in visual density between mature specimens of horsechestnut and thornless honey locust.

Figure 8-16. Visual canopy density of a mature thornless honey locust.

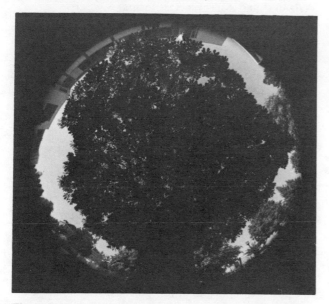

Figure 8-15. Visual canopy density of a mature horsechestnut.

Measuring shading coefficients is extremely complicated due to the constant movement of shadow patterns and changes in the quantity and quality of solar radiation. Currently, no consensus exists as to which procedures can provide reliable information with the least amount of effort and money. However, researchers are attempting to solve this problem as well as to provide shading coefficients for a greater number of species. Because designers are specifying planting of young trees but planning for mature vegetation, they would benefit from more information describing how the shading coefficients of a single species with and without leaves varies as it develops and matures. Canopy density also varies among trees as a seasonal response to moisture conditions. Some deciduous trees in Florida lose many or all of their leaves in the dry summer period. Evergreens in Arizona become more open when subject to drought

stress. Leaf drop and physiological adaptations such as leaf folding reduce the amount of exposed surface area. Little is known of the effects these changes have on canopy density. Further research is also needed on the effects of cultural practices on shading coefficients. For example, Holzberlein (1979) recommends an oval pruning pattern to reduce twig shading during the leafless season. Frequent pruning necessary to maintain an oval form may result in a profusion of branches, as occurs when a tree is pollarded. This could have a negative effect by lowering the shading coefficients of the leafless plant.

Designers and planners should also consider the shading coefficients of vegetation without leaves. The trunks, branches, and twigs of trees can intercept large amounts of solar radiation. Heisler et al. (1981) found shading coefficients of .40 for leafless elms and .50 for leafless London plane trees, while Westergaard (1982) has reported that the visual density of most leafless deciduous trees ranges between .60 and .70 (shading coefficients), or a 30% to 40% blockage of winter sunlight. A solar control planting design that intends to provide solar control and solar access when the plants approach maturity may obstruct solar access for years before that time. For example, if young transplants are located south of the structure to shade the roof, several years must pass before trees grow tall enough for lower branches to be pruned for solar access. Although the canopy density of trees generally increases with age, significant shading may still occur.

When winter shading is unavoidable, plants with low shading coefficients when in leaf and high shading coefficients when leafless should be selected. Research on the impact of tree shade on home heating and cooling costs is incipient. Heisler (In Preparation) and Thayer, Maeda, and Zanetto (1983) report on energy cost tradeoffs for trees to the south of homes (see Chapter Seven). The author (In Preparation) is currently developing an interactive Shadow Pattern Program for microcomputers that calculates shadow patterns on buildings from trees located anywhere around a structure. It will front-end a building energy analysis program to derive the effects of shade on annual space heating and cooling costs. Table 8-3 lists the calculated shading coefficients of selected leafless landscape trees.

Foliation Period

Foliation period, the average period when a plant is in leaf, should be considered in relation to the local overheated period when plants are selected for solar control and solar access. The ideal synchronization of leaf season and overheated period would result in the plant reaching full leaf just as average temperatures exceed 70F (21C). Full leafless condition should be reached when average temperatures drop below 70F (21C). Unfortunately, few plants are that cooperative.

Changes in air temperature and photoperiod stimulate certain hormonal changes within plants that initiate and regulate the processes of leaf-out and leaf abscission. A plant generally takes several weeks to go from bud break to full leaf, and from full leaf to a leafless condition. The interaction of site and microclimatic factors affect the response of plants to these and other important environmental clues. Foliation periods display an elasticity that parallels human comfort needs. In a cold spring, the leaves arrive later and after a long, warm summer they last longer. Despite such variations, a consistency of response can be attributed to each species due to genetic similarities that regulate the amount of warmth and light required to initiate bud break or how much cold and light reduction are necessary to cause leaf abscission. Plant species can be arranged in a sequential order by their long-term average time for leaf-out and leaf-drop, despite the fact that these times change year to year.

Hammond, Zanetto, and Adams (1980), McPherson (1981c), and Ticknor (1982) have categorized landscape trees according to foliation period characteristics for California, Utah, and Oregon, respectively. Table 8-3 lists the approximate times of foliation and defoliation for selected trees.

From these data, it is clear that the foliation period of most trees exceeds the duration of the regions' overheated period. In northern Utah, for example, the overheated period extends from May 22 to Sept. 27. Most trees have achieved full leaf-out by mid-May but do not begin dropping leaves until late October. Therefore, in Utah and many other parts of the country, it is most desirable to select trees that are late to leaf-out and early to drop their leaves if solar access is a concern. In warm, sunny areas where solar control is of prime importance, the designer may select species that leaf-out early and drop their leaves late. Of course, evergreens have the longest foliation period and are frequently used for solar control in Florida, Arizona, and southern California.

Foliation characteristics of plants used to shade outdoor spaces may differ from those used to shade buildings. A patio located in a "hot pocket" facing south might be used earlier in the spring if the tree shading it is one that does not leaf-out early. If the patio remains warm into the fall, a tree that does not drop its leaves early would be more appropriate. By manipulating foliation period and canopy density, landscape architects can control seasonal changes in the microclimates of outdoor spaces.

The role of microclimatic factors in determining foliation period is also important to consider. A plant located in a benign microclimate, sheltered from wind and cold, may have a foliation period three to six weeks longer than that of a similar plant in an exposed location. This unavoidable extension of the foliation period can be mitigated through the selection of species with short foliation periods.

Cultural practices also influence foliation period (Wagar, 1982). To delay time of leaf-out and encourage early leaf-drop, heavy watering and fertilizer applications should be avoided in the spring and fall. Unpruned trees generally lose their leaves before recently pruned trees. Thus, trees should not be pruned until after they have lost their leaves. This practice will not only promote earlier defoliation but also will increase the leafless shading coefficient.

Research is now being conducted in California to develop plants with low shading coefficients when in leaf and high leafless shading coefficients for a variety of foliation periods. In the near future, nurseries may supply plants specifically selected and bred for their energy-conserving capabilities. It is up to designers and planners to make creative use of recent data regarding canopy density and foliation periods. This information can provide an opportunity for new syntheses and greater control (independent of mechanical systems) over the environments we create.

Height-to-Canopy Bottom

As previously mentioned, the height from the ground to the canopy bottom is important to consider when selecting trees for solar control and solar access. Trees with low branching scaffolds (primary support limbs issuing from the trunk) may occlude solar radiation during the winter, especially if the trees are located to the south of the structure. Trees branching high above the ground can effectively obstruct the summer sun and still allow the lower angle winter sun to strike the wall. Trees located around two-story homes must begin to branch higher above the ground to provide both solar control and solar access than if they shaded a one-story home. However, thermal mass associated with solar gaining surfaces is usually located on the first floor for structural support reasons, and therefore, extended shading of second stories is usually less harmful than is blocking of solar access to first floor windows.

The need to prune trees for solar access can be reduced by selecting species whose height-to-canopy bottom conforms to shading geometry requirements. For example, the American elm and cottonwood typically begin to branch much higher than littleleaf linden at maturity. The location and spacing of scaffold branches on young stock will not change as they grow unless an external force intervenes or self-pruning occurs. Designers have the opportunity to control this variable when selecting or specifying plants to be purchased and when developing maintenance programs. In any case, one can specify a desired height-to-canopy bottom range that will assure adequate solar control and solar access.

Size and Form

The size and form of a plant directly affect the area covered by its shadow pattern. It may take several shrubs or small trees to shade an amount of surface area equal to what one large tree can shade. Trees with broad round forms cast wide shadows ideal for solar control. In contrast, tall narrow trees cast paltry summer shadows and long winter shadows that may conflict with a neighbor's solar access (Zanetto, 1978). Since the cooling effect of plant shade is partially a result of the percentage of surface area shaded, the interaction of plant size and form with the sun's daily and seasonal path should be utilized to determine how best to shade as large an area as possible, when and where high temperatures create uncomfortable conditions.

Growth Rate

The faster a plant grows, the sooner maximum shading efficiency will be achieved and the shorter the payback period. Unfortunately, most plants with rapid growth rates are also weak wooded, posing a hazard to person and property. The silver maple, box elder, and willow are examples. Invasive or water-seeking roots are another undesirable trait shared by most rapid growers. The damage invasive roots can wreak on foundations and utilities has been well publicized (Aldous, 1979) and should dissuade designers from using offending species where problems could occur. For these reasons, most rapid growers are not the first plants one would choose to locate near a structure. However, some trees are fast growing when young but subsequently slow down and develop strong wood. Most notable among these are the ashes, sycamores, and honey locusts. Rapid growth may be coaxed from slower growing species through heavier than normal applications of water and fertilizer, although this does require additional expenditures of time, money, and energy.

A second option is to plant large trees with moderate growth rates. The major advantages of large transplants is that their aesthetic, functional, and energy-saving attributes are synchronized with the life span of the structure and benefits are realized earlier. The life span of most city structures is estimated to be 50 years, whereas trees mature in 30 to 50 years. Thus, trees planted to shade a new structure reach their full potential at about the same time the building nears obsolesence (Baer & Gordon, 1972). Other researchers, however, maintain that urban landscapes change so rapidly that young transplants never have a chance to reach maturity. In either case, large transplants do provide an immediate effect that rapid growers cannot.

A third way to reduce the payback period is to interplant a mixture of faster and slower growing species in what is called a successional or rotational planting. Rapid growers begin to provide shade in a matter of years, while simultaneously serving as nurse plants to the shade tolerant slow growers. In about 10 years, the slower growers are large enough to provide adequate shade once the rapid growers are thinned out. The advantage of this type of planting is that a high level of shading efficiency is achieved relatively soon and sustained for a long period of time without the hazards and high maintenance costs associated with the culture of only rapid-growing species, or the high initial costs required to plant large trees.

Life Span

Life span is closely related to growth rate in that most rapid growers are short-lived, whereas most slow growers are long-lived. The life span of the plant should be related to that of the structure it will shade. Impermanent structures, like mobile homes, may benefit most by quick shade from rapid growers with short life spans. Plants with long life spans should be used near institutional structures (schools, hospitals, etc.) that have longer operational periods.

Other

As is the case with all plantings, cultural and maintenance requirements, ornamental features, and relative cost and availability of prospective species cannot be neglected. Without an ecological fit between plant and site, survival may not be possible. The plants' preferences and tolerances to different soils, degrees of exposure, irrigation regimes, and extreme temperatures should all be determined. Tolerance to de-icing salts, air pollutants, soil compaction, and other environmental stresses are equally important. Maintenance requirements to consider when selecting a plant for solar control include wood strength, invasive roots, pruning requirements, litter drop, and susceptibility to insects and disease. The ornamental attributes of plants are important because they can contribute to the overall design concept, or if improperly used, detract from the design's visual unity. The energy-conscious designer's goal should be to mesh ecological and aesthetic sensitivity and the intrinsic beauty of these living organisms with the functional shading requirements of the site.

One will rarely find a single plant that meets all the criteria described above. The designer must evaluate which factors are most important in view of the client's preferences and his or her own experiences. In many cases, a single plant can provide several functional benefits. For example, a drought-tolerant conifer located to the northwest of a building can provide shade from the late afternoon summer sun, block winter winds, conserve water, offer cover and food for certain wildlife, and enhance the privacy of a nearby patio. It can also function aesthetically by adding color to the winter landscape. Thus, final plant selection for a holistic design should be based upon a careful analysis of the total contribution a given plant will make to the landscape, and not solely upon its ability to control solar radiation.

Prototypical Designs

General patterns of plant location for solar control will vary from region to region and to a lesser extent from site to site in response to meso- and microclimatic differences. The purpose of this concluding section is to illustrate similarities and differences between prototypical designs for the same one-story residence located in four cities representing different climatic regions. Important climatic data are first presented and then the design is interpreted. Tree dimensions were obtained from techniques for precision planting described in Appendix C. The solutions presented are simplistic in that they address only the issues of solar control, solar access, and wind control. It is up to the landscape designer to integrate these considerations with other functional, ecological, and aesthetic program components. Several observations can be made regarding the designs:

1. Distances of trees from the structure can increase as trees are located progressively further to the northeast and northwest. Because of higher solar altitude angles when the sun is near its zenith (late morning and early afternoon), trees must be located closer to the home to provide solar access and solar control during midday hours. If placed south of the home and far from the structure, trees must be very tall and begin to branch abnormally high above the ground.
2. As site latitude decreases, the critical areas to shade shift to the north. For example, in northern latitudes it is most important to shade southeast-, southwest-, and west-facing windows, as well as the roof. In southern latitudes the sun's path is higher in the sky so it becomes more important to shade east-, west-, and northwest-facing windows, as well as the north roof.
3. The dilemma posed by the need to provide solar control without significantly reducing natural ventilation can be solved by using vines or shrubs to shade walls in conjunction with high-branched trees to shade windows.
4. In northern latitudes, low-branching conifers located to the north of due west can effectively block both unwanted summer sun and winter winds. Foundation plantings of evergreen vines and shrubs also serve this purpose. In southern latitudes the location of this azimuth angle at which solar access becomes unimportant is further to the south.
5. Locating solar collectors on the east side of the roof allows for more extensive shading of the southwest roof and wall surfaces. This placement enhances the peak load cooling effect.

Honolulu, Hawaii: Hot-Humid Region

The climate of Honolulu is dominated by intense solar

radiation, however, the warming effects are mitigated by consistent summer tradewinds from the northeast as well as the moderating influence of the Pacific Ocean. Although the overheated period extends throughout the year, temperatures are seldom below 70F (21C) or above 85F (29C). High relative humidity is a problem particularly in areas near the mountains where precipitation is greater and lush vegetation reduces convective cooling. Sites located near the ocean are drier but receive more solar radiation. In both cases designers should avoid locating vegetation that isolates living areas from the refreshing tradewinds.

Because Honolulu is south of the Tropic of Cancer the sun's path travels north of the zenith in midsummer. This suggests that north-facing surfaces, especially roofs, need to be shaded for protection. Provision of solar access to south-facing surfaces is also important. At present there are more solar collectors per capita in Hawaii than in any other state.

Planting Design

1. Shrubs and trees to the east deflect cooling breezes into living spaces and their shade keeps the home from warming up early in the day (Figure 8-17). Trees located about 20 ft (6.1 m) east of the home should begin to branch 12 ft (3.7 m) above the ground. A dense canopy and smooth surface (as occurs when pleached into a hedge) will simultaneously promote natural ventilation and cooling from shade.

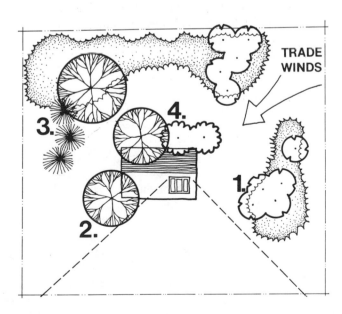

Figure 8-17. Planting design — Honolulu, Hawaii.

2. This tree is located to shade the southwest wall and roof while not interfering with the solar skyspace to the south. Trees located 10 to 20 ft (3-6.1 m) from a one-story home at this azimuth angle (230°) in Honolulu should branch 12 to 18 ft (3.7-5.5 m) above the ground. Shading of the roof is desirable provided strong-wooded litter-free species are selected. Any tree located north of west-southwest (245° azimuth) should branch to the ground because solar access to windows is no longer necessary.

3. Low-branching, tall evergreens should be located to the west and northwest to block afternoon sunlight. These plantings are critical to human comfort because of the unpleasant conditions that result from a combination of hot afternoon temperatures and intense summer insolation on west- and north-facing walls and roof. Select plants with very dense canopies and plant them close together to form a continuous barrier to the sun.

4. In Honolulu the sun shines on north-facing building surfaces all day from early June to late July. Because the altitude angle of the sun is very high throughout most of this time, trees should be located to cast shade on the north-facing roof. In the example they are located five to fifteen ft (1.5-4.6 m) north of the home and should begin to branch above the eaves to avoid impinging on the wall. Tall, wide-spreading, and strong-wooded species are most desirable.

Phoenix, Ariz.: Hot-Arid Region

The climate of hot-arid regions such as Phoenix is characterized by very hot summers and moderately cool winters. Average summer maximum temperatures are well above 100F (38C) and minimum temperatures average 70F to 80F (21-27C). Solar radiation is very strong due to low water vapor content in the atmosphere and the high elevation. Shading of ground and building surfaces from March to December is a very effective means of improving human comfort in this region. Summer breezes travel east to west in a reversing valley flow pattern, but are not generally strong or cool enough to provide much respite.

Winter conditions in Phoenix are mild with mean temperatures ranging from 50F to 60F (10C-16C) and sometimes reaching 80F (27C). Because this is one of the sunniest places in the United States there is great potential for use of photovoltaics in the future.

Planting Design

1. Three trees are located east of the home to shade the wall and windows from morning sunlight (Figure 8-18). Trees planted 20 ft (6.1 m) east of northeast from the residence should branch about six ft (1.8 m) above the ground and reach a height of 25 ft or more (6.6 m). Low-branching trees such as these may inhibit cooling breezes from the east. The trees planted 15 ft (4.6 m) to the southeast (110° azimuth) should branch 10 ft (3 m) above the ground and achieve an ultimate height of 30 ft (9.1 m).

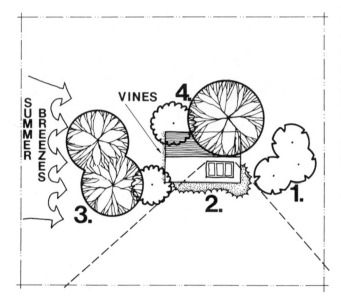

Figure 8-18. Planting design — Phoenix, Ariz.

2. The south side of the home is devoid of trees that will block solar access. Shrubs are located to shade the south wall surface.

3. Two trees are shown southwest of the home. The closest one shades the roof, wall, and perhaps the air conditioner. It branches just above the eaves and will reach 25 ft (7.6 m) in height. The second is further from the residence (20 ft) and must be taller to provide both shade and solar access to windows (10 ft to canopy bottom and 50 ft tall). In the example, cooling breezes are from the west and desirable, however, the afternoon sun is not. If the breezes are not important to cooling, dense-, low-branching trees are preferred for locations north of 250° azimuth. In this case, a high-branching tree taller than 30 ft (9.1 m) is selected and located to the northwest to allow for air flow under the canopy and still provide some shade. Vines are planted to grow up the west

walls for additional protection from low angle sunlight.

4. Because of the high altitude angle of the summer sun in Phoenix the north-facing roof can become very hot if left unshaded. Some of this heat is transferred into living areas below. Thus, several large, strong-wooded trees should be located to partially shade the roof and outdoor living areas north of the home.

Minneapolis, Minn.: Cold Region

Cold winters and warm summers typify the climate of Minneapolis. Cooling is of secondary importance to reducing heat loss in this region. Mean temperatures in the winter are well below freezing and are often combined with strong northwesterly winds. Wind protection is a prime concern during the heating period. Although cloud cover often limits winter sunshine it is still important to design for solar access so that available sunlight is effectively utilized.

Summers are short in Minneapolis, but the combination of very warm temperatures and high humidity often create conditions warranting solar control and natural ventilation. Shading is effective from June to mid-September, and care should be taken to utilize the cooling summer breezes from the south-southeast.

Planting Design

1. Three trees placed to the east-southeast block morning summer sun without blocking solar access or cooling summer breezes (Figure 8-19). Trees 10 to 15 ft (3-4.6 m) from the east wall should begin to branch 12 ft (3.7 m) above the ground and grow to 30 ft (9.1 m).

2. Shade on the south- and west-facing surfaces reduces late afternoon temperatures inside the home. A tree located 15 ft (4.6 m) off the southwest corner (240° azimuth) should begin to branch 12 ft (3.7 m) above the ground and attain an ultimate height of at least 30 ft (9.1 m). A taller tree will shade more of the roof surface.

3. Trees located south of due west should branch high enough above the ground to allow sunlight to enter west-facing windows during late fall when heating is required. They should also block late afternoon summer sun. If placed 25 ft (7.6 m) from the west wall they should begin to branch 10 ft (3 m) above the ground and be at least 25 ft (7.6 m) tall. These dimensions are reduced if trees are located closer to the wall. Many fruit trees are appropriate for shading

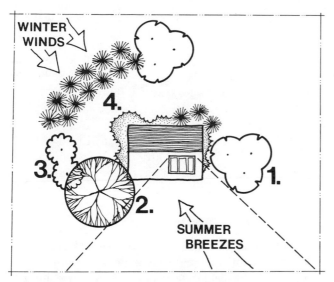

Figure 8-19. Planting design — Minneapolis, Minn.

west walls if placed about 15 ft (4.6 m) from the home.

4. In Minneapolis, air temperatures are above 70F (21C) when the sun is north of due west and therefore solar access is not required. Low-branching conifers not only intercept late afternoon sunlight but also provide wind protection. They should be placed 30 to 50 ft (9-15 m) from the home as described in Chapter Nine. A foundation planting of evergreen vines, coniferous shrubs, or densely branched deciduous shrubs may also reduce winter heat loss and summer heat gain from north- and west-facing walls.

Atlanta, Ga.: Temperate Region

The climate of Atlanta is temperate, with cool winters; hot, humid summers; and long, pleasant springs and falls. Shading is beneficial from mid-April to late October even though frequent cloud cover reduces the amount of direct solar radiation. Although summers are humid and hot (80F to 90F) consistently high wind speeds (6-10 mph) offer excellent potential for natural cooling. Wind directions frequently shift during the summer, so on-site observations are needed before deciding which areas should remain relatively unobstructed to promote natural cooling.

Prevailing winter winds are from the northwest and strong enough to require wind protection measures. Mean winter temperatures range from 40F to 50F (4-10C), but maximums may exceed 70F (21C). Vegetation should not obstruct solar access.

Planting Design

1. Early morning sunlight will strike windows from

the northeast during midsummer (Figure 8-20). This can result in excessively warm temperatures indoors unless shade is provided. Shrubs, vines,

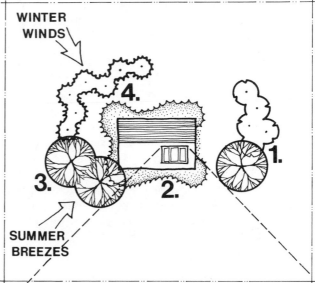

Figure 8-20. Planting design — Atlanta, Ga.

or a massing of small trees 20 ft tall (6.1 m) will keep the home cooler later into the day. A larger tree 20 ft (6.1 m) to the southeast also accomplishes this purpose. It should begin to branch 15 ft (4.6 m) above the ground and grow to 45 ft (13.7 m).

2. During the middle of days in late summer, solar control from overhangs may not shade the lower south-facing wall surfaces. Shrubs can effectively block this unwanted solar radiation while still permitting solar gain through windows during the winter.

3. In this example, it is assumed that prevailing summer breezes are from the southwest. To allow for natural ventilation and at the same time shade the south- and west-facing roof and walls it is necessary to use relatively high-branching, medium-sized trees. The tree located 10 ft (3 m) from the home (240° azimuth) should branch above the eaves and reach an ultimate height of 35 ft (10.7 m). The second tree is shown 20 ft (6.1 m) from the home (260° azimuth) and should grow to 40 ft (12.2 m).

4. As was the case in Minneapolis, trees located north of due west should branch nearly to the ground and also provide winter wind protection. Because of less severe winters in Atlanta, dense deciduous plantings or broadleaf evergreens may

be used instead of conifers. Trees planted 25 ft (7.6 m) from the structure should reach a minimum height of 30 ft (9.2 m) to provide adequate shade. Foundation plantings along the north- and west-facing walls also serve a dual purpose by providing wind protection and solar control.

Conclusions

Shade from trees, shrubs, and vines can significantly reduce temperatures inside protected structures and hence improve comfort and reduce space cooling costs during the overheated period. To maximize potential savings, designers should carefully consider when and where to shade. Improperly located vegetation may actually increase space heating costs by blocking solar access, and have relatively little effect on space cooling costs. Analysis techniques and design guidelines presented in this chapter, Appendix C, and Chapter Seven make it possible for designers to judiciously select and precisely locate vegetation both for solar control and for solar access. Finally, it should be emphasized that solar control is but one of many elements that comprise the planting design process. The energy-conscious designer's challenge lies in the skillful integration of this component with all others to create landscapes that are attractive, functional, energy conserving, and appropriate to their context and purpose.

Acknowledgment

Appreciation is extended to Gordon Heisler and Howard Wiig for their reviews and suggestions. Art work was done by David Socwell, Paul Sorey, and Lee Klopfer.

CHAPTER NINE
Planting Design for Wind Control

GORDON M. HEISLER
USDA Forest Service
University Park, Pennsylvania

MUCH research has been done on the use of trees and other vegetation for control of wind. However, most of this research was directed to the use of shelterbelts to improve crop microclimate or protect farmsteads, and only a small portion pertains directly to the problem of modifying wind to enhance livability or conserve energy in buildings typical of today's built environment. In studies evaluating windbreak effects on energy use, some difficulty always exists in extrapolating the results to other sites, climates, and buildings. In studies using wind tunnels or other models, a question remains of similarity with the full-scale environment. Nevertheless, we can piece together much information from existing studies that will be pertinent to landscape design for wind control to save energy, the main purpose of this chapter.

Energy savings by control of wind accrue primarily through reductions in wind-induced air infiltration, but also to some extent by reductions in convective heat transfer at building surfaces. Enhancement of cooling through breeze control may also lead to energy savings. This chapter proceeds from a brief discussion of heat transfer processes in buildings to basic mechanisms of windbreak effects on windflow and air temperature. With this as background, a section follows surveying some of the studies of windbreak effects on energy savings and breeze control. A brief discussion of methods of economic evaluation of windbreak energy savings and then other benefits leads naturally to recommendations for design of windbreaks, including evaluation of wind climatology, tree density and spacing, space requirements, and

species selection. Finally, two design examples are illustrated.

Tree windbreaks are primarily emphasized because most small buildings are constructed on nonforested sites. But much of the discussion pertains also to full forest cover or even to scattered trees because these affect microclimate similarly, although to a greater or lesser degree than windbreaks. Fences may also be used in the landscape to achieve effects similar to windbreaks, especially where space is limited.

Heat Transfer Processes Influenced by Wind

The transfer of heat into and out of a building takes place by one of the three basic heat transfer mechanisms — conduction, convection, and radiation, described in Chapter Four. Some further discussion of these processes as they pertain to buildings is useful for understanding wind effects on building energy use.

Heat Transmission

Heat is transmitted through a building structural assembly by a combination of the three basic heat transfer processes. Consider a frame house with an exterior wall composed of wall board, 2 x 4-in. (5.1 x 10.2-cm) studs with insulation between them, sheathing, sheathing paper, and an exterior siding material (Figure 9-1, see next page). Heat is transferred from other walls and objects in the room to the surface of the wallboard by radiation, and from the room air by convection to the thin boundary layer of still air adjacent to the surface, followed by conduc-

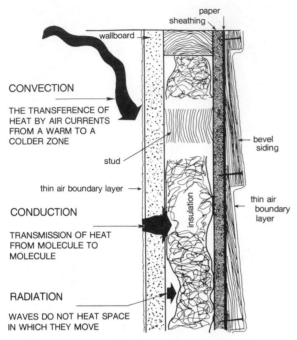

Figure 9-1. Cross section of a typical frame wall and modes of heat transmission. Adapted from: (Sherwood & Hans, 1979)

tion through the still air layer. Conduction carries heat through the wallboard. If there are gaps in the insulation, heat is transferred by radiation, and if the gaps are small, by conduction through still air. If the gaps are large, air warmed at the inside of the wallboard moves upward, that cooled by the sheathing moves downward, and these two flows may mix to greatly accelerate heat transfer through the wall. Heat transfer through sheathing, sheathing paper, and siding is by conduction. Through the studs from wallboard to sheathing, heat transfer is by conduction, and from the outer surface of the wall to the atmosphere, heat is transferred in the same manner as at the interior surface — by radiation, conduction, and convection (ASHRAE, 1977; Sherwood & Hans, 1979).

"U" and "R" values. Thermal transmittance (U) is the heat transmission per unit area expressed in Btu hr^{-1} ft^{-2} (or W m^{-2}) through a body or structure (such as a wall) and its thin boundary films of fluids (usually air) on each side, divided by the difference between the temperatures of the environments on either side of the body or structure. The effectiveness of insulation is commonly described by R, which is essentially the reciprocal of U, except that R does not include the boundary films. The R value of a typical wall as described above is about 12, and a conventionally insulated ceiling has an R of about 20.

Heat transfer through windows. Heat is transferred through windows into buildings as solar radiation (see

Chapter Eight) and into and out of buildings by conduction. The relatively great importance of heat loss or gain by conduction through windows is indicated by their low R values — only about 1.0 for a single pane and about 1.6 for double panes.

Wind effects on transmission heat loss. The U value of windows and walls includes a contribution for the thin surface boundary layer of still air. The thickness of this layer and the rate of heat convection at the outside of the layer depend partly on wind speed. For a reduction in wind speed from 15 mph (6.7 m sec^{-1} down to 5 mph (2.2 m sec^{-1}), U for insulated walls is decreased only about 1%. Hence, windbreaks have a relatively small effect on U values for walls. For windows, windbreaks have a greater effect. A reduction in wind speed from 15 to 5 mph would decrease effective U about 9% for double-pane windows and about 13% for single-pane windows (Figure 9-2).

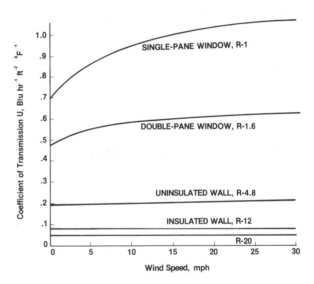

Figure 9-2. The effect of wind speed on coefficients of heat transmission for walls and windows.

Air Infiltration

Some flow of air into and out of houses is necessary for the health of occupants. However, especially in cold weather, the rate of this flow, or "infiltration," is far in excess of that required for ventilation, and large heat losses result. Air may infiltrate a building through cracks around doors and windows, directly through small pores in walls, through open doors or windows, or through other openings. Air infiltration is a response to pressure differences between inside and outside air, and infiltration increases as the pressure differences increase. The pressure differences are caused by wind or by air density differences, the latter due to temperature differences. The primary influence of windbreaks in reducing energy needs is by wind speed reductions and corresponding reductions in air infiltration.

Wind-induced air infiltration. In wind-induced air infiltration, air flows around or over a building creating regions in which wind pressure on the building exterior is above or below general atmospheric pressure, which is also the average pressure on interior surfaces. The distribution of air pressures on the walls of a model house in a wind tunnel (Figure 9-3) indicates a typical

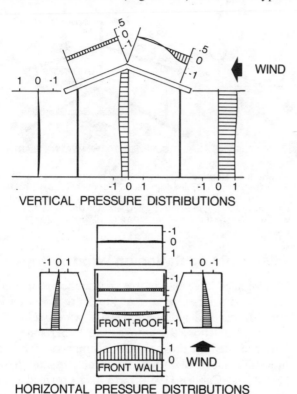

Figure 9-3. Pressure distribution (relative magnitude of pressure indicated by hatched area) on surface of test house in wind tunnel. Units (-1, 0, 1) depict magnitude of local pressure relative to average pressure over the model. From: (Buckley, Harrje, Knowlton, & Heisler, 1978)

distribution of inflow and outflow surfaces. Wind pressures are highly positive on the front wall, and nearly zero (the same inside and outside) on the lee wall. Air would tend to enter through the front wall and leave through side walls and the lee roof.

Although wind tunnel results graphically illustrate wind pressure over a house, the wind tunnel only approximates the real world. In particular, the initial flow was laminar in the wind tunnel from which Figure 9-3 was derived, whereas wind in the atmosphere is turbulent. In a real atmosphere, the pressure distributions and surfaces of exfiltration shift with changes in wind direction. More important, tur-

bulent fluctuations in wind speed cause corresponding fluctuations in pressure on exterior surfaces. These fluctuations could cause a pulsating flow through openings in the surfaces, but the role of turbulence in affecting air infiltration in buildings is complex and has only recently been addressed by engineering research (e.g., Blomsterberg & Harrje, 1979).

Temperature-induced air infiltration. Temperature-induced air infiltration is primarily effective in winter when warm air inside a building is relatively light and it rises and flows out of any openings in the upper levels of the building, while cold, dense outside air flows into the building through lower level openings. This is known as the "chimney" or "stack" effect in engineering literature. With temperature differences acting alone, a neutral pressure level exists where there is no pressure difference between inside and out (Figure 9-4). At other levels, the pressure difference

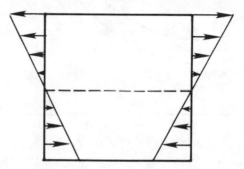

Warm interior, cold exterior, no wind

Figure 9-4. Idealized pressure-difference distribution (indicated by arrows) across the walls of a building (shown in section) due to inside-to-outside air temperature differences with cold outside temperatures. Adapted from: (Sinden, 1978)

depends on the distance from the neutral pressure level and the difference ($\triangle$T) between temperatures of inside and outside air (ASHRAE, 1977; Mattingly, Harrje, & Heisler, 1979). The rate of air infiltration in buildings is generally related in a linear way to $\triangle$T.

Wind and temperature together. Some experimental data suggest that when wind and temperature differences work together to cause air infiltration, the net result is not a simple addition of the two effects; nevertheless analysis of other data suggests that addition is sufficient to describe the net result (Hunt, 1980, summarizes research on this problem). Generally, wind-induced air infiltration is at least approximately proportional to the square of wind speed. The result of this is that at low wind speeds of a few miles per hour, doubling of wind speed will change the rate of infiltration only slightly, whereas at higher wind speeds, a doubling of wind speed increases air infiltration dramatically, and high rates of air infiltration are possible. Figure 9-5 illustrates additive wind and temperature effects on air infiltration in a mobile home.

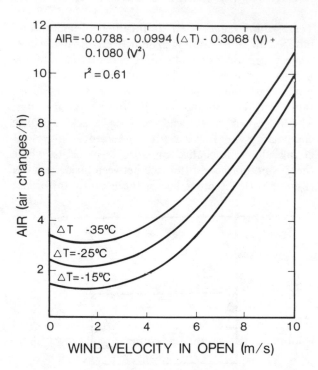

Figure 9-5. Relationship between winter air infiltration rate (AIR) in a mobile home and the wind velocity (V) and temperature differences (△ T) between inside and outside air. outside air. From: (DeWalle, Heisler, & Jacobs, 1983)

Relative importance of air infiltration heat loss. Some idea of the relative importance of heat transfer by air infiltration and conduction through different parts of a house envelope (external walls, roof, and windows) is indicated by estimated values for a reference house during a typical heating season in Madison, Wis. (Figure 9-6). Air infiltration averaged 33% of the total heat loss, and this is consistent with other "rule-of-thumb" estimates (Mattingly et al., 1979). On cold windy days, heat losses due to air infiltration may account for one-half or more of the total heat loss, and inside air may be exchanged with outside air at the rate of several changes per hour. Houses in windy climates and in exposed windy locations tend to have particularly high air infiltration rates. In these situations, windbreaks can be highly effective in saving energy. Within developments of closely spaced houses where considerable vegetation already exists, the effect of added windbreaks generally would be small.

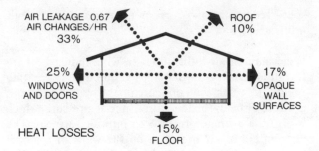

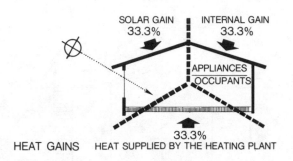

Figure 9-6. Heating season energy balance for a 6 Btu ft⁻² (Degree F day)⁻¹ (37.9 kilojoule m⁻² [degree C day]¹) house at Madison, Wis. Potential and internal gain factors are estimated assuming 100% use and 72F (22C) indoor design temperature, with double-glazed south windows at 10% of floor area. From: (Sherwood & Hans, 1979)

Effects of Vegetation on Wind

Windbreaks have fascinated researchers for many years, and a large volume of literature exists on the many direct and indirect effects of windbreaks. Van Eimern, Karschon, Razumova, and Robertson (1964) have provided the most complete summary of this vast literature, much of it in German or Russian. Jensen (1954) and Caborn (1957) have also provided extensive literature reviews and have reported on their own experimentation on windbreak effects. Beginning in 1941, Naegeli reported on a classical series of wind measurements (11 of Naegeli's papers, mostly in German, are cited by Van Eimern et al., 1964), which have provided basic data often referred to by others and used in reanalysis for evaluating aerodynamic effects of windbreaks. Read (1964) provides a good summary of the numerous reports on benefits, design, and methods of planting and maintenance of shelterbelts on the Great Plains. Plate (1971) has more recently evaluated findings on the aerodynamic effects of windbreaks.

Aerodynamic Action of Windbreaks

Windbreaks reduce average wind speed horizontally in three ways. First, they absorb some of the wind's energy by frictional drag as the moving air passes through and around them. Second, they deflect wind to higher levels (Figure 9-7). And third, windbreaks change relatively smooth, horizontally directed air

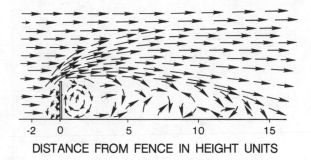

DISTANCE FROM FENCE IN HEIGHT UNITS

Figure 9-7. Idealized streamlines of air flow around and through a permeable fence. Adapted from: (Finney as cited by Van Eimern et al., 1964)

flow in random directions. That is, more turbulence is created. The degree to which these three processes work with windbreaks of various structures differs somewhat.

Windbreak Effects on Mean Wind

The effect of windbreaks in reducing average horizontal wind has been investigated in many studies (Van Eimern et al., 1964). Most have shown that the extent of windbreak protection is proportional to height. This may not be strictly true for very tall windbreaks, but proportionality is normally assumed and distance from the windbreak is often expressed in units of windbreak height (H) when windbreak effects are described.

Figure 9-8 illustrates wind measurement results for

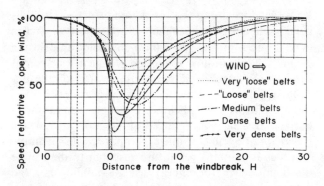

Figure 9-8. Average wind speed at shelterbelts of different degrees of permeability (Naegeli, 1946, cited in Caborn, 1957).

the condition of wind perpendicular to a long, narrow windbreak on a flat plane with no other nearby obstructions. A windbreak usually begins to exert a measurable influence on air flow between about 3 and 10 H from the upwind edge. Windspeed is sharply reduced near the windbreak, and a minimum is reached within 10 H of the downwind edge. Minimum

wind speed may be as low as 10% of open wind. Wind recovers gradually to the open speed and reaches it between 20 and 50 H downwind. For uniformly vertical windbreaks, this same pattern of reduction with distance generally applies at any height from near the ground to about 0.75 H.

Other important aspects of windbreaks affect mean flow. For many purposes, including assessment of effects on building energy use, the distance to which a windbreak reduces mean wind by an amount great enough to have practical significance — say 20% of open wind — is more important than the total distance over which a measurable reduction occurs. Another useful measure is the overall effectiveness of the windbreak. This can be evaluated as the sum or average of all reductions at 1-H intervals in the lee of the windbreak. Yet another and perhaps more useful measure for landscape design is the average wind reduction between the windbreak and 10 H downwind, that is, the average reduction at 10 points, 1 H, 2 H, etc., to 10 H (Heisler, Miller, & Toedter, In Preparation). This measure is closely related to overall windbreak effectiveness in reducing horizontal winds, is easily calculated from most existing data, is useful in describing the effectiveness of shorter windbreaks, and covers the zone of greatest reduction.

The size of the maximum reduction is closely related to windbreak density. An impermeable windbreak provides the largest maximum reduction in horizontal windspeed, with less dense windbreaks providing proportionately smaller maximum reductions. Figure 9-8 illustrates the finding of some research that the distance between the windbreak and the point of maximum reduction is small for very dense or impermeable windbreaks and for very porous ("loose") windbreaks, whereas for medium-density windbreaks, this distance is greatest.

Several wind tunnel studies (summarized by Van Eimern et al., 1964) suggest that windbreaks with medium geometric permeability of between 20% and 40% with many small openings produce the greatest overall reduction in horizontal wind. Geometric "permeability" is not particularly pertinent or measurable for tree windbreaks. For most vegetative windbreaks in leaf and with no large openings or spaces between plants, the maximum reduction is usually between 60% and 85%, and reductions greater than 20% occur to 15 or 20 H downwind.

The cross-sectional width-to-height ratio and the shape of the windbreak as a whole also may affect performance, though these factors are much less important than density. Several studies (Van Eimern et al., 1964) suggest that for windbreaks of equal overall density, wind speed in the lee of the windbreak recovers more quickly as the windbreak width increases. However, density and shape effects are difficult to separate because as windbreaks become wider they also become more dense overall.

Windbreak effectiveness is diminished as the incidence angle of the wind departs from the perpendicular. Although different studies have reached different conclusions as to the magnitude of the reduced effectiveness for particular wind angles (Seginer, 1975b), the reduction in distance over which winds are reduced by 20% or more ("protected distance") is approximately proportional to the cosine of the angle between the wind direction and a line perpendicular to the windbreak. Hence, winds at a 60° angle from the normal to a windbreak would have a protected distance of about one-half that of perpendicular winds.

Windbreak effectiveness is somewhat greater when the flow of approaching wind is relatively smooth than when the flow is turbulent. Turbulence causes greater mixing of air in the lee of the windbreak, and the downward flux of horizontal momentum is enhanced. That is, fast-moving air at higher levels is brought down to lower levels more quickly if the approach wind is more turbulent. Two factors that can increase turbulence of the approach wind are the roughness of the ground surface and atmospheric instability, which occurs on sunny days when the ground is heated and rising warm air creates turbulence. In one experiment with a 50% porous fence, the protected distance (distance with 20% or greater reduction) decreased from about 20 H when the ground surface was a smoothly harrowed field to about 15 H when the field was plowed (Seginer, 1975b). In another experiment with the same fence, protected distance decreased from about 22 H with a stable atmosphere to about 10 H with a very unstable, turbulent atmosphere (Seginer, 1975a).

When wind must flow through a constricted space, its velocity increases. Such constrictions created by large buildings lead to serious high-speed wind problems that may be alleviated with tree windbreaks (Durgin & Chock, 1980). If wind flows through gaps in windbreaks, velocity is also accelerated (Figure 9-9). Buildings downwind of the gap may have high air infiltration rates. If such a gap cannot be filled, it may be possible to plant new trees up- and downwind of the gap (Figure 9-10) to eliminate the problem. Designers should avoid creating unnecessary gaps in windbreaks.

Turbulence Behind Windbreaks

As previously noted, turbulence may affect both air infiltration and convective heat transfer. No definitive study of the relationship of turbulence intensity in the

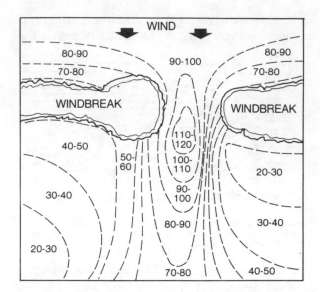

Figure 9-9. Wind is accelerated through a gap in a windbreak. Numbers indicate percentage of open wind. From: (Naegeli, cited by Caborn, 1957)

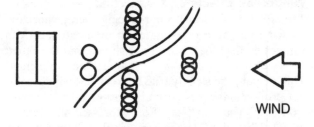

Figure 9-10. Possible solution to the problem of a driveway through a windbreak. Wind tunnel results showed the solution was highly successful. (Harrje, Buckley, & Heisler, 1982)

lee of windbreaks to that of the undisturbed flow has been made under full-scale conditions. Several studies (Van Eimern et al., 1964) have suggested that in the vicinity of maximum reduction in mean horizontal wind, turbulence is *increased* above that of the undisturbed flow. Another study (Gandemeer, 1979) has found that at 3 H behind a hedge, where mean horizontal wind was reduced about 50%, turbulence was *reduced* by 50% or more, compared with open turbulence. It remains for future research to determine the significance for energy use in buildings of the degree of turbulence and spatial distribution of turbulence behind windbreaks. DeWalle and Heisler (1983) have speculated that differences in turbulence may have accounted for the occurrence of maximum reductions in air infiltration in a mobile home at 1 H downwind of a windbreak, whereas the maximum reduction in mean horizontal wind was at 2 H.

Wind within Forests

Wind within forests is important because many homes are built on forested sites from which only a few trees

170

have been removed. In forests, wind is reduced much below wind in the open. Figure 9-11 provides measurements that directly compare wind in forests with wind in the open at the same level, and the relationship between forest and open winds can be inferred from the many measurements of vertical wind profiles in and above forests (Figure 9-12). The percentage of wind speed reduction by a forest, compared with the open, depends on the distance into the forest from the upwind edge (Figure 9-11), height above the ground, and stand structure and species composition. Some measurements of average wind speed in a mature deciduous forest (DeWalle et al., 1983) illustrate the difference between the leafless and in-leaf condition. At a point about 130 ft (40 m) into the stand from the edge facing the prevailing wind direction, average wind speed at the 6-ft (2-m) height was reduced about 40% below open wind speed in the winter, and about 62% in the summer. As Figure 9-11 indicates, wind reductions near the ground (at the 4.6-ft [1.4-m] height, in this case) are about 90% at locations well into dense forests.

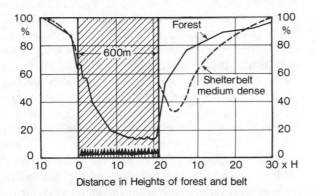

Figure 9-11. Relative wind speed upwind, within, and downwind of a coniferous forest (average height 92 ft [28 m]) compared to windspeed upwind and downwind of a medium-density tree belt. (Naegeli, 1954, as cited in Van Eimern et al., 1964)

Effects of Forests and Windbreaks on Temperature and Humidity

The effects of forests and windbreaks on air temperature and humidity are variable depending upon time of day, amount of cloudiness, available moisture in soil and groundcover, wind speed, and height above the ground. Air temperature differences between an open area and a forested or windbreak-protected zone are due to different degrees of mixing of air by turbulence, modifications in evaporation and transpiration, and effects of the vegetation on longwave and shortwave radiation.

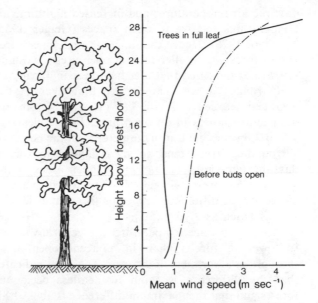

Figure 9-12. Wind profile within and above a deciduous forest. From: (Geiger, 1965)

Windbreaks

Within the area of greatest wind reductions near a windbreak, air temperatures may be about 5F (about 3C) warmer on clear days (Van Eimern et al., 1964; Woodruff, Read, & Chepil, 1959). On clear nights, most of the protected zone behind windbreaks is slightly cooler. The effect of evaporational cooling by the trees in a windbreak seems to be generally overridden by the air-mixing effects. That is, air cooled by a narrow windbreak is quickly mixed with the large volumes of air moving through the windbreak site, and hence the evaporational cooling is not usually significant on the site.

Because temperatures may either be cooler or warmer in the protected zone, the average effect on energy use is probably negligible in most instances. However, where vegetation is immediately adjacent to buildings, this may not be true because the ground and building surfaces are shaded and no strongly sun-heated surface provides heat to the air between the building and the vegetation. Because of the radiation reductions and possibly because of evaporational cooling, in summer we would expect cooler temperatures in this space, sometimes referred to as the "dead air zone." Parker (1981) has reported on experiments near Miami, Fla., in which surface temperatures of a mobile home shaded by adjacent shrubs were up to 24F (13C) cooler than surfaces without nearby shrubs, and air temperatures within the shrubs were as much as 13F (7C) cooler.

Forests

Forests are generally characterized by reduced

daytime air temperatures and increased nighttime air temperatures relative to open spaces (Geiger, 1965; Yoshino, 1975). Hence the range of air temperatures within forests is smaller than in open areas. Yoshino (1975) has indicated that a cedar forest in Japan had daily ranges in air temperature that over a year averaged between 1.8F and 3.6F (1C and 2C) smaller than temperatures in an open area. Forest clearings 1.5 to 2.0 times greater in diameter than the height of surrounding trees tend to have higher maximum daytime temperatures than either open areas or the surrounding forests. Geiger (1965) has cited an example where the difference between a forest and clearing was as much as 9.7F (5.5C).

Monthly average temperatures are generally slightly lower in forests than in adjacent open areas throughout all or most of the year. Table 9-1 indicates that the difference is small for leafless deciduous forests and that the maximum difference is about 1.8F (1C).

Table 9-1. Decrease in Mean Monthly Air Temperatures (°C) in Forests Compared to Open Areas

Forest	Jan.	April	July	Oct.	Annual Average
Deciduous	0.07	0.00	0.80	0.52	0.31
Conifers	0.67	0.73	0.78	1.02	0.85
Japanese Cedar	0.16	0.11	0.38	0.16	0.23

From: (Yoshino, 1975)

These temperature effects are seen in large forests rather than in small groves of trees. For buildings sited in or adjacent to large forests, the significance of the temperature effect would depend upon the climatic region and season of the year. Generally, the forest effects on radiation and wind would have a larger impact on energy use than the effects on air temperature.

Evaluations of Windbreak Energy Savings

Bates (1945a) seems to have been the first to evaluate the effect of windbreaks on energy use in buildings; he used 4 x 4-ft (1.2 x 1.2-m) test units as model houses. Harrje et al. (1982); Mattingly and Peters (1977); and Woodruff (1954) have used wind tunnel models to estimate windbreak effect on energy use for heating. Harrje et al., and Mattingly and Peters have also evaluated tree effects on the basis of an index of wind-

induced air infiltration derived from pressure distributions over the surface of model houses. Mobile homes have also been used as test units to evaluate forest and windbreak effects on energy use (DeWalle, 1980; DeWalle & Heisler, 1983; DeWalle et al., 1983). The only experimental evaluation of windbreak effects on air infiltration for full-scale buildings has been by Mattingly et al. (1979).

Flemer (1974) has compared fuel consumption in a New Jersey house before and after a white pine windbreak was installed. After the trees reached the height of the house, he reported an average winter fuel saving of 10% more than that before the windbreak. This seems to be the only published record of actual fuel savings from windbreaks planted near a full-sized house.

Estimated potential seasonal energy savings range from 3% for a townhouse (Mattingly et al., 1979) to 40% (Bates, 1945a). The 3% figure was probably unusually low because the windbreak, consisting of ten 25-ft (7.6-m) white pine trees, protected only one wall of the townhouse and that wall was already partly protected by a 5-ft (1.5-m) fence. The ten trees also would have saved energy in adjacent house units, but this was not measured. The 40% savings estimate is unusually high because it assumed a quite leaky house built in the 1930s located in the center of a grove of trees and thus protected on all sides from the high winds of the northern Great Plains. Probably more typical of actual potential savings in the majority of small buildings is the estimate by DeWalle et al. (1983) of a 12% seasonal savings with a single-row evergreen windbreak. For an average frame house, air infiltration (which accounts for most of the energy savings by windbreaks) produces about one-third of the winter heat loss. Hence, a 50% reduction in air infiltration — probably about the maximum possible with windbreaks on all sides — would lead to about a 17% heating fuel saving.

Economics of Windbreaks

To be more meaningful, estimates of savings must be converted to dollar values and compared to estimates of the cost of planting and maintaining the plant material over its life span. The most useful comparison is between the present value of future savings and maintenance versus the cost of installing the planting material. The present value of future savings can be computed from the discount formula: $PV = FV(1 + i)^{-n}$, where i is the interest rate. The present value (PV) of a monetary savings (FV) at some time n years in the future is defined as the amount of money that would have to be invested at the present time to earn the actual amount of the savings (FV) by the future (nth) year.

DeWalle (1980) estimated typical annual savings from a windbreak as 15% of the heating bill, or $158 per year, for a house at 45°N latitude (Maine). Using reasonable assumptions for 1978 economic conditions, allowing only five years for a windbreak to reach an effective height, and assuming 7% interest, he estimated that the present value of energy savings over a 20-year effective windbreak life was $1,192. This was less than the estimated $1,500 for planting a windbreak of 6.6-ft-tall (2-m), balled and burlapped coniferous trees. DeWalle concluded that an initial investment for smaller three- or four-year-old windbreak planting stock would be economical because of the smaller initial investment, even though benefits are received later than those from larger planting stock.

The results of economic analyses vary with the assumptions regarding future economic conditions. The monetary benefit of a windbreak depends on the relationship between the rate of increase or decrease in fuel cost (fuel escalation rate, FER) and the interest rate on alternative investments. The difficulty of arriving at appropriate assumptions for future fuel costs and interest rates has become apparent during the last decade. At present, it seems reasonable to guess that over the next two decades, fuel costs might escalate about as fast as the interest rate one might earn on investments, that is, FER will equal i.

With the assumption that FER = i, the fuel escalation cancels the effect of discounting future savings to the present time with the present value formula, and present value of savings in some future year is equal to the actual dollar savings at the future time. If we go back to DeWalle's example and assume equal interest and fuel escalation rates (and ignore changes in the value of the dollar due to inflation), the 1978 present value of the savings estimated by DeWalle would be increased from $1,192 to $2,370. Planting the larger trees for $1,500 would then be economically beneficial.

Economic analyses of windbreak benefits also can consider the change in windbreak effectiveness with growth of the trees. As an example, we might evaluate relative potential savings of planting trees of three different sizes for a windbreak to protect a one-story house with a present annual heating bill of $1,000. To begin, we estimate that a fully developed windbreak of 12 trees will save 15% of the energy used for heating. Table 9-2 gives the estimated cost for purchase and planting of 12 trees. Professional planting is assumed for the 5- and 10-ft (1.5- and 3-m) trees, but homeowner planting is assumed for the seedling-size trees. Maintenance cost is expected to be small relative to savings and is omitted for simplicity.

We might estimate the percentage savings over time as in Figure 9-13. For 18- to 24-in.-tall (0.46- to 0.61-m) seedlings, some years are required before they gradually become effective. In a wind tunnel study, Harrje et al. (1982) have found that an index of wind-induced air infiltration decreases about linearly with height of trees in a windbreak. Tests were run with models to represent trees between 15 and 40 ft (4.6 and 12.1 m) in height protecting a house 25 ft (7.6 m) tall. Figure 13 assumes a linear increase in tree height and in savings between 7 and 15 years after planting, and then a gradual tapering off of the increase in effectiveness until full effectiveness is reached at 15% in year 20. The curves assume that all three planting

Table 9-2. Estimated Savings over 20-year Life Cycle and Payback Time for Windbreaks of 12 Trees of Different Initial Size

Tree size at planting	Present value of fuel savings over 20 years	Estimated cost of planting	Present net value of 20-year windbreak investment	Discounted payback time, years
Assumption 1, fuel escalation rate = 0%, interest rate = 4%				
Seedling	$ 765	$ 60	$ 705	9
5-ft	1,295	780	515	14
10-ft	1,765	2,400	-635	20
Assumption 2, fuel escalation rate = interest rate				
Seedling	1,370	60	1,310	8
5-ft	2,110	780	1,306	15
10-ft	2,690	2,400	290	18
Assumption 3, fuel escalation rate = 8%, interest rate = 4%				
Seedling	2,453	60	2,393	8
5-ft	3,504	780	2,724	10
10-ft	4,258	2,400	1,858	14

sizes will have equal growth rates and that the seedlings would have grown to 5 ft (1.5 m) in 5 years and 10 ft (3 m) in 10 years. If energy savings are assumed to level off at 15% for all three sizes, the relative benefits can be evaluated over only the 20 years required for the seedlings to be fully effective. In future years, benefits are equal for the three sizes.

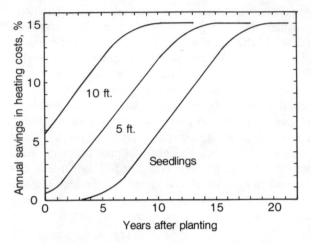

Figure 9-13. Estimated annual savings in heating costs with a windbreak protecting a conventional ranch-style house with trees planted as seedling, 5-ft-tall (1.5-m) and 10-ft-tall (3-m) conifers.

To evaluate trends in savings if fuel cost increases and interest rates differ, three sets of assumptions are used: (1) FER = 0%, i = 4%; (2) FER = i; and (3) FER = 8%, i = 4%. In this analysis, the inflation rate is assumed to be zero, so FER and i are real rates. A real interest rate of 4% is near the center of the range of pessimistic and optimistic forecasts. With assumption 2, FER and i would be any equal percentage above the inflation rate.

Except for the 10-ft (3-m) trees in assumption 1, the plantings all pay for themselves within 20 years. Shortest payback times and greatest net return on the investment (largest present net value) occur with assumption 3, in which FER exceeds i by the greatest amount. With all three assumptions, the seedlings pay for themselves in the shortest time. However, the largest net return in the long run occurs with 5-ft (1.5-m) trees under assumption 3. Energy saving is usually only one of several benefits of trees, and their planting and management is often well justified by the other benefits.

Vegetation for Enhancing Ventilation

Where natural ventilation rather than air conditioning is relied on for cooling of buildings during the overheated season, landscape designers should con-

sider the effect of tree arrangements on predominant summer breezes (Parker, 1983). Because the distribution of wind directions usually changes with the seasons (see Chapter Five), most of the winter winds may be blocked by windbreaks, whereas summer winds are not greatly interfered with or perhaps are even enhanced. It has been suggested (for example, Moffat & Schiler, 1981) that funnel-shaped tree arrangements might be used to "funnel" breezes toward a building, though this idea seems not to have been tested. Although wind speed may be increased through gaps in windbreaks (Figure 9-9), it is not clear that a funneling arrangement would have a net positive effect on ventilation, given the usual variations in wind direction and air turbulence.

Wind tunnel tests indicate that wind is accelerated beneath the crowns of trees that have branches pruned from the ground to part-way up the bole. This can be used to enhance ventilation if trees are close to open windows and pruned to just above window height (White, 1954). Thus, trees on the south side of a building, while providing only a small amount of shade in summer unless they overhang the roof, may potentially enhance ventilation by southern breezes.

Effect of Windbreaks on Snow Distribution

Depending upon their placement, windbreaks can be either a bane or benefit in affecting snow distribution. The most common design goal is to place windbreaks so they do not cause drifts that obstruct sidewalks and driveways. In some situations, windbreaks can be used as snow fences to catch blowing snow and deposit it out of the way. Because snow is deposited in the zones of low wind velocity and scoured away from zones of high velocity, drift patterns vary with windbreak density. As density decreases, drifts become wider and shallower. A formula by Bekker (cited in Caborn, 1957) has been suggested for computing drift patterns to the lee of windbreaks:

$$L = \frac{36 + 5H}{K}$$

The formula was derived for porous fences where L = length of the drift parallel to wind direction in feet, H = fence height in feet, and K = 1 for 50% fence densities and K = 1.28 for 70% densities. Bekker suggested that an extra 16 ft (about 5 m) be allowed for experimental error. This formula simply indicates the approximate extreme drift length and probably is not particularly useful for landscape design with tree windbreaks.

For moderately dense one-row conifer windbreaks, the major snow drifts will tend to be in a zone about 3 or 4 H wide bracketing the downwind point of maximum wind reduction. For one-row conifer windbreaks that are dense, particularly near the ground, snow will drift closer to the windbreak. With windbreaks of two, three, or more widely spaced rows of dense shrubs or conifer trees with branches down to the ground, a deep drift will form within or just to the lee of the windbreak, and with wider windbreaks the drift will not extend beyond the lee edge. Conversely, if a narrow windbreak has low density near the ground, drifts will be shallow, long, and centered far to the lee. Shrubs may be used to alleviate snow drift problems or to act as snow fences in many situations (Figure 9-14) because most blowing snow moves in a zone near the ground. Bates (1945b) and Robinette (1972) provide further discussion of snow control with vegetation.

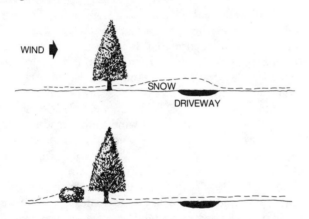

Figure 9-14. Shrubs used to modify snow drift patterns and improve the effectiveness of windbreaks in reducing wind speeds.

Other Benefits of Windbreaks

Noise Control
Wide windbreaks, (33 ft [10 m] or more) definitely reduce some noise from sources such as highway traffic. However, because of the many variables controlling propagation of sound outdoors, the value of only one or two tree rows in controlling noise is less certain. Certainly, narrow tree belts are less effective in noise control than well-constructed wood or concrete barriers. To be useful in noise control, plantings must be as dense as possible and must screen the noise source from view (see Cook, 1980; Heisler, 1977; Herrington, 1974; Reethof & Heisler, 1976).

Screening
Windbreaks and the function of visual screening are generally compatible. Some tree species useful for screens, in order of decreasing density according to Robinette (1972) are arborvitae, eastern hemlock, Douglas fir, white spruce, and white pine. Some of the hard pines, such as red pine, would be generally less optically dense than the species listed above. Although white pine is not the most dense, it is often the best screen tree because of its rapid growth. Recommended spacing for trees in screens is 1½ to 2 ft (0.46 to 0.61 m) (Robinette, 1972). These spacings would quickly provide a dense hedge for screening views at pedestrian height, but are closer than necessary for windbreak protection of buildings. Visual density of a row of screening trees is generally increased with the regrowth that occurs after side trimming as a hedge. Trimming also can be used to keep a tree row within bounds of the available space.

Wildlife
Windbreaks create favorable habitats for many species of wildlife enjoyed by homeowners, particularly birdlife. Windbreaks provide birds with food, cover, and nesting sites. Many homeowners enjoy backyard birdfeeders, and these are generally more successful with the wind protection and nearby cover afforded by windbreaks. The variety of birdlife increases with the number of vegetation strata available in the habitat (Gill, DeGraaf, & Thomas, 1974). Hence, windbreaks with several species that grow at different rates, together with a row of shrubs, will provide the best bird habitat. Desirable shrubs for northeastern wildlife are described by Gill & Healy (1974). Sources of further information on improving wildlife habitat include an article for homeowners, "Invite wildlife to your backyard" (Thomas, Brush, & DeGraaf, 1973), and books such as *The Backyard Bird Watcher* (Harrison, 1979) and *Songbirds in Your Garden* (Terres, 1953).

Air Purification
Many types of vegetation have the ability to purify air (Dochinger, 1980; Smith, 1980, Smith & Dochinger, 1976), but the effectiveness of vegetation for pollution control has not been well documented with field studies. Tree belts and windbreaks along roads remove dust and other particulates such as lead (Heichel & Hankin, 1977) by reducing windspeed and allowing suspended particles to fall in much the same way that snow is deposited in drifts, and by impaction of particles on the trees themselves. On a year-round basis, conifers are more effective than deciduous species in removing dust (Dochinger, 1980). McCurdy (1980) offers suggestions for design of greenbelts for control of pollution from highways. To be effective in

removing pollutants, trees obviously must be tolerant of the pollutants they absorb. A useful guide to pollution tolerance has been published by the USDA Forest Service (1973).

Design to Control Wind for Energy Conservation

Windbreak Location for Heat Energy Saving

Optimum windbreak location depends on the pattern of wind speeds and wind direction at the site, the house-to-windbreak distance for minimizing air infiltration and convective heat loss, and the maintenance of solar access.

Wind climatology. The most important place to locate windbreaks for heat energy saving is upwind from the building in the direction of the highest frequency of strong winter winds. For much of the U.S., this is the west and northwest. However, winds vary from city to city and region to region. Local topography and structures can channel winds so that the wind distribution at a particular site may differ from the regional trend (see Chapter Five). The distribution of winds greater than about 7 mph (6 knots or 3 m sec⁻¹) is of most consequence for windbreak planning. Where possible, complete wind distributions averaged over a number of years (see Chapter Five) should be used in site planning.

Windbreak length. Generally, heat loss reduction with a windbreak increases as the length of the windbreak is increased to protect a longer perimeter of the building, or to protect the building from winds from a wider range of directins. But wind tunnel tests (Harrje et al., 1982) suggest that even one or two conifers may provide savings for an otherwise exposed house.

Maintaining solar access. Maintenance of solar access is an important consideration in windbreak placement and in management of existing trees on a site. Where windbreaks are indicated for the south side of a house because prevailing winter winds are from that direction, the windbreak must be quite far from the house to avoid shade and loss of solar heat in winter (Figure 9-15). At 40⁰ latitude, trees taller than about one-half of the distance between the tree and the house provide significant shade during large portions of the heating season. At 50⁰ latitude, the same is true for trees taller than one-third the distance between the tree and house. Hence, for houses with large windows on the south that could provide solar heat, windbreaks in that direction may be inefficient. Although east and west windows are less important for solar input than south-

facing windows, there is still a significant potential for obtaining solar heat during the heating season through windows on these walls.

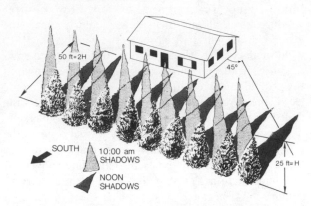

Figure 9-15. Shadows of a windbreak on the south side of a house at 40⁰ latitude on Dec. 21. Tree height is one-half of the tree-to-house distance.

House-to-windbreak distance. The optimum distance for reducing air infiltration and convective heat loss often has been considered the distance between a windbreak and the point of maximum reduction in windspeed — frequently taken as 3 H to 7 H for moderately dense windbreaks. Studies of mean pressure distributions on a house model (Harrje et al., 1982) with laminar flow in a wind tunnel tend to also indicate that 3 H to 7 H is optimum for house-to-windbreak distance. However, other studies indicate closer house-to-windbreak distances are optimum. Woodruff's (1954) wind tunnel study, in which turbulent flow and actual heat loss in a house model were simulated, showed maximum heat energy use reductions at 2 H behind a 10-row windbreak. A study by DeWalle and Heisler (1983) suggests that maximum heat energy and air-infiltration reductions in a mobile home occur at 1 H behind a one-row white pine windbreak, though maximum windspeed reductions are at 2 H in the lee of the windbreak.

To maximize the long-term effectiveness of windbreaks at latitudes between 35⁰ and 50⁰, east or west windbreaks should be planted about 50 ft (15 m) from a house where possible. Windbreaks grow to a partially effective height long before reaching their mature height. At 50 ft (15 m) from a house a windbreak will begin to be effective when it is 5- to 10-ft (1.5- to 3-m) tall, but it will not shade east or west walls until becoming much taller. Windbreaks on the north side of a building will not interfere with solar access, and they can be effective when planted close to the building. For home sites where drifting snow is a problem, such as in wide-open spaces in the Plains states, windbreaks should be farther from buildings to ensure that snow is not deposited around the buildings (Read, 1964).

Species Selection for Windbreaks

The choice of plant species for wind control should include not only the effectiveness in controlling wind, but also a host of other tree characteristics that include growth rate, insect and disease resistance, maintenance considerations, ornamental features, and tree life span. These factors and more are highlighted in a valuable reference, Dirr's *Manual of Woody Landscape Plants* (1977). Foster (1978) has useful plant lists for various purposes including windbreaks.

There is no perfect species for windbreaks and certainly no one species is best for every situation. Essentially all coniferous species can provide effective wind protection. The ideal species would be fast growing, visually dense, and have stiff branches that do not self-prune readily. Species tolerant of shade, such as hemlock and most species of spruce, usually are dense and slow to self-prune. Most pines are less dense and self-prune more readily. White pine is intermediate in shade tolerance, density, and tendency to self-prune. Unfortunately, most shade-tolerant species tend to be slow-growing.

Colorado spruce is probably the best of all species for dense, stiff branches. In wind tunnel tests with four species, spruce offered the most wind resistance followed by Scotch pine and Douglas fir, which were about equal, and western hemlock, which offered substantially less resistance (Raymer, 1962). Hemlock crowns are dense, but the thin, flexible branches "streamline" in the wind, thus reducing resistance. Based on density and branch stiffness, white spruce should be nearly as effective as Colorado spruce, and Norway spruce just a bit less effective than white spruce. Nevertheless, Norway spruce may be the best spruce to plant for windbreaks because it is faster growing than white or Colorado spruce. White pine also ranks highly as a windbreak tree because although it is not quite as dense and stiff as the spruces, it is the fastest-growing conifer over much of the country. After a species is selected, fast-growing varieties or cultivars of that species should be sought.

Coniferous trees are generally far more effective than leafless deciduous trees as windbreaks, but leafless deciduous trees do provide good wind protection in some circumstances. Dense deciduous trees in leaf may reduce wind about as effectively as conifers, but when leaves fall, deciduous trees lose about 50% of their effectiveness. Single rows of leafless deciduous species planted 1 ft (0.3 m) apart and pruned as hedges have provided wind reductions comparable to reductions by coniferous windbreaks (Sturrock, 1969), but it may be difficult to achieve such reductions with deciduous windbreaks sufficiently tall to fully protect buildings. Fast-growing deciduous species, such as hybrid poplars, may be planted close together in a row adjacent to conifer rows to form a visual screen quickly and provide a bit of extra wind protection in winter. The poplars can be removed as the conifers mature. Quite substantial winter wind reduction may be possible with multiple wide-spaced rows of hybrid poplars planted close together (less than a meter apart) in the row, though I know of no test of such an arrangement.

Species should be fitted to soil and other site features. For example, spruces are generally better for shallow soils or poorly drained sites because of their shallow, wide-spreading root systems. The pines are superior for sandy soils. Hemlock may be grown successfully in partial shade. White pine is subject to "wind burn" on exposed sites until it becomes established, and may initially need some wind protection itself. Arborvitae is especially subject to damage from strong winds, ice, and snow. Spruce and fir are generally resistant to damage from heavy snow, but are prone to stem breakage or uprooting in heavy winds. On windy sites, larger size planting stock must be guyed until roots have developed sufficiently.

Another consideration is insect and disease resistance. For example, gall aphids may be a serious problem with spruces. Spraying and pruning can eliminate, or at least alleviate, the problem, but this requires conscientious maintenance. White pines can be killed by blister rust, and white pine weevil may also attack this species, resulting in deformity and reduced height growth.

Planting Arrangement

In most residential situations, space will limit windbreaks to narrow strips — one or two rows of trees. Close spacing will speed development of windbreak effectiveness. A spacing of 6 ft (2 m) on center or even closer can be used for pines, spruces, and fir; and 3 or 4 ft (1 m) can be used for columnar species such as arborvitae. At close spacing, crowns will close together more quickly than when trees are planted at wider spacings, and full effectiveness will be reached sooner. Height growth of trees in single-row windbreaks is not reduced at close spacings and in fact may be enhanced somewhat (Van Haverbeke, 1977).

Where there is sufficient space, a second row of trees should be added. Again if there is sufficient space, the distance between rows may be made much wider than the spacing between trees to enhance windbreak effectiveness. The larger space will reduce competition of lower inside branches for light. These branches will be retained longer to assist in blocking wind. A spacing of 10 to 12 ft (3 to 4 m) between rows is about right for pine, spruce, and fir (Figure 9-16). With only one or two tree rows, creating an excessively dense windbreak need not be of much concern.

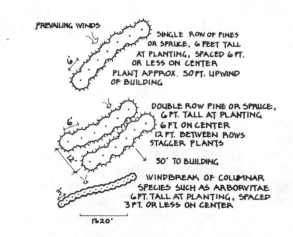

Figure 9-16. Suggested spacing of trees within windbreaks.

If space is insufficient for wide spacing between rows, two rows will still be more effective than one. Staggering the trees in the rows will increase effectiveness in reducing winds at right angles to the windbreak. Where space is just barely sufficient for a row of narrow trees, a windbreak design may include plans for side pruning the trees to create a tall hedge. Soon after a light pruning, regrowth will restore or even enhance wind reduction effectiveness. Most species will endure or benefit from pruning, but hemlock is especially adaptable to pruning.

Planting in distinct rows of single species need not be adhered to strictly. A more free-form grouping or naturalistic arrangement will be equally effective if there are no gaps in the arrangement. A mixture of species is often visually more appropriate, and will also avoid the risk of high susceptibility to insects and diseases associated with monocultures.

In the planting design process, extra consideration should be given to growth-promoting features, since rapid height growth of tree windbreaks will enhance their economic benefit. Especially important is soil moisture control. This may be accomplished by a wide, mulched bed or a tilled area around the trees. On some sites it may be possible and desirable to increase soil moisture by diverting run-off water from roofs or parking lots to the windbreak trees. Drip irrigation systems are especially appropriate for windbreak trees because water is applied directly to

the trees' root zone and not to surrounding weeds. This may reduce the need for weed control and improve plant establishment and survival rates.

Design Examples

Two design examples will illustrate the application of design for wind control. For other design examples, see Center for Landscape Architectural Education and Research (1978), Moffat & Schiler (1981), and Robinette (1977).

Single Residence

As an example of the principles of wind control, the following describes a design for wind control for an existing one-story house on a square-shaped half-acre lot in northeastern New Jersey (Figure 9-17, see next page). The house is on the north side of an east-west street. The owners wish to have play, garden, and patio areas behind the house. Other houses are to the west, north, and east, and screening views from the backyard in these directions is desirable. Existing plantings are limited to several specimen trees on the front lawn and low shrubs along the foundation on the south. Adjacent lots have only sparse landscaping that provides little wind reduction.

The house was built in the 1960s, before energy conservation became an important consideration in residential construction. On the north, floor-to-ceiling windows and a sliding-glass door facing the patio allow high rates of heat loss. Although steps have been taken to control energy use by tightening the house and adding insulation, space-conditioning costs remain high. The owners have been easily persuaded to incorporate energy-conserving features into new landscape plantings which they have decided to install to provide visual screening and a more visually pleasing home. The cost of the new plantings will be at least partly repaid as energy savings accrue. Both heat energy and cooling energy savings are also of interest.

The first planning step is to evaluate the wind regime. We can use average wind data from the Newark airport, which is about 15 miles away in a similar topographic setting (U.S. Weather Bureau, 1962). January and July may be used as design dates for the heating and cooling season. Table 9-3 (see page 180) shows the wind direction frequency distributions for these months. In winter, we should particularly provide protection from the high-speed winds out of the northwest. In summer, winds from the southeast are most common, and keeping this direction unobstructed should be a design goal. Had wind control been considered in the original design, the garage

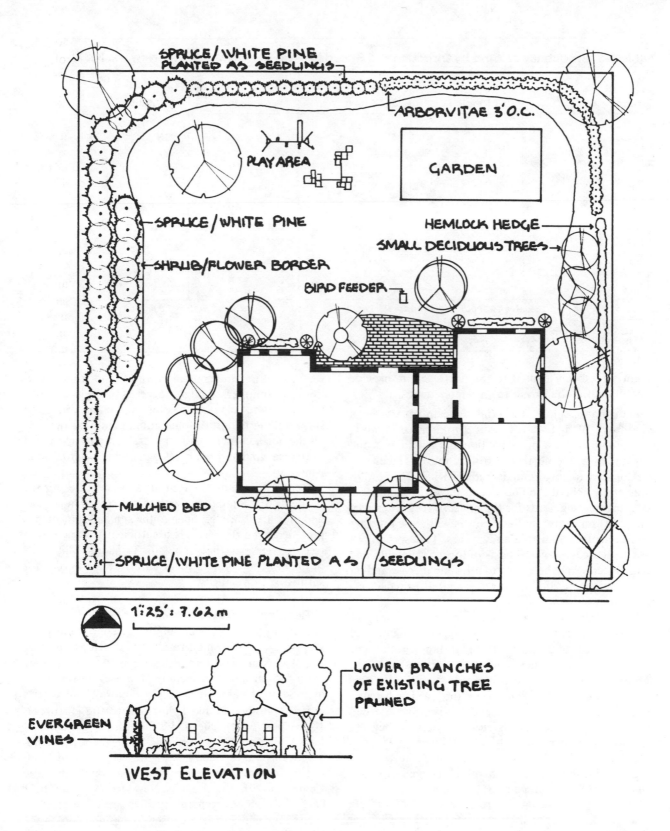

SPRUCE/WHITE PINE
PLANTED AS SEEDLINGS

ARBORVITAE 3' O.C.

PLAY AREA

GARDEN

SPRUCE/WHITE PINE

HEMLOCK HEDGE

SMALL DECIDUOUS TREES

SHRUB/FLOWER BORDER

BIRD FEEDER

MULCHED BED

SPRUCE/WHITE PINE PLANTED AS SEEDLINGS

1":25': 7.62 m

LOWER BRANCHES
OF EXISTING TREE
PRUNED

EVERGREEN
VINES

WEST ELEVATION

Figure 9-17. An energy-saving landscape design for a one-story house on a half-acre (0.2-ha) lot in New Jersey. (Trees shown as they would appear about 5 to 10 years after planting)

179

Table 9-3. Frequency of Wind by Direction and Speed for Two Design Months for Newark, N.J.[a]

Wind direction	January		July	
	0-7.5 mph	> 7.5 mph	0-7.5 mph	> 7.5 mph
N	**[b]	****	*	**
NNE	**	*******	**	****
NE	***	***	*	****
ENE	*	**	*	**
E	**	*	**	*
ESE	*	*	*	**
SE		*		**
SSE	*	*	**	*****
S	*	**	**	****
SSW	***	***	****	********
SW	******	***	********	******
WSW	****	****	****	*****
W	**	******	***	***
WNW	*	************	*	******
NW	*	***********	*	*****
NNW	*	*********	*	****
CALM	*		**	
	Mean speed = 11.1 mph = 9.6 knots		*Mean speed = 8.8 mph = 7.6 knots*	

aBased on 10-year data, 1951-1960, from U.S. Weather Bureau (1962).
bEach asterisk = 1% of time.

might have been located to the northwest to provide protection for the house from winter winds.

The major plant material investment is in a windbreak of 5- to 6-ft (about 2-m) spruce or white pine along the west property boundary with a second row added to the northwest of the house. These trees are located to immediately reduce wind for the outdoor areas behind the house, and they will soon begin reducing heating needs for the house. Trees are spaced 6 ft (2 m) on center so that crowns will close together for full protection within a few years. Tree species can be selected partly on the basis of local availability and cost. Species may be mixed to alleviate disease and insect problems of monoculture, as well as to reduce esthetic monotony.

To complete the screening and wind protection, we use 18- to 24-in.-tall (.46- to .51-m) planting material to reduce cost of planting. The planting of white pine or spruce is extended to the south and east with the smaller stock. Columnar arborvitae spaced 3 ft (1 m) on center are used adjacent to the garden because space is limited. These will eventually provide excellent wind protection and screening, though they are not fast-growing. Along the east boundary, space is also limited and there is competition from a shade tree. Here a shade-tolerant hemlock hedge is used for wind control and screening.

Trees for solar control are placed in appropriate locations around the house as suggested in Chapter Eight. Existing shrubs along the south border of the house are pruned low each fall to maintain solar access in winter. Shrubs are planted along the east and

west to aid in wind control in winter and solar reductions in summer, though there is a trade-off here because some solar input is lost in winter. Evergreen shrubs along the north foundation, columnar conifers on the north corners, and an evergreen vine are added to reduce wind and not block significant solar input in winter.

Generally, the different needs and amenities for the residents are compatable with this design. The garden and play areas are left open to the sun and screening is provided. The driveway is a sufficient distance from tree barriers so that snow drifts should not be a problem. The conifers form an attractive border for shrubs or flower beds.

A Residential Development

We are asked to provide an energy-conserving landscape design for a small residential development near Topeka, Kan. The infrastructure is already decided upon — a group of conventional houses on small lots along a road paralleling a busy highway that carries mostly automobile and light-truck traffic (Figure 9-18, see next page). The land is flat, former agricultural land with no nearby obstacles to obstruct the wind. Topeka averages 5,200 heating degree days and 1,260 cooling degree days per year (National Climatic Center, 1979), thus, as in New Jersey, both heat energy and cooling energy savings are of interest.

January and July are chosen as design months for wind control (Table 9-4). In January, wind speeds and frequencies are rather evenly distributed around the compass. Winds directly from the north and directly

180

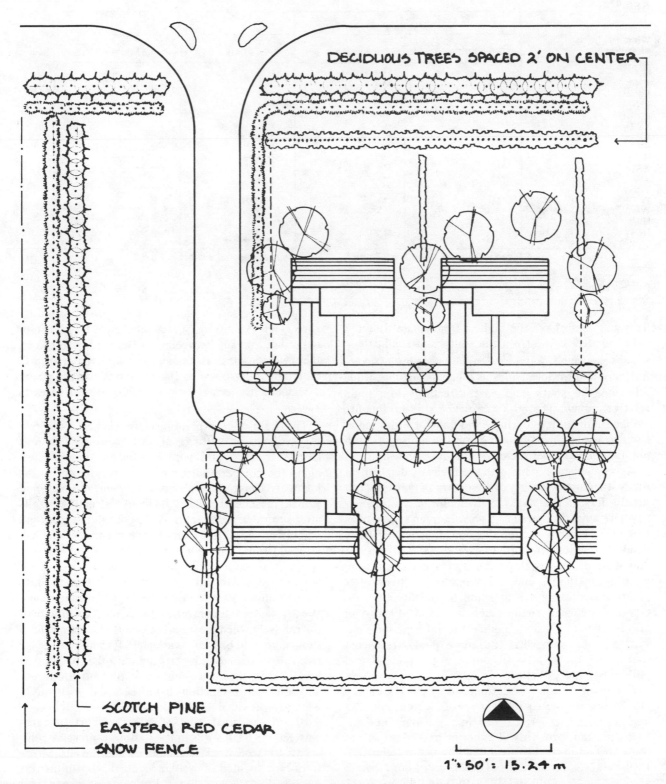

DECIDUOUS TREES SPACED 2' ON CENTER

SCOTCH PINE
EASTERN RED CEDAR
SNOW FENCE

1" = 50' = 15.24 m

Figure 9-18. An energy-saving landscape design for a residential development near Topeka, Kan. (Trees shown as they would appear about 5 to 10 years after planting.)

181

Table 9-4. Frequency of Wind by Direction and Speed for Two Design Months for Topeka, Kan.[a]

Wind direction	January		July	
	0-6.5 knots	> 6.5 knots	0-6.5 knots	> 6.5 knots
N	***b	***********	***	****
NNE	*	***	*	**
NE	*	***	***	*
ENE	**	**	***	**
E	***	***	******	***
ESE	**	**	***	**
SE	**	**	***	***
SSE	*	**	**	****
S	***	********	*******	***************
SSW	**	******	**	*******
SW	***	***	**	**
WSW	*	*	*	*
W	**	***	*	*
WNW	**	****	*	*
NW	**	******	*	*
NNW	*	******	*	*
CALM	*******		************	
	Mean speed = 8.4 knots = 9.7mph		*Mean speed = 6.8 knots = 7.8 mph*	

aBased on 10-year data, 1965-1974, from National Climatic Center (1979).
bEach asterisk = 1% of time.

from the south have the highest frequencies. In July, winds tend to come from the south and southeast.

A year-round balance is achieved by blocking northern and western winds as much as possible, while allowing the south and east directions to remain relatively open. The 80 x 125-ft (24 x 38-m) lots are rather small to develop full wind control with vegetation, so we augment plantings on the house lots with plantings on the perimeter of the development.

Agreements are made with the highway department for a staggered planting of two rows of 4-ft-tall (1.2-m) conifers on the 50-ft (15-m) highway right-of-way to abate noise and serve as a visual screen. These trees will also serve to shelter the houses from northerly winds. These plantings are to extend 200 ft (61 m) east and west of the development. For species selection, planting methods, and maintenance of trees after planting, we can refer to some of the literature on Great Plain shelterbelts (such as Read, 1964; Van Haverbeke, 1977) and modify the information considering our somewhat different goals, restricted space, the high value of our "crop" (people and buildings), and esthetics.

Following recommendations of Van Haverbeke (1977), we decide to use a row of Scotch pine and another of eastern red cedar in these plantings anticipating that growth will equal or exceed growth of these species in tests of field windbreaks in Nebraska. In those tests, three-year-old seedlings of both species grew to between 13 and 14 ft (4.0 and 4.3 m) in 12 years after planting. Spacing between the trees within

rows is 6 ft (1.8 m) for Scotch pine and 4 ft (1.2 m) for red cedar. Spacing between the rows is 12 ft(3.7 m), so they will develop as single rows and the trees will maintain full crowns to the ground for many years. The space between rows will be mowed during early years.

The right-of-way plantings are backed by a row of seedlings or cuttings of fast-growing deciduous trees such as hybrid poplar, willows, or green ash along the northern border of the lots adjacent to the highway. These are spaced at 2-ft (.6-m) intervals and will be pleached so that a hedgelike structure results after several growing seasons. The deciduous trees will quickly provide a full visual screen in summer and will also add some winter wind protection.

For protection from westerly winds, a row of eastern red cedar and a row of Scotch pine are also planted about 60 ft (18 m) west of the entrance road. We are somewhat concerned about snow drifting onto the roadway when the trees are taller. During winter, a snow fence will be located about 15 ft (5 m) west of the tree row to reduce snow drifting onto the road and to form a drift that will supply moisture for the trees.

Additional protection from easterly or westerly winds is provided by tall hedges between the back yards of the north row of houses. Shorter hedges between the back yards in the south row preserve solar access to large areas of glazing on south walls. Shade trees are located for solar control in summer as described in Chapter Eight. For example, shade trees on the north side of the street through the development are selected from species that will be small sized at maturity so that solar access to houses on the north side of the street will not be impeded. Groundcover and shrubs are used to add greater interest to the primarily functional plantings shown in Figure 9-18.

Summary

High wind speeds increase air infiltration rates and also to some extent increase convective heat transfer at building surfaces, thus leading to large amounts of energy use for heating buildings. For buildings of conventional construction, total air infiltration may account for about one-third of the total heat load, though much of the infiltration may be due to the temperature difference between inside and outside air. Temperature-induced air infiltration increases approximately linearly with the inside-to-outside temperature difference, but wind-induced air infiltration increases approximately in proportion to the square of wind speed.

Windbreaks of one or two rows of closely spaced coniferous trees generally produce medium-density windbreaks with maximum reductions of 60% to 75% at about two to four tree heights to the lee of the windbreak, and with reductions of 20% or more extending to 15 or 20 tree heights downwind and up to a height of about 75% of the height of the windbreak. Very dense or solid wind barriers produce larger reductions in horizontal wind speed, though these reductions occur over a shorter distance and more turbulence is produced than when wind barriers are of medium density.

Hence, windbreaks may greatly reduce air infiltration in locations that would be otherwise exposed. Estimates of potential energy savings by tree windbreaks range as high as 40% of total energy use, although 10% to 15% is probably a more realistic estimate of potential energy savings for houses with conventional construction.

In designing windbreaks or in placing buildings in relation to existing wind barriers on the site, the average distribution of wind speeds and directions throughout the heating and cooling seasons should be considered. Windbreaks should be perpendicular to the direction of high-speed winds, and should be upwind from the building in the direction of stronger winter winds, usually west or northwest in the U.S.

Even short windbreaks may be effective, though savings generally increase with protection from a greater range of directions.

For maximizing effectiveness over the life of a tree windbreak to be planted on the east or west sides of a building, a good windbreak-to-building distance is about 50 ft (15 m). Windbreaks on the north side of a building will not interfere with solar access, and they can be effective when close to the building. For buildings with large windows on the south that could accept solar heat, windbreaks should be a sufficient distance so that these apertures are not shaded.

Tree windbreaks are more effective when they are tall and relatively dense. While species such as Colorado spruce produce excellent barriers once they reach sufficient size, less dense but faster-growing species such as Norway spruce or many of the pines may be more cost effective. Species may be mixed to improve esthetic interest. Trees can be closely spaced within the rows; 6 ft (1.8 m) on center or even less. If more than one row is used, the spacing between rows should be greater than that between trees. When energy savings are balanced against cost of planting, net returns over many years may be greater when large-size trees are planted, though payback times may be shorter when small-size trees are planted.

Windbreaks may serve a number of other functions in the landscape including screening, snow drift control, enhancement of wildlife habitat, directing summer breezes, moderating wind for outdoor human comfort, reducing noise, and purifying air. Landscape design using windbreaks not only should consider energy conservation, but also should integrate the other functional and esthetic benefits. Especially when the other benefits are added to energy savings, windbreaks for exposed sites in temperate to cool climates generally become a very attractive investment.

Acknowledgments

Lee Herrington, Greg McPherson, and David R. Miller (Associate Professor and Extension Forester, University of Connecticut) reviewed the manuscript and made many helpful suggestions. David Gansner and Owen Herrick of the Northeastern Forest Experiment Station made suggestions for the section on economics of windbreaks.

CHAPTER TEN
Water-Conserving Landscape Design

ROBERT L. THAYER, JR., ASLA
THOMAS RICHMAN
University of California, Davis
Davis, California

Waste not, want not, is a maxim I would teach,

Let your watchword be dispatch, and practice what you preach;

Do not let your chances like sunbeams pass you by,

For you never miss the water till the well runs dry.

— Rowland Howard, 1876

OBSERVING the rapid population movement to the southern and western "sun-belt" states, some modern historians have suggested that if America had been settled from west to east, instead of east to west, we would not be the nation of sun worshippers we are. Migrating across the great western deserts and dry plains, our ancestors, had they come from the west coast toward the east, would have screamed "hallelujah" at the sight of rain and humid environments. They would have developed a deep cultural sense of water as a precious resource, and would have filled the landscape with systems and images which reflected this preciousness. The individual and national consciousness would be keenly aware of the necessity of water for life, and people would use it wisely, as if their lives depended on it. Because the culture would have rooted in a region of limited water supply, traditions of efficient water use would be inbred. Even after these hypothetical pioneers had reached the last frontier in Maine or Georgia, joyously celebrating the plentiful water supply in the promised land, they would still understand the importance of water management as a facet of a balanced relationship with the earth.

As it happened, however, the founders of this country arrived from a humid European homeland and disembarked from their tall-masted ships in the humid eastern portions of the expansive New World. They brought with them cultural images and preferences concerning water use which were easily adapted to the new home. Clean, fresh water was plentiful and there was plenty of energy to manipulate it to serve society's needs. Thus, along with the birth of America was born a cultural attitude and tradition of water as a limitless resource, the exploitation of which being only limited by the peoples' ingenuity and efforts.

So rivers became thoroughfares for commerce and depositories of waste products. Dams were erected to control their flow, prevent flooding, store water, and generate power. Deep shafts were punctured into the earth so that water lying beneath the surface could be extracted and put to use. Huge channels were cut to redirect the meandering course of rivers, to straighten them, and in some cases, even to reverse their direction of flow. As time went by, water was manipulated to carry waste products directly from the house or business into sewers and then to rivers or oceans. The expansion of cheap energy sources enabled people to find new ways of enjoying larger and larger quantities of water: for personal hygiene, for expression of social status, for domestic chores, for pleasure. The citizens dreamed and struggled to acquire a house surrounded by lush landscapes, with swimming pools and fountains. They discovered it was easier to hose down the driveway, using hundreds of gallons of cheap water, than it was to get out a broom. If by chance the area in which they chose to live did not supply the requisite water, they undertook monumental engineering challenges, building aqueducts to carry water hundreds of miles so they could make the desert green and grassy, thus perpetuating their cultural tradition.

All of this activity left its mark upon the land. Furthermore, it generated patterns of living that required vast expenditures of both water and energy. The cultural attitudes developed over time remain today as motives for society's use of water. Yet, the situation today is different from what is once was. Lanscape architects, as the professionals with primary responsibility for land and resource planning and management, must understand water: Its uses, its sources, its symbolic value, its limitations.

This chapter will explore the importance of water as an element of the landscape. The correspondence of water and energy use will be demonstrated and it will be shown that saving water also saves energy. With this connection established, the focus will shift to residential and community water use, stressing the significance of water in the landscape. A brief discussion of plant materials appropriate for water-conserving landscapes will be included. Moving from the technical to the conceptual, the chapter will examine the attitudes, perceptions, and images that act to fashion the "ideal landscape." Finally, specific tools for the design of water-conserving landscapes will be developed, and three scenarios, ranging in degree of innovation, will be offered to suggest ways by which designers and planners can contribute to the conservation of a precious resource and the creation of a new cultural tradition, more appropriate and satisfying for the times.

The National Water Crisis

Present trends in water use indicate conclusively that Americans must adjust their attitudes and policies if they are to avoid a shortage of both water quality and quantity in the near future. Recent cover articles in popular magazines such as *Forbes* (1979) and *Newsweek* (1981) attest to the growing awareness that, like the energy crisis of the present, water looms as the next critical commodity in which demand will exceed supply, unless present circumstances are altered.

Groundwater

Society uses two basic sources of water. The first is above-ground water stored in lakes, rivers, snowpacks, and reservoirs. This water also seeps into the soil and is stored in large underground lakes or aquifers, the second source of water. This underground water supply accumulates over centuries, remaining pure and clean in realtively sterile underground pools. The groundwater of the United States is a vast resource with an estimated volume far greater than all of the nation's lakes and reservoirs, a volume equivalent to about 35 years of surface run-off nationwide (U.S. Water Resources Council, 1978). America's use of water so greatly exceeds its above-ground supply that a full one-quarter of its annual water is taken from underground wells, about 82 billion gallons each day. This withdrawal exceeds the rate of recharge by 21 billion gallons per day, thus diminishing the supply of this high-quality underground water source (*Newsweek,* 1981). The U.S. Water Resources Council warned in 1978 that "diminishing artesian pressure, declining spring and streamflow, land subsidence, and salt-water intrusion all indicate long-term excessive use of ground waters." The Council identified problem areas in every region of the nation, including the Gila River Basin (Arizona and New Mexico), the High Plains of the central states, the San Joaquin Valley of California, the Susquehanna River Basin, Southeast Georgia, the Houston-Galveston area, and the island of Oahu, Hawaii (Figure 10-1). Some experts predict that if present trends continue, the largest of these underground aquifers, the Ogallala of the High Plains, will be exhausted by the turn of the century (*Forbes,* 1979).

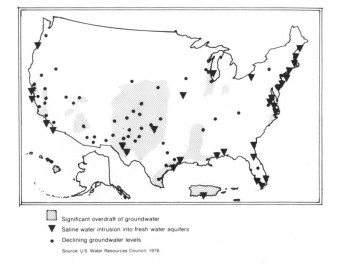

Significant overdraft of groundwater
▼ Saline water intrusion into fresh water aquifers
• Declining groundwater levels
Source: U.S. Water Resources Council, 1976

Figure 10-1. Areas of U.S. groundwater problems.

Besides causing potential water shortages, this withdrawal of underground water creates large airspaces in areas once filled with water. The land resting on these depleted underground lakes often subsides as the weight of the land is no longer supported by water. For example, land within a 40-mile radius of downtown Houston has subsided as much as nine feet due to the depletion of the underground water table, causing sewer lines to change direction and allowing waters from Galveston Bay to flood neighborhoods (Boykin, 1982). In California's San Joaquin Valley, land has subsided more than 30 ft (9m) due to 50 years of groundwater pumping (*Newsweek,* 1981).

In addition to the diminishing amount of available groundwater, the quality of water also is deteriorating. Pumping of groundwater in coastal areas creates suction, which draws saline water into the aquifers from the sea, thus making groundwater unsuitable for agricultural or domestic uses. Figure 10-1 shows saline water intrusion into freshwater aquifers found near urban areas along the entire U.S. coastline. Large-scale agricultural application of pesticides and other chemicals from industrial sources are being discovered in groundwater supplies all across the country, especially in California and New England where agricultural and industrial use of groundwater is most intense. The chemicals typically found in groundwater include trichloroethylene (TCE), chloroform, DBCP, and other confirmed carcinogens, along with hazardous chemicals such as arsenic (Boykin, 1982). An official of the California Department of Food and Agriculture estimates that 35% of the wells in the Central Valley of California are contaminated with the pesticide DBCP (Maddy, 1982). Even water-rich Illinois faces severe problems of aquifer contamination and depletion (Krohe, 1982). Compounding this problem of groundwater degradation is that in the cool, dark environment of the aquifer, the natural biological cleansing processes take place extremely slowly, if at all. As one Environmental Protection Agency official put it, "The contamination of groundwater is almost irreversible. Once it's done, there's damned little you can do about it" (*Newsweek,* 1981).

Surface Water

As the underground water resource rapidly reaches its usable limits, so too are the limits to development of surface water being discovered. The sheer costs of building large-scale water projects such as dams and aqueducts, as well as the energy costs of transporting water over great distances, have caused a marked increase in public resistance to the development of surface water. Californians overwhelmingly rejected a June 1982 ballot initiative that would have approved construction of a multibillion dollar canal designed to carry water from the humid northern part of the state to the urban and agricultural interests in the arid south. The Great Plains states of Iowa and Nebraska threatened in late 1981 to sue South Dakota in an attempt to block its plan to sell Missouri River water to an energy development corporation that wanted to construct a pipeline for the transport of coal slurry from Wyoming to Alabama (*Business Week,* 1981). In the Appalachian community of Brumley Gap, Va., residents joined forces with the Sierra Club and other groups early in 1979 to take legal action against the local power company's plans to dam their valley for the production of hydroelectric power (*Time,* 1979). Clearly, a national consensus is emerging that expresses a desire to retreat from the days of grand and extravagant water projects.

The water shortage is not caused by a lack of rain. The nation uses only about 2.5% of the rainfall it receives. Unfortunately, as far as society's needs are concerned, the rain falls either at the wrong time or in the wrong place. With the increased movement of people to the sunbelt, the demand for water far exceeds the natural rainfall in these arid and semi-arid regions. Yet, the new homeowners in Phoenix, Escondido, and San Antonio bring with them the desire for acres of green grass, swimming pools, and elaborate fountains to which they were accustomed in the East and Midwest. In addition to this residential demand for water, the sunbelt states also host a thirsty and highly profitable agriculture, which uses up to 90% of the water in some areas (U.S. Water Resources Council, 1978). This demographic shift from the humid East to the arid Southwest has given the western states the first experience with problems of increasing water demand in the face of constantly dwindling supplies. Yet, as we have seen, the entire nation faces limits and challenges to water use and development.

Water Demand

Even as the difficulties of providing adequate water increase, so too does the public demand for it. Figure 10-2 shows that water demand has increased steadily as the luxuries and complexities of society have grown. The per capita water use remained fairly constant for centuries until the Industrial Revolution, when the use of water for hygiene and industry skyrocketed.

Analysis of residential as opposed to total water use reveals that increasing per capita residential use for

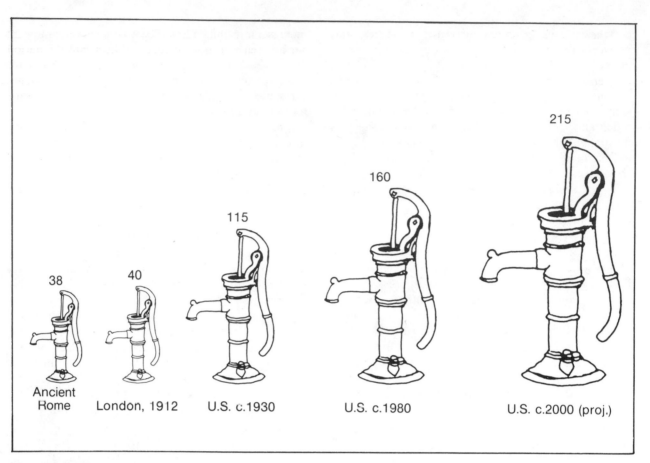

238   40   115   160   215

Ancient   London, 1912   U.S. c.1930   U.S. c.1980   U.S. c.2000 (proj.)
Rome

Figure 10-2. Historical trends in residential water use (gallons per capita per day). From: (Milne, 1976; State of California, 1979)

bathing, washing clothes, landscape irrigation, and other needs contributes a large share of this overall increased demand. A John Hopkins University study (Linaweaver, 1967) has shown residential water use increasing more than 100% in 40 years, from 35 gallons per capita per day (gpcd) in 1924, to 80 gpcd in 1967. A more recent study (Milne, 1979) has estimated about 140 gpcd of residential water use in the average American home. Furthermore, this trend seems to be continuing as levels of income rise nationally, studies having suggested that water use increases with income (State of California, 1979).

Clearly, then, all the major factors of water use and availability in the United States are acting together to force a reevaluation of our attitudes about the use of water. The arid and semi-arid regions of the West have experienced the first shortages of water as populations expanded beyond the region's indigenous water supply. Yet even the eastern states are faced with shortages of water, both in quantity and quality. The rising costs of treating, transporting, and storing water also contribute to the difficulty. And, finally,

the public's demand for lush, water-thirsty landscapes, even where inappropriate, increases residential demand and symbolizes a national consciousness out of touch with the true environmental and monetary costs of water.

Water and Energy

Water is, in the jargon of economists, a "free good," a commodity so common and plentiful that enough exists for everyone without scarcity for anyone. Although this perhaps is true, when one considers the tiny fraction of rainfall society actually collects and uses the processes used to deliver water to the user make the cost of water significant; these costs are reflected primarily in the cost of energy. It takes energy to pump water from the source, to purify it, to transport it, to heat or cool it, and finally, to cleanse it after it has been used. A large component of energy is also embodied in the facilities (canals, dams, pumps, treatment plants, etc.) needed to perform these services. As energy costs rise, so do the costs of water, and the saving of water carries with it the added bonus of energy savings. Further, the reduction of water use at the beginning of the water cycle reduces the amount of energy needed in subsequent steps as well; each gallon saved in the delivery system represents one less gallon of wastewater to be treated later on. This "multiplier effect" of water savings indicates the substantial impact water conservation can have on energy use.

Pumping

One gallon of water weighs about eight pounds. Water's sheer weight and bulk makes its transport a significant energy consumer. The city engineer of Davis, Calif., estimates that one-half of the city's corporate electricity bill is spent in pumping water from area wells; half of this water is used to irrigate residential landscapes (Pelz, 1982). This indicates the significance of energy in landscape irrigation: It represents one-fourth of the city's total electricity bill. A study for the development of Burke Centre, Va. (Land Design/Research Inc., 1979), has found that "it takes as much energy at the generator to create electricity for water and sewer needs" as for all of the other electrical uses of the community. In fact, the fastest growing item in the nation's water budget is the energy needed to pump water from one place to another (Milne, 1979).

Treatment and Delivery

After water is pumped from the source, it must be purified before it can be delivered to the users. Water treatment represents about 10% of the total water energy budget (Nusbaum, 1976), but this does not include the embodied energy costs in the manufacture and supply of treatment chemicals. Once purified, the delivery of water from the treatment plant to the user requires significant energy expenditures, varying according to the distance of the users from the source.

Perhaps the most extreme example of a long-range water delivery system is the California State Water Project, which delivers water from lakes and reservoirs in northern California to agricultural and urban interests in semi-arid southern California. It takes about 2,900 kwh to deliver one acre-foot of water to the Los Angeles area via this system (Minton, 1982). At 1982 electrical rates this comes to about $13/acre-foot. Yet utilities and the State of California are presently renegotiating their contracts to adjust for the increasing costs of producing energy. In 1985, this same acre-foot will cost about $80, and by the turn of the century an acre-foot of water delivered to Los Angeles through the State Water Project is expected to cost more than $230. This represents a nearly 20-fold increase in energy cost within a 20-year period. Other water delivery systems may not be as extensive, but all will be subject to the same economic spiral, and the saving of water will become an increasingly significant means of reducing society's total energy demand.

Wastewater Disposal

After water is used, it must be purified before it is returned to the biosphere. The cost of wastewater treatment, the last factor in the water-energy budget, is also currently increasing, but for two reasons. First, the cost of the energy required to treat wastewater is rising, and second, effluent standards are becoming stricter, thus necessitating more thorough (and more energy-intensive) treatment of wastewater (Reid, 1976).

Water Pricing

Every time a tap is opened, all these steps must be completed, each using large amounts of energy in the process. If energy is so expensive, why is water so cheap? In the Los Angeles metropolitan area, with its sophisticated and energy-intensive water system, a single dollar buys about 15,000 gallons of pure tapwater (State of California, 1979). Reid's 1976 study of wastewater treatment determined the national average cost to be less than 0.8 cents per thousand gallons. Clearly, society is not pricing water according to its true value.

There are two major reasons for this. First, the water that is withdrawn from underground aquifers over and above the amount replaced by natural rainfall represents a water resource lost forever. This type of water withdrawal is called water "mining" by hydrologists, because the water is removed from the land, never to be replaced. Further, once an aquifer is depleted, recharging is practically impossible because the structure of the underground cavity is usually destroyed (*Newsweek*, 1981). Yet this well water is sold at some of the cheapest rates: A person simply sinks a well and pays the cost of pumping. The true value of the irreplaceable water resource is not represented in the short-range price.

The pricing structure of water is the second contributor to its unnaturally low cost. Throughout our history, federal and state governments have subsidized the various water projects necessary to supply water, primarily to encourage and facilitate economic growth. Thus the energy costs embodied in the dams, canals, processing plants, and other large-scale projects are not reflected in users' direct water costs. All of these factors tend to defeat the natural market mechanism of a free economy to set a reasonable price for water. In the words of the *California Water Atlas* (State of California, 1979):

> An elaborate set of subsidies encourages this [market system-frustrating] behavior. Federal water projects, for example, obtain subsidies through extraordinarily inexpensive financing arrangements and long-term repayment terms which may extend over 30 or 40 years. Where water projects generate hydroelectric power, the revenues from energy sales . . . subsidize the cost of water delivery. And in many local projects property tax revenues are used to pay off portions of the development costs of a water system and thereby mask the true cost of water to the consumer. (p. 79)

Furthermore, the method of calculating a consumer's water bill contributes to the prevailing cheapness of water and its waste. Many communities charge residential water customers a flat rate for water, regardless of the amount used. Not surprisingly, these communities exhibit water use that is often double that of neighboring communities that meter the amount of water used and charge by the unit. This extra water consumed in flat-rate areas is most often used for increased landscape irrigation (Linaweaver, 1967). In agriculture and industry, the pricing structure for large-scale water users often reduces the per-unit cost of water as the quantity demanded increases. This rate structure, known as the decreasing block rate, is widely used by water companies today (Milne, 1976) and serves to reward extravagant and wasteful water practices in large-scale water-consuming activities.

The water and energy crises are inextricably linked. The development of water resources is usually not limited so much by the absolute availability of water, but by the costs of making existing water available to meet the users' needs. In irrigation, for example, the high cost of electricity needed to run the pumps limits the amount of water farmers can economically draw from their wells. As the water table recedes and the aquifer is depleted, more energy is required to lift the water from the deeper level, thus increasing the per-unit cost of water. Conservation of water and maintenance of the water table would reduce the energy needed to irrigate the soil. California's State Water Project, which delivers water through canals to agricultural and urban users, consumes almost as much electricity to pump water around the state as do all the people of Los Angeles (*Newsweek*, 1981).

In some areas, especially the southwestern states, the absolute quantity of water is limited. In all parts of the nation, pure usable water itself is becoming increasingly scarce. The energy required to provide the water becomes more costly. The nation's willingness and ability to construct large-scale water systems is diminishing. From every point of view, water conservation appears to be the best and easiest means for assuring adequate water supply and saving a significant fraction of the nation's energy budget.

Residential Water Use

Estimates for per capita water use vary widely according to climate, season, and socio-economic factors, but in general, the average American uses about 100 to 150 gallons of water per day in the residence for washing, bathing, flushing toilets, drinking, cooking, landscape irrigation, and other miscellaneous tasks. In the eastern states, about 25% of total residential water is applied outside the home, primarily for landscape irrigation. In the west, landscape irrigation accounts for more than 50% of residential water demand (Milne, 1976). The demand for this irrigation water is also much more income-elastic than demand for the water used inside the home. Milne (1976) has found that both wealthy and poorer communities have similar indoor water consumption, but the outdoor water use in upper class neighborhoods far exceeds that of the lower classes, primarily because of the affluence expressed in expansive, lush landscapes. It is in the arena of residential landscapes that landscape architects can have the greatest, most immediate influence on domestic water conservation.

Significant water savings can be achieved in residential landscapes with far greater ease than in most of the other major categories of water use. A New Mexico study (Flack, 1977) has found that through increased efficiency in watering techniques, plant water requirements could be reduced by as much as 47%. During the drought of 1976-77, landscaping firms and government agencies in California reported a 25-90% reduction in water use for landscape plantings due to efficient irrigation and changes in maintenance practices (California Department of Water Resources, 1979). In addition to the great potential savings through boosting efficiency, recycled water can be used for irrigation. By using water for more than one function, less water needs to be treated, pumped, and disposed of in the water cycle. Flack (1977) has found that although public attitudes generally oppose using recycled water for direct bodily contact (drinking, washing, etc.), its use for irrigation purposes is acceptable. The collection of "greywater," that is, all of the wastewater of a residence except that which carries solid wastes, can be an extremely effective method of recycling water within the residential environment. Greywater, if properly collected, carries almost no harmful organisms, and the phosphates from household soaps, when applied to the soil along with the recycled water, benefit the soil and plants. These soaps must be biodegradable, however (Milne, 1976).

Many options can minimize residential water use, from waterless toilets to low-volume shower heads, all of which merit consideration in the larger picture of water conservation. Ideally, architects, planners, landscape architects, and government agencies will all work together to implement total systems that promote responsible and appropriate water use.

Water-Conserving Landscape Design

Short of this, however, water-conserving landscape design can achieve immediate savings. The large percentage of water used outdoors can be reduced dramatically without any sacrifice of personal hygiene or comfort. Whether through improved maintenance or replacement of thirsty lawns and shrubs with drought-tolerant plants, water conservation in the landscape will significantly improve society's overall water and energy balance.

Furthermore, the gradual transformation from the monotony of green grass, which carpets so much of the present landscape, to a more ecologically appropriate and varied water-conserving landscape will help to create in the public's mind the idea of water as a precious natural resource. This consciousness of water use, as demonstrated in the landscape, will in turn set the stage for greater, more significant shifts in water policy and attitudes throughout society. The landscape architect can perform a valuable public service by working toward the design and implementation of landscapes that demonstrate the potential of water conservation. With concrete examples of responsible water use as part of their daily experience, people will become more aware of the need to conserve water. They will also grow comfortable through gradual exposure to the new ideas and practices that are the foundation of the water-conserving landscape image.

Attitudes, Perceptions, and Images

Historical Background

Much of the designed landscape in the United States today owes its aesthetic origins to the romantic traditions of the eighteenth-century English landscape revolutionaries like Lancelot Brown and Humphrey Repton. The English pastoral image, elaborated in the U.S. by Fredrick Law Olmsted and other nineteenth-century landscape architects, persists to this day in our dependence upon lawn and informal groupings of trees and shrubs. Derived from the picturesque treatment of English country estates with ample greenswards and informal vistas of distant scenery, the typical residential and recreational landscape has shrunk considerably but has maintained much of the character of its cultural predecessors. Houses or buildings are set in the center of an expanse of turfgrass, highlighted by groves and specimen trees, and punctuated with foundation and focal shrubs and bedding plants. The expansive front lawn has become a prestige symbol, romantically harkening to past eras of conspicuous status and wealth. Although more climatically adaptable to the eastern United States with its ample rainfall, the idealized pastoral landscape has been unreservedly transported to the arid west, where it is far less appropriate. This romantic, water-loving landscape has taken root in places like Colorado, California, and Arizona, where it survives only with the support of extensive water development and delivery systems, cheap energy, and large numbers of recent migrants from the East Coast who bring their landscape aesthetic expectations to the new region. Even in the East, where significantly less irrigation is required to support this ideal landscape, the facade of the English landscape tradition is beginning to wear a little thin. People are questioning the suitability of intensive energy expenditures for fertilizing, mowing, pruning, and manicuring a landscape image that seems more a relic of the past than a bellwether of the future.

Maintaining the vestigial organ of Anglo-Saxon landscape heritage — the suburban front lawn — has become a symbol-based subculture. For the work-harried executive mowing the lawn on Saturday, it provides both a visible concrete achievement (in contrast to work's often intangible frustrations) as well as a visual indicator of "keeping one's life in order." A trim, healthy lawn represents a well-maintained self-image for the suburbanite and his family (Figure 10-3, see next page). Lawn mowing seems often to be a masculine endeavor. Perhaps this too is a cultural holdover from the days of the country gentleman tending his estate. Since most suburban lot sizes are somewhat regulated, it is no longer the area of turfgrass in front of the house but the degree of its manicure that evokes an image of status and sparks the Saturday morning lawn-mowing ritual.

Weeds, brown spots, grasses going to seed, and heterogeneous groundcover areas have no place in such a landscape. All manner of mowers, trimmers, pesticides, herbicides, sprinkler irrigation hardware, fertilizers, and even green dyes are enlisted to maintain the turf garden ideal. Energy and water inputs are

191

Figure 10-3. A vestige of our English heritage — the suburban front lawn.

not only acceptable, but essential supplements, for this is a landscape of conspicuous consumption. In addition to homeowners with their front lawns, corporations with their symbolic headquarters and communities with their neighborhood parks embrace the "clean and green" convention, which is exalted by the landscape industry and suppliers as the only desirable landscape alternative.

There do exist, however, individuals and small groups who are working to overcome the inertia of this landscape tradition and create a more appropriate and satisfying landscape image. These include the native plant societies, some ecologists, horticulturists, landscape architects, and urban agriculturists. These people are innovators — people whom comunication scientist E.F. Rogers (Rogers & Shoemaker, 1971) describes as venturesome, eager to try new ideas, and willing to take the risks of public rejection and disapproval. Today's landscape innovators have one thing in common: a desire to reverse the trend toward excessive resource consumption (i.e., water and energy) necessitated by "maladapted" (Dubos, 1965) landscape treatments.

With this positive approach, a countermovement of "conspicuous nonconsumption" (Thayer, 1980) has begun that attempts to visibly and publicly demonstrate alternatives to the status quo, in hopes of contributing to the general welfare. This process of altering landscape design to create more resource-conservative landscapes is easily described by borrowing from theories of environmental aesthetics, innovation diffusion, and landscape history.

Aesthetics, Innovation, and Revolution

The landscape has many "meanings," from the abstract form, texture, and color composition to the heavily symbolic overtones discussed above. Much of the way designed landscape appears can be attributed to its role in elaborating the idealized way people view

the world. These landscapes historically owe their existence to the romantic fantasies and whims of aristocratic clients who hired landscape architects and designers to make their landscape dreams come true. The everyday, real image is fluid, functional, often ugly, and apt to change rapidly or even violently due to technological, economic, or political influences. The ideal image is a vision of how the world should be, not how it actually is. The ideal image is grounded in tradition and nostalgia, and is a protection against the harsh experiences of the uncertain and often painful real image. The ideal image provides support and security against the shock and discomfort of everyday life. The tension between the ideal and the real is exemplified by the large fountains gracing a Phoenix subdivision. These fountains, with their large plumes of water evaporating in the desert air, testify to the landscape ideal of the new homeowners, while the reality of the dams, aqueducts, pumping stations, and energy expenditures necessary to provide this water remains hidden from view. Although out of sight, this dependence on a complex water system cannot totally escape the homeowner's mind: The ideal and real images strike an uneasy dissonance. Or consider the difference between the ideal image presented by the City of San Anselmo, Calif., which placed a life-sized plastic deer astride the entrance to its newly remodeled Mission-style Town Hall (Figure 10-4), and the reality of the human population expansion in the area, which necessitates the periodic capture and relocation of large numbers of deer to wildlife preserves far from the urban center.

Figure 10-4. The real versus the ideal — San Anselmo, Calif., Town Hall.

Periodically throughout history, what people know as visual reality and what they hold as visually ideal grow so divergent that a state of cognitive dissonance (Festinger, 1957) occurs and the public senses the impotence of traditional idealized images. New forms created by innovative artists and designers revolutionize the aesthetic norms and move the ideal image into closer congruence with reality. Examples of this type of design revolution can easily be seen in the breakdown of the French Baroque garden as exemplified by Versailles. The English Landscape School was largely a style of landscape design intended to be more respectful of "nature" and to replace the elaborate, costly, and pompous French formality, thus bringing the ideal image of the landscape more into harmony with the realities of the undulant English topography. In architecture, the Bauhaus movement of Gropius and his colleagues was a radical aesthetic departure from archaic neoclassicism in an attempt to bring building design into closer harmony with the advancing industrial and economic realities. Figure 10-5 illustrates the historic pattern of the relationship between ideal and real images.

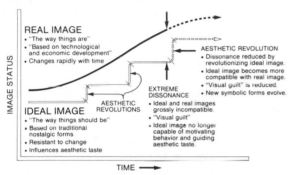

Figure 10-5. Mental images and esthetic revolution. From: (Thayer, 1980)

Present Crisis and Innovation Diffusion

The present resource crisis — energy, water, soil — represents another dramatic shift in the real image. We acknowledge that our technological activities will exhaust our supply of fossil fuels and tax our water systems, but we persistently cling to nostalgic land-use patterns and designs. Parks and subdivisions glorify a clean, green, resource-intensive appearance (Figure 10-6). Technological manifestations in the landscape are downplayed or hidden completely. Irrigation heads are a turflike green color and pop out of sight when not in use, power lines are buried, and air conditioners are hidden in an attempt to disguise or visually minimize in the landscape the technologies we somehow dislike, but can't seem to live without. These attempts to mitigate the visual impact of technology on the landscape derive from a desire to preserve the integrity of our aesthetic images in spite of sweeping technological and cultural change. Yet even though the visual constituents are preserved, the symbolic meanings of these traditional resource-dependent

Figure 10-6. Clean, green, and wasteful — apartment complex in southern California.

landscapes are unable to eliminate the uneasy dissonance we feel between our ideals and our impressions of reality. The images must change: An aesthetic revolution is necessary and is already underway — one that will renovate our ideal image to one more compatible with the realities of our present culture and its water and energy supplies.

How does this revolution work? What role do designers and planners play? The aesthetic revolution begins with physical innovations created by designers who are unafraid to take visual "risks." These innovators experiment with actual physical design alternatives that save water and energy. They consider not only functional operation and practical implementation, but they also concern themselves with the esthetic nuances implied by their ideas. Some design approaches will fail to achieve public acceptance. The first attempts at water-conserving landscapes will likely experience growing pains, just as the fledgling solar industry's first houses were often crude and visually awkward. Yet like the automobile, the flush toilet, the solar panel, and other innovations, the water-conserving landscape will follow a predictable pattern of diffusion into the social framework:

1. It will be *visibly differentiable* from traditional landscape styles.
2. It will *function to save water* and energy.
3. It can be *tested and adopted* by the public on a trial bases.
4. It will ultimately begin to *symbolize* a new attitude toward resources.

Rogers (1971) has identified groups within society according to their willingness and ability to accept innovations. First are the *innovators,* who experiment with the problem and develop initial alternatives. Soon to join them and adopt their innovations are the *early adopters*, who are somewhat more traditional, yet flexible. These are the opinion leaders in the community where views are respected and emulated by the next group, the *majority*, who approach the innovation with varying degrees of deliberateness (early majority) or skepticism (late majority). Sooner or later, however, if an innovation is to be successfully diffused into society, the majority follow the lead of the early adopters and themselves adopt the innovation. Last to accept the innovation are the *laggards*. This group is conservative, oriented to the past, and suspicious of change. By the time the laggards adopt an innovation, it has become part of the mainstream.

Landscape designers and planners will achieve greater results when proposing water-conserving plans if they are aware of their clients' attitudes toward innovation. This chapter will later describe three scenarios for water-conserving landscapes and offer design examples appropriate for various clients ranging from early adopters to laggards. Although some water savings are possible through minor manipulations of the traditional landscape image (scenario 1), this approach serves only the most conservative client. It will have little or no visible impact on esthetics and will do the least to diffuse water-conserving innovations into common practice. Although radically different approaches (scenario 3) may initially seem extreme, they are necessary as visual indicators and stimulants of change, just as the gardens of Stowe in 1750 or the architecture of Le Corbusier in the 1930s were critical to their respective aesthetic movements. *Without a physical, imageable manifestation in the landscape, water conservation has little chance of helping to influence public opinion and alter resource-wasting habits.*

Visual Meanings

Just as any new visual stimulus acquires "meaning" in terms of its use and context, new approaches to water-conserving landscape design will result in new symbolic meanings for landscape elements. For example, the drought of 1976-77 in California was felt no worse than in Marin County, which managed to reduce its water consumption by a dramatic 53% (State of California, 1979). During this crisis lawns were allowed to die and turn brown out of the necessity to direct water for more critical uses. Subsequently, a brown lawn became a symbol of its owners' environmental and social consciousness, while homeowners still irrigating their lawns were treated with disdain. This is a most extreme example, one representing an abrupt and perhaps overly rapid change in aesthetics. Nevertheless, the process of transferring symbolic status from lawns and other water intensive landscape forms to new water-

conserving alternatives is a major goal worthy of the landscape architect's attention. By advocating water-conserving residential, recreational, commercial, corporate, and public landscapes, the designer can not only help to save a significant amount of water and energy but can also embody and visually express the values of "conspicuous nonconsumption" in a thoughtful, innovative, and publicly acceptable manner.

Major hurdles facing landscape architects include unrealistic water pricing, lagging public opinion, and inadequate education. As a profession, landscape architects have hesitated to take visual risks in the landscape for fear of negative public response. Public preconceptions of drought-tolerant landscapes may be far more extreme and formidable than the actual alternatives the profession could generate, but the risk is seldom taken — turfgrass and exotics are often chosen and the issues of water conservation and client education are ignored. Landscape architects must remember that even Olmsted, the great champion of the English landscape tradition, rejected turfgrass and exotics when designing for an arid environment. His design of Stanford University in 1890 featured oases of tropical and subtropical plantings, surrounded by a gravel courtyard. Olmsted reasoned that in the Mediterranean climate of California irrigated lawn areas were inappropriate and, in spite of pressure from his clients, insisted on a planting plan in harmony with the environmental realities (Turner, 1976). Landscape architects need to emulate this attitude of flexibility and innovation if they are to succeed in replacing the common misconceptions of water-conserving landscapes (Figure 10-7) — cacti and boulders — with a new aesthetic imagery (Figure 10-8, see next page).

Figure 10-7. An unfortunate stereotype of the drought-tolerant garden — excessive use of inert materials with minimum vegetation.

Figure 10-8. A better drought-tolerant landscape image — more plants, greater diversity, and minimal water consumption.

Public Response to Alternatives

In an attempt to test the acceptability of several water conserving-landscape alternatives, the author (1982) conducted a controlled study of public response to eight nearly identical test landscapes wherein only irrigation rates and groundcover materials varied. Each test landscape measured 10 x 20 ft, and also included a tree, several common shrubs, garden screen fencing, and a viewing bench (Figure 10-9). Eight groups of 21

Figure 10-9. Subject viewing a test landscape in a study of human response to water conserving gardens. From: (Thayer, 1982)

subjects each viewed one test landscape per group and responded to a questionnaire that measured overall preference for each garden and appropriateness of each garden for specific landscape situations.

All test gardens were equally watered during the establishment of the plant material. The experimental watering regime commenced after the winter rains had

ceased. The questionnaire was administered at the end of the summer dry season. Subjects were drawn from a population of adult male and female homeowners in Santa Clara County, Calif. Groundcovers included mown turgrass (tall fescue), coyote bush (*Baccharis pilularis*), redwood bark chips, and decomposed granite (Figure 10-10). Experimental irrigation schedules included *typical* (4 in./month), *reduced* (2 in./month), and *no additional* irrigation.

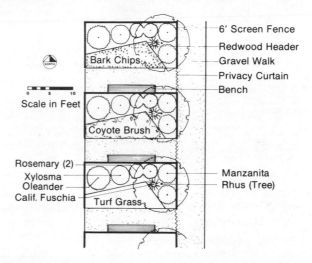

Figure 10-10. Plan view of test landscapes. From: (Thayer, 1982)

The general hypothesis was that subjects would find certain test landscapes with reduced irrigation and alternative groundcovers as aesthetically and functionally acceptable as normally irrigated landscapes with mown turf. Subjects viewed and evaluated only one test landscape and were told nothing that might bias their responses. A rigorous test of significance was applied to the questionnaire results, which are shown in Table 10-1 (see next page).

Results were provocative. Statistically, subjects found the test landscapes with 50% reduced irrigation and alternative groundcovers (coyote brush, redwood bark, decomposed granite) as acceptable as the typically irrigated control landscape with turfgrass. While irrigated turfgrass was preferred for landscapes subject to human contact such as sitting or lying down, the turfgrass landscape with 50% reduced irrigation was least liked for most landscape uses. Surprisingly, when asked about the shrubs in the various experimental plots, subjects reported no significant differences in visual quality between shrubs under normal, reduced, or even non-irrigated conditions.

Generalizations about these experimental results are restricted by the nature of the research method,

195

Table 10-1. Mean Preference Scores for 8 Experimental Landscapes.

| | Treatment | | | | | | Mean preference score[x] | | | | |
| | Irrigation | | | | | | | | | | |
Landscape code	regime (2nd year)	Groundcover	1	2	3	4	Query[z] 5	6	7	8	9
A	None	Bark chips	.33ab[y]	-.50ab	.25a	-2.20a	.90a	-1.20a	.25ab	.85a	.55a
B	None	Coyote brush	.38ab	-.19ab	.76a	-1.81a	.62a	-.57a	-.43a	.76a	.38a
C	Bimonthly	Turfgrass	-.48a	-1.24a	.42a	-1.71a	-.19a	-1.24a	-.62a	-.19a	.43a
D	Bimonthly	Decomposed granite	.86ab	-.43ab	1.00a	-1.67a	1.10a	-.33a	.67ab	1.14a	.85a
E	Bimonthly	Bark chips	1.38 b	.14ab	1.05a	-2.00a	1.38a	-.14a	.57ab	1.10a	.86
F	Bimonthly	Coyote brush	1.38 b	.10ab	1.10a	-2.33a	1.29a	.15a	.76ab	1.05a	1.19a
G	Biweekly	Turfgrass	1.38 b	1.10 b	.96a	.55 b	1.21a	.10a	1.29 b	1.80a	1.40a
H	Biweekly	Decomposed granite	.81ab	.35ab	.96a	-1.33a	.90a	.10a	.65ab	1.29a	1.45a

[x]Mean response to questions listed expressed as a value between bipolar opposite scores (-3.0 = "dislike very much", + 3.0 = ((like very much").
[z]1. "Overall, how do you *like* this landscape?"
2. "Specifically, how well do you like the *groundcover* in the setting?"
3. "Specifically, how well do you like the *shrubs* in the setting?"
4. "How comfortable would you find this landscape for *sitting or lying* upon?"
5. "How comfortable would you find this landscape for *viewing* from a lawn, path, street, or bench?"
6. "How well would you like this landscape as part of your *front yard*?"
7. "How well would you like this landscape as part of your *back yard*?"
8. "How well would you like this landscape as part of your *neighborhood park*?"
9. "How well would you like this landscape as part of your *street or highway corridor*?"
[y]Mean separation by Newman-Keuls multiple comparison, 5% level.
From: (Thayer, 1982)

subject pool, and geographic region. Differences in public attitudes and responses could occur if the experiment were reproduced under different circumstances. However, it seems clear that for areas of restricted rainfall, a water-conserving approach to landscape design in which turf is restricted to areas of active human use and contact is appropriate. Landscaped buffers, passive use areas, and zones used primarily for visual or focal areas can be put to groundcovers requiring less irrigation or, in some cases, no additional irrigation whatsoever.

Obviously, more work is needed on ways of measuring and increasing public acceptance of water conserving landscapes. Conservation education programs aimed at diffusing new landscape design approaches should be adopted as public policy. What is of more urgent need, however, are descriptions of specific techniques and methods by which water can be saved in the designed landscape. Following are some examples of such information.

Plants and Water

Perhaps the most visible, direct facet of design in which the landscape architect works is in the selection of plant materials. The landscape architect also bears responsibility for site planning, grading, drainage, and other factors of design relating to water, and genuine water savings can be achieved through better understanding of these principles. However, judicious selection of plant materials can often be the simplest, most immediate contribution of landscape designers to water conservation.

The key to selecting plants for the water-conserving landscape is to choose plant materials that can be given a climate and growing condition duplicating, as far as possible, their native environment. Two categories of plants exist that meet these criteria for the water conserving landscape: native plants and "adapted" plants.

Native Plants

Native plants are species and varieties indigenous to the area of the landscape. These plants are ideally suited for local conditions because they have evolved in the area without irrigation or other human influences. If given a situation similar to their native growing climate, they are unsurpassed for care-free landscape value because they thrive in the vicissitudes of the regional climate. In addition to their ease of maintenance and minimal need for irrigation, native plants also provide the aesthetic benefit of regional identity. Every geographical area has its own particular native plant communities, and the artful manipulation of these various species in the built environment provides landscapes unique to each area, thus giving people a greater sense of "place."

Native plants must be carefully selected, however. Not all plants native to a region have the same cultural requirements. California, for example, is a semi-arid region. Yet certain California natives, like the white alder (*Alnus rhombifolia*) are native to streambanks in the hills, and require significant irrigation when cultivated in most California landscapes. The landscape architect must be aware of these microclimate variables and consider each native species individually. Another difficulty with native plants arises from their growth characteristics, which may not fulfill public expectations. Most drought-tolerant plants are slower growing than common cultivars. They often exhibit a more irregular and rugged form than the clipped hedges and shrubs of our cultural tradition. Many natives depend on long taproots for their drought resistance and therefore must be planted in the field from small containers to allow natural development of the root system. Furthermore, although many of the native plants can survive with little or no irrigation when mature, because they are planted from containers into the landscape, they require regular irrigation and maintenance until they become established. Yet these difficulties are not shortcomings of the plant material itself, but stem from public attitudes and expectations, which through education and example can be influenced by landscape architects and other landscape professionals.

Adapted Plants

The second category of plants for the water-conserving landscape is the "adapted" plants; plants not native to the region of their landscape use, but to regions with similar climates. The wide array of plants from Mediterranean climates around the world that are common in California represent adapted plants. These include species that have become so well adapted to the California environment that they have naturalized and even become pests in some areas (e.g., *Eucalyptus, Ailanthus*). These adapted plants have tremendous landscape potential, for they provide variety of form and color while retaining the cultural benefits of native plants. Some of the more popular "adapted" plants found in California include the rockrose (*Cistus*) from the Mediterranean region, the *Gazania* from South Africa, and *Grevillea* from Australia.

Our traditional landscape image is, as pointed out, largely a product of the English landscape palette adapted to the humid northeastern United States. There the English yew (*Taxus*), turfgrass, and other components of the romantic landscape can be grown with little trouble. In this way, our society was able to adopt and adapt its ideal landscape image from the English tradition with only minor modification. Yet this image persists even in the arid and semi-arid regions of the country, where these plants must be supported by large water and energy inputs.

Thus, plants which are "adapted" to one region of the country are "maladapted" to others. Birches, turf, and rhododendrons may be appropriate for the Atlantic seaboard, but not in Houston, Tex. Similarly, the traditional landscape elements of the Spanish colonial period — yucca, juniper, and cacti — may thrive in the arid southwest, but would be inappropriate in St. Louis, Mo. Every site has its own unique macro- and microclimate. To produce a successful water-conserving planting plan, the designer must be fully aware of the cultural needs of each plant. With this awareness, selections from the available native and adapted plants can be made according to design and program specifications, with the confidence that they will fulfill the intended vision.

Designing Water-Conserving Landscapes

The design of water-conserving landscapes follows the same time-tested process inherent to all landscape architecture — a simultaneous consideration of site factors and program needs and the cyclical process of matching physical landscape features to the most appropriate land uses, and vice versa. However, water-saving landscape design is best achieved by placing a greater degree of emphasis on two areas: the physical ecology of plants and plant communities in relation to micro site conditions, and the human ecology of land uses in relation to potential need for additional water or irrigation above that which naturally occurs.

The first concept — ecological planting design — emphasizes a thorough examination of the water, soil, sunlight, wind, and other micro-environmental factors in relation to plant communities, whether strictly native or adapted to the region. "Natural landscaping" is a term frequently used to describe such considerations, and although somewhat misleading as a label, is aimed at matching the specific microsite and climate condition with plants native to those conditions. The logic here is sound; plants ideally suited to climate, soil, sun, wind, and other site conditions require less energy, water, and maintenance to grow and thrive than exotics. They may in some cases constitute the beginning of a plant community that evolves to make a pleasing landscape with little further investment in resources or manpower. Diekelmann and Schuster (1982) have written extensively on this subject. Both water and energy can be saved by adhering to principles of ecological planting design.

197

The second concept — the human ecology of water use — adds a new twist to the design process in that it requires the site to be analyzed according to predicted or planned human use intensity. The underlying assumption is that water is most "needed" in the landscape in places where people use the land most intensively for practical or esthetic reasons. By examining areas within the site according to the potential frequency and types of human activity, areas of water-use intensity, or "hydrozones," can be established to enable the designer to maximize the functional efficiency and psychological effect of water and energy applications to the landscape. *Through hydrozonic landscape planning and design, the water use within a given site is varied in proportion to the varying use intensities of different portions of the site.* In this way, energy is also conserved, because saving water saves the energy inherent to water delivery systems, pruning and mowing, and other maintenance factors. Detailed land use, space utilization, circulation patterns, and other variables that determine water needs are important factors in the design program and must be considered throughout the planning process if the hydrozonic approach is to succeed. The hydrozone concept can be applied at any scale, and gives designers and land use planners a powerful means of understanding and explaining the relationship between water and human use intensity.

Hydrozones

The *principal hydrozone* represents the area within the site that experiences both the greatest human impact upon the land and the largest subsequent water and energy use. On the residential scale, the principal hydrozone is generally coincidental with the back yard lawn area where people have the most direct contact with the landscape — where they play, run, sit, or lie down to relax. On the community scale, the principal hydrozone is found in local parks and gathering places such as urban plazas and spaces around well-used public buildings. Intensive human activity in the principal hydrozone justifies the greatest water and energy use here. The principal hydrozone resembles the "mini-oasis" referred to by Duffield and Jones (1981).

Areas that are visually important but less physically manipulated by human activity are contained in the *secondary hydrozone*; often including areas for passive recreation, space delineation, or focal interest. In the residence, this might be a prominent shrub and flower bed near the main entrance; in the community, this often includes focal plantings within parks or around public buildings, entrance plantings, or other

moderately water-intensive landscape accents. The secondary hydrozone, while not as directly contacted by the users, has enough significance to merit some water and energy inputs.

The *minimal hydrozones* are the areas of the site that receive little or no human use, and therefore justify little irrigation or related energy expenditure. These include buffer zones, distant views, and directional delineators such as median strips and highway embankments. These areas, according to the hydrozonic approach, are matched with landscape material that survives with only slightly more water than natural rainfall.

Finally, the *elemental hydrozone* describes the area of the site that receives only natural rainfall and no supplementary water supply. Here the human use intensity is lowest. At the regional scale, the elemental hydrozone is represented by the natural or undeveloped landscape, with little or no human influence. At the residential level, utility areas, mulched parkways, unirrigated plants, or naturally existing vegetation belong to the elemental hydrozone.

By differentiating the site into its principal, secondary, minimal, and elemental hydrozones, the designer or planner is able to put the water where it is needed and to avoid extravagant use of water in areas little used or appreciated. Inherent to the hydrozonic planning concept is the need to carefully evaluate the area required for each zone and to limit the size of the principal and secondary hydrozones (which consume the most water and energy) to what is absolutely necessary for the fulfillment of the designer's program. Table 10-2 (see next page) illustrates a matrix used to evaluate potential hydrozones.

Thus, wasting water on the areas where people have little contact, impact, or exposure to the landscape is unnecessary. Utilizing water where it is most needed and appreciated results in little change in esthetic potential or loss of visual quality. The principal hydrozone — the area of water expenditure on such things as turf, fountains, swimming pools, or well-irrigated crops — becomes more dominant and visually precious in the landscape. Water features, areas of turfgrass, or productive vegetable gardens are visually emphasized "water use nodes" of human activity.

Implementing the Hyrdrozone Concept

The designer wishing to save water can use the concept of "down-zoning": When in doubt, relegate a certain landscape area to the next lowest hydrozone. For example, if a rural highway interchange only receives sporadic auto traffic and no direct human contact (by other than perhaps an occasional hitchhiker), it need

198

Table 10-2. Matrix of Hyrdozone Values

	Human contact	Visual importance	Water & energy needs
Principal hydrozone	Direct, intense, active.	Conspicuous	Greatest
Secondary hydrozone	Less direct, less intense, more passive.	Conspicuous	Reduced
Minimal hydrozone	Little	Less conspicuous	Slight
Elemental hydrozone	None	Inconspicuous	None

Figure 10-11. Fenced-off water treatment plant (top) and civic center fountain (bottom) with lots of lawn but no people using it.

not be included in the principal or secondary hydrozone, but instead should be assigned to the minimal hydrozone.

A question could arise at this point about whether this technique unduly restricts human use. By reducing areas such as turf, which can be used for sitting, runing, lying down, or play, does the designer make the landscape less functional and enjoyable? Hardly. For example, irrigated turfgrass surrounding a sewage treatment plant and bounded by a chain link fence does not receive enough human use to warrant the water and energy expended upon it (Figure 10-11). Instead, by placing such an area in a minimal hydrozone during the planning stages and designing it with less water-intensive plant and landscape materials, the designer can achieve the same or even greater level of visual clarity and quality than the original turfgrass lawn.

Indeed, skillful application of the hydrozone concept may enable landscape architects to transform the problem of water and energy shortage into an opportunity. By identifying areas of greatest human impact, and designing them with plant and landscape materials that invite and encourage human activity, designers can provide people with a more visually understandable and "readable" space. Today, the typical urban or suburban setting gives no clue regarding human use intensity. The front lawn, punctuated by shrubs and trees, looks exactly the same and requires exactly the same water and energy inputs as the heavily utilized private garden in the rear, yet is little used. The front lawn exists primarily as a status symbol, a visual badge of suburban confederacy. By downzoning the front yard from a primary to a secondary or minimal hydrozone, it can be designed to more accurately reflect its traditional purpose as a visual complement to the house and a reflection of the homeowner's way of life (Figure 10-12, see next page). In other applications as well — the subdivision, the public gathering place, the community (Figure 10-13), and the regional land use study (Figure 10-14) — the hydrozone concept can be used to bring diversity and visual clarity to the landscape.

Some may argue that the concept of hydrozones threatens the traditional landscape aesthetic of "green grass and trees around me," and prevents people from enjoying the landscape as they are accustomed. Though hydrozonic design may change the *potential* use of an area, analysis will reveal that the actual use remains unchanged. People could picnic on a grass parking strip, but they rarely do, so the actual use would remain unchanged even if the area were paved.

As shown later in this chapter, significant water and energy savings can be realized through improved irrigation and maintenance practices. If a client or designer desires a traditional landscape image, different maintenance practices in the various hydrozones can provide some water and energy savings without sacrificing the visual integrity of the landscape. In other situations, areas that may not be contacted directly by the users, but which have important functions requiring water and energy inputs (e.g., fire buffer zones, microclimate modification, etc.) can be identified and appropriately zoned.

Even regions with enough rainfall to support a lush landscape benefit from the hydrozonic approach, for areas of high use intensity can be differentiated from

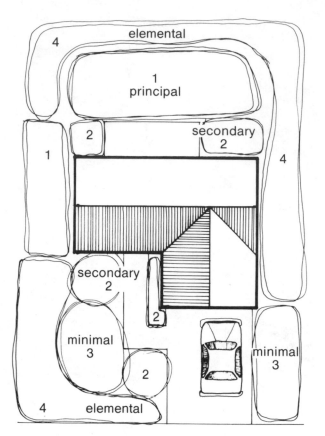
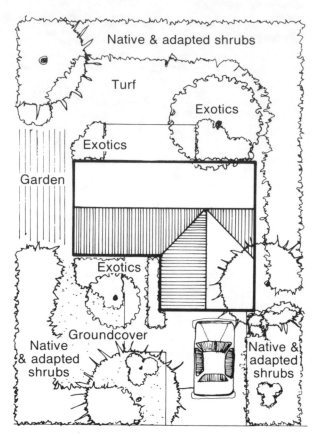

Figure 10-12. Hydrozone concept applied to a suburban lot.

Figure 10-13. Hydrozone concept applied to community scale.

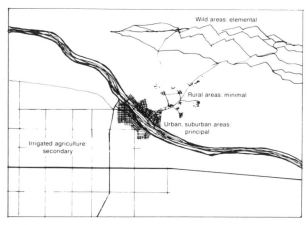

Figure 10-14. Hydrozone concept applied to regional scale.

low-use areas. If water savings are less important, energy savings can be realized through differentiation of the designed landscape. For example, a large turf area may, with sufficient rainfall, remain entirely as turf, but be zoned into areas of close mowing and un-mowed meadow, according to human use intensity. The closely mown area will also receive supplemental irrigation when necessary, frequent fertilization, maintenance, and other energy inputs. The unmown area, because it is less used, would be classified as a less intensive maintenance zone, and would require fewer energy additions to survive. Thus hydrozoning saves maintenance energy and brings diversity into the landscape, even in situations where dramatic water savings are not sought. The hydrozone concept does not dictate design, but presents a defensible, rational process by which a water-conserving landscape design can be achieved.

200

Techniques for Managing the Principal Hydrozone

Landscaped areas in the principal hydrozone, where most human impact occurs, must be kept intact through some expenditure of water and energy. However, careful management programming can minimize the additional water necessary even in this zone. For swimming pools, covers can be placed on the water surface when the pool is not in use to conserve heating energy and reduce evaporative losses. For water features requiring electrical or mechanical energy to operate, renewable energy sources can provide power for water motion as is done in the Flint River Park in Flint, Mich., where water is pumped by means of a series of windmills and an Archimedes screw driven by the river's natural current.

Most commonly, however, designers are faced with the necessity of establishing and sustaining viable areas of turfgrass in the principal hydrozone — playing fields, parks, etc. Several approaches can reduce the amount of water needed to maintain healthy, attractive turf:

Choose the right species of turfgrass. As might be expected, warm-season grasses such as Bermuda, hybrid Bermuda, and zoysia grass are all more drought-tolerant than their northern, cool-season counterparts. Closely following these grasses, however, is tall fescue, a course but durable turf for active play. Next in the order of decreasing drought tolerance comes bluegrass, perennial ryegrass, bentgrasses, St. Augustine grass, and dichondra, a common lawn substitute. Several "native grasses" such as annual ryegrass, wheatgrass, and buffalo grass have considerable resistance to drought.

The choice of a grass species, however, depends on many other factors unrelated to water conservation. Bermuda grasses, zoysia, and St. Augustine grasses all go dormant and turn brown in areas with markedly cool winters. Tall fescue is considerably drought-tolerant and will retain color in the winter months, but is somewhat coarser than the turf people often expect. Tall fescue can be managed at a finer texture by being seeded more heavily than normal, causing thinner blades due to more competition among individual plants. Kentucky bluegrass and mixtures of bluegrass, ryegrass, and fescue are perhaps the most popular turfgrasses in the nation, but require considerably more water, especially if soil preparation is inadequate. Crested wheatgrass, blue grama, and buffalo grass are all western natives which, after establishment, will require less freqeuent watering but should not be considered true substitutes for the other species

listed. They will stand some foot traffic but will not provide the popular "green carpet" image and should therefore be considered for the secondary or minimal hydrozone, away from heavy human use.

The use of "native" grasses is a highly regional phenomenon. In most areas of California, native grasses can no longer compete with the multitude of imported grasses, weeds, and thistles. In Colorado and the Rocky Mountain states, buffalo grass and grama grasses are combined with other adapted grasses into "foothills" blends, which have been successfully used in rural open spaces and parks. Designers in various regions should consult local agricultural and horticultural extension specialists to determine the best grasses for saving water.

Mow at the proper height. Most turfgrass should be maintained at a height of two inches or more. Research has shown that turf mown higher will resist drought more effectively due to a more substantial root structure. When they are well-irrigated, longer turf blades will transpire more water than the same turf mown closer to the ground. Where turf must be of high visual quality and frequent irrigation is possible, mowing at a two-inch height seems logical. When turf is to withstand a reduced irrigation schedule, either through voluntary or involuntary means, mowing at three or four inches will allow the turf to withstand drought with less impact on appearancc.

Apply fertilizer adequately, but do not overfertilize. Danielson and his colleagues (1981) have reported that turfgrass irrigation can be reduced to 70% of maximum ET (evapotranspiration) with no significant loss in color if fertilization regimes are maintained. In fact, turf under slightly reduced irrigation with sufficient nitrogen will develop stronger root systems for drought resistance instead of the normally high flush of top growth found with irrigation rates approaching maximum ET. (This seems to be a natural adaption of the plant to adverse conditions.) Phosphorus is important for root development, while potassium aids in the natural resistance to drought. If fertilization rates as well as irrigation are reduced, loss of visual quality and color occur at an earlier stage. Overfertilization causes the turfgrass to flush with top growth at the expense of root development, making the turf less resistant to drought.

Aerate soil and remove thatch. Turfgrass with a heavy level of thatch feels spongy, and irrigation water is prevented from moving down into the root zone, often running off onto pavement where it is wasted. While a minimum thatch layer (about one-half inch) is necessary to keep roots cool and reduce advective water loss from the soil, too much thatch is detrimental. Aeration of the soil, particularly for turf established on heavy clays, is necessary for adequate root growth and drought resistance. Foot traffic will compact soil that has been soaked with water, impairing aeration and dramatically reducing soil air spaces. Since mechanical aeration takes energy, a reduced irrigation regime will allow heavily used turfgrass to be supported by soil with less moisture, more air spaces, and better bearing resistance.

Manage irrigation. Fine-tuning irrigation scheduling, application rates, controllers, and moisture sensors can account for 30% to 50% savings over the average turf irrigation requirements, with virtually no significant change in landscape appearance or image. A common problem with turf irrigation systems is application of water at a rate greater than that which can be readily absorbed; a situation leading to rapid buildup of a layer of water, which then runs off laterally. In heavy soils, water should be applied slowly for long periods of time, with substantial time between waterings. If the type of irrigation heads cannot provide slow application rates, they should be replaced with low volume heads, or operated by "syringing," that is, repeated short applications separated by adequate time intervals to enable all applied water to be used. Lighter, sandier soils will require more frequent irrigation at higher application rates to keep roots from drying out. Over the life of a turfgrass planting requiring an irrigation system, installing automatic irrigation timers is highly advisable. Automatic turf control technology is now solid-state, with every conceivable feature available, including rain and soil moisture sensors that will override irrigation programs to reduce unneeded water. An improperly programmed controller may waste water, but a properly programmed electronic controller can save water and maintenance energy far in excess of its initial cost.

Irrigation schedules will vary according to the water conservation requirements. During a drought, when irrigation water is scarce, restricted, or simply not available, turf can be allowed to go dormant and turn brown if the root system is substantial and can store enough nutrients to produce new growth when irrigation is resumed. Turfgrasses that have been watered deeply will develop more extensive root systems than those watered frequently and at shallow depths. If turf survival is paramount, irrigation can be reduced to levels far below that required for maintenance of green color.

Landscape Alternatives for the Secondary and Minimal Hydrozones

Some of the management and design techniques previously described for turfgrasses can be adapted to plantings of less water-intensive native grasses in the secondary or minimal hydrozones. For the most part, however, these zones call for plantings other than relatively shallow-rooted grasses that require more frequent watering. Alternatives include trees, shrubs, woody and herbaceous groundcovers, organic and inorganic mulches and, of course, paving.

Tree cover. Generally speaking, trees are the natural climax landscape in regions receiving more than 20-in. of rainfall per year. In the eastern and midwestern United States, the climax landscape is a forest (hardwood or softwood, depending on site and climate conditions). Even in areas receiving less than 20 in. of rainfall, groves of trees can be established with minimum additional irrigation. California's Central Valley has many dense forests and woodlots of eucalyptus trees planted for fuel wood in regions of 15 in. of rainfall or less.

Tree stands often are overlooked as landscape treatments for the secondary and minimal hydrozones, partly because of expense and partly because landscape architects tend to consider trees as specimens. The expense of planting many trees in a grove or woods can be buffered by planting smaller nursery stock, planting from seed, or allowing natural succession to take place where possible. On an area basis, trees will transpire approximately as much water as an equivalent area of turf. However, trees generally tap sources of water in soil far deeper than grass roots and therefore can survive longer periods of drought without irrigation. Many trees native to the American west need no additional water when established. Some adapted species, such as the eucalypti of California, actually suppress weeds and understory growth through deposition of leaf and bark litter containing acids and oils. Consequently, some very useful, drought-tolerant landscapes result; shade is provided, yet the understory is free for moving about and adequate for passive recreation, such as picnicking.

For secondary hydrozones, a grove of native or well-adapted trees, planted to a density approaching that of an orchard, will provide a water-saving alternative. When greywater recycling becomes more acceptable, these groves can provide shade, fruit, understory recreation space, and even biomass for direct or indirect fuel production. Mulches can be applied for the first few years of establishment to keep tree groves free of weeds. In addition, tree stands can be more easily irrigated with simpler, more efficient equipment. In areas where rainfall is sufficient to produce tree stands naturally, no irrigation and only selective removal of unwanted species is necessary to allow natural forest cover to evolve.

Shrubs and woody groundcovers. The most obvious alternatives for the secondary hydrozone are shrubs native or adapted to the site and climate conditions. Shrubs like rhododendrons in the hills of North Carolina, junipers in the Rockies, Oregon grape in certain areas of Oregon, coyote brush for the California foothills, sagebrush for the Arizona desert, and wild blueberries for the coast of Maine are examples of low-maintenance native plantings for their respective sites. Of course, selecting species of water-conserving shrubs and woody groundcovers will depend on close approximation of natural communities and locations in the developed landscape. In the California foothills, shrub chapparal associations consisting of manzanita, ceanothus, toyon, chamise, and wild buckwheat cover the landscape and can be replicated almost entirely in deliberately planted landscapes with similar site conditions. These shrubs are all adapted to waterless summers and can be successfully established in well-drained soils with minimum irrigation. Drought-tolerant, woody shrubs often depend on extensive root systems to take up water deep in the soil. Until roots are established, most drought-tolerant shrubs need water, as does any ornamental shrub. Many a native shrub has died in the landscape because of failure by the misinformed homeowner or contractors to provide adequate water for root establishment. However, not all shrubs native to arid and semi-arid landscapes are drought-resistant. Alders, willows, cottonwoods, and wild grape all occur in riparian environments with ample year-round soil moisture and cannot be expected to survive without additional irrigation. Shrubs are native or adaptable to xeric, mesic, or hydric sites, but rarely all three. (Some willows will withstand complete inundation as well as complete drought for brief periods). Shrubs able to tolerate both shade and drought are less easily found, although not impossible to find if one searches for the appropriately analogous natural conditions. For shady locations, shrubs commonly thought to require more water often can be used in water-saving landscapes simply because evaporation and transpiration are reduced with increasing shade.

With exceptions, notably the California chaparral,

shrubs rarely exist only in association with other shrubs, but are often found as pioneer species after fires, in the understory of larger trees, or in riparian or high altitude associations with trees, grasses, or herbaceous groundcovers. Regional- and site-specific characteristics will suggest ways of using shrubs and woody groundcovers in the design of water-saving landscapes.

Herbaceous groundcovers. Nationwide, a multitude of herbaceous groundcover plant material is available, much of which in contrast to lawns can reduce water use. Choices range from vetches and clovers, which need some water, to succulent stonecrops, ice plants, and other water-storing herbs. Cultivated from forms found native in arid and semi-arid environments worldwide, many drought-tolerant herbaceous groundcovers spread quite rapidly.

Herbaceous groundcovers have some advantage over turf in that they require a lesser degree of accuracy in irrigation coverage than turf, which must be evenly irrigated across a given area. Groundcovers planted on 18- to 48-in. centers can be irrigated with shrub spray heads or, better still, drip systems. Pitt et al. (1982) estimated that for a selected location in Maryland, groundcover can be established requiring half the irrigation of an equivalent area of turf, and consuming roughly 25% of the energy over a period of five years (see Chapter Eleven). Although groundcovers are not maintenance free, they require less maintenance as they become established. Many can be grown from cuttings, reducing the price per square foot to reasonable levels. Some groundcovers can stand moderate foot traffic — clover, for example, can be used in many places where a lawn might normally be considered. Clover will consume less water and fix soil nitrogen. It can be turned into the soil as an amendment, can be maintained with only very infrequent mowing, and is pleasant enough to sit or lie upon.

Some groundcovers grow so vigorously that they are hard to contain in small planter areas. Generally, the faster a groundcover grows, the larger an area it should occupy. Algerian ivy (*Hedera canariensis*) has been known to spread from groundcover beds all the way up 100-ft palm trees in southern California. Water, of course, can be restricted to curtail growth, but choice of groundcover material should relate to the need for trimming and confining plants to definite borders.

In the Midwest, allowing the native prairie grasses and herbaceous plants to reestablish in developed landscapes has been successful. Darrel Morrison's plan (1975) for the CUNA Mutual Insurance Society in Madison, Wis., is a good example of the use of a prairie border between native woodlands and manicured turfgrass and illustrates a zoned or graded approach to water and energy requirements. Although merely not mowing a Kentucky bluegrass lawn and allowing whatever prairielike plant association to evolve has been attempted before with mixed success, courts in the states of Wisconsin and Maryland have set legal precedents allowing grasses in ornamental landscapes to grow to their natural height. Prairie landscapes must be carefully developed, however, since many of the native grasses and plants that might have composed an original prairie ecosystem may have long since retreated from the developed area. What may invade a disturbed site instead are quack grasses, Canada, Russian, or star thistle, bindweed, ragweed, or other aggressive weeds, depending on geographical area. These must be controlled, often at great expense. The California Department of Transportation is experimenting with methods of controlling weeds in its dryland plantings along highway corridors. In some cases, biannual mowing is sufficient to control star thistle and other noxious plants. Fire has been successfully used in restoring prairie and meadow plantings, although the problems of using controlled burning are obvious. Chemical weed control is possible but a direct waste of nonrenewable energy.

Mulches. Mulching can significantly reduce plant water consumption, particularly in areas of the minimal hydrozone where the ground must be covered and kept tidy and weed free but is not apt to be very visually important. Mulches may be organic (bark or wood chips, nut shells, peatmoss, pine needles) or inorganic (gravel, rock, plastic, etc.). Mulches have several functions worth emphasizing:

1. *Soil temperature modification and insulation.* Mulches keep soil cooler in summer and warmer in winter and can often aid in preventing frost damage to roots. By lowering soil temperatures in summer, mulches reduce direct evaporation of soil moisture to the air.
2. *Reduction of advective drying of the soil.* By reducing wind speeds close to the soil layer, mulches prevent extra evaporation of soil moisture that would normally result from wind drying.
3. *Weed suppression.* Mulches reduce growth of weeds, either by extra-large pore spaces that are too big to support root growth (as in bark chips or gravel) or by direct suffocation (plastic). Weeds that normally grow on the surface — and waste water — are retarded, thus keeping more

moisture available in the soil for desired plants.
4. *Reduction of soil compaction.* By absorbing and redistributing bearing loads applied at localized point sources (e.g., foot traffic), subsoil underneath the mulch retains good structure and avoids compaction that otherwise would rob the soil of pore spaces, water-holding capacity, and plants' ability to resist drought.
5. *Improvement of soil structure by organic mulches.* As organic mulches decompose, they add organic material to the soil, improving soil structure and nutrient accessibility. However, as woody mulches decompose, they may temporarily reduce soil nitrogen as it is consumed in the decomposition process. This can be offset by using initial soil fertilization before mulching or mulches that decompose very slowly, such as redwood bark.

Mulches are not without problems. Some organic mulches are fine enough to be blown by the wind. Others, such as shredded newspaper, white gravel, deep red volcanic cinders, may meet with some resistance (perhaps justifiable) from an esthetic standpoint. Extremely light-colored inorganic mulches such as white gravel increase glare and reflected light and do not blend well with most landscape compositions. Although some mulches, such as redwood bark or medium-textured wood chips, can be walked on or even used to sit on, others offer little resistance to foot traffic. The ubiquitous black plastic sheet mulch buried under wood chips is hardly worth installing, for it inevitably shows through disturbances in the top bark layer and has rather negative esthetic connotations. Of greater merit are the various organic fabrics used for erosion control. Soil cement mixtures and polymeric soil additives have been used to control weeds with varied success. Gravel and river rock can be effective, but smaller gravels will quickly fill with ambient soil particles brought by wind or water runoff and will evolve into a good growth medium for weeds. Generally, a 4-in. layer of mulch is required to be an effective weed suppressant. Anything less invites frustration.

Paving. At first mention, the suggestion of paving as an alternative water-saving groundcover may bring on shudders of protest. However, the logic of paving a small portion of a site and putting the remainder to drought-tolerant groundcover merits consideration and offers a significant alternative to a fence-to-fence expanse of turf. In fact, even turf is inappropriate in locations where continual or heavy traffic occurs.

Surprisingly enough, one of the most water-conserving landscape treatments is a wood deck; it succeeds in shading out weeds, stands up under traffic, cools the soil beneath, reduces soil moisture evaporation, and allows rainwater to fall through its cracks and buildup the soil-water profile.

Water Management

Water management is the cornerstone of water-conserving landscape design, regardless of the hydrozone in question. Following are techniques that have broad application and substantial potential for water conservation.

Drip and subterranean irrigation. In areas of the country requiring additional irrigation to support ornamental plant growth, drip and subterranean irrigation systems are becoming more reliable and popular. Technically referred to as low-volume irrigation, the various systems deliver water at low pressures (about 20 psi) and low flow rates (one gallon per hour for each emitter) directly to the root zones of plants. Pioneered in Israel where water is precious, drip or "trickle" irrigation systems often consist of one or more valves, antisiphon devices, pressure regulators, and a system of half-inch black polyethylene hose extending into the landscaped areas. Microtubing, or ⅛-in. "spaghetti," transfers water from the main lines to the root ball of the plant. Emitters dissipate pressure by various techniques including vortex swirling of the water in tiny chambers, and can be connected either at the end of the microtubing or between the main lines and the microtubing. Occasionally, emitters are mounted in the main lines that run directly past the root areas to be watered, eliminating the need for microtubing. Small, low-volume misters, spray heads, and tubing with microperforations also are available. Most drip components can be assembled with only a small hole punch for use in placing emitters on pressure lines. Polyethylene hose is quite flexible and can be easily meandered about to conform to the most complex garden shapes. The system is "tinkertoy-like" in that it can be changed and altered quite readily as plants grow, are replaced, or establish themselves until they no longer need irrigation. Prices are not low, but are currently competitive with standard sprinkler systems and are bound to drop as the market expands.

Drip or low-volume irrigation systems can be used to advantage for all types of plantings other than lawns, which are better off with standard sprinkler systems due to coverage requirements. Drip systems are ideal for trees, shrubs, groundcover, vines, and even hanging plants which can be irrigated by means of small microtubing spurs from main lines. Major advantages of drip systems are as follows:

1. Water is applied directly and only to the roots of the plants. Nonplanted soil areas are not watered and subsequent weeds are not a problem.
2. Soluble fertilizer can be injected into the system and taken directly to where it is most useful.
3. Water is applied at a very slow rate, which enables it to be easily utilized by plants even in heavy soils.
4. Because the area of surface wetting is small, little evaporative losses occur.
5. Because water flow rates are small (60 emitters require only one gpm of flow), pressure losses due to pipe friction are minimal, making pipe sizing less critical to design performance. One-half-inch pipe is the universal main for residential scale systems.
6. Low-pressure operation allows snap-together and friction-type fittings, eliminating the need for screw threads, glue, or thrust blocking.
7. Codes allow low-pressure lines to be placed on the surface rather than deeply buried, eliminating considerable installation cost and effort.

Drip systems do have disadvantages, however. Occasionally, since flows are low, emitters are small, and water is apt to contain precipitates, clogging can occur. Filtering at the source and occasional flushing of the lines can reduce the problem. Drip irrigation does not rinse the leaves of shrubs and groundcovers as do conventional sprinkler systems. Drip tubing, if visible, could be considered unsightly due to its snake-like appearance.

Many of these disadvantages can be minimized by burying main lines or setting mains, emitters, and microtubing directly on grade and covering the system with a medium-coarse mulch that would cover the system, prevent casual vandalism, protect the emitters, and reduce ultraviolet radiation damage to the system components. Small, U-shaped pieces of stiff wire can be used to pin down the drip tubing against minor expansion, contraction, or jarring. Nevertheless, drip irrigation is estimated to save between 30% and 50% of the water required by the conventional method to irrigate plants.

A recent development in low-volume irrigation is the subterranean, or buried, irrigation line. Like drip systems, subterranean irrigation systems rely on low-flow, low-pressure characteristics to deliver water underground, right to the root zones of plants. Installation costs of trenching, etc., are more than for drip

205

and conventional irrigation (more pipe trenches are required); but there are advantages. Subterranean irrigation systems have been used successfully to irrigate lawns: Grids of buried soaker tubing are placed according to soil characteristics to provide even wetting of the grass root zone. Since the systems are buried, little vandalism can occur. However, it is difficult to check emitter flow rates, wetting, or even whether the system has been left on or off.

For both drip and subterranean irrigation, emitter spacing depends upon the clay content of the soil. Heavy soils absorb water more slowly, causing a wider wetted profile, necessitating wider spacing for emitters. Sandy soils require closer spacing due to the lack of lateral movement of water. Timing of water application is also critical. In saline soils, drip systems can be allowed to operate at low levels almost continuously, thereby allowing the salts to leach down through the soil pores and away from root zones. This feature has contributed to the success of crop production in Israel where saline water is a problem.

Rainwater harvesting. The collection and use of rainwater for irrigation can provide a significant amount of a site's water needs. Milne (1976) has suggested that, even allowing for evaporation, the average world rainfall (26.3 in./year) collected from an 1800-ft^2 area could meet a person's domestic water demands. Although rainwater collected from urban areas is probably not potable because of the concentration of pollutants (Jenkins & Pearson, 1978), rainwater harvesting for landscape use is feasible and becoming more economical. Short of actually collecting and storing rain, new methods of channeling rainwater can contribute to water conservation. Downspouts leading to perforated drainpipes buried in the ground can help to sustain the soil-water profile. Open channel drainage and catch basins eliminate the need for costly subsurface storm drainage systems and help to further increase water percolation into the soil (Figure 10-15). These systems also provide a strikingly different visual and environmental landscape image by creating riparian habitats and plantings within the urban setting. Locating landscape plants in areas where surface drainage water collects eliminates the need for extensive irrigation.

Greywater cycling. If water can be used more than once, then each cycle of reuse represents water conserved. Recycling water within a household or a site is both practical and economical with current technology. Most water-recycling systems collect all

Figure 10-15. Open-channel drainage, which saves water and provides sensory interest.

of the water except that used to flush solid wastes into sewers. The collected water, greywater, consists of water used for bathing, cooking, clothes washing, etc. It can be stored and then used either for toilet flushing or for irrigation with minimal treatment. Figure 10-16 (see next page) illustrates how recycling of greywater in the integral urban house can reduce water consumption. Reid (1976) has concluded that such a system shared among a housing cluster could significantly reduce the costs of installing and maintaining a large septic system. Unfortunately, current institutional barriers and archaic plumbing codes prevent more widespread adoption of greywater cycling.

The previously described techniques will enable the landscape architect to design a water-saving landscape that achieves the same design effect for much less water and energy. In the following section, several alternative landscape schemes are offered that employ a number of these recommended alternatives.

Three Scenarios for Water-Conserving Landscape Design

To better understand the application of the hydrozone concept to water-conserving landscape design, consider a moderate-income housing project, still in the planning stage. The developer-management company calls on the designer to provide a master plan and planting and management plans. The basic site planning and architecture have already been determined. This site could exist in any region of the United States; thus by correctly identifying and determining the needs and desires of the client, the designer can suggest water-conserving landscape approaches that exist along a continuum of slight-to-radical innovation. Figure 10-17 (see page 208) graphically presents such approaches. The following scenarios suggest three positions the designer may take, depending on the

Per Capita Consumption of Water at the Integral Urban House (August)

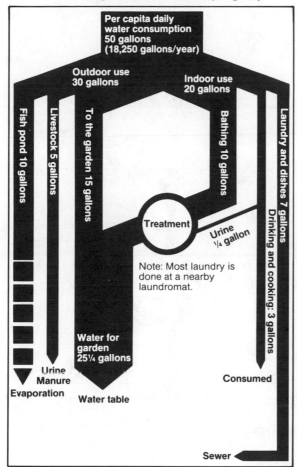

Typical Water Consumption in a Suburban California House

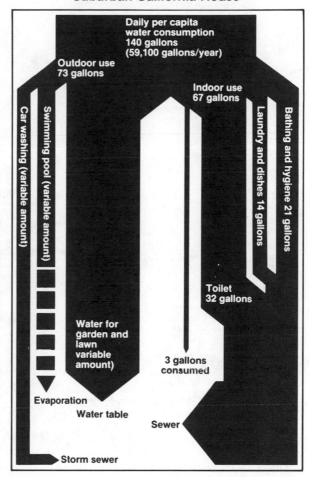

Figure 10-16. Per capita consumption of water — a typical suburban California house compared to the Integral Urban House. Adapted from: (Farallones Institute, 1979)

client's attitude and receptiveness to new ideas. Figure 10-18 (see page 209) shows how the case study site is analyzed by hydrozones.

Scenario 1: Traditional Design Solution

The client wants a traditional landscape image and recognizes the need to minimize energy and water use, but is unwilling to deviate from conservative landscape design (Figure 10-19, see page 210).

- Reduce irrigation to save water and reduce frequency of mowing, pruning.
- Utilize deep watering to encourage deep roots, save labor, and increase drought tolerance.
- Establish a proper irrigation schedule, installing automatic irrigation controllers.
- Mulch the soil around the base of plants.
- Maintain adequate watering basins around plants.

- Moderate fertilizer applications.
- Install low-volume sprinkler heads.
- Substitute some unused turf areas (e.g., parking strips, utility areas, etc.) with mulch or paving.

Scenario 2: Moderate Innovation

The client recognizes need to adjust landscape image and is willing to entertain new ideas and design solutions as long as they aren't too "far-out" or provocative. The client sees himself as responsible and forward-looking, but does not want to alienate any potential buyers (Figure 10-20, see page 211).

Options:

- Implement management practices outlined in scenario 1.
  Limit turf areas and water features to the primary hydrozone only.

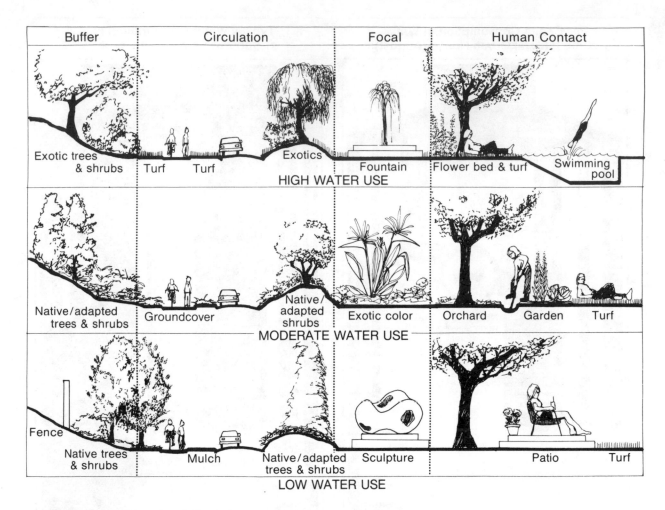

Buffer	Circulation	Focal	Human Contact

Exotic trees & shrubs · Turf · Turf · Exotics · Fountain · Flower bed & turf · Swimming pool

HIGH WATER USE

Native/adapted trees & shrubs · Groundcover · Native/adapted shrubs · Exotic color · Orchard · Garden · Turf

MODERATE WATER USE

Fence · Native trees & shrubs · Mulch · Native/adapted trees & shrubs · Sculpture · Patio · Turf

LOW WATER USE

Figure 10-17. Water use relating to human use — three approaches.

- Limit thirsty ornamentals and flower beds to the secondary hydrozone.
- Select native or adapted groundcover for areas without foot traffic.
- Select native and adapted plants where feasible.
- Specify drip and/or subterranean irrigation systems for shrub beds, groundcover, and tree plantings.
- Consider porous paving materials to increase water percolation.

Scenario 3: Radical Innovation

The client wants to adopt innovations, is concerned with water and energy crises, and wants the project to reflect the latest in design solutions. He wants to explore new ideas and technologies and sees radical innovation as the only means of remaining viable in light of coming social and economic changes (Figure 10-21, see page 212).

Options:

- Implement practices outlined in scenarios 1 and 2.
- Establish alternative renewable energy sources (e.g., wind, solar, etc.).
- Develop rainwater harvesting, open channel drainage, and catch basins.
- Explore greywater cycling systems for landscape irrigation.
- Tolerate a moderate amount of naturalized plant material to exist within cultivated areas to minimize expenditures for herbicides and maintenance.
- Allow portions of lawn to remain unmowed and to be managed as meadow.
- Plant primarily with native and adapted plants.
- Use portions of the site for food production, orchards, vegetable gardens, and vineyards.

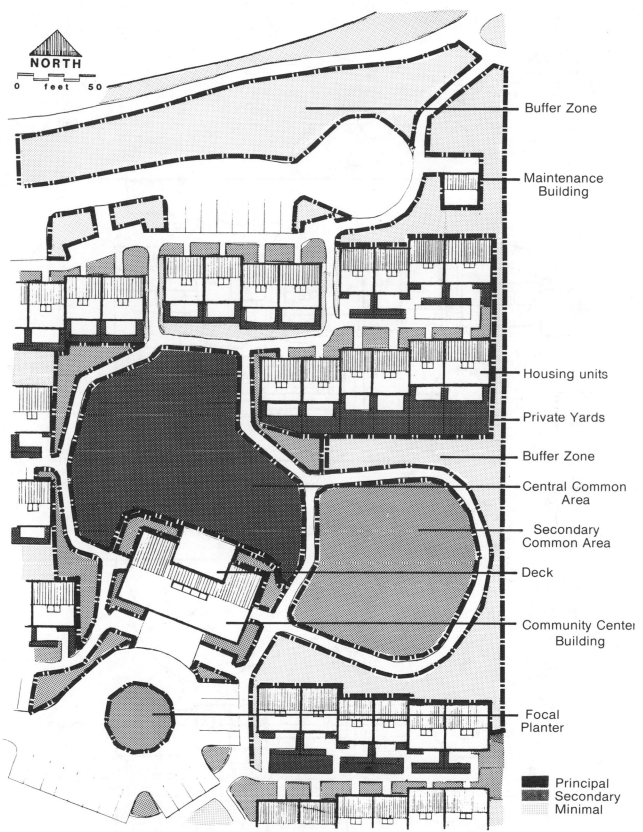

NORTH

0 feet 50

Buffer Zone

Maintenance Building

Housing units

Private Yards

Buffer Zone

Central Common Area

Secondary Common Area

Deck

Community Center Building

Focal Planter

Principal
Secondary
Minimal

Figure 10-18. Landscape development analyzed by hydrozones.

209

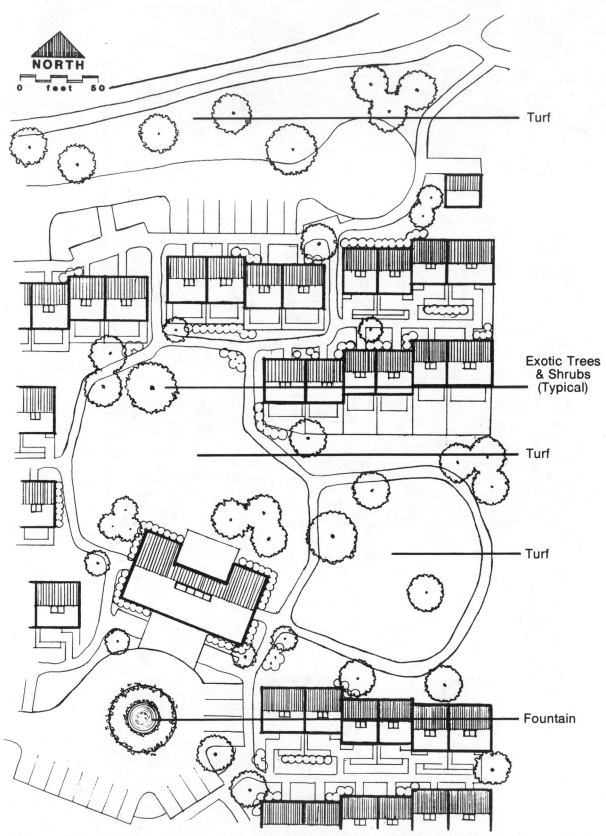

NORTH

0 feet 50

Turf

Exotic Trees
& Shrubs
(Typical)

Turf

Turf

Fountain

Figure 10-19. Traditional landscape imagery — turfgrass with trees and foundation shrubs.

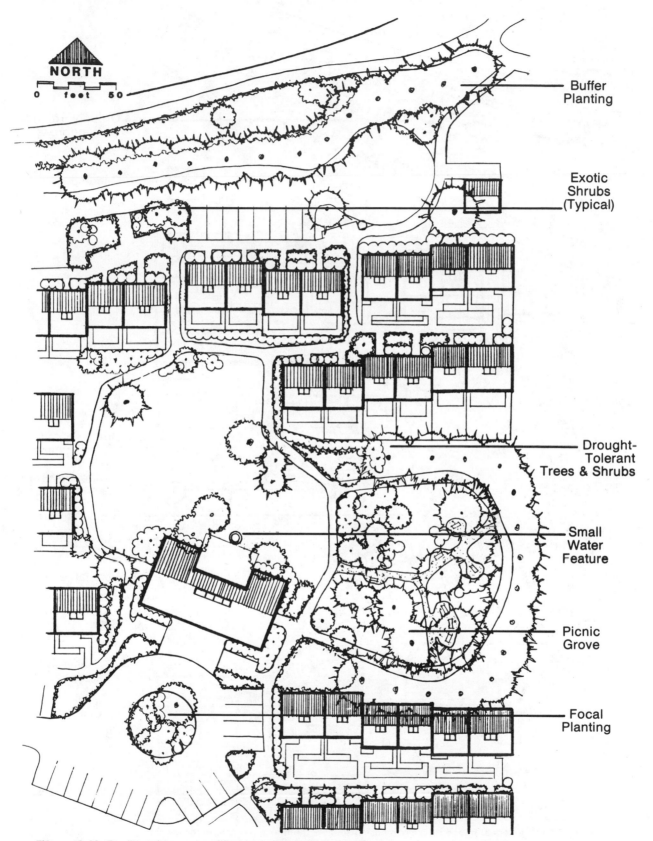

NORTH

0   feet   50

Buffer
Planting

Exotic
Shrubs
(Typical)

Drought-
Tolerant
Trees & Shrubs

Small
Water
Feature

Picnic
Grove

Focal
Planting

Figure 10-20. Traditional image modified by hydrozonic approach.

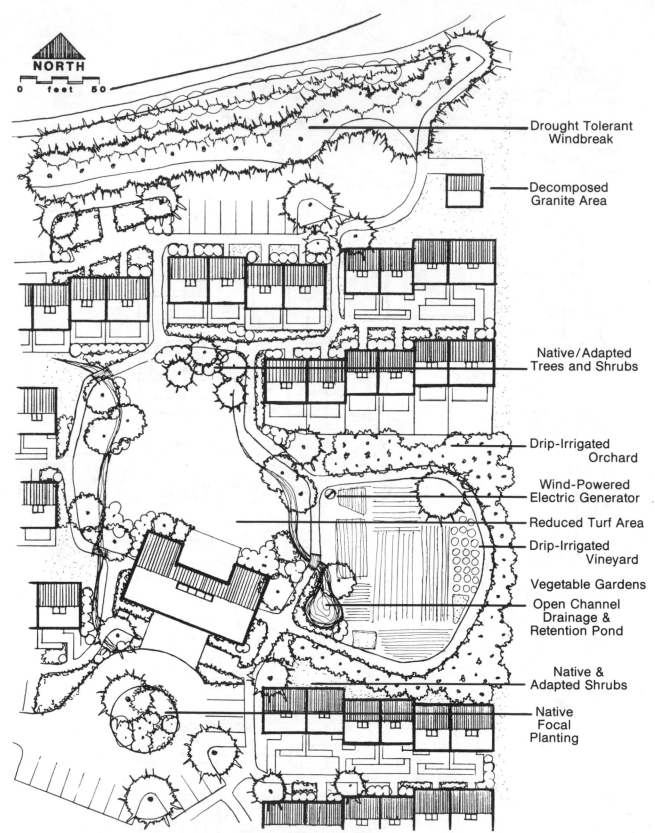

NORTH

0 feet 50

Drought Tolerant
Windbreak

Decomposed
Granite Area

Native/Adapted
Trees and Shrubs

Drip-Irrigated
Orchard

Wind-Powered
Electric Generator

Reduced Turf Area

Drip-Irrigated
Vineyard

Vegetable Gardens

Open Channel
Drainage &
Retention Pond

Native &
Adapted Shrubs

Native
Focal
Planting

Figure 10-21. Traditional image radically modified to save the maximum amount of water.

212

- Use mulches instead of cultivated groundcovers in the elemental hydrozone (especially in arid climates).

Conclusions

Water conservation significantly conserves energy. Achieving real savings is a tremendously complex task, involving social, political, and economic decisions on all levels. Yet designers and planners can encourage water savings while simultaneously shaping public attitudes toward water conservation. Landscape architects pride themselves in being stewards of the land and its resources. In terms of site-scale design to save water, landscape architects have failed in practice to live up to what they believe themselves to be in theory. The public and the profession need a new process, a new esthetic, based more on design and resource integration and less on romantic nostalgia. The hydrozone concept provides both a framework for rational design and a foundation for new landscape imagery. From this, an honest and lasting landscape tradition reflecting conservation values will emerge.

CHAPTER ELEVEN
Conservation of Embodied Energy through Landscape Design

DAVID G. PITT
University of Maryland
College Park, Maryland

L ANDSCAPE planners and designers — be they landscape architects, architects, urban and regional planners, engineers, nurserymen, or landscape contractors — are inherently involved in fitting society's needs for physical use of the environment onto the physical resource base of the landscape. Historically, objectives in establishing relationships between humans and their environments have focused on solutions that maximize usefulness and esthetic enjoyment for society. During the 1960s, planners and designers realized that the human-environment relationships they create can have substantial positive and negative effects on the physical and biological properties of the environment, a consequence first identified a century earlier by Fredrick Law Olmsted. In the aftermath of the OPEC nations' embargo on oil flowing into the United States during the winter of 1973-74, landscape planners and designers began to examine the implicit and explicit effects of their professional intentions on the consumption of fossil fuel sources of energy.

Other chapters in this volume examine landscape planning and management techniques as methods for minimizing the fossil fuel requirements of space conditioning; i.e., maintaining human comfort in both interior and exterior environments. This chapter focuses on embodied fossil fuel energy in landscape planning and design; the fossil fuel consumption that occurs in the manufacturing of landscape materials and in the processes of implementing and maintaining design

solutions. The quantity of energy embodied in a landscape is a direct by-product of choice of materials, facility layout, and other design decisions. Two concepts are important to understanding and evaluating embodied energy in landscape planning and design: direct versus indirect consumption of energy and the British thermal unit (Btu) as a measure of energy consumption.

Direct and Indirect Energy Consumption

Energy can be consumed either directly or indirectly. Direct consumption occurs for example when gasoline is burned in an engine to propel a car from one point to another. Indirect consumption occurs when a product is purchased that requires energy in its manufacture. Several forms of direct energy consumption exist in the construction and maintenance of landscape plans and designs; two examples include the combustion of gasoline to operate a lawn mower and the use of an electric pump to draw and deliver irrigation water. Indirect fossil fuel energy consumption in landscape construction and maintenance takes place every time a bag of fertilizer, lime, or pesticide is applied to the land; every time a pallet of bricks or cubic-yard of sand is laid; and every time concrete is used as a paving surface. Although the purchase and the use of these items may involve no direct fossil fuel energy consumption, energy is required in their manufacture. Thus, when they are purchased and used in the landscape, an indirect consumption of energy occurs.

The British Thermal Unit as a Measure of Energy Consumption

Energy consumption is often measured and compared in terms of the British thermal unit (Btu). A Btu represents the amount of energy required to raise the temperature of one pound of water (approximately two cups of water) from 39.2F (4C) to 40.2F (4.5C). Both direct and indirect energy consumption can be expressed in terms of Btus. For example, the Btus directly consumed in the combustion of a gallon of gasoline range from 110,000 to 140,000 depending upon the octane rating of the gas. The manufacture of one pound of nitrogen fertilizer requires 33,500 Btus which are indirectly consumed when the fertilizer is purchased and applied to the land.[1] By converting the energy that is directly consumed in landscape construction and maintenance to Btus, along with the energy that is consumed in the manufacture of materials used in landscape construction and maintenance, it is possible to compare the energy requirements of alternative landscape planning and design solutions *before* they go into the ground. Such an analysis permits designers and planners to reduce, or at least to consider, the energy consumption requirements they build into their designs.

Scope of the Chapter

The following sections of this chapter examine the fossil fuel energy that is directly or indirectly consumed (in terms of Btu equivalents) in the implementation and maintenance of landscape designs. The chapter focuses on the residential site in temperate and arid climates. A case study illustrates the application of major points presented in the chapter.

Embodied Energy in Site Planning and Design

Embodied energy considerations enter the site design process at two stages: during formulation of the conceptual or preliminary design, and in the specification of plant and construction materials to implement a final design. A design concept generally specifies a pattern of visual mass-to-space relationships to be established in facilitating human use of the landscape. In the context of this discussion, mass-to-space can be thought of as the ratio of open landscape area to landscape occupied by vegetation. Mass-to-space relationships are critical determinants of embodied energy requirements in site design because the creation and maintenance of open space generally implies considerably higher fossil fuel input than does the creation and maintenance of vegetative mass. The more intensive human use occurring in developed open spaces requires the specification of landscape materials that are more resilient to human use. As the following discussion and case study demonstrate, the higher the resiliency of a landscape material, the more intense are its embodied energy requirements.

BTU Consumption in Landscape Construction and Maintenance

As a prelude to evaluating the embodied energy consequences of a design decision, a site designer must have an understanding of the Btus inherent to the selection of commonly used landscape materials. As noted earlier, these Btus may be consumed directly (e.g., the 124,000 Btus consumed through the combustion of a gallon of gasoline to propel a lawnmower) or indirectly (e.g., when materials requiring Btus in their manufacture are selected for use in a design).

Until recently, quantification of energy consumption in landscape construction and maintenance was scant. However, a recent report (National Capital Region, National Park Service, 1981) that was compiled from many sources lists direct and indirect energy consumption of various materials used in landscape construction and maintenance. Table 11-1 presents the Btus directly or indirectly consumed by more than 50 materials and pieces of equipment commonly used in landscape construction and maintenance.

---

[1] For purposes of comparison there are 5.82 million Btus in a barrel of crude oil.

Table 11-1. Btu Consumption by Materials Used in Landscape Construction and Maintenance

Material	Consumption
Fuel and engine/motor operation	
1 Gallon of gasoline	124,000
1 Gallon of diesel fuel	140,000
1 Kilowatt-hour of electricity	11,300
1 Horsepower-hour of gasoline engine operation	8308
1 Horsepower-hour of diesel engine operation	6160
Irrigation water	
1 Gallon of water pumped 100 feet of lift by electricity and distributed through buried permanent sprinkler system	4.3
1 Gallon of water pumped 100 feet of lift by electricity and distributed through hand moved sprinkler system	4.3

1 Gallon of water pumped 100 feet of lift by electricity and distributed through traveler sprinkler system	6.3
1 Gallon of water pumped 100 feet of lift by electricity and distributed through trickle sprinkler system	3.5
1 Acre-inch of water pumped 100 feet of lift by electricity and distributed through buried permanent sprinkler system	116,830
1 Acre-inch of water pumped 100 feet of lift by electricity and distributed through hand moved sprinkler system	116,830
1 Acre-inch of water pumped 100 feet of lift by electricity and distributed through traveler sprinkler system	171,170
1 Acre-inch of water pumped 100 feet of lift by electricity and distributed through trickle irrigation system	95,095
Fertilizer and soil amendments	
Manufacture of 1 pound nitrogen fertilizer	33,500
Manufacture of 1 pound phosphorous fertilizer (P_2O_5)	3150
Manufacture of 1 pound potassium fertilizer (K_2O)	2950
Manufacture of 1 pound lime	3750
Manufacture of 1 pound sulfur	47,916
Manufacture of 1 pound inorganics	4356
Pesticides	
Manufacture of 1 pound toxaphene insecticide	24,552
Manufacture of 1 pound methyl parathion insecticide	67,716
Manufacture of 1 pound 2,4-D herbicide	40,788
Manufacture of 1 pound 2,4,5-T herbicide	57,024
Manufacture of 1 pound trifluralin herbicide	87,120
Manufacture of 1 pound glyphosate herbicide	187,704
Manufacture of 1 pound paraquat herbicide	194,040
Manufacture of 1 pound propanil herbicide	97,020
Manufacture of 1 pound MCPA herbicide	53,856
Manufacture of 1 pound methyl bromide fungicide	287,100
Manufacture of 1 pound petroleum	90,684
Manufacture of 1 pound xylene	18,374
Construction materials	
Manufacture of 1 pound PVC plastic	51,600
Manufacture of 1 pound polyethylene plastic	59,400
Manufacture of 1 pound steel	33,700
Manufacture of 1 pound aluminum	140,000
Manufacture of 1 pound portland cement	3,555
Manufacture of 1 pound crushed stone	28
Manufacture of 1 cubic foot crushed stone	3,111
Manufacture of 1 pound gravel	2,222
Manufacture of 1 pound sand	8
Manufacture of 1 cubic foot sand	889
Manufacture of 1 cubic foot concrete (½" aggregate)	97,509
Manufacture of 1 pound asphalt	294
Manufacture of 1 cubic foot asphalt	42,630
Manufacture of 1 pound brick	3,450
Manufacture of 1 brick	14,662
Manufacture of 1 sq. foot brick	65,981
Manufacture of 1 board foot pressure treated southern pine finished lumber[a]	3,236
Equipment and machinery	
Manufacture of 1 tractor, mower, etc. per horsepower of engine	10,515,200
Manufacture of 1 diesel engine per horsepower of engine	3,970,000
Manufacture of 1 electric motor per horsepower of motor	1,980,000
Manufacture of 1 buried permanent sprinkler system per irrigated acre	31,818,000
Installation of 1 buried permanent sprinkler system per irrigated acre	1,369,000
Manufacture of 1 hand moved sprinkler irrigation system per irrigated acres[b]	9,201,000
Installation of 1 hand moved sprinkler irrigation system per irrigated acres[b]	42,000
Manufacture of 1 traveler sprinkler irrigation system per irrigated acre	14,421,000
Installation of 1 traveler sprinkler irrigation system per irrigated acre	57,000
Manufacture of 1 trickle irrigation system per irrigated acre	26,065,000
Installation of 1 trickle irrigation system per irrigated acre	273,000

[a]This figure was calculated for the author by the wood products utilization section of the Maryland Forest Service, Annapolis, Md. All other figures on this table were obtained or derived from *Energy Conservation Concepts in Managing Urban Parks*, a publication prepared for the National Park Service, U.S. Department of the Interior. (See references for full citation.)

[b]These figures are based on manufacture and installation of a hand-moved sprinkler system suitable for agricultural use. In all probability, they considerably overestimate the energy consumption required for the manufacture and installation of a hand-moved sprinkler system used in a residential context.

Embodied Energy Requirements of Various Site Design Components

The Btu estimates presented in Table 11-1 describe the energy consumption required for manufacturing the raw materials used in constructing and maintaining landscape designs. However, before these data can be used to estimate the embodied energy requirements of a site design, the materials (and their energy requirements) must be combined and examined from the perspective of how they are normally used in the landscape. For example, site designers often divide their designs into square feet of turf, square feet of brick patio or wood deck, square feet of shrub or tree mass, etc. Turf maintenance involves input of fertilizer, herbicides, gasoline, and may involve irrigation water. Brick patio construction (assuming dry joint construction) requires brick, sand, and treated lumber. Wooden decks usually imply input of concrete for post footings and various fasteners in addition to treated lumber. Tables 11-2 to 11-6 present translations of the raw material energy requirements given in Table 11-1 into embodied energy requirements of various components of a typical site design. These data include analyses of the embodied energy requirements for 1,000 ft^2 of turf (Table 11-2), groundcover plants (Table 11-3), shrub masses (Table 11-4), tree masses (Table 11-5), and brick, concrete, asphalt, gravel, and wood decking surfaces at appropriate thicknesses and strengths for detached residential and other extensively used landscapes (Table 11-6). The analyses assume a residential context in which all construction and maintenance labor except mowing is manual and do not involve fossil fuel energy inputs. The data in

Tables 11-2 through 11-6 do not include the direct and indirect energy consumption involved in equipment manufacture or transportation.

Calculations for the embodied energy requirements of the vegetative components of a site design have been dichotomized into requirements characteristic of designs in a temperate climate and a hot arid climate. In calculating embodied energy requirements for groundcover, shrub, and tree masses in hot arid climates, the vegetative masses are differentiated into two groups. The first, oasis-type plants (principally exotic subtropical species such as palms), are adaptable to normal temperature but not to low soil moisture regimes. The second are drought-tolerant plants that, once established, acclimate themselves both to heat and low moisture. All calculations assume use of standard landscape construction (Carpenter, 1976) and landscape maintenance practices. Because maintenance inputs for groundcover, shrubs, and trees diminish as plants mature, the embodied energy requirements presented in Tables 11-3, 11-4, and 11-5 represent average annual Btu consumption for the first 10 years of landscape establishment.

A comparison of the energy requirements of turf (Table 11-2) with those for groundcover plants (Table 11-3), shrub masses (Table 11-4), and tree masses (Table 11-5) reveals that throughout the life of all materials, turf has a considerably higher energy requirement than do groundcover plants, shrubs, or trees. The annual energy consumption needed to maintain 1,000 ft^2 of turf in a temperate climate (239,088 Btus) is 4.4 times greater than the average annual energy consumption required to maintain

Table 11-2. Btu Consumption Required Annually in Temperate and Arid Climates to Maintain 1,000 Ft^2 of Turf in a Residential Setting[a]

Maintenance requirement	Annual Btu consumption	
	Temperate climate	Arid climate
Fertilization[b]	172,050	100,500
Herbicide application[c, d]	18,546	18,546
Irrigation[e]	10,728	93,870
Mowing[f]	37,764	34,636
Total	239,088	247,552

[a]These figures do not include the indirect consumption of energy required for mower, spreader, and irrigation system manufacture or installation. They also do not include any direct energy consumption involved in transporting machinery or equipment. The figures assume use of a cool-season grass in the temperate climate and a warm-season grass in the arid climate.

[b]Fertilizer input in temperate climates are calculated on the basis of an annual application of 3 lb nitrogen per 1,000 ft^2 in a nutrient ratio of 3:1:2 (N:P:K) plus a triennial application of 50 lb lime per 1,000 ft^2. Annual turf fertilization for arid climates is also assumed to be 3 lb nitrogen per 1,000 ft^2. However, phosphorus and potassium inputs are not needed since they produce insignificant effects on plant growth and development in many arid climate soils. Lime is unnecessary in alkaline arid climate soils.

[c]Herbicide requirements for turf in both temperate and arid climates are assumed at 15 lb Dacthal-75 (DCPA) per acre. Btu equivalents for Dacthal-75 are unavailable but have been estimated using those for MCPA in Table 11-1.

[d]Insecticides and fungicides are applied as needed. Requirements depend on plant species, pest characteristics, and site conditions and are too variable to permit a generalization. When needed, these inputs will substantially increase the embodied energy requirements (Parker, 1981).

[e]These figures are based on the assumption that temperate climates receive 40-42 in. rainfall per year, while arid climates receive 8-12 in. per year. Annual irrigation needs of four acre-inches in temperate climates are based on the sporadic nature of growing-season rainfall. Arid climate turf management objectives are based on maintaining summer-long green grass that requires 35 acre-inches per year. Irrigation is assumed to involve pumping water 100 ft of lift from a well with electricity and distribution via a hand-moved sprinkler.

[f]These figures are based on the assumption that a 3-hp mower is used, which consistently cuts an 18-in. swath at 2 mph including turns. Cool-season grasses in temperate climates are assumed to require 24 mowings annually, while warm-season grasses in arid climates are assumed to require 22 mowings annually.

1,000 ft² of groundcover. In a hot arid climate, turf consumes 1.5 times as much energy as an equal area of oasis-type groundcover, and 2.7 times as much as drought-tolerant groundcover. A comparison of the energy requirements of turf with those of shrubs (Table 11-4) and trees (Table 11-5) reveals even further the embodied energy consumption savings inherent to selecting materials other than turf. Temperate-climate turf consumes 4.8 times as much energy as temperate-climate shrubs and 4.6 times as much as trees on a per-unit-area basis. Similarly, arid-climate turf consumes 1.5 times as much energy as oasis-type shrubs, 3.6 times as much as drought-tolerant shrubs, 1.5 times as much as oasis-type trees, and 2.9 times as much as drought-tolerant trees.

Substantial reductions in embodied energy requirements are also apparent when comparing the use of drought-tolerant plants with the use of oasis-type plants in arid climates. In comparing ground surfaces, for example, turf (an oasis-type plant) and oasis-type groundcovers consume 2.7 and 1.8 times as much energy, respectively, as drought-tolerant ground-

Table 11-3. Average Annual Btu Consumption Required to Maintain 1,000 Ft² of Groundcover Plants in a Residential Setting over First 10 Years of Establishment in Temperate and Arid Climates[a]

| | Annualized Btu consumption | | |
| | | Arid climate | |
Maintenance requirement	Temperate climate	Oasis-type plants	Drought-tolerant plants
Fertilizer[b]	42,030	67,000	40,200
Herbicide[c, d]	2,000	2,000	2,000
Irrigation[e]	10,728	93,870	48,276
Total	54,758	162,870	90,476

aFertilizer, herbicide, and irrigation inputs will vary depending on stage of landscape development. These figures do not include the indirect consumption of energy required for mower, spreader, and irrigation system manufacture or installation. They also do not include any direct energy consumption involved in transporting machinery or equipment.

bFertilizer inputs in temperate climates are calculated on the basis of 3 lb nitrogen per 1,000 ft² applied in a nutrient ratio of 1:1:1 (N:P:K) in the first year of establishment, 3 lb nitrogen per 1,000 ft² applied in ratio of 1:0:0 in the second year and triennially thereafter. Fertilizer inputs for oasis-type plants in arid climates assume an annual application of 2 lb nitrogen per 1,000 ft² applied in a 1:0:0 ratio (see note b, Table 11-2). Fertilizer inputs for drought-tolerant plants in arid climates assume annual applications of 2 lb nitrogen per 1,000 ft² applied in 1:0:0 nutrient ratio for the first two years and biennial applications of 2 lb nitrogen thereafter.

cHerbicide is assumed to be applied at a rate of 5 lb Surflan 75 W (Oryzalin) per acre during the first two years of establishment. Thereafter, the groundcover plants will control weeds through shading and competition. Btu equivalents for Surflan 75 W are not available but have been estimated using those for trifluralin in Table 11-1.

dInsecticides and fungicides are applied as needed. Requirements depend on plant species, pest characteristics, and site conditions and are too variable to permit a generalization. When needed, these inputs will substantially increase the embodied energy requirements (Parker, 1981).

eFour acre-inches of irrigation are assumed necessary each year in temperate climates due to the sporadic nature of growing-season rainfall. Annual irrigation needs for oasis-type plants in an arid climate are assumed equivalent to those of turf in arid climates; i.e., 35 acre-inches. For the first three years of establishment, drought-tolerant plants in arid climates are assumed to require 35 acre-inches of irrigation. For years four to six, these needs diminish to 25 acre-inches. In year seven and annually thereafter, drought-tolerant plants in arid climates are assumed to have acclimated to natural rainfall and have no irrigation requirements.

Table 11-4. Average Annual Btu Consumption Required to Maintain 1,000 Ft² of Shrub Mass in a Residential Setting over First 10 Years of Establishment in Temperate and Arid Climates[a]

| | Annualized Btu consumption | | |
| | | Arid Climate | |
Maintenance requirement	Temperate climate	Oasis-type plants	Drought-tolerant plants
Fertilization[b]	36,204	63,650	16,750
Herbicide Application[c, d]	3,000	3,000	3,000
Irrigation[e]	10,728	93,870	48,276
Total	49,932	160,520	68,026

aFertilizer, herbicide, and irrigation input will vary depending on stage of landscape development. These figures do not include the indirect consumption of energy required for mower, spreader, and irrigation system manufacture or installation. They also do not include any direct energy consumption involved in transporting machinery or equipment. Figures assume a free-standing shrub mass that is not underplanted with groundcover or turf.

bTemperate climate shrub fertilization is assumed to be a triennial application of 3 lb nitrogen per 1,000 ft² in a nutrient ratio of 10:6:4 (N:P:K). Fertilization of oasis-type shrubs in arid climates is assumed at 1 lb nitrogen per 1,000 ft² for the first year of establishment and 2 lb nitrogen per 1,000 ft² annually thereafter. Drought-tolerant shrub fertilization inputs for arid climates are assumed at a biennial rate of 1 lb nitrogen per 1,000 ft². In both temperate and arid climates other inputs may be required (e.g., sulfur) but these requirements vary with plant species and site conditions and cannot be generalized.

cHerbicide is assumed to be applied at a rate of 5 lb Surflan 75 W (Oryzalin) per acre during the first three years of establishment. Thereafter, the shrubs will control weeds through shading and competition. Btu equivalents for Surflan 75 W are not available but have been estimated using those for trifluralin in Table 11-1.

dInsecticides and fungicides are applied as needed. Requirements depend on plant species, pest characteristics, and site conditions and are too variable to permit a generalization. When needed, these inputs will substantially increase the embodied energy requirements (Parker, 1981).

eFour acre-inches of irrigation are assumed necessary each year in temperate climates due to the sporadic nature of growing-season rainfall. Annual irrigation needs for oasis type plants in an arid climate are assumed equivalent to those of turf in arid climates, i.e., 35 acre-inches. For the first three years of establishment, drought-tolerant plants in arid climates are assumed to require 35 acre-inches of irrigation. For years four to six, these needs diminish to 25 acre-inches. In year seven and annually thereafter, drought-tolerant plants in arid climates are assumed to have acclimated to natural rainfall and have no irrigation requirements.

Table 11-5. Average Annual Btu Consumption Required to Maintain 1,000 Ft² of Tree Mass in a Residential Setting over First 10 Years of Establishment in Temperate and Arid Climates[a]

Maintenance requirement	Annualized Btu consumption		
	Temperate climate	Arid climate	
		Oasis-type plants	Drought-tolerant plants
Fertilization[b]	36,204	63,650	33,500
Herbicide Application[c,d]	5,000	5,000	5,000
Irrigation[e]	10,728	93,870	48,276
Total	51,932	160,520	86,776

[a]Fertilizer, herbicide, and irrigation input will vary depending on stage of landscape development. These figures do not include the indirect consumption of energy required for mower, spreader, and irrigation system manufacture or installation. They also do not include any direct energy consumption involved in transporting machinery or equipment. Figures assume a free-standing tree mass that is not underplanted with shrubs, groundcover or turf.

[b]Temperate climate tree fertilization is assumed to be a triennial application of 3 lb nitrogen per 1,000 ft² in a nutrient ratio of 10:6:4 (N:P:K). Fertilization of oasis-type trees in arid climates is assumed at 1 lb nitrogen per 1,000 ft² for the first year of establishment and 2 lb nitrogen per 1,000 ft² annually thereafter. Drought-tolerant tree fertilization inputs for arid climates are assumed at 1 lb nitrogen per 1,000 ft² for year one, 2 lb nitrogen per 1,000 ft² for years two, three, and four, respectively, and a biennial application of 1 lb nitrogen per 1,000 ft² thereafter.

[c]Herbicide is assumed to be applied at a rate of 5 lb Surflan 75 W (Oryzalin) per acre during the first five years of establishment. Thereafter, the trees will control weeds through shading and competition. Btu equivalents for Surflan 75 W are not available but have been estimated using those for trifluralin in Table 11-1.

[d]Insecticides and fungicides are applied as needed. Requirements depend on plant species, pest characteristics, and site conditions and are too variable to permit a generalization. When needed, these inputs will substantially increase the embodied energy requirements (Parker, 1981).

[e]Four acre-inches of irrigation are assumed necessary each year in temperate climates due to the sporadic nature of growing season rainfall. Annual irrigation needs for oasis-type plants in an arid climate are assumed equivalent to those of turf in arid climates, i.e., 35 acre-inches. For the first three years of establishment, drought-tolerant plants in arid climates are assumed to require 35 acre-inches of irrigation. For years four to six, these needs diminish to 25 acre-inches. In year seven and annually thereafter, drought-tolerant plants in arid climates are assumed to have acclimated to natural rainfall and have no irrigation requirements.

Table 11-6. Btu Consumption Required to Manufacture Materials for 1000 Ft² of Various Paving Surfaces[a]

Material	Btu consumption
Brick (laid on 1 inch of sand)	66,055,083
Concrete (4 inch slab, not including reinforcing bars)	32,503,000
Asphalt (4 inch thickness)	14,209,986
Wood decking[b]	13,787,234
Gravel (8 inches deep including sub-base)	1,488,740

[a]These figures do not include any direct consumption of energy required for delivery of materials nor any direct consumption involved in installation.

[b]This figure is based on use of 4 x 4-in. posts set 22 in. in the ground on a concrete footing 8 in. deep and 12 in. in diameter. 4 x 6-in. beams spanning not more than 6 ft are spaced not more than 6 ft apart. 2 x 6-in. joists and headers are spaced 16 in. on center, and 2 x 6-in. decking boards are spaced 3/16-in. apart. The lower edge of the joists and header are raised 3 in. off the ground, and the deck surface is raised 10 in. off the ground. Kiln-dried, pressure-treated southern pine lumber is used exclusively. The figure is exclusive of any steps or railings.

covers. Furthermore, over a 10-year period, turf and oasis-type groundcovers in an arid climate consume 1.6 and 1.1 times as much, respectively, as an equal area of gravel (Table 11-6). Similarly, oasis-type shrubs and trees consume 2.4 and 1.8 times as much energy, respectively, as drought-tolerant shrubs and trees.

Among the five paving surfaces presented in Table 11-6, 1,000 ft² of brick has the highest energy requirement for manufacture (66 million Btus) while the 1,000 ft² of gravel represents the lowest indirect consumption of energy (1.5 million Btus).

As the fossil fuel sources of energy needed to manufacture or maintain brick, concrete, and grass become more scarce, it is tempting on the basis of the data presented in Tables 11-2, through 11-6 to conclude that the landscapes of the future will contain only groundcover plants, shrubs, trees, and gravel. These are indeed the most energy-efficient materials. However, common sense and the following residential

case study suggest the impracticability of the indiscriminate application of such a concept.

Residential Case Study

The process of accounting for the embodied energy requirements in site design is best illustrated through a case study. The following case study presents a brief description of a residential site and its surroundings, a statement of the owner's objectives, and a final design for landscape rehabilitation. Using the data presented in the Tables 11-2 through 11-6, the embodied energy requirements associated with the landscape materials used in the existing and proposed case study designs are then examined. Finally, the embodied energy costs and conservation benefits of selecting landscape materials other than those specified in the final design are analyzed.

Description of Site

The site selected for this case study (Figure 11-1, see

next page) is a 9,011-ft² lot located in a Maryland suburb of the Washington, D.C., metropolitan area. A 26x35-ft brick two-story Cape Cod house sits 48 ft back from the street in an orientation facing due east. Manmade landscape features on the site include a driveway extending from the street to an attached carport, a concete walk connecting the carport with the front porch, a small metal back stoop, a storage shed, and a 3½-ft-high chain-link fence around the back yard.

The existence of 17 shade trees (6½- to 24-in. caliper) on the site was one factor motivating the present owner to purchase the house. Foundation plantings exist adjacent to the entry walk, and shrub masses are located at the northwest corner of the lot, near the corner formed by the rear porch and basement stairwell and adjacent to the air conditioner compressor on the north side of the house. All other areas on the site are covered with turf. Much of the turf is in poor condition due to dense shading from the trees.

An 8-ft change in vertical elevation exists from the front door down to the street. The front lawn has a uniform 5-8% slope except for a 30% bank adjacent to the street sidewalk. The driveway, the only pedestrian approach to the house, has a uniform slope of 11%. The awkwardness of this slope, especially in the winter, is a problem the owner would like resolved in rehabilitating the site. The back yard has a fairly uniform cross-pitch of 3-4% running from north to south. Soils on the site consist of 18 to 24 in. of sandy loam underlain by clayey subsoil. No drainage problems presently exist on the site.

The present owners are quite friendly with neighbors on both the north and south sides, but relations with adjacent property owners to the west are undefined. Deed restrictions preclude the use of fencing higher than four feet.

Table 11-7 presents an estimate of the average annual energy consumption required to maintain the present landscape. The Btu consumption estimate for turf is calculated by multiplying the square footage of turf in the existing landscape, as illustrated in Figure 11-1, by the annual per-square-foot energy requirement of temperate-climate turf, as derived from Table 11-2. The groundcover and shrub estimates are based on the square footage of beds illustrated in Figure 11-1 multiplied by the average annual per-square-foot energy requirement of temperate-climate groundcover and shrub beds presented in Tables 11-3 and 11-4, respectively. Maintenance of the 6,463 ft² of turf, 506 ft² of shrubs, and 28 ft² of groundcover currently existing in the landscape requires an average annual energy consumption of slightly more than 1,572,000 Btus.

Owner's Design Objectives

Most of the present owner's design objectives for landscape rehabilitation result from previous owners having made no attempt to define usable outdoor spaces. Objectives for the front yard include:

- Improving pedestrian access from the street to the front door and from the carport and driveway to the front door. Presently, all foot traffic must negotiate the rather steep drive. Access along the walk adjacent to the house is impaired by overgrown shrub material and a carport roof-support post.
- Creating a gathering space wherein guests may be greeted or several people might have casual conversation.
- Reducing exposure to low morning sun in the summer without totally blocking the winter sun.
- Creating some commonality and flow between the size of indoor living room spaces and outdoor spaces for greeting, sitting, or pedestrian access.
- Maintaining continuity in construction materials and architectural detailing of the house with the design in the landscape.
- Maintaining informal pedestrian access and visual links with neighbors on both the north and the south sides of the property.

Table 11-7. Average Annual Btu Consumption Required to Maintain Existing Case Study Landscape over 10 years[a]

Landscape element	Average annual Btu consumption	
Front yard		441,088
Maintenance of 1,785 ft² of turf	426,772	
Maintenance of 256 ft² of shrub mass	12,783	
Maintenance of 28 ft² of groundcover	1,533	
Back yard		1,131,436
Maintenance of 4,678 ft² of turf	1,118,454	
Maintenance of 260 ft² of shrub mass	12,982	
Total average annual energy consumption		1,572,524

[a]Maintenance requirements of proposed trees are fulfilled through maintenance of shrub, ground cover, and turf underplantings.

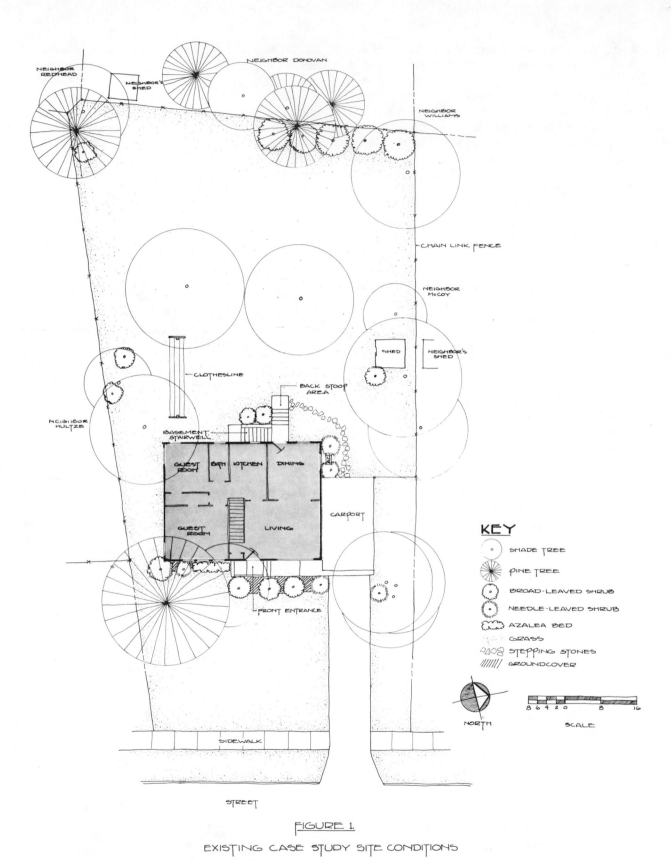

KEY

○ SHADE TREE

✳ PINE TREE

❀ BROAD-LEAVED SHRUB

❁ NEEDLE-LEAVED SHRUB

◎ AZALEA BED

GRASS

⌀⌀⌀ STEPPING STONES

///// GROUNDCOVER

NORTH

SCALE
8 6 4 2 0   8   16

FIGURE 1.

EXISTING CASE STUDY SITE CONDITIONS

Figure 11-1. Residential case study site showing existing landscape.

Objectives for the back yard include:

- Allowing family meals to be extended out of the dining room onto an immediately adjacent portion of the landscape. The existing back stoop severely constricts this flow.
- Creating an outdoor area suitable for entertaining 10 to 12 people. This space should appear as a natural extension of the indoor and outdoor dining areas.
- Creating an area suitable for various lawn games and the free play of young children.
- Locating all utility and service functions in the landscape to the rear of the carport and screening them from other portions of the yard.

- Maintaining access from the carport to the back door, from the back door to the basement stairwell and from the yard through the existing gate into the southerly neighbor's yard.
- Defining access among the various spaces to be created in the yard.
- Defining visual linkages with both the northern and southern neighbors while at the same time providing more privacy.
- Blocking the flow of winter wind from the northwest corner of the lot around the house.

Figure 11-2 illustrates these objectives as a design concept.

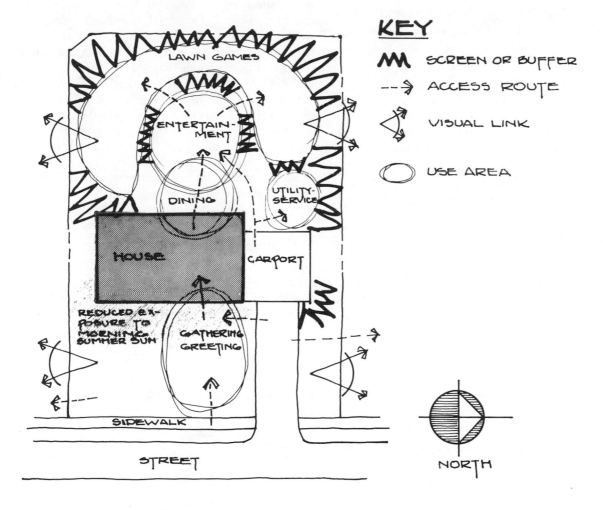

FIGURE 2.

CASE STUDY DESIGN CONCEPT

Figure 11-2. Residential cast study design concept.

223

Proposed Design Rehabilitation

As Figure 11-3 (see next page) illustrates, the final design prepared to guide landscape rehabilitation proposes the establishment of several new landscape features:

- A brick pedestrian circulation system in the front yard. The stair, walkway, and sitting area combination eases negotiation of the 11% slope in the driveway; provides more accessible connections between the street, driveway, and front door; enables the gathering of small groups of people; and harmonizes the landscape with the architectural design of the house. Planters are used to define key pivots in the circulation system, and access is maintained to both neighbors.

- A series of planting beds for those portions of the east and north sides of the house that receive no intensive use.

- A 10 x 12-ft treated southern pine deck that allows the dining room to flow out into the back yard.

- A brick patio that extends the character of the deck out under the large existing trees for back yard entertaining.

- Brick walkways linking the carport, relocated storage shed and compost pile, patio, deck, and basement stairwell.

- Shrub and understory tree masses that provide definition for the deck, patio, and lawn area and define circulation among these areas.

- Evergreen tree and shrub masses adjacent to the property lines that define the lawn play area, provide needed privacy without destroying all visual links to the neighbors, and block the winter wind.

Proposed Design-Embodied Energy Requirements

Translating the proposed landscape design into embodied energy requirements necessitates calculating the area covered or materials needed for each of the new landscape elements. Multiplying these area measurements and materials estimates by the per-square-foot or unit energy requirements found in Tables 11-2 through 11-6 produces an estimate of the fossil fuel energy requirements involved in the manufacture, installation, and maintenance of the various landscape elements.

Assuming that implementation of the design will be done entirely by manual labor (a reasonable assumption in a residential context), the direct energy consumption involved in the installation of the design (e.g., operation of power tools and equipment) can be eliminated from consideration. Thus, the energy costs of the design fall into two categories: those involved in manufacturing the treated lumber and brick paving used in the deck, planters, walks, and patios; and those involved in establishing and maintaining various forms of vegetation. Table 11-8 presents the Btu consumption required to manufacture the construction materials used in the rehabilitation of the front and back yards of the case study design. Table 11-9 (see page 226) presents an average annual estimate of the Btus needed to maintain the turf, groundcover, and shrubs illustrated in Figure 11-3.

Manufacturing the treated lumber and brick paving required for all walks, patios, decks, and planters included in the design will consume a total of 56,288,987 Btus. Average annual energy consumption involved in the maintenance of all vegetative portions of the design will be 1,089,716 Btus.

Table 11-8. Btu Consumption Required to Manufacture the Construction Materials Used in Case Study Design

Landscape element	Materials required	Btus consumed	
Front yard			18,238,418
Patio and walks	240.0-ft² brick paving	15,853,320	
	55.1-board-feet treated lumber edging	178,304	
Steps	28-ft² brick paving	1,849,540	
	65.2-board-feet treated lumber	210,987	
Planter	45.2-board-feet treated lumber	146,267	
Back yard			38,050,569
Patio and walks	540.0 ft² brick paving	35,669,700	
	131.0-board-feet treated lumber	423,916	
Deck	526.4-board-feet treated lumber	1,703,430	
	2.6-ft³ concrete	253,523	
Entire yard			56,288,987

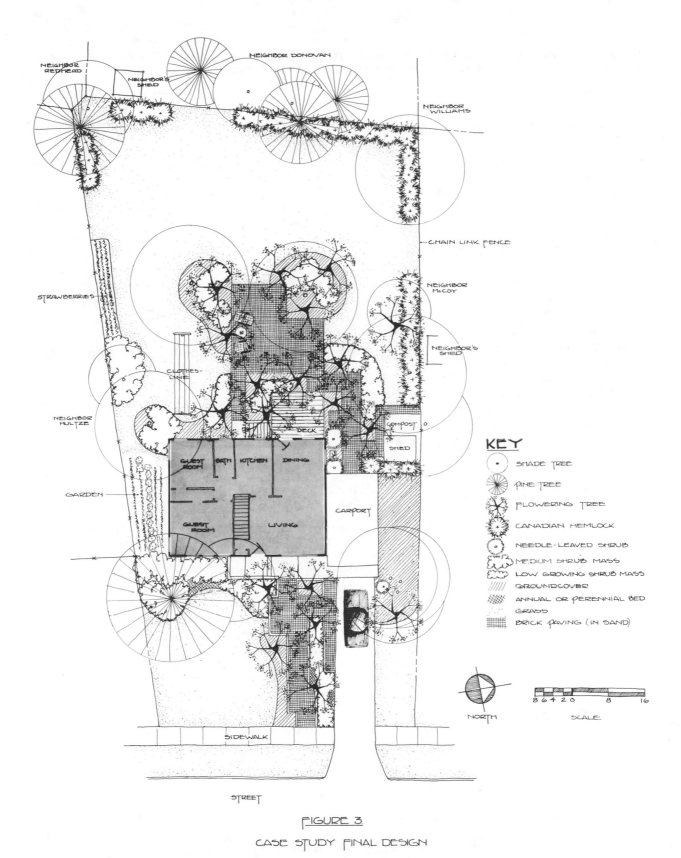

KEY

- ⊙ SHADE TREE
- ⊛ PINE TREE
- ✳ FLOWERING TREE
- ✦ CANADIAN HEMLOCK
- ◉ NEEDLE-LEAVED SHRUB
- ◌ MEDIUM SHRUB MASS
- ◌ LOW GROWING SHRUB MASS
- ▨ GROUNDCOVER
- ▦ ANNUAL OR PERENNIAL BED
- ▦ GRASS
- ▦ BRICK PAVING (IN SAND)

NORTH

SCALE
8 6 4 2 0   8   16

FIGURE 3.

CASE STUDY FINAL DESIGN

Figure 11-3. Final redesign of the residential case study site.

225

Table 11-9. Average Annual Btu Consumption Required to Maintain Vegetative Portion of Revised Case Study Landscape over First 10 Years of Landscape Establishment[a]

Landscape element	Average annual Btu consumption	
Front yard		335,732
Maintenance of 1,293 ft² of turf	309,141	
Maintenance of 254 ft² of groundcover	13,908	
Maintenance of 254 ft² of shrub mass	12,683	
Back yard		753,984
Maintenance of 2,846 ft² of turf	680,444	
Maintenance of 360 ft² of groundcover	19,713	
Maintenance of 1,078 ft² of shrub mass	53,827	
Total average annual energy consumption		1,089,716

[a]Maintenance requirements of proposed trees are fulfilled through maintenance of shrub, ground cover and turf underplantings.

Existing Vs. Proposed Design Energy Requirements

Assuming manual labor will be used exclusively for construction, and ignoring any direct energy consumption involved in delivery of materials, over a 10-year period the construction and maintenance of the proposed design will require a total of 67,186,147 Btus. Continued maintenance of the existing landscape over a 10-year period will require 15,725,240 Btus. Thus, a gross comparison of maintaining the site as it presently exists with establishing and maintaining the proposed design suggests that the rehabilitated landscape will consume 4.3 times as much energy as the existing design.

However, using such a gross comparison of the energy requirements inherent to the existing and the proposed designs as a basis for design decision making ignores two critical points: The client is dissatisfied with the landscape as it presently exists and 56,288,987 Btus or 83.8% of the 10-year consumption required for the establishment and maintenance of the rehabilitated landscape are tied up in the patios, decks, walkways, and raised planters. All of these elements are relatively permanent property improvements needed to fulfill the owner's desire for a more useful landscape. Once the fixed energy costs of installing these improvements in the landscape are absorbed, none of the construction materials will involve very sizable energy requirements on an annual basis.

Given the fairly permanent nature of the construction needed to improve the utility of the case study landscape, it is perhaps more realistic to compare the two designs on the basis of the energy consumption required for annual maintenance. As Table 11-7 illustrates, continued maintenance of the existing landscape in its present condition will require 1,572,524 Btus annually. This rate of consumption is 1.44 times higher than the 1,089,716 Btus required annually to maintain the proposed design once it has become established. When compared on the basis of Btus required per square foot of vegetative area to be maintained, the 179 Btus per square foot required for maintenance of vegetation in the proposed design is 25% more efficient than the 224 Btus per square foot required for the existing landscape.

Energy Consumption Vs. Landscape Utility

Given the case study's design concept illustrated in Figure 11-2, the indirect energy requirements for materials could have been considerably reduced by selecting a less consumptive paving surface. As Table 11-6 illustrates, brick is one of the most consumptive of all paving surfaces. Had concrete been selected instead of brick, the energy indirectly consumed by the 808 total square feet of paving surface would have been reduced from 53,372,560 to 26,262,424 Btus. Had gravel been selected, the indirect consumption in paving surface manufacture would have been 1,202,902 Btus. However, neither paving surface fulfills the client's design objectives as adequately as brick. Concrete would provide a suitable walking surface but it would not meet the client's desire to harmonize landscape and architectural materials. Concrete would provide none of the color and textural enrichment to the design inherent to brick. Gravel is considerably less suitable than brick as a walking surface in heavily trafficked areas, especially given the barefooted nature of much of the pedestrian circulation that occurs in the summer around the home. Substitution of treated southern pine decking for the brick would have reduced the indirect energy consumption tied up in paving areas from 53,372,560 Btus to 11,140,085 Btus and produced a visually and functionally acceptable solution. However, this would involve substantial excavation to bring the deck down to grade level.

Further reductions in annual energy consumption required for maintenance may be realized by reducing the areal extent of turf in the yard. Indeed, had groundcover been substituted for turf throughout the design, average annual consumption would have been reduced from 1,089,716 Btus to 326,774. However, such a concept would have totally ignored the client's desire for a lawn sports and a children's free play area, because groundcover lacks the resiliency needed to accommodate such intensive uses.

Arid Climate Adaptation of Case Study Design
As other contributors to this volume have suggested, site design in an arid climate is subject to climatic influences vastly different from those in temperate zones (see Chapter Four). The contrast of the Vermont farmhouse with the Spanish hacienda of the American southwest testifies to the influence of climatic variation on environmental design objectives as well as material selection. Since landscape materials and design objectives, especially those relating to energy conservation, vary across climatic regions, direct inter-regional comparison of designs is generally not feasible.

For the purpose of comparing the relative embodied-energy requirements of oasis-type landscapes and drought-tolerant landscapes, the site and client of the temperate-climate case study have been relocated to an arid climate context. Assuming the *concept* of the temperate-climate case study as presented in Figure 11-3 can be implemented in an arid climate with different plant species, a basis can be established for making such a comparison. Table 11-10 compares the average annual Btu consumption of the case study design as adapted to an arid-climate oasis landscape with an adaptation based on drought-tolerant plants.

The groundcover and shrub mass Btu consumption calculations in Table 11-10 are developed by multiplying their respective areal measurements from Figure 11-3 by their respective areal unit rate of Btu consumption from Tables 11-3 and 11-4. Turf Btu consumption is similarly calculated from Figure 11-3 and Table 11-2. For the drought-tolerant arid landscape adaptation, it is assumed that all turf areas in Figure 11-3 will be replaced with decomposed granite screenings, a material resilient enough to accommodate the intensive play it will receive. Btu consumption required for the mining and processing of granite screenings is assumed equivalent to that required for gravel. The Btu consumption of 1,000 ft² of granite as presented in Table 11-6 is averaged over a 10-year life span. This average calculation for gravel over 10 years is used as the average annual Btu consumption for decomposed granite.

The figures in Table 11-10 suggest that annual maintenance of the oasis-type landscape will consume 1.8 times as many Btus as will annual maintenance of the drought-tolerant landscape. Most of the oasis landscape's increased energy consumption is a byproduct of the electricity needed to fulfill its high irrigation requirements. The largest absolute saving of the drought-tolerant adaptation over the oasis adaptation is obtained through the replacement of turf with decomposed granite. However, the largest relative reduction in Btu consumption is produced by the replacement of oasis-type groundcover and woody plant materials with drought-tolerant varieties. The shift from turf to granite represents a 39.9% reduction in Btu consumption while the shift in groundcover and shrub masses represents savings of 44.4% and 57.6%, respectively. These figures are comparable to the findings of a recently conducted empirical comparison of energy and water consumption in oasis and drought-tolerant landscapes in Arizona (Center for Environmental Studies, 1977). Table 11-10 illustrates the dramatic energy savings provided by turf reduction in arid climates while highlighting the importance of adapting the total landscape to the minimal rainfall conditions that characterize dry environments.

Table 11-10. Average Annual Btu Consumption Required to Maintain Arid Climate Adaptation of Case Study Landscape over First 10 Years of Landscape Establishment[a]

Landscape element	Average annual Btu consumption	
	Oasis-type plants	Drought-tolerant plants
Front yard		
Maintenance of 1,293 ft² of turf and granite[b]	320,085	192,494
Maintenance of 254 ft² of groundcover	41,364	22,981
Maintenance of 254 ft² of shrub mass	40,772	17,279
Back yard		
Maintenance of 2,846 ft² of turf and granite[b]	704,533	423,695
Maintenance of 360 ft² of groundcover	58,633	32,571
Maintenance of 1,078 ft² of shrub mass	173,041	73,332
Total average annual energy consumption	1,338,433	762,352

[a]Maintenance requirements of proposed trees are fulfilled through maintenance of shrub, ground cover, and turf underplantings.
[b]Calculations based on turf maintenance Btu requirements (see Table 11-2) are used for oasis-type plant adaptation. Calculations based on gravel Btu manufacture requirements (see Table 11-6) averaged over 10-year life span are used for drought-tolerant plant adaptation.

Case Study Implications

The energy comparisons presented in this case study illuminate three critical issues relative to embodied-energy consumption and the selection of materials for use in site-scale landscape design.

1. The least consumptive landscapes are not always the most attractive or the most functional. Had this been true, the case study design alternative consisting of gravel walks and patios and no turf would have been selected for implementation. Thus, the desire to reduce embodied-energy consumption in site planning and design must be tempered by the necessity of satisfying the client's functional and esthetic needs. If construction materials were priced according to the intensity of energy input required for their manufacture, the marginal difference in material cost might prove sufficient to alter client needs and desires. However, with brick costs presently about six times as high as gravel costs on a per-square-foot basis, the cost differential does not, in most cases, justify the substitution of the less desirable paving surface. In spite of this financial constraint, the case study illustrates that materials less consumptive of energy can be successfully substituted into a design in areas where low levels of use intensity occur.

2. Sizable reductions in the average annual energy consumption required for landscape maintenance can be realized by carefully examining the level of use intensity in the landscape and by thinking of shrub and groundcover beds as vehicles for defining intensively used areas and directing circulation among these areas. The skillful designer will take advantage of the spatial definition and screening potential these beds offer to add intrigue and make the yard seem considerably larger than it actually is and simultaneously to mask unwanted portions of the landscape from view. In concert with the canopies of shade trees and the vertical stature of evergreen trees, carefully designed shrub and groundcover beds can also help create, furnish, and separate specific outdoor rooms within the yard (e.g., patio, lawn sports area, children's play, etc.), direct the movement of people from one space to another, and help reduce the flow of the chilling winter wind around structures. In addition to providing these visual and functional benefits, such beds also will reduce considerably the area covered with turf and consequently the amount of energy required for landscape maintenance. This is evidenced by the 25% reduction in Btu consumption per square foot of maintained vegetation realized in the maintenance of the proposed case study design as compared with the existing design.

3. In arid climates, embodied-energy requirements for landscape construction and maintenance can be greatly reduced by selecting drought-tolerant plant species to accomplish design objectives (see Chapter Ten). Furthermore, replacement of turf with other highly resilient ground surfaces (e.g., the granite screenings used in the drought-tolerant adaptation) will help reduce embodied-energy requirements of designs in arid regions. Turf reduction objectives must, however, take into account the potentially negative microclimatic effects of the turf substitute. For example, granite has a higher albedo than turf and offers no evaporative cooling of air temperature. Hence, it is possible that an expansive use of granite may actually increase the heat load on structures in the landscape. The resulting increase in direct consumption of energy for space conditioning could offset the savings in embodied energy that decomposed granite apparently provides. A "mini-oasis" compromise (Jones, 1981) of small areas of turf immediately adjacent to structures and more expansive use of turf substitutes further away from buildings may help reduce embodied-energy and irrigation requirements without creating space-conditioning problems.

Conclusions

One of the primary objectives in site planning and design is to increase the overall utility of the landscape to the user. Increasing the utility of the landscape implies creating spaces and selecting materials that will facilitate and withstand the intensity of human activity occurring in the landscape. When evaluated as a surface for intensive use, groundcover plants and shrubs (the most energy-efficient vegetative materials) prove to be unable to accommodate intense foot traffic. Similarly, the impermanent nature of gravel (the least consumptive paving surface) makes it appropriate only for very low levels of traffic.

A direct relationship exists between the amount of energy required to manufacture or maintain materials (be they vegetative or manmade) and the ability of these materials to withstand high intensities of use (i.e., their resilience to human use). Highly resilient surfaces (e.g., brick, concrete, and turf) require considerable energy in their manufacture, installation, and maintenance. Conversely, materials that have low energy requirements are considerably less resilient. Use of a material having low resilience in a situation of high-intensity activity will ultimately require additional energy inputs in the form of repair or replacement.

The positive relationship between the resilience and the energy requirements of landscape materials suggests that material selection should be based on a careful consideration of the location and intensity of human activity. In a site design context, this means defining where foot traffic is likely to be highest and selecting materials for these areas that will withstand the level of use they will receive. For such high-use areas as a main approach walk or a patio, a highly resilient material such as brick or concrete is needed. Similarly, for a major play area, the resiliency of turf makes it a better selection than groundcover plants.

What most people and many designers fail to realize is that the intensity of use is not uniformly distributed across the landscape. Therefore, it is not always necessary for every walk to be constructed of a highly resilient material that also has high-embodied-energy requirements. Gravel and even mulched walkways are often sufficient to handle foot traffic on service paths. Similarly, the entire back yard in a residential setting need not always be covered with the energy extravagance that is manifest in turf. Areas in the yard that are seldom used or are too heavily shaded for successful turf development could be converted to planting beds consisting of shrub and groundcover materials whose energy requirements are substantially less than those of turf.

The previous chapter in this volume ("Water-Conserving Landscape Design") introduced the concept of hydrozones as a means for reducing irrigation needs in the landscape. Just as the hydrozone concept relates irrigation needs directly to the intensity of use occuring in the landscape, so also must embodied energy requirements be related to use intensity. The selection of landscape materials to reduce consumption of embodied energy must begin with a careful analysis of intended human use of the landscape. Intensity of use determines the resilience that will be required of the material. Resilience, in turn, determines the energy that will be required in the material's manufacture, installation, and maintenance. Although it is not practical to eliminate materials having substantial embodied-energy requirements from the landscape, it is feasible to reduce their areal expanse. Careful consideration of the intensity of human use received by all parts of the landscape and the material resilience required to support various uses will permit the substitution of groundcover plants, shrubs, and gravel in areas that might otherwise be covered with turf or brick.

Acknowledgments

Standard landscape maintenance practices were established through personal communications with Dr. Francis R. Gouin, Extension Horticulturist, and Dr. Thomas Turner, Extension Turf Management Specialist, both with the University of Maryland Cooperative Extension Service; Dr. Charles Sacamano, Extension Horticulturist, Dr. William R. Kneebone, Extension Agronomist, and Mr. Stanley Heathman, Extension Weed Control Specialist, all with the University of Arizona Cooperative Extension Service. All footnotes in Tables 2 through 5 are attributable to these sources. Illustrations for this chapter were prepared by William Gould.

Alternative Futures 4

CHAPTER TWELVE
Community Design Case Study:
Oak Hills

E. GREGORY McPHERSON
Utah State University

ROBERT HRABAK
Kron-Hrabak Inc.

DAVID SOCWELL
Allred, Soffe & Associates

THE primary purpose of the Oak Hills case study is to demonstrate design principles and analytical methods that authors have cited throughout this text. A case study approach provides the realistic context needed to achieve this end. Practitioners may discover procedures and results that can be directly applied to their work. Landscape architects may also find that the results from this study further enhance their understanding of expected costs and potential benefits associated with different energy-conserving site design strategies.

The method used in this study follows that cited in Chapter Two and documented in the Center for Landscape Architectural Education and Research's *Site and Neighborhood Design for Energy Conservation: Five Case Studies*(CLAER, 1981). In each case study, energy cost comparisons were made between a conventional site design and a redesign or energy plan that incorporated various energy-conserving site design principles. Calculations indicated that implementation of the energy plans could result in substantial savings in embodied energy (20% to 30%) and annual operational energy costs (10% to 15%). Results for three case studies are described in more detail in Chapter Two.

The advantage of modifying a conventional plan by employing feasible energy conservation options is that options can be applied quickly without repeating the entire planning process. One disadvantage is that not all energy conservation options are evaluated. Energy options assessed in this case study are the effects of reduced road width, driveway, and parking areas on embodied-energy use and site development costs, and the effects of improved building and window orientation, and massing of the structures on energy costs for space heating. A second possible drawback of this method is that with a poorly conceived program or conventional plan, the application of some promising options may not be practical. In the Oak Hills case study the number of options explored were limited because the program and location of the major collector road remained similar in both plans. However, these similarities provide a basis for comparison of the plans so that potential energy savings can be viewed in relation to a base line case.

The Oak Hills case study begins with a description of site analysis techniques used as a basis for generating the energy plan. Development programs and site designs are presented and compared. Energy-conserving site design principles used at the site-specific scale are illustrated as enlargements of representative portions of the site. Techniques for calculating costs for site development, embodied energy, and operational energy for both plans are described, as are the results of these analyses.

Site Analysis

Located in the Wasatch Mountains near Salt Lake City, Ut., at approximately 40°N latitude, 112°W longitude, the 812-acre case study site is part of a much larger proposed development. It was selected because of the diversity of land uses and facilities sited on it in the conventional plan. Because the clients requested that the exact location and name of the proposed development remain confidential, the case study team assigned the name Oak Hills to the site.

Landscape architects employed by Land Design, Inc., of Salt Lake City collected data on soils, slope, and vegetation prior to developing their site plan (the conventional plan). The case study team used these data to limit the number of factors influencing location of various land uses on the site.

Soils and Vegetation

Soil characteristics do not limit the site development. Soils over the entire site are suitable for all types of proposed development. Mature stands of gambel oak and big-tooth maple cover much of the site, both dominant species of the Chaparral Zone, which lies between 5000 and 7500 ft in the Wasatch Range. Both design teams assumed that the site was covered by thickets of these tall shrubs.

Climate

Meso- and microclimatic data were collected and evaluated for use in site design and as input for the DLOAD software package used to calculate space heating costs. Table 12-1 gives mean monthly and annual temperatures and heating degree-days for a nearby site (within 60 miles) at approximately the same elevation (5950 feet). There are no cooling degree-days. The large number of heating degree-days suggests that reducing space-heating costs is a high design priority.

Upper air flows are generally from the north and northwest during the winter, and south to southeast during the summer. However, the dense thickets,

which extend up to 25 ft (7.6 m) above the ground and cover the site, are likely to moderate air flows near the surface. Clearing vegetation during site development will significantly alter both synoptic and diurnal air movement patterns. The most consistent flows will be down-canyon breezes during the evenings and mornings, and up-valley flows during the afternoons. Air flows up and down natural drainages will not be strong and may provide natural cooling to nearby structures during July and August.

Buildings located on ridgetops occasionally will be exposed to strong winds, a liability during the winter. Retention of existing vegetation will reduce the impact. Cool thermal belts also will occur in depressions where cold air pockets exist. Existing vegetation should minimize the drifting of snow, however, snow drop zones may occur downwind (south) of ridges and clearings.

Elevation, Slope, and Aspect

The site exhibits a high degree of topographical relief. Figure 12-1 (see next page) shows elevation bands ranging from 5600 to 6350 ft (1707 to 1935 m). Both design teams developed slope maps, of primary importance for locating buildable sites in the conventional plan. The design team working on the energy plan also created an aspect map to determine which parts of the site had an orientation favorable for solar collection. The site has few flat areas or south-facing slopes.

Solar Flux

The amount of solar radiation received at the earth's surface is influenced both by angle of slope and angle of slope orientation. The design team overlayed the slope and aspect maps to identify the relative amount of insolation on different portions of the site. Table 12-2 (see next page) gives selected combinations of slope and aspects.

Values ranging from 1 (best) to 5 (unacceptable) were assigned to each matrix cell based on the relative amount of available insolation and relative development cost. The building suitability matrix integrates solar flux with traditional development cost factors to locate sites most suitable for development of structures that will use solar energy. For example, portions of the site with slopes greater than 30% were

---

Table 12-1. Mean Monthly and Annual Temperatures and Heating Degree Days.

Month	Jan.	Feb.	Mar.	Apr.	May	Jun.	Jul.	Aug.	Sept.	Oct.	Nov.	Dec.	Ann.
Temperature (°F)	22	25.5	32.1	41.4	50.7	58.3	65.3	63.3	55.5	45.9	32.7	24.1	43.1
Heating degree days (65F base)	1333	1100	1026	690	443	227	46	71	282	592	960	1237	8007

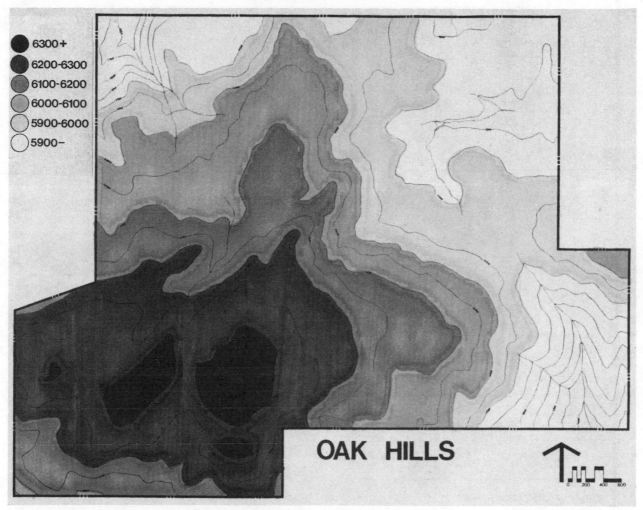

Figure 12-1. Map of elevations showing obvious mountain terrain.

Symbol	Elevation
●	6300+
●	6200-6300
●	6100-6200
●	6000-6100
○	5900-6000
○	5900-

OAK HILLS

Table 12-2. Building Suitability Matrix[a]

SLOPE		Aspect				
(%)	NE, N, NW	E	SE	S	SW	W
0-5	2	2	1	1	1	2
6-10	3	2	1	1	1	2
11-20	3	2	2	1	2	2
21-30	4	3	2	2	2	3
31-40	5	5	4	4	4	5
> 40	5	5	5	5	5	5

aKey: 1 = best; 2 = good; 3 = acceptable; 4 = poor; 5 = unacceptable

categorized as poor or unacceptable, regardless of orientation, because of high development costs. Areas with less steep slopes but orientations other than south, southeast, or southwest were categorized as less suitable for building than those with the preferred orientation. The matrix was used to develop a building suitability map (Figure 12-2, see next page).

Development Programs and Site Designs

Table 12-3 (see page 237) shows the Oak Hills development programs for the conventional and energy plans. In both plans, 42% (341 acres) of the site (812 acres) has been developed and 58% (471 acres) remains as open space. The energy plan has 141 more single family units (1522) than the conventional plan (1381). The average density of these units is slightly greater in the energy plan (5.8 DU/Ac. vs. 5.6 DU/Ac.). Single-family units occupy 30% and 32% of the site in the conventional and energy plan, respectively. Other buildings occupy 7% of the site in both plans. Roads, including cul-de-sacs, cover 6% of the site in the energy plan and 6.8% of the site in the conventional plan.

Site Designs

Figures 12-3 and 12-4 show site designs for the con-

Figure 12-2. Lightest colored areas receive the most solar radiation and are most desirable locations for housing that uses solar energy.

ventional and energy plan, respectively. The primary difference between the conventional and energy plans is that in the energy plan all residential structures are oriented within a 30-degree azimuth range of true south. In the conventional plan, units are sited without regard for solar orientation or access. Figure 12-5 (see page 240) reflects this for typical attached single-family units taken from the same location on both plans. It also shows the clustering of units around parking courts in the energy plan, as opposed to the use of cul-de-sacs and private drives in the conventional plan, thus reducing the amount of paved surface area and increasing open space. In the energy plan, 1.5 parking places are provided per unit as compared with 1.15 in the conventional plan.

The collector, which runs from the southwest to the northeast corner of the site, was not relocated.Most traffic will enter and leave through the northeast corner. In the energy plan, the office complex, community center, and condominiums are relocated near

the entrance to the site to reduce vehicular traffic through the site. Commuters can stop for sundries on their way home from work without having to retrace their path (Figures 12-3 and 12-4, see pages 238, 239). A pedestrian and bicycle path system links residences in the southern portion of the site with offices and a community center. It also provides alternative access to the school, which is more conveniently located in the center of the site. The golf course layout resembles that of the conventional plan and occupies areas less suitable for development. Residential units are located adjacent to fairways where practical. Conflicts between golfers and autos are reduced by one-half in the energy plan. This solution is less expensive than is construction of underpasses for golfers.

In each plan the case study team compared the number of units located in areas designated best and good, and poor and unacceptable by overlaying each plan on the building suitability map (Figure 12-2). In both plans, 39% of the units are located in areas with

Table 12-3. Oak Hills Development Programs

Type	Density (Units per acre)		Number of Acres		Number of Units		Unit size[a] (sq. ft.)	
	Conv. plan	Energy plan	Conv. plan	Energy plan	Conv. plan	Energy plan	Conv. plan	Energy plan
Single family units								
Single family detached	2.2	2.2	34.1	36.4	76	79	2,400	2,400
Single family attached (external garage)	5.9	5.8	188.6	190	1104	1100	1,600	1,600
Single family attached	9.2	9.5	21.9	36	201	343	1,600	1,600
Total (single family units)	5.6	5.8	244.6 (30%)	262.4 (32%)	1381	1522		
Other buildings								
Resort hotel	33.1	31.0	12.1	12.9	400	400	139,200	147,000
Community center			8.8	8.8			92,500	101,000
Professional office			15.6	15.8			156,800	164,000
Resort condominiums	88.1	104.6	5.7	4.8	502	502	64,800	64,400
School			14.3	14.2			56,000	58,000
Clubhouse			2.6	1.8			5,000	5,000
Total (other)			59.1 (7%)	58.3 (7%)	902	902	514,300	539,400
Other land uses								
Collector road			10.7	8.3				
Loop roads			26.0	12.2				
Cul-de-sac[b]			(18.7)	(28.1)				
Total roads			36.7 (4.5%)	20.5 (2.5%)				
Total developed space			340.4 (42%)	341.2 (42%)				
Total open space			471.6 (58%)	470.8 (58%)				
Total project area			812	812	2283	2424		

aSize for all "Other buildings" shown as ft² per floor.
bCul-de-sac road length is included in calculation of acreage for each building type.

little or moderate slope and desirable slope orientation for solar access. However, 16% of the units in the conventional plan are to be built on 20% to 30% slopes with a north orientation and slopes steeper than 30%, whereas only 10% of those in the energy plan are in these categories. The majority of units in both plans are located in areas designated only as acceptable for building because the rugged topography and unfavorable orientations make the site as a whole less than ideal for development of buildings designed to utilize solar energy.

Energy-Efficient Cluster

Figure 12-6 (see page 241) shows an enlarged site plan for a typical cluster of attached units in the energy plan. Solar access, solar control, wind control, and hydrozonic landscaping principles have been incorporated into the design.

Figure 12-7 (see page 243) shows shadow patterns from buildings (dark gray) and vegetation (light gray). Shadow pattern templates were used (see Chapter Seven) and building placement was arranged to permit south-wall solar access. Figure 12-8 (see page 244) illustrates in section how the location of carports and vegetation have been controlled to protect the solar skyspace as defined by the bulk plane height limit (27°). Native vegetation to the north is retained to control winter winds (see Chapter Nine).

The first priority for solar control is to shade east- and west-facing windows and walls (see Chapter Eight). This is accomplished with native vegetation and fruit trees planted in rows (Figure 12-6). South walls are shaded by shrubs, which can easily be pruned for solar access. Garden space is located at the end of each auto court (screened by a hedge of berries) to further promote community cohesiveness and self-sufficiency.

Figure 12-9 (see page 245) shows three hydrozones selected for the site (see Chapter Ten). Areas that receive intensive use comprise the primary hydrozone and are covered with turf, which will be frequently irrigated and maintained. The secondary hydrozones consist of focal plantings at the entries and in the auto courts. Attractive turf substitutes such as ground covers and mulch are used to reduce water and maintenance requirements while still projecting a mini-oasis image. Wildflowers, native grasses, shrubs, and trees surround, and, in places, meander into the site. These areas are the elemental hydrozones and receive no supplemental irrigation.

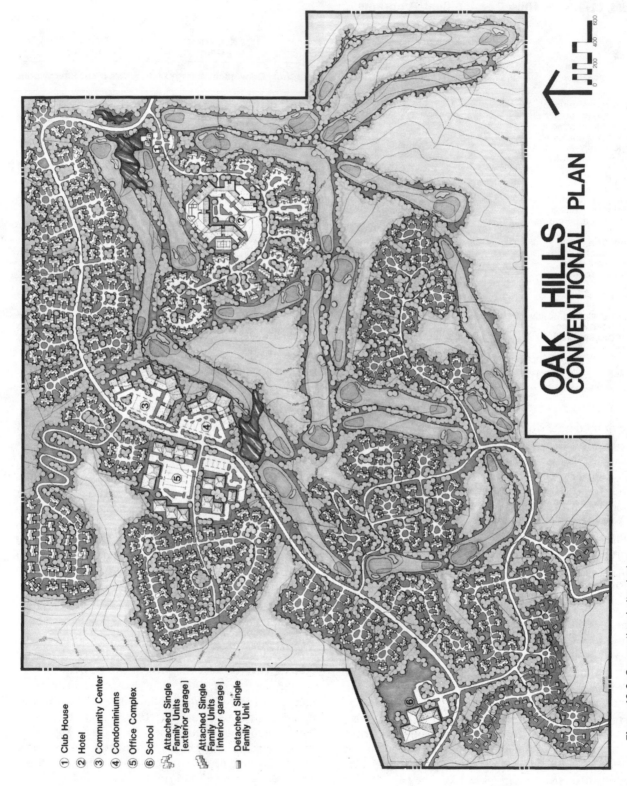

① Club House
② Hotel
③ Community Center
④ Condominiums
⑤ Office Complex
⑥ School
Attached Single Family Units [exterior garage]
Attached Single Family Units [interior garage]
Detached Single Family Unit

OAK HILLS
CONVENTIONAL PLAN

0 200 400 600

Figure 12-3. Conventional site design.

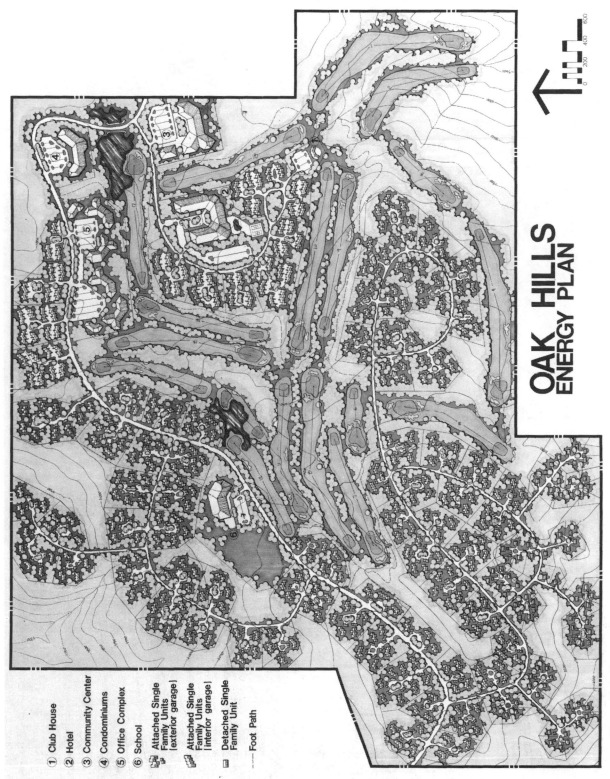

① Club House
② Hotel
③ Community Center
④ Condominiums
⑤ Office Complex
⑥ School

🏘 Attached Single
Family Units
(exterior garage)

🏘 Attached Single
Family Units
(interior garage)

▫ Detached Single
Family Unit

----- Foot Path

OAK HILLS
ENERGY PLAN

Figure 12-4. Energy plan.

239

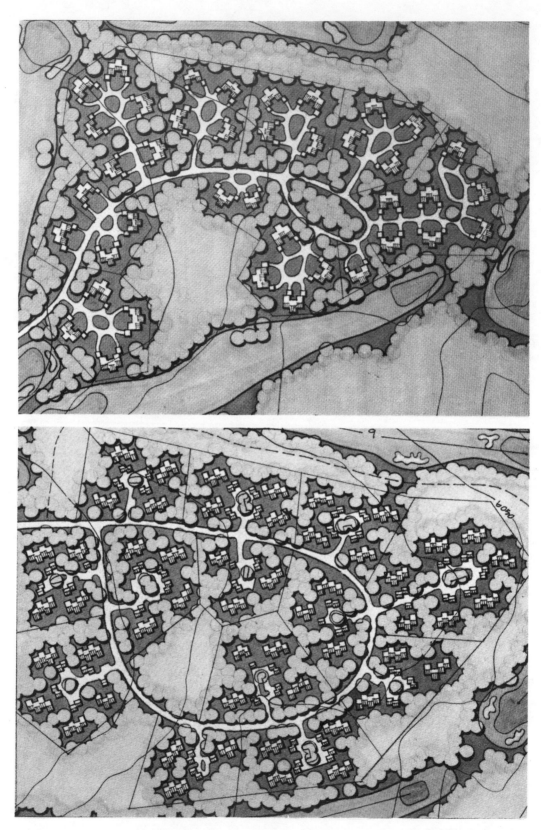

Figure 12-5. Representative examples of siting of single-family attached units in the conventional plan (above) and energy plan (below).

240

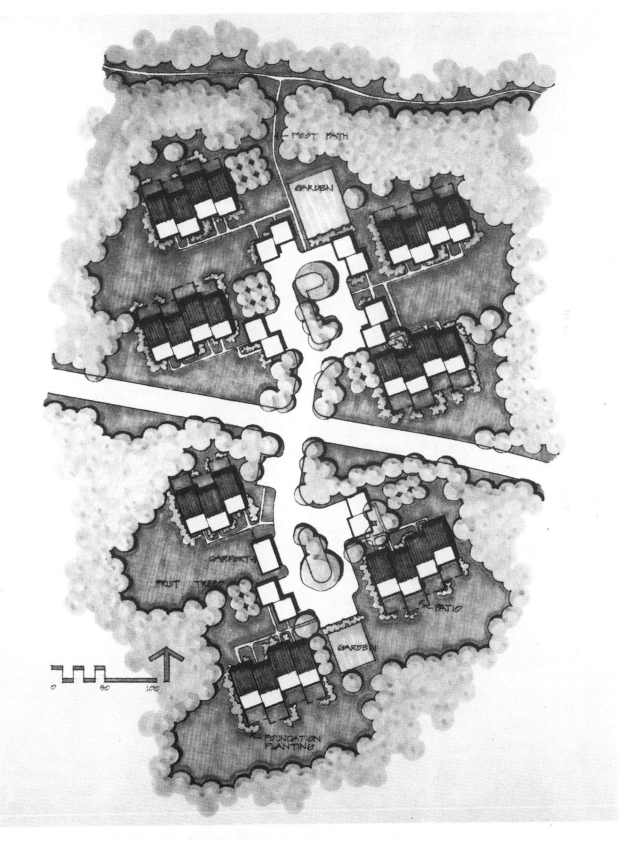

Figure 12-6. Typical siting of attached units clustered around auto courts.

241

Embodied-Energy and Installation Cost Comparison

Infrastructure elements that embody energy can be classified as belowground and aboveground (see Chapter Eleven). Storm sewers, sanitary sewers, and water lines are examples of belowground infrastructure. Roads, curbs, and walks are aboveground site infrastructure elements. The following examines embodied-energy and installation costs associated with asphalt surfacing of roads, driveways, and parking facilities. In the conventional plans for the Greenbrier and Radisson case studies, roads and driveways consume 35% of the total energy embodied in site infrastructure. They account for 31% of the total site development costs in the Radisson plan (CLAER, 1981).

Asphalt comes from crude petroleum and is used as a binder for aggregate for road surfaces. Approximately 587,500 Btu/ton are consumed in the process of extracting and manufacturing asphalt for road surfaces (Smith, 1981). Energy is required to extract crude oil and transport it to a refinery. Once at the refinery, energy is required to heat the oil and run it through the refining process. Lighter fractions are removed and asphalt is the heavier residual material.

Asphalt itself embodies potential energy that could be used for fuel. About 38 million Btu/ton of asphalt can be released when it is diluted with oil and burned (Smith, 1981). This energy is permanently lost to society when asphalt is used as a paving material rather than as a fuel.

Table 12-4 (see page 246) shows dimensions, embodied-energy costs, and installation costs of asphalt surfaces for the conventional and energy plans at Oak Hills. Embodied energy for roads can be saved by reducing either the thickness of the slab or the width of the pavement. Because reducing the thickness of the slab would require greater long-term maintenance, this option was excluded. Reducing the street width may require modification of subdivision regulations; however, precedents have been established for changes of this nature.

Dimensions in Table 12-4 are quantity take-offs obtained with planimeters. Linear measurements were converted into surface area (square feet). Embodied energy totals were calculated by determining embodied-energy per-unit-area (Btu/ft²) using figures cited (notes a and b) and multiplying these by the total surface area. Energy costs were found using the figures and assumptions given in c. Installation costs were derived by multiplying costs-per-unit-area ($/ft²) by total surface area.

Road length for the energy plan is 26,850 ft greater than the conventional plan due to more cul-de-sacs. The length of loop roads is less in the energy plan. Reductions in road widths offset the increased length of roads in the energy plan. Road surface area is 15% less for the energy plan. This translates into an embodied energy savings of 1.53 x 10¹⁰ Btu, or $89,386 in oil equivalent dollars (assuming an oil price of $34/-barrel). Road installation costs are $575,165 less for the energy than for the conventional plan. This amounts to a savings of $546 per single-family dwelling unit.

Single-family detached homes are located closer to access roads in the energy plan, which reduces driveway length. In the energy plan, single-family attached units are clustered around auto courts with adjacent carports. As a result, driveway surface area is reduced by 39% for these units as compared with those in the conventional plan. Increased visitor parking is provided in the energy plan. The design team decided that the convenience associated with this amenity outweighs the resulting increase in energy and installation costs. However, despite increased pavement for visitor parking, the energy plan results in a small savings in embodied-energy and installation costs for driveways and parking. Embodied-energy and installation costs are $9 and $84 less, respectively, when compared to the conventional plan on a per-dwelling-unit basis.

In the energy plan, costs associated with parking facilities for other buildings including the club house, hotel, community center, condominiums, office complex, and school are reduced by 7%. This was achieved by providing designated parking spaces for small cars, which reduces the surface area of each lot.

In sum, site design changes in the energy plan result in 15% less paved surface area. This represents a 25%, or 1.73 x 10¹⁰ Btu, reduction in embodied energy consumption, which is an oil-equivalent savings of $101,116. Total installation costs are reduced from $3,299,050 ($2,389/DU) in the conventional plan to $2,608,326 ($1,714/DU) in the energy plan, a 21% savings ($690,724) for the entire development. When the design team calculated the effects of these design changes on a per unit basis they considered only those costs associated with roads, driveways, and parking that will be passed on to future homeowners. Costs for other parking facilities (i.e., office complex, club house, hotel, etc.) were excluded. Reductions in asphalt surface area resulted in a 34% ($94) savings in embodied energy and a 30%, or $675, savings in installation costs per dwelling unit.

242

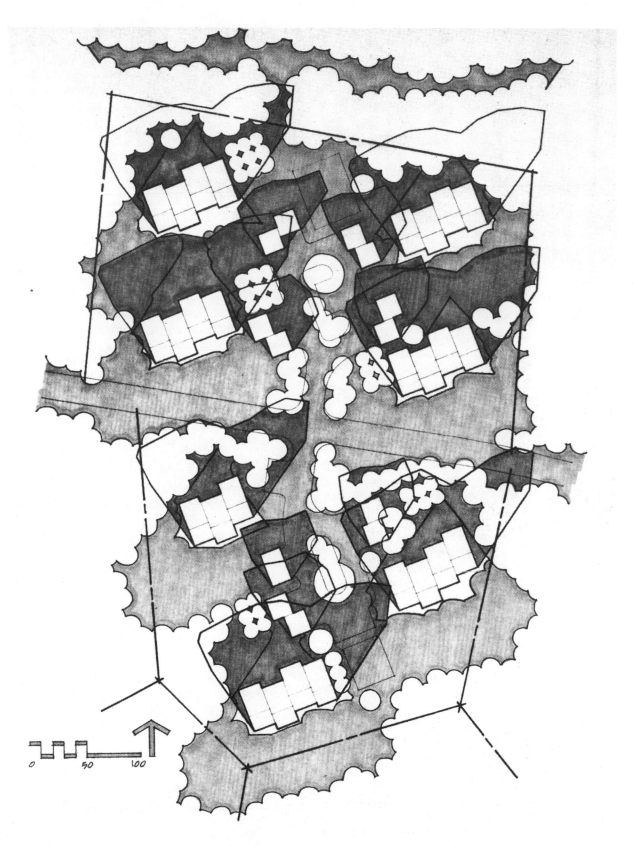

Figure 12-7. A shadow pattern plan depicting shadows from vegetation (light gray) and buildings (dark gray).

243

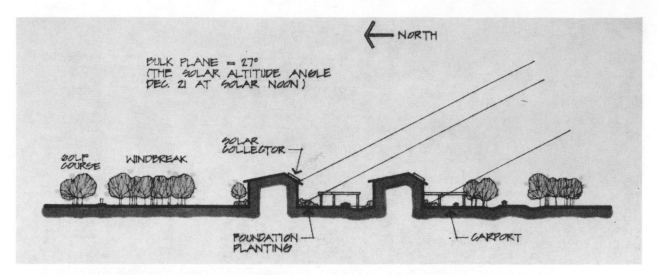

Figure 12-8. Section view illustrates use of the bulk plane to ensure south wall solar access.

Operating Energy Analysis

The conventional and energy plans were evaluated to determine the effects of improved building orientation, massing, and distribution of glazing on annual heating costs. Ideally, such an analysis would be conducted at an earlier phase in the design process than is indicated in this case study. Energy conservation options found to be energy efficient, economical, and marketable could then be implemented in the site plan.

Procedures

DLOAD, a building energy analysis microcomputer program, was used to estimate annual space-heating costs of prototypical single-family residential units in each plan. Although it is beyond the scope of this chapter to present a detailed account of assumptions, inputs, and procedures specific to DLOAD, a general description of steps taken in the simulation is offered to illustrate the type of data needed and methods required to perform such an analysis.

Like many popular correlation tools, DLOAD uses detailed simulations to empirically correlate important design parameters and weather data groups with the monthly fraction of the heating load supplied by solar energy (Klein, 1983). The monthly and annual output variable is termed solar savings fraction (SSF), which is the fraction of the heating load met by solar energy. SSF is then used as an intermediate variable for calculating auxiliary heating requirements. Two volumes of the *Passive Solar Design Handbook* (Los Alamos Scientific Laboratory, 1980; Jones, 1983) describe related heat transfer equations and other aspects of the method in detail.

Weather data. Weather data used as input to DLOAD included mean monthly temperatures and heating degree-days. Data approximating that of the site were found in *Climatological Design Indices for Utah* (Hubbard & Richardson, 1979) and are shown in Table 12-1. Data on average daily solar radiation on a horizontal surface for each month for Salt Lake City were also utilized.

Building prototypes. Four similar building prototypes were defined for each plan:

1. Single-family detached.
2. Single-family attached with detached garage.
3. Single-family attached with internal garage and south entry.
4. Single-family attached with internal garage and north entry.

Thermophysical properties and dimensions of each prototype were recorded on data sheets. Factors (and their values) remaining constant for all prototypes were:

- Air infiltration (1 air change/hour).
- R-value wall (11).
- R-value ceiling (19).
- Slab on grade, perimeter R-value (5).
- Glass transmission U-value (.56, double pane with storms).
- Heating fuel (gas @ $.45/100 ft³).
- Thermostat setting (65F).
- Rate of internal heat gain (80 MBtu/day).

Input factors that changed with prototype follow:

- Length
- Width

244

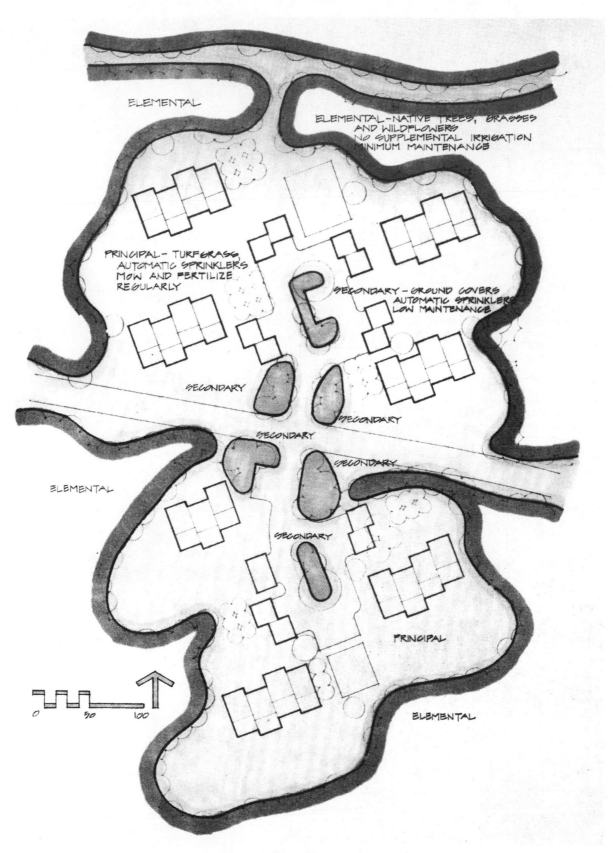

ELEMENTAL

ELEMENTAL—NATIVE TREES, GRASSES
AND WILDFLOWERS
NO SUPPLEMENTAL IRRIGATION
MINIMUM MAINTENANCE

PRINCIPAL— TURFGRASS
AUTOMATIC SPRINKLERS
MOW AND FERTILIZE
REGULARLY

SECONDARY— GROUND COVERS
AUTOMATIC SPRINKLERS
LOW MAINTENANCE

SECONDARY

SECONDARY

SECONDARY

SECONDARY

ELEMENTAL

SECONDARY

PRINCIPAL

ELEMENTAL

0   50   100

Figure 12-9. Primary, secondary, and elemental hydrozones.

245

Table 12-4. Embodied-Energy and Installation Cost Comparison for Pavement

Item	Length (linear ft) Conv. plan	Length (linear ft) Energy plan	Road width (linear ft) Conv. plan	Road width (linear ft) Energy plan	Total Surface Area (square ft) Conv. plan	Total Surface Area (square ft) Energy plan	Total embodied energy (10^{10} Btu) Conv. plan	Total embodied energy (10^{10} Btu) Energy plan	Energy costs (crude oil equiv.)[c] Conv. plan	Energy costs (crude oil equiv.)[c] Energy plan	Installation costs[d] Conv. plan	Installation costs[d] Energy plan
Roads												
Collector[a]	9,000	9,000	52	40	468,000	360,000	1.25	.95	$ 73,032	$ 56,066	$ 533,520	$ 410,400
Loop[a]	24,940	17,660	48	30	1,197,120	529,800	3.19	1.41	186,354	82,382	1,304,717	603,972
Cul-de-sac[b]	27,100	61,230	30	20	813,000	1,224,600	1.08	1.62	63,104	94,656	609,750	918,450
Total	61,040	87,890			2,478,120	2,114,400	5.52	3.99	322,490	233,104	2,507,987	1,932,822
per DU	44.2	57.7			1,794	1,389	4.00×10^7	2.62×10^7	234	153	1,816	1,270
Drives/parking[b]												
Driveway SFD	60	24	10	10	45,600	18,960	6.05×10^8	2.51×10^8	3,536	1,462	34,200	14,220
Driveway SFA	35	18.4	10	10	434,350	265,512	5.76×10^9	3.57×10^9	33,660	20,842	325,763	199,134
Parking bay SFA[e]	6	20	5	5	31,200	110,000	4.14×10^8	1.46×10^9	2,414	8,534	23,400	82,500
Total					511,150	394,472	6.78×10^9	5.28×10^9	39,610	30,838	383,363	295,854
per DU					370	259	4.91×10^8	3.47×10^6	29	20	278	194
Other parking[b]					543,600	506,200	7.21×10^9	6.71×10^9	42,126	39,168	407,700	379,650
Total					3,532,870	3,015,072	6.919×10^{10}	5.189×10^{10}	$404,226	$303,110	$3,299,050	$2,608,326
per DU[f]					2,558	1,981	5.010×10^7	3.409×10^7	293	199	2,389	1,714

[a]Assumes 4" asphalt (AC-20 Petroleum Asphalt @ .1386 gal/ft²; 192,235 Btu/gal)

[b]Assumes 2" asphalt (AC-20 Petroleum Asphalt @ .069 gal/ft²; 192,235 Btu/gal). From: (Center for Advanced Computation, and R.G. Stein and Associates, undated)

[c]Assumes projected price of crude oil @ $34/barrel; 5.82 x 10⁶ Btu/barrel of crude oil. From: (DOE/EIA-0173, 1982)

[d]Asphalt Installation Costs (ft²)

	Cost	
	2"	4"
Materials:		
1. Asphalt-$25/ton	.30	.60
2. Prime coat RC-250-$1/gal	.03	.03
3. Gravel base-$4/ton, 6" thick	.15	.15
4. Hauling-10 miles-gravel $1.75/ton-mile	.04	.04
asphalt $1.85/ton-mile	.01	.01
Labor:		
5. Finish grade and apply asphalt	.07	.10
6. Profit and overhead	.15	.21
Total	$.75	.14

[e]In the conventional plan, .15 parking bay is provided for visitors per unit of attached housing. In the energy plan, .5 parking bay is provided for visitors per unit of attached housing.

[f]All per-dwelling-unit calculations are based on single-family unit totals (conv. plan = 1381, energy plan = 1522).

(From: Smith, 1981)

- Floor-to-ceiling height
- Number of stories
- Glazing (ft^2) on each wall (S, E, W, N)

In this case study, the volume of corresponding prototypes remained the same, whereas glazing was redistributed to allow units in the energy plan to utilize more available solar energy gained from improved orientation. Thus, two-story, south-facing, single-family detached units in each plan have the same dimensions (40 x 30 ft) and area to heat, but glazing as a percentage of wall area is different, as Table 12-5 shows.

Table 12-5. Glazing as Percent of Wall Area

	Conventional plan	Energy plan
South wall	10%	20%
East wall	7.5%	5%
West wall	7.5%	5%
North wall	10%	2.5%

Assumptions regarding thermophysical properties are conservative, owing to the readily available improvements in flame technologies and in R-19/R-38 construction with substantially reduced air infiltration (.5 air change/hour). These assumptions have been retained to best indicate the role and magnitude of impact that slight adjustments to glazing orientation, building orientation, and building placement can have as practiced by the landscape architectural profession on a conventional building program. Reliance on state-of-the-art mechanical systems, building enclosure and sealing technologies, and radical departures from generally commercialized housing types was felt to obscure firm conclusions regarding the marginal impact of landscape decisions.

Despite these intentions, some alteration of the physical structure parameters and mix of structure types is inevitable if the design is to remain plausible and realistic in adapting to improvements in siting. The gain of 141 total units is indicative of this difficulty, and has been minimized in the comparative statistics on per-unit performance shown in the following tables.

Quantity take-offs. The first quantity take-off describes orientation of reference walls (the longest wall) for each prototype. This is achieved by counting the number of units of each prototype whose reference wall is nearest each orientation category. For example, in the Oak Hills energy plan 79, 1100, 122, and 132 units of prototypes 1, 2, 3, and 4, respectively,

were oriented within 30^0 east of true south. Twenty-eight units of prototype 3, and 61 units of prototype 4, were oriented within 30^0 west of true south. When the orientation of attached units is determined, the reference wall is the longest wall of the structure. This is frequently the shortest wall of each unit.

The second quantity take-off lists how many structures contain the same number of attached units for each attached-unit prototype. Table 12-6 (see next page) shows this information collected for the energy plan.

Simulation. Energy performance simulations were run for each of the structural variants with their appropriate orientation categories. Table 12-6 shows 11 structural variants in the energy plan. DLOAD treats structures oriented within 30^0 east or west of south as one orientation category. Thus, in the energy plan the orientation category does not affect the number of structural variants. In the conventional plan, five of the eight structural variants were simulated at more than one building orientation.

DLOAD output consisted of tables delineating monthly and annual solar savings fraction and auxiliary heating requirements (MMBtu). Annual total auxiliary heating requirements for each structural variant were multiplied by the number of units comprising that variant and converted into space-heating costs. Subtotals of each variant in a plan were added to derive total energy costs.

Results

Results from Table 12-7 (see next page) illustrate that the energy plan has a net total savings of 8.4 billion Btu/year or 7% ($37,800). Annual operational energy savings range from 13% to 16% ($53 to $85) on a per-unit basis for the different unit types. Average per-unit savings is 15.7% due to the preponderance of units in the single family attached-exterior garage prototype.

Table 12-8 (see next page) compares per-unit energy consumption for different structural variants found in the conventional and energy plans. The increasing number of units per structure and the decreasing energy consumption in both plans correlate, thus indicating the value of creating larger structures that reduce the surface-to-volume ratio of each unit in climate with long heating seasons.

The savings are comparable with overall averages, but tend to have reduced potential as the structures increase in size. Indeed, a major and seemingly hidden factor behind the 15.7% overall reduction on a per-unit basis is the shift to more aggregated attached units in the energy plan. This shift, when controlled in the above comparison, is reduced to a weighted savings of 13.7%, or about one-sixth less. Thus, even for

Table 12-6. Quantity Take-Offs: Energy Plan

Unit type	Numbers of units per structure						Totals
	1	3	4	6	6	7	
Prototype 1 (SFD)	79 (79)						79 (79)
Prototype 2 (attached garage)		24 (8)	1076 (269)				1100 (277)
Prototype 3 (SFA-south entry)			8 (2)	55 (11)	66 (11)	21 (3)	150 (27)
Prototype 4 (SFA-north entry)			4 (1)	35 (7)	126 (21)	28 (4)	193 (33)

Number of structures shown in parentheses below number of units.

Table 12-7. Operating Energy Cost Comparison

Unit type	Total DUs		Total energy use (billion Btu/yr)		Per unit performance (MMBtu/yr)		Per unit annual savings
	Conv. plan	Energy plan	Conv. plan	Energy plan	Conv. plan	Energy plan	Energy plan
Single family detached Costa	76	79	11.3 $ 50,850	10.2 $ 45,900	148.4 $667	129.3 $582	13% $85
Single family attached Exterior garage (cost)	1104	1100	93.6 $421,200	78.6 $353,700	85 $383	71.4 $321	16% $62
Single family attached Interior garage (cost)	201 ———	343 ———	16.6 $ 74,700	24.3 $109,350	83.8 $372	71 $319	14% $53
Totals*b*	1381	1522	121.5 $546,750	113.1 $508,950			

*a*All cost calculatpons assume 1983-84 residential gas prices of 45¢/therm ($4.50/MMBtu) inclusive of all fees and taxes.
*b*Total savings equal to 8.4 billion Btu/yr or $36,800.

Table 12-8. Comparison of Variant Types of Attached Units Controlled for Density

Unit type	Average unit energy consumption (MMBtu/yr)		Savings (%)
	Conv. plan	Energy plan	
SFA — exterior garage			
3-unit structure	87.7	77.0	12
4-unit structure	84.0	71.3	15
Avg. units/structure	3.68	3.97	
SFA — interior garage			
4-unit structure	83.8	72.6	13
5-unit structure	79.8	71.1	11
6 unit structure	77.0	71.0	8
Avg. units/structure	4.02	5.72	

this "controlled" comparison, as much as 15% of the aggregate per-unit savings is attributable to longer and larger structures. Better siting for solar energy utilization and improved distribution of glazing to collect more solar energy account for the remaining energy savings found in the Oak Hills energy plan.

Summary

Reductions in width of roads and other asphalt surfaces resulted in an embodied-energy savings of 1.73×10^{10} Btu (25%) for the Oak Hills energy plan. Improved orientation, window locations, and packing of units in larger structures resulted in an annual savings of 8.4×10^9 Btu (7%) for space heating costs. Assuming that calculated savings of embodied energy represent a third of those achievable through other means (i.e., curbs, walks, utilities), total embodied-energy savings would equal 5.19×10^{10} Btu. Given this assumption, in 6.2 years annual savings in space heating will equal initial embodied energy savings. Thus, over a 30-year project life, an initial savings of 5 Btu in embodied energy is equivalent to a 1 Btu reduction in operating energy. Although landscape architects should not neglect to implement site design options that reduce consumption of embodied energy, greater emphasis should be placed upon siting and landscaping of buildings to promote energy conservation and solar energy use. Some design solutions that reduce embodied energy, such as reducing road width and eliminating sidewalks, may also reduce pedestrian safety and mobility or otherwise have an adverse effect on the users' quality of life. Energy-conserving design options that influence siting and landscaping do not have the same potential to detract from the visual image and quality of life factors that affect a development's marketability and liveability.

Conclusions of this study regarding embodied energy, space heating, and passive site design correspond with results cited in Chapter Two from case studies conducted in other climate zones. This study also confirms the legitimate role of the landscape architectural profession to continue pushing back areas of uncertainty and quantifying the benefits of energy-conserving site design.

Acknowledgments

The authors wish to thank Larry Wegkamp for his valuable suggestions offered during manuscript review, and Land Design, Inc. for their cooperation.

CHAPTER THIRTEEN
The Ecological City: Closing the Loop

DAVID MORRIS
Institute for Local Self-Reliance
Washington, D. C.

Experience is a good teacher, but she sends in terrific bills.

— *Minna Antrim*

FOR the past century our designers, engineers, builders, and financiers have constructed a nation based on the principle of *separation*. Cheap energy and cheap disposal costs made transportation and environmental concerns unimportant. The result has been a fractured society where the three parts of the development equation, production, consumption, and disposal, take place many miles away from one another.

We separated production and consumption: the farm from the kitchen, the workplace from the worker, the power plant from the appliance. By 1975 labor traveled on average 20 miles to work. Energy in the form of electricity traveled more than 200 miles before it performed useful work. Food traveled more than 1000 miles before it was consumed. We separated production and consumption from disposal. Toxic wastes were buried far from the factory. Garbage and sludge were dumped into remote landfills or rivers.

The legacies of the era of separation surround us. Such ubiquitous devices as the flush toilet, the uninsulated attic, the interstate freeway system, single-use zoning, and high rise buildings are some of the consequences. Our great population and commercial centers became concentrated islands of consumption, wholly dependent on imports. Cities like Salinas, Kans., or Bellingham, Wash., (population 50,000), import 100 tons of food, 500 tons of fuel and more than 31,000 tons of fresh water every day. To facilitate this tremendous flow of materials, more than a quarter of our urban land is devoted to roadways for trucks, cars, and busses. Electrical grids criss-cross our urban skies. Gas and water pipelines form an underground network. Like the giant organism it has become, the city disposes of equally large quantities of potentially valuable wastes. Salinas and Bellingham dispose of more than 20,000 tons of fertilizer and soil conditioner (human waste) annually and 50,000 tons of raw materials (solid wastes).

Like a living creature, the city pulsates with energy, creating giant heat islands. Satellite photographs show our heavily populated areas literally glowing in the dark.

Long distribution systems and the fragmentation of the production-consumption-disposal loop are inherently inefficient. And so long as energy and disposal costs were nominal these inefficiencies were unimportant. However, the 1500% increase in oil prices in the 1970s and the growing willingness of societies to regulate their disposal practices changed the underlying assumptions. Almost overnight transportation costs became an important part of the production equation. Disposal costs became formidable. Centralized systems had to compete with decentralized systems. Systems that removed the supplier from the consumer had to compete on more even terms with systems that brought the supplier and the consumer into proximity. Central power plants had to compete with rooftop solar cells. Mid-east oil had to compete with heat recovery technologies and gentle heat pumps that extract the warmth from nearby soils and groundwater. Remote suppliers of virgin materials had to compete with local recyclers as a source of raw materials.

In the new age, distribution lines will be shorter and the wastes of one system will become the raw materials of another. Integration will become a new design principle for architects, engineers, and economists alike. The old fragmented, inefficient, dependent city will give way to the new integrated, efficient, and self-reliant city.

The Integrated City

The discovery of the value of integration has been occasionally serendipitous. For example, when Portland, Ore., undertook a massive study of potential energy savings in the late 1970s, an unexpected finding was that 5% of projected energy could be saved by reviving neighborhood grocery stores. Single-use zoning had forced residents to drive to a commercial area to buy a pack of cigarettes, a gallon of milk, a loaf of bread. To reduce gasoline consumption, Davis, Calif., enacted an ordinance that allowed people to work in their homes.

Across the nation entirely new industries have been created to design integrated systems. Higher energy prices have made it more economical to capture the city's waste heat, that is, to turn the glow the satellites could see back in on ourselves by internally consuming the energy. Indeed, the fastest growing segment of the $20-billion conservation and alternative energy industry is the business of "shared savings." Engineering firms contract with a manufacturer or office building owner to capture the enterprise's waste heat for useful operations and split the savings.

After we extract the maximum value from the resources inside the building (and buildings have now been built that have no furnaces — "zero energy" houses warmed by body heat and waste heat of appliances and lights), we search for new fuel sources that might be nearby. The warmth of the soil and groundwater present such an opportunity. Sweden already sells large water heat pumps that can extract useful energy from water no more than two degrees above freezing. Groundwater and soil below the freeze level maintain an almost constant temperature year round, usually 15 to 20 degrees above freezing. Several commercial complexes are now heated by the soil upon which they are built. Several German cities extract heat from the water they flush from their toilets. Households send the water to the sewage plant where a giant heat pump extracts the warmth and sends it back via a district heating system to the resident.

Heat pumps take advantage of the earth's furnace. Solar cells take advantage of the furnace that burns 93 million miles away from us. The sunlight that falls on rooftop photovoltaic devices pushes electrons across a junction and sets up an electrical current that can power devices within the house. The idea that the rooftops and sides of buildings can actually become power plants is the next step in the evolving awareness of integrated systems. The first step occurred when architects realized that in warm climates black rooftops burdened building-cooling systems. Davis, Calif., for example, enacted a city ordinance that mandated light-colored rooftops to reflect the sun's heat. Solar cells help us conceive of the roof not only as a barrier to the weather but as a device for converting parts of the environment into useful work.

The technological dynamic is driven by basic economics. Yet it carries with it a psychological and institutional dynamic.

In Phoenix, Ariz., an enterprising subdivision developer sells homes equipped with photovoltaic rooftops. Solar cells are not yet competitive with purchased utility power, although they are already competitive for applications in remote areas, such as mountain peaks for powering communication facilities, and will be competitive at the grid-connected household level by 1987 or 1988. The Department of Energy has subsidized these homes to determine how the technologies operate in a working environment. Nine-hundred square feet of solar cells generate a surplus of electricity for an energy-efficient house on a year-round basis. What can be done with the surplus electricity? The developer, John Long, has offered each buyer the choice of one of three models of converted electric vehicles. The moral? When the rooftop becomes a power plant, the automobile becomes a household appliance!

Indeed, the home and the car form a symbiotic relationship. When the car's batteries are depleted, it plugs into the house for recharging. In case of a utility blackout during cloudy days, the car's storage batteries could provide emergency power for the house.

The value of real estate may change when the rooftop generates significant wealth. In 1983 a 900-square-foot array generates the equivalent of $1000 a year in electricity. Consider that roof rent. The rule of thumb in real estate is that the value of a property is worth 10 times its rental value. Therefore a home on the north side of the street facing south may soon be worth at least $10,000 more than the identical home on the south side of the street facing north. As real estate values shift, property tax assessments will shift. By the end of this century the phrase, "born on the wrong side of the street," will be to an integrated society what "born on the wrong side of the tracks" was to a fragmented society.

In 1984 the Wisconsin Electric Power Company concluded that since two thirds of the fuel it burned in its large power plants went off as waste heat the company was in effect producing more heat than electricity. It petitioned the state legislature to allow the creation of several new subsidiaries. WisPark would develop industrial parks, linked into a district heating system to the nearby power plants. WisVest would use the cash flow of the utility to back bonds issued to finance the infrastructure of these new industrial parks.

A Brooklyn, N.Y., apartment and commercial complex called Starrett City is another example of the dynamics of the age of integration. Starrett City houses 20,000 people. Built in 1974, it is not connected to the electrical grid system. Instead, the complex has its own power plants. The waste heat from the plants warms the water and the buildings. Starrett City imports natural gas to fuel the power plants. In the late 1970s its building managers worried about possible disruptions in the natural gas supply. They sought new sources of fuel.

Across the street sits one of New York City's sewage treatment plants. In 1984 Starrett City and the City of New York signed a barter agreement. Starrett City would pipe some of its waste hot water to the sewage plant. The warm water allows New York to reduce the amount of oil used to warm the digesters. The digestion process generates methane gas, quite similar to natural gas. The sewage plant pipes the methane back to Starrett City to fuel its power plants. In addition, the sewage plant sends its effluent water across the street to provide make-up water for the boilers, thus reducing the need for cooling towers and allowing Starrett City to use its water supply for potable purposes.

The agreement will save both parties hundreds of thousands of dollars annually. The higher price of fuel made it economical for Starrett City to seek cheaper sources and for engineers to design the technologies needed to extract the methane inexpensively. In doing so the relationship between apartment complex and sewage plant changes from a one-way relationship to a partnership. The wastes of one process become the raw materials of another. Such is the way of the ecological city.

In October 1983 Modesto, Calif., Mayor Peggy Mensinger turned a valve and methane from the city's sewage plant filled gas pumps. With the help of Pacific Energy Corporation, Modesto can now run its entire city fleet from this by-product of sewage digestion. Three miles of pipelines connect the plant to "gas" stations at the police headquarters, the public works truck depot, and city hall. Methane fuel has many advantages, one of which is its impact on air pollution. As one of the engineers working for Pacific Energy Corporation happily observes, "You can breathe the exhaust." In several smog-ridden sections of California, that can be an important consideration.

The citizens of Modesto may soon view their relationship to the sewage plant in a different light. After all, a family of four is "generating" the equivalent of 15 gallons of gasoline. That's a different kind of tax to pay for city services. In the modern parlance, Modesto is a city that is "getting its shit together."

Sometimes integration provides multiple benefits. That appears to be the case with Ted Taylor's ice ponds. Taylor is a physicist who worked at Los Alamos on the first atomic bomb and later became one of those most active in the fight against nuclear proliferation. In the late 1970s he explored the potential of solar energy. Unlike most of his colleagues he preferred the opportunities offered by the "coolth" of night and winter air. A garden-variety hose sprays a fine mist of water into the cold air. The droplets freeze and fall into a cavity dug out of the ground, where the slush is covered by an insulating cover. The ice water cools nearby buildings.

The Prudential Insurance company's office complex in Princeton, N.J., is cooled in this fashion. Taylor sees dairies as the primary market. Dairies use electricity year-round to cool milk. Ice ponds in states like New York or Wisconsin or Minnesota have paybacks of 1 to 3 years.

Ice ponds may solve two problems at once. The mid-Atlantic region is experiencing water shortages. Long Island, N.Y., and northern New Jersey have polluted their ground-water supplies. Taylor has proposed the construction of an "iceberg" on Long Island. The workability of the concept is based on the different melting points of seawater and freshwater. Saltwater would be sprayed into the air, much like freshwater to create gigantic icebergs. Saltwater melts before freshwater. The salt washes off, leaving potable water behind. The fastest melt naturally occurs in August, the month the demand for air conditioning and water is greatest.

Again and again we discover that a step toward in-

253

tegration usually leads us toward an entirely different dynamic. For example, in the late-1970s architects made houses more energy efficient by reviving the practice of burrowing underground, using the warmth and the wind protection of the soil as a wall material. Earth-sheltered homes now number perhaps 4,000 and increase by about 1000 a year. A few commercial structures also have been built underground, but most are relatively shallow — only a story or two. Now civil engineers are teaming up with geologists to build structures that take advantage of the limestone and sandstone underpinnings of some cities. Drill through the limestone and dig out the sandstone. The limestone becomes a very strong ceiling. Spray on a modest adhesive and the sandstone becomes an adequate wall.

The 150,000-square-foot Civil and Mineral Engineering Building on the urban campus of the University of Minnesota in Minneapolis illustrates the advantages of underground structures. The bottom floor is more than 100 feet underground. The building cost half that of a surface building. Indeed, once the builders got below the limestone layer, expanding the mined space became very inexpensive. The operating costs of the building are low. The temperature of underground sandstone is 52F year-round. Indeed, as the warmth of the building escapes into the surrounding stone it warms that stone up. Over the years the building will become surrounded by what David Bennett, the principal architect on the project, calls a "thermal balloon." By 1986 the building should reach temperature equilibrium with the surrounding earth, and from then on the prime source of heat will be lights, office machinery, and human bodies.

Dr. Fairhurst of the Underground Space Center points out that even though the excavation costs were lower than surface level building, the small size of the building increased its cost per square foot. Moreover, since the excavation was vertical a very expensive modern bucket brigade was needed to take out the sand. But many river-based cities, such as Minneapolis' sister city Saint Paul, are built on bluffs. Rivers run through or near downtown. Construction crews could excavate horizontally, through the bluff, and easily carry out the sand onto waiting barges. In fact, cities downstream from Minneapolis have already expressed interest in using this material as fill to expand their usable land area. Fairhurst estimates an unfinished construction cost of $8/ft². Saint Paul is currently exploring the possibility of constructing millions of square feet of low-cost storage, industrial, and transportation space under downtown.

Science fiction stories of the 1950s sometimes described the city of the future as having industries and power plants located underground. The industries were almost entirely automated and the waste heat from these processes flowed upwards to the surface office buildings and residences.

Kansas City is built over still-active mines. More than 5000 acres already have been mined, and 2 to 3 million square feet a year are added. Ten years ago Kansas City began to recover this space. More than 20 million square feet already are used. Taking a cue from Ted Taylor, Kansas City found that it could capture the winter's cold in underground stone pillars. The cold pillars cut the cost of storing vegetables so much that Kansas City is attracting vegetable growers to move their storage facilities from Chicago, where high-priced electricity cools the food.

Integration Does Not Mean Self-sufficiency

As biologist Russell Anderson has written, self-reliance is "the capacity for self-sufficiency, but not self-sufficiency itself. Self-reliance represents a new balance, not a new absolute." Once again the energy industry provides a good example. As mentioned above, a 900-square-foot rooftop covered with high-efficiency solar cells can provide more electricity than an energy-efficient house consumes year-round. Unfortunately, the electricity is not produced exactly when it is needed. Therefore the homeowner must either store the power in costly batteries or rely on outside power plants. The electric grid system was established precisely because of its economic benefits. A century ago the electric power industry began by selling complete power plants. Only later were companies (utilities) created that sold the electricity itself. The rationale behind interconnecting is that the electric grid becomes an efficient storage system that reduces the need for each building to have power plants sufficient to meet their peak demand. Not everyone uses electricity at the same time. Utilities call this the "diversity" factor. It means that 10 houses do not need 10 times the plant capacity of one house, if they are connected.

In the late 1970s at MIT a computer analysis was done of photovoltaic homes in different regions of the United States. Whether in Seattle or Tucson or Buffalo the study concluded that the optimum arrangement was where the home "exported" about 50% of the electricity it produced and "imported" 50% of what it consumed. The economics of interdependence was one of the reasons Congress enacted the Public Utilities Regulatory Policies Act of 1978 (PURPA). Upheld by the Supreme Court in 1982 and again in

1983, PURPA abolished the century-old monopoly that utilities had over the generation of electric power. An electric utility must purchase power from independent producers at a price equal to that it would have had to pay to generate a new unit of electricity. The independent power generation industry has grown from zero in 1979 to about $3 billion in 1984. At the present growth rate, and provided that the construction schedules of central power plants have been severely cut back by the late 1980s, greater investments will be made in small power plants that are independently owned than in large, central power plants.

PURPA eliminated a monopoly. It created a monopsony, economic jargon for a situation in which there is one buyer. Under the law independent producers cannot sell their electricity to anyone but the utility. The next step in the democratization of our electric system is to eliminate the monopsony and transform the grid into a giant marketplace. The utility will become a giant switching system, like the telephone company. At MIT the Homeostatic Energy Group has been designing systems whereby microprocessor-based technology is used to monitor supply and demand in five-minute intervals. Prices fluctuate accordingly. The producer who tries to sell electricity in the early morning hours when there is a glut of power will receive a lower price than the producer who has power to sell at the peak late afternoon hours. We will all remain consumers. But we will also assume the role of producers. Alvin Toffler, author of *Future Shock* and *The Third Wave*, calls these new entities "prosumers."

Of course, one can become overly optimistic over how widely accepted integration as a basic design principle has been. Institutions built up over a century do not easily change in the light of recent developments. Nor do ways of thinking. While promising, the new techniques are still embryonic. Long Island's restaurants serve ducks raised in Wisconsin, when fifteen years ago Long Island Duckling was a much sought-after dish. Macroengineers are busily designing a system to divert the Mississippi to irrigate west Texas drylands. In late 1983 Los Angeles contracted to buy 400 MW of electricity from British Columbia, more than 1000 miles away. San Francisco tried to truck its garbage a hundred miles away to Yolo County (Yolo County refused however). Washington, D.C., tried to resolve its sludge problem by sending it via barge to Haiti (Haiti politely declined).

And while Ted Taylor proposes his urban iceberg, the first commercial venture was established in 1983 to tow an iceberg from the north pole to Saudi Arabia to provide fresh water. The old ways die hard.

But they are dying. For we are discovering the costs involved in such systems. It now costs twice as much to deliver electricity or food as it takes to generate or grow it. Economically strapped cities now hungrily eye roads that reduce their tax revenue by taking land out of production. The costs of pollution from car exhausts and the additional burdens on sewage systems from road run-off run into the millions of dollars for even modest cities. In 1980 Arizona decided that it was more appropriate to use water for the more "valuable" residential or commercial sectors than for agriculture. By 2006 any remaining agricultural land may be purchased by the state if a "higher" use for water can be found. However, even by the early 1980s planners discovered that a decreased agriculture meant increased sandstorms. Hundreds of tons of dust must be trucked out of Arizona cities each year. The bill for shorter lived air conditioners because of dust stuck in the compressors and the cost of cleaning bills have not even been calculated.

However, the bill for hazardous waste dumping has been calculated. In some cases it is total. The entire city of Times Beach, Mo., disappeared because of hazardous wastes. Samuel Epstein estimates that the national cost of cleaning up just the existing hazardous waste dumps is greater than the national military budget.

The costs of fragmented systems burden the nation. The benefits of integrated systems encourage new technologies and new techniques that move production and consumption back together. The city as nation becomes a working metaphor.

The City as Nation

While architects and engineers devise ingenious ways to extract the maximum value from local resources, economists and planners relish the economic development spinoffs. Infrared cameras can take pictures of the heat loss from entire communities. Imagine a camera that could photograph the flow of capital. Take a picture of the city. The largest outflow of dollars pays for taxes. Much of that money comes back into the city in the form of social services, highway funds, social security, aid to hospitals, schools, or the city government, etc. The next largest outflow pays for energy. A city of 50,000 will spend about $1500 for energy for every man, woman, and child in 1984. More than $75 million leaves the city for imported fuels and electricity.

Very little of that money returns. Whereas 40 cents on the dollar spent on the typical basket of goods stays in the local economy, only 5 to 15 cents of the energy dollar does so. (The full dollar would remain in the local economy only if all the steps in the production process were local; for example, if bread were baked by local merchants who hired local residents and bought the flour from local mills and the mills processed local wheat and the investors were local, etc.) Thus our city of 50,000 pays a penalty of at least 25 cents on the dollar, or $15 million, because it spends the money on energy rather than for some other purpose. That may be equivalent to the city's general budget, or the payroll of its largest employer. Energy dollars hemorrhage hard-earned capital from the local economy. A city that reduces this "leakage" gains in several ways. The investment in energy efficiency can itself promote local employment. The diversion of money that would have been exported into more local business can also create jobs. By the author's calculation, a 20% reduction in imported energy would have reduced the unemployment rate by a full percentage point or more in Kalamazoo, Mich., in 1983.

Thus energy efficiency becomes the cornerstone of an effective economic development strategy. But efficiency in its broader definition is really the objective. The community is viewed as a nation. The objective is to reduce its imports, increase its exports, and extract the maximum amount of useful work from local resources. Each profession has its own jargon to describe this process. Economists call it "capturing the value added." Ecologists call it "closing the loop." I call it "local self-reliance." Once again integration becomes a basic design principle.

Take the case of Hagerstown, Md., population 40,000. Not only does it use methane from its sewage plant to fuel city vehicles, but it captures the fertilizer value of its sludge. This is possible because in the mid-1970s the city forced its 114 industrial customers to eliminate the heavy metals they were dumping into the municipal sewage plant by installing treatment systems at their plants.

Under the aegis of Mike McGauhey, director of its Water Pollution Control Department, 600,000 hybrid poplar trees were planted on 500 acres of city-owned land in 1982. Fertilized by the sludge the poplars grow to 14 feet in two years and thereafter grow from stumps. The first harvest should occur in mid 1984. The city expects initially to chip the wood and burn it to generate electricity for sale to the local power company. As the technologies for converting cellulose into alcohol improve, the pulp may be converted into liquid fuels. The residue of that process is a high protein animal feed. McGauhey estimates that 100 head of hogs and cattle could be raised from the residue of 600,000 hybrid poplars.

If the wood is burned for electric power, the waste heat might be used to warm a greenhouse for vegetable production. A Viennese firm has offered to build a Growth Chamber, a vertical greenhouse that uses hydroponics (a soil-less growing technique). One acre under a Growth Chamber could produce 100 times the vegetables of an acre of soil. McGauhey eyes the nearby military bases as the market for this food.

The sewage plant cost the city $2 million a year in 1978. By 1985 it might be generating a net profit. In 1978 it was viewed as a disposal site. Today it is viewed as a production plant, a hybrid gas well/fertilizer factory/tree farm/power plant/hog farm. Such is the value of integration.

The human waste stream offers opportunities. Even more so does the solid waste stream. As energy prices have increased, so has the value of recycled materials. The enormous amount of energy required to convert a tree into paper is embodied in that paper, therefore substantially less energy is needed to recycle that paper into a new product, thus reducing its price. Moreover, industries that use scrap tend to use less water and create less air pollution. The latter is important to a society that imposes restrictions on pollution from industrial plants.

The recycling industry began as a volunteer-based, environmentally motivated effort in the late 1960s. Today it has become a multibillion dollar industry. Dun and Bradstreet predicts that by the year 2000, the recycling industry may be the world's second largest, next to agriculture.

Cities are the repositories of post-consumer and commercial scrap. They dump hundreds of millions of tons of raw materials into landfills every year. Every household disposes of about two tons of increasingly valuable materials each year. A city the size of San Francisco throws away more paper each year than is produced by a large commercial timber stand, more copper than is extracted from a small commercial mine, and more aluminum than from a modest bauxite mine. Municipal sanitation departments may soon be renamed "Departments of Mining and Materials."

Clearly, cities do not produce materials; they dispose of used commodities. New materials must always replenish their supply. Yet modern technologies allow us to recycle commodities many times. Paper can be recycled ten times before it loses its fiber value. Even then it can be recycled for progressively lesser value uses, such as for animal feed or soil conditioner.

One of the intriguing aspects of scrap industries is their size. Factories that use scrap not only use less water and less energy and are less polluting than those that use virgin materials, but they are also much smaller. For example, the only profitable areas of the steel industry are those that use electric arc furnaces and 100% scrap. The industry calls these "mini-mills" or sometimes even "neighborhood mills." The annual output of a typical mini-mill might be 200,000 tons, a drop in the bucket compared to the giant integrated works at Sparrows Point in Baltimore, Md., which produces tens of millions of tons a year. Thus, recycling industries not only get their materials locally but they can also serve regional markets. And because of their relatively nonpolluting nature, they can be sited in or near urban areas.

The City and Region

When Hagerstown, Md., Camden, N.J., or Duluth, Minn., begins to use sludge for its fertilizer value or when cities like St. Paul, Minn., develop extensive farmers markets for local growers, the links between urban and rural areas are strengthened. Rising energy prices increase transportation costs. In the Twin Cities these extra costs add about 15% to the price of California carrots over Minnesota carrots. Sludge can reduce the expense of artificial natural-gas-based fertilizers, but only if the farmer is near the source.

Indeed, science and technology may soon transform the economic foundations of our rural communities. Many of our smaller cities depend on the economic health of their surrounding farming communities. For the past five years the price farmers receive for their crops has not equalled their production costs. More and more attention is being directed at raising the value that farmers can receive per acre of cropland and toward diversifying their markets. This is reminiscent of the 1930s when the agricultural depression spurred Henry Ford to bring together 300 agriculturalists, scientists, and business people to form the Farm Chemurgic Council. Ford believed that the way out of the farm depression was to find industrial uses for agricultural materials. In 1942 Ford's own scientists were the first to convert soybeans to plastics. He dreamed of producing postwar automobiles whose plastic seatcovers would be made from farm products.

The precipitous drop in oil prices after World War II delayed this scientific dynamic. The four research centers established in the early 1940s to research industrial uses for agricultural materials turned their efforts elsewhere. However, the rise in oil prices in the 1970s and the advances in the biological sciences spurred a revival in this research. Remember the radio commercial in the mid-1970s that catalogued the number of products that were made from petroleum? Desks, lamps, cups, bathtubs, floors, chairs, radios, toothbrushes, clothing, medicines; the voice droned on. In fact, anything that can be made from petroleum can be made from plant matter. In 1925 85% of our industrial chemicals were made from fermentation by microbes and 13% from wood distillation. Only 2% came from coal and less than one-tenth of one percent from petroleum. By 1945 50% came from petroleum and another 21% from coal. Today the pendulum is swinging the other way. Our enhanced ability to harness the tiny microbe and rising petroleum prices may soon combine to transform America from a hydrocarbon-based economy to a carbohydrate-based economy.

Already agriculture is replacing the fuel markets. In 1982 wood fuel produced more energy than all of our nuclear power plants. Alcohol fuels now displace 0.5% of our vehicular fuel market. Ethanol is not yet competitive with gasoline but it is already competitive with the lead additives used to enhance octane ratings. As the federal government tightens its lead requirements to meet goals for reduced air pollution, ethanol will become even more competitive. In 1983 Illinois became the first state to approve the use of ethanol as an airplane fuel. Because the high octane rating needed for airplane fuels makes them very expensive, ethanol fuel is already competitive for this potentially vast market.

Fuel is an important market. But the chemical value of an organic compound is worth about three times its fuel value. Already starch is beginning to replace petroleum as the basis for some products. Starch-based plastics have a highly desirable feature: they are biodegradable. For example, starch-based polyethylene has been used as a mulch for vegetable farms in Florida. This mulch is more expensive than that derived from petroleum, but unlike conventional plastics, it degrades over the growing season. The $100 per acre the farmer saves from not having to dispose of the petroleum-based mulch more than offsets its somewhat higher initial cost. An English firm, Coloroll, Ltd., introduced hospital laundry bags made of starch-based plastics in 1979. Hospital personnel can dump all disease-ridden and dirty clothes, etc., into the bag and dump the entire bag into the laundry. The bag dissolves in the wash.

In late 1981 AE Staley, the largest producer of corn syrup, opened a pilot plant in Decatur, Ill., which produces methyl glucoside, a widely used plasticizer for rigid foams, paints, and adhesives by fermenting corn rather than by synthesis from hydrocarbons. The company says that on a per-pound basis corn as a feedstock costs half as much as petroleum. Its target is the five-billion-pound market for foams, adhesives, paints, and detergents. As a vice-president of the company proclaimed, "The possibility of creating a chemical industry based on sugar and starch as a supplement to the petrochemical industry seems at hand."

As we switch to a carbohydrate economy, the economic foundations of rural areas may change. The dynamics of what Russell Buchanan of Soil and Land Use Technology, Inc., calls "botanochemical" complexes may be far different from those of petrochemical complexes. Petrochemical plants import their raw materials over thousands of miles in part because transportation costs are minimal. But agricultural commodities are bulky and expensive to transport. So processing facilities will be located near their raw material sources. Once again the principle of integration dominates industrial planning.

Botanochemical complexes will produce many products for diversified markets: fuels, chemicals, animal feed, human food, fertilizer. Already some cooperative farm associations have constructed processing plants that extract multiple products from corn, including foams, adhesives, and detergents. They get two and three times the value out of the corn than they would have if they had used corn only for animal feed. Moreover, these diversified markets reduce their reliance on any one market. If the food market is depressed, they can process more raw material into fuel. If the fuel market is depressed, they can process more into chemicals. This stabilizes income and allows them to better plan ahead.

The Community of the Future

Science fiction stories invariably ask what the community of the future will look like. But science fiction is quickly becoming science fact. Consider that the fastest growing part of our national economy is computers. Microprocessors are made from silicon, which comes from sand. The housing is made from plastics, which can come from plant matter. What is a computer? A bucket of sand and a few pounds of plant matter. And an enormous amount of ingenuity and technical know-how. In fact, the fastest growing segment of the computer and electronics markets is software. Software is the art of providing instructions for the computer to process information. What is the driving force behind software? The person sitting before a computer thinking up more efficient ways of doing things. What fuels that person? Food calories. Ironically we have come full circle. A society which two hundred years ago was based on agriculture is once again becoming based on agriculture. Now modern science allows us to extract ever greater value from these materials.

We are fast moving from an economy based on iron ore and petroleum to one based on sand, plant matter, solar energy, and recycled goods. It is interesting that each of these has a decentralizing dynamic. Sand is the only commodity produced by every state in the country and by most of our counties. Plant matter grows widely over the earth's surface, and solar energy is most economically harnessed through decentralized conversion technologies.

We often hear the metaphor "the global village." Yet equally valid is the metaphor "a globe of villages." The community of the future will not only be part of an international economic system but will be independent of that system in basic ways. It will be increasingly self-sufficient in materials production but will become increasingly interdependent on the rest of the world for information, entertainment, and knowledge. We will trade information globally, but we will trade materials regionally. Planetary commerce will consist of electrons but not molecules.

Microprocessors will monitor our usage and reorient our technologies. We see such examples today: solar cells rotate to follow the sun's path, and shades rise and fall depending on the angle of the sun. Lights turn off when the room is no longer occupied. Warmth is extracted from our soils and our groundwater. More than 80% of our solid and human waste streams is potentially recyclable. Tires that formerly made excellent habitats for mosquitoes, or littered the countryside can be pulverized and recreated as shoes, flooring, and roadways.

How far can we go toward extracting useful energy from local resources? Consider a vignette from the lives of Henry Ford and Thomas Edison, two of America's greatest inventors and entrepreneurs. One day Ford came to his friend Edison's house for dinner. He noticed the gate was hard to push. Given Edison's mechanical genius and penchant for perfection Ford wondered why he would allow such a faulty mechanism. After dinner he raised the question. Edison answered with a smile that the gate was attached to a pump. When a visitor swung the gate open a gallon of water was pumped into a storage tank. Everyone in Edison's neighborhood had a white picket fence. But only Edison was extracting useful work from each visitor.

That story reminds us that "waste" is only a resource for which we haven't yet found use. Think of the amount of waste we could harness. A friend once wondered aloud if we might one day be able to capture for useful effect the kinetic energy of children in a nursery. Why not? Piezoelectric crystals are materials that generate electricity when subjected to pressure.

Imagine a layer of piezoelectric crystals under the floor of nurseries? Or roadways? No process is 100% efficient, but what would happen if we could recapture 25% of wasted kinetic energy?

Integration raises interesting institutional questions. For example, what is the nature of future utilities? Already shopping centers, industrial parks, and offices are using groundwater heat pumps; some are reinjecting the warm water back into the aquifers. Who regulates these subterranean projects? The water department? The public works department? When solar technologies sprout on every rooftop, who guarantees the owner's access to sunlight? The city? The marketplace?

Some of the most important issues concern equity. The new integrating technologies will be purchased first by the wealthy. The last to be served will be the poor and the elderly. Certainly life-cycle costing makes little sense to a 70-year-old; two-year payback periods are irrelevant to the person who cannot qualify for any loan. The poor inherit the hand-me-downs of society. They inherit the used houses, the used cars, the used refrigerators. Because of the major changes in energy prices and environmental considerations in the past decade, the difference between the costs of owning old and new products is enormous. If we don't do something the poor will inherit a physical stock that they cannot afford to operate.

To resolve this dilemma we might redefine the term "social security." In 1984 the average social security recipient will receive about $2500 a year. Some of that income may soon be taxed. Given the changes in social security in the past few years, it appears certain that future increases may not keep up with the cost of living. On the other hand, the 900-square-foot photovoltaic array at present electricity prices will generate more than $1000 a year ($2000 in New York City or Honolulu). That can be considered after-tax income. Moreover, electric prices will probably rise at least faster than the average cost of living; perhaps much faster.

The social security recipient receives money generated from those now paying into the system and from the revenues generated from the social security trust fund. Assuming a 10% return on investment, the $2500 a year assumes $25,000 in the trust fund. A 900-square-foot photovoltaic system should cost less than $25,000 by 1988. Which would we prefer? To be given a pension based on political whim and constantly depreciating in value, or a productive asset that is self-controlled and appreciating in value?

One final point. What holds true for the poor in this country may be equally valid for the developing nations. Certainly as the United States has enacted strict environmental regulations based on the social costs of cleaning up our wastes, the products that don't meet those standards have been exported abroad. Developing countries live so close to the economic edge that a cheaper first cost almost always has a higher importance even though it burdens future generations with massive clean-up costs. If communities in the United States learn to live within their natural resource budget and still maintain a high standard of living, the technologies developed to do this may be appropriate for the developing world. If Tucson or Phoenix learn to produce their basic goods and services in an environment that lacks water (rather than importing water from California or Washington), the techniques developed to do this can become a major export to equatorial countries.

The principle of integration affects not only the way we design our communities but the way we design our businesses. Low-cost, computer-assisted design and computer-assisted manufacturing are already broadening the functions of the typical landscape architectural office into engineering and planning. No longer is the designer interested only in form and function of individual structures but in systemic design of entire communities and in the economic impact of those designs. Computer-assisted modeling helps us to track the most indirect implications of our designs, and computer assisted graphics help to translate the esoteric techniques of modeling into information accessible to a broad segment of our citizens. This in turn allows community residents to participate in designing their futures.

Our cities are becoming giant laboratories and research and development centers. It is there that the future is being tested and refined. A strategy of import substitution helps to "incubate" new knowledge-intensive technologies that can become a lucrative export commodity with a beneficial worldwide impact. The United States is blessed with an abundance of natural resources, a moderate climate, and a huge technological capacity. Developing countries often lack all three. They can develop the scientific capacity, but by a quirk of nature they can never expand their natural resource base. By extracting greater amounts of useful energy from local resources, communities in the United States can help developing nations to do more with what they have and thereby raise their standards of living. The global village transmits the information; the globe of villages provides the technologies. Integration and local self-reliance become the governing design principles.

259

Conclusion

Energy is a means to an end; fuels are important only inasmuch as they perform useful work. We don't need oil, natural gas, or coal. We need to warm our bodies to 98.6F, to turn the wheels of our cars, to melt raw materials so they can be transformed into usable commodities, to provide the electricity needed to run our computers. Planners and designers are learning that we can apply human ingenuity to extract useful work from local resources. To do so means that we must treat the soil, groundwater, air flows, and our waste flows in a much more integrated fashion. When the household becomes a power plant and the city becomes a mine then site planning takes on a different and more systemic flavor.

The planner must be technically proficient. Yet of equal or perhaps even more importance, the plan must be driven by a coherent vision. We now have the technical capability to meld cherished values that emphasize community with a new and superior definition of efficiency. That blend of science and ethics will not inevitably occur. We live in a period of great change, yet change cannot always be equated with progress. Bertrand Russell once wrote, "Change is scientific, progress is ethical. Change is indubitable, whereas progress is a matter of controversy."

Progress is value-laden. The changes in natural resource economics in the past twenty years and the dynamics of modern science make it possible for us to choose a future that is not an extrapolation of the present. Will we have change or progress? We can't yet know, but the seeds of a new way of doing things have been planted in our urban centers.

Appendices 5

Appendix A-1

Table A-1. Potential Modifications to Planning Process to Reflect Need for Energy Conservation

Steps in conventional project	Possible additional steps or modifications for energy-oriented project
Phase I Project initiation	
A. Assemble team	— Include someone on team with good overall knowledge of energy considerations
B. Set preliminary goals	— Include energy-related goals
C. Set initial schedule, organization and assignments	— Allow time/budget for analysis of energy concerns
Phase II Basic reconnaissance/inventory	
A. Conduct preliminary market studies	— Identify uses and combinations of uses "needed" for energy conservation and include in market studies

B. Identify site opportunities, collect initial site date, e.g.:
  • ownership
  • likely cost
  • zoning
  • utility availability
  • access
  • soils
	— Collect additional data needed for analysis of major energy impacts and energy conservation potentials, e.g.:
	  • general topography and slopes
	  • transportation availability
	  • availability of groundwater
	  • energy systems available
	  • solar, wind, and other potential energy sources

C. Review public decision environment
  • types and complexity of controls
  • agencies involved in approval process
	— Identify attitudes toward energy conservation
	— Identify agencies who might be most involved in major energy-related decisions; e.g. power companies, water quality agencies, etc.

D. Review financing environment	— Identify attitudes pro and con regarding the financing of energy-related facilities and innovative developments
Phase III Establish program/needs	
A. Review results of Phase II and establish project goals	— Identify energy-related goals, options/techniques to be used
B. Develop initial development program(s)	— Include major uses/facilities required for energy conservation/production
C. Develop preliminary budget	— Include allowances for major energy-related investments — Identify when such investments would be required
D. Test for financial and market feasibility	— Evaluate potentials for cost recovery through energy conservation and impacts on sale/rent returns

E. Test for management feasibility	— Consider augmenting/modifying team to obtain capabilities required, e.g.:
	  • skills in energy production/use
	  • skills in selected types of development
	  • etc.

F. Establish program and budget	— Consider energy saving service and operational concepts and determine impact on program

G. Review and select site(s)	— Assure use of energy conservation/use criteria in site selection, e.g.; potentials for:
	  • mixed use development
	  • clustering and/or higher densities
	  • on-site energy generation

Phase IV Concept or schematic planning	

A. Detailed site survey
  • topography
  • drainage
  • soils
  • utilities
  • easements
  • covenants/restrictions
	— Collect special data needed for energy-related planning at overall project scale, e.g.:
	  • slopes and earthform windbreaks
	  • tree cover
	  • wind directions/strength
	  • sun access

B. Integrate and analyze site data, identify:
  • buildable/unbuildable areas
  • points of access
  • views in and out of site
  • drainage/flood patterns
  • areas required for drainage retention
  • business centers
  • mixed use developments
	— Include analyses of energy-related conditions, e.g.:
	  • north and south slopes
	  • natural windbreaks
	  • areas where special energy facilities (e.g. central heating) might be located
	  • areas which might accept special forms of construction, e.g.; below-grade construction

(Continued on next page)

C. Develop designs for prototype "building blocks" of project:
- typical building clusters
- neighborhoods
- business centers
- mixed use developments

- areas to be preserved in present form to conserve "embodied" energy and/or to maintain natural energy conserving features
- Include types of building blocks which are oriented to both energy conservation and markets
- Size and design prototypes to reflect energy conserving concepts/principles
- Define locational guidelines that reflect energy conservation needs

D. Develop alternate locations (schematic) plans) for major building blocks and systems of project
- major access points and circulation routes
- major drainage facilities
- major open space systems
- areas for development, by type (building blocks)
- major utility corridors

- Reflect analyses of energy-related site conditions in locational plans
- Seek to minimize amount or length of systems in relation to amount of development provided
- Coordinate systems to achieve multiple purposes, including creation, preservation and enhancement of energy conservation potentials, e.g.:
  - optimum use and protection of south slopes
  - maximize values of open space and vegetation
  - minimize pavements, earth moving, etc.
- Include community and "energy" production and distribution systems where appropriate

Phase V   Evaluation/Selection/Refinement

A. Test and evaluate alternative schematic plans
- conformance with regulations
- cost
- marketability/marketing
- fiscal impact
- environmental impact
- scheduling/staging

- If changes in regulations are needed to implement energy objectives, note and explore potentials for change
- Evaluate energy consumption of alternatives including both embodied energy as well as ongoing usage
- Perform life-cycle costing on significant energy consumption features of the plan
- Evaluate tax, financing, and related implications of alternatives, with special reference to energy saving tax benefits, subsidies.

B. Select and obtain approval of preferred plan
- development team
- financial institutions
- public agencies

C. Prepare development schedule and marketing plan
- systems
- building blocks
- market segments/priorities

D. Convert selected schematic plan into a master plan
- refine/revise
- document
- obtain formal approvals

- If special energy saving features are involved which require public or financial institution approval and/or which are eligible for public subsidy, prepare documentation required to obtain needed approvals and subsidy
- Where appropriate, plan to test energy saving features in early stages of project for feasibility and market potential

Phase VI   Implementation Planning and Design

A. Conduct more detailed surveys of first priority development areas

- Include design features important to planning for energy conservation at cluster and site scale, e.g.:
  - slopes
  - sun access
  - conditions affecting microclimate

B. Prepare schematics for necessary first segments of overall system plans

C. Develop prototype designs for individual buildings and/or building groups

- If appropriate, include plans for community or group energy generation facilities
- Apply concepts and principles required to permit energy conservation, e.g.:
  - south orientation
  - shielding from undesirable winter winds and access to cooling breezes
  - protection of sun access

D. Refine market analysis for first stage development

- Identify concerns which will affect marketability of energy saving features, e.g.:
  - reliability
  - costs vs. returns
  - resale value

(Continued on next page)

E. Prepare detailed analysis of first stage development area
- buildable/unbuildable area
- views
- drainage
- access
- utility access

— Include analyses related to energy conservation, e.g.:
- areas affected by summer/winter winds
- sun exposure/protection

F. Prepare first stage development plan alternatives
- access systems
- drainage
- utilities
- building locations
- locations and types of landscaping

— Reflect principles and analyses related to energy conservation in site planning
— Include any common or joint use facilities for energy generation or conservation

G. Evaluate and select plan
- costs
- marketability

— Evaluate energy consumption/conservation potentials
— Evaluate initial as well as life-cycle costs
— Identify tax, financing and related implications

H. Proceed with design of individual structures and groups of structures
- building plans
- system plans
- lanscape plans

— Include energy saving designs in buildings as appropriate, consider and evaluate and test various options
— Include community or group energy systems as appropriate
— Carefully relate buildings and site to optimize energy and cost savings
— Provide special landscape design features required to help conserve energy, e.g.:
- windbreaks and channeling of wind
- selective reflection and/or absoprtion of sun
- preservation of sun access

I. Proceed with design of supporting systems
- streets
- utilities
- open space
- drainage

— Adjust standards to achieve an optimum balance of energy and cost savings and functional capability
— Include, as appropriate, energy-related systems, e.g.:
- community energy systems
- pedestrian and bicycle facilities

Adapted from: (Barton-Aschman, 1981)

Appendix A-2

Table A-2. Listing and Classification of Energy Conserving Options

Development feature and action	Embodied energy	Maintenance	Vehicular use	Vehicular energy	Local energy prod.	Wind protection/use	Sun protection/use	Energy use/loss	Community	Neighborhood	Cluster design	Building design	Operations
1. Functions													
1.1 Mix of uses													
1.1.1 Disperse public services			x						x	x			
1.1.2 Disperse retail services			x						x	x			
1.1.3 Disperse job opportunities			x						x	x			
1.1.4 Provide for local gardening/food production			x		x				x	x	x		
1.2 Location of uses													
1.2.1 Locate related functions close together			x						x	x			
1.2.2 Locate higher densities close to best transportation			x						x	x			
1.2.3 Locate higher densities on south slopes/lower density and open space uses on north slopes							x		x	x			
2. Services													
2.1 "Public" safety													
2.1.1 Consolidate/integrate safety and emergency services	x	x							x	x			x
2.2 Communications													
2.2.1 Provide telephone shopping			x						x	x			x
2.2.2 Provide cable communications			x						x	x			x
2.2.3 Provide neighborhood communications center			x						x	x			x
2.3 Waste Collection													
2.3.1 Efficient waste collection/haulage			x						x	x			x
2.3.2 Reclamation of waste materials					x				x	x			x
2.4 Delivery													
2.4.1 Consolidate/coordinate delivery systems (e.g., package pickup center)			x						x	x			x
2.4.2 Reduce/consolidate mail systems			x						x	x			x
3. Systems													
3.1 Circulation													
3.1.1 Use conservative development standards	x	x								x	x		
3.1.2 Use conservative street patterns	x	x	x						x	x			
3.1.3 Provide walking/cycling path system			x						x	x	x		
3.1.4 Provide preferential treatment to energy-efficient transport			x	x					x	x	x		x
3.1.5 Reduced/optimized traffic controls				x						x	x		x
3.1.6 Restrict auto access			x							x	x		x
3.2 Utilities													
3.2.1 Use efficient utility layouts	x				x				x	x	x		
3.3 Lighting													
3.3.1 Use efficient lighting					x				x	x			x
3.4 Access													
3.4.1 Provide public transit to major destinations			x						x				x
3.4.2 Provide ridesharing facilities/services			x						x	x			x
3.4.3 Provide park/ride facilities			x						x	x			x

267

Table A-2. Listing and Classification of Energy Conserving Options (Continued)

Development feature and action	Embodied energy	Maintenance	Vehicular use	Vehicular energy	Local energy prod.	Wind protection/use	Sun protection/use	Energy use/loss	Community	Neighborhood	Cluster design	Building design	Operations
3.4.4 Provide jitney/para-transit service			x							x			x
3.4.5 Provide neighborhood transportation centers			x							x			x
3.5 Heating/cooling systems													
3.5.1 Develop cluster systems					x						x		
3.5.2 Develop district systems					x					x			
3.5.3 Use groundwater heat exchangers					x						x	x	
3.5.4 Use "neighborhood" fuel source					x				x	x			x
3.5.5 Use congeneration plant					x				x	x			
3.5.6 Pumped water power generation					x				x	x			
3.5.7 Develop waste recovery power/heat/system					x				x	x			
3.6 Water systems													
3.6.1 Develop dual (potable/non-potable) water system		x								x	x		
3.6.2 Require/use water-saving devices	x	x								x	x	x	x
3.6.3 Store/use storm water	x	x							x	x	x		
3.6.4 Reuse "white water"	x	x									x	x	
3.6.5 Use pond or other supply to meet peak emergency needs	x									x	x		
3.7 Electrical system													
3.7.1 Develop wind power to produce electricity					x				x	x			
3.7.2 Solar energy to produce electricity						x			x	x			
3.8 Storm water system													
3.8.1 Maximize existing swales for runoff	x	x							x	x	x		
4. Site features													
4.1 Land form													
4.1.1 Use natural earth form, minimize earth work	x									x	x	x	
4.1.2 Preserve/create features that provide windbreaks	x					x				x	x	x	
4.1.3 Preserve/create forms that use and protect from sun	x						x			x	x	x	
4.1.4 Balance cut/fill	x		x						x	x	x	x	
4.2 Landscape planting/materials													
4.2.1 Use reduced maintenance materials		x								x	x		
4.2.2 Plant to provide winter windbreaks						x				x	x		
4.2.3 Plant to utilize summer breezes							x			x	x		
4.2.4 Preserve useful natural vegetation	x								x	x	x	x	
4.2.5 Landscape to screen paved areas from sun							x				x		
4.2.6 Landscape to screen buildings from pavement reflection							x				x		
4.2.7 Landscape to shade building/or provide solar access							x				x	x	
4.3 Water areas/ways													
4.3.1 Water retention to reduce storm runoff	x	x								x			
4.3.2 Create/use water areas to moderate climate						x	x			x	x		
4.3.3 Preserve/use natural waterways	x	x							x	x			
4.4 Pavements													
4.4.1 Reduce pavement areas	x	x					x		x		x		
4.4.2 Modify pavement design (permeable, less reflective)	x						x		x		x		

Table A-2. Listing and Classification of Energy Conserving Options (Continued)

Column groups — **Objective**: *reduce* (Embodied energy, Maintenance, Vehicular use, Vehicular energy); *optimize* (Local energy prod., Wind protection/use, Sun protection/use, Energy use/loss). **Scale/Time design phase**: Community, Neighborhood, Cluster design, Building design, Operations.

Development feature and action	Embodied energy	Maintenance	Vehicular use	Vehicular energy	Local energy prod.	Wind protection/use	Sun protection/use	Energy use/loss	Community	Neighborhood	Cluster design	Building design	Operations
4.5 Parking													
4.5.1 Reduce parking supply	x	x	x						x		x		
4.5.2 Preferential treatment to energy-efficient users			x	x					x		x		x
4.5.3 Location of parking to north of building to reduce reflected solar radiation							x		x	x			x
5. Buildings													
5.1 Arrangement													
5.1.1 Cluster	x	x	x		x					x	x	x	
5.1.2 Shelter winter winds/open to summer breezes						x				x	x	x	
5.1.3 Reduce building setbacks						x				x	x	x	x
5.1.4 Maximize natural light into buildings							x					x	x
5.1.5 Orient to sun/preserve solar access							x					x	x
5.2 Location													
5.2.1 Lee of water to benefit from climate modification						x				x	x		
5.2.2 Lee of natural windbreaks						x				x	x		
5.2.3 Avoid "pockets" of wind-temperature extremes						x	x		x	x			
5.2.4 Concentrate on south slopes							x		x	x			
5.3 Basic building design/construction													
5.3.1 Optimize room orientation/grouping activity						x	x					x	
5.3.2 Minimize "skin" to volume ratio						x	x					x	
5.3.3 Use berms, below-grade space						x	x				x	x	
5.3.4 Optimize roof design/orientation						x	x					x	
5.3.5 Optimize roof overhang shading of glazing in summer							x					x	
5.3.6 Use architectural elements (walls, fences, decks, awnings, wings, shading eaves)						x	x		x	x			
5.3.7 Optimum exterior insulation, vapor barriers, caulking						x	x			x			
5.3.8 Use vestibules, air locks, double doors, etc.						x		x		x			
5.3.9 Insulate between interior temperature zones								x		x			
5.3.10 Group functions with same HVAC and lighting requirements								x		x			
5.3.11 Insulation of hot water heater and pipes, and HVAC duct work								x		x			
5.3.12 Increase wall cavity for added insulation								x		x			
5.3.13 Insulate slab foundation								x		x			
5.3.14 Building height to optimize wind protection					x	x	x		x	x			
5.4 Fenestration													
5.4.1 Selective placement of glazing							x	x		x			
5.4.2 Optimum shading of glazing							x			x	x		
5.4.3 Use of natural lighting/skylights							x	x		x	x		
5.4.4 Use of drapes, blinds, interior shutters							x	x		x	x		

Table A-2. Listing and Classification of Energy Conserving Options (Continued)

Development feature and action	Embodied energy	Maintenance	Vehicular use	Vehicular energy	Local energy prod.	Wind protection/use	Sun protection/use	Energy use/loss	Community	Neighborhood	Cluster design	Building design	Operations
5.4.5 Double/triple glazing							X	X				X	
5.4.6 Operable/inoperable windows						X		X				X	X
5.5 *Lighting*													
5.5.1 Color schemes to permit lower light levels								X				X	X
5.5.2 Reduced light levels								X				X	X
5.5.3 Efficient light fixtures								X				X	
5.5.4 Photovoltaic or other automatic control of lights								X				X	X
5.5.5 Reduce decorative lighting								X				X	X
5.6 *HVAC systems (sources)*													
5.6.1 Passive solar heating					X							X	X
5.6.2 Water source heat pump					X							X	
5.6.3 Evaporative cooling					X							X	
5.6.4 Natural cooling/ventilation					X							X	X
5.6.5 Air/heat pump transfer systems								X				X	X
5.6.6 Heat recovery on exhausts								X				X	X
5.6.7 Greenhouse for heat storage					X			X				X	X
5.6.8 Active solar heating/convective loop					X			X				X	X
5.6.9 Wood burning/direct combustion					X			X				X	X
5.6.10 Water cooled lummaires					X			X				X	X
5.6.11 Return air through light fixtures					X			X				X	X
5.7 *HVAC systems (operations)*													
5.7.1 Clock/automatic thermostats								X				X	
5.7.2 Economizer cycle on HVAC								X				X	
5.7.3 Attic ventilation								X				X	X
5.7.4 Variable air volume efficiency								X				X	
5.7.5 Reduce comfort levels								X					X
5.7.6 Building temperature zoning								X				X	X
5.7.7 Optimize multi-use systems								X				X	
5.7.8 Eliminate control overlap								X				X	
5.7.9 Multistage systems								X				X	
5.7.10 Insulate duct work								X				X	
5.7.11 Reduce duct work distances								X				X	
5.7.12 Air transfer systems to transfer energy with building								X				X	
5.8 *Water systems*													
5.8.1 Mixing valves								X				X	
5.8.2 Flow reducers								X				X	
5.8.3 Individual metering								X				X	
5.8.4 Reduce line distances								X				X	
5.8.5 Insulate lines	X							X				X	
5.8.6 Lower thermostat settings								X					X
5.8.7 Low water use toilets/appliances/bath/facilities								X				X	
5.8.8 Instant water heaters								X				X	
5.8.9 Automatic closing valves								X				X	
5.8.10 Domestic hot water/heat reclaimer								X				X	X
5.8.11 Active solar water heating system					X			X				X	
5.9 *Electrical systems*													
5.9.1 Individual metering								X				X	
5.9.2 Automatic load shedding								X				X	
5.9.3 Microprocessor control								X				X	

Development feature and action	Objective reduce				Objective optimize				Scale/Time design phase				
	Embodied energy	Maintenance	Vehicular use	Vehicular energy	Local energy prod.	Wind protection/use	Sun protection/use	Energy use/loss	Community	Neighborhood	Cluster design	Building design	Operations
5.10 Appliances/mechanical													
5.10.1 Microprocessor controls								x				x	
5.10.2 Lower/higher thermostat settings								x					x
5.10.3 Use high efficiency appliances/ mechanical systems								x				x	x
5.10.4 Capture waste/heat/ humidity								x				x	x
5.10.5 Natural dish/clothes drying, etc.								x					x
5.10.6 Cold water washing								x					x
5.10.7 Match equipment size and use								x				x	x

Adapted from: (Barton-Aschman, 1980)

Appendix B-1

B-1. Conversion Factors and Abbreviations

Length	cm	M	in	ft
1 cm =	1	0.01	0.3937	0.03281
1 M =	100	1	39.37	3.281
1 in =	2.540	0.0254	1	0.08333
1 ft =	30.48	0.3048	12	1

Area	cm	M	in	Ft
		Square		
1 sq cm =	1	0.0001	0.1550	0.001076
1 sq m =	1000	1	1550	10.76
1 sq in =	6.452	0.000645	1	0.00694
1 sq ft =	929	0.09290	144	1

Weight/mass

1 gm = 0.002205 lb   1 Kgm = 2.205 lb
1 lb = 453.6 gm   1 lb = 0.4536 Kg

Speed

1 Km/hr = 0.2778 M/sec = 0.6214df mph = 0.700 knots
1 mph = 1.609 Km/hr = 0.4470 m/sec = 1.14 knots

Other

1 Btu = 1055 Joule = 252.0 cal = 0.000293 KwHr
1 cal = 0.003969 BTU = 4.187 Joule
1 cal/cm^2/min = 1 Ly/min

Abbreviations

Btu	=	British thermal unit
cal	=	gram calorie
cm	=	centimeter
ft	=	foot
gm	=	gram
in	=	inch
Km	=	Kilometer
Ly	=	Langley
M	=	Meter
min	=	minute
mph	=	mile per hour
sec	=	second

Appendix B-2

B-2. Solar Radiation Equations

1) Wavelength, period, wavenumber

$$L = P/C = 1/N$$

where

L	=	wavelength	cm
P	=	period	sec
C	=	speed of light	cm/sec
N	=	wavenumber	

273

B-2. Solar Radiation Equations (Continued)

2) Direct beam radiation equations:
   a) The altitude angle (ALT) is the height of the sun above the horizon and is given by:

$$ALT = ARC \ SIN[\ COS(L)COS(D)COS(H)+SIN(L)SIN(D)]$$

where

   L = latitude angle
   D = declination angle of sun (0 at equinox,
       −22.5 winter solstice, 22.5 summer solstice)
   H = hour angle: degrees to sun in sun's arc
       or 15 x hours from solar noon; (− in AM, + in PM)

   b) the zenith angle: angle between the sun and the zenith:

$$Z = 90 - ALT$$

   c) the azimuth angle is the angle to the sun from S; − to E, + to W:

$$AZM = ARC \ SIN[\ COS(D)SIN(H)/COS(ALT) \ ]$$

   d) hours and angle from solar noon to sunrise (SR) and sunset (SS):

$$H = ARC \ COS[TAN(L)TAN(D) \ ]$$

where

$$H/15 = time \ to \ SR \ and \ SS$$

and

$$AZM = ARC \ COS[\ SIN(D)/COS(L) \ ]$$

where
   AZM is the angle to the point of sunrise or sunset on the horizon (− to E, + to W):
   e) the angle (B) between the sun's ray and the normal to any surface of slope P and aspect (angle from S) A (both in degrees):

$$B = ARC \ COS \ [\ SIN(P)COS(ALT)COS(Z-A)+COS(P)SIN(ALT) \ ]$$

Appendix B-3

B-3. Soil Temperature Equations

The soil thermal properties are combined to provide the damping depth:

$$D = [2k/Cw] \ ^{-1/2}$$

where

   k = thermal conductivity
       cal/cm / C/cm
   C = volumetric heat capacity
       cal/cm / C
   w = angular velocity — for daily wave = 7.27 x 10 rad/sec

D is the depth at which the ratio of the temperature wave at depth D to the amplitude of the surface wave is 1/e or 37%

If the surface temperature wave is described by:

$$Tsur = Tave + Tamp \ SIN(wt)$$

where

   t   = time (sec)
   Tsur = temperature at surface at time t,
   Tave = average temperature,
   Tamp = amplitude of temperature wave,
then the temperature at depth Z is given by:

$$Tz = Tave + Tsur \ EXP(-Z/D)SIN(wt - Z/D)$$

B-3. Soil Temperature Equations (Continued)

where

T_z = the temperature at depth Z and time t

EXP = the exponential function. EXP($-Z/D$) = the fractional reduction to the surface temperature wave and

$-Z/D$ = the phase lag in radians.

B-4. Local Climatological Data

LOCAL
CLIMATOLOGICAL DATA
Monthly Summary

NATIONAL WEATHER SERVICE OFC

JAN 1983
SYRACUSE, NEW YORK 14771
HANCOCK INTERNATIONAL AIRPORT

LATITUDE 43° 07' N   LONGITUDE 76° 07' W   ELEVATION (GROUND) 410 FEET   TIME ZONE EASTERN   WBAN #14771

ISSN 0198-3687

JAN 1983
SYRACUSE, NEW YORK

OBSERVATIONS AT 3-HOUR INTERVALS

JAN 1983, SYRACUSE, NEW YORK 14771

WEATHER CODES

* TORNADO	2L FREEZING DRIZZLE	1PH ICE PELLET SHOWERS
T THUNDERSTORM	S SNOW	A HAIL
Q SQUALL	SW SNOW SHOWERS	IF ICE FOG
R RAIN	SG SNOW GRAINS	GF GROUND FOG
RW RAIN SHOWERS	SP SNOW PELLETS	BD BLOWING DUST
ZR FREEZING RAIN	IC ICE CRYSTALS	
L DRIZZLE	IP ICE PELLETS	

BN BLOWING SAND
BS BLOWING SNOW
BY BLOWING SPRAY
K SMOKE
H HAZE
D DUST

CEILING: UNL INDICATES UNLIMITED.
WIND DIRECTION: DIRECTIONS ARE THOSE FROM WHICH THE WIND BLOWS, INDICATED IN TENS OF DEGREES FROM TRUE NORTH; I.E., 09 FOR EAST, 18 FOR SOUTH, 27 FOR WEST. AN ENTRY OF 00 INDICATES CALM.
SPEED: THE OBSERVED AVERAGE ONE-MINUTE VALUE. EXPRESSED IN KNOTS (MPH=KNOTS X 1.15).

PAGE 2

EXTREME FOR THE MONTH - LAST OCCURRENCE IF MORE THAN ONE
T TRACE AMOUNT
- HEAVY FOG VISIBILITY 1/4 MILE OR LESS.
BLANK ENTRIES DENOTE MISSING OR UNREPORTED DATA

DATA IN COLS 6 AND 12-15 ARE BASED ON 7 OR MORE OBSERVATIONS AT 3-HOUR INTERVALS. RESULTANT WIND IS THE VECTOR SUM OF WIND SPEEDS AND DIRECTIONS DIVIDED BY THE NUMBER OF OBSERVATIONS. ONE OF THREE WIND SPEEDS IS GIVEN UNDER A MILE OF WIND PASSES A STATION DURING THE DAY. FASTEST MILE - HIGHEST RECORDED SPEED FOR WHICH A MILE OF WIND PASSES STATION (DIRECTION IN COMPASS POINTS). FASTEST OBSERVED ONE MINUTE WIND SPEED - HIGHEST ONE MINUTE SPEED (A / DEGREES). PEAK GUST - HIGHEST INSTANTANEOUS WIND SPEED (A / APPEARS IN THE DIRECTION COLUMN). ERRORS WILL BE CORRECTED AND CHANGES IN SUMMARY DATA WILL BE ANNOTATED IN THE ANNUAL PUBLICATION.

I CERTIFY THAT THIS IS AN OFFICIAL PUBLICATION OF THE NATIONAL OCEANIC AND ATMOSPHERIC ADMINISTRATION, AND IS COMPILED FROM RECORDS ON FILE AT THE NATIONAL CLIMATIC DATA CENTER, ASHEVILLE, NORTH CAROLINA, 28801

ACTING DIRECTOR
NATIONAL CLIMATIC DATA CENTER

NATIONAL
ENVIRONMENTAL SATELLITE, DATA
AND INFORMATION SERVICE

NATIONAL
CLIMATIC DATA CENTER
ASHEVILLE NORTH CAROLINA

noaa
NATIONAL OCEANIC AND ATMOSPHERIC ADMINISTRATION

276

B-4. Local Climatological Data (Continued)

OBSERVATIONS AT 3-HOUR INTERVALS — JAN 1983 14771 SYRACUSE, NEW YORK

HOUR L.S.T	SKY COVER (TENTHS)	CEILING IN HUNDREDS OF FEET	VISIBILITY MILES (TENTHS)	WEATHER	AIR °F	WET BULB °F	DEW POINT °F	REL HUMIDITY %	DIRECTION	SPEED (KNOTS)	SKY COVER (TENTHS)	CEILING IN HUNDREDS OF FEET	VISIBILITY WHOLE MILES / 16THS MILE	WEATHER	AIR °F	WET BULB °F	DEW POINT °F	REL HUMIDITY %	DIRECTION	SPEED (KNOTS)	SKY COVER (TENTHS)	CEILING IN HUNDREDS OF FEET	VISIBILITY WHOLE MILES / 16THS MILE	WEATHER	AIR °F	WET BULB °F	DEW POINT °F	REL HUMIDITY %	DIRECTION	SPEED (KNOTS)
				DAY 19										DAY 20										DAY 21					
01	10	38	4	SWF	-04	-04	-07	87	35	11	8	23	10		00	00	09	65	25	3	0	UNL	10		-01	-01	-05	83	19	4
04	10	45	5	SWF	-05	-05	-09	83	35	4	7	23	10		-01	-02	-11	62	00	0	0	UNL	10		-01	-03	-14	74	07	4
07	3	UNL	7		-03	-05	-16	95	00	0	0	UNL	10		00	00	13	75	00	0	4	UNL	10		-04	-04	-04	95	03	4
10	2	UNL	10		-03	-03	-11	68	00	0	2	UNL	10		00	00	-10	64	00	0	6	UNL	6	F	04	04	00	83	08	4
13	8	25	7		06	05	03	66	00	14	10	UNL	15		11	09	-04	50	26	5	9	UNL	7		25	22	13	60	00	4
16	8	20	2	R SW	07	07	03	83	29	15	10	UNL	15		10	09	01	67	27	7	10	UNL	10		25	22	12	55	30	4
19	8	23	4	SW	03	03	01	83	36	4	10	UNL	10		06	06	02	83	00	0	10	UNL	10		11	11	08	88	00	0
22	7	32	7		-02	-02	-06	83	00	0	10	UNL	10		03	03	-01	83	00	0	0	UNL	7		09	06	03	60	00	0
				DAY 22										DAY 23										DAY 24					
01	6	UNL	7		09	09	08	96	00	5	10	50	10		30	27	21	69	06	10	10	5	1	RF	33	33	32	98	00	0
04	5	UNL	7		08	08	05	87	00	0	10	40	5	ZR	29	28	26	89	07	12	10	2	LF	35	35	35	100	26	12
07	4	UNL	7		01	01	00	95	00	0	10	19	3	ZLF	30	29	28	92	07	8	10	4	SF	33	33	32	96	25	9
10	8	250	5	F	10	10	07	88	09	6	10	4	2	ZRF	31	31	30	96	07	7	10	13	6		34	33	32	92	25	13
13	10	200	6		24	21	13	63	06	7	10	4	2	ZRF	32	32	31	96	08	8	10	15	7		35	33	31	85	25	13
16	10	120	10		30	26	18	61	08	4	10	17	5	RF	32	32	32	100	08	4	10	17	7		35	33	31	85	25	10
19	10	80	10		30	27	20	64	07	9	10	25	5	F	33	33	32	96	09	6	10	17	6	RWF	34	34	32	92	25	11
22	10	80	10		29	26	23	69	08	10	10	4	1	F	32	32	32	100	00	0	10	9	7		35	34	32	89	25	11
				DAY 25										DAY 26										DAY 27					
01	10	17	7		35	33	31	85	24	15	10	7	4	SW	25	23	17	72	29	13	10	UNL	10		16	15	11	81	05	4
04	10	32	7	RW	36	34	31	82	24	12	10	10	2	SW	23	23	21	92	07	8	8	UNL	10		16	16	13	88	15	4
07	10	32	7		35	33	31	85	24	14	10	4	1/2	SW	20	18	11	68	28	10	0	UNL	25		15	15	14	96	05	4
10	10	25	7		35	33	30	82	24	13	8	3	2	SW	18	15	-04	88	28	10	0	UNL	7		18	18	14	89	08	3
13	10	15	1	8 S	36	33	29	75	26	13	8	27		SW	22	15	10	60	27	11	4	UNL	8		30	25	15	54	26	7
16	10	15	4		32	30	28	79	24	12	10	50	10		20	17	08	60	29	9	4	UNL	15		24	21	13	51	26	4
19	10	50	10		32	30	26	79	24	22	10	50	10		17	16	12	80	00	0	10	UNL	10		21	19	12	68	12	4
22	7	40	10		26	23	20	79	25	11	10	UNL	10		16	15	10	84	11	4	10	UNL	10		18	17	13	80	00	0
				DAY 28										DAY 29										DAY 30					
01	8	65	10		11	11	09	92	10	5	3	UNL	10		16	14	14	92	04	4	10	UNL	7		28	26	20	72	06	7
04	0	UNL	7		08	08	07	96	06	5	2	UNL	10		13	13	13	100	03	4	10	UNL	200	7		29	27	22	69	07	6
07	3	UNL	7		09	09	07	91	10	6	4	UNL	7		21	20	17	84	05	4	10	UNL	200	7		33	30	24	70	07	10
10	3	UNL	7		19	17	12	74	08	8	5	UNL	7		31	20	17	64	10	5	10	230	7		41	36	29	62	13	7
13	5	UNL	15		28	25	17	64	07	7	10	UNL	10		34	30	23	64	10	5	10	15	5	RF	36	35	33	89	10	6
16	6	45	10		31	27	19	61	07	6	10	UNL	10		34	30	26	60	07	4	10	10	5	RSF	33	33	32	96	07	6
19	4	UNL	10		23	21	14	69	06	8	10	UNL	10		31	29	24	75	08	7	10	8	1	RSF	33	33	32	96	00	0
22	2	UNL	10		18	17	13	81	05	3	10	UNL	10		30	28	23	75	07	5	10	25	2	RSF	33	33	33	100	00	0
				DAY 31																									
01	10	32	7	RSF	35	35	34	96	21	6																				
04	10	50	7	S	34	33	32	92	24	8																				
07	10	19	7	S	34	33	31	89	24	10																				
10	10	15	7	SWF	34	32	30	89	24	13																				
13	10	15	7		34	32	30	85	24	13																				
16	10	20	7		34	32	30	85	25	12																				
19	10	20	7		33	32	30	89	25	12																				
22	10	32	7		32	32	29	85	25	12					SYRACUSE N Y					03	01									

PAGE 3

SUMMARY BY HOURS

HOUR L.S.T	SKY COVER (TENTHS)	STATION PRESSURE (INCHES)	AIR TEMP °F	WET BULB °F	DEW POINT °F	REL HUMIDITY %	WIND SPEED (MPH)	DIRECTION	SPEED (MPH)
			AVERAGES					RESULTANT WIND	
01	8	29.63	22	21	17	83	7.7	27	2.4
04	8	29.64	21	19	16	84	7.6	30	2.0
07	8	29.65	20	19	16	85	7.3	27	2.0
10	8	29.67	22	21	18	83	8.9	25	2.4
13	8	29.63	26	25	20	74	10.1	27	4.4
16	8	29.63	25	23	19	75	9.5	26	4.0
19	8	29.64	24	23	19	82	8.0	26	2.9
22	8	29.64	22	22	18	82	8.3	29	2.5

HOURLY PRECIPITATION (WATER EQUIVALENT IN INCHES) — JAN 1983 14771 SYRACUSE, NEW YORK

DATE	A.M. HOUR ENDING AT												P.M. HOUR ENDING AT												DATE
	1	2	3	4	5	6	7	8	9	10	11	12	1	2	3	4	5	6	7	8	9	10	11	12	
1							T																		1
2																									2
3	T	.01	T	T	T	T	T	T	T	.01	.01	T	T	.01	.01	T		T	T	.01	.01	T	3
4																									4
5																									5
6																									6
7		T		T		T	T	T		.01	T		T		.01	T	T			T	T		7
8																									8
9	T	T	T	T			.01	.02	T	T						T	.01	T	T		.08	.09	9
10																	T	.01	T	T		10
11	.10	.05	.02	.01	T		.02	.01	T			.01	T	.01								11
12	T	T		T	T		T	T	T	T	.01	.01	.02	.01	T					T	12
13	T	T	T	T	T	T	T	T														T	13
14																									14
15		.03	.01	.01	T	T		.01	.01	T	T	.01	.01	.02	T		.01	.02	.01	.01	T	.01	15
16	.02	.01	.01	.01				.01	.01	T		T	.01			.01	T		.01	.01		.01	16
17	T	T					.01	.02	.02	.02	T	T	T		.01		T			.01		.01	17
18	T	T		.01	T	T	T						T	T			T					T	18
19	T			.01	T	T	T	T															19
20																									20
21																									21
22																									22
23	T		T	.01	.01	T	T		.09	.09	.07	.06	.04	.04	.03	.03	.03	T	.01	.01		T	T	23
24			T		.04	.01	.01	.01	.01	T		T	T		T			T			.01	T	24
25							T		T	.01	.01	T	T						T	.02	T	T	25
26	.01	T		.01	.01	T	T	T	.01	T	.01	T											26
27																									27
28																									28
29																									29
30													T	.02	.03	.02	.02	.02	.01	.01	.02	.03	30
31																									31

MAXIMUM SHORT DURATION PRECIPITATION

TIME PERIOD (MINUTES)	5	10	15	20	30	45	60	80	100	120	150	180
PRECIPITATION (INCHES)	00.03	00.06	00.07	00.09	00.11	00.15	00.16	00.16	00.17	00.21	00.25	00.27
ENDED: DATE	10	10	10	10	10	10	10	11	11	11	11	11
ENDED: TIME	2240	2246	2250	2305	2315	2325	2345	0005	0025	0040	0114	0140

THE PRECIPITATION AMOUNTS FOR THE INDICATED TIME INTERVALS MAY OCCUR
AT ANY TIME DURING THE MONTH. THE TIME INDICATED IS THE ENDING TIME
OF THE INTERVAL. DATE AND TIME ARE NOT ENTERED FOR TRACE AMOUNTS.

SUBSCRIPTION PRICE AND ORDERING INFORMATION AVAILABLE FROM:
THE NATIONAL CLIMATIC DATA CENTER, FEDERAL BUILDING
ASHEVILLE, NORTH CAROLINA 28801
ATTN: PUBLICATIONS

SYRACUSE, NEW YORK
USCOMM - NOAA - ASHEVILLE, NC   505

U.S. DEPARTMENT OF COMMERCE   AN EQUAL OPPORTUNITY EMPLOYER
NATIONAL CLIMATIC DATA CENTER
FEDERAL BUILDING
ASHEVILLE, N.C. 28801

POSTAGE AND FEES PAID
U.S. DEPARTMENT OF COMMERCE
COM 210

U.S.MAIL

FIRST CLASS

277

B-5. Table for Calculating 2 Hourly Temperatures

MONTHS			JAN	FEB	MAR	APR	MAY	JUN	JUL	AUG	SEP	OCT	NOV	DEC
T MAXIMUM														
T MINIMUM														
AVERAGE RANGE														
S VALUES														
TIME	J, N, D AP. AU	F,MA,S,O MY,JN,JL	2 Hourly Temp. = T min + [S x Range]											
1 a.m.	.13 / .17	.13 / .12												
3 a.m.	.07 / .10	.06 / .08												
5 a.m.	.04 / 0	0 / 0												
7 a.m.	0 / .10	.07 / .26												
9 a.m.	.16 / .49	.38 / .60												
11 a.m.	.55 / .77	.68 / .82												
1 p.m.	.83 / .95	.89 / .93												
3 p.m.	1 / 1	1 / 1												
5 p.m.	.69 / .94	.91 / .96												
7 p.m.	.38 / .71	.62 / .75												
9 p.m.	.25 / .41	.32 / .37												
11 p.m.	.19 / .27	.20 / .22												

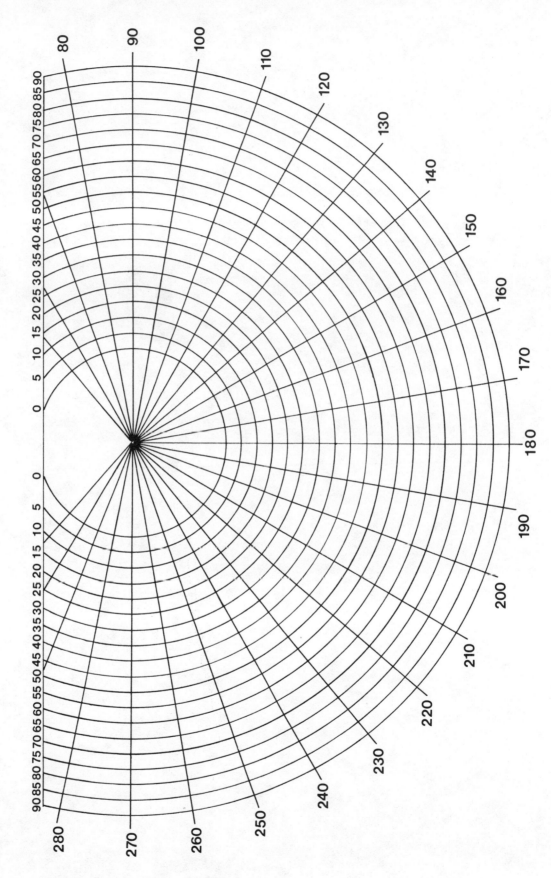

B-6. Elevation Angles Figure

Appendix C

Precision Planting for Solar Control and Solar Access

E. GREGORY McPHERSON
Utah State University
Logan, Utah

Landscape architects should have a methodology for locating plants to provide solar control and solar access. Although the process may at first appear involved, ultimately it is not too difficult. Designers who master it will have at their disposal a valuable tool for solar control planting design. The basic premise of the process is to maximize year-round energy savings by locating the foliage mass so that it obstructs solar radiation when shading is needed, but allows insolation to pass under the canopy and strike the structure for winter heat gain. The foliage mass is precisely located by determining the position of the sun when shading is needed. The first task is to determine the extent of the overheated period.

The Overheated Period

Olgyay and Olgyay (1957) define the average overheated period as that when cooling measures are needed, or more specifically for the temperate region, when temperatures are above 70F (21C). If the effect of humidity is important, wet bulb temperatures can be plotted on a psychometric chart to ascertain the temperature-humidity condition at which cooling is needed (Novell, 1981).

A simple method for determining two-hourly temperatures based on monthly average temperatures was referred to in Chapter Five. This method provides information necessary for calculating the overheated period. The approximate beginning and ending of the overheated period can be determined by noting the

first and last months when temperatures exceed 70F (21C). May and September are the first and last overheated months for Salt Lake City (Table C-1).

Table C-1. Two-hourly temperatures for Salt Lake City, Utah (F).

MONTHS		JAN	FEB	MAR	APR	MAY	JUN	JUL	AUG	SEP	OCT	NOV	DEC
T MAXIMUM		37	42	51	62	72	82	92	90	80	66	49	40
T MINIMUM		18	23	30	37	45	52	61	59	50	39	28	23
AVERAGE RANGE		19	19	21	25	27	30	31	31	30	27	21	17
TIME / S VALUES (J,N,D / AP,AU)	(EMASO / MY,JN,JL)	colspan 2 hourly Temp. = Tmin + [S x Range]											
1 a.m. — .13 / .17	.13 / .12	20	25	33	41	48	56	65	64	54	43	31	25
—	—	19	24	31	40	47	54	63	62	52	41	29	24
3 a.m. — .07 / .10	.06 / .08	19	23	30	37	45	52	61	59	50	39	29	24
5 a.m. — .04 / 0	0 / 0	18	24	31	40	52	60	69	62	52	41	28	23
7 a.m. — 0 / .10	.07 / .26	21	30	38	49	61	70	80	74	61	49	31	26
9 a.m. — .16 / .49	.38 / .60	28	36	44	56	67	77	86	83	70	57	40	32
11 a.m. — .55 / .77	.68 / .82	34	40	49	61	70	80	90	88	77	63	45	37
1 p.m. — .83 / .95	.89 / .93	37	42	51	62	72	82	92	90	80	66	49	40
3 p.m. — 1 / 1	1 / 1	31	40	49	61	71	81	91	88	77	64	42	35
5 p.m. — .69 / .94	.91 / .96	25	35	43	55	65	75	84	81	73	56	36	29
7 p.m. — .38 / .71	.62 / .75	23	29	37	47	55	63	72	71	60	48	33	27
9 p.m. — .25 / .41	.32 / .37	22	27	34	44	51	59	69	67	56	44	32	26
11 p.m. — .19 / .27	.20 / .22												

The first and last day of the overheated period can be quickly calculated through interpolation using the equations below:

$$n = \frac{(Tx - 70)30}{Tx - Tz}$$

$$D_1 = D - n$$

$$D_2 = D + n$$

where:

n = number of days from 15th of the overheated month,

D = 15th day of the overheated month,

D_1 = first day of the overheated period,

D_2 = last day of the overheated period,

Tx = maximum hourly temperature of the overheated month,

Tz = maximum temperature of the previous month (if solving for D_1), or the succeeding month (if solving for D_2).

The first and last day of the overheated period for Salt Lake City are May 9 and Oct. 6, respectively, as shown below:

1. Solve for the first day of the overheated period (D_1) where:

D = May 15

Tx = 72F

Tz = 62F

$$n = \frac{(72 - 70)30}{72 - 62} \qquad n = 6$$

$D1$ = (May) 15 − 6 $\qquad$ $D1$ = May 9

2. Solve for the last day of the overheated period (D_2) where:

D = Sept. 15

Tx = 80F

Tz = 66F

$$n = \frac{(80 - 70)30}{80 - 66} \qquad n = 21$$

D_2 = Sept. 15 + 21 $\qquad$ D_2 = Oct. 6

For the purposes of precision planting, the hours when temperatures are 70F (21C) or above must be calculated. This is done by determining the time when temperatures reach 70F (21C) for the first and last time of each overheated month. Interpolate using the following equations:

$$n = \frac{(70 - Tz)120}{Tx - Tz}$$

$$t_1 = H_1 + n$$

$$t_2 = H_2 - n$$

where:

n = number of minutes from the overheated hour,

t_1 = time overheating begins,

t_2 = time overheating ends,

Tx = first overheated 2-hourly temperature (if solving for t_1), or last overheated 2-hourly temperature (if solving for t_2),

Tz = 2-hourly temperature proceeding overheating (Tx) if solving for t_1, or 2-hourly temperature succeeding overheating (Tx) if solving for t_2,

H_1 = hour when Tz occurs for first overheated time (t_1),

H_2 = hour when Tz occurs for last overheated time (t_2).

The example below illustrates that the overheated period extends from 8:20 a.m. to 9:30 p.m. on Aug. 15 in Salt Lake City.

1. Solve for the first time overheating occurs on August 15 (t_1) where:

Tx = 74

Tz = 62

H_1 = 7 a.m.

$$n = \frac{(70 - 62)120}{12} \qquad n = 80$$

t_1 = 7 a.m. + 80 $\qquad$ $t2$ = 8:20 a.m.

2. Solve for the last time overheating occurs on August 15 (t_2) where:

Tx = 71

Tz = 67

H_2 = 11 p.m.

$$n = \frac{(70 - 67)120}{4} \qquad n = 90$$

t_2 = 11 p.m. - 90 $\qquad$ t_1 = 8:20 a.m.

The extent of the overheated period for the 15th of each overheated month can be easily calculated. The equations above were used to calculate the overheated hours for Salt Lake City shown below:

Day	Overheating begins	Overheating ends
May 15	1:00 p.m.	5:20 p.m.
June 15	9:00 a.m.	7:50 p.m.
July 15	7:10 a.m.	10:20 p.m.
Aug. 15	8:20 a.m.	9:30 p.m.
Sept. 15	11:00 a.m.	7:28 p.m.

Before the overheated period is depicted graphically, the beginning and ending hours must be converted from local standard time to local solar time (the time that would be read from a sundial oriented south, measured from solar noon, the moment when the sun is highest in the sky). Because local standard time is usually slightly different than local solar time, the following correction should be made:

1. Determine the longitude of the locality and the longitude of standard time meridian (75° for Eastern Standard Time; 90° for Central Standard Time; 105° for Mountain Standard Time; 120° for Pacific Standard Time; 135° for Yukon Standard Time; 150° for Alaska-Hawaii Standard Time).
2. Multiply the difference in longitudes by four minutes/degree. If the locality is east of the standard meridian, add the correction minutes; if it is west, subtract them.

In the example, Salt Lake City (112° longitude) is 7° west of the 105° Mountain Standard Time meridian. This difference multiplied by four minutes/degree results in a correction of−28 minutes. For complete accuracy, the equation of time for each date in question should also be added, but this is not necessary because its effect is small (±15 minutes). Following are the corrected beginning and ending times of overheating for Salt Lake City:

Day	Overheating begins	Overheating ends
May 15	12:32 p.m.	4:52 p.m.
June 15	8:32 a.m.	7:22 p.m.
July 15	6:42 a.m.	9:52 p.m.
Aug. 15	7:52 a.m.	9:02 p.m.
Sept. 15	10:32 a.m.	7:00 p.m.

The overheated hours for each day in the overheated period are depicted in solar time by drawing a graph locating the hours of the day (1 to 24) on the horizontal axis and every fifth day of the overheated period on the vertical axis. The points corresponding to the time overheating begins and ends for the 15th of each overheated month are then plotted as shown in Figure C-1. The overheated hours are assumed to extend from 2 p.m. to 4 p.m. on the first and last overheated day, and these points are plotted. All points that represent the time when overheating begins are connected. The line should reach its left most location at approximately Aug. 1, because overheating begins earliest on the day average temperatures are greatest. This time must be estimated because it has not been calculated. The lines connecting June 15 to July 15 and Sept. 15 to Aug. 15 are extended at their same respective angles until they intersect. Intersection should occur at approximately Aug. 1. The same procedures are used to draw a line connecting points representing the times when overheating ends. The result is two lines that gradually separate from each other until approximately Aug. 1,

the warmest day of the year, and then begin to converge as they approach the last day of the overheated period. The area within these lines is the period when cooling is required. Figure C-1 illustrates the overheated period for Salt Lake City, Utah. Previously calculated overheated hours are used.

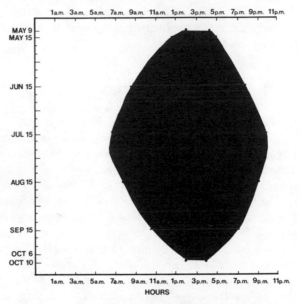

Figure C-1. The overheated period for Salt Lake City.

This method of calculating the overheated period substitutes simplicity for rigorous accuracy. Deviations of 30 to 60 minutes from normal may result due to any or all of the following:

1. Use of average daily temperature curves for each month based upon average monthly maximum and minimum temperatures instead of recorded three-hourly observations.
2. Failure to account for different times of sunrise and sunset due to horizon lines that are not flat.
3. Estimations of when the warmest day of the year occurs and the overheated hours of the first and last days.

McPherson (1980) describes techniques to eliminate most of these inaccuracies, but given the variable nature of other solar control parameters (e.g., different foliation periods, growth rates, microclimatic effects, etc.), the method just presented reaches a suitable compromise between the need for precision and the need for prompt design solutions.

The Shading Mask

To determine the position of the sun when shading is needed, a temporal definition of the overheated period must be translated into one that is spatial. Translation

283

is achieved by transferring the overheated period onto a sun angle chart for the latitude using the steps described below. Bennett's (1978) sun angle charts are used in the following example, although several others work equally well (List, 1949; Mazria, 1979).

Two time periods are first defined. Time Period 1 extends from the first day of the overheated period to June 21; Time Period 2 begins June 21 and extends to the last day of the overheated period. In the example, the two time periods are:

Time Period 1 = May 9-June 21
Time Period 2 = June 21-Oct. 6

These time periods must be defined to avoid confusion when plotting the shading masks on the sun angle chart. Every sun path line on the chart (except June 21 and Dec. 22) represents the sun's path on two dates.

The solar path for the first day of the overheated period is located. Interpolation may be necessary. As previously mentioned, the overheated period for this day is assumed to be 2:00 p.m. to 4:00 p.m. On the sun path for that day (May 9), these times are located and two large dots are placed to represent them. They are then connected along the sun path with a dashed line as Figure C-2 (see next page) illustrates. The next sun path line corresponds to May 20. The first and last overheated hour are determined for that day. In the example, these times would be 11:45 a.m. and 5:30 p.m. for May 20. The dots are positioned at the appropriate places on the sun path and connected to the previously placed dots by a broken line. This procedure is repeated for each sun path whose date is included in Time Period 1. Some overheating requiring shading occurs after sunset. Plotting is done only until sunset on the chart. If desired, more accuracy can be obtained by plotting additional points demarcating the overheated periods for dates halfway between those listed on the sun angle chart. The following times are plotted as points for corresponding dates in Figure C-2:

Time Period 1

Date	t1	t2
May 9	2:00	4:00
May 20	11:45	5:30
June 21	8:10	8:10

Once all the dots are plotted and connected, the overheated period for Time Period 1 is defined. Shading of the area will increase graphic clarity.

The process is repeated on the same sun angle chart for Time Period 2, except all dots are connected with a solid line. In the example for Salt Lake City, the following times would be plotted for the corresponding dates:

Time Period 2

Date	t1	t2
June 21	8:10	8:10
July 23	6:30	10:00
Aug. 12	7:15	9:10
Aug. 27	8:30	8:20
Sept. 10	9:45	7:30
Sept. 23	11:30	6:00
Oct. 6	2:00	4:00

Figure C-2 illustrates the Shading Masks for both time periods, as if they were overlaid on a light table. The symmetry of the sun's path around June 21 is not duplicated by the overheated period. Due to the earth's heat lag effect, Time Period 1 is shorter in duration than Time Period 2. Because each line (except the highest and lowest) on the sun angle chart represents two dates when the sun has the same path, the shading mask for Time Period 1 represents not only the sun's position during part of the overheated period (May 9 to June 21) but also the mirror image of this time (June 21 to Aug.6). The latter representation is inaccurate because the overheated hours per day are longer after June 21 than before.

A similar problem occurs for Time Period 2 (June 21 to Oct. 6). In this case, the mirror image represents the sun's position between March 8 and June 21. Use of the shading mask for Time Period 2 would result in shade two months before the overheated period begins. In the example, the shading mask for Time Period 2 overlaps the mask for Time Period 1. The area of overlap represents the sun's position when shading is always needed. In architectural parlance, fixed shading devices are required. Movable shading devices are best suited for use during the remainder of Time Period 2. Because deciduous plants function like movable shading devices, the designer can use a composite of the two shading masks without seriously reducing solar heat gain in the spring. Deciduous trees are mostly leafless during the time prior to the beginning of the overheated perod when shading is provided (March 6 to May 9). Selecting species with high leafless shading coefficients that are also late to leaf-out will further maximize heat gain. Air temperatures are increasing during this transition period so that the price paid for shading prior to the overheated period is small compared to the comfort and energy savings that accrue from the shade plants will cast near the end of the overheated period. These, then, are several reasons for using the shading mask

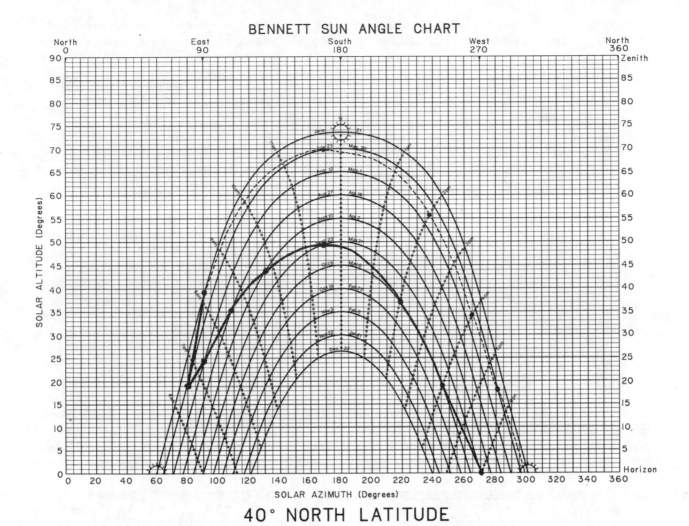

BENNETT SUN ANGLE CHART

40° NORTH LATITUDE

Figure C-2. Shading mask for Time Periods 1 and 2.

for Time Period 2 if it encompasses that of Time Period 1; otherwise, a composite of both may be required. Shading masks are flexible tools, and each designer should determine when shading is appropriate and inappropriate.

Elevation Angles

Once the shading mask is drawn, the necessary lower and upper elevation angles defining the space the foliage mass must occupy to block the sun can be determined for any azimuth angle. Referencing these critical elevation angles is facilitated by transfering the shading mask onto the elevation angles diagram.

An elevation angles figure (Figure C-3, see next page) is created by first drawing a series of concentric hemispheric lines that correspond to solar altitude angles (5° increments). Then lines are drawn that radiate from a center. These lines represent solar

azimuth angles (10° increments). The lowest and highest azimuth angles needed are those which the shading mask intersects. A blank elevations angle figure is located in Appendix B-6.

Before the elevation angle figure is plotted, the shading mask is used to determine the lowest and highest altitude angle for each azimuth angle. Ten degree azimuth angle increments are used. The following altitudes angles were found for Salt Lake City using Figure C-2.

Azimuth angle	Lowest altitude angle	Highest altitude angle
70°	0	0
80°	19	19
90°	24	38

(Continued on next page)

Azimuth angle	Lowest altitude angle	Highest altitude angle
100°	30	49
110°	36	57
120°	41	63
130°	44	67
140°	46	70
150°	48	71
160°	49	73
170°	49	73
180°	49	74
190°	48	73
200°	45	73
210°	41	71
220°	37	70
230°	31	67
240°	24	63
250°	16	57
260°	8	49
270°	0	38
280°	0	25
290°	0	12
300°	0	0

until two elevation angle points have been recorded for every 10° change in solar azimuth angle. These lines are connected and shaded in the interior to finish the elevation angles figures as shown for Salt Lake City in Figure C-3. Elevation angle figures (Figures C7-C19) for selected U.S. cities are provided at the end of this Appendix.

The inner boundary of the darkened region in the elevation angles figure represents the lowest elevation angles of the overheated period. This line corresponds to the required distance from the ground to the bottom of the canopy. Trees with branches lower than this will block solar radiation during the underheated period. Trees that begin to branch higher than this will allow unwanted insolation to strike the structure during the overheated period. The outer boundary line represents the highest elevation angles during the overheated period. This line corresponds to the required tree height. Trees that do not reach this height will not provide shade to the structure during the entire overheated period. Trees taller than this will cast longer winter shadows than are necessary, which may violate the solar access of neighboring structures.

Design Application

Once an elevation angles diagram is produced for a region, it can be used in various ways: to evaluate the

Once the altitude angles are recorded, the elevation angle figure is drawn. Two dots are placed on the figure at the appropriate locations along the corresponding azimuth angle line. This is continued

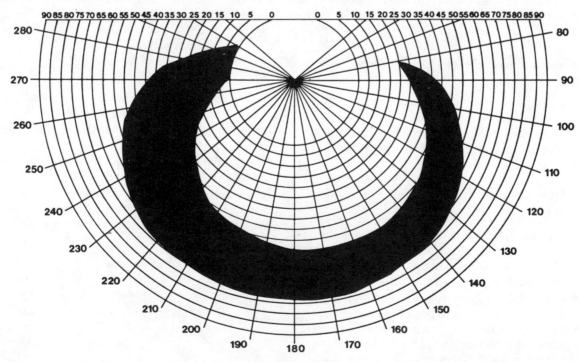

Figure C-3. Elevation angle figure for Salt Lake City, Utah.

shading effectiveness of existing vegetation, to assist in selecting a plant for a predetermined location, or to locate a given plant species for optimal solar control. The following examples illustrate how a landscape architect can apply this design tool for each of these purposes. The elevation angles diagram for Salt Lake City is used (Figure C-3). Problems are solved using a graphic method; however, a mathematical method can be employed with equal success. McPherson (1980) describes how the following trigonometric equations are used in the computational problem-solving approach:

where:

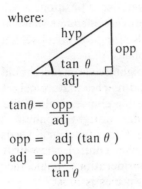

$$\tan\theta = \frac{opp}{adj}$$

$$opp = adj\,(\tan\theta)$$

$$adj = \frac{opp}{\tan\theta}$$

Example 1. A client desires to know how effectively an existing tree provides shade and solar access to a passive solar home opposite it. The tree is located 15 ft (4.5 m) south of the east edge of the residence. The canopy begins 10 ft (3.9 m) above the ground and the tree is 50 ft (15 m) tall with a 30-ft (9.1 m) crown diameter as Figure C-4 shows.

First, the azimuth angle of the tree is determined. The center of the residence is located and a line that extends from this point through and beyond the tree trunk is drawn. A protractor is used to determine the azimuth angle, which is 120° in the example.

A section showing the structure and the tree is drawn. The land slopes away from the home at a gradual 6% grade. The overhang and windows on the south wall are illustrated.

The elevation angles figure is consulted. At 120° azimuth, the inner boundary, which corresponds with desired height to canopy bottom, is 41°, and the outer boundary, which corresponds with desired tree height, is 63°.

Using the protractor, a line is drawn that rises from the ground at 41° tangential to the canopy bottom (line A). In the example, this line strikes the ground about 8 ft (2.4 m) south of the home, which indicates that the canopy is too low to permit solar access shortly after the overheated period ends. A second line (line B) is now drawn at the same angle (41°) through the top of the window. The canopy should not extend below this

line if complete solar access to the south facing window is desired. In this example, the landscape architect should recommend that the lowest branches of the tree be pruned up an additional 11 ft (3.4 m).

A line is drawn tangential to the north edge of the tree crown that rises at 63° from the ground plane (line C). Approximately half of the roof is shaded when the sun is at its highest altitude angle at this azimuth. As the altitude angle becomes lower, more of the roof will be shaded.

The tree effectively provides solar control during the overheated period. However, solar access during the fall and spring is not provided because the canopy is too close to the ground. Up-pruning and thinning of the lower branches are recommended.

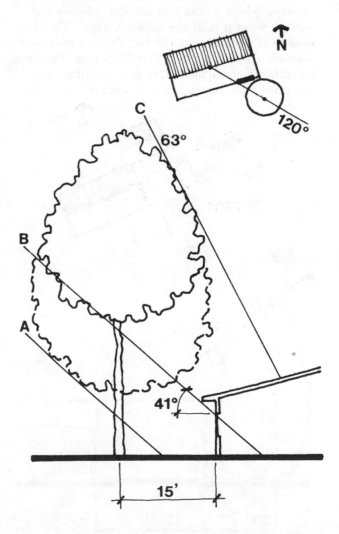

Figure C-4. Example 1. Existing tree needs to be pruned up for solar access.

287

Example 2. The client would like a solar control planting to reduce direct and reflected solar radiation that create uncomfortably high late afternoon temperatures in the west side of the residence. Plants must be located at least 25 ft (7.6 m) from the structure because of the intervening driveway, as Figure C-5 shows.

First, the azimuth angles defining the front and end of the proposed planting area are determined with a protractor. In this example, the azimuth angle is 270° at the front of the planting area and 298° at the end. Vegetation located here will shade the west-facing window and wall.

The elevation angles figure is used to find the lower and upper elevation angles for each azimuth angle. The lower and upper angles for 270° azimuth are 0° and 38°, respectively. They are both 0° at 298° azimuth, which means that the sun is below the horizon when it is at this azimuth angle. Therefore, shading is unnecessary. The fact that the lower angle for both azimuth angles is 0° indicates that the sun is not this far north when heat gain is desired and therefore solar access is not a concern.

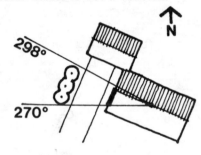

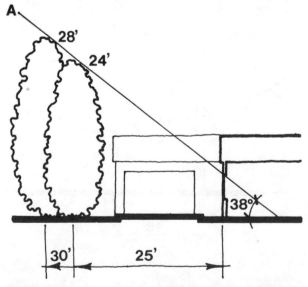

Figure C-5. Example 2. Trees located to the west must be tall enough to block late afternoon sun and branch to the ground.

A section showing the proposed planting area and the one-story structure is drawn. Using the protractor, a line is drawn tangential to the top of the window that rises at a 38° angle, as line A in Figure C-5 shows. Now the vertical distance is measured from the ground to this line at 25 ft (7.6 m) and 30 ft (9.1 m) from the home. To fully shade the window, the plant located at 270° azimuth must be at least 24 ft (7.3 m) tall if planted 25 ft (7.6 m) from the home and 28 ft (8.5 m) tall if planted 30 ft (9.1 m) away. In addition, the plant should branch to the ground to block low-angle solar radiation. Because the upper elevation angle becomes progressively smaller at positions north of 270° azimuth, plants that provide adequate shade at the 270° azimuth angle will also function effectively at points further north in the planting area.

Plants that the designer might recommend should branch close to the ground and reach a mature height of at least 20 ft (6.1 m). Possible choices include the American arborvitae, red cedar, upright Japanese yew, and buckthorn tallhedge. Other functional needs (e.g., year-round screening, wind control, snow-drift control, etc.) and esthetic considerations should then be used to determine which species is most appropriate for the area.

Example 3. The client has purchased a 12-ft (3.7 m) red maple (50-ft (15-m) mature height) and would like to plant it in a location where its maximum solar control potential can be obtained. Although the residence is not a passive solar design, solar access through south-facing windows is desired.

As discussed in Chapter Eight, the red maple should be located to provide shade on Aug. 1 at 3:00 p.m. The corresponding azimuth angle can be found through interpolation on the sun angle chart for 40° north latitude. In this case, the tree should be placed at an azimuth of 255°. Figure C-6 (see next page) shows the azimuth line along which the red maple should be placed.

A section of the site and structure is drawn, and the lower and upper elevation angles determined for 255° azimuth from the elevation angles figure. They are 13° and 53° respectively. A line is drawn tangential to the top of the window that rises at 13° (line A in Figure C-6). A second line is drawn also tangential to the top of the window that rises at 53° (line B). A tree whose canopy reaches this line will shade the window and partially shade the roof except on a few days near the summer solstice.

The tree cannot be placed closer than 15 ft (4.6 m) or further than 30 ft (9.1 m) from the residence because of the sidewalk and driveway. Vertical measurements are made from the ground to lines A

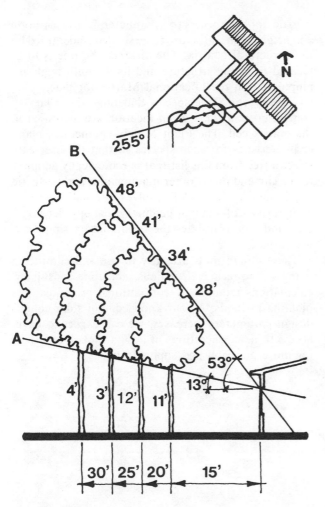

Figure C-6. Example 3. Canopy dimensions vary with distance from the structure in this example of trees located to provide maximum solar control and solar access.

and B at 15 (4.6 m), 20 (6.1 m), 25 (7.6 m), and 30 ft (9.1 m) from the home to determine heights from the ground to canopy bottom and minimum mature tree heights, as Figure C-6 shows. These heights may also be calculated using the second trigonometric equation.

The required tree height increases as horizontal distance from the structure increases. Required height from the ground to canopy bottom also increases, but at a slower rate. The advantages of placing the red maple 15 ft (4.6 m) from the home instead of 30 ft (9.1 m) are as follows:

1. Assuming a growth rate of 1.5 ft (45 m) a year, the tree 15 ft (4.6 m) away will reach an effective height of 28 ft (8.5 m) in 10.6 years, but if located 30 ft (9.1 m) from the home, it will take 24 years to reach an effective height of 48 ft (14.6 m).

2. If located at 15 ft (4.6 m), the tree will shade a greater expanse of the southwest-facing wall

than will the same tree located 30 ft (9.1 m) from the home.

3. In both cases, the trees must be pruned up high enough to permit a relatively unobstructed view out of the windows. It may be easier to prune a tree up to 11 ft (3.4 m) than 14 ft (4.3 m).

4. At 15 ft (4.6 m) from the structure, the tree will shade the home's entry during the mid to late afternoon and part of the driveway in the morning. The tree located 30 ft (9.1 m) away will shade the driveway more effectively than the entry.

Given this information, the designer can assess the merits of locating the red maple at each position in the context of the entire design scheme, as well as solar control. If optimum solar control effects are desired, the tree should be located 15 ft from the building, along the 255° azimuth line.

These three examples illustrate that design for solar control can be based upon empirically derived information applied in a systematic manner. Landscape architects who implement the precision planting process no longer need to rely upon general guidelines (e.g., plant deciduous trees to the south) or intuition alone. As a result, landscape architects who use this design tool can easily integrate solar control considerations into the planting design process and provide clients with landscapes that conserve more energy than ever before.

Other Design Tools for Solar Control

Space does not permit a detailed description of all the solar control design tools available to landscape architects. A brief review of several of the most pertinent and promising design tools follows. Interested professionals should contact the authors for more information.

The Florida Cooperative Extension Service has recently published circulars for eleven regions within the state, *Factors for Determining Shading Patterns in Florida,* by D. E. Buffington, S. S. Sastry, and R. J. Black. Each circular demonstrates through examples how precise shadow locations can be determined by using azimuth angles and shade projection factors. The twelve tables at the end of the circular present the shade projection factors (which are multiplied by the height of the shading object to calculate shadow length) for each daylight hour of four days in every month. These circulars provide homeowners and designers with an easy-to-use tool for calculating the effectiveness of various shading devices.

J. Alan Wagar (1982) has developed one of the most

precise solar control computer programs to date. SOLAR PLOT and its interactive version SOLPLOT were written in FORTRAN and are now available for use with microcomputers. The programs aid designers by calculating required canopy height for vegetation located opposite windows or other vertical surfaces. The operator defines latitude, the azimuth angle the surface faces, window dimensions, and the dates and hours for which specific solar control effects are desired. Output consists of coutour lines that correspond to minimum and maximum canopy height surfaces for the predetermined design dates and hours. The programs' accuracy and the ease with which a variety of shading conditions can be analyzed make them extremely valuable design tools.

McPherson (1981b) has developed a Solar Control Matrix System (SOLMAT) that provides designers with a simple and quick method for locating and selecting trees for shading and solar access. SOLMAT is based on a FORTRAN program listing tree species that pass several solar control criteria tests. This output is translated into four matrices for designers who do not have access to a computer. The orientation and height of the structure to be shaded is identified on the Structural Matrix. The distance the tree is to be located from the structure and its azimuth angle is pinpointed on the Locational Matrix for that structural type. Tree species that meet the solar control criteria for a given location are identified in the matrix cell. The Plant Matrix enumerates plant characteristics for each species so that the user can select a tree from this list that is ecologically adapted to the site and meets other maintenance and aesthetic requirements. SOLMAT resolves internally the complexities of shading geometry, canopy density, etc., and then translates the results into a simple-to-use format.

These design tools are easy to use and eliminate many of the technical, tedious, and time-consuming calculations required by conventional precision planting methods. As our knowledge of solar control design parameters increases, we can expect to have access to new generations of design tools that will be far more powerful and sophisticated.

Elevation Angle Figures for 12 U.S. Cities.

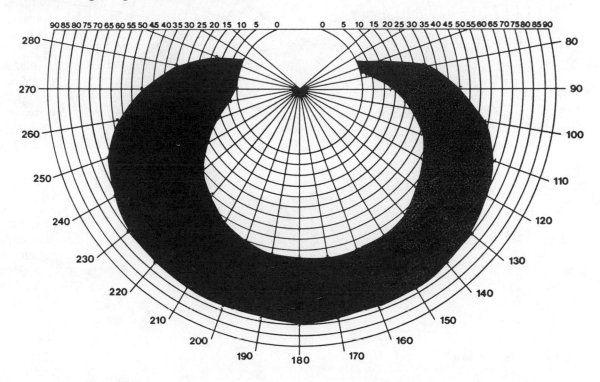

Figure C-7. Atlanta, Ga.

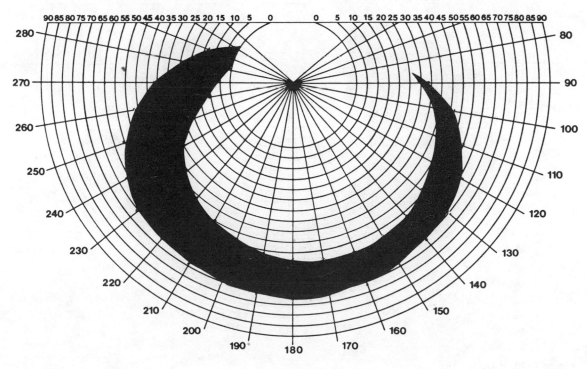

Figure C-8. Boston, Mass.

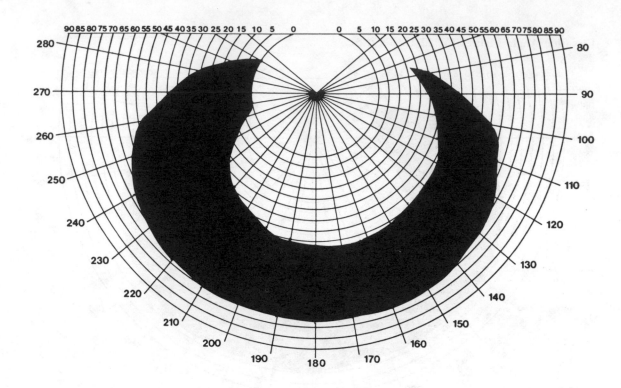

Figure C-9. Fresno, Calif.

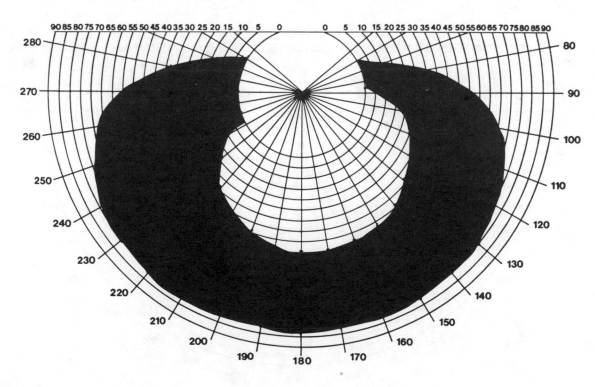

Figure C-10. Houston, Tex.

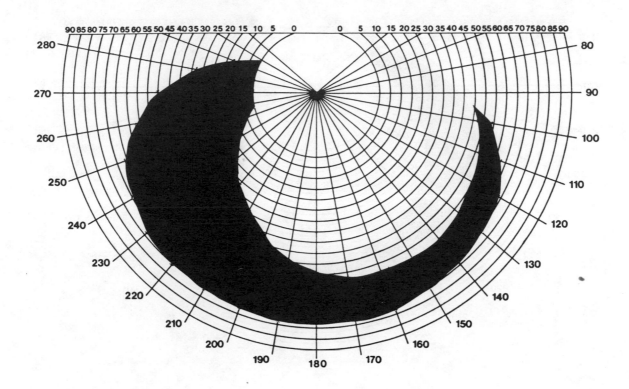

Figure C-11. Los Angeles, Calif.

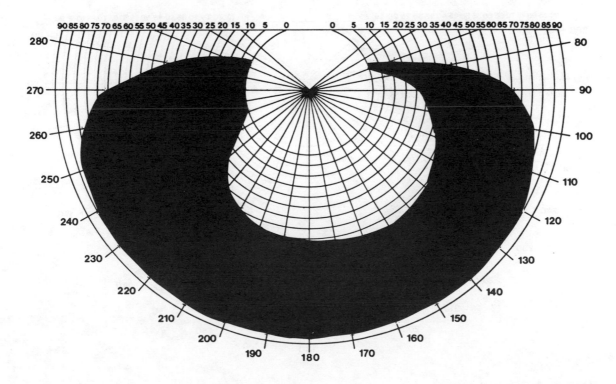

Figure C-12. Miami, Fla.

293

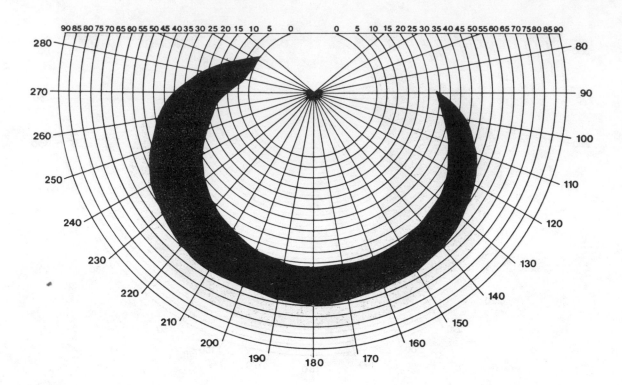

Figure C-13. Minneapolis, Minn.

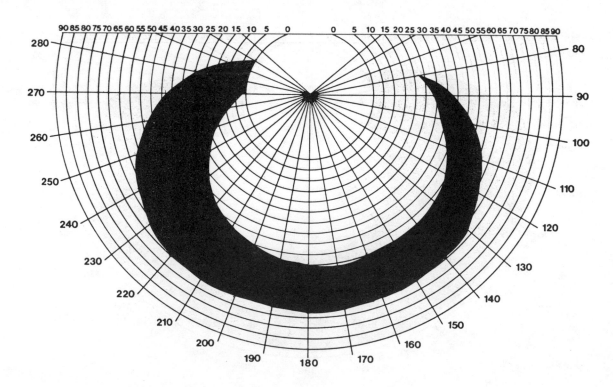

Figure C-14. Philadelphia, Pa.

294

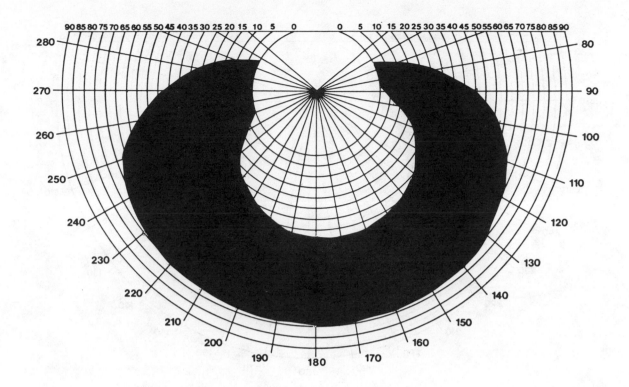

Figure C-15. Phoenix, Ariz.

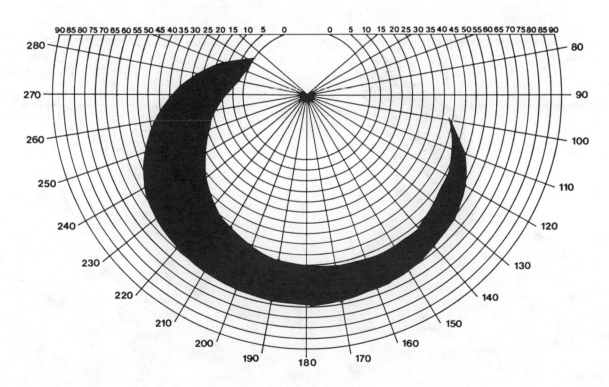

Figure C-16. Portland, Ore.

295

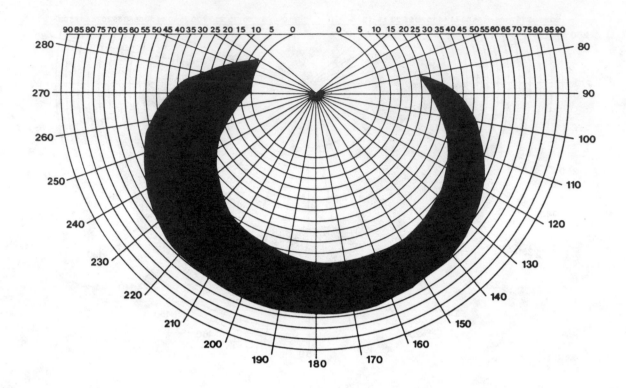

Figure C-17. Salt Lake City, Utah.

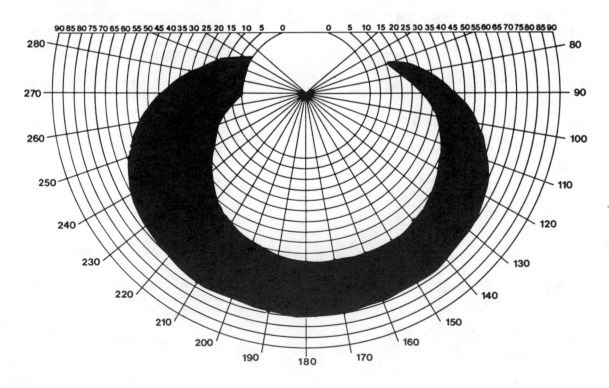

Figure C-18. St. Louis, Mo.

Annotated Bibliography

Planning and Energy Management

Barton-Aschman Associates, Inc. (1980). *Overview of energy-conserving development planning and design techniques based on five case studies* (ANL/CNSV-TM-59). Argonne, IL: for Argonne National Laboratory and the U.S. Department of Energy. (NTIS)

An excellent comparison of the five DOE sponsored case studies and overview of a comprehensive planning process for energy conservation. Seven appendices contain valuable case study examples of many energy conservation options.

Brookhaven National Laboratory/State University of New York. (1977). *Land use and energy utilization.* Springfield, VA: NTIS.

This study explores the quantitative relationships between alternative land use patterns and their resultant energy and fuel demands as well as the impact of these demands on the regional and national energy supply.

Erley, D., Mosena, D., & Gill, E. (1979). *Energy efficient land use* (Report No. 341). Chicago, IL: American Planning Association.

Discusses and illustrates energy-saving concepts of site selection, topography, vegetation, and landscaping. The report also covers basic planning principles related to housing density, land-use integration, and transportation.

Erley, D., & Mosena, D. (1980). *Energy conserving development regulations: Current practice* (Report No. 35). Chicago, IL: American Planning Association, for Argonne National Laboratory.

The study discusses development practices that save energy and presents examples of regulations implemented by communities throughout the country.

Hittman Associates Inc. (1978). *Comprehensive community energy planning* (Vols. 1-3). Columbia, MD: U.S. Department of Energy.

A methodology and workbook to assist community officials and staff with development and evaluation of energy conservation programs.

Jacobs, J. (1970). *The economy of cities.* New York: Vintage Press.

This classic examines the role of city economies in the national economy and develops a new theory for the way the development process occurs. Jacobs weaves case studies with a conceptual framework to explain why some cities develop healthy, diversified economies while the growth of others is stunted or distorted.

Knowles, R. L. (1974). *Energy and form.* Cambridge, MA: MIT Press.

This award-winning book begins with an historical analysis of the ecological-energy networks of several primitive American cultures. Theoretical principles are applied in a case study (Owens Valley, Calif.) and presented as form generators of future communities.

Living Systems. (1977). *Davis energy conservation report.* Davis, CA: City of Davis.

This report describes the Davis Energy Conservation Project including the Energy Conservation Building Code, planning for energy conservation, climate analysis, public education programs, and solar homes. Although the analysis and program are specific to Davis, this report provides an excellent model for programs that can be done anywhere in the U.S.

Real Estate Research Corporation. (1978). *Working papers on marketing and market acceptance.* Washington, DC: U.S. Department of Housing and Urban Development.

A two-volume work examining the potentials and problems of marketing solar homes. Contains information on financing, marketing, characteristics of solar purchasers and builders, and the impact of lending institutions on consumers.

Ridgeway, J. (1979). *Energy efficient community planning.* The J.G. Press, Inc.

An overview of the efforts of Seattle, Wash., Davis, Calif., Northglenn, Colo., and Hartford, Conn., plus specific programs of other U.S. cities. Gives a good review of what has been done.

Sizemore & Associates. (1978). *Methodology for energy management plans for small communities: Final report.* Atlanta, GA: U.S. Department of Energy.

A detailed report on how to do an energy audit and energy-management plan for a small community. Includes flow charts and a comprehensive questionnaire for use in the energy audit.

Smith, C. B. (1981). *Energy management principles.* New York: Pergamon Press.

A comprehensive text on general principles of energy management, including building and site energy audits, energy efficiency analyses, management of heating, cooling, and electrical loads, and the economics of efficient energy use.

Spirn, A. W. (1984). *The granite garden: Urban nature and human design.* New York: Basic Books.

This book is one of the first to present a comprehensive and coherent picture of the natural environment of the city — its air, its natural water supply, the ground on which it is built — and explains how knowledge of urban nature may help to create better surroundings for us all. Spirn examines the costs we pay for largely ignoring the natural environment and gives examples of cities that have reduced their operating costs by designing themselves more in harmony with nature.

Stein, B. A., & Hodax, M. B. (1976). *Competitive scale in manufacturing: The case of consumer goods.* Cambridge, MA: Center for Community Economic Development.

One of the few books that examines in detail the proposition that small manufacturing plants can produce cost-competitive goods. Stein and Hodax explore a dozen industries, from dressmaking to shoe making to appliance manufacturing. In each they identify the minimum efficient plant size. Their conclusion is that many cities provide large enough internal markets for these manufacturing facilities.

Stobaugh, R., & Yergin, D. (1979). *Energy future.* New York: Random House.

A very lucid and well-grounded treatise on the role of solar and renewable energy development in solving the nation's energy problems. A good overview of America's energy issues in a political context.

Site Planning and Design

Byrne, R. M., & Howland, L. (1980). *Background information summary.* Washington, DC: The Urban Land Institute.

This report describes how passive solar techniques, including proper orientation, shading, and material choice can reduce a structure's energy load by 25-50%. The report also states that up to 60% energy savings can be expected from a combination of energy-conscious site design and provisions of relatively sophisticated individual and community systems. Site design alone can provide up to 30% savings without increases in development costs.

Center for Landscape Architectural Education and Research. CLAER. (1981). *Site and neighborhood design for energy conservation: Five case studies* (ANL/CNSV-TM-99). Argonne, IL: Argonne National Laboratory and the U.S. Department of Energy.

This volume contains most of the information reported in the five individual case study reports. Comparisons regarding development plans, team structure, methodological approaches, and implementation programs are included. This book contains a wealth of information, but poor organization and the lack of an index require the to exercise patience and persistence.

County Council of Sussex. (1973). *A design guide for residential areas.* London: Anchor Press, Ltd.

An excellent British example of good neighborhood planning. Includes design standards for narrow streets, pedestrian walkways, and a wide variety of key planning elements. Excellent illustrations.

De Chiara, J., & Koppelman, L. (1975). *Manual of housing planning and design criteria.* Englewood Cliffs, NJ: Prentice Hall.

An excellent handbook on housing and subdivision design. Emphasis is on conventional practices.

Foster, R. S. (1978). *Homeowner's guide to landscaping that saves energy dollars.* New York: David McKay.

A rather comprehensive treatment of use of site design and plant materials for climatic modification. It is written for the average homeowner and contains no references, but some professionals may find it useful.

Howland, L., & Silverman, J. (1980). *Focus on energy conservation: A second project list.* Washington, DC: The Urban Land Institute.

The report discusses solar housing in Boulder, Colo., which designers estimate can achieve a 20% energy saving as a result of site planning and energy conservation. The project list also cites Reston, Va., as a community that has achieved significant energy savings as a result of sensitive site planning, which includes cluster development, extensive use of natural vegetation, and mixed land use.

Hutchison, B. A., Taylor, F. G., Wendt, R. L., & The Critical Review Panel. (1982). *Use of vegetation to ameliorate building microclimates: An assessment of energy conservation potentials* (No. 1913). Oak Ridge, TN: Oak Ridge National Laboratory, U.S. Department of Energy. (NTIS)

This report evaluates the space-conditioning energy conservation potentials of landscapes. The physical bases for vegetative modifications of climate are discussed, and results of past studies are reviewed. The state of the art of energy-conserving landscape designs is assessed and recommendations are presented for further research.

Land Design/Research, Inc. (1976). *Cost effective site planning.* National Association of Home Builders.

This book provides basic guidelines for energy conservation through proper site selection and planning. Twenty-five plans for varying densities are presented. Cluster and conventional plans are compared in terms of site costs and land utilization.

Land Design/Research, Inc. (1980). *Planning for housing: Development alternatives for better environments.* National Association of Home Builders.

This report shows how several fundamental concepts of mixed land use, compact development and better use of existing landscape resources are basic to the development of attractive, energy-efficient residential neighborhoods.

Lang, R., & Armour, A. (1982). *Planning land to conserve energy: 40 case studies from Canada and the United States.* Ottawa, Canada: Environment Canada.

An extremely valuable casebook for planners and designers. Forty well-documented examples of energy-oriented planning practices are presented. Topics covered include community energy profiles, municipal plans and policies, new communities and residential development, non-residential land use, and land use and development controls.

Living Systems. (1980). *Planning solar neighborhoods.* Sacramento, CA: California Energy Commission.

The best book yet on comprehensive design of solar neighborhoods, authored by solar experts with considerable experience. Aimed primarily at California conditions, it can be extrapolated easily to other climatic and physiographic regions. The book describes major climate regions and offers strategies for building design, neighborhood site planning, and landscape design for solar protection and energy conservation on a region-by-region basis.

Lynch, K. (1971). *Site planning.* Cambridge, MA: MIT Press.

A classic text on site planning that should be read by every energy-conscious designer.

McClenon, C., & Robinette, G. O. (Eds.). (1977). *Landscape planning for energy conservation.* Reston, VA: Environmental Design Press.

A guide for planning with vegetation and landforms. Includes sections on site selection and analysis and site planning for solar architecture. A number of case studies are given for various climatic regions.

Moffat, A. S., & Schiller, M. (1981). *Landscape design that saves energy.* New York: William Morrow and Co.

This book presents the basics of climatic analysis and offers specific design guidelines for four climate zones. Primarily for homeowners but also of interest to professionals.

Ontario Ministry of Housing. (1980). *Residential site design and energy conservation.* Ontario, Canada: Author.

This report shows that a traditional low-density subdivision could save 15-20% of the energy needed for space heating by selecting housing with better energy efficiency, orienting the buildings to receive the most sun and least wind effect, arranging landscaping as a shelter, and increasing major southerly windows.

Planning Collaborative Inc. (1983). *Tumbler Ridge: Energy-efficient subdivision and community designs.* Vancouver, British Columbia: Research report prepared for the Canada Mortgage and Housing Corporation.

A study that assesses the costs and benefits of community design principles for energy conservation applied to a new resource community in northern British Columbia. Proposed design patterns to achieve solar access, wind protection, and reduced capital costs for infrastructure are presented graphically and thoroughly evaluated.

Real Estate Research Corporation. (1974). *The costs of sprawl.* Washington, DC: U.S. Government Printing Office.

Energy consumption is reduced 44% in high-density planned communities as compared to low-density sprawl communities. The reduction reflects variations in residential power consumption by housing type and decrease in automobile use in high-density planned areas.

Robinette, G. O. (1972). *Plants/people/and environmental quality.* Washington, DC: U.S. Department of the Interior, National Park Service.

A graphic presentation showing how to use plants as environmental planning elements for modifying the impact of wind, solar radiation, air pollution, noise, and visual blight.

Sterling, R., Carmody, J., & Elnicky, G. (1981). *Earth sheltered community design: Energy efficient residential development.* New York: Van Nostrand Reinhold.

An excellent examination of all aspects of community design including site analysis, infrastructure design, and siting of various types of energy-efficient design. Case studies are used effectively to illustrate important concepts.

Urban Land Institute. (1981). *Energy-efficient community development techniques* (C. S. Crane & J. D. Steller, Jr., Eds.). Washington, DC: Author.

The best organized and most useful analysis of the five DOE SAND case studies available to date. Project data, team methodologies, conservation options, energy costs and savings are presented in a consistent format with salient points summarized. The report also contains an excellent energy bibliography and glossary.

Energy-Efficient Architecture

A.I.A. Research Corporation. (1978). *Regional guidelines for building passive energy conserving homes.* Washington, DC: U.S. Government Printing Office.

A description and analysis of thirteen climatic regions for the continental United States and Hawaii. The building guidelines range from climatic and conceptual considerations to choice of materials and details. Well illustrated.

Anderson, B. (1976). *The solar home book.* Harrisville, NH: Cheshire Books.

One of the best books on passive and solar home concepts and design in print. It also gives a good introduction to solar hot water systems. Well written with excellent illustrations. Appendices contain much technical information.

Bainbridge, D., Corbett, J., & Hofacre, J. (1979). *Village homes solar house designs.* Emmaus, PA: Rodale Press.

A concise presentation of site design principles and numerous architectural plans from the much publicized solar neighborhood in Davis, Calif.

Clark, K. N., & Paylore, P. (Eds.). (1980). *Desert housing: Balancing experience and technology for dwelling in hot arid zones.* Tucson, AZ: Office of Arid Lands Studies, University of Arizona.

An excellent collection of essays on desert housing and energy conservation from world-renowned authors. Contains a chapter on landscape architecture for arid zones. A must for every designer working on projects in desert climates.

Eccli, E. (1976). *Low cost energy efficient shelter for the owner and builder.* Emmaus, PA: Rodale Press.

An excellent design manual on energy efficient houses for anyone considering designing and building a home. Includes many money-saving suggestions as well as excellent sections on windows, doors, vents, and other key house components ignored in many books. Valuable for builders and architects.

Leckie, J., Masters, G., Whitehouse, H., & Young, L. (1975). *Other homes and garbage.* San Francisco: Sierra Club Books.

This book covers a wide variety of information on self-sufficient residential energy systems such as wind, water, and methane, as well as solar. The book includes a fairly good chapter on climatically adapted architecture and also provides a good introduction to active systems. The explanation of the ASHRAE methodology for calculating heat loss and heat gain of buildings is well done.

Mazria, E. (1979). *The passive solar energy book.* Emmaus, PA: Rodale Press.

Excellent. A well-organized and easy-to-comprehend collection of passive solar principles and applications. Its key asset is a presentation of a series of rules of thumb for sizing the various elements. The illustrations are a delight. The new "Professional" edition contains additional appendices of great value.

Olgyay, V., & Olgyay, A. (1963/1973). *Design with climate: Bioclimatic approach to architectural regionalism.* Princeton, NJ: Princeton University Press.

This is a classic on climatically adapted building design and planning. It is not a design handbook but does provide principles of climatic variables and their interaction with building design and siting.

Pearson, J. (1978). *Hawaii home energy book.* Honolulu, HA: The University Press of Hawaii.

This book is a delightful primer on home energy conservation for hot, humid climates. It addresses a range of energy options including solar control, ventilation, landscaping, and architectural design.

Sherwood, G. E., & Hans, G. E. (1979). *Energy efficiency in light-frame wood construction* (No. FPL 317). Madison, WI: Forest Products Laboratory, U.S. Forest Service.

This report first discusses improving the thermal performance of a house by careful planning and design. It also provides technical information on thermal properties of construction materials and basic engineering design principles. It contains one of the best discussions available on moisture condensation problems.

Watson, D. (1979). *Energy conservation through building design.* New York: McGraw-Hill.

Written by leading authorities in their fields, this book addresses every aspect of the efficient use of energy in building design, including planning and engineering. It is not limited to new building design, but includes methods of analyzing existing structures and ways to reduce their energy consumption by both controlled usage and retrofitting measures.

Watson, D., & Labs, K. (1983). *Climatic design: Energy efficient building principles and practices.* New York: McGraw-Hill.

The authors present eight basic climatic design techniques and describe their application to site planning and building design. Climatic data for 20 U.S. cities are presented in a very useful format.

Climate and Design

ASHRAE. (1981). *Handbook of fundamentals and product directory.* New York: Author.

This standard reference for thermal analysis methodology presents detailed information on thermal properties of materials. The handbook also contains excellent data on climatic design conditions, solar radiation, and window-shading methods. Unfortunately, there are no sections specifically directed towards designing solar buildings. In addition, a large portion of the book consists of nonapplicable information on refrigeration and industrial heating and cooling systems.

Bird, R. E., & Hulstrom, R. L. (1981). *A simplified clear sky model for direct and diffuse insolation on horizontal surfaces.* Golden, CO: Solar Energy Research Institute.

Detailed and technical comparison of several simple, broadband insolation models currently in use, and based upon this comparison, presentation of a simplified model. This report may be of use to designers of solar energy systems in locations where insolation data are lacking.

Egan, D. M. (1975). *Concepts of thermal comfort.* Englewood Cliffs, NJ: Prentice-Hall.

A well-illustrated basic text on the interaction between weather, construction materials, architectural mechanical systems, and human comfort.

Geiger, R. (1975). *The climate near the ground.* Cambridge, MA: Harvard University Press.

A detailed scientific text that covers the principles of microclimatology, mainly in agricultural and forestry applications. Much of the theory is applicable to building design and planning, but the format is difficult to use.

Givoni, B. (1976). *Man, climate, and architecture.* London: Elsevier.

A most comprehensive technical book on human comfort and the thermal performance of buildings. It contains excellent quantitative descriptions of the thermal performance of building materials and design features such as ventilation and window shading. This book is useful for those who want a detailed understanding about the interactions of people, buildings, and climate.

Loftness, V. E. (1977). *Identifying climatic design regions and assessing climatic impact on residential building design* (Tech. Paper No. 1). Washington, DC: AIA Research Corporation.

Climatic data from 130 U.S. Cities are analyzed to establish predominant residential design conditions. The potential of other climatic forces to shift conditions into the comfort zone is assessed. Maps illustrate predominant design conditions and identify regionally available climatic forces for increasing natural comfort.

Loftness, V. E. (1982). Using climate/energy graphics to establish energy conscious design priorities. In *Proceedings of the 7th National Passive Solar Conference.* Newark, DE: American Solar Energy Society.

This paper describes a pre-design climatic analysis tool. It translates a combination of typical conditions, coincident conditions, and diurnal variations into design guidelines for building massing, siting, organization of spaces, enclosure design and opening design, as well as mechanical systems integration.

Lowry, W. P. (1969). *Weather and life.* New York: Academic Press.

Introductory text on biometeorology provides detailed information on the physical environment, including radiation, temperature, moisture, and wind. Also expands the energy budget concept and includes data collection and instrumentation.

Peterson, J. T. (1969). *The climate of cities: A survey of recent literature.* Raleigh, NC: U.S. Department of Health, Education, and Welfare, the National Air Pollution and Control Administration.

Brief review of literature on city climatology, particularly the differences between urban and rural climates. Although dated, the information is still valid.

Reifnsyder, W. E., & Lull, H. W. (1965). *Radiant energy in relation to forests.* Washington, DC: U.S. Department of Agriculture, Forest Service Technical Bulletin No. 1344.

Reviews the fundamentals of short- and long-wave radiation, radiation measurement, and certain radiation relationships important in the forest. Three aspects of the forest-energy relationship are discussed: transpiration, snow melt, and growth.

Rosenberg, N. J. (1974). *Microclimate: The biological environment.* New York: John Wiley and Sons.

Provides basic material pertaining to the biological, physical, and ecological principles of the microclimate. In addition, considerable attention is given to the ways in which the microclimate can be beneficially altered.

Schroeder, M. J., & Buck, C. C. (1970). *Fire weather.* Washington, DC: U.S. Department of Agriculture, U.S. Government Printing Office.

Although this book is intended for people interested in forest fires, it is one of the few general meteorology texts focusing on the weather at the earth's surface. Particularly useful is the detailed discussion of surface winds and their interaction with topography.

Strock, C., & Kozel, R. (1976). *Handbook of air conditioning, heating, and ventilating.* New York: Industrial Press.

An engineering manual similar to ASHRAE except that it is much easier to read and use. The climatic data section is excellent and contains much information not contained in ASHRAE or other standard references. The book also contains sections on thermal properties of materials and heat transfer equations. Overall, this is an excellent and very useful handbook.

U.S. Department of Commerce. (1974). *Climatic atlas of the United States.* Asheville, NC: Publications Unit, National Climatic Center.

An extremely useful compendium of maps and data that illustrate climatic variations in the United States.

Watt Engineering, Ltd. (1978). *On the nature and distribution of solar radiation.* Washington, DC: U.S. Department of Energy, Government Printing Office.

A comprehensive collection of information on solar radiation including working formulas, insolation models, and sun path diagrams.

Solar Control and Solar Access

Burke, K. H., & Lemans, B. N. (1980). Simplified solar easements. *Solar Law Reporter, 2*(2).

A clear discussion of solar easements: what they are and how they can be established. The *Solar Law Reporter* is an excellent journal for those who desire to keep abreast of current developments in solar law.

Erley, D., & Jaffe, M. (1980). *Site planning for solar access: A guidebook for residential developers and site planners.* Chicago, IL: American Planning Association, U.S. Government Printing Office.
A comprehensive document discussing legal and planning tools for solar access. It discusses in greater detail some concepts and techniques presented here in Chapter Seven. An excellent resource.

Fregonese, J. A. (1980). *Ashland Oregon's solar strategy.* Ashland, OR: City of Ashland Planning Department.

Ashland's prototypical "solar setback" approach to protecting solar access to new and infill development in a hilly environment. Contains a good graphic technique of considering sloped sites in projecting shadows to determine minimum solar setbacks.

Hayes, G. D. (1979). *Solar access law.* Cambridge, MA: Ballinger.

This is the most comprehensive volume on the legal aspects of solar access protection. A valuable book for those involved in legal analysis of solar access alternatives.

Heisler, G. M. (1982). Reductions of solar radiation by tree crowns. In *The Renewable Challenge, Proceedings of the Annual Meeting.* Newark, DE: American Section, International Solar Energy Society.

One of the most technically thorough and scientifically sound discussions of the effects of tree crowns on solar radiation values.

Jaffe, M., & Erley, D. (1979). *Protecting solar access for residential development: A guidebook for planning officials.* Chicago, IL: American Planning Association, U.S. Government Printing Office.

A companion document to *Site Planning for Solar Access,* produced for national distribution through the Departmnent of Housing and Urban Development. Emphasizes legal and planning tools for solar access protection.

Knowles, R. L. (1981). *Sun rhythm form.* Cambridge, MA: MIT Press.

A book describing in detail Knowles's concepts for utilizing solar envelope zones to protect solar access, particularly in developed urban areas. Includes examples of work from the author's graduate students who prepared urban design concepts in direct response to solar envelope configurations.

Kohler, J., & Lewis, D. (1981). Let the sun shine in. *Solar Age, 6*(11).

A brief but important article establishing the fact that solar collectors lose efficiency in nearly direct proportion to the amount they are shaded. An important article for researchers exploring foliar density effects on solar access and building energy performance.

Olgyay, V., & Olgyay, A. (1957). *Solar control and shading devices.* Princeton, NJ: Princeton University Press.
A classic work that focuses on solar radiation as a key climatic influence. Describes the overheated period, shading mask, architectural applications, and shading effects of vegetation.

Oregon Appropriate Technology, Inc. (1982). *The Eugene-Springfield solar report.* Eugene, OR: City of Eugene.
Describes a practical method of determining the amount and value of existing solar access in communities. A good practical application of solar access theory to a real situation.

Parker, J. H. (1981). *Uses of landscaping for energy conservation.* Tallahassee, FL: Governor's Energy Office.
Presents research results on the effects of shading on energy use for air conditioning. Parker presents guidelines for precision landscaping to save energy in Florida. The report also contains an energy analysis of residential landscapes and a list of recommended native plants.

Spirn, A. W., & Santos, A. N. (1981). *Plants for passive cooling: A preliminary investigation of the use of plants for passive cooling in temperate humid climates.* Department of Landscape Architecture, Harvard University, Technical report for Oak Ridge National Laboratory, Solar and Special Studies Section, Oak Ridge, TN.
A useful collection of imaginative solar control strategies for designers. Textual descriptions are limited but there are many nicely illustrated examples.

Wind Control

Bates, C. G. (1945). Shelterbelt influences II. The value of shelterbelts in house heating. *Journal of Forestry, 43,* 176-196.
Describes early measurements of wind effects on energy use for heating houses. A thorough series of ments and analyses was carried out using 4 x 4-ft (1.2 x 1.2-m) cubical structures as model houses.

Center for Landscape Architectural Education and Research. (1978). *Options for passive energy conservation in site design.* (Prepared for U.S. Department of Energy Contract No. EC-77-C-01-5037). Reston, VA: Author.
Using mostly brief excerpts and illustrations, reviews some of classical literature pertaining to air flow principles (pp. 32-46), wind control, and energy saving through site selection and design and use of fences and vegetation (pp. 71-91). Both heating- and cooling-energy savings are included. Design examples that include wind control for individual buildings or groups of buildings are given.

DeWalle, D. R., Heisler, G. M., & Jacobs, R. E. (1983). Forest home sites influence heating and cooling energy. *Journal of Forestry, 81,* 84-88.
Describes results of a series of experiments using small mobile homes as test units to evaluate the effect of forested home sites on heating and cooling energy use.

Harrje, D. T., Buckley, C. E., & Heisler, G. M. (1982). Building energy reductions: Optimum use of windbreaks. *Journal of Energy Division, Proceedings of the American Society of Civil Engineers, 108,* 143-154.
Describes a series of wind-tunnel experiments to evaluate the relative effects of different tree arrangements on wind-induced air infiltration.

Hunt, C. M., King, J. C., & Treschsel, T. R. (Eds.). (1980). *Building air change rate and infiltration measurements* (ASTM Special Publication 719). Philadelphia: American Society for Testing and Materials.
A series of papers that present the state of the art on air infiltration in buildings and methods of measurements. The treatment is highly technical and intended for those with a special interest in recent research on the topic.

Van Eimern, J., Karschon, R., Razumova, L. A., & Robertson, G. W. (1964). *Windbreaks and shelterbelts* (WMO-No. 147.TP.70). Geneva, Switzerland: World Meteorological Organization.
A thorough review of world literature on windbreak and shelterbelt influences on air flow and agricultural crops.

Woodruff, N. P. (1959). *Shelterbelt and surface barrier effects on wind velocities, evaporation, house heating, and snowdrifting* (Technical Bulletin 77). Manhattan, KS: Kansas Agricultural Experimental Station.

Describes wind tunnel experiments to evaluate effects of shelterbelts, including effects on heating energy use.

Water Conservation

California, State of. (1979). *The California water atlas*. Sacramento, CA: Author.

A work of publishing art, superb graphics. The history, condition, and future of water use in the state most dependent upon water management. Immensely valuable to experts and laymen alike.

Diekelmann, J., & Schuster, R. (1982). *Natural landscaping: Designing with native plant communities*. New York: McGraw-Hill.

Sound advice on the design and implementation of landscapes using native plant materials. Well-developed, step-by-step processes presented in clear graphic form. Emphasis on East coast and Midwestern plant communities.

Duffield, M. R., & Jones, W. D. (1981). *Plants for dry climates: How to select, grow and enjoy*. Tucson, AZ: H.P. Books.

This magazine-style publication emulates the highly successful Ortho and Sunset formats. Regional maps for southwestern states identify different types of arid and semi-arid climates. Useful plant lists and many color photographs aid in plant selection.

Farallones Institute. (1979). *The integral urban house*. San Francisco: Sierra Club Books.

Presents a blueprint for realizing an ecologically sustainable urban society. Treats water conservation at the individual dwelling unit level, as well as other energy parameters. Sections on livestock, gardening, etc., may seem superfluous but merit thought in the big picture.

Linaweaver, F. P. (1967). *A study of residential water use*. Washington, DC: U.S. Department of Housing and Urban Development.

Though dated and a bit academic, the most quoted source in the literature on water conservation.

Milne, M. (1976). *Residential water conservation* (Report No. 35). Davis, CA: California Water Resources Center.

Excellent overview of water use and potential savings in the residential sector. Much discussion devoted to water-saving devices within the home, but there remain substantial information and insight of benefit to landscape architects.

Molison, B. (1978). *Permaculture* (Vols. 1 & 2). Stanley, Tasmania, Australia: Targari Books.

Highly detailed and utopian approach to creating a "permanent agriculture" based on renewable resources and energy conservation. Volume 2 deals most specifically with landscaping.

Morrison, D. G. (1975, October). Restoring the mid-western landscape. *Landscape Architecture. 65*(6), 398-403.

Case study of the author's successful attempt to restore the prairie landscape on a Wisconsin site.

Newsweek. (1981, February). Are we running out of water? *97*(8).

Provocative cover story explores water use trends throughout the U.S. Excellent orientation and discussion of current problems and policies.

Rogers, E. M., & Shoemaker, F. F. (1971). *Communication of innovations, a cross-cultural approach* (2nd ed.). New York: The Free Press.

Exploration of the way innovations are assimilated into societies. Worthwhile reading for anyone interested in trying to initiate change.

Thayer, R. L., Jr. (1982, August). Public response to water conserving landscapes. *HortScience, 17* (4).

Experimental study indicating that the public is willing to accept esthetic alternatives to turfgrass under certain conditions.

U.S. Water Resources Council. (1978). *The nation's water resources, 1975-2000*. Washington, DC: U.S. Government Printing Office.

The definitive source on U.S. water problems, trends, and use. Four volumes, copiously mapped, graphed, and illustrated. Everything you ever wanted to know about water in America.

Embodied Energy

Batty, J. C., Humad, S. N., & Keller, J. (1975). Energy inputs to irrigation. *Journal of the Irrigation and Drainage Division* in *Proceedings of the American Society of Civil Engineers, 101* (IR4):201-215.

Provides specifications on Btu consumption involved in manufacture of various metals and plastics used in landscape construction materials, manufacture of engines and manufacture and installation of various types of irrigation systems.

Busey, P., & Burt, E. (1981, March). Turf management energy use is reevaluated in Florida. *Weeds, Trees and Turf*, pp. 37-42.

Examines energy savings in warm-season turf management that may be realized through use of improved and less water consumptive species of grass and improved techniques of turf culture.

Falk, J. H. (1976). Energetics of a suburban lawn ecosystem. *Ecology, 57:* 141-150.

Outlines through a case study the energy flows of a California suburban lawn. Examines both natural flows and fossil fuel energy inputs required for turf management.

Gilley, J. R., & Watts, D. G. (1977). Possible energy savings in irrigation. *Journal of the Irrigation and Drainage Division* in *Proceedings of the American Society of Civil Engineers. 103* (IR4):455-457.

Examines energy conservation potentials that can be realized in agricultural irrigation systems.

National Capital Region, National Park Service. (1981). *Energy conservation concepts in managing urban parks.* Washington, DC: U.S. Department of the Interior, National Park Service; and U.S. Department of Energy.

A comprehensive examination of fossil fuel energy inputs required for maintenance of urban parks. Examines conservation alternatives and contains extensive bibliography on the subject of embodied energy in landscape planning and design.

Office of Energy Research and Planning. (1974). *Energy study.* Portland, OR: State of Oregon.

Provides specifications of Btu consumption involved in manufacture of aluminum, paperboard, and brick.

Parker, J. H. (1982). An energy and ecological analysis of alternative residential landscapes. *Journal of Environmental Systems,* LL(3): 271-288.

Examines energy flows in hot, humid landscapes. Presents analyses of embodied-energy requirements of several alternative landscape design concepts.

Pimental, D., Hund, L. E., Bellotti, A. C., Furster, M. J., Okan, I. N., Shules, O. D., & Whitman, R. J. (1973). Food production and the energy crisis. *Science, 182*:443-449.

Provides specifications for Btu consumption involved in manufacture of fertilizers and pesticides.

Stanhill, G. (1974). Energy and agriculture: A national case study. *Agro-Ecosystems,* L: 205-217.

Provides specifications for Btu consumption involved in manufacture of fertilizers.

Steinhart, J. S., & Steinhart, C. E. (1974). Energy use in the U.S. food system. *Science, 184*:307-316.

Provides specifications for Btu consumption involved in manufacture of fertilizers. Examines fossil fuel energy inputs in food production.

The Asphalt Institute. (1979). *Energy requirements for roadway pavements* (IS-173). College Park, MD: Author.

Provides specifications for Btu consumption involved in manufacture of cement, lime, sand, gravel, and asphalt products.

References

(Numbers at end of each reference indicate chapter(s) in which reference is cited.)

Aldous, T. (Ed.). (1979). *Trees and buildings: Complement or conflict?* London: RIBA Publications Limited and the Tree Council. **VIII**

Alexander, C. (1979). *The timeless way of building.* New York: Oxford University Press. **VI**

Alexander, C., Ishikawa, S., Silverstein, M., Jacobson, M., Fiksdahl-King, I., & Angel, S. (1977). *A pattern language.* New York: Oxford University Press. **VI**

Allen, L. F. (1852). *Rural architecture.* New York: Moore. **I**

American Planning Association. (1980). *Solar access — guidebook for California communities.* Sacramento, CA: California Energy Commission. **VII**

American Society of Heating, Refrigerating, and Air Conditioning Engineers (ASHRAE). (1977). *ASHRAE Handbook, 1977 Fundamentals.* New York: Author. **IX**

Argonne National Laboratory. (1979). *Community systems: Energy saving programs for communities.* Argonne, IL: Author. **II**

Baer, W. C., & Gordon, P. (1972). Tree planting reconsidered: An argument for big transplants. *Landscape Architecture, 62,* 236-239. **VIII**

Bailey, L. H. (Ed.). (1907-1909). *Cyclopedia of American agriculture* (4 vols.). New York: Macmillian. **I**

Bainbridge, D., Corbett, J., & Hofacre, J. (1979). *Solar houses of Village Homes.* Emmaus, PA: Rodale Press. **VI**

Barber, J. W. (1848). *Historical collections of every town in Massachusetts, with geographical descriptions.* Worcester, MA: Lazell. **I**

Barnaby, C., Caeser, P., Wilcox, B., & Nelson, L. (1977). *Solar for your present home.* Sacramento, CA: California Energy Commission, 1977. **VII**

Barton-Aschman Associates, Inc. (1980). *Overview of energy-conserving development planning and design techniques based on five case studies* (ANL/CNSV-TM-59). Argonne, IL: Energy and Environmental Systems Division, Argonne National Laboratory, (NTIS). **III**

Bates, C. G. (1945a). Shelterbelt influences II. The value of shelterbelts in house heating. *Journal of Forestry, 43,* 176-196. **IX**

Bates, C. G. (1945b). *The windbreak as a farm asset* (Farmers' Bulletin 1405). Washington, D.C.: U.S. Department of Agriculture. **IX**

Battelle Pacific Northwest Laboratory. (1981). *Wind energy resource atlas* (12 vols.). Richland, WA: Author. (NTIS) **III**

Belknap, D., & Furtado, J. (1968, January). The natural land unit as a planning base. *Landscape Architecture, 58*(2), 145-147. **VI**

Bennett, R. (1978). *Sun angles for design.* Bala Cynwyd, PA: Author. **VIII, C**

Berdahl, P., Grether, D., Martin, M., & Wahlig, M. (1978). *California solar data manual.* Sacramento, CA: California Energy Commission. **VII**

Blomsterberg, A., & Harrje, D. T. (1979). Approaches to evaluation of air infiltration energy losses in buildings. *ASHRAE Transactions, 85* (Part 1), 797-814. **IX**

Borg, W., & Gall, M. (1979). *Educational research.* New York: Longman. **III**

Boykin, J. (1982). Liquid life: The water beneath us. *The Stanford Magazine, 10*(1), 10-21. **X**

Bray, R. K. (1982). *Effectiveness of vegetation in energy conservation.* Unpublished master's thesis, University of Georgia, Athens, GA. **VIII**

Brown, R. H. (1948). *Historical geography of the United States.* New York: Harcourt. **I**

Bryan, H. (1982, September). Seeing the light. *Progressive Architecture, 63*(9), 251-254. **VI**

Buckley, C. E., Harrje, D. T., Knowlton, M. P., & Heisler, G. M. (1978). *The optimum use of coniferous trees in reducing home energy consumption* (Report PU/CES 71). Princeton, NJ: Princeton University Center for Environmental Studies. **VI, IX**

Buffington, D. E. (1978). Value of landscaping for conserving energy in residences. In *Proceedings of the Florida State Horticultural Society. 91,* 92-96. **VII**

Buffington, D. E. (1979). Economics of landscaping features for conserving energy in residences. In *Proceedings of the Florida State Horticultural Society. 92,* 216-220. **VII, VIII**

Buffington, D. E., & Black, R. J. (1981). Life-cycle costing of plant materials for residential energy conservation. In *Proceedings Florida State Horticultural Society. 94,* 205-208. **VIII**

Buffington, D. E., Sastry, S. K., & Black, R. J. (undated). *Factors for determining shading patterns in Florida* (Circular No. 505-516). Florida Cooperative Extension Service, Gainesville, FL: University of Florida. **C**

Bureau of Research. (1979). *Houses and climate: An energy perspective for Florida builders.* Tallahassee, FL: Governor's Energy Office. **III**

Burke, K. H., & Lemons, B. N. (1980). Simplified solar easements. *Solar Law Reporter, 2*(2). **VII**

Business Week. (1981, October). A pipeline that is inciting a water war. *27*(11), 59-60. **X**

Caborn, J. M. (1957). *Shelterbelts and microclimate.* Edinburgh, Scotland: H. M. Stationery Office. **IX**

California, State of. (1979). *The California water atlas.* Sacramento, CA: Author. **X**

California Department of Water Resources. (1979). *Plants of California landscapes* (Bulletin 209). Sacramento, CA: State of California. **X**

Calthorpe, P., & Benson, S. (1979). The solar shadow: A discussion of issues eclipsed. In *Proceedings of the 3rd National Passive Solar Conference.* Newark, DE: American Section of the International Solar Energy Society. **III, VI**

Cannell, M. G. R. (1982). *World forest biomass and primary production data.* London: Academic Press. **III**

Capen, O. B. (1905). Country homes. *Country Life, 8,* 58-61. **I**

Carpenter, J. D. (Ed.). (1976). *Handbook of landscape architectural construction.* Washington, D. C.: Landscape Architecture Foundation. **XI**

Carroll, T. C., Hathans, R., Palmedo, P. F., & Stern, R. (1976). *The planner's energy workbook: A user's manual for exploring land use and energy utilization relationships.* Brookhaven National Laboratory. **II**

Center for Advanced Computation, & R. G. Stein and Assoc. (undated). *Energy in building construction.* Washington, D.C.: Energy Research and Development Administration, Contract No. E (11-1)-2791. **III, XII**

Center for Environmental Studies. (1977). *Microclimate, architecture, and landscaping relationships in an arid region: Phoenix, Arizona* (Research paper No. 4). Tempe, AZ: Arizona State University. **VIII, XI**

Center for Landscape Architectural Education and Research. (1978). *Options for passive energy conservation in site design.* (Prepared for U.S. Dept. of Energy, Contract No. EC-77-C-01-5037). Reston, VA: Author. **IX**

Center for Landscape Architectural Education and Research. (1981). *Site and neighborhood design for energy conservation: Five case studies* (ANL/CNSV-TM-99). Argonne, IL: Energy and Environmental Systems Division, Argonne National Laboratory. (NTIS) **II, III, VI, VIII**

Cleveland, H. W. S. (1873). *Landscape architecture as applied to the wants of the west.* Chicago: Jansen. **I**

Congressional Budget Office. (1977). *Urban transportation and energy: The potential savings of different modes.* Washington, D.C.: U.S. Government Printing Office. **III**

Cook, D. I. (1978). Trees, solid barriers, and combinations: Alternatives for noise control. In Hopkins, G. (Ed.) *Proceedings of the National Urban Forestry Conference* (Vol. 1 ESF Publication 80-003). Syracuse, NY: State University of New York, College of Environmental Science and Forestry. **IX**

Corbett, M. (1981). *A better place to live.* Emmaus, PA: Rodale Press. **III, VI**

Corbett, M., & Corbett, J. (1979). Village Homes: A neighborhood designed with energy conservation in mind. In *Proceedings of the 3rd National Passive Solar Conference.* Newark, DE: American Section of the International Solar Energy Society. **VI**

Cunningham, M. P. (1952, January). The use of the grapevine. *House Beautiful, 51,* 30-31. **I**

Danielson, R. E., Feldhake, C. M., & Hart, W. E. (1981). *Urban lawn irrigation and management practices for water saving with minimum effect of lawn quality.* Fort Collins, CO: Colorado Water Resources Institute. **X**

Daryanani, S., & Lull, W. (1982). Passive solar energy in commercial buildings. *Buildings, 76,* 104-110. **VIII**

DeChiara J., & Koppelman, L. (1975). *Manual of housing planning and design criteria.* Englewood Cliffs, NJ: Prentice-Hall. **III**

Deering, R. B. (1956). Effect of living shade on house temperatures. *Journal of Forestry, 54,* 399-400. **VIII**

DeWalle, D. R. (1978a). Manipulating urban vegetation for residential energy conservation. In Hopkins, G. (Ed.) *Proceedings of the National Urban Forestry Conference* (Vol. 1 ESF Pub. 80-003). Syracuse, NY: State University of New York, College of Environmental Science and Forestry. **II, IX**

DeWalle, D. R. (1978b). *Residential energy conservation using urban trees and forests, A problem analysis.* University Park, PA: Institute for Research on Land and Water Resources, Pennsylvania State University. **II**

DeWalle, D. R., & Heisler, G. M. (1983). Windbreak effect on air infiltration and space heating in a mobile home. *Energy and Buildings, 5,* 279-288. **II, IX**

DeWalle, D. R., Heisler, G. M., & Jacobs, R. E. (1983). Forest home sites influence heating and cooling energy. *Journal of Forestry, 81,* 84-88. **II, VIII, IX**

Dick, E. (1937). *The sod house frontier.* New York: Harper. **I**

Diekelmann, J., & Schuster, R. (1982). *Natural landscaping: Designing with native plant communities.* New York: McGraw-Hill. **X**

Dillman, D. (1979). *Mail and telephone surveys: The total design method.* New York: Wiley and Sons. **III**

Dirr, M. A. (1977). *Manual of woody landscape plants.* Champaign, IL: Stipe Publishing Co. **IX**

Dochinger, L. S. (1980). Interception of airborne particles by tree plantings. *Journal of Environmental Quality, 9,* 265-268. **IX**

Dubos, R. (1965). *Man adapting.* New Haven, CT: Yale University Press. **X**

Duckworth, E., & Sandberg, J. (1954). The effect of cities upon horizontal and vertical temperature gradients. *Bull. American Meteorological Society, 35,* 198-207. **VIII**

Duffield, M. R., & Jones, W. D. (1981). *Plants for dry climates: How to select, grow and enjoy.* Tucson, AZ: H.P. Books. **X**

Durgin, F. H., & Chock, A. W. (1980). *A brief review of pedestrian level winds.* Cambridge, MA: The Wright Brothers Memorial Wind Tunnel-M.I.T. **IX**

Dwight, T. (1821/1969). *Travels in New England and New York.* Cambridge, MA: Harvard University Press. **I**

Eisentadt, M. M. (1982). Access to solar energy: The problems and its current status. *Natural Resources Journal, 22,* 21-52. **VII**

Elliott, D. L. (1979). Meterological and topographical indicators of wind energy for regional assessments. *Proceedings of the Conference on Wind Characteristics and Wind Energy Siting* (PNS-3214). Richland, WA: Pacific Northwest Laboratory. **III**

Energy Research and Development Administration. (1977). *Life cycle costing emphasizing energy conservation: Guidelines for investment analysis.* Washington, D.C.: Division of Construction Planning and Support. **III**

Erley, D., & Jaffe, J. (1979). *Site planning for solar access. A guidebook for residential developers and site planners.* Chicago, IL: American Planning Association, U.S. Department of Housing and Urban Development. **VII, VIII**

Erley, D., & Mosena, D. (1980). *Energy conserving development regulations: Current practice* (Report No. 352). Chicago, IL: American Planning Association. **III**

Estienne, C. (1616). *Maison rustique, or, the countrey farme.* London: Joslip. **I**

Fanger, P. O. (1970). *Thermal comfort: Analysis and applications in environmental engineering.* New York: McGraw-Hill. **IV**

Federer, C. A. (1976). Trees modify the urban microclimate. *Journal of Arboriculture, 2,* 121-127. **VIII**

Ferber, R. (Ed.). (1974). *Handbook of marketing research.* New York: McGraw-Hill. **III**

Festinger, L. (1975). *A theory of cognitive dissonance.* Evanston, IL: Row, Peterson. **X**

Fitch, A. M. (1949, October). How you can use House Beautiful's climate control project. *House Beautiful, 91,* 142-143. **I**

Flack, J. E. (1977). *Achieving urban water conservation, a handbook.* Fort Collins, CO: Colorado Water Research Institute. **X**

Flemer, W., III. (1974). The role of plants in today's energy conservation. *American Nurseryman, 89,* 39-45. **IX**

Forbes, (1979, August). Water: The next crisis. **X**

Foster, R. S. (1978). *Homeowner's guide to landscaping that saves energy dollars.* New York: David McKay. **IX**

Fregonese, J. A. (1980). *Ashland, Oregon's solar strategy.* Ashland, OR: City of Ashland Planning Department. **VII**

Fregonese, J. A. (1983). *The SUNDIAL program.* Ashland, OR: Orion Compugraphics. **VII**

Gandemeer, J. (1979). Wind shelters. *Journal of Industrial Aerodynamics, 4,* 371-389. **IX**

Gardner, T. J. (1982). *The effect of five species of shade trees on the interception of summer and winter insolation.* Unpublished Masters Thesis, Ohio State University, Columbus, OH. **VIII**

Gates, D. M. (1980). *Biophysical ecology.* New York: Springer-Verlag. **IV, VIII**

Geiger, R. (1965). *The climate near the ground.* Cambridge, MA: Harvard University Press. **IX**

Gergacz, J. W. (1982). Legal aspects of solar energy: Statutory approaches for access to sunlight. *Environmental Affairs, 10*(1), 1-36. **VII**

Gill, J. D., & Healy, W. M. (1974). *Shrubs and vines for northeastern wildlife* (General Technical Report NE-9). Upper Darby, PA: USDA Forest Service. **IX**

Gill, J. D., DeGraaf, R. M., & Thomas, J. W. (1974). *Forest habitat management for non-game birds in central Appalachia* (Research Note NE-192). Upper Darby, PA: USDA Forest Service. **IX**

Gipe, P. (1981a). Power in the wind: An introduction. *Solar Age, 6*(4). **III**

Gipe, P. (1981b). Sources of wind data. *Solar Age, 6*(5), 35-36. **III**

Goodman, L. J., & Love, R. N. (Eds.). (1981). *Biomass energy projects, planning and management.* New York: Pergamon Press. **III**

Gordon, E. (1949, October). What climate does to you and what you can do to climate. *House Beautiful, 91,* 31. **I**

Greenbriar Associates. (1980). *Energy conserving site design — Greenbriar case study, Chesapeake, Virginia* (DOE/CS/24216-1). Washington, D.C.: U.S. Department of Energy, U.S. Government Printing Office. **II**

Hammond, J., Zanetto, J., & Adams, C. (1981). *Planning solar neighborhoods.* Sacramento, CA: California Energy Commission. **VI, VII, VIII**

Hammond, J., Hunt, M., Cramer, R., & Neubauer, L. (1974). *A strategy for energy conservation.* Davis, CA: City of Davis. **VI**

Hamrin, J. G. (1978). *Low energy consuming communities: Implications for public policy.* Unpublished doctoral dissertation, University of California, Davis, Davis, CA. **VI**

Hannon, B. M. (1977). *Energy use for building construction.* Springfield, VA: (NTIS Nos. 2791-3, 2791-4). **III**

Hansen, D. G., & Mandraes, D. R. (1979). Cost effectiveness of landscaping for energy savings: A case study. In *Proceedings of the Fourth National Passive Solar Conference* (pp. 476-479). Newark, DE: American Section of the International Solar Energy Society. **VIII**

Harrison, G. H. (1979). *The backyard bird watcher*. New York: Simon and Schuster. **IX**

Harrje, E. T., Buckley, C. E., & Heisler, G. M. (1982). Building energy reductions: Optimum use of windbreaks. *Journal of Energy Division, Proceedings of the American Society of Civil Engineers, 108,* 143-154. **IX**

Harwood, C. (1977). *Using land to save energy*. Cambridge, MA: Ballinger. **VI**

Hayes, D. (1977). *Rays of hope — The transition to a post-petroleum world*. New York: W. W. Norton. **II**

Hayes, G. B. (1979). *Solar access law*. Cambridge, MA: Ballinger. **VII**

Heichel, G. H., & Hankin, L. (1972). Retention of particulate lead on foliage and twigs of a white pine windbreak. In Northeastern Forest Experiment Station, *Proceedings of the Conference on Metropolitan Physical Environment* (General Technical Report, NE-25). Upper Darby, PA: USDA Forest Service. **IX**

Heisler, G. M. (1977). Trees modify metropolitan climate and noise. *Journal of Arboriculture, 3,* 201-207. **IX**

Heisler, G. M. (1982). Reductions of solar radiation by tree crowns. In *Progress in Solar Energy* (pp. 133-138). Newark, DE: American Section of the International Solar Energy Society. **VII, VIII**

Heisler, G. M. (In Preparation). *Effect of individual trees on the solar radiation climate of small buildings*. University Park, PA. **VIII**

Heisler, G. M., Halverson, H. G., & Zisa, R. P. (1981). Solar radiation measurements beneath crowns of open-grown trees. In *15th Conference on Agriculture and Forest Meteorology and 5th Conf. on Biometeorology*. Boston, MA: American Meteorology Society. **VIII**

Heisler, G. M., Miller, D. R., & Toedter, R. M. Classification of windbreak effectiveness. To be submitted to *Agricultural Meteorology*. **IX**

Henderson, A. (1978). *Architecture in Oklahoma*. Norman, OK: Point Riders Press. **I**

Herrington, L. P. (1974). Trees and acoustics in urban areas. *Journal of Forestry, 72,* 462-465. **IX**

Hill, G. G. (1901). *Practical suggestions for farm buildings*. Washington, D.C.: U.S. Government Printing Office. **I**

Hirst, E. (1974a). Automobile energy requirements. *Transportation Engineering Journal, 44.* **III**

Hirst, E. (1974b). *Direct and indirect energy costs for automobiles*. Oak Ridge, TN: Oak Ridge National Laboratory. (Report No. ORNL-NSF-EP-64) **III**

Holzberlein, T. M. (1979). Don't let the trees make a monkey of you. In *Proceedings of the Fourth National Passive Solar Conference* (pp. 416-419). Newark, DE: American Section of the International Solar Energy Society. **VIII**

House and Garden. (1948, March). Vines with a purpose, *93,* 114-115. **I**

Howard, E. (1902). *Garden cities of tomorrow*. Cambridge, MA: MIT Press. **VI**

HSM & Company. (1981). *A strategy to provide and protect solar access*. Portland, OR: Solar Access Alliance. **VII**

Hubbard, K. G., & Richardson, E. A. (1979). *Climatological design indices for Utah*. Logan, UT: United States Department of Agriculture. **XII**

Hubka, T. C. (1977, December). The connected farm buildings of southwestern Maine. *Pioneer America, 9,* 143-178. **I**

Hulstrom, R. L. (1981). *The solar radiation energy resource atlas of the United States*. Golden, CO: Solar Energy Research Institute, U.S. Government Printing Office (061-000-00570). **III**

Hunt, C. M. (1980). Air infiltration: A review of some existing measurement techniques and data. In C. M. Hunt, J. C. King, & T. R. Trechsel (Eds.) *Building air change rate and infiltration measurements* (ASTM Special Publication 719). Philadelphia, PA: American Society for Testing and Materials. **IX**

Hutchinson, B. A., Taylor, F. G., Wendt, R. L., & The Critical Review Panel. (1982). *Use of vegetation to ameliorate building microclimates: An assessment of energy conservation potentials* (No. 1913). Oak Ridge, TN: Oak Ridge National Laboratory, Environmental Sciences Division. **II, VII, VIII, IX**

Illlustrated Annual Register. (1880). Wind power, *8,* 126-129. **I**

Illustrated Annual Register. (1866). Woodland and timber crop, *4*, 256-265. **I**

Inman, R. E., Salo, D. J., & McGurk, B. J. (1977). *Silvicultural biomass farms: Site specific production studies and cost analyses* (MTR 7347) (Vol. IV). McClean, VA: Mitre/Metrek. **III**

Issacs, R. R. (1948). The neighborhood theory, an analysis of its adequacy. *Journal of the American Institute of Planners.* **VI**

Ise, J. (1936). *Sod and stubble: The story of a Kansas homestead.* New York: Harcourt. **I**

Jaffe, M. (1980). A commentary on solar access: Less theory, more practice. *Solar Law Reporter, 2*(2). **VII**

Jaffe, M., & Erley, D. (1979). *Protecting solar access for residential development.* Chicago, IL: American Planning Association, U.S. Department of Housing and Urban Development. **VII**

Jenkins, D., & Pearson, F. (1978). *Feasibility of rainwater collection systems in California.* Davis, CA: California Water Resources Center. **X**

Jennings, J. (1982). Winter shading from deciduous trees. *Eugene — Springfield solar report.* Eugene, OR: Oregon Appropriate Technology. **VIII**

Jensen, M. (1954). *Shelter effect.* Copenhagen: Danish Technical Press. **IX**

Johnson, B. D., McBee, J. K., & Tasselli, J. T. (Undated). *Solar absorption through vegetation: A two-season study.* Unpublished technical report. Virginia Polytechnic Institute and State University, Blacksburg, VA. **VIII**

Johnson, S. W. (1806). *Rural Economy.* New York: Riley. **I**

Jones, R. W. (Ed.). (1983). *Passive solar design handbook, volume three: Passive solar design analysis and supplement.* Newark, DE: American Solar Energy Society. **XII**

Jones, W. D. (1981). Making desert plants work for you. *Desert Plants, 3*(1), 18-28. **VII**

Kern, B., Kern, K., Mullan, J., & Mullan, O. (1982). *The earth sheltered owner built home.* North Fork, CA: Mullein Press. **VI**

Kerr, V. N. (1979). New Mexico's solar rights act: The meaning of the statute. *Solar Law Reporter, 1*(4). **VII**

Klein, S. A. (1983). Computers in the design of passive solar systems. *Passive Solar Journal, 2*(1), 57-64. **III, XII**

Knapp, C. L., & Stoffel, T. L. (1982). *Direct normal solar radiation data manual.* Golden, CO: Solar Energy Research Institute, U.S. Government Printing Office (061-000-0059). **III**

Knapp, C. L., Stoffel, T. L., & Whitaker, S. D. (1980). *Insolation data manual.* Golden, CO: Solar Energy Research Institute, U.S. Government Printing Office (060-000-00489-1). **III**

Knowles, R. L. (1981). *Sun rhythm form.* Cambridge, MA: MIT Press. **VI, VII**

Kohler, J. (1983). Home size hydro power, a practical case study. *Solar Age, 8,* 34-39. **III**

Kohler, J., & Lewis, D. (1981). Let the sun shine in. *Solar Age, 6,*(11). **VI, VII**

Kosloff, L. H. (1982). *Approaches to solar access: Easements and zoning for shade control.* Unpublished paper, King School of Law, University of California, Davis, California. **VII**

Krohe, J., Jr. (1982, June, July, August). Water as a resource in Illinois. *Illinois Issues.* **X**

Labs, K. (1979, October). Underground building climate. *Solar Age.* **VI**

Labs, K. (1981). Direct-coupled ground cooling: Issues and opportunities. In *Proceedings of the International Passive and Hybrid Cooling Conference* (pp. 131-135). Newark, DE: International Solar Energy Society. **III**

Laechelt, R. L., & Williams, B. M. (1976). *Value of tree shade to homeowners* (Bulletin No. 2450). Montgomery, Washington, D.C.: U.S. Department of Energy. (NTIS) **II, III, X**

Land Design/Research Inc. (1979). *Energy conserving site design case study: Burke Center, Virginia.* Washington, D.C.: U.S. Department of Energy. (NTIS) **II, III, X**

Langewiesche, W. (1949, October). How to pick your private climate. *House Beautiful, 91,* 146-150. **I**

Langewiesche, W. (1950, July). How to manipulate sun and shade. *House Beautiful, 92,* 42-45, 91-94. **I**

Laurie, M. (1975). *An introduction to landscape architecture.* New York: American Elsevier. **VI**

Libbey-Owens-Ford., Co. (1975). *Sun angle calculator.* Toledo, OH: Author. **VII**

Linaweaver, F. P. (1967). *A study of residential water use.* Washington, D.C.: U.S. Department of Housing and Urban Development. **X**

List, R. J. (1949). *Smithsonian meteorological tables*. Washington, D.C.: Smithsonian Institution Press. **C**

Living Systems. (1977). *Davis energy conservation report: Practical use of the sun*. Davis, CA: U.S. Dept. of Housing and Urban Development Innovative Project #B-75-51-06-001. **VIII**

Loftness, V. (1977). *Identifying climatic design regions and assessing climatic impact on residential building design*. Technical Paper No. 1. Washington, D.C.: AIA Research Corporation. **III**

Los Alamos Scientific Laboratory. (1980). *Passive solar design handbook, volume two: Passive solar design analysis*. Los Alamos, NM: Author. **VI, XII**

Los Angeles, City of. (1980). *Solar envelope zoning: Application to the city planning process*. Los Angeles, CA: Author. (NTIS) **VII**

Lunde, P. J. (1982). Payback time. *Solar Age, 7*(7), 63-64. **III**

Lynch, K. (1971). *Site planning*. Cambridge, MA: MIT Press. **III**

Maddy, K. (1982, July). Pesticides threaten groundwater supply. *The California Aggie*, Davis, CA. **X**

Marsh, G. P. (1864/1965). *Man and nature: Or, physical geography as modified by human action*. Cambridge, MA: Harvard University Press. **I**

Mattingly, G. M., Harrje, D. T., & Heisler, G. M. (1979). The effectiveness of an evergreen windbreak for reducing residential energy consumption. *ASHRAE Transactions, 85,* (Part 2), 428-444. **IX**

Mattingly, G. M., & Peters, E. F. (1977). Wind and trees: Air infiltration effects on energy in housing. *Journal of Industrial Aerodynamics, 2,* 1-19. **IX**

Mayhew, A. (1973). *Rural settlement and farming in Germany*. New York: Harper & Row. **I**

Maynard, S. T. (1905, September). Laying out the grounds of a country home. *Country Life, 9,* 13-14. **I**

Mazria, E. (1979). *The passive solar energy book*. Emmaus, PA: Rodale Press. **III, C**

McAdams, W. (1982). The evolution of building strategies: Communico's efforts in Santa Fe. *Passive Solar Journal, 2*(1), 29-44. **III**

McClenon, C., & Robinette, G. O. (Eds.). (1977). *Landscape planning for energy conservation*. Reston, VA: Environmental Design Press. **III, VII, IX**

McCurdy, T. (1980). Open space as an air resource management strategy. In G. Hopkins (Ed.) *Proceedings of the National Urban Forestry Conference* (Vol. 1, Publication 80-003). Syracuse, NY: State University of New York, College of Environmental Science and Forestry. **IX**

McHarg, I. (1969). *Design with nature*. Garden City, NY: Natural History Press. **III, VI**

McHarg, I. L., & Sutton, J. (1975, January). Ecological plumbing for the Texas coastal plain. *Landscape Architecture, 65*(1), 78-89. **VI**

McMillin, C. W. (Ed.). (1978). *Complete tree utilization of southern pine: Proceedings of a symposium*. Madison, WI: Forest Products Research Society. **III**

McPherson, E. G. (1980). *The use of plant materials for solar control*. Unpublished master's thesis, Utah State University, Logan, UT. **VIII**

McPherson, E. G. (1981a). The effects of orientation and shading from trees on inside and outside temperatures of model homes. In Bowen, A., Clark, E., & Labs, K. (Eds.). *Proceedings of the International Passive and Hybrid Cooling Conference* (pp. 369-373). Newark, DE: American Section of the International Solar Energy Society. **II, VIII**

McPherson, E. G. (1981b). A methodology for locating and selecting trees for solar control in Utah. In *Proceedings of the 1981 Annual Meeting* (pp. 72-76). Newark, DE: American Section of the International Solar Energy Society. **VII, VIII**

McPherson, E. G. (1981c). *The use of trees for solar control in Utah*. Research report available from the Utah Energy Office, Room 3000, State Office Bldg., Salt Lake City, UT 84114. **VIII, IX**

McPherson, E. G. (1983). Personal correspondence. Logan, UT. **V**

McPherson, E. G. (In Preparation). A shadow pattern program for building energy analysis. Logan, UT. **VIII**

Milne, M. (1976). *Residential water conservation* (Report No. 35). Davis, CA: California Water Resources Center. **X**

Minton, J. (1982). California Department of Water Resources, personal correspondence. **X**

Moffat, A. S., & Schiler, M. (1981). *Landscape design that saves energy.* New York: William Morrow and Company. **VII, IX**

Montgomery, D. A., Heisler, G. M., & Keown, S. L. (1982). Solar blocking by common trees. In *Proceedings of the 7th National Passive Solar Conference.* Newark, DE: American Solar Energy Society. **VIII**

Morrison, D. G. (1975, October). Restoring the midwestern landscape. *Landscape Architecture. 65*(6), 398-403. **X**

Mumford, L. (1965). The garden city idea and modern planning. In E. Howard, *Garden cities of tomorrow.* Cambridge, MA: MIT Press. **VI**

National Association of Home Builders. (1974). *Land development manual.* Washington, D.C.: Author. **III**

National Capital Region, National Parks Service. (1981). *Energy conservation concepts in managing urban parks.* Washington, D.C.: U.S. Department of the Interior, National Parks Service, U.S. Department of Energy. **XI**

National Climatic Center. (1979). *Airport climatological summary, Topeka, Kansas, Municipal-Philip Billard Airport.* In Climatology of the United States No. 90 (1965-1974). Asheville, NC: National Oceanic and Atmospheric Administration. **IX**

National Oceanic and Atmospheric Administration. (1977). *Climatic atlas of the United States.* Asheville, NC: National Climatic Center. **III, IV, VII**

National Well Water Association. (undated). 500 W. Wilson Bridge Road, Worthington, OH 43805. **III**

Newsweek. (1981, February). Are we running out of water? 97(8). **X**

Nisbet, F. J. (1977). Shelterbelts: Keeping the wind out and fuel bills down. *Country Journal, 4,* 48-53. **II**

Nordham, D. (Ed.). (1981). *Microcomputer methods for solar design and analysis.* Golden, CO: Solar Energy Research Institute. **III**

Novell, B. (1981). A simple design method for shading devices and passive cooling strategies based on monthly average temperatures. In A. Bowen, E. Clark, & K. Labs (Eds.) *Proceedings of the International Passive and Hybrid Cooling Conference* (pp. 392-396). Newark, DE: American Section of the International Solar Energy Society. **III, V, C**

Nusbaum, W. E. (1976). Inventory of energy use in water supply systems. *Energy conservation in the design of water quality control systems.* **X**

O'Callaghan, P. W. (1978). *Building for energy conservation.* New York: Pergamon Press. **II**

Odum, H. T. (1976). Developing a steady state for man and land: Energy procedures for regional planning. *Science for Better Environment,* Proceedings of the International Congress on Human Environment, Kyoto, Japan, 353-361. **III**

Odum, H. T., & Bayley, S. (1975). A model for understanding the relationships of money, energy, and survival value. In Conner, & Loehman (Eds.), *Economics and decision making for environmental quality.* Gainesville, FL: University of Florida Press. **III**

Olgyay, V. (1963/1973). *Design with climate* (4th ed.). Princeton, NJ: Princeton University Press. **IV, VI, VII, VIII**

Olgyay, A., & Olgyay, V. (1957/1976). *Solar control and shading devices.* Princeton, NJ: Princeton University Press. **VIII, C**

Oregon Appropriate Technology, Inc. (1982). *The Eugene-Springfield solar report.* Eugene, OR: City of Eugene. **VII**

Otawa, T., Schoen, D. A., & Justham, S. A. (1982). *A wind resource prospecting study for Indiana.* Muncie, IN: Center for Environmental Design, Research, and Service, Ball State University. **III**

Parker, J. H. (1981). *Use of landscaping for energy conservation.* Final Report, STAR Project 78-012, Tallahassee: Florida State University System. **II, VIII, IX**

Parker, J. H. (1982). An energy and ecological analysis of alternate residential landscapes. *Journal of Environmental Systems, 11*(3), 271-288. **II, XI**

Parker, J. H. (1983). Landscaping to reduce the energy used in cooling buildings. *Journal of Forestry, 81,* (82-84, 105). **IX**

Pelz, D. (1982). Personal correspondence, Director of Public Works, Davis, CA. **X**

Perry, C. (1929). *Regional survey for New York and its environs.* New York: Russell Sage Foundation. **VI**

Peterson, J. T. (1969). *The climate of cities: A survey of recent literature.* Raleigh, NC: U.S. Department of Health, Education, and Welfare, the National Air Pollution and Control Administration. **V**

Pickens, B. L. (1950, July). How to live at peace with the Gulf Coast climate. *House Beautiful, 92,* 102-106. **I**

Pitt, D. G., Gould, W., & Green, J. E. (1982a). A new approach to conservation — Energy consumed by the landscape. *American Nurseryman, 155*(3), 60-71. **II, X**

Pitt, D. G., Gould, W., & Green, J. E. (1982b). A new approach to conservation — A case study. *American Nurseryman, 155*(3), 74-75. **II, X**

Plate, E. J. (1971). The aerodynamics of shelterbelts. *Agriculture Meteorology, 8,* 203-222. **IX**

Plimpton, F. T. P., Jr. (1961, September). Plant a windbreak. *Horticulture, 39,* 456. **I**

Raymer, W. G. (1962). *Wind resistance of conifers* (NPL Aero Report/1008). London: National Physical Laboratory, Physics Division. **IX**

Read, R. A. (1964). *Tree windbreaks for the central Great Plains* (Agriculture Handbook No. 250). Washington, D.C.: U.S. Government Printing Office. **IX**

Real Estate Research Corporation. (1971). *Selling the solar home* (HUD-PDR-296-2). Washington, D.C.: U.S. Department of Housing and Urban Development, U.S. Government Printing Office. **III**

Reethof, G., & Heisler, G. M. (1976). Trees and forests for noise abatement and visual screening. In F. S. Santamour, H. D. Gerhold, & S. Little, (Eds). (General Technical Report NE-22). *Better Trees for Metropolitan Landscapes Symposium Proceedings.* Upper Darby, PA: USDA Forest Service. **IX**

Reid, G. W. (1976). *An exploratory study of possible energy savings as a result of water conservation practices.* Norman, OK: University of Oklahoma, (prepared for U.S. Department of Commerce). **X**

Reifsnyder, W. E., & Lull, H. W. (1965). *Radiant energy in relation to forests* (U.S. Department of Agriculture — Forest Service Technical Bulletin No. 1344). Washington, D.C.: U.S. Government Printing Office. **IV, VIII**

Reiman Buechner Partnership. (1979). *Energy conserving site design case study: Radisson, New York.* Washington, D.C.: U.S. Department of Energy. (NTIS). **II, III**

Richman, A., & Chapin, F. S. (1977). *A review of the social and physical concepts of the neighborhood as a basis for planning residential environments.* Chapel Hill, NC: Department of City and Regional Planning. **VI**

Ridgeway, J. (1979). *Energy-efficient community planning: A guide to saving and producing power at the local level.* Emmaus, PA: J.G. Press. **III**

Riordan, E. J., & Hiller, R. (1980). Describing the solar space in a solar easement. *Solar Law Reporter, 2*(2). **VII**

Robinette, G. O. (1972). *Plants/people/and environmental quality.* Washington, D.C.: U.S. Department of Interior. **IX**

Robinson, J. S. (Ed.). (1980). *Fuels from biomass: Technology and feasibility.* Park Ridge, NJ: Noyes Data Corp. **III**

Rogers, E. M., & Shoemaker, F. F. (1971). *Communication of innovations, a cross-cultural approach* (2nd ed.). New York: The Free Press. **X**

Rondon, J. (1980). *Landscaping for water conservation in a semi-arid environment.* City of Aurora, CO. **X**

Ross, M., & Williams, R. (1977, February). The potential for fuel conservation. *Technology Review,* pp. 49-57. **II**

Royal Dutch Touring Club. (1978). *Woonerf: A different approach to environmental management in residential areas and the related traffic legislation.* The Hague, The Netherlands: Author. **VI**

Rudofsky, B. (1964). *Architecture without architects.* New York: Museum of Modern Art. **VI**

Ruegg, R. T., McConnaughey, J. S., Sav, G. T., & Hockenbery, K. A. (1978). *Life cycle costing: A guide for selecting energy conservation projects for public buildings.* Washington, D.C.: National Bureau of Standards, NBS Building Science Series 113. **III**

Rutman, D. B. (1967). *Winthrop's Boston: A portrait of a puritan town, 1630-1649.* Boston: Beacon. **I**

Schiler, M. (1979). *Computer simulations of foliage effects on building energy load calculations.* Unpublished master's thesis, Cornell University, Ithaca, NY. **VII, VIII**

Schoner, B., & Uhl, K. P. (1975). *Marketing research: Information systems and decision making* (2nd. ed.). New York: Wiley & Sons. **III**

Seginer, I. (1975a). Atmospheric stability effect on windbreak shelter and drag. *Boundary-Layer Meteorology, 8,* 383-400. **IX**

Seginer, I. (1975b). Flow around a windbreak in oblique wind. *Boundary-Layer Meteorology, 9,* 133-141. **IX**

Shenandoah Development, Inc. (1980). *Energy conserving site design case study: Shenandoah, Georgia.* Washington, D.C.: U.S. Department of Energy. (NTIS) **III**

Sherwood, G. E., & Hans, G. E. (1979). *Energy efficiency in light-frame wood construction* (Research Paper FPL 317). Madison, WI: Forest Products Laboratory, USDA Forest Service. **IX**

Smalley, E. V. (1893, September). Isolation of life on prairie farms. *Atlantic, 72,* 378-382. **I**

Smith, D. R. (1981). *Life cycle cost and energy comparison of grass, pavement and asphalt* (Order No. a-4331-4). Dayton, OH: City Manager's Office, Box 22. **XII**

Smith, W. H. (1980). Urban vegetation and air quality. In G. Hopkins (Ed.) *Proceedings of the National Urban Forestry Conference* (Vol. 1, ESF Publication 80-003). Syracuse, NY: State University of New York, College of Environmental Science and Forestry. **IX**

Smith, W. H., & Dochinger, L. S. (1976). Capability of metropolitan trees to reduce atmospheric contaminants. In F. S. Santamour, H. D. Gerhold, & S. Little (Eds.) *Better trees for metropolitan landscapes* (General Technical Report NE-22). Upper Darby, PA: USDA Forest Service, Northeastern Forest Experiment Station. **IX**

Solar Age. (1983). Rating the site survey tools. *Solar Age, 8*(6), 14-16. **III**

SolarCal Local Government Commission. (1981). *Solar access ordinances — A guide for local governments.* Sacramento, CA: Author. **VII**

Solar Energy Research Institute. (1980). *Analysis methods for solar water heating and cooling applications.* Golden, CO: Solar Energy Research Institute. **III**

Spirn, A. W., & Santos, A. N. (1981). *Plants for passive cooling: A preliminary investation of the use of plants for passive cooling in temperate humid climates.* Department of Landscape Architecture, Harvard University, Technical report for Oak Ridge National Laboratory, Solar and Special Studies Section, Energy Division, Oak Ridge, TN. **VIII**

Stein, C. (1957) *Toward new towns for America.* New York: Reinhold Publishing. **VI**

Stein, R. G. (1977a). *Architecture and energy.* Garden City, NY: Anchor Press/Doubleday. **III**

Stein, R. G. (1977b). Energy cost of building construction. *Energy and Building, 1,* 27-29. **III**

Steinitz, C., Parker P., & Jordan, L. (1976). Hand-drawn overlays: Their history and prospective uses. *Landscape Architecture, 6* (9), 444-445. **III**

Sterling, R., Carmody, J., & Elnicky, G. (1981). *Earth sheltered community design: Energy efficient residential development.* New York: Van Nostrand Rheinhold Co. **III, VI**

Stilgoe, J. R. (1981, January). New England coastal wilderness. *Geographics Review, 71,* 33-50. **I**

Stilgoe, J. R. (1982a). *Common landscape of America, 1580 to 1845.* New Haven, CT: Yale University Press. **I**

Stilgoe, J. R. (1982b). Suburbanites forever: The American dream endures. *Landscape Architecture, 72,* 88-93. **I**

Stobaugh, R., & Yergin, D. (1979). *Energy future.* New York: Random House. **II, VII**

Stoeckeler, J. H., & Williams, R. A. (1949). Windbreaks and shelterbelts. *Trees: Yearbook of agriculture, 1949,* Washington, D.C.: U.S. Government Printing Office. **I**

Sturrock, J. W. (1969). Aerodynamic studies of shelterbelts in New Zealand — 1: Low to medium height shelterbelts in mid-Canterbury. *New Zealand Journal of Science, 12,* 754-776. **IX**

Swanson, M. (1980). *Energy conserving site design case study: The Woodlands, Texas.* Washington, D.C.: U.S. Department of Energy. (NTIS) **III**

Terres, J. K. (1953). *Songbirds in your garden.* New York: Thomas Y. Crowell. **IX**

Tetra Rech, Inc. (1975). *Energy use in contract construction industry.* Arlington, VA: Author. **III**

Thayer, R. L., Jr. (1977, May). Designing an experimental solar community. *Landscape Architecture, 67*(3), 223-228. **VI**

Thayer, R. L., Jr. (1980). Conspicuous non-consumption: The symbolic aesthetics of solar architecture. In R. Stough & A. Wandersman (Eds.) *Optimizing environments: Research, practice and policy,* Washington, D.C.: Environmental Design Research Association. **X**

Thayer, R. L., Jr. (1981a). *Solar access: It's the law!* Davis, CA: Institute of Governmental Affairs, University of California, Davis. **VII**

Thayer, R. L., Jr. (1981b). Landscape planting for energy conservation. *Solar Engineering, 6*(10).**VII**

Thayer, R. L., Jr. (1981c). Designing and evaluating energy efficient landscape plantings. *Solar Engineering, 6*(11). **VII**

Thayer, R. L., Jr. (1982). Public response to water conserving landscapes. *HortScience, 17*(4). **X**

Thayer, R. L., Jr. Unpublished manuscript. SOLAX: Microcomputer solar access control of trees in solar developments. Davis, CA. **VII**

Thayer, R. L., Jr., & Zanetto, J. (1982). *Energy conservation guidelines for mobile home communities.* Oceanside, CA: City of Oceanside. **VI**

Thayer, R. L., Jr. Zanetto, J. A., & Maeda, B. (1983). Modelling the effects of deciduous trees on thermal performance of solar and non-solar houses in Sacramento, California. *Landscape Journal, 2*(2), 155-164. **II, VII**

The Country Gentleman. (1864, September). Shade trees for barn yards, *24,* 144. **I**

The Garden. (1927, September). Windbreaks in small gardens, *91.* **I**

Thomas, J. W., Brush, R. O., & DeGraaf, R. M. (1973). Invite wildlife to your backyard. *National Wildlife Magazine, 11,* 5-16. **IX**

Thoreau, H. D. (1985/1961). *Cape Cod.* Boston, MA: Crowell-Appollo. **I**

Ticknor, R. L. (1981). Selecting deciduous trees for climatic modification. *American Nurseryman, 153*(1), 10-88. **VIII**

Time. (1979, February). In Virginia: Brumley Gap takes on a dam site, *113*(9), 5-6. **X**

Toth, R. (1974). *A planning and design process.* Unpublished manuscript. Department of Landscape Architecture and Environmental Planning, Utah State University, Logan, UT. **III**

Trewartha, G. T. (1968). *An introduction to climate.* New York: McGraw-Hill Book Co. **V**

Troth, H. (1905, February). Windbreaks for country homes. *Country Life, 7,* 363-366. **I**

Turner, P. V. (1976). *The founders and the architects: The design of Stanford University.* Palo Alto, CA: Stanford University Press. **X**

Underground Space Center, University of Minnesota. (1978). *Earth sheltered housing design.* Minneapolis, MN: Author. **VI**

Untermann, R., & Small, R. (1977). *Site planning for cluster housing.* New York: Van Nostrand Reinhold Co. **VI**

U.S. Department of Agriculture. (1973). *Trees for polluted air.* Washington, D.C.: Author. **X**

U.S. Department of Energy/Energy Information Administration. (1981). *Residential energy consumption survey: 1979-1980 consumption and expenditures, Part 1: National data* (DOE/EIA-0262/1). Washington, D.C.: U.S. Government Printing Office. **III**

U.S. Department of Energy/Energy Information Administration. (1982a). *Short term energy outlook, Volume 1 — Quarterly projections* (DOE/EIA/-0202 (82/1Q). Washington, D.C.: U.S. Government Printing Office. **II**

U.S. Department of Energy/Energy Information Administration. (1982b). *1981 Annual report to Congress, Volume 3 — Energy projections* (DOE/EIA/-0173 (81)/3. Washington, D.C.: U.S. Government Printing Office. **II**

U.S. Department of Energy/Energy Information Administration. (1983 & 1984). *Residential energy consumption survey: Consumption and expenditures, April 1981 through March 1982* (2 vols.) Part 1: National data (DOE/EIA-0321/1), Part 2: Regional data (DOE/EIA-0321/2). Washington, D.C.: U.S. Government Printing Office. **III**

U.S. Department of Energy/Energy Information Administration. (1983). *Residential energy consumption survey: Regressional analysis of energy consumption by end use* (DOE/EIA — 0431). Washington, D.C.: U.S. Government Printing Office. **III**

U.S. Department of Energy/Energy Information Administration. (1984). *Annual energy outlook 1983* (DOE/EIA-0383). Washington, D.C.: U.S. Government Printing Office. **II**

U.S. Department of Transportation. (1977). *UTPS-Urban transportation planning system.* Washington, D.C.: U.S. Department of Transportation. **III**

U.S. Water Resources Council (1978). *The nation's water resources, 1975-2000* (Vols. 1-4). Washington, D.C.: U.S. Government Printing Office. **X**

U.S. Weather Bureau. (1962). *Decennial census of United States climate — summary of hourly observations, Newark, NJ* (Climatography of the United States No. 82-88). Washington, D.C.: U.S. Government Printing Office. **IX**

Van Eimern, J., Karschon, R., Rasumova, L. A., & Robertson, G. W. (1964). *Windbreaks and shelterbelts* (WMO-No. 147.TP.70). Geneva, Switzerland: World Meteorological Organization. **IX**

Van Haverbeke, D. F. (1977). *Conifers for single-row field windbreaks* (Research Paper RM-196). Fort Collins, CO: Rocky Mountain Forest and Range Experiment Station. **IX**

Van Wijk, W. R. (1963). *Physics of plant environment.* Amsterdam: North Holland Publishing Co. **IV**

Wagar, J. A. (1982). *Using vegetation to control sun and shade on windows.* Berkeley, CA: USDA Forest Service, Pacific Southwest Forest and Range Experiment Station. **VII, VIII, C**

Waggoner, P. E., Pack, A. B., & Reifsnyder, W. E. (1959). *The climate of shade* (Bulletin No. 626). Storrs, CT: Agricultural Experiment Station. **VIII**

Wasitynski, C. (1982, March/April). The energy dimension. *Sierra,* pp. 30-31. **II**

Watson, D., & Labs, K. (1983). *Climatic design: Energy efficient building principles and practices.* New York: McGraw-Hill. **VI**

Webb, W. P. (1931). *The great plains.* New York: Ginn. **I**

Wegley, H. C., Montie, M. O., & Drake, R. L. (1980). *A siting handbook for small wind energy conversion systems* (PNL-2521). Richland, WA: Pacific Northwest Laboratory. **III**

Westergaard, C. J. (1982). *The relative ability of various shade trees to block or filter direct solar radiation in the winter.* Unpublished master's thesis, Cornell University, Ithaca, NY. **II, VI, VIII**

White, L. P., & Plaskett, L. G. (1981). *Biomass as fuel.* New York: Academic Press. **III**

White, R. F. (1954). *Effects of landscape development on the natural ventilation of buildings and their adjacent areas* (Research Report No. 45). College Station, TX: Texas Engineering Experiment Station. **IX**

Williamson, J. F. (Ed.). (1979). *New western garden book.* Menlo Park, CA: Lane Publishing Co. **VII**

Wood, W. (1634). *New England's prospect.* London: Bellamie. **I**

Woodruff, N. P. (1954). *Shelterbelt and surface barrier effects on wind velocities, evaporation, house heating, and snowdrifting* (Technical Bulletin 77). Manhattan, KS: Kansas Agricultural Experimental Station. **IX**

Woodruff, N. P., Read, R. A., & Chepil, W. S. (1959). *Influence of a field windbreak on summer wind movement and air temperature* (Technical Bulletin 100). Manhattan, KS: Kansas Agricultural Experiment Station. **IX**

Wyman, D. (1939, February). Natural screens and windbreaks. *Real Gardening, 1,* 78-85. **I**

Yoshino, M. M. (1975). *Climate in a small area.* Tokyo: University of Tokyo Press. **IX**

Younger, V. B. (1981, Summer, Fall). Water use and turf quality of warm-season and cool-season turfgrasses. *California Turfgrass Culture, 31*(3) (4). **X**

Zanetto, J. (1978). The location and selection of trees for solar neighborhoods. *Landscape Architecture, 68*(6), 514-517. **VII, VIII**

Zanetto, J. (1983). Personal Correspondence. Davis, CA. **III**

Zanetto, J., & Harding, D. (1981). Earthshelter: Performance evaluation of a northern California residence. In *Proceedings of the 6th National Passive Solar Conference.* Newark, DE: American Section of the International Solar Energy Society. **VI**

Zanetto, J., & Thayer, R. L., Jr. (1983). Street tree retrofits: Energy conservation in Davis. *Landscape Architecture, 73*(2). **VI, VII**

Zuccheto, J. (1975). Energy-economic theory and mathematical models for combining systems of man and nature, case study: The urban region of Miami, Florida. *Ecological Modelling, 1,* 241-268. **III**

Biographies of Contributing Authors

Dr. Gordon Heisler has been a Forest Meteorologist with the Northeastern Forest Experiment Station of the U.S. Forest Service since 1972, and has been stationed on the Penn State campus, University Park, Pennsylvania, since 1978. He has degrees in Forestry from Pennsylvania State and Yale, and a Ph.D. in Forest Influences from the State University of New York, College of Environmental Science and Forestry in Syracuse. Much of his research has been concerned with the effects of windbreaks and shade trees on energy use for heating and cooling buildings.

Dr. Lee P. Herrington received his education in Forestry and Biometeorology from the University of Maine and Yale University. After two years as the senior meteorologist with Melpar, Inc., he joined the faculty at the State University of New York, College of Environmental Science and Forestry. Since that time he has been active in research, teaching, and continuing education in the areas of forest meteorology, urban micrometeorology, and thermocomfort. In recent years his interest has been directed toward urban microclimate and the role that vegetation can play in improving the thermocomfort of people in urban environs.

Robert Hrabak is Assistant Environmental Scientist in the Energy and Environmental Systems Division at Argonne National Laboratory. He received a Bachelor of Architecture degree from the University of Kentucky in 1972, and a Master of City Planning in Urban Design from Harvard University in 1974. He served as a regional planner in Baltimore from 1975 to 1977. Since joining Argonne Laboratory he has engaged in energy conservation research and managed the Site and Neighborhood Design (SAND) case studies. Current activities focus on the documentation and the development of methodological tools to facilitate efficient identification and evaluation of energy conservation strategies in the development process.

Greg McPherson is a Research Associate with the Forest Resources Department at Utah State University. He received a Master of Landscape Architecture degree from Utah State in 1980 and taught courses in plant materials, planting design, and residential design as a Lecturer with the Department of Landscape Architecture and Environmental Planning from 1981 to 1983. His research into various aspects of energy efficient site design has resulted in a number of publications, workshops, and consulting projects. He will be pursuing a Ph.D. in Urban Forestry at the College of Environmental Science and Forestry at SUNY-Syracuse.

David Morris holds degrees in Industrial and Labor Relations (B.S., Cornell), Political Science (M.A., University of Florida), and Urban Planning (Ph.D., Union Graduate School). He is the author of *Self-Reliant Cities* (Sierra Club Books) and *The New City States* (Institute for Local Self-Reliance). His book *Neighborhood Power* (1975) was voted one of the top two books on neighborhoods ever written in a survey conducted by the University of Pittsburgh. His most recent book is *Be Your Own Power Company* (Rodale Press, 1983). Morris is a regular columnist for *Solar Age* magazine. Articles he has authored have appeared in major journals and newspapers. He lectures widely on decentralist development strategies and advises numerous cities on ways to implement such strategies.

David G. Pitt is Associate Professor and Extension Specialist in Landscape Architecture and Regional Development in the Department of Horticulture at the

University of Maryland, College Park, Maryland. He has authored several extension publications and trade journal articles on landscape design as a means for energy conservation. Additional research interests reflected in his publications include the identification and management of perceived values in the landscape, and the interface between public interest and private rights in land management. He is currently investigating the factor's associated with landowner's decisions to participate in Maryland's agricultural land preservation program.

Thomas A. Richman graduated Phi Beta Kappa from Stanford University in 1980 with a degree in English and Classics. After working in residential landscape design in Santa Barbara, California, he enrolled at the University of California, Davis, where he received a Bachelor of Science degree in Landscape Architecture. While at Davis, he won an ASLA Student Honor Award, was chosen "outstanding senior student" by the faculty, and worked as a research assistant to Professor Thayer. His current work as a private consultant includes landscape design and construction management for a 35 acre hospital in Northern India.

David E. Socwell graduated Cum Laude from Utah State University in 1983 with a Bachelor's of Landscape Architecture degree. While attending the university he served as a teaching and research assistant and won a number of scholastic awards. These include the American Society of Landscape Architects' Honor Award, and a third place award of merit in the International Federation of Landscape Architects' Renewable Resources competition. He is currently an Associate in the design firm of Allred, Soffe and Associates, Inc. His work has included research and evaluation, master planning, and site design responsibilities for several large scale multi-use projects in Summit County, Utah.

Professor John R. Stilgoe (Ph.D.) teaches in the Departments of Landscape Architecture and Visual & Environmental Studies at Harvard University. Author of *Common Landscape of America, 1580 to 1845* and *Metropolitan Corridor: Railroads and the American Scene* (both Yale University Press) and many scholarly articles, he is presently writing a book on the evolution of American suburbs. With his wife and sons he lives far south of Boston on a farm with mature windbreaks.

Robert L. Thayer, Jr., is Associate Professor of Landscape Architecture, Department of Environmental Design, and Research Landscape Architect in the Experiment Station, College of Agriculture and Environmental Sciences, University of California, Davis. His research and professional work encompass solar utilization and energy conservation in land planning, water conservation planning, and public attitudes toward resource-conserving landscape innovations. He has recently completed two computer simulation studies of the effects of trees on energy performance of houses and has been a consultant to the City of Portland, Oregon, during development of municipal solar access ordinances. He has published widely in scholarly and technical journals and is the recipient of awards for Research in the 1981, 1982, and 1983 ASLA Professional Awards Program. He also received the ASLA Bradford Williams Medal in 1978.

James Zanetto is a self-employed architect and planner in Davis, California. He received a Bachelor of Architecture degree from the University of Southern California in 1971, and a Masters of Landscape Architecture degree from the University of California at Berkeley in 1976. From 1977 to 1981 he worked for Living Systems in Winters, California and co-authored two solar planning manuals for residential developers and designers. Other publications have appeared in *Landscape Architecture* and the *Landscape Journal*. His practice specializes in climatically adapted architecture, planning, and landscape design. He and his family reside in a passive solar, earthsheltered home that he designed and built.

Subject Index